The
Course
of
United States
History

Volume II: From 1865

The
Course
of
United States
History

Volume II: From 1865

Edited by

David Nasaw
City University of New York
College of Staten Island

The Dorsey Press

Chicago, Illinois 60604

© THE DORSEY PRESS, 1987

ISBN 0-256-03552-0
Library of Congress Catalog Card No. 86–71919

Printed in the United States of America

1 2 3 4 5 6 7 8 9 0 MP 4 3 2 1 0 9 8 7

To Peter and Daniel

Preface

This book has been designed as a supplementary reader for college students in introductory U.S. history courses. It includes essays, chapter-length excerpts, primary documents (most of them complete and unabridged), and original commentaries by Richard Current, Eric Foner, Lloyd Gardner, David Garrow, James Gilbert, James Henretta, Walter LaFeber, Stephen Nissenbaum, Neal Salisbury, Kathryn Kish Sklar, Susan Ware, Sean Wilentz, and R. Jackson Wilson.

I have made use in this reader of a very old technique for introducing students to the study of history. I have included primary documents in each chapter and asked master teachers who are experts in their fields to comment on the documents as they would in their own classrooms. These original commentaries analyze and explain the meaning, purposes, and rhetorical strategies that make the documents so revealing.

Many of these documents are already American classics: John Winthrop's "A Model of Christian Charity," the Declaration of Independence, Washington's "Farewell Address," Lincoln's "Gettysburg Address." Others are included because they capture an important moment in our history and can provide students with a sense of being present as history is being made. The "Address" of the South Carolina Colored State Convention, Henry Cabot Lodge's Senate speech on the "Philippine Islands," the "Truman Doctrine" message to Congress, Martin Luther King's "I Have a Dream" speech, and Ronald Reagan's "Acceptance" speech to the Republican Convention in Dallas belong in this category.

Framing the documents and commentaries are articles and chapter-length excerpts. I used a few simple criteria in selecting these readings: Is the selection readable and will it interest students in introductory courses? Is the subject matter such that college students should be acquainted with it? Are the interpretations and research current? Each reading is followed by questions designed to stimulate classroom discussion.

When U.S. history textbooks were heavily slanted toward traditional political history, it was incumbent on "readers" to fill in the social history side of the story. Textbooks have changed substantially in the past decade. They now include much more social and cultural history than ever before and supplement their narratives with anecdotal material and biographical sketches of the people, famous and not so famous, who have contributed to the making of our nation's history. This change in the texts has made it possible for us to design a new kind of anthology, one that by integrating social and political history in new ways will highlight for our students the explanatory power, imagination, and excitement of good historical writing.

David Nasaw

Contents

List of Illustrations   *xi*

Chapter One   **The Civil War**   **1**

Frederick Douglass and Abraham Lincoln,
Nathan Irvin Huggins   2
Fighting the Civil War, *T. Harry Williams*   15
Document:
Abraham Lincoln, "The Gettysburg Address";
commentary by R. Jackson Wilson   35

Chapter Two   **Reconstruction**   **46**

Slaves No More, *Leon F. Litwack*   47
Document:
Addresses from the South Carolina Colored
State Convention; *commentary by Eric Foner*   65
Blacks and the Politics of Redemption, *Mary
Frances Berry and John W. Blassingame*   81

Chapter Three   **A Changing Social Order**   **97**

Understanding the Populists, *James Turner*   98
The Progressives and the City, *Paul Boyer*   113
Document:
Jane Addams, "The Subjective Necessity for
Social Settlements"; *commentary by Kathryn
Kish Sklar*   135

Chapter Four   **A New World Power**   **152**

Capitalists, Christians, Cowboys, *Emily S.
Rosenberg*   153
Document:
Henry Cabot Lodge, Speech to the United
States on the Philippine Islands; *commentary
by Lloyd Gardner*   175
Managing the War, *Barry D. Karl*   196

Chapter Five	**Between the Wars**	**212**

Piety, Profits, and Play: The 1920s; Bruce
Barton; Henry Ford; Babe Ruth, *Warren
Susman*   213
The Superfluous People of the Great
Depression, *Caroline Bird*   237
Document:
Franklin Delano Roosevelt, First Inaugural
Address; *commentary by Susan Ware*   253
Black Americans and the New Deal, *Harvard
Sitkoff*   266

Chapter Six	**War and Postwar**	**281**

From World War to Cold War, *Thomas G.
Paterson*   282
Document:
Harry S. Truman, Address on Foreign Economic
Policy, Delivered at Baylor University, March 6,
1947, and Special Message to the Congress on
Greece and Turkey: The Truman Doctrine,
March 12, 1947; *commentary by Walter LeFeber*   297
Postwar Families, *James Gilbert*   316

Chapter Seven	**American Dreams, American Nightmares**	**331**

Black Women and the Civil Rights Movement,
Paula Giddings   332
Document:
Martin Luther King, "I Have a Dream" Speech;
commentary by David J. Garrow   351
The War in Vietnam, *Walter LaFeber*   362

Chapter Eight	**Toward the Twenty-First Century**	**378**

The New Feminism, *William H. Chafe*   379
The New Urban Crisis, *Richard C. Wade*   397
Document:
Ronald Reagan's Second Acceptance Speech to
Republican Nominating Convention;
commentary by James Gilbert   409
Index   i
About the Contributors   xvii
About the Editor   xviii

List of Illustrations

Photographs of Abraham Lincoln   34
Harper's Weekly illustration "The First Vote"   64
Jane Addams   134
Henry Cabot Lodge   174
President Franklin Roosevelt   252
World Journal Tribune cartoon "There Are Such"   296
Leaders of the August 28, 1963, March on Washington   350
Ronald Reagan at the 1984 Dallas Convention   408

Chapter One

The Civil War

NATHAN IRVIN HUGGINS

Frederick Douglass and Abraham Lincoln

Was the Civil War a war to preserve the union or a war to end slavery? Abraham Lincoln left no doubt as to where he stood on the subject. "My paramount object," he wrote in the summer of 1862, "is to save the Union and is not either to save or to destroy Slavery."

Frederick Douglass took a quite different view of the "object" of the war. From the outset, he viewed it "as a means to end slavery." Douglass did not want the slaves to be considered simply as the "cause" of the fighting or the "contraband" of war; he wanted them to take their place on the battlefield alongside white northern troops. "He knew," as Nathan Huggins recounts in the following selection, "that only by black involvement could abolition become the chief war aim. The more blacks participated, shifting the balance, the more they could be certain of affecting their future."

In this excerpt from his biography of Frederick Douglass, former slave, abolitionist orator, and black leader, Nathan Huggins describes the conflict between Lincoln and Douglass over the causes, course, and ultimate meaning of the Civil War. During the war itself, the two leaders disagreed often on the most fundamental of questions. But Lincoln's assassination brought them together as Douglass, once the President's steadfast opponent, joined the chorus of praise for the man he now described as not only a great president "but a friend to black people."

Along with most Americans of his time, Frederick Douglass had a providential view of American history. It had been no accident that the continent became available to Europeans when it did. Human progress was being marked

Nathan Irvin Huggins is a professor of history and Afro-American studies at Harvard University and the author of several books including *Black Odyssey: The Afro-American Ordeal in Slavery* and *Slave and Citizen: The Life of Frederick Douglass,* from which the following selection has been excerpted.

out in the new-world settlement, and in the United States one could find a nation breaking free from the corruption and tyranny of the old world, founding itself on natural law. It had been in God's design to give men, at a precise moment in history, a vision of the divine ordinance and a chance to realize it in the United States. With its Declaration of Independence as the expression of natural law, the Constitution should have translated its ideals and principles into republican institutions suited to a divine purpose.

Many Americans articulated this sense of providence in expansionism under the slogan Manifest Destiny, in which superior Anglo-American institutions were to be brought to the service of other peoples in the hemisphere. Most, however, saw this ordained progress as ideational rather than territorial. It was for the American nation to be true to its ideals and create a society in which all men could live in prosperity and peace. The promise of America was the perfectability of society and the perfectability of man in the creation of the ultimate in social evolution: a Nation of Nations.

Douglass, like most black leaders, held to this view of America seeing a special providence in the presence of the African in America. God would not have suffered such an enormity as the slave trade were it not ultimately to serve some higher end. Some, with a missionizing turn of mind, saw that ultimate purpose to be the return of the Afro-American to Africa to bring Christianity to a pagan people along with the benefits of civilization. Douglass, however, saw it differently. The African was the ultimate test of American civilization. The American had a higher calling: to achieve the will of God in this world. But to do that, he must see the sin against God of slavery and racisim and accept the Afro-American as a man, a citizen, and a brother. Only then could the American civilization come into its own.

Douglass's faith in the righteousness of this view, in the essential moral capacity of every man, and in the certainty that evil would not go unpunished sustained him in the long, arduous, and frustrating struggle against slavery and racism. A people, no matter how arrogant and self-assured, could not for long work against the laws of God and nature without retribution. The American people had good and evil before them in the starkest of terms: the idealism of the Declaration of Independence and the unmitigated evil of slavery. All of human history might well be seen to have led to this dramatic confrontation. To be uncertain of the outcome was to be faithless in divine design and purpose.

The events of the 1850s sorely tried Douglass's certainty of a guiding providence. The coming of the Civil War revived his faith, not so much in people as in the power of historical forces to resolve contradictions. No one wanted it but the war came. Northerners, and even Republicans, had seemed willing to give up any worthwhile principle, ignoring human rights, for peace. Nevertheless, the war came.

Antislavery advocates had been predicting a crisis of union all along. The fundamental contradictions of a free society resting on slave labor had bound Americans in a logic of events that had to lead to this point. Even a Southerner, Hinton Rowan Helper, had come to see by 1857 that slavery was necessarily destructive to Southern society. While his book, *The Impending Crisis of the South,* was an economic rather than a moral critique, it nevertheless predicted a crisis. The view of inevitabilty was echoed in William H. Seward's rhetoric, the "irrepressible conflict," and even in Abraham Lincoln's "house divided." The war, when it came, seemed merely to bear out what Douglass had known all along: the laws of nature and the logic of events would lead to this unless Americans willingly took the radical path, abolishing slavery and combating racial prejudice. . . . But the war could not be allowed merely to take its course; the issues needed to be correctly understood by national leaders, and the prosecution of the war had to be pressed unrelentingly toward the eradication of slavery.

There was little in Abraham Lincoln's conception of the war and its issues to cheer Douglass. True, Lincoln had been fast in his refusal to compromise with secessionists; and he had been firm in holding to the Republican party's policy on exclusion of slavery from the territories, but he would have left the slave to his master and the fugitive to his fate with slave hunters. Lincoln would hold to no principles more compelling than the Union itself. For those, like Douglass, who had never found virtue in a union based on slavery, Lincoln's position could inspire little confidence.

Douglass saw his role as bringing the nation to see the war as against slavery and for freedom, and to bring blacks, both slave and free, into the war as active combatants. Although he would be frustrated and annoyed at the slowness of Lincoln, he remained convinced throughout that the war would be revolutionary, and would itself be the best educator of conservative leaders.

Seeing the war as a means to end slavery, Douglass was anxious that it be carried at once into the heartland of the South. He had always seen the four million enslaved blacks as the Achilles's heel of the American nation. With the South's secession, the vulnerability was the Southern Confederacy's alone. The quickest way to end the rebellion was to strike at the South's vitals, to arm the slave and free black volunteers, and the Confederacy would be bound to collapse at once. Knowing that Republicans like Lincoln had as Whigs and Democrats been able to accommodate themselves very well to slavery in the Old South, he was fearful that unless blacks became a part of the war, Northern and Southern conservatives would make a peace that left the status of blacks unchanged.

Abraham Lincoln would have had it that way if he could. He was unwilling to view the war as inevitably revolutionary. He believed that he could best save the Union by raising no challenges to existing institutions and prejudices. He rested his strategy on the Border States—Delaware, Missouri, Maryland, Tennessee, and Kentucky. Their presence within the Union would be ready proof of the possible coexistence of slavery with the new administration. They represented a moderate alternative to the extremism of secession. As Lincoln understood it, the principle which held border-state moderates to the national government was that of preserving the Union, and only that. To encourage the thought that the government's war had any other end but to save the Union would be to alienate those moderates. . . .

From Lincoln's first call for volunteers, Northern blacks pressed to be enlisted in the Army. Some suggested schemes of using Northern blacks to organize slave revolts. Lincoln, however, had no intention of recruiting black soldiers, fearing both the border-state reaction and a negative effect on Northern white enlistments; using black troops and provoking slave insurrections might be a way to win a war, but it was hardly a way to preserve a white man's Union.

The war, as Douglass saw it, had a momentum of its own and would not be confined to the convenient limits Lincoln desired. Once the die had been cast, once the slave states seceded and the Confederacy had established itself in defense of the slave system, it was futile to look for moderate positions which would have denied Southerners a share in the nation's future on their own terms. In time expediency would force Lincoln beyond his war of limited liabilities into one that would redefine the nation altogether. But he could not be hurried by Douglass or abolitionists or even radicals within his own government. . . .

As 1862 began, the government had not moved very far on the question of slavery. Douglass was disappointed. Beginning in the fall of 1861 his lectures and editorials hammered away at the notion that slavery was the central issue in the "rebellion." It had to be attacked frontally. Throughout the winter and spring of 1862 his message was the necessity for "instant and Universal Emancipation."

He was greatly impressed by a change in public sentiment. His entire career on the public platform had brought him to expect hostility and even violence from white audiences. Now, the hisses and the catcalls were gone, and he was listened to with respectful attention. There was not only a new-found respect but a general acceptance of his central premises: that the evil of the slave power was the root cause of the war, and that a cessation of slavery was necessary to end the war. As he saw it, the Northern public was far in advance of Lincoln and his government; Washington needed to get the message. . . .

Whatever Lincoln's dreams of other ways out—that blacks would go away or that moderate Southerners would prevail in the notion that the Union was a value transcending all others—he had at last to confront slavery or give up the war. The military circumstances of the war forced this choice upon him. European governments were tempted to support the Confederacy in deference to their own industrial interests; they could hardly find the cause of the Union compelling. And as the war moved into its second year, Northerners became impatient and resentful of its costs, and the need for decisiveness became imperative.

By July 1862 Lincoln seemed to have accepted the inevitable. On July 22 he announced to his cabinet that he intended to proclaim all slaves free in those states still in rebellion on 1 January 1863. He refrained from any public statement, however, and continued to pursue a course of cautious reserve. He awaited the appearance of a military victory. On September 22, following Robert E. Lee's setback at Antietam, he issued the preliminary proclamation of his intentions.

Making it clear that he had not adopted abolitionist ideas, Lincoln was careful to reiterate in the proclamation that the purpose of the war was the restoration of the Union and that he intended still to work for compensation for those who voluntarily freed their slaves. He did declare, however, that "the Executive Government of the United States . . . will do no act . . . to repress such persons . . . in any effort they make for their actual freedom," thus removing the confusion of policy toward fugitives within Union lines, and implying an official indifference to slave insurrections. Yet slavery would remain untouched in those states still part of the Union. All of Tennessee was omitted as well as those portions of Virginia and Louisiana that were under the control of the Union army. In fact, the proclamation would do little beyond what Congress had done in the Second Confiscation Act.

Douglass was in no way deceived that Lincoln's edict would actually break the chains of any slaves. He was saddened by the grudging way the president came to do what Douglass knew to be right; he had done the deed "like an ox under the yoke, or a Slave under the lash." Douglass noted that Lincoln had delayed for three months the effect of his proclamation, presumably still willing to leave slavery untouched if Southerners were willing to lay down their arms. And in his annual address to Congress on December 1 Lincoln gave every sign that he hoped to be excused from the obligation to fulfill his pledge.

Despite these reservations, Douglass told his readers that they would witness a momentous day on January 1. Lincoln could not go back on his word, and the Confederates would give him no excuse to back out. Once that edict took effect, the "national ship" would be swung around into "the trade winds of the Almighty." It could never turn back and live. The proclamation would add "four millions to the strength of the Union, . . . establish the moral power of Government," and kindle anew the enthusiasm of the friends of freedom. The war would be based at last on the defense of freedom over slavery—the only grounds on which it credited a people and a nation to struggle.

On the night of December 31 Douglass took part in a vigil at Tremont Temple in Boston. There were over three thousand in the audience awaiting official word from Washington. The old abolitionist crowd was there. There were speeches by Douglass, J. Sella Martin, the black preacher William Wells Brown, a fugitive from slavery, and Anna E. Dickinson, the women's rights advocate. It was well after ten at night before a man came through the crowd, yelling, "It is coming! It is on the wires!" The crowd erupted in cheers; there were prayers of thanksgiving, and the joyous celebration spent itself only with the dawn.

January 1863 was a month of jubilee celebrations for blacks across the country, and Douglass traveled over two thousand miles speaking at gatherings from Boston to Chicago. He reflected deeply on recent events; one of his first childhood questions had been why black people were slaves, and he had wondered if they would be forever. "From that day onward, the cry that has reached the most silent chambers of my soul, by day and by night has been How long! How long oh! Eternal Power of the Universe, how long shall these things be?" Now, it seemed, the handwriting was on the wall.

The use of black troops in the Union army followed the Emancipation Proclamation. The edict announcing that freed slaves would be received into the army was not clear how they would be used. Early in 1863 Congress passed a resolution authorizing the enrollment of blacks into the military service. . . .

For Douglass the martial role for blacks was crucial. If the war could be waged without regard to black men, slave and free, then there could be little argument about the justice of their oppression. He knew that only by black involvement could abolition become the chief war aim. The more blacks participated, shifting the balance, the more they could be certain of affecting their future.

He published his stirring editorial, "Men of Color to Arms," which was to be reprinted in newspapers throughout the North and used as a way to encourage recruitment. He urged black men to put aside their questions about the duplicity of the government and its tardiness in calling them. The time had come and black men must enlist: "Liberty won by white men would lose half its luster. 'Who would be free themselves must strike the blow.'" He called cowardly that cynicism which dismissed this as the "white man's war," which claimed that blacks would be "no better off after than before the war." This was the hour of black men, and they must act. "I am authorized to assure you," he wrote, "that you will receive the same wages, the same rations, the same protection, the same treatment, and the same bounty, secured to white soldiers." The entire reputation of the race rested upon the willingness of black men to take up arms. "The chance is now given you to end in a day the bondage of centuries, and to rise in one bound from social degradation to . . . common equality with all other varieties of men." He called to them in the spirit of the black insurrectionists who had given their lives for liberty: Denmark Vesey, Nat Turner. He did not forget Shields Green and John Copeland who had followed John Brown.

In March Douglass began a recruiting tour of western New York. His sons, Charles and Lewis, were among the first to join the Massachusetts 54th. But Northern black men were not automatic recruits; they could point to little in their experiences with white men and the government to give them confidence or a sense of loyalty. The decade of the 1850s followed by Lincoln's mean and grudging spirit had nearly shattered their morale as citizens. Douglass hammered away, nevertheless, at the necessity for them to act as citizens whatever others would have them be. Popular prejudice considered them cowardly and unmanly; manhood required them to serve in the army. White Americans would deny them citizenship; only by assuming the responsibility of citizens could they rightfully challenge that denial. The rights of black men were in question; learning the use of arms was the surest way to claim and defend their rights. Oppression and prejudice had undermined black men's self-respect; enlistment and martial valor would regain it. An army of black men, in the final analysis, would be the best guarantee against a "pro-slavery compromise at the end of the war." Douglass had fair success in his efforts. By the end of May, the all-black 54th Regiment sailed from Boston harbor for South Carolina.

Douglass found, as he continued his recruitment efforts, that he was more and more embarrassed by the disparity between his assurances to black men and the realities of their army service. . . . Black troops, when they were paid at all, were paid as laborers rather than as combat troops. They suffered insults and harassment at the hands of Union army officers and men. When captured by the Confederate army, they were treated as slaves and fugitives rather than as prisoners of war. They were denied honors they had earned, and they were not promoted into commissioned ranks.

From the beginning Douglass had warned that black troops would suffer annoyances: their mistakes amplified, and their successes ignored. But he had believed that their valor, despite these abuses, would triumph over both slavery in the South and prejudice in the North. He had not been prepared, however, for systematic discrimination, purposeful and official insult by the Union army and the government.

There came reports of Confederate atrocities against black soldiers, and the national government did nothing. The story was that Confederates refused to treat black troops by the conventions of war. Jefferson Davis had, on 23 December 1863, declared that slaves captured in arms would be treated as felons rather than as prisoners of war. Prisoners wounded in a battle had little chance of surviving, and others were likely to be sold into slavery rather than imprisoned. Word of massacres was everywhere to be heard. Some were untrue, but others, like the shooting of twenty noncombatant teamsters at Murfreesboro, were genuine. The horror stories multiplied with reports of new engagements in which blacks played a major role: Port Hudson, Milliken's Bend, Fort Wagner. Still there was not even a word of official protest from Washington. How different it had been when two white officers had been threatened with execution at Richmond; the national government promised to retaliate and nothing happened. For Douglass it was an old story, recalling to him his youth in slavery. The saying went: "Half a cent to kill a Negro and half a cent to bury him." In protest Douglass ended his recruitment efforts.

He informed Major G. L. Stearns, the man charged with recruiting blacks for the Massachusetts regiment, of his grievances. Stearns urged Douglass to go to Washington and lay his complaints before the president. Through Stearns an audience with Lincoln was arranged for early August.

Douglass could not have helped being awed by the momentous and symbolic character of his meeting with the president. Twenty-five years had passed since his escape from slavery; his beginnings in bondage remained sharply etched in his mind. His sense of personal obligation to those who remained in chains was never more keen than during the war years. As a free man he had been reminded at every turn that he and his people were despised by the vast majority of white Americans. Even this president, with whom he was to talk, had shown no sign that he did not share in that general contempt. And yet the audience with the president marked the distance he had traveled from servitude to public celebrity.

There was more here than pride of personal accomplishment, although there was that too. Douglass, from his first days as an antislavery speaker, understood himself to be—both in his own view and that of those who looked on—a representative of his people. Representative, not in his being a typical black man or a spokesman for a cause, but in that his very person and life symbolized the black American inspiring respect. Thus, his meeting with Lincoln was fraught with meaning far beyond the specifics of their discussion.

Any apprehension he may have had about how he would be received was quickly put to rest. He was admitted at once on presenting his card. Lincoln rose to greet him, shook his hand, and put him at his ease. He was direct and frank with Douglass, but in every way treated him with respect. The president was neither officious, patronizing nor condescending; that went a long way with Douglass. "Honest" was the word that came to his mind to describe the president. Thus, he found some satisfaction in an interview which on every other score was disappointing.

Douglass urged three matters on the president. Black soldiers should receive the same pay and bounties as white soldiers. The government should protect black soldiers as readily as whites; they should be exchanged as prisoners the same as others, and protected from inhuman treatment; and the United States government should promise to retaliate the murder of captured black soldiers. Finally, he asked that distinguished and valorous service by black soldiers be rewarded as with white soldiers and that promotions, including commissions, go to those so deserving.

Lincoln answered that the use of black soldiers had not been a popular move, that unequal pay seemed to him a necessary concession to smooth the way over popular prejudice. In time, he promised, the pay would be equal. In any case, he argued, black people had more to gain from their service in the army than others and might be content to suffer for a time a difference in pay. He confessed that he did not know what to do about Confederate treatment of black soldiers. While he deplored their policy, he could not bring himself to the kind of retaliation that would arbitrarily hang some Confederate soldier who was at hand for the deeds of those out of reach. He did promise, however, to sign any commission recommended by Secretary of War Edwin M. Stanton.

Lincoln gave no ground in the interview. Even on the matter of commissions he had not said that he would instruct the War Department to commission black officers. . . . Lincoln had no intention of standing in advance of what he thought to be white public opinion on race. But Douglass came away satisfied with the character of the man, his honesty and humanity. Douglass's faith in what he called the "educating tendency" of the war, that events would pull Lincoln and the nation further than they dreamt of going, persuaded him to take up once again his recruiting efforts.

There were, in fact, some tangible changes. On July 30 Lincoln issued an order stating that for every Union prisoner killed in violation of the rules of war, a Confederate prisoner would be similarly executed; and for every Union soldier enslaved or sold into slavery, a Confederate soldier would be put to hard labor. He had been slow to act, but he acted. Douglass, before the December meeting of the American Anti-Slavery Society, quoted the president as saying: "remember that Milliken's Bend, Port Hudson, and Fort Wagner are recent events; and that these were necessary to prepare the way for this very proclamation of mine." Lincoln may not have been willing to engage in the fact of retaliation, but he seemed ready to use the threat of it; this mollified Douglass and other black men. . . .

By the end of the war some 200,000 black men had served in the Union army and navy. Whatever Lincoln's words to Douglass meant, very few of them became officers during the war. General Benjamin Butler had commissioned seventy-five in the three regiments he raised in 1862, but most of them were replaced by white men under General Nathaniel P. Banks. At the end of the war, six sergeants of the Massachusetts 54th and 55th Regiments were promoted to lieutenant. An indepenent Kansas light-artillery battery had three black officers. Eight black surgeons were commissioned as majors, and in February 1865 Martin R. Delany was commissioned Major of Infantry and ordered to recruit an *"armée d'Afrique"* in South Carolina. Excluding chaplains, not more than one hundred blacks received commissions during the war.

Throughout the war, Douglass was deeply torn. He saw the administration as inclined to hedge on principles having to do with black people. Failing the press of expediency, Douglass knew that blacks would be left high and dry by Lincoln and his government. Yet Lincoln was all they had, and Douglass knew he was better than many they might have. At least he seemed to have a personal integrity. Douglass remained persuaded that the events of history had a way of carrying men beyond themselves. The war was an opportunity for black men to shape its aims and determine their future as well. Shakespeare's words came to his mind, and he never tired of quoting them:

> There is a tide in the affairs of men,
> Which, taken at the flood, leads on to fortune.

He stressed to his audience what to him was the real message of these words:

> We must take the current when it serves
> Or lose our ventures.

Thus, he was circumspect in his criticism of the Lincoln administration lest his words reinforce the cynicism of alienated black men. Understandably, many wondered how they would profit from serving a Union whose most fervent hope was to be a white man's country.

Cautious as he was, he could have no illusions. . . . With 1863 coming to an end, the unexpected length of the war and its awful cost began to take its toll on Northern white sentiment. There was every reason to fear that the government and the people lacked the resoluteness to finish a war to end slavery if some accommodation short of that could be found. As Douglass saw it, only the steadfastness of the Confederacy kept the war going at all. If exhaustion opened them to compromise, the cause of the black people would be cast aside. . . .

He could understand the impatience and gloom that pervaded the North. What had been predicted to be a ninety-day war was going into its third year. The human cost had mounted to over 200,000, the debt incurred by the war was like "a mountain of gold to weight down the necks of our children's children." But the fearful thing was that the public might rush to a peace of accommodation leaving fundamental issues untouched, setting the stage for resumption of conflict at a later time.

It was no surprise to him that Democratic party members, now calling themselves men of peace, were charging the Republicans with conducting an abolitionist war. To Douglass's chagrin, the Republicans found this embarrassing. The Democrats, he charged, had for thirty years supported slavery: in the war with Mexico, in the annexation of Texas, in the Fugitive Slave Law. They found no principle in the right of *habeas corpus* when it came to fugitive slaves, or in states' rights when it came to personal liberty laws, but they supported such principles in the cause of the Confederacy and its Northern sympathizers. To Douglass, the Democrats' call for peace was treason pure and simple. Yet, the Democrats' subversion troubled him less than the Republican's duplicity and irresolution: "We have much less to fear from the bold and shameless wickedness of the one than from the timid and short-sighted policy of the other."

The truly loyal man, in Douglass's view, had to take an uncompromising stand on four points: that the aim of the war was the abolition of slavery; that there would be "consent to no peace, which shall not be . . . an Abolition peace"; that everyone in the country be entitled to the same rights, protection, and opportunities; and, since the white race should have "nothing to fear from fair competition with the black race," that black men should be invested "with the right to vote and to be voted for."

As yet neither Lincoln nor the Republicans had come to accept even the first two planks of this platform, and Douglass must have known that even his abolitionist friends would shrink from putting their support behind the third and fourth. To his mind, Lincoln's public statements were in no way different from those of the late Stephen Douglas, who expressed indifference if slavery were voted up or down. Yet it was a deception to fancy the reestablishment of the Union, for "that old Union . . . we shall never see again while the world standeth."

The war had to be fought for a new kind of national unity, not shamed by slavery, not belying the Declaration of Independence, in which patriotism would not conflict with justice and liberty, in which sections and sectional interests would be erased.

The new nation he envisioned would transform the South so that the "New England schoolhouse" takes the place of "the Southern whipping-post." We want a country, he said, "in which no man shall be fined for reading a book, or imprisoned for selling a book . . . where no man may be imprisoned or flogged or sold for learning to read, or teaching a fellow mortal how to read"; that liberty, freedom, and national unity had to be the object of the war or else it would be little better than a "gigantic enterprise for shedding human blood."

The war, he thought, might be a part of the nation's Manifest Destiny, forcing a reorganization and a unification of the country's institutions into a true national unity; not a union but a nation. He felt a divine energy at work, for it was only as the government took its grudging steps in the direction of liberty had "the war prospered and the Rebellion lost ground." Humanity and justice did not win at each moment; they were often overpowered. But "they are persistent and eternal forces" against which it was fearful to contend. They constituted a force in nature, and the rulers had only to "place the Government fully within these trade winds of Omnipotence," and the Confederacy would be doomed.

Antislavery work was never more needed. "The day that shall see the Rebels at our feet," he said, "will be the day of trial." The moral character of the nation would then be tested, and it would prove true to its calling only if it held firm on the esssential issues: "No war but an Abolition war; no peace but an Abolition peace; liberty for all, chains for none; the black man a soldier in war, a laborer in peace; a voter in the South as well as in the North; America his permanent home, and all Americans his fellow-countrymen."

With such a sense of the "Mission of the War," Abraham Lincoln's policies continued to trouble Douglass. Early in 1864 his discontent with the president was most intense. He wrote to English friends hoping they would help expose from abroad the shame and *"the swindle"* of the government's abolitionism. The administration's policy remained to *"do evil by choice, right by necessity."* Lincoln, he noted, was presently to pocket veto the Wade-Davis Bill, which would have restricted the organization of Southern state governments to those with a "loyal majority." The president preferred his own plan which called for only ten percent. Douglass warned his English friends that Lincoln had no intention of extending the franchise to blacks in the South. He thought it dishonorable to invest rebels with political power and hold it from those loyal to the government: "To hand the Negro back to the political power of his master." . . .

The gloom in Washington was thick [in the summer of 1864]. There was no sign that the Confederacy was weakening. Indeed, the Capitol had been shaken by Jubal Early's thrust at Washington which brought confederate troops almost within sight. With it all, the administration was facing a national election which might well turn the Republicans out.

Earlier, Frederick Douglass had given his support to a call by radical Republicans and abolitionists for a convention to oppose the renomination of Abraham Lincoln. The convention met on May 31 in Cleveland, nominating John C. Frémont for president and John Cochrane, a nephew of Gerrit Smith, for vice president. The platform called for the uncompromised prosecution of the war, a constitutional amendment to prohibit slavery, a one-term presidency, postwar reconstruction by Congress rather than the executive, and the confiscation of confederate lands to be redistributed to loyal soldiers and actual settlers.

On 8 June 1864 the Republicans, under the name of the National Union Party, met in Baltimore. They nominated Lincoln to stand for reelection and Andrew Johnson, the War Democrat from Tennessee, for vice president. There was no great enthusiasm for Lincoln, but the party had little alternative. The platform and public statements from the convention carefully disassociated the party from any identification with abolitionists or the cause of black Americans. . . .

Throughout August it seemed there would be a Democratic victory. Indeed, Lincoln wrote a formal memorandum outlining his proposed role during the interim between the election and the inauguration in the event of a Democratic victory at the polls. But in early September the tide of war turned clearly in the Union's favor. Atlanta fell to General Sherman on September 3, giving Lincoln the military victory he sorely needed. He was reelected handily.

After the election Douglass again took up the lecture circuit. Now, with the collapse of the Confederacy imminent, he could extend his tour into regions he never before dared go. He went into Virginia for the first time, and he gave six lectures in Baltimore. This "homecoming" was a personal triumph to Douglass as a free man of stature and repute. His visit was also the occasion of an emotional reunion with his half-sister, Eliza, who in the thirty years since last he saw her had managed to buy her freedom along with that of her nine children.

Abraham Lincoln was assassinated on April 15. Frederick Douglass was among those to eulogize him. Most black Americans had come to look upon him as a great president and a friend to black people. However far that was from the truth, and however grudgingly he moved to support the interests of Afro-Americans, they would join in his celebration as the Great Emancipator.

Douglass, of course, knew better. He had been one of the president's severest critics while he lived. He knew that Lincoln did very little for Afro-Americans, slave or free, and that what he did was grudging, calculated, and expedient. He may well have become educated to a more generous view of Afro-Americans had he lived, and Douglass would not be wrong in seeing himself as the president's educator. But surely Douglass would have preferred several other men to Lincoln. And he knew that had the president lived to serve out his term, there would be nothing in his program of reconstruction to applaud. Lincoln would not have been an advocate of suffrage for the freedman or any other major reform in the South. Chances were that he would continue flirting with colonization schemes or encourage plans to make freedmen wards of the community.

Yet, Douglass eulogized him, attributing to the dead president qualities which he had found lacking in the living one. And Douglass was not alone. As a martyr Lincoln could be a more effective reformer than he would have been in life. If one could identify him with the cause of freedom and justice for the black man, one could go a long way toward claiming principles in his name which he would hardly have staked his life or career on.

In the spring of 1865 Frederick Douglass played his part in the creation of the Lincoln myth. As is so often the case with myths, this one came to have more vitality than the real man. In time Douglass came to forget there was a difference.

QUESTIONS FOR DISCUSSION

1. Why did Douglass believe it so important that blacks take part in the war?

2. What do you think were the root causes of Lincoln's reluctance to free the slaves?

3. Why did Douglass, "one of the president's severest critics while he lived," eulogize him after death and, in so doing, contribute to the building of the Lincoln myth?

T. HARRY WILLIAMS

Fighting the Civil War

"The Civil War," as T. Harry Williams tells us in the following selection, "was a great dramatic experience and a searing national tragedy." It was also a "pivotal event" in the history of the American people. The outcome of the war—and the events that transpired during it—"determined to a large extent the direction the nation would take in the future."

This was a war whose outcome was decided not only by soldiers and their generals, but by the men and women who produced and transported the weapons and supplies that sustained the armies in the field. The war pitted army against army, industry against industry, and railroad against railroad. In the end, it was the North's material advantages in industry and transportation facilities, as well as its superior reserves of manpower, that spelled the difference between victory and defeat.

The Civil War was the first American war in which the government had to resort to national conscription to raise mass armies. Though thousands of young men voluntarily enlisted in the armies and state militias at the outbreak of hostilities, their numbers—and the length of their enlistments—were not at all sufficient to fight the war to its conclusion, especially as that conclusion, to the surprise of so many on both sides, would not be reached until almost four years had passed and more than 600,000 lives lost.

No other American conflict—indeed, no other episode in our history—has so gripped the popular imagination as has the Civil War, the struggle between the United States and the Confederate States, the North and the South. It is the most written about, read about, and known about of all our wars.

T. Harry Williams died in 1979 while he was completing work on *The History of American Wars,* from which the following excerpt has been taken. Williams taught history at Louisiana State University for many years and was the author of several books, including *Lincoln and his Generals* and *Huey Long,* the winner of the Pulitzer Prize and National Book Award in 1970.

From *The History of American Wars: From 1745 to 1918,* by T. Harry Williams, pp. 199-218, 219-227, 245–259. Copyright © 1981 by T. H. W. Inc. Reprinted by permission of Alfred A. Knopf, Inc.

The reasons for the war's enduring hold have been speculated on by many observers, including some who have admitted its fascination even while lamenting the national preoccupation with it. Critics have suggested that this war prompts attention merely because its story possesses unusual human interest and rare drama, and without conceding to their opinion, it must be said that the conflict had these qualities. It offers the reader an unparalleled cast of military characters—heroes and greats, might-have-been greats, and failures. It also offers speculative suspense—fateful battles that either side might have won, when, in contrast to later wars, men rather than machines clearly controlled the fighting.

More perceptive commentators have conjectured that the war has the attraction of a great tragedy. For the first and only time in their history Americans were unable to resolve differences between themselves through the normal political process and resorted to four years of bloody war. In this view the Civil War represents a national failure. It is a crimson gash across the success story that is American history, an episode that should not have happened, that "strange and sad war" in the memorable phrase of the poet Walt Whitman.

The Civil War *was* a great dramatic experience and a searing national tragedy. But drama and pathos in themselves would never have ensured the place it has obtained in the public consciousness. There is something more. The American people, with a sound instinct, have sensed that this war was the pivotal event in their history. It determined to a large extent the direction the nation would take in the future. One of the war's results, the abolition of slavery, settled an issue that had brought on the conflict but left a new problem, the place of the black race in American society, to be dealt with by later generations. But the political result was never questioned after 1865: it was decided forever that the Union was indivisible. Even the defeated side accepted the verdict, an outcome that has not always occurred after civil struggles. Indeed, the ties of union were strengthened by the war, a development that intrigued a former Confederate general. Contemplating in the early 1900s the nation that had emerged from the war, Edward Porter Alexander was led to write: "Its bonds were not formed by peaceable agreements in conventions, but were forged in the white heat of battles, in a war fought out to the bitter end, and are for eternity."

Previous conflicts had only minor effects on the structure of American society. Afterward, the position of the United States might be more secure vis-à-vis other nations or its pride or boundaries might be enlarged, but the basic social institutions remained essentially the same as before the war. The Civil War, however, compelled change in important areas of national life and left in its wake altered or new institutions.

The war forced change through its dimensions. The first big American war, it was also the first big American undertaking of any kind. The people of the United States, at least those of the majority North and to a lesser extent those of the minority South, were called on to do something that had never been required of them before—to put forth a supreme effort to achieve an objective so precious that every resource had to be employed and every obstacle had to be overcome. In the North the object was to maintain intact the Union, the great American experiment in popular government, which when threatened with destruction suddenly assumed hitherto unexpressed values, both mystical and material, in the minds of men. To preserve the Union, the Northern people would submit to controls from the central government that prior to the war they would have considered abhorrent—if they had even conceived that such restraints could exist.

Before the war the average citizen was, of course, conscious that a government existed in Washington, but he was unlikely ever to feel its hand as he went about his everyday activities. He paid no taxes to the government, because it did not have to levy general duties to sustain its modest functions; it could derive what revenue it needed by selling public lands or collecting import tariffs, exactions that affected only a small portion of the population. He handled little national currency, except coins, because the government issued hardly any paper notes of its own; most money consisted of notes put out by state banks. He could pass a lifetime without encountering directly the force of a federal law or even seeing a federal enforcement official, because only a few national laws applied to the ordinary citizen and only a small number of federal employees were retained to administer these laws. The absence of centralism in the political system was reflected in the social system. American society, viewed as a whole, was loosely and locally organized; its institutions were characterized by an absence of mass and a lack of shape.

The amorphous structure was ill fitted to conduct a great war or, indeed, any large undertaking, and under the strains of the Civil War its institutions and organization underwent important changes. In each section, or nation, the principal agent of change was the central government, but the men in that government were themselves often only the agents of forces beyond their control, of the implacable demands of the war. Thus the two presidents, Abraham Lincoln in the North and Jefferson Davis in the South, at times proposed measures they did not wish to advance but that seemed necessary to victory. The Civil War revealed a significant and an ominous truth about great wars—like the even more encompassing world conflicts of the twentieth century, it enforced its own conditions on the human beings who thought they could direct it.

The most important change caused by the war was a greater concentration of power in government. In both sections it was realized that this struggle would require a more centralized direction than had been necessary in previous conflicts, nothing less than a mobilization of mass endeavor to attain a mass result, and the central governments almost immediately gathered large new powers unto themselves. The Northern government was more successful in this centralization than was the Southern, and some of the accretions of authority were retained even after the nation was reunited in 1865. . . .

By far the most striking exercise of central power, and to many people in both sections a frightening exercise, evolved out of the need of the rival governments to raise mass armies. Each government initially assumed it could enlist adequate forces by calling for volunteers, the traditional American method of mobilization, and in the first year of the war, when martial enthusiasm ran high and the war promised to be a short and glorious one, volunteering did serve to fill the ranks. But soon enlistments dwindled, and it became evident that the volunteer system would not provide the mass armies the war was going to require. Forced by the manpower crisis to act drastically, both governments resorted to conscription, the Confederate States in 1862 and the United States a year later—the first time in an American war that national conscription was employed. Although the draft was accepted in both sections, its enforcement was a wrenching experience to people who had hardly known the authority of government; it seemed wrong for the hand of government to reach into a community, pick up a young man, and dress him in uniform. Almost as alarming was the action of both administrations in suspending civil law and placing opponents of the war under military arrest. The American people were learning a hard fact about war, that if its stakes are great enough, customary liberties have to be sacrificed to maintain national existence. . . .

Historians of the Civil War are often criticized, sometimes with justice, for exaggerating the importance of the conflict. Perhaps most controversial is their claim that the struggle was the first of the modern wars. However, these historians are trying seriously to view the Civil War from other than a domestic perspective, to place it against the backdrop of general military history. Specifically, they regard it as a harbinger of the greater conflicts of the twentieth century, the two world wars.

The Civil War seems modern because many of the features that distinguish modern wars initially appeared in it. It was the first conflict in which the massive productive capacities of the Industrial Revolution were placed at the disposal of the military machine. It witnessed the first prominent use of mass production of goods to sustain mass armies, mass transportation on railroads, and telegraphic communication between different theaters and on the battlefield. It saw also the first use of such devices of the future as armored warships, breech-loading and repeating rifles, rifled artillery, land and sea mines, submarines, balloons, precursors of the machine gun, and trench warfare. It is true that some of the innovations had appeared in previous wars. The government of Revolutionary France, for one example, had raised mass armies, and some of the "new" weapons had been employed in earlier conflicts. Nevertheless, the fact remains that in no previous war had so many of the methods and weapons made possible by modern industry been so apparent. In its material manifestations alone, in its application of the resources of technology to the business of killing, the Civil War presaged the later world wars.

The Civil War also antedated the twentieth century in a more important way, in the spirit in which it was fought. This was not a struggle to induce another nation to recognize a maritime right or cede a border territory, as were the War of 1812 and the Mexican War. The Civil War was a war of ideas, the North standing for nationalism and, later, for emancipation, and the South for local-ism and slavery. Because it involved great and emotional ideals, it was a war of unlimited objectives. The North was aiming to restore the Union by force; the South was trying to establish its own independence by force. Between these purposes there could be no compromise, no partial triumph for either side. One or the other had to achieve a complete victory.

The totality of these objectives led some historians to call the Civil War a total war. The label is somewhat exaggerated, as neither side put forward the absolute effort required of many nations in World War I or World War II. Citizens were conscripted and industry was encouraged to shift to war produc-tion, but this was not the complete mobilization of resources that characterizes total war. Still, the Civil War missed totality by but a narrow margin. It became a rough and ruthless war, involving in its lethal path the civilian populations, especially those in the South. Because new and deadlier weapons were avail-able, it was more destructive of lives and property than any previous American war. If it was not the first modern war, it was ominously prophetic. . . .

Some modern Civil War scholars have marveled that Southerners ever thought they could prevail against an adversary so superior in material re-sources. Looking at the indicators of physical strength in the two sections, these historians have concluded that the Southern venture in independence was conceived in reckless disregard of reality and was foreordained to fail.

The supporters of this interpretation overlook an important fact, that the Confederacy, for all the odds against it, was able to carry on the struggle for four years. But there is a measure of logic in their argument. All the great material advantages were on the side of the United States, or the North, and these advantages did influence the outcome of the war. This material superi-ority was apparent as the war began and became more obvious and more important the longer it continued.

First of all, the North had a substantial advantage in population and hence a large manpower reservoir from which to draw its armed forces. The twenty-three "loyal" states had a population of over 21 million, whereas the popula-tion of the eleven Confederate states was but 9 million. However, these totals give a somewhat misleading impression of the relative strength of the two sections. The Northern aggregate included over half a million people in the Pacific coast states, an area too distant from the conflict to provide a direct contribution to the military effort, and the inhabitants of the four loyal slave states, which sent thousands of recruits to the Confederate armies. On the other side, the total Confederate population included over 800,000 in Tennes-see, whose eastern mountains contained a pro-Union population, and an in-determinable number of Union partisans in the mountain areas of other states where slavery was almost unknown. Complicating the problem of evaluating Confederate strength was the presence in the Southern population of over 3 million slaves, so that the white, or military, population was less than 6 million.

If the slaves are counted in the Southern total, the Confederacy faced human odds of more than two to one. If the slaves are subtracted, the odds were almost four to one.

However the disparity is calculated, it is evident that the North enjoyed a substantial advantage in manpower. But the South was able to offset its inferiority in total numbers by making real, if indirect, use of its slave population. Not only did slaves serve as military laborers and in other capacities in the armed forces, but by their assured presence as agricultural laborers they freed a large number of white men for military service. Morever, the South mobilized its forces somewhat more quickly than the North, and until 1863 maintained armies that were not appreciably smaller than those of the North. It is true that after 1863 Northern armies increased in size while Southern forces decreased, but until that time the Confederates possessed such strength that they might conceivably have won a decision on the field. Finally, at all stages of the conflict the North had to divert large portions of its armies to the maintenance of long lines of communication in the invaded South and to the garrisoning of occupied areas. Preponderance of numbers in itself has never guaranteed victory in war, especially if the superior side must invade and hold a large hostile area—as witness the failure of Britain to conquer the American colonies.

More marked than the North's edge in manpower was the superior potential of its economy to provide the matériel of war. In the North were 81 percent of the nation's factories and 67 percent of the farms. Even this overwhelming preponderance does not convey an adequate appreciation of the South's backwardness in production. The great majority of the region's factories were small establishments, actually not factories but shops, the average plant representing a modest capital investment and employing but a few workers; more serious, the typical factory was not mechanized but relied on hand labor, which had a limited productive capacity. In contrast, the more numerous Northern factories were, usually, larger in capital investment, in number of workers employed, and in annual value of products. But the most important difference between the rival industrial systems was that the larger Northern plants had installed labor-saving equipment that increased vastly their productive potential. Machines, such as the reaper, drill, and thresher, were also in use on Northern farms; such devices were unknown in Southern agriculture.

The importance of the North's greater economic potential was soon apparent. During the first year of the war both sides had to purchase arms and other supplies in Europe, but by 1862 the Northern industrial system had converted to producing war goods, and after that year Northern reliance on Europe practically ceased. The South, in contrast, never achieved self-sufficiency. Although the Confederacy's industrial capacity was expanded, it was not able to provide its armies with anything like the amount and variety of goods they required, and was even less able to satisfy the wants of the civilian population for consumer goods. For every step forward the South took in production, the North took several that were much longer.

Few persons in either section in 1861 foresaw the role that Northern industry would play in the war. One who did was former army officer William T. Sherman, later to become a Northern general. Sherman warned a Southern friend: "You are rushing into war with one of the most powerful, ingeniously mechanical and determined peoples on earth—right at your door. You are bound to fail." There was some exaggeration in his prediction but much truth. Economic inferiority alone did not doom the South to defeat, any more than did inferiority in size of population. But inadequacy did contribute mightily to the eventual result and was a major reason for the Confederate downfall. After 1863 Southern morale sagged badly from the realization that the South faced a foe with apparently limitless resources.

Still another advantage possessed by the North was its transportation facilities, superior in every way to those of the South. The North had more and better inland-water transport, in the form of steamboats and barges, and more surfaced roads and wagons and animals. But the North's greatest advantage lay in its railroads, which had become the dominant form of transportation in the country before the war. The North had over 20,000 miles of railroads, whereas the South, comprising at least as large a land area, had but slightly more than 9,000 miles. However, the superiority of the Northern system was even more marked than the trackage totals indicate. Many of the Northern lines had been built by big companies and were "through" roads, providing continuous connections between distant points. In contrast, the Southern roads had largely been constructed by small concerns and were short lines; a railroad map of the region reveals long gaps between key places. The few through lines that existed, like the connection between Richmond and Memphis and that between Richmond and the Carolinas, ran close to the land border or the sea and were highly vulnerable to Northern raiders.

Both rail systems performed prodigious feats during the war, especially in moving troops vast distances from one theater to another. The Northern network was able to bear easily the burden placed upon it; rolling stock that became unusable was quickly replaced, the total trackage was even extended somewhat. But the Southern system gradually broke down under the unusual strains and by 1864 was almost in a state of collapse. Locomotives, freight cars, and rails simply deteriorated and became unusable; other stock was destroyed or damaged by Northern raiders. None of the equipment could be replaced. Before the war Southern roads purchased their rolling stock from Northern factories or from the few large Southern ironworks that cast rail supplies. The war cut off the Northern source and diverted the Southern source; Southern iron plants turned to producing armaments and did not make a single car during the war.

The prostration of the rail system affected the Confederacy's war-making ability in several adverse ways. During the last half of the war it became increasingly difficult to move large bodies of troops any distance by rail, even to shift men within one theater. Equally serious, it became harder to transport food and other bulk supplies from producing centers to the armies or to the cities and towns that depended on outside sources for sustenance. The problem of feeding soldiers and civilians became especially acute the longer the war continued. Agricultural production declined as Federal forces occupied or devastated large areas and as thousands of slaves deserted the plantations and farms to flock into the camps of the invaders. But despite the drop, the South up to near the end was probably producing enough food to meet its minimum wants. Often, however, the provender could not be carried by the railroads to where it was needed, so hunger afflicted the armies and large sections of the civilian population. Although the privation was severe, its effect was more psychological than physical, intensifying the mood of hopelessness that grew on the populace after 1863. The collapse of the railroad system was not a decisive factor in causing Confederate defeat, but it was an important force in weakening the Confederate will to fight.

A final advantage enjoyed by the North was its preponderant sea power. At the beginning of the war the United States Navy numbered some 90 ships of all types, not all of them serviceable, and a personnel of 9,000, a small force compared to the squadrons of the larger European powers and inadequate to perform the task first demanded of it, to blockade the long Southern coast. However, rapid expansion converted the navy into one of the major sea forces of the world and enabled it to play a major part in the conflict—by 1864 it numbered approximately 670 ships of all types and boasted a service of over 50,000 men. The Confederacy had no navy, but it set out immediately to build one. It was never able to match the North's superior construction facilities, however, being able to put together but about 130 vessels that enlisted a personnel of only 4,000 men or so, and Northern sea power remained dominant throughout the war.

The Northern navy performed two important strategic functions. First, it attempted to seal off the Confederacy from intercourse with the outside world. The effect of this effort has been questioned by some historians, who have pointed out that a large number of vessels slipped in and out of the blockade. There can be no doubt that the blockade was "leaky"; it was impossible to close off completely the extensive coastline. However, most of the ships entering Southern ports were small craft that rarely carried heavy equipment like armaments and that often brought in luxury items to dipose of at a high profit. And fewer and fewer of these vessels got through as the navy became ever stronger and was able to tighten its stranglehold. The consequence of its labor has been stated aptly by historian D. P. Crook: "The blockade forced the Confederacy to breathe through a constricted windpipe, and the effort became more debilitating with time."

Northern naval power also supported Federal land forces operating in the Western theater, the region between the Appalachian Mountains and the Mississippi River. In this area the invading Federals advanced along the larger rivers, which were navigable to small ships of war and transport vessels, and the navy moved with the army, carrying supplies and joining in attacks on Confederate strongpoints. The combined assaults were the first large amphibious operations in American military history and represented a new degree of cooperation between the land and sea services.

The sheer weight of Northern material superiority has persuaded observers that the result of the war was inevitable. The odds against the South were indeed great, but not so preponderant as to render the cause of the Confederacy hopeless. As previously indicated, Confederate armies might have achieved such decisive victories before 1863 as to force recognition of Southern independence—if fortune had shifted her favor on one field or another. Even without a smashing military success, the Confederacy might have secured its policy goal simply by tiring the North out, by convincing the enemy that it could not be conquered. The South was fighting for something concrete, something easy for its people to support. It wanted only to be independent; it had no aggressive designs on the North. For its part, the North was fighting for an abstract principle, to maintain the Union, and this was a goal the North could abandon without incurring direct harm. The United States could have peace and still be independent by simply quitting the war. That the Northern citizenry did not succumb to this temptation can be ascribed to several factors—to the fact that the military situation never seemed to be completely hopeless, to the leadership of President Lincoln, but primarily to its own determination to see the war out.

At the start of hostilities the majority of ordinary folk in both sections, and most of the leaders, thought the war would not last long. One big successful battle would convince the other side that it was beaten, the predictions ran, and the war would be over within a year or even less. These cocksure opinions sprang in part from American memories of the short Mexican War but fundamentally from the feeling of superiority that each section had developed about itself, or from the converse of this, the conviction each one held that the other was inferior and hence would be an easy victim. Thus, in the North many observers forecast that the "rebels" would be whipped "before the next cotton crop," and in New York City men were knocked down in the streets for merely suggesting that Southerners might fight well. In the South, where the conditions of plantation culture encouraged men to think of themselves as knights without peer, confidence in the result was even higher, and more unreal. Southerners dismissed as unimportant the North's greater resources, particularly its ability to raise more troops; those "popinjays" and "scurvy fellows" of the cities could not possibly be a match for the "hot blooded, thoroughbred, impetuous men" of the Confederacy. "Let them come South and we will put our negroes to the dirty work of killing them," one newspaper trumpeted.

More thoughtful men in both sections did not indulge in these fantasies. The two presidents especially, Lincoln and Davis, realized that the war was likely to be a long and hard-fought struggle, and their concern was reflected in the manpower policies they recommended to their respective congresses. Lincoln after Fort Sumter called on the states to provide 75,000 militia for three months' service, the maximum period allowed under existing law. His action was intended as only a symbolic assertion of the purpose of the government to uphold the Union. He knew the militia could not be utilized in a long war, but with Congress not in session he decided to summon every force available to him. In his determination he employed even a power denied to him by the Constitution, the stipulation that only Congress can augment the size of the armed forces. By proclamation he authorized an increase of 23,000 men in the regular army and the enlistment of 42,000 volunteers for three years. He asked Congress to legalize his acts when it convened in regular session in July and further induced it to provide him authority to raise a total of 500,000 volunteers for three years' service. Because of Lincoln's insistence the North was off to a good start. It had called into being a large force that could be held under arms for a significant period of time, and avoided the error of creating a short-term army for a short war. Undoubtedly the great majority of congressmen who accepted the president's recommendation believed that the conflict would take much less than three years.

President Davis was not so fortunate in dealing with his Congress. Although he earnestly and frequently warned that the war would be a long one, not many heard him. The first military legislation enacted by the Confederate Congress provided for enlistment of only 100,000 men, for a service of twelve months. Later laws authorized Davis to accept up to 500,000 volunteers for terms of not less than one year or more than three years, and as many as would volunteer for the duration. But the damage was already done. Over 300,000 came forward in 1861, as contrasted with 600,000 in the North, but at least one-third and possibly two-thirds of them enrolled under the twelve-month law and were slated for discharge in the spring of 1862.

Both governments thus appreciated that this war was going to be more encompassing than any previous American conflict; nothing like these hosts had been contemplated in earlier struggles. But in choosing a method to mobilize troops they were not so realistic. Both administrations assumed that they could raise and then maintain armies of sufficient size by calling for volunteers, the traditional way of creating a fighting force, but one that had been developed for smaller wars. The volunteer system turned out enough men in 1861, when martial enthusiasm and expectations of a brief war ran high in both sections, but as 1862 dawned, much of the earlier ardor was fading. Now the signs were obvious that the war was going to be a long, hard struggle. Volunteering fell off badly in both sections, but the decline affected more adversely the Confederacy, the side with the smaller manpower resources.

As the spring of 1862 approached, the Confederacy seemed threatened by a dissolution of its armies, and this in the face of expected large Northern offensives. Despite urgent appeals from Richmond, few volunteers were coming forward to augment the ranks or to replace men who were leaving. And many were threatening to depart. The twelve-month men, trained and battle–hardened veterans, showed little disposition to reenlist. Their attitude was that they had done their bit—and now they would go home and rest for a time while others took up the burden. Where to find the "others" was the problem that worried the government.

The Confederacy met the crisis with bold action. At Davis's recommendations, Congress enacted in April a measure imposing conscription on the white male population, the First Conscription Act, the numbered title being applied later to distinguish it from subsequent draft laws. The act declared that all able-bodied white males between the ages of eighteen and thirty-five were liable to military service for three years and would be called up at the will of the central authority. In an equal assertion of power, designed to retain veterans in service, the measure decreed that men already in the army were to continue for three years from the date of their enlistment, getting credit for one year but having to serve two more. As the war continued, Congress enacted two additional draft bills, each a response to a worsening manpower situation. The Second Conscription Act (September, 1862) extended the upper age of men liable to service to forty-five years. The Third Conscription Act (February, 1864) fixed the lower and upper age limits at seventeen and fifty. In its desperation the Confederacy was said to be reaching toward "the cradle and the grave."

With its larger manpower resources, the North was able to maintain its armies by relying on volunteers longer than its adversary. But by the latter part of 1862 Washington was also having difficulty in inducing sufficient men to come forward, and the president and legislative leaders began to consider that conscription might be necessary. However, action was slow in coming; not until March, 1863, did Congress finally enact a draft measure. Entitled the Enrollment Act, it declared that all able-bodied males between the ages of twenty and forty-five if unmarried, and between twenty and thirty-five if married, were liable to be called up for service for three years. Ironically, in view of the differing constitutional traditions of the two sections, the Northern law did not provide for as great an exertion of national authority as did its Southern counterpart of the previous year. It did not actually impose a direct draft but held forth the threat of conscription in order to stimulate enlistments. Each state was divided into enrollment districts and at a call for troops was assigned a quota of men to be raised based on its population. If a state or a district could fill its quota, by offering cash bounties or through other appeals, it escaped the draft completely. If the quota was not met, the government stepped in to draft enough men to make up the difference. The state naturally exercised great efforts to avoid the necessity for national interposition, and some states and many districts went through the war without ever seeing conscription agents.

The men in the two governments who drew the draft laws were attempting to provide a method of mobilization without benefit of precedents from the American past. Conscription had been employed in colonial times to maintain the militia, it is true, but then it had been invoked by local governments and in wars that forced men into service for only very limited periods of time. For the kind of conflict the Civil War was becoming, the modest practices of the colonial era offered little direction, and needing a model, legislators turned to the laws of European nations with long experience with conscription. They took from these measures the principal provisions of their own acts and also the European usage of exempting some men from service, a procedure that was partly favoritism to the richer classes but also recognition of the fact that some citizens had to be held out of uniform to perform vital functions on the home front.

The Northern conscription act, because it was intended to work indirectly, allowed few exemptions, occupational or any other kind. Ranking national and state officials and clergymen could claim deferment, and so also could a son of a dependent widow or of dependent parents. However, it was possible to escape service by purchasing exemption. A man who was called up could hire a substitute to go in his place, or, if he did not feel such an urgent rush of patriotism, could remain at home simply by paying the government a "commutation" fee of $300.

In contrast, the several Confederate draft laws provided numerous exemptions. A conscripted Southerner could escape service by employing a substitute. But, unlike a similarly situated Northerner, he could not get off by paying a cash commutation. The fee in the North set a maximum top price on substitutes, but the Southern law had no such brake, so the price demanded by proxies mounted ever higher as the war continued, reflecting both a decreasing pool of manpower and an increasing supply of depreciated paper currency. It eventually reached as high as $10,000 and became a form of escape that only the wealthiest could afford.

Most Confederate exemptions were allowed to men assumed to be in an occupation important to the war effort. Although the purpose of the government was laudable, and its practice strikingly modern in anticipating the later principle of "selective service," it erred badly in choosing those to be deferred. The laws permitted too many occupational exemptions and included numerous groups that by no realistic standards could be said to be performing necessary war work. Moreover, although the intention was more unconscious than deliberate, some of the exemptions had the effect of relieving from service men in the upper classes. Thus, exemption was extended to railroad employees, workers in mines, foundries, and furnaces, telegraph operators, and doctors and druggists, individuals who were obviously important on the home front. But it was granted also to Confederate and state officials and clerks, factory owners, college presidents and professors, lower school teachers with twenty or more pupils, militia officers certified by their governors as needed locally, and newspaper editors. The most overt example of class favoritism was a provision exempting one white man on each plantation containing twenty or more slaves, referred to scornfully by non-slaveholders as the "twenty-nigger law." The various indulgences allowed to the upper groups aroused wide and bitter class discontent and caused many ordinary men to say, as some in the North said too: "It's a rich man's war but a poor man's fight."

To many people in both sections conscription came as a new and ominous exercise of national power, a startling interference with traditional freedom of choice. The majority accepted it as something disagreeable that had to be endured to achieve victory, but minorities denounced the draft as unnecessary or unjust or unconstitutional, and often as all of these. In the North resistance was strongest in the poorer sections of cities, among laborers who considered that the draft law discriminated against men of their class, and among immigrants who had come to America partly to escape conscription in their own lands. . . .

Although the opponents of conscription were moved by different influences, they shared one belief: all of them objected to fighting to free slaves or to elevate in the slightest way the condition of blacks. Usually critics of conscription limited themselves to denouncing it in speeches or the press. But occasionally feelings among the poorer classes boiled up to such a point that violence erupted. The most spectacular instance occurred in New York City in 1863. Excited by news that a new draft call had been issued, mobs of protesters rioted for four days, killing a number of whites and blacks and holding parts of the city in their grip until dispersed by troops sent in by the national government.

In the South, opposition to drafting did not take a violent turn. But a form of passive resistance developed, beginning in the summer of 1863, when military reverses convinced many people that the war could not be won, and becoming stronger as subsequent reverses pointed to the inevitable end. Thousands of men who were called up did not report, remaining hidden at home by friends or families or taking to the hills or woods to escape detection by government agents. Thousands already in the army deserted, going home to see to their families, or joining other evaders congregated in foothill areas in such numbers as to be able to defy attempts by the government to bring them back. A woman who saw such men trudging by her door in 1865 wrote in anguish in her diary: "I am sure our army is silently dispersing. Men are moving the wrong way, all the time. . . . They have given the thing up."

Another form of resistance was a kind of legal sabotage of the draft laws, a method of opposition that reflected the Southern tendency to define the rightness or wrongness of every issue, including even military policy in a desperate war, in constitutional terms. Southerners who in the old Union had fought the centralizing tendencies of the government did not lose this habit now they had a government of their own. Many of them opposed Confederate authority when it sought to exercise certain powers in connection with the war effort, being most aroused by the adoption of conscription, which in their view was an unconstitutional use of power. These states' righters, as they were called, controlled the governments of Georgia, South Carolina, and North Carolina, and the governors in these states used a variety of methods to impede enforcement of conscription. . . .

The draft policies of the two governments seem defective if compared to later practices. They contained too many loopholes that facilitated too many evasions. But their architects were pioneering in a new form of mobilization, whereas the framers of modern laws had the benefit of the Civil War experience. The Union and Confederate acts should not be judged by their shortcomings but by their results, and those were impressive. Both sides raised [troops] by drafting and by volunteering large numbers of men. The statistical methods used by the two governments do not permit an accurate statement of the total numbers enlisted, including, as the records do, men who enrolled for short terms or joined up several times under different names to claim bounties. But it is possible to estimate with reasonable accuracy the number of men who served for a meaningful period, three years. The appraisals indicate that 1,500,000 long-term soldiers served in the Union armies and that 900,000 such men served in the Confederate forces. The latter total was an exceptionally high percentage of troops to be raised out of a white population of 6 million.

The Confederacy got its maximum strength onto the field at an early date in the war and then saw it drain away, whereas the strength of the Union began gradually but increased steadily. The South, resorting to conscription first, had 500,000 men under arms at the end of 1862 and during the first half of the following year. At the end of 1863, 465,000 men were carried on the army rolls, but not more than 230,000 were actually present for duty. The situation grew even worse during the desperate year of 1864. At its close, only 200,000 were on the rolls and probably not more than half were present for duty; an estimated 100,000 men had deserted and gone home. The Union armies, in contrast, expanded constantly. Conscription had the anticipated effect of spurring enlistments, and in 1864 the North had 500,000 men in service and hundreds of thousands more waiting in enrolled reserves. The arithmetic of manpower at last caught up with the Confederacy.

When military historians refer to manpower in conflicts before the Civil War, they are referring to white manpower. Black men had served in the earlier wars but never in numbers large enough to influence the outcome, or to cause whites to appreciate their contribution. The Civil War was the first struggle in which blacks participated in substantial numbers and the first in which their presence helped to determine the result. Admitted reluctantly into Northern armies, they won commendation of their efforts from civil and military leaders, including President Lincoln.

The Northern Congress authorized the executive branch to employ "persons of African descent" in the armed forces in the summer of 1862. Although black and abolitionist leaders had urged that Negroes be given a chance to prove their worth in combat, the appeals were not the primary influence in moving the government to act. Rather, it was responding to increasing demands from whites that blacks be compelled to share the perils of battle. Why should white blood be shed when black blood was available, was a question being asked by more and more whites.

Even after the doors were opened, the government moved slowly to enlist blacks. Not until 1863, when emancipation was proclaimed as an objective of the war, was there an active recruitment policy, concentrated in occupied areas of the South and on the former slave population. The War Department sent an officer of general rank to the lower Mississippi Valley to raise troops from among the freedmen of the area, and this man eventually organized fifty regiments. Also active in enlisting former slaves were some state governments, which sought by this method to fill the quotas assigned to them in troop calls and thus to escape the draft; agents of the northeastern states offering generous bounties were especially successful in this endeavor. So effective were the combined programs of the federal and state governments that of approximately 180,000 blacks enlisted about 65 percent were raised in Southern states.

Black soldiers, whether freedmen or free men from Northern states, suffered various discriminations. They served in segregated units and were initially paid less than white soldiers, although the monetary discrepancy would be eliminated. They also had to serve under white line officers, the government refusing to entrust them to leaders of their own race; only one hundred blacks were commissioned as officers, and none attained a rank higher than major. Used at first as laborers or rear-zone troops, black regiments were eventually placed in battle by officers who came to have confidence in them or who were forced by a lack of white troops to use them. They acquitted themselves well in various engagements, winning a grudging but increasing respect from whites. Whatever their performance, blacks added important manpower to the Union armies when more strength was needed. Lincoln declared several times that without this accession the war could not be maintained.

From the beginning of the conflict, the Confederacy made important use of its slave manpower. . . . The mere presence of the slaves as agricultural laborers freed a larger percentage of white men to fight than would otherwise have been available. Slaves also were impressed to serve as military laborers, and they comprised half or more of the work force in the larger armament plants and of military hospital staffs. But this indirect participation did not seem enough to some. As the war wore on and white manpower ran down, various military and civilian leaders suggested that the Confederacy should exploit this unused source of strength, should employ blacks as soldiers. The proposal horrified most whites. A general in the western army reflected a common reaction in denouncing "this monstrous proposition . . . revolting to Southern sentiment, Southern pride, and Southern honor."

The resistance to using black soldiers crumbled only in the face of impending defeat, when the white leadership realized it had no alternative but to call slaves into service. In February 1865, Congress authorized President Davis to requisition 300,000 black troops, a quota being assigned to each state based on its slave population. The act did not promise that slaves who fought would be freed after the war; Davis, however, wrote in his instructions to the War Department that no man was to be asked to fight as a slave but, with the consent of his master, was to go into service free. But the decision to accept black soldiers came too late to help the Confederacy. Before the government could take action to implement the law, the war was over.

In both sections the decision to employ black manpower had been forced by the demands of the war—the totality of the conflict compelled use of all human resources. These demands also caused the use of another group hitherto excluded from participation in war making, women. Although women were not permitted to serve directly in the military forces, they rendered important support doing work that otherwise would have had to be performed by men. Dorothea Dix, who had been pioneering for two decades in better treatment for the insane, spent the Civil War years as superintendent of women hospital nurses. Thousands of women served as nurses and aides in hospitals, as workers in textile and other factories, and as clerks in government offices. They also were active in the various private organizations that sprang into being to minister to the wants of soldiers, such as the United States Sanitary Commission in the North. The appearance of these groups was yet another indication of total involvement demanded by the war. . . .

Both sides used a variety of weapons during the war, but generally they were the same ones. These arms, which came into use and were tested during the 1850s, were employed without important alteration throughout the conflict. Several new weapons were introduced, but produced in such small quantity as to have no significant effect on the course or the outcome of the war.

The basic small-arms weapon of the infantry soldier was the rifle musket, a single-shot, muzzle-loading piece with a range of about half a mile, but most effective at 300 yards or less. Although several models of this weapon had been developed and were used during the war, the parts in them were essentially standard, and the guns could be produced in mass by the tooling machines available to manufacturers. Models of breech-loading and repeating rifles had been developed before the war, and the advantages offered by these weapons, a longer range and a faster rate of firepower, were apparent to ordnance officers. But despite their superiority, only a modest number of breech-loaders and repeaters were contracted for during the conflict. The failure to produce larger quantities was usually ascribed to the conservatism of ordnance bureaucrats, but these men had sound reasons for concentrating on turning out rifle muskets. An extensive retooling process was required to fabricate breech-loaders and repeaters in quantity, and neither government could afford to take the time to make the transition. Each one wisely decided to rely on the weapon it could already produce in mass amounts.

Because of the distinction between field and heavy artillery, there was no basic artillery weapon. The most widely used fieldpiece of the war was the "Napoleon," a single-shot, muzzle-loading gun with a range of a mile, but most effective at half that distance or less. Pulled to a field by horses, a battery or batteries of Napoleons spewed forth shell, case shot, and canister and were effective dealers of death in the cramped spaces in which most of the battles of the war occurred. Rifled guns were also employed in the field service but in relatively small numbers. Although they had approximately twice the range of the Napoleons, they were no more effective than the latter at close distances, if as much so, and because of elementary sighting devices they were inefficient in searching out a remote or concealed foe. They were most frequently used to "soften up" an enemy position by bombarding it before the infantry attacked.

The heavier artillery was employed against fortifications, permanent or field, and in naval engagements. Most of the heavy pieces were muzzle-loading, single-shot smoothbores, the Rodmans, or Dahlgrens developed before the war or models similar to them. Rifled cannon were also introduced, the most effective being the Parrott gun, which also was developed before the war. Although the rifled pieces had no faster rate of firepower than the smoothbores, being also single-shot muzzle-loaders, they possessed longer ranges, some of them being able to hurl a projectile as far as four to five miles. But at anywhere near their maximum range they were erratically inaccurate and were, like the rifled field cannon, unable to "locate" a distant or concealed target.

The weapons that came into use during the 1850s produced much greater firepower than anything possessed by armies in earlier conflicts—a force on the defensive could now strike attackers with artillery and musket shot almost from the time the latter started to move out. Students of tactics realized the threat that the new weapons posed for advancing infantry and considered the possibility of adopting a more dispersed or extended formation to make the attackers a less inviting target. But baffled by the problem of controlling large bodies of men beyond voice or vision, commanders continued to rely on a relatively rigid and close line formation. The number of lines was reduced from three to two but the men still moved forward in a dense conformation. The favored attack formation was in a "column of brigades," three brigades of a division aligned from front to back, and it was believed that the brigades, striking in successive waves, would be able to carry an enemy position.

Attackers in a Civil War battle usually opened by bombarding an enemy position to cripple opposing artillery and prepare the way for advancing infantry. Hardly ever was a bombardment effective. The defending infantry, employing rifle muskets, could keep artillery at a distance of a mile or more, and at this range the fire of cannon was ineffective. Consequently, when the attacking infantry finally moved out it encountered an unshaken enemy and received devastating fire from artillery and muskets the moment it started to advance.

As the attacking lines went forward, officers attempted to keep them parallel, perfectly dressed. One reason for this effort was that if a line halted to fire it could deliver a more massed volley if held parallel; more important, a regular line would have a maximum shock impact when it struck the defenders. Sometimes the insistence on maintaining uniformity had eerie results—men hit by bullets fell in parallel positions. A Confederate officer at Gettysburg saw a sight he described as "sickening and heart-rending." He counted seventy-nine rebels "laying dead in a straight line. I stood on their right and looked down their line. It was perfectly dressed. Three had fallen to the front, the rest had fallen backward, yet the feet of all these dead men were in a perfectly straight line." The principal result of adhering to a rigid line was tremendous casualty rates; men advancing in this formation were a vulnerable target and in hard-fought battles went down in windrows. Many units in both armies sustained total losses, killed and wounded, of 40 to 80 percent in a single engagement; at Gettysburg two out of every ten Union soldiers and three out of every ten Confederates were hit by bullets. The aggregate of service deaths on both sides was 618,000, a number almost equal to the deaths in all other American wars combined.

Frontal assaults in lines did not often succeed in Civil War battles. If the defenders were roughly equal in number and in a strong position, they could issue a fire that would shatter the attackers short of the defensive line or, if the latter continued, that would prevent them from making a real breakthrough; even a smaller defensive force, if sheltered by field fortifications, could usually hold off an attack. The attackers, raked by artillery fire from the first and then by artillery and musket fire, tended to lose their formation; the successive lines ran together and approached the defenders bunched into a crowd and thus lost much of their shock effect. Even if a penetration was made, the surviving attackers were too few to exploit it into a breakthrough, and their reserves were too distant to aid them. Subject to a counterattack, the penetrating force had to retire or risk capture. The problem of the attackers was expressed aptly by a Confederate private at Gettysburg. Referring to the inability of the rebels to gain a foothold on Cemetery Ridge, he said: "It ain't hard to get on that ridge, the hell of it is trying to stay there."

Despite the failure of most frontal assaults and the frightful losses incurred in the dressed-line advances, generals continued to rely on the traditional formation throughout the war. They could always hope an attack would succeed, as some assaults did, and they remained convinced that only a close-order formation would assure them control of their troops. Some commanders adopted a modified version of the frontal attack. Feigning an advance on their front, they attempted to pass a force around the flank of the defenders, thus forcing the latter to abandon their prepared position and fight on less favorable ground. Other generals experimented with new and more extended formations. One innovation came to be called the advance by "rushes"; it probably originated by chance and was then employed by officers who saw its efficacy. An example of its use occurred in the Federal assault on Fort Donelson. Two lines of infantry coming under heavy fire lay down, the second forming on the left of the first. When the enemy fire abated, the line rose and rushed forward until pinned down again by fire. Rising and rushing in this manner, the attackers eventually carried the position with slight loss.

Another development was to strengthen the line of skirmishers, who ordinarily had no other mission than to feel out the enemy position. A general might advance half the strength of regiments in the front line of advance while holding the rest in support. This arrangement gave skirmishers for the first time a combat mission but enabled officers to retain a measure of control over the whole body of troops.

The various tactical innovations modified but did not seriously disturb the dominant role of firepower in the war. To the end, the plunging shot of artillery and muskets ruled most fields. Indeed, in the closing campaigns armies disappeared into the earth, both attackers and defenders digging into entrenchments before engaging in operations. Long forgotten were the parade-ground formations and the cheering crowds and the hopes of easy victory of 1861.

QUESTIONS FOR DISCUSSION

1. Why do historians so often refer to the Civil War as the "first modern war"?

2. What was the reaction, North and South, to conscription?

3. Compare Williams' and Huggins' discussions of the role of black soldiers in the war.

4. Provide at least one example of the ways in which the war, in Williams' words, "determined to a large extent the direction the nation would take in the future."

Many of Abraham Lincoln's contemporaries thought he was an ugly man, and even his supporters could hardly claim that he was handsome. But in the long run, he was able to turn this potential liability into a great asset. His stalking frame became a symbol of his public role as a simple man who had become a great democratic leader. And his rugged face became the most immediately recognizable one Americans have ever known. These photographs catch the deep change in Lincoln's image wrought by the Civil War. In the first, he is very much the earnest and watchful politician campaigning to be president in June of 1860—serious enough, but with no obvious depth. In the second, he is the figure he so much wanted history to remember: deeply marked by the sorrows of war, staring distantly, but with a thoughtful smile. This photograph, taken just four days before his death, is the picture of a man who has endured much, but has not surrendered hope or determination. *(Photos courtesy the Chicago Historical Society)*

Abraham Lincoln:
The Gettysburg Address

Commentary by R. Jackson Wilson

For the friends of the Union, the Fourth of July, 1863, came less in celebration than in anxiety, and even dread. The news that trickled in from the battlefields was scattered and uncertain. Abraham Lincoln and the people he had led into Civil War had the gravest kinds of reasons to be concerned. Out in the West, at Vicksburg on the Mississippi, a Union army led by Ulysses S. Grant seemed unable to budge the Confederate forces that were holding the last southern stronghold on the river. Even worse, in the East, the Union was being invaded: Robert E. Lee had brought an enormous army across the Potomac, north through Maryland, and into Pennsylvania.

Lee was probably headed for the important railroad center of Harrisburg, and there was every reason to believe that he might capture it. Between him and Washington there would still be a lot of Union power. But what might a victorious southern army of almost 100,000 men do next? Philadelphia was not out of Lee's reach. He might even head for New York City. Only one thing was clear: Lee's soldiers had beaten the armies of the Union soundly at Fredericksburg in December, then again in May at Chancellorsville. Now there were rumors of a great battle at the Pennsylvania town of Gettysburg, and if Lee won another victory there, no one could trust in the survival of the Union.

During the next couple of days, the telegrams and newspaper reports began to take shape. By July 7, it was plain that the Union had been preserved. At last came details of Vicksburg's surrender to Grant on July 4. And at Gettysburg, after terrible fighting on the first three days of the month, Lee had abandoned his invasion. He had started the difficult work of withdrawing his beaten army through the rain and mud, back toward the Potomac and the defensive safety of Virginia. Lee had not held back at Gettysburg. Twenty-three thousand of his boys and men had been killed, wounded, or captured trying to take the low hills outside the town. Now there was nothing for him to do but try to get his broken force home. He could only pray that the Union commanders did not realize that if they attacked him now, they could smash his army—and with it every Confederate hope.

And so, on the night of July 7, Washington celebrated a kind of delayed Independence Day. A crowd led by a brass band came to the White House to serenade the president. In a time when presidents of the United States still walked the streets of the capital, tipping their hats to people they passed, it would have been very rude of Abraham Lincoln not to come to a window to greet the crowd and make a little speech.

Lincoln was a very experienced stump speaker, and he knew that his audience would respond well if he connected the Union victories with the Fourth of July. He also was a bit of a mystic, and so he asked the crowd to consider what an omen it was that Vicksburg's surrender and Lee's retreat came on Independence Day. Was there a providence in the fact that the only two signers of the Declaration of Independence who later became presidents, John Adams and Thomas Jefferson, had died within hours of each other on July 4, 1826? Or that another president had died five years later, also on July 4? Surely, he said, these events were "peculiar," "remarkable," and "extraordinary." Surely this "glorious theme" was a grand "occasion for a speech." But, the president told the crowd, "I am not prepared."

And if anyone needed proof that Lincoln really was not prepared to make a speech that night, the strongest evidence was that he had not done his arithmetic. When he began to speak of 1776 and independence, he talked like a man spinning yarns on the back porch after supper. He asked, "How long ago is it?" And his answer was both approximate and awkward: "Eighty-odd years since. . . . That was the birthday of the United States of America." A few months later, Lincoln would step to the front of a speaker's platform at Gettysburg with a couple of small sheets of paper in his hands, put on some reading glasses, and prove that he did know how to subtract 1776 from 1863, knew that exactly eighty-seven years had passsed between the Declaration of Independence and the battle of Gettysburg. He would prove more than that, too. He would show that he understood the awesome difference between saying "Eighty-odd years since," and saying "Four score and seven years ago." This time he *was* prepared, and the result was the two-minute masterpiece of the American language that would become known as the Gettysburg Address.

What took Lincoln to Gettysburg was a ceremonial exercise, one of those occasions on which politicians and orators claim the center of the stage. The battlefield had been cleaned up. The thousands of Union dead had been dug out of the shallow graves where they had been laid in groups of four, five, and six, depending on the clusters in which they had been found after the battle. A cemetery had been created by the states that had had units in the Union forces (the land had cost the states a little over $2,000—well under a dollar for each man who had defended it with his life). Now it was time to dedicate the ground.

A grand ceremony had been planned. There would be a printed program, a procession, three bands, a platform of dignitaries, and a main speaker who was supposed to be one of the greatest orators in America: Edward Everett. There would be hymns and prayers and dirges. Fine words would ring out, again and again, in trembling intonations: "Almighty God . . . hallowed . . . consecrated . . . in vain . . . freedom . . . republic . . . our fathers"—these and a dozen more of the most sacred verbal tokens of the Union cause. (It would not matter, of course, that these same verbal tokens would have been just as plentiful at any similar ceremony in the Confederacy. What mattered, for this day, was that the Union keep as firm a hold on such language as its soldiers had kept on the terrain last July.) Then, when the ceremony was almost over, after the procession and the bands, the prayers, and a two-hour speech by Everett, the president would be called upon for what the program listed as "Dedicatory Remarks." His real job was simply to be present, to formally dedicate the cemetery. In fact, the invitation to speak at all had been almost insulting: He had been asked, rather pointedly, to make "a few dedicatory remarks."

What Lincoln did on that platform on November 19, 1863, was to work a bit of verbal magic. Instead of a few harmless remarks at the end of a long ceremony, he managed to utter sentences that the supporters of the Union would soon come to regard as a sacred declaration of a holy cause. In his speech he pointed backward to the Declaration of Independence; but the Gettysburg Address would gain a status that rivaled the Declaration itself. In the long run, Lincoln's "government of the people, by the people, and for the people," would become as familiar as the Declaration's "All men are created equal."

The Address was in many ways a conventional schoolmaster's nightmare. Lincoln violated one "rule" after another. His verbs skipped from one tense to another, and then another. The speech had only ten sentences—taking an average of 12 seconds each to speak aloud—but these ten were littered with thirteen uses of the word "that," two of them coming one after another, in an awkward "that that." Each of the last four sentences contained the word "here." Worst of all, the Address repeated big words, at a time when genteel convention condemned repetition and favored the introduction of elaborate synonyms instead. The first sentence was built around the words "nation," "conceived," and "dedicated"; the second sentence contained these same three words. In fact, "dedicate" or "dedicated" cropped up in five of Lincoln's ten sentences.

But schoolmasters do not always know best. In truth, the Address was a remarkable work of art. It would be difficult to imagine a more careful verbal architecture than the one Lincoln had shaped. His repetitions were all quite deliberate, and one of them, *dedicate,* was a key to his strategy. He had prepared a speech built on reversals and oppositions. And the idea of "dedication" was one of the main things the speech meant to reverse. Repeating the word did not signify a lack of skill or a thin vocabulary. On the contrary, it was evidence of superb command of language. In the simplest terms, what Lincoln said at Gettysburg was that he and the crowd had come to dedicate a cemetery, which meant to formally declare that it was holy, consecrated ground. But they could not really do what they had come to do, since the men who had died there had already dedicated it, made it holy—hallowed—and consecrated. And so it must be that the president and the audience had not really come to dedicate at all, but *to be* dedicated. This put Lincoln in a splendid position. He had been given formal authority only to dedicate the cemetery. But he could not do that. Well, then he could do something much grander: He could tell the people what *they* ought to be dedicated *to.* This deftly redefined the meaning of the official program's promise that he would make "Dedicatory Remarks." He had not come to cut ribbons, but to define the very purpose of the Union's war.

Lincoln's trick on the word *dedicate*—almost a pun, but a profound one— played directly into a second skillful reversal. He had come to a place of death. Men had died there and had been buried. In fact the Union dead had been buried once, hurriedly, when the fighting was done, then dug up for a second burial in a carefully laid out semicircle. The thousands of Confederate dead were still scattered around the huge battlefield, mostly in unmarked graves. (This was a Union cemetery, after all. The Confederates would wait seven years for the first attempts to identify their bodies, and return them to Virginia, or Georgia, or South Carolina.) But the vocabulary Lincoln chose to emphasize was not the vocabulary of death, but of conception and birth. His opening sentence was about the way the "fathers" had "brought forth" the nation. The had "conceived" it. And he ended with the promise of a "new birth of freedom."

This use of the lexicon of conception and birth in a place whose function was death was related to a third opposition that completed Lincoln's plan. He began by talking about the past, and did so with an exaggerated precision, as though part of his purpose was to accurately date the Declaration of Independence. But "four score and seven" was Biblical language, designed to suggest something much more grand than a nagging precision about dates. And his last phrase—equally Biblical in tone—pointed not to the past but to the future: "shall not perish from the earth." He began in the past tense, used the present tense in the middle of the Address, and then ended in the future tense. The implicit message was perfectly clear: the cause of the Union was not grounded in some event that had occurred eighty-seven years before, nor in some temporary clash of interests between North and South, but was a cause for all time, as enduring as the other things—mostly religious—the audience might associate with words like "hallow" and "consecrate."

For all these ingenious verbal strokes—the play on the meanings of "dedicate," the talk of birth in this sanctuary of death, the facing about from the definite past to the indefinite future—Lincoln may have had a variety of mixed motives. But his main purpose was to make a statement of Union war aims that would be beyond any possible controversy. He was claiming for the Union nothing less than what he thought was the deepest and most central message of the American experience. But he was very careful to limit this claim to what he was confident his audience—and most voters in the North—could easily accept. And so he said nothing about slavery, nothing about the constitutional question of secession, nothing about the treason of the rebellious Confederacy, and above all nothing about what would happen to the South and to slavery when the war was over. He carefully avoided anything that might cause even a ripple of debate in the North. He was reaching for the highest possible ground, far above that particular battleground and cemetery, and far above disagreements and controversies over the legality of secession, the future of black people in America, or the conduct of the war. But he was trying to make that ground narrow as well as high, limited to one concept—liberty—and one proposition—equality—that he could hold out to the crowd as the unquestionable premises on which their Union had been brought forth. When he took off his reading glasses, put away his two sheets of paper, and walked slowly back to his chair on the crowded platform, he had no way of knowing whether he had succeeded.

The Gettysburg Address

Fourscore and seven years ago, our fathers brought forth upon this continent a new nation, conceived in liberty and dedicated to the proposition that all men are created equal.

Now we are engaged in a great civil war, testing whether that nation—or any nation, so conceived and so dedicated—can long endure.

We are met on a great battle-field of that war. We are met to dedicate a portion of it as the final resting-place of those who have given their lives that that nation might live.

It is altogether fitting and proper that we should do this.

But, in a larger sense, we cannot dedicate, we cannot consecrate, we cannot hallow, this ground. The brave men, living and dead, who struggled here, have consecrated it, far above our power to add or to detract.

The world will very little note nor long remember what we say here; but it can never forget what they did here.

It is for us, the living, rather, *to be dedicated,* here, to the unfinished work that they have thus far nobly carried on. It is rather for us to be here dedicated to the great task remaining before us; that from these honored dead we take increased devotion to that cause for which they here gave the last full measure of devotion; that we here highly resolve that these dead shall not have died in vain; that the nation shall, under God, have a new birth of freedom, and that government of the people, by the people, for the people, shall not perish from the earth.

Commentary: Part II

Just as the crowd thought Lincoln might be completing a brief opening statement, the president had *stopped* talking. When they realized he was finished, the people applauded—not wildly, as they had for Everett's grandiose oration, but about as firmly as they would for any president making any speech. The real impact of the Gettysburg Address was not on the audience in the cemetery, but on the rest of the nation. And, in an important sense, the Gettysburg Address did not exactly *happen* that afternoon at half past two. As an event, rather than just a collection of spoken words, the Address really took place gradually, as people read and reread it, then began to memorize and repeat it in clubs and churches and schools. At Gettysburg on November 19, there was little drama. Only as days and months passed did it become clear what Lincoln had done there. He had given the Union its war creed.

The process took a little time. Even what he had said, exactly, was not immediately known for certain. Everett, the professional orator, had released copies of his long speech to the press far enough in advance that all the major papers could print it, word for word. But Lincoln had still been working on his speech late the previous night. When he gave it, he had the only copy in the world in his own hands. So the speech had to be taken down by reporters on the spot, and the result was that some important newspapers printed versions of it that differed considerably from what really had been said. And these versions were copied by many of the papers in smaller towns and cities. The Philadelphia *Inquirer,* for example, got the first couple of sentences right, but made hash of what came next. "We are met to dedicate it," Philadelphians read, "on a portion of the field set apart as the final resting place of those who gave their lives for the nation's life; but the nation must live, and it is altogether fitting and proper that we should do this." Toward the end of the speech, the *Inquirer* had Lincoln wallowing in this clumsy mess: "We owe this offering to our dead. We imbibe increased devotion to that cause for which they here gave the last full measure of devotion." And this garbled version of the speech was even reprinted in the newspaper of Gettysburg itself.

But Lincoln was lucky. The Civil War is often called the first "modern" war, because of the way both sides used modern methods of transportation and communication to mobilize whole societies, rather than just armies for the field. For civilians, one thing that had become mobilized was the news. The telegraph had led to the creation of an organization called the Associated Press, the first electronic media "network." Most city newspapers had access to the Associated Press's telegraphed version of what the president had said. And it just happened that the reporter who sent out that version was careful and accurate.

But even when Lincoln's phrases were known, and known accurately, there were other, powerful obstacles to those words becoming a verbal national monument. He was a president who had been elected by a minority of the popular vote. Until that July of Gettysburg and Vicksburg, the war had not gone well. Casualties were high and victories few. He had issued a proclamation emancipating slaves in rebel-held territory. But a majority of his northern constituents were still not ready to fight an "abolitionist" war for the liberation of a people most of them considered racially inferior. Also, Lincoln was the president of a Union in which there were still two parties, and the Democrats were already gearing up for next year's election. At this point, it was not at all clear that Lincoln could even win reelection, much less become a national hero whose words could be engraved in stone and chanted aloud by generations of school children. The splendid national unity Lincoln was appealing for in his speech was very far from a reality.

And so the initial reception of the Gettysburg Address was mixed. Democratic papers accused Lincoln of making a stump speech, designed to set off his campaign for reelection. In nearby Harrisburg—a town that had probably been saved from Lee's army by the battle of Gettysburg—it was reported that the president had "acted without sense," and made some "silly remarks." Even a paper in Lincoln's home town, Springfield, Illinois, was equally harsh. And from what may have been the most influential newspaper in the world, *The Times* of London, came this ugly assessment: "The ceremony was rendered ludicrous by some of the sallies of that poor President Lincoln. . . . Anything more dull and commonplace it wouldn't be easy to produce."

On the other side, from newspapers and magazines that supported the Republican party, came predictable praise. The speech, it seemed to these commentators, was "a perfect gem," "a splendid oration," given "from the heart to the heart." But even some of the papers that praised the speech did so in terms that were nearly insulting. The Detroit *Advertiser and Tribune* commented that Everett's oration had been "noble," but that the president had caught the "spirit of the day" with the "unstudied pathos that amimates a sincere but simple-minded man." And from a friendly British magazine came the haughty judgment that Lincoln might be "something more than a boor"; had any king in Europe spoken more "royally" than "this peasant's son"?

If Lincoln's purpose had been to persuade, he had—as he himself felt—failed. Those who opposed him before the speech still opposed him. And those who were already his supporters remained so. In this respect, there is a curious similarity between the Gettysburg Address and the Emancipation Proclamation he had issued a year earlier. The Emancipation Proclamation did not immediately free a single slave. It simply declared that all the slaves in *Confederate* territory were free. It applied only to those places where it could not be enforced. But, in the long run, the Emancipation Proclamation signaled a profound change in the course of American history. From the time Lincoln signed it, one thing was clear: If the North won the war, slavery would be ended. And so it was with the Gettysburg Address. It probably caused no change of mind or heart in a single member of its immediate audience. And the Americans in its larger audience were already convinced anyway that the Declaration of Independence was a fine document, and that government of the people, by the people, and for the people was an excellent thing–in theory at least.

Lincoln did not present himself at Gettysburg as a debater, arguing for a point with logic and evidence. He was not arguing for the *truth* of the proposition that all men were created equal. Instead, he was speaking like a high priest at a religious ritual, raising that proposition up so that people could look upon it once more and reaffirm their "dedication" to it. More than that, he was claiming that what the Civil War was "testing" was exactly that old and familiar proposition. If the Union failed, then the proposition would be proved false, not in some abstract and philosophical way but by a cruel, irreversible test of experience.

Little wonder, then, that the tired crowd at Gettysburg was not suddenly converted to a novel sense of themselves and their war. The chemistry through which Lincoln's brief "dedicatory remarks" became a great speech required something more than the mere delivery of the sentences. It was only as Union forces drove deeper and deeper into the Confederacy, only as the triumph of what Lincoln called "the work" became the certain result of one battle after another, that an assertion of principle as plain and simple as he had made could be transformed into an authoritative national text. From Gettysburg, aided by Union victories in the field, Lincoln moved on to a triumphant re-election. And then, with victory grasped, he passed on to martyrdom. And with each of these steps, the ten sentences he had spoken at the cemetery took on more and more meaning. By the time he was buried, the Gettysburg Address was ready to be chiseled into marble.

And this was possible because he had made a strategic decision at Gettysburg, a decision that helped his speech to become an unchallenged statement of political doctrine. He had defined the meaning of the war in a way that could gain the broadest possible consent, not only during the fighting but during the coming peace. From the beginning of the war, Lincoln had groped for a formula that could unify the North, and mobilize the moral energy necessary to sustain the terrible struggle. At first, he had tried defining the war as a simple effort to maintain the Union as a political fact. In this formulation, the moral question of slavery was irrelevant. He had said this very carefully in a public letter in 1862: "If I could save the Union without freeing any slave, I would do it, and if I could save it by freeing all the slaves, I would do it, and if I could do it by freeing some and leaving others alone, I would also do that." But later that same year, he had gone to the other extreme: the Emancipation Proclamation had made the Civil War a war against slavery.

Neither of these formulas had worked. A war for the simple idea of the political Union might have attracted enough support to sustain public opinion through one or two defeats and a few thousand casualties. But as it became clear that the defeats would be many, and the casualties in the tens and even hundreds of thousands, something more than the purely political principle of Union was needed. On the other hand, a war against slavery was attractive only to an earnest minority—black and white—in the North who were willing to see their sons die so that black men and women might be free; such a definition of war aims went too far for most people.

What Lincoln used at Gettysburg was a middle way of defining the war. The Union armies, he claimed, were fighting for much more than mere political nationality. "Liberty" and "equality" were at stake. During the years to come, white Americans in both the North and the South would engage in a long, bitter, and inconclusive debate over just what the connection was between the war and slavery, and over what degree of responsibility the Union ought to take for the social well-being of the freed blacks. But Lincoln stopped well short of this problem at Gettysburg. He laid down no doctrine and proposed no program for dealing with this awesome problem. He left it to history. And by doing this, he enabled whites and blacks, North and South, to read what they wished into phrases like "conceived in liberty" and "created equal."

Lincoln also had worked carefully with the second person plural pronouns, "we," "our," and "us." He talked of "our fathers" in an extremely loose way. He ignored the fact that the founding fathers had included many slaveholders who were the ancestors not of the Union dead, but of those Confederate boys whose bodies still lay about the battlefield in their "temporary" graves. And he ignored the fact that the United States already had a large number of citizens whose "fathers" had been born and died thousands of miles away, in Europe or Asia—and that many of these immigrants bitterly opposed the war, and voted Democratic. He also made no reference to the Afro-American "fathers" of the millions of slaves waiting for freedom. Instead, he spoke of the fathers casually, as though a citizen's biological ancestry were of no importance. What was implied, plainly, was that simply being a citizen of the Union gave every man equal claim on the ancestral achievement of Independence and Union. And being an opponent of the Union would deprive a person of any share of what had been "brought forth" in 1776, even if his grandfather had actually signed the Declaration of Independence.

Lincoln had also played very effectively on a colossal vanity in his public. He told them that as citizens of the Union—no matter who their real fathers had been, they had a unique and exclusive claim on democracy. On their resolve and on their victory, he said, depended the fate not just of the Republic, but of the very idea of popular government. It was not just their nation that was being tested. It was "any nation so conceived." And if they failed, democracy would never survive anywhere in the world.

Behind this simple appeal to patriotism, and to the ideals of the founding fathers, lay a truly revolutionary strategy. On the surface, Lincoln had seemingly looked to the past for the principles that gave meaning to the war. But he had subtly worked those principles into something quite new. In the founding of the Republic, he said, the Union had been the creation of men committed to liberty and equality; in his beginning sentences, the nation was the offspring of these men and their principles. But he went on to invert that idea. He transformed the Union from a creation or an offspring into a creative principle. In the beginning, liberty and equality had generated the Union. Now the Union—and only the Union—could generate liberty and equality. And if the Union failed, liberty and equality would fail, everywhere and forever.

The fathers had thought of the government they were creating as something they *made,* or "instituted." Lincoln was helping to mold a different conception of nationhood, one that would triumph in Europe and America by the end of the nineteenth century. He and his audience were participants, whether they realized it or not, in a historical process even larger than the Civil War and the end of the American slavery. Lincoln's two-minute masterpiece was one among the many emerging formulations that defined the nation as something that could take men. This idea, whose first great expression may have been Napoleon Bonaparte's efforts to take the French Revolution by force of arms into the rest of Europe, went far beyond old-fashioned and legalistic notions of "sovereignty." It would take different shapes in the various nations of the transatlantic world. But whatever shape it took, the idea that the nation-state is the source and creator of values, rather than their expression or outcome, fused the two distinct notions of government and nationality into one potent doctrine. The doctrine might operate in the world for better or for worse, but it would become the ultimate appeal of political leaders who wanted to stir their people to action.

Lincoln was probably not thinking in such historical terms as he pondered what to say at Gettysburg. For the moment, at least, his appeal was as profound as it was simple. The mere fact of citizenship, not only for those who were born into it but also for those who claimed it as immigrants and perhaps even as freed slaves, transformed an individual. Being a citizen made a man free and equal, and bound him together in liberty and equality with all the other spiritual descendants of the founding fathers. Only the Union made democracy possible, and that Union must be tended in devotion and preserved in valor, for without it democratic government would surely "perish from the earth."

Chapter Two

Reconstruction

LEON F. LITWACK

Slaves No More

"To describe the end of slavery in the South is to re-create a profound hu-
man drama." So writes Leon Litwack in the preface to Been in the Storm So
Long, *his magisterial book on "the aftermath of slavery."*

As we have seen, Abraham Lincoln declared early and often that the Civil
War was being fought to save the Union, not to destroy slavery. But slavery
was destroyed in the course of that war: not all at once by the stroke of the
pen that signed the Emancipation Proclamation, but piece by piece.

Some slaves were "freed" by northern troops and others freed themselves by
running away from their masters. For the vast majority, however, freedom re-
mained a wish rather than a reality until the final defeat and surrender of the
southern troops. When it came, that long-sought freedom would change not
only the legal status of the former slaves, but the web of social relationships
that had depended on the existence of the "peculiar institution."

In the following selection, Leon Litwack focuses our attention on the South
in the period immediately following the collapse of the Confederacy when for-
mer slaves and former masters confronted the first and perhaps the most vital
question of Reconstruction, "What, then, was 'freedom' and who was 'free?'"

O n the night of April 2, 1865, Confederate troops abandoned Richmond.
The sudden decision caught Robert Lumpkin, the well-known dealer in slaves,
with a recently acquired shipment which he had not yet managed to sell. Desperately, he tried to remove them by the same train that would carry Jefferson
Davis out of the Confederate capital. When Lumpkin reached the railway station, however, he found a panic-stricken crowd held back by a line of Confederate soldiers with drawn bayonets. Upon learning that he could not remove
his blacks, the dealer marched them back to Lumpkin's Jail, a two-story brick

---

Leon Litwack is a professor of history at the University of California, Berkeley. The following selection is from *Been in the Storm So Long: The Aftermath of Slavery,* the winner of the
1979 Pulitzer Prize for history.

From *Been in the Storm so Long,* by Leon Litwack, pp. 167–220. Copyright © 1979 by Leon
F. Litwack. Reprinted by permission of Alfred A. Knopf, Inc.

house with barred windows, located in the heart of Richmond's famous slave market—an area known to local blacks as "the Devil's Half Acre." After their return, the slaves settled down in their cells for still another night, apparently unaware that this would be their last night of bondage. For Lumpkin, the night would mark the loss of a considerable investment and the end of a profession. Not long after the collapse of the Confederacy, however, he took as his legal wife the black woman he had purchased a decade before and who had already borne him two children.

With Union soldiers nearing the city, a Confederate official thought the black residents looked as stunned and confused as the whites. "The negroes stand about mostly silent," he wrote, "as if wondering what will be their fate. They make no demonstrations of joy." Obviously he had not seen them earlier that day emerging from a church meeting with particular exuberance, "shaking hands and exchanging congratulations upon all sides." Nor had he heard, probably, that familiar refrain with which local blacks occasionally regaled themselves: "Richmond town is burning down, High diddle diddle inctum inctum ah." Whatever the origins of the song, the night of the evacuation must have seemed like a prophetic fulfillment. Explosions set off by the retreating Confederates left portions of the city in flames and precipitated a night of unrestrained looting and rioting, in which army deserters and the impoverished residents of Richmond's white slum shared the work of expropriation and destruction with local slaves and free blacks. Black and white women together raided the Confederate Commissary, while the men rolled wheelbarrows filled with bags of flour, meal, coffee, and sugar toward their respective shanties. Along the row of retail stores, a large black man wearing a bright red sash around his waist directed the looting. After breaking down the doors with the crowbar he carried on his shoulder, he stood aside while his followers rushed into the shops and emptied them of their contents. He took nothing for himself, apparently satisfied to watch the others partake of commodities long denied them. If only for this night, racial distinctions and customs suddenly became irrelevant.

Determined to reap the honors of this long-awaited triumph, white and black Yankees vied with each other to make the initial entry into the Confederate capital. The decision to halt the black advance until the white troops marched into the city would elicit some bitter comments in the northern black press. "History will show," one editor proclaimed, "that they [the black troops] were in the suburbs of Richmond long before the white soldiers, and but for the untimely and unfair order to halt, would have triumphantly planted their banner first upon the battlements of the capital of '*ye greate confederacie.*'" Many years later, a former Virginia slave still brooded over this issue. "Gawdammit, 'twas de nigguhs tuk Richmond," he kept insisting. "Ah ain't nevuh knowed nigguhs—even all uh dem nigguhs—could mek such uh ruckus. One huge sea uh black faces filt de streets fum wall tuh wall, an' dey wan't nothin' but nigguhs in sight." Regardless of who entered Richmond first, the black newspapers and clergymen perceived the hand of God in this ironic triumph. The moment the government reversed its policy on black recruitment it had doomed the Confederacy. And now, "as a finishing touch, as though He would speak audible words of approval to the nation," God had delivered Richmond—"that stronghold of treason and wickedness"—into the hands of black soldiers. "This is an admonition to which men, who make war on God would do well to take heed."

To the black soldiers, many of them recently slaves, this was the dramatic, the almost unbelievable climax to four years of war that had promised at the outset to be nothing more than a skirmish to preserve the Union. Now they were marching into Richmond as free men, amidst throngs of cheering blacks lining the streets. Within hours, a large crowd of black soldiers and residents assembled on Broad Street, near "Lumpkin Alley," where the slave jails, the auction rooms, and the offices of the slave traders were concentrated. Among the soldiers gathered here was Garland H. White, a former Virginia slave who had escaped to Ohio before the war and now returned as chaplain of the 28th United States Colored Troops.

> I marched at the head of the column, and soon I found myself called upon by the officers and men of my regiment to make a speech, with which, of course, I readily complied. A vast multitude assembled on Broad Street, and I was aroused amid the shouts of ten thousand voices, and proclaimed for the first time in that city freedom to all mankind.

From behind the barred windows of Lumpkin's Jail, the imprisoned slaves began to chant:

> Slavery chain done broke at last!
> Broke at last! Broke at last!
> Slavery chain done broke at last!
> Gonna praise God till I die!

The crowd outside took up the chant, the soldiers opened the slave cells, and the prisoners came pouring out, most of them shouting, some praising God and "master Abe" for their deliverance. Chaplain White found himself unable to continue with his speech. "I became so overcome with tears, that I could not stand up under the pressure of such fullness of joy in my own heart. I retired to gain strength." Several hours later, he located his mother, whom he had not seen for some twenty years.

The white residents bolted their doors, remained inside, and gained their first impressions of Yankee occupation from behind the safety of their shutters. "For us it was a requiem for buried hopes," Sallie P. Putnam conceded. The sudden and ignominious Confederate evacuation had been equaled only by the humiliating sight of black soldiers patrolling the city streets. For native whites, it was as though the victorious North had conspired to make the occupation as distasteful as possible. Few of them could ever forget the long lines of black cavalry sweeping by the Exchange Hotel, brandishing their swords and exchanging "savage cheers" with black residents who were "exulting" over this dramatic moment in their lives. After viewing such spectacles from her window, a young white woman wondered, "Was it to this end we had fought and starved and gone naked and cold? To this end that the wives and children of many dear and gallant friends were husbandless and fatherless? To this end that our homes are in ruins, our state devastated?" Understandably, then, local whites boycotted the military band concerts on the Capitol grounds, even after Federal authorities, in a conciliatory gesture, had barred blacks from attendance.

Four days after the entry of the Union troops, Richmond blacks assembled at the First African Church on Broad Street for a Jubilee Meeting. The church, built in the form of a cross and scantily furnished, impressed a northern visitor as "about the last place one would think of selecting for getting up any particular enthusiasm on any other subject than religion." On this day, some 1,500 blacks, including a large number of soldiers, packed the frail structure. With the singing of a hymn, beginning "Jesus my all to heaven is gone," the congregation gave expression to their newly won freedom. After each line, they repeated with added emphasis, "I'm going to join in this army; I'm going to join in this army of my Lord." But when they came to the verse commencing, "This is the way I long have sought," the voices reached even higher peaks and few of the blacks could suppress the smiles that came across their faces. Meanwhile, in the Hall of Delegates, where the Confederate Congress had only recently deliberated and where black soldiers now took turns swiveling in the Speaker's chair, T. Morris Chester, a black war correspondent, tried to assess the impact of these first days of liberation: the rejoicing of the slaves and free blacks, the tumultuous reception accorded President Lincoln when he visited the city, the opening of the slave pens, and the mood of the black population. "They declare that they cannot realize the change; though they have long prayed for it, yet it seems impossible that it has come."

It took little time for the "grapevine" to spread the news that Babylon (as some blacks called it) had fallen. When black children attending a freedmen's school in Norfolk heard the news, they responded with a resounding chorus of "Glory Hallelujah." Reaching the line "We'll hang Jeff Davis to a sour apple tree," one of the pupils inquired if Davis had, indeed, met that fate. The teacher told her that Davis was still very much alive. At this news, the pupil expressed her dismay "by a decided pout of her lips, such a pout as these children only are able to give." Still, the news about Richmond excited them. Most of the children revealed that they had relatives there whom they now hoped to see, several looked forward to reunions with fathers and mothers "dat dem dere Secesh carried off," and those who had neither friends nor relatives in the city were "mighty glad" anyway because they understood the news to mean that "cullud people free now."

When the news reached a plantation near Yorktown, the white family broke into tears, not only over the fall of Richmond but over the rumor that the Yankees had captured Jefferson Davis. Overhearing the conversation, a black servant rushed through the preparation of the supper, asked another servant to wait on the table for her, and explained to the family that she had to fetch water from the "bush-spring." She walked slowly until no one could see her and then ran the rest of the way. Upon reaching the spring, she made certain she was alone and then gave full vent to her feelings.

> I jump up an' scream, "Glory, glory, hallelujah to Jesus! I's free! I's free! Glory to God, you come down an' free us; no big man could do it." An' I got sort o' scared, afeared somebody hear me, an' I takes another good look, an' fall on de groun', an' roll over, an' kiss de groun' fo' de Lord's sake. I's so full o' praise to Masser Jesus. He do all dis great work. De soul buyers can neber take my two chillen lef' me; no, neber can take 'em from me no mo'.

Several years before, her husband and four children had been sold to a slave dealer. Her thoughts now turned to the possibility of a reunion.

Only a few miles from the Appomattox Courthouse, Fannie Berry, a house servant, stood in the yard with her mistress, Sarah Ann, and watched the white flag being hoisted in the Pamplin village square. "Oh, Lordy," her mistress exclaimed, "Lee done surrendered!" Richmond had fallen the previous week, but for Fannie Berry this was the day she would remember the rest of her life.

> Never was no time like 'em befo' or since. Niggers shoutin' and' clappin' hands and singin'! Chillun runnin' all over de place beatin' tins an' yellin'. Ev'ybody happy. Sho' did some celebratin'. Run to de kitchen an' shout in de winder:

> > Mammy, don't you cook no mo'
> > You's free! You's free!

Run to the henhouse an' shout:

> > Rooster, don't you crow no mo'
> > You's free! You's free!
> > Ol' hen, don't you lay no mo' eggs,
> > You's free! You's free!

Go to de pigpen an' tell de pig:

> > Ol' pig, don't you grunt no mo'
> > You's free! You's free!

Tell de cows:

> > Ol' cow, don't you give no mo' milk,
> > You's free! You's free!

Meanwhile, she recalled, some "smart alec boys" sneaked up under her mistress's window and shouted, "Ain't got to slave no mo'. We's free! We's free!"

The day after the celebration, however, Fannie Berry went about her usual duties, as if she hadn't understood the full implications of what had transpired. And as before, she permitted her mistress to hire her out. Finally, the woman for whom she was working told her she was now free, there was no need to return to her mistress, and she could stay and work for room and board. "I didn't say nothin' when she wuz tellin' me, but done 'cided to leave her an' go back to the white folks dat furst owned me."

Unlike many of their rural brethren, who evinced a certain confusion about the implications of freedom and when to claim it, the blacks in Richmond had little difficulty in appreciating the significance of this event. And they could test it almost instantly. The promenaded on the hitherto forbidden grounds of Capitol Square. They assembled in groups of five or more without the presence or authorization of a white man. They sought out new employers at better terms. They moved about as they pleased without having to show a pass upon the demand of any white person. "We-uns kin go jist anywhar," one local black exulted, "don't keer for no pass—go when yer want'er. Golly! de kingdom hab kim dis time for sure—dat ar what am promised in de generations to dem dat goes up tru great tribulations." And they immediately seized upon the opportunity to educate themselves and their children, to separate their church from white domination, and to form their own community institutions.

Less than two years after the fall of Richmond, a Massachusetts clergyman arrived in the city with the intention of establishing a school to train black ministers. But when he sought a building for his school, he encountered considerable resistance, until he met Mary Ann Lumpkin, the black wife of the former slave dealer. She offered to lease him Lumpkin's Jail. With unconcealed enthusiasm, black workers knocked out the cells, removed the iron bars from the windows, and refashioned the old jail as a school for ministers and freedmen alike. Before long, children and adults entered the doors of the new school, some of them recalling that this was not their first visit to the familiar brick building.

Despite the immediate gratification experienced by the black residents of Richmond, the death of slavery proved to be agonizingly slow. That precise moment when a slave could think of himself or herself as a free person was not always clear. From the very outset of the war, many slaves assumed they were free the day the Yankees came into their vicinity. But with the military situation subject to constant change, any freedom that ultimately depended on the presence of Union troops was apt to be quite precarious, and in some regions the slaves found themselves uncertain as to whose authority prevailed. The Emancipation Proclamation, moreover, excluded numbers of slaves from its provisions, some masters claimed to be unaware of the emancipation order, and still others refused to acknowledge it while the war raged and doubted its constitutionality after the end of hostilities. "I guess we musta celebrated 'Mancipation about twelve times in Harnett County," recalled Ambrose Douglass, a former North Carolina slave. "Every time a bunch of No'thern sojers would come through they would tell us we was free and we'd begin celebratin'. Before we would get through somebody else would tell us to go back to work, and we would go. Some of us wanted to jine up with the army, but didn't know who was goin' to win and didn't take no chances."

Outside of a few urban centers, Union soldiers rarely remained long enough in any one place to enforce the slave's new status. Of the slaves in her region "who supposed they were free," a South Carolina white woman noted how they were "gradually discovering a Yankee army passing through the country and telling them they are free is not sufficient to make it a fact." Nor was the protection of the freedman's status the first priority of an army engaged in a life-and-death struggle. When the troops needed to move on, many of the blacks were understandably dismayed, confused, and frightened. "Christ A'mighty!" one slave exclaimed in late 1861 when told the troops were about to depart. "If Massa Elliott Garrard catch me, might as well be dead—he kill me, certain." Even if Union officers assured him of his safety, the slave had little reason to place any confidence in the word of someone who would not be around on that inevitable day of reckoning. . . .

Widespread dismay at the impending departure of the Yankees reflected not only the prevailing uncertainty about freedom but the very real fear that their masters or the entire white community might wreak vengeance on them for any irregular behavior during the brief period of occupation. In a Mississippi town near Vicksburg, a number of slaves had joined with the Yankees to plunder stores and homes, apparently assuming that the soldiers would be around to protect them. But now the troops were moving on, leaving the looters with their newly acquired possessions and all the slaves, regardless of what role they had played in the pillaging, at the mercy of the whites who felt betrayed and robbed. With "undisguised amazement," the blacks watched the soldiers leave, and within hours one of them caught up with the Yankee columns and reported that a number of his people had already been killed. On a plantation near Columbia, South Carolina, the master and mistress waited until the Yankees departed and then vented their anger on a young slave girl who had helped the soldiers to locate the hidden silverware, money, and jewelry. "She'd done wrong I know," a former slave recalled, "but I hated to see her suffer so awful for it. After de Yankees had gone, de missus and massa had de poor gal hung 'till she die. It was something awful to see." With similar swiftness, a slaveholder who was reputedly "very good to his Negroes" became so enraged over the behavior of a black that the moment the Yankees left the area he strung him up to the beams of a shed. . . .

What, then, was "freedom" and who was "free"? The fluctuating moods of individual masters, unexpected changes in the military situation, the constant movement of troops, and widespread doubts about the validity and enforcement of the Emancipation Proclamation were bound to have a sobering effect on the slaves' perceptions of their status and rights, leaving many of them quite confused if not thoroughly disillusioned. The sheer uncertainty of it all prompted blacks to weigh carefully their actions and utterances, as they had earlier in the war, even in some instances to disclaim any desire to be free or to deny what the Yankees told them. "Sho' it ain't no truf in what dem Yankees wuz a-sayin',"Martha Colquitt recalled her mother telling her, "and us went right on living just like us always done 'til Marse Billie called us together and told us de war wuz over and us wuz free to go whar us wanted to go, and us could charge wages for our work."

Only with "the surrender," as they came to call it, did many slaves begin to acknowledge the reality of emancipation. The fall of Richmond and the collapse of the Confederacy broke the final links in the chain. With freedom no longer hanging on every military skirmish, slaves who had shrewdly or fearfully refrained from any outward display of emotion suddenly felt free to release their feelings and to act on them. Ambrose Douglass, who claimed to have celebrated emancipation every time the Yankees came into Harnett County, North Carolina, sensed that this time it was different, and he proposed to make certain. "I was 21 when freedom finally came, and that time I didn't take no chances on 'em taking it back again. I lit out for Florida." The day the war ended, Prince Johnson recalled, "wagon loads o' people rode all th'ough de place a-tellin' us 'bout bein' free." When the news reached Oconee, Georgia, Ed McCree found himself so overcome that he refused to wait for his master to confirm the report of Lee's surrender: "I runned 'round dat place a-shoutin' to de top of my voice."

In the major cities and towns, far more than in the countryside, the post-Appomattox demonstrations resembled the Jubilees that would become so firmly fixed in black and southern lore. If only for a few days or hours, many of the rural slaves flocked to the nearest town, anxious to join their urban brethren in the festivities and to celebrate their emancipation away from the scrutiny of their masters and mistresses. When news of "the surrender" reached Athens, Georgia, blacks sang and danced around a hastily constructed liberty pole in the center of town. (White residents cut it down during the night.) Although urban blacks had enjoyed a certain degree of autonomy in the past, military occupation afforded them the first real opportunity to express themselves openly and freely as a community, unhampered by curfews, passes, and restrictions on assemblages. Even before Appomattox, many of them made full use of such opportunities.

The largest and most spectacular demonstration took place in Charleston, less than a month after Union occupation. More than 4,000 black men and women wound their way through the city streets, cheered on by some 10,000 spectators, most of them also black. With obvious emotions, they responded to a mule-drawn cart in which two black women sat, while next to them stood a mock slave auctioneer shouting, "How much am I offered?" Behind the cart marched sixty men tied together as a slave gang, followed in turn by a cart containing a black-draped coffin inscribed with the words "Slavery is Dead." Union soldiers, schoolchildren, firemen, and members of various religious societies participated in the march along with an impressive number of black laborers whose occupations pointed up the important role they played in the local economy—carpenters, butchers, tailors, teamsters, masons, wheelwrights, barbers, coopers, bakers, blacksmiths, wood sawyers, and painters. For the black community of Charleston, the parade proved to be an impressive display of organization and self-pride. The white residents thought less of it. "The innovation was by no means pleasant," a reporter wrote of the few white on-lookers, "but they had sense enough to keep their thoughts to themselves."

Less than a week after the end of the war, still another celebration in Charleston featured the ceremonial raising of the United States flag over the ruins of Fort Sumter. Far more dramatic than any of the speeches on this oc-casion was the presence of such individuals as William Lloyd Garrison, the veteran northern abolitionist, for whom this must have been a particularly sat-isfying day. Robert Smalls, the black war hero who had delivered a Confederate steamer to the Union Navy, now used that same ship to convey some 3,000 blacks to Fort Sumter. On the quarterdeck stood Major Martin R. Delany, who had once counseled emigration as the only alternative to continued racial oppression and enslavement and who would soon take his post as a Freed-men's Bureau agent in South Carolina. Next to Delany stood another black man, the son of Denmark Vesey, who some thirty-three years before had been executed for plotting a slave insurrection in Charleston.

Nearly a week after the fall of Richmond, the Confederate dream lay shat-tered. When the news reached Mary Darby, daughter of a prominent South Carolina family, she staggered to a table, sat down, and wept aloud. "Now," she shrieked, "we belong to Negroes and Yankees." If the freed slaves had reason to be confused about their future, their former masters and mistresses were in many instances absolutely distraught, incapable of preceiving a future without slaves. "Nobody that hasn't experienced it knows anything about our suffering," a young South Carolina planter declared. "We are discouraged: we have noth-ing left to begin new with. I never did a day's work in my life, and don't know how to begin." Often with little sense of intended irony, whites viewed the downfall of the Confederacy and slavery as fastening upon them the ignominy of bondage. Either they must submit to the insolence of their servants or ap-peal to their northern "masters" for protection, one white woman wrote, "as if we were slaves ourselves—and that is just what they are trying to make of us. Oh, it is abominable!" . . .

Although the time and manner varied from place to place, the majority of masters eventually got around to informing their slaves that emancipation had become the law of the land. Occasionally, they did so under the compulsion of a Federal order, upon the visitation of a Freedmen's Bureau officer, or at the demand of their own slaves. Usually, the master himself decided how and when to make the announcement. When he sent out the word for his slaves to assemble the next day, nearly everyone knew what to expect. "There was little, if any, sleep that night," Booker T. Washington recalled. "All was excitement and expectancy." Except perhaps for the coming of the Yankees, it was like no other day in their lives. Outside the Big House, the master waited for them on the front porch, often with his entire family standing beside him. To the very end, he would invariably act the role of the patrician, even as he presided over the dispersion of his flock and the sundering of traditional and even intimate ties. Observing how their master "couldn't help but cry" or "couldn't hardly talk," some former slaves confessed to having felt a certain compassion for him at this moment, putting the best possible face on his previous treatment of them. "We couldn't help thinking about what a good marster he always had been," a former Georgia slave recalled, "and how old, and feeble, and gray headed he looked as he kept on a-talkin' that day." Such sentiments were not shared by all slaves, not even on the same plantation, and each black had a different way of recollecting a master's or mistress's tears at the moment of emancipation. "Missy, she cries and cries, and tells us we is free," a former Louisiana slave recalled, "and she hopes we starve to death and she'd be glad, 'cause it ruin her to lose us."

Once the slaves had been assembled for the master's announcement, most of them stood quietly and anxiously, waiting to hear how he would choose to tell them of their freedom. Some of them remained apprehensive, recalling that the only previous occasion for such a gathering had been to tell them they had been sold. Before his master could say a word, Robert Falls remembered questioning him in a mocking manner, "Old Marster, what you got to tell us?" His mother quickly warned him that he would be whipped but the slave owner decided instead to use the outburst to make his point. As Falls recalled his words:

> No I wont whip you. Never no more. Sit down thar all of you and listen to what I got to tell you. I hates to do it but I must. You all aint my niggers no more. You is free. Just as free as I am. Here I have raised you all to work for me, and now you are going to leave me. I am an old man, and I cant get along without you. I dont know what I am going to do.

In less than ten months, he was dead. "Well, sir," Falls explained, "it killed him."

What the slaves recalled most vividly, "jes like it yestiddy," was the manner in which the master recognized their freedom, both his words and temperament at that moment. The way he imparted the information revealed much about his state of mind, the kind of relationship he thought he enjoyed with his slaves, and how he viewed the future. He first read to them some official-looking paper setting forth the details of emancipation. It might have been the Emancipation Proclamation itself or a recent Federal circular; in any event, the language was cold, detached, bureaucratic, and often incomprehensible. After the formal reading, Silas Smith of South Carolina remembered, "us still sets, kaise no writing never aggrevated us niggers way back dar." Since such a moment called for absolute clarity, most masters obliged with their own explanation, and those were the words the slaves had waited to hear. "We didn't quite understand what it was all about," a former Missouri field hand recalled, "until he informed us that it meant we were slaves no longer, that we were free to go as we liked, to work for anyone who would hire us and be responsible to no one but ourselves." As if to underscore the significance of his remarks, and perhaps in some instances to commemorate the slave's graduation to a different status, some masters ceremoniously presented to each of them "de age statement," which included his or her name, place of birth, and approximate age or date of birth. "I's 16 year when surrender come," Sam Jones Washington told an interviewer many years later. "I knows dat, 'cause of massa's statement. All us niggers gits de statement when surrender come."

To free his blacks was not to surrender the convictions with which he had held them as slaves. In explaining to them the circumstances that now made freedom necessary, most masters made it abundantly clear that their actions did not flow from some long-repressed humanitarian urge. "We went to the war and fought," a Texas planter declared, "but the Yankees done whup us, and they say the niggers is free." That was the typical explanation, as most ex-slaves recalled it: they were now free "'cause de gov'ment say you is free" or "'cause the damned Yankees done 'creed you are." If some slaves had felt that only "massa" could free them, many masters insisted that the Yankees had set them free. That they chose to view emancipation in these terms was perfectly consistent with their own self-image. "I have seen slavery in every Southern State," a prominent Virginian concluded in June 1865, "and I am convinced that for the slave it is the best condition in every way that has been devised." The "tens of thousands" of old men, women, and children he expected would now starve for lack of support only made him that much more certain. "A Farmer now has to pay his hands and he will keep none but such as will work well, women with families and old men are not worth their food and they are being turned adrift by the thousands." As many masters viewed this moment, then, if they had acted from humanitarian considerations, they would have retained slavery, because of the protection and sustenance it afforded a people incapable of caring for themselves.

If slaveholders felt morally reprehensible or guilt-ridden, they evinced no indication of it at the moment they declared their blacks to be free. Nothing in the postwar behavior and attitudes of these people suggested that the ownership of slaves had necessarily compromised their values or tortured their consciences. . . . Rather than confess any misgivings about their slaveholding past, most masters at this moment viewed themselves as decent men, good Christians who had performed a useful, necessary, and benevolent task, fulfilling an obligation to an inferior people which more than compensated for the labor they had received in return. There was nothing for which they needed to apologize. As George A. Trenholm proudly told the Chamber of Commerce of Augusta, Georgia, in early 1866, "Sir, we have educated them. We took them barbarians, we returned them Christianized and civilized to those from whom we received them; we paid for them, we return them without compensation. Our consciences are clear, our hands are clean." . . .

Where the master assembled the blacks to tell them they were no longer his slaves, the reactions he provoked gave rise to the legendary stories of a

"Day of Jubilo," in which crowds of ecstatically happy blacks shouted, sang, and danced their way into freedom. Large numbers of former slaves recalled no such celebration. Although not entirely myth, the notion of a Jubilee, with its suggestion of unrestrained, unthinking black hiliarity, tends to neglect if not demean the wide range and depth of black responses to emancipation, including the trauma and fears the master's announcement produced on some plantations. The very nature of the bondage they had endured, the myriad of experiences to which they had been exposed, the quality of the ties that bound them to their "white folks," and the ambivalence which had suffused those relationships were all bound to make for a diverse and complex reaction on the day the slaves were told they no longer had any masters or mistresses.

Capturing nearly the full range of responses, a former South Carolina slave recalled that on his plantation "some were sorry, some were hurt, but a few were silent and glad." From the perspective of the mistress of a Florida household, "some of the men cried, some spoke regretfully, [and] only two looked surly and had nothing to say." Although celebrations seldom followed the master's announcement, numerous blacks recalled taking the rest of the day off, if only to think through the implications of what they had been told. Still others, like Harriett Robinson, remembered that before the master could even finish his remarks, "over half them niggers was gone." But the slaves on an Alabama plantation stood quietly, stunned by the news. "We didn' hardly know what he means," Jenny Proctor recalled. "We jes' sort of huddle 'round together like scared rabbits, but after we knowed what he mean, didn' many of us go, 'cause we didn' know where to of went." None of them knew what to expect from freedom and they interpreted it in many different ways, explained James Lucas, a former slave of Jefferson Davis, who achieved his freedom at the age of thirty-one.

> Dey all had diffe'nt ways o' thinkin' 'bout it. Mos'ly though dey jus' lak me, dey didn' know jus' zackly what it meant. It was jus' somp'n dat de white folks an' slaves all de time talk 'bout. Dat's all. Folks dat ain' never been free don' rightly know de *feel* of bein' free. Dey don' know de meanin' of it. Slaves like us, what was owned by quality-folks, was sati'fied an' didn' sing none of dem freedom songs.

How long that sensation of shock or incredulity lasted would vary from slave to slave. "The day we was set free," remembered Silas Shotfore, "us did not know what to do. Our Missus said we could stay on the place." But his father made one decision almost instantly: no matter what they decided to do, they would do it somewhere else.

Suspicious as they might be of the white man's pronouncements, some blacks were initially skeptical, thinking it might all be a ruse, still another piece of deception calculated to test their fidelity. With that in mind, some thought it best to feign remorse at the announcement, while others needed to determine the master's veracity and sought confirmation elsewhere, often in the nearest town, at the local office of the Freedmen's Bureau, or on another plantation.

When his master explained to him that he was now a free man, Tom Robinson refused to believe him (" 'You're jokin' me,' I says") until he spoke with some slave neighbors. "I wanted to find out if they was free too. I just couldn't take it all in. I couldn't believe we was all free alike."

Although most slaves welcomed freedom with varying degrees of enthusiasm, the sense of confusion and uncertainty that prevailed in many quarters was not easily dispelled. The first thought of sixteen-year-old Sallie Crane of Arkansas was that she had been sold, and her mistress's reassurance that she would soon be reunited with her mother did little to comfort her. "I cried because I thought they was carrying me to see my mother before they would send me to be sold in Louisiana." The impression deliberately cultivated by some masters that the Yankees intended to sell freed slaves to Cuba to help defray war costs may have had some impact. Not matter what they were told, a former North Carolina slave recalled of the master's announcement, he and his mother were simply too frightened to leave the premises. "Jes like tarpins or turtles after 'mancipation. Jes stick our heads out to see how the land lay."

Nor did some slaves necessarily welcome the news when they fully understood its implications for their own lives. The sorrow which some displayed was not always pretense. To those who were reasonably satisfied with their positions and the relations they enjoyed with the white family, freedom offered no immediate cause for rejoicing. "I was a-farin' pretty well in de kitchen," Aleck Trimble remarked. "I didn't t'ink I eber see better times dan what dem was, and I ain't.". . .

The mixed emotions with which slaves greeted their freedom also reflected a natural fear of the unknown, along with the knowledge that "they's allus 'pend on Old Marse to look after them." For many blacks, this was the only life they had known and the world ended at the boundaries of the plantation. To think that they no longer had a master or mistress, while it brought exuberance and relief to many, struck others with dismay. "Whar we gwine eat an' sleep?" they demanded to know. And realizing they could not depend on the law or on other whites for protection, who would now stand between them and the dreaded patrollers and "po' buckra"? After hearing of their freedom, Silas Smith recalled, "de awfulest feeling" pervaded the slave quarters that night as they contemplated a future without masters or mistresses. "You felt jes' like you had done strayed off a-fishing and got lost." Fifteen years after emancipation, Parke Johnston, a former Virginia slave, vividly recalled "how wild and upset and *dreadful* everything was in them times."

> It came so sudden on 'em they wasn't prepared for it. Just think of whole droves of people, that had always been kept so close, and hardly ever left the plantation before, turned loose all at once, with nothing in the world, but what they had on their backs, and often little enough of that; men, women and children that had left their homes when they found out they were free, walking along the road with no where to go.

*   *   *   *   *

The uncertainties, the regrets, the anxieties which characterized many of the reactions to emancipation underscored that pervasive sense of dependency— the feeling, as more than one ex-slave recalled, that "we couldn't do a thing without white folks." Slavery had taught black people to be slaves—"good" slaves and obedient workers. "All de slaves knowed how to do hard work," observed Thomas Cole, who had run away to enlist in the Union Army, "but dey didn't know nothin' 'bout how to 'pend on demselves for de livin'." Of course, the very logic and survival of the "peculiar institution" had demanded that nothing be done to prepare slaves for the possibility of freedom; on the contrary, they had been taught to feel their incapacity for dealing with its immense responsibilities. Many years before the war, a South Carolina jurist set forth the paternalistic ideal when he advised that each slave should be taught to view his master as "a perfect security from injury. When this is the case, the relation of master and servant becomes little short of that of parent and child." The testimony of former slaves suggests how effectively some masters had been able to inculcate that ideal and how the legacy of paternalism could paralyze its victims. . . .

Upon hearing of their freedom, some slaves instinctively deferred to the traditional source of authority, advice, sustenance, and protection—the master himself. Now that they were no longer his slaves, what did he want them to do? Few freed blacks, however, no matter how confused and apprehensive they may have been, were altogether oblivious to the excitement and the anticipation that this event had generated. At the moment of freedom, masses of slaves did not suddenly erupt in a mammoth Jubilee but neither did they all choose to be passive, cowed, or indifferent in the face of their master's announcement. Outside of the prayer meetings and the annual holiday frolics, plantation life had afforded them few occasions for free expression, at least in the presence of their "white folks." If only for a few hours or days, then, many newly emancipated slaves dropped their usual defenses, cast off their masks, and gave themselves the rare luxury of acting out feelings they were ordinarily expected to repress.

Once they understood the full import of the master's words, and even then perhaps only after several minutes of stunned or polite silence, many blacks found they could no longer contain their emotions. More importantly, they felt no need to do so. "That the day I shouted," was how Richard Carruthers of Texas recalled his emancipation. Booker T. Washington stood next to his mother during the announcement; many years later he could still vividly recall how she hugged and kissed him, the tears streaming down her face, and her explanation that she had prayed many years for this day but never believed she would live to see it. Freedom took longer to reach Bexar County, Texas, where the war had hardly touched the lives and routines of the slaves. But Felix Haywood, who worked as a sheepherder and cowpuncher, recalled how "everybody went wild" when they learned of freedom. "We all felt like horses and nobody had made us that way but ourselves. We was free. Just like that, we was free."

If neither words nor prayers conveyed the appropriate emotions, the newly freed slaves might draw on the traditional spirituals, whose imagery easily befitted an occasion like emancipation. The triumph had come in this world, not in the next. The exuberance and importance of such a moment also inspired updated versions of the spirituals and songs especially composed for the occasion. Out in Bexar County, Felix Haywood heard them sing:

> Abe Lincoln freed the nigger
> With the gun and the trigger;
> And I ain't goin' to get whipped any more.
> I got my ticket,
> Leavin' the thicket,
> And I'm a-headin' for the Golden Shore!

Harriett Gresham, who had belonged to a wealthy planter in South Carolina, remembered hearing the guns at Fort Sumter that inaugurated the war, as well as the song that sounded the death of slavery:

> No slav'ry chains to tie me down,
> And no mo' driver's ho'n to blow fer me.
> No mo' stocks to fasten me down,
> Jesus break slav'ry chain, Lord.
> Break slav'ry chain, Lord,
> Break slav'ry chain, Lord,
> Da Heben gwinter be my home.

"Guess dey made 'em up," Annie Harris said of many of the songs she heard in those days, "'cause purty soon ev'ybody fo' miles around was singin' freedom songs."

Although the classic version of the Jubilee featured large masses of people, some newly freed slaves only wanted to be alone at this moment. Neither fear of the master nor deference to his feelings entirely explains this preference. Overwhelmed by what they had just heard, some needed a momentary solitude to reflect on its implications and to convince themselves that it had really happened, while others simply preferred to express themselves with the least amount of inhibition. Lou Smith recalled running off and hiding in the plum orchard, where he kept repeating to himself, "I'se free, I'se free; I ain't never going back to Miss Jo." After hearing of his freedom, an elderly Virginia black proceeded to the barn, leaped from one stack of straw to the other, and "screamed and screamed!" Although confined to bed, Aunt Sissy, a crippled Virginia slave, heard the celebration outside, limped out the door, and then simply stood there praying. "Wouldn't let nobody tetch her, wouldn't set down. Stood dere swayin' fum side to side an' singin' over an' over her favorite hymn."

> Oh, Father of Mercy
> We give thanks to Thee
> We give thanks to Thee
> For thy great glory.

Like Aunt Sissy, many slaves viewed their deliverance as a sign of divine intervention. God's will had been heeded, if belatedly, and in this act lay final proof of His omnipresence. Few expressed it more eloquently than the Virginia black woman who looked upon emancipation as something approaching a miracle. "Isn't I a free woman now! De Lord can make Heaven out of Hell any time, I do believe." In addressing his Nashville congregation, a black preacher interpreted emancipation as a result of his people having kept the faith, even when it appeared as though there was no hope and that the Lord had forsaken them.

> We was all like de chil'en of Israel in Egypt, a cryin' and cryin' and a gronin' and gronin', and no Moses came wid de Lord's word to order de door broke down, dat we might walk t'rough and be free. Now de big ugly door is broke down, bress de Lord, and we know de groans of de captive is heard. Didn't I tell you to pray and not to faint away, dat is not to doubt, and dat He who opened de sea would deliber us sure, and no tanks to de tasker massas, who would nebber let us go if dey could only hab held on to us? But dey couldn't—no dey couldn't do dat, 'cause de Lord he was wid us, and wouldn't let us be 'pressed no more. . . .

*   *   *   *   *

Despite the debilitating effects of dependency and the confusion which persisted over the precise nature of their new status, the freedmen were neither helpless, easily manipulated, nor frightened into passivity. Although some still deferred to the advice of the old master, many did not. During slavery, they had often survived only by drawing on their own inner resources, their accumulated experience, and the wisdom of those in their own ranks to whom they looked for leadership and counsel. Upon being told of their freedom, the blacks on many plantations retired to their quarters to discuss the announcement, what if any alternatives were now open to them, and the first steps they should take to test their freedom. On a plantation in Georgia, for example, where the owner had asked his former slaves to remain until they finished the current crop, they discussed his proposal for the next several days before reaching a common decision. "They wasn't no celebration 'round the place," William Hutson recalled, "but they wasn't no work after the Master tells us we is free. Nobody leave the place though. Not 'til in the fall when the work is through."

The possibilities that suddenly presented themselves, the kinds of questions that freedom posed, the sheer magnitude of this event in their lives could not always be readily absorbed. Recounting his own escape to freedom, more than two decades before the war, William Wells Brown never forgot the strange sensations he experienced: "The fact that I was a freeman—could walk, talk, eat and sleep as a man, and no one to stand over me with the blood-clotted cowhide—all this made me feel that I was not myself." For the newly emancipated blacks, however, most of whom chose to remain in the same regions in which they had been slaves, the problems they faced were far different and more formidable than those which had confronted the fugitives upon reaching the North. Experiencing her first days of freedom, a Mississippi woman voiced that prevailing uncertainty as to how to give meaning to her new status: "I used to think if I could be free I should be the happiest of anybody in the world. But when my master come to me, and says—Lizzie, you is free! it seems like I was in a kind of daze. And when I would wake up in the morning I would think to myself, Is I free? Hasn't I got to get up before daylight and go into the field to work?"

The uncertainties plagued both blacks and whites. Under slavery, the boundaries had been clearly established and both parties understood them. But what were the proper boundaries of black freedom? What new forms would the relationship between a former slave and his former master now assume? How would the freed blacks be expected to interact with free whites? Neither the blacks nor the whites were altogether certain, though they might have pronounced views on such matters. Now that black freedom had been generally acknowledged, it needed to be defined. The state legislatures, the courts, and the Federal government offered some direction. But freedom could ultimately be defined only in the day-to-day lives and experiences of the people themselves. "De day of freedom," a former Tennessee slave recalled, the overseer came out into the fields and told them that they were free. "Free how?" they asked him, and he replied, "Free to work and live for demselves." In the aftermath of emancipation, the newly freed slaves would seek to test that response and answer the question for themselves.

QUESTIONS FOR DISCUSSION

1. Why are the "legendary stories" of "Day of Jubilo" celebrations more mythic than real?

2. Why was news of emancipation greeted with "mixed emotions" and "confusion and uncertainty" by so many slaves?

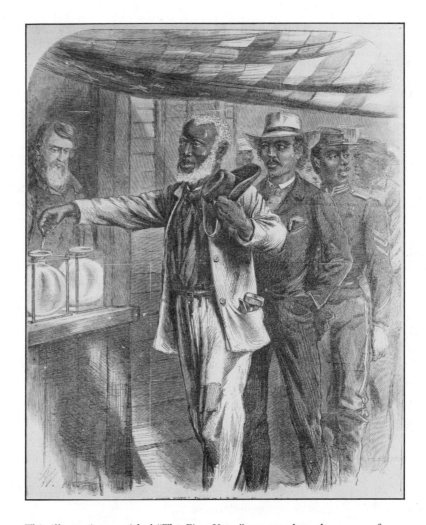

This illustration, entitled "The First Vote," appeared on the cover of *Harper's Weekly* on November 16, 1867. The voters lined up before the ballot boxes represent the three groups from which the black political leadership would emerge: the former slave artisan (note the tools in the pocket of the first man in line), the urban free negro, and the soldier. *(The Bettmann Archive)*

Addresses from the South Carolina Colored State Convention

Commentary by Eric Foner

The first state-wide black convention in the history of South Carolina assembled in Charleston's Zion Church in November 1865. Four-and-one-half years had passed since the Civil War began in Charleston harbor, and nine months since Union troops occupied the city, resulting in the social revolution of emancipation. The most widely publicized of several state-wide black conventions held in the South that year, South Carolina's meeting revealed blacks' attitudes and aspirations and the nature of an emerging black political leadership at the dawn of freedom.

The fifty-two delegates represented many strands of this country's black experience. More than half had been born free, reflecting the size and prominence of Charleston's prewar free black community. Generally light of skin and often well educated and prosperous, the city's free persons of color had always been conscious of the gap separating them from the slaves who formed the vast majority of the state's black population. Against lengthening odds, they had attempted to maintain a middle ground between black and white, but in 1865 many cast their lot with the freedmen.

Several of the delegates had come to South Carolina from homes in the North; their presence illustrated how, during the Reconstruction period following the Civil War, the South became a place of opportunity for talented blacks whose opportunities in northern states were limited by racial prejudice. Perhaps the best known was Martin R. Delany. Called by historians the "father of black nationalism" because of his advocacy during the 1850s of black emigration to Africa or the Caribbean, Delany had helped recruit black troops during the Civil War and became one of the few blacks to be commissioned as an officer. In 1865, he was employed by the Freedmen's Bureau, the federal agency established to provide relief to destitute freedmen, protect blacks' legal rights, and assist in the adjustment to free labor. A Charleston newspaper referred to him as "the Patrick Henry of his race." Another black northerner was Philadelphia-born Jonathan Gibbs, a Dartmouth-educated Presbyterian minister who had been sent South to help establish black schools. And, of course, former slaves were present including William Beverly Nash, a hotel servant before emancipation, and Jacob Mills, a Charleston butcher.

South Carolina's black convention was one of a series that assembled throughout the South in 1865 and 1866. All told, several hundred delegates attended these gatherings, some selected by local meetings especially convened for the purpose; others by churches, fraternal societies, Union Leagues, and black army units; still others simply self-appointed. In one North Carolina county, blacks in 1866 held an election to choose between two candidates who had conducted "a regular canvass" for delegate.

The South Carolina delegates were typical of those who attended these conventions; generally free urban mulattoes and skilled former slaves took the lead, and ministers, former soldiers, and those born in the North played a prominent role. The gathering also reflected the uneven nature of black political mobilization in 1865, for in nearly every state, organization progressed much faster in the cities, where most free blacks lived and the Army and Freedman's Bureau offered protection, than in the rural black belt where most of the former slaves resided. The South Carolina delegates came mainly from Charleston and the surrounding counties; many "up-country" areas were not represented at all.

On occasion, tensions between various components of the black community surfaced during convention debates. The official *Proceedings* contained a discreet reference to the "spirited discussion" inspired by a resolution referring to blacks' making "distinctions among ourselves." By and large, however, the convention was harmonious, with delegates devoting their time to considering issues that united the black community rather than dividing it.

The sudden emergence of political organization was part of a larger movement among blacks to establish their autonomy from white control. Before the Civil War, free blacks had created a network of institutions—churches, schools, mutual benefit societies—that flourished despite the constant surveillance of whites, while slaves had forged a culture centered on the family and the "invisible institution" of the slave church. With emancipation, these institutions were consolidated and liberated from white supervision. Blacks took initiatives to reunite spouses separated by slavery and rescue their children from court-ordered "apprenticeship" arrangements whereby former slaveowners sought to retain, in part, an unfree labor force. They removed themselves from churches dominated by whites and established their own schools and benevolent societies. Political organization was nurtured by this flourishing network of churches, schools, and fraternal societies, which united the free-born and former slaves. It was by no means coincidental that the South Carolina convention met in a black church, for the church had become the focal point of the black community.

At the same time, blacks emerging from slavery tried to define the economic terms of their freedom, to take control of their working lives and gain access to the resources of the South. As in other areas of their lives, blacks sought autonomy in their economic relationships, and in a rural society, autonomy meant land. "Their great desire," wrote one Georgia plantation owner, "seems to be to get away from all overseers, to hire or purchase land, and work for themselves." Many blacks insisted they had earned a right to the land by two-and-a-half centuries of unrequited toil. In some parts of the South, they refused to sign labor contracts or to leave plantations, maintaining instead that the property rightfully belonged to them. Often, planters called in federal troops or the Freedmen's Bureau to evict them. The contest over land was most intense on South Carolina's Sea Islands near Charleston, from which planters had fled early in the war, and in the adjacent "low country," where General William T. Sherman had ordered forty acres of land provided to every black family. Andrew Johnson, who succeeded to the presidency after Lincoln's assassination, ordered this land restored to its former owners, but blacks had no intention of surrendering it without a struggle.

The delegates who assembled at Charleston were fully aware of these economic conflicts, but, partly because free urban blacks dominated the gathering, they received little attention. The convention's memorials to the people of South Carolina, the legislature, and Congress demanded for blacks the same right to pursue a livelihood as whites enjoyed, but referred only obliquely to the land issue, reminding Congress of the government's "pledges" regarding land. Many delegates, especially blacks from the North and the better off free-born, were strongly influenced by the "free labor" ideology of the national Republican party. They believed individuals should work hard to acquire property, not be given it by the government. Their own experience of achieving prosperity in the face of adversity convinced successful free blacks that the freedmen needed, not government assistance, but only an equal chance. Thus delegates emphasized blacks' right to competitive equality but made no mention of more far-reaching policies, like government-sponsored land distribution, that would have been necessary so that former slaves did not emerge into freedom as impoverished, landless laborers.

Political, not economic concerns, dominated the convention, for the delegates' primary aim was to stake blacks' claim to equal citizenship in the American republic. In drafting their resolutions and memorials, they drew upon what historian Vincent Harding calls the "Great Tradition" of black protest, articulated by northern free blacks before the Civil War. Grounded in an affirmation of Americanism, this tradition insisted that blacks formed an integral part of the national community, and as such were entitled to the same rights and opportunities white citizens enjoyed. Blacks now contended that the logical and essential corollary of the end of slavery was the eradication of all color discrimination, complete equality before the law, and the enfranchisement of the black population.

The convention expressed a broad aspiration for equality, demanding for blacks the full gamut of opportunities and privileges enjoyed by whites, ranging from access to education to the right to bear arms, sit on juries, establish newspapers, assemble peacefully, and "develop our whole being by all the appliances that belong to civilized society." These were not "special favors," but simple justice, privileges essential to the very meaning of freedom. While forthright in claiming civil and political equality, their tone was conciliatory rather than confrontational, assuring South Carolina's whites of blacks' "spirit of meekness" and consciousness of "your wealth and greatness, and our poverty and weakness." "We are Americans by birth," they insisted, echoing the prewar "Great Tradition," "and we assure you that we are Americans in feelings." Against discrimination based on race, they counterposed an irrefutable logic: "We simply desire that we shall be recognized as men," and "why should we suffer on account of . . . color?" Rather than glorying in the South's defeat or the abolition of slavery, they held out to South Carolina whites "the right hand of fellowship."

As in other parts of the South, the preoccupation of the South Carolina black leadership was what the delegates called "the inestimable right of voting for those who rule over us in the land of our birth." In a democratic political culture, the ballot symbolized more than simply the right to choose public officials—it defined the public community, a community in which blacks insisted they deserved a place. In justifying their demand for legal and political equality, blacks drew upon traditions deeply rooted in their own experience. Many in 1865 insisted that the participation of 200,000 black soldiers in the Civil War had earned blacks full recognition as citizens. Others couched their beliefs in the language of black religion. As slaves, blacks had come to think of themselves as analogous to the Jews in Egypt, an oppressed people whom God, in the fullness of time, would deliver from bondage. The Civil War they viewed as God's instrument of deliverance, and Reconstruction another step in a divinely ordained progress toward full equality.

Most of all, blacks appealed to republican traditions shared by all Americans. They referred to the heritage of the American Revolution, whose ideals they eloquently invoked. The South Carolina delegates cited the "immortal Declaration of Independence" (especially the maxim "that all men are created equal"), the Constitution, and the general democratic principles of the larger political culture, in support of their own demands. This, they believed, would most effectively make their case before white society. No taxation without representation, government based on the consent of the governed—these doctrines should apply to blacks as well as whites. America could only live up to its own creed by absorbing blacks fully into the civil and political order.

Thus, the delegates combined an insistent demand for equal rights with a conciliatory tone, reflecting the political situation toward the end of 1865. In May, President Johnson had announced a Reconstruction plan that restored southern whites to local power but did not offer blacks a role in the political system. Constitutional conventions had met throughout the South to ratify the end of slavery, but none even considered extending the franchise to blacks. Congress, moreover, had not yet met to deliberate upon Reconstruction.

Powerless at home and uncertain of how national policy would evolve, the South Carolina delegates addressed themselves to several different audiences simultaneously and shaped their rhetoric to make the broadest appeal. They hoped to influence the white citizens and legislature of their own state and the authorities in Washington. But beyond this, their resolutions were directed toward public opinion at large, especially that of the Republican North, which was determined that the fruits of the Civil War, including emancipation, be confirmed in Reconstruction. And, of course, the convention addressed blacks themselves. Although the vast majority of former slaves were illiterate, the proceedings and resolutions (reprinted in pamphlet form and in sympathetic newspapers) would be read aloud at black gatherings, both reflecting and shaping the ongoing development of black politics.

The convention's mixture of radicalism and moderation also mirrored the indecision of an emerging class of black political leaders still finding its voice in 1865, and dominated by urban free blacks, ministers, and others who did not always feel the bitter resentments of rural freedmen, having often enjoyed harmonious relations with at least some members of the white community. But the demand for political equality was indeed a radical departure, especially in a state like South Carolina where some 60 percent of the population was black. In 1865, only six northern states, all with minimal black populations, allowed blacks to vote. In other societies that had abolished slavery, no precedent existed for incorporating the former slaves as full and equal citizens so quickly after emancipation.

Black suffrage would have radically transformed the political structure of the South, and it is not surprising that virtually no one within the white community advocated such a course. Instead, the legislatures that convened at the end of 1865 adopted "Black Codes," severely restricting blacks' economic opportunities by requiring them to sign yearlong contracts for plantation labor or face fines and jail sentences for "vagrancy."

The leaders of Presidential Reconstruction believed that emancipated blacks must remain a subordinate plantation labor force, with only those legal rights that white society felt it desirable to grant. Already in November 1865, it was clear South Carolina would follow this path. Thus, in addition to pleading its case before the people of the state, the black convention appealed to Congress for assistance. The Civil War had taught blacks to view the federal government as their protector. They now insisted that Washington must not abandon those who had become free to the mercy of their former owners.

The South Carolina convention was only one of many black protests against the course of Presidential Reconstruction that would help convince the Republican North that further national action was required to guarantee the fruits of the Civil War—"loyal" government in the South and protection of the basic rights of the emancipated slaves. When Congress did act, in 1867, a black leadership was ready to step onto the stage of politics.

Address of the Colored State Convention to the People of the State of South Carolina

Fellow Citizens:—We have assembled as delegates representing the colored people of the State of South Carolina, in the capacity of State Convention, to confer together and to deliberate upon our intellectual, moral, industrial, civil, and political condition as affected by the great changes which have taken place in this State and throughout this whole country, and to devise ways and means which may, through the blessing of God, tend to our improvement, elevation, and progress; fully believing that our cause is one which commends itself to all good men throughout the civilized world; that it is the sacred cause of truth and righteousness; that it particularly appeals to those professing to be governed by that religion which teaches to "do unto all men as you would have them do unto you."

These principles we conceive to embody the great duty of man to his fellow man; and, *as men,* we ask only to be included in a practical application of this principle.

We feel that the *justness* of our cause is sufficient apology for our course at this time. Heretofore we have had no avenues opened to us or our children— we have had no firesides that we could call our own; none of those incentives to work for the development of our minds and the aggrandizement of our race in common with other people. The measures which have been adopted for the development of white men's children have been denied to us and ours. The laws which have made white men great, have degraded us, because we were colored, and because we were reduced to chattel slavery. But now that we are freemen, now that we have been lifted up by the providence of God to manhood, we have resolved to come forward, and, like MEN, speak and *act* for ourselves. We fully recognize the truth of the maxim that "God helps those who help themselves." In making this appeal to you, we adopt the language of the immortal Declaration of Independence, "that all men are created equal," and that "life, liberty, and the pursuit of happiness" are the right of all; that taxation and representation should go together; that governments are to protect, not destroy the rights of mankind; that the Constitution of the United States was formed to establish justice, to promote the general welfare, and

70

secure the blessings of liberty to all the people of this country; that resistance to tyrants is obedience to God—are American principles and maxims; and together they form the constructive elements of the American Government.

We think we fully comprehend and duly appreciate the principles and measures which compose this platform; and all that we desire or ask for is to be placed in a position that we could conscientiously and legitimately defend, with you, those principles against the surges of despotism to the last drop of our blood. We have not come together in battle array to assume a boastful attitude and to talk loudly of high-sounding principles or unmeaning platforms, nor do we pretend to any great boldness; for we know your wealth and greatness, and our poverty and weakness; and although we feel keenly our wrongs, still we come together, we trust, in a spirit of meekness and of patriotic good-will to all the people of the State. But yet it is some consolation to know (and it inspires us with hope when we reflect) that our cause is not alone the cause of five millions of colored men in this country, but we are intensely alive to the fact that it is also the cause of millions of oppressed men in other "parts of God's beautiful earth," who are now struggling to be free in the fullest sense of that word; and God and nature are pledged in its triumph. We are Americans by birth, and we assure you that we are Americans in feeling; and, in spite of all wrongs which we have long and silently endured in this country, we would still exclaim with a full heart, "O America! with all thy faults we love thee still."

> Breathes there a man with soul so dead
> Who never to himself hath said—
> "This is my own, my native land!"
> Whose heart hath ne'er within him burned
> As home his footsteps he hath turned,
> From wandering in a foreign strand?

Thus we would address you, not as enemies, but as friends and fellow-countrymen, who desire to dwell among you in peace, and whose destinies are interwoven, and linked with those of the American people, and hence must be fulfilled in this country. As descendants of a race feeble and long oppressed, we might with propriety appeal to a great and magnanimous people like Americans, for special favors and encouragement, on the principle that the strong should aid the weak, the learned should teach the unlearned.

But it is for no such purposes that we raise our voices to the people of South Carolina on this occasion. We ask for no special privileges or peculiar favors. We ask only for *even-handed Justice,* or for the removal of such positive obstructions and disabilities as past, and the recent Legislators have seen fit to throw in our way, and heap upon us.

Without any rational cause or provocation on our part, of which we are conscious, as a people, we, by the action of your Convention and Legislature, have been virtually, and with few exceptions excluded from, first, the rights of citizenship, which you cheerfully accord to strangers, but deny to us who have been born and reared in your midst, who were faithful while your greatest trials were upon you, and have done nothing since to merit your disapprobation.

We are denied the right of giving our testimony in like manner with that of our white fellow-citizens, in the courts of the State, by which our persons and property are subject to every species of violence, insult and fraud without redress.

We are also by the present laws, not only denied the right of citizenship, the inestimable right of voting for those who rule over us in the land of our birth, but by the so-called Black Code we are deprived the rights of the meanest profligate in the country—the right to engage in any legitimate business free from any restraints, save those which govern all other citizens of this State.

You have by your Legislative actions placed barriers in the way of our educational and mechanical improvement; you have given us little or no encouragement to pursue agricultural pursuits, by refusing to sell to us lands, but organize societies to bring foreigners to your country, and thrust us out or reduce us to a serfdom, intolerable to men born amid the progress of American genius and national development.

Your public journals charge the freedmen with destroying the products of the country since they have been made free, when they know that the destruction of the products was brought about by the ravages of war of four years duration. How unjust, then, to charge upon the innocent and helpless, evils in which they had no hand, and which may be traced to where it properly belongs.

We simply desire that we shall be recognized as men; that we have no obstructions placed in our way; that the same laws which govern white men shall direct colored men; that we have the right of trial by a jury of our peers, that schools be opened or established for our children; that we be permitted to acquire homesteads for ourselves and children; that we be dealt with as others, in equity and justice.

We claim the confidence and good-will of all classes of men; we ask that the same chances be extended to us that freemen should demand at the hands of their fellow-citizens. We desire the prosperity and growth of this State and the well-being of all men, and shall be found ever struggling to elevate ourselves and add to the national character; and we trust the day will not be distant when you will acknowledge that by our rapid progress in moral, social, religious and intellectual development that you will cheerfully accord to us the high commendation that we are worthy, with you, to enjoy all political emoluments—when we shall realize the truth that "all men are endowed by their Creator with inalienable rights," and that on the American continent this is the right of all, whether he comes from the east, west, north or south; and, although complexions may differ, "a man's a man for a' that."

ZION CHURCH, Charleston, S.C., }
November 24, 1865.   }

Address to the Legislature of the State of South Carolina

To the Honorable Senate and House of Representatives of the State of South Carolina in General Assembly Met:

Gentlemen:

We, the colored people of the State of South Carolina, do hereby appeal to you for justice.

The last four years of war have made great changes in our condition and relation to each other, as well as in the laws and institutions of our State. We were previously either slaves, or, if free, still under the pressure of laws made in the interest and for the protection of slavery.

But the events of the past four years have destroyed this state of things. Our State has been called upon to remodel her Constitution from its very foundation and first principles; and, as we have been, and still are, deeply affected by all these changes in interests of vital importance to us, we have resolved, in the Convention which we have called together to consider our interests, to petition your Honorable body for justice.

We ask that those laws that have been enacted, that apply to us on account of our color, be repealed. We do not presume to dictate to you, gentlemen; but we appeal to your own instincts of justice and generosity. Why should we suffer on account of the color that an all-wise Creator has given to us? Is it possible that the only reason for enacting stringent and oppressive laws for us is because our color is of a darker hue?

We feel assured, gentlemen, that no valid reason can exist for the enactment and perpetuation of laws that have peculiar application to us.

We are now free. We are now *all* free. But we are still, gentlemen, to a certain extent in your power; and we need not assure you with what deep concern we are watching *all* your deliberations, but especially those that have peculiar reference to us.

We would ask your Honorable body for the right of suffrage and the right of testifying in courts of law. These two things we deem necessary to our welfare and elevation. They are the rights of every freeman, and are inherent and essential to every republican form of government.

Our appeal is based on justice; but we do not rely solely upon that: we appeal to your *generosity.* Grant us the opportunity of elevating ourselves.

It is for you to say whether we shall become useful citizens or dissatisfied subjects; whether you will become the generous helpers of the weak, and thereby add to your strength, or whether you will weaken yourselves by oppressing those who mean well to all.

We do sincerely hope that you will grant your petitioners their desires. We are natives of this State, and we feel assured that nothing is needed to render our future relations mutually beneficial but the bestowment of the rights we ask.

ZION CHURCH, Charleston, S.C.,
November 24, 1865.

Memorial
To the Senate and House of Representatives of The United States, in Congress Assembled

Gentlemen:

We, the colored people of the State of South Carolina, in Convention assembled, respectfully present for your attention some prominent facts in relation to our present condition, and make a modest yet earnest appeal to your considerate judgment.

We, your memorialists, with profound gratitude to almighty God, recognize the great boon of freedom conferred upon us by the instrumentality of our late President, Abraham Lincoln, and the armies of the United States.

> The fixed decree, which not all Heaven can move,
> Thou Fate, fulfill it; and, ye Powers, approve.

We also recognize with liveliest gratitude the vast service of the Freedmen's Bureau, together with the efforts of the good and wise throughout our land to raise up an oppressed and deeply injured people in the scale of civilized being, during the throbbings of a mighty revolution which must affect the future destiny of the world.

Conscious of the difficulties that surround our position, we would ask for no rights or privileges but such as rest upon the strong basis of justice and expediency, in view of the best interests of our entire country.

We ask first, that the strong arm of law and order be placed alike over the entire people of this State; that life and property be secured, and the laborer as free to sell his labor as the merchant his goods.

We ask that a fair and impartial construction be given to the pledges of government to us concerning the land question.

We ask that the three great agents of civilized society—the school, the pulpit, the press—be as secure in South Carolina as in Massachusetts or Vermont.

We ask that equal suffrage be conferred upon us, in common with the white men of this State.

This we ask, because "all free governments derive their just powers from the consent of the governed;" and we are largely in the majority in this

State, bearing for a long period the burden of an odious taxation, without a just representation. We ask for equal suffrage as a protection for the hostility evoked by our known faithfulness to our country's flag under all circumstances.

We ask that colored men shall not in every instance be tried by white men; and that neither by custom or enactment shall we be excluded from the jury box.

We ask that, inasmuch as the Constitution of the United States explicitly declares that the right to keep and bear arms shall not be infringed—and the Constitution is the Supreme law of the land—that the late efforts of the Legislature of this State to pass an act to deprive us of arms be forbidden, as a plain violation of the Constitution, and unjust to many of us in the highest degree, who have been soldiers, and purchased our muskets from the United States Government when mustered out of service.

We protest against any code of black laws the Legislature of this State may enact, and pray to be governed in peaceful convention, to discuss the political questions of the day; the right to enter upon all avenues of agriculture, commerce, trade; to amass wealth by thrift and industry; the right to develope our whole being by all the appliances that belong to civilized society, cannot be questioned by any class of intelligent legislators.

We solemnly affirm and desire to live orderly and peacefully with all the people of this State; and commending this memorial to your considerate judgment. Thus we ever pray.

CHARLESTON, S.C., November 24, 1865. ⎫
Zion Presbyterian Church   ⎬
                                                                ⎭

=====   Commentary: Part II   =====

In March 1867, convinced that the governments created under Presidential Reconstruction had failed to protect the basic rights of blacks and white Unionists, Congress decreed universal manhood suffrage for the South, inaugurating a period of black political participation known as Radical Reconstruction. Temporary military rule was established and new constitutional conventions were held, establishing state governments resting on the principle of equal civil and political rights for all. Throughout the South, governments controlled by the Republican party (with blacks playing a major role) came to power in 1868 and 1869. In no state were black leaders as prepared politically as in South Carolina, and nowhere would they play so significant a role in attempting to implement the egalitarian ideas formulated in 1865.

It is remarkable how many convention delegates of 1865 went on to hold positions of prominence in Radical Reconstruction. Jonathan Gibbs, who by 1867 had moved to Florida, became that state's secretary of state and superintendent of public education; Francis L. Cardozo served as South Carolina's secretary of state and treasurer; and Jonathan J. Wright became the only black to sit on a state supreme court during Reconstruction. Four 1865 delegates went on to sit in Congress: Richard H. Cain, an Ohio-educated minister who came to the state as a missionary in 1865; Robert C. DeLarge, a free-born Charleston tailor; Joseph H. Rainey, a barber whose parents had purchased their freedom before the Civil War; and Alonzo J. Ransier, who also held the post of South Carolina's lieutenant governor.

Twelve delegates also sat in South Carolina's Constitutional Convention of 1868, which drafted a new frame of government that democratized the state for black and white alike. It established the first public school system in South Carolina's history, reformed the archaic system of legislative representation, expanded the rights of women, made many local offices elective rather than appointive, and established a state land commission to assist the poor of both races in acquiring property. And thirteen of the delegates served in the legislature, which during the years of South Carolina Reconstruction (1868–1877) swept away the Black Codes and legal discrimination, enacted sweeping civil rights laws, reformed the system of taxation so that men of property would bear the highest burden, and took steps to develop the state's economy and repair the damage done by the Civil War. The implementation of this economic program was marred by corruption—railroad companies and other economic interests bribed state and local officials to gain advantages for themselves—but taken together, the policies of Reconstruction marked an unprecedented effort to modernize and democratize the state. The demands of the 1865 black convention had been enshrined in law.

Compared with 1865, however, the political mobilization of the black community during Radical Reconstruction was far more extensive and deeply rooted. In 1867, with the coming of black suffrage, a wave of political activism swept across the rural South. The meteoric rise of local black political activity was reflected in the growth of the Union League, which served, as one member described it, as "a political school for the people," an institutional structure which blacks could utilize to voice their own grievances and aspirations. Meetings were generally held in a black church or school, a member's home, or, if necessary, secretly in the woods or fields. Issues of the day were discussed, Republican newspapers read aloud (since the vast majority of former slaves were illiterate), and political strategies weighed. Moreover, unlike the conventions of 1865, the leagues took a keen interest in economic issues. Their leaders assisted freedmen in contract disputes with white employers and sometimes helped organize strikes of plantation workers.

The Union Leagues generated a new class of local black political leaders, most of them former slaves who had not been involved in the first wave of organization in 1865. In the black belt, where few free blacks had lived before the Civil War, ex-slave teachers, preachers, artisans, and former soldiers now came to the fore in politics. Indeed, these lines of occupation and social function often overlapped: preachers and teachers earned their living in part as laborers; politicians helped organize churches; schools served as meeting houses for the Union League.

The political ideology of the "Great Tradition" now spread into the rural South and was expanded to reflect the experience of humble former slaves. The importance of equal civil and political rights was stressed again and again, but so too were economic concerns neglected in 1865. The claim to land had found little expression at the early black conventions, but in 1867 demands for land animated black politics. State Republican conventions found themselves divided between "confiscation radicals" who demanded that the property of Confederate planters be divided among the poor (black and white), and more moderate voices, appalled by the possibility of interference with property rights.

The outcome of this debate reveals a great deal about the limits within which black politics could operate during Reconstruction. Northern Republicans, with the exception of a few Radicals like Congressman Thaddeus Stevens, rejected the idea of land distribution entirely. Southern white Republicans— both "carpetbaggers" from the North and "scalawags," or native southerners— looked to a program of economic development that depended on massive investment from the North, investment certain to be discouraged by a land redistribution policy. Blacks themselves, moreover, were divided on the land question. Like South Carolina, Louisiana had a large antebellum free black population that took a leading role in Reconstruction politics. At the Louisiana Republican convention, according to one newspaper, "all the freedmen, *save one,* were in favor of confiscation," while "the white and free-born colored members" opposed.

The confiscation debate underscored both the radical potential inherent in Reconstruction, and the limits within which black politicians were forced to operate. Both the approval of the national Republican party and allies among local whites were crucial for success, even in states with black majorities such as Louisiana, Mississippi, and South Carolina. Everywhere but in South Carolina, blacks remained junior partners within the party. Only in South Carolina did blacks dominate the constitutional convention and legislature, and even here all the Reconstruction governors were white.

Nonetheless, on the local level, numerous enclaves of genuine black political power existed during Reconstruction. Reporter Edward King, traveling across the South in 1873 and 1874, encountered many such examples—black aldermen and city councilmen in Petersburg, Houston, and Little Rock, parish jury members in Louisiana, black magistrates in the South Carolina low country. One focal point of black politics was Beaufort, South Carolina, the heart of low-country black life, whose streets were lined with the graceful homes of prewar rice planters. "Here the revolution penetrated to the quick," King observed. "One of the most remarkable revolutions ever recorded in history had occurred. A wealthy and highly prosperous community has been reduced to beggary; its vassals have become its lords."

The existence of black and sympathetic white local officials often made a real difference in the day-to-day lives of the freedmen, ensuring that blacks accused of crimes would be tried before juries of their peers rather than by whites alone, as under Presidential Reconstruction, and enforcing fairness in such prosaic aspects of local government as road repair, public employment, tax assessment, and poor relief. In South Carolina, in 1876, rice plantation workers held a series of successful strikes, aided by the support of local officials. Black judges and juries would not convict them of interfering with planters' rights; the black militia could not be used against them; the Republican governor, needing black votes in a difficult reelection campaign, did not heed local whites' pleas for assistance. Thus, as the 1865 convention had predicted, the vote proved a weapon blacks could use effectively in pursuing their own interests.

For some black politicians, as for many whites in nineteenth-century America, official position became a means of social advancement. Politics was one of the few areas of dignified work open to black men of talent and ambition, and compared with other opportunities, the rewards of even minor office could seen dazzlingly high. The salaries of legislators, sheriffs, justices of the peace, and other officials far outstripped those most blacks could ordinarily command. Many South Carolina black leaders came to politics from positions of relative comfort, but others were able to translate office into significant personal gain. Former slave John A. Chestnut, an 1865 convention delegate who went on to serve in the state's constitutional convention and legislature, had acquired real and personal property worth nearly $1,000 by 1870. William Beverly Nash, the former hotel servant, owned a brick-making establishment and coal yard worth over $5,000.

For many black leaders, however, politics brought little personal wealth. Even the most prominent found it difficult to translate political standing into a major share in their state's economic resources. A Charleston streetcar company formed by leading black politicians, including several 1865 convention delegates, failed. The black community was too poor to subscribe capital for such a venture, and whites shunned it entirely. Political participation could sometimes severely damage one's financial standing. South Carolina Union League and militia leader Henry Johnson, a bricklayer and plasterer by trade, remarked, "I always had plenty of work before I went into politics, but I have never got a job since." Other political leaders faced even more serious dangers. Political violence, so pervasive in large parts of the Reconstruction South, was often directed precisely at local political leaders. No South Carolina convention delegate seems to have been a victim, but they knew that in 1868, a prominent black political organizer in the state named Benjamin Randolph was assassinated while campaigning. As Reconstruction wore on and white opponents organized Ku Klux Klan violence to oppose it, many a local Republican organization saw its leaders murdered, assaulted, or forced to flee their homes.

As Republican organizations were disrupted by violence, and northerners became more and more reluctant to intervene in the South to protect black rights, one by one the Reconstruction governments were overthrown. With the irrevocable end of Reconstruction in 1877, the nation appeared to repudiate the ideal of racial equality expressed by the 1865 South Carolina black convention. Within a generation, blacks were stripped of the rights guaranteed them in the 1860s. The Fourteenth and Fifteenth Amendments to the federal

Constitution, guaranteeing, respectively, equality before the law and political rights for blacks, were reduced to nullities as one state after another disenfranchised its black population. Legalized segregation emerged as a new system of racial domination, and the flourishing black school systems established during Reconstruction were starved for funds. Political power once again reverted to those who believed the only role for blacks in southern society was that of dependent plantation laborer.

With blacks effectively barred from voting and holding office, politics could no longer serve as an effective vehicle for either personal or community advancement for men like those who had gathered in 1865. The few remaining black politicians ceased to exercise real power, apart from a handful of men dependent on federal patronage. A few blacks representing the low country continued to serve in the state legislature, and occasionally in Congress, until the turn of the century. However, in 1895, South Carolina adopted a new constitution designed to strip blacks of the right to vote. Men of ambition in the black community now found other outlets for their talents, whether in education, business, the church, or the professions.

In retrospect, Reconstruction appears not only as an unprecedented attempt to construct an interracial democracy from the ashes of slavery, but one of those rare historic moments embodying genuine possibilities for far-reaching social change. In a sense, the failure of Reconstruction was a twofold tragedy. On the one hand, demands for civil and political equality for blacks, such as those voiced by the South Carolina convention of 1865, did not represent an entirely adequate response to the legacy of emancipation, for Reconstruction failed to solve the pressing economic problems of the former slaves. On the other hand, the nation's failure to live up to these lofty goals was a disaster for black America, and profoundly affected the future development of the society as a whole. Nearly a century would pass before another generation of black southerners would renew the demand that America live up to its professed principles.

MARY FRANCES BERRY AND JOHN W. BLASSINGAME

Blacks and the Politics of Redemption

For the freedmen, as we have seen in the previous selection, emancipation brought with it a measure of confusion and uncertainty. The Union had been preserved and slavery had been destroyed. But what did it all mean? When and how would the seceded states be allowed back into the Union? Would the freedmen be afforded all the rights and privileges that white citizens enjoyed? How would they be protected from those who sought to restrict their freedom?

Primary among the questions that remained to be answered were the political ones. Would the freedmen be given the right to vote and to hold office? Emancipation did not automatically carry with it the rights to suffrage. Freed blacks had been fighting for decades without success for the right to vote in the northern states.

For reasons that had as much to do with the political needs of the Republican Party as the demands of justice, the freedmen were given the rights to vote and hold office by the Reconstruction Act passed by Congress in 1867. By 1877, however, this brief period of black political participation came to an end as southern "whites forced blacks out of the political arena while the national government acquiesced."

When we take into consideration the brevity of their participation, their general inexperience, the divisions among them, the perfidy of white Republicans in the South, and the lack of support in the North, "it is phenomenal," Mary Frances Berry and John W. Blassingame conclude in the following selection, "that blacks were as successful as they were."

Mary Frances Berry is a former Assistant Secretary of Health, Education and Welfare and the author of several books. **John W. Blassingame** is Professor of History, African, and Afro-American Studies at Yale University and the author of *The Slave Community: Plantation Life in the Antebellum South*. The following excerpt is taken from *Long Memory: the Black Experience in America*.

From *Long Memory: The Black Experience in America* by Mary Frances Berry and John W. Blassingame. Copyright © 1982 by Oxford University Press, Inc. Reprinted by permission.

Jeffersonian Democracy, Jacksonian Democracy, Progressivism, and many of the other labels frequently used in describing American politics had virtually no meaning for blacks. For long periods of time, white men excluded Afro-Americans from the body politic. Throughout most of their sojourn in America, blacks confronted the unshakeable white belief that Chief Justice Rogert B. Taney expressed succinctly in his 1857 decision in the Dred Scott case. According to Taney, . . . American blacks "had for more than a century been regarded as beings of an inferior order . . . so far inferior that they had no rights which the white man was bound to respect."

Confronting such white supremacists as Taney, blacks argued that both the Declaration of Independence and the Constitution had been perverted. Until white men lived up to the ideals embodied in these documents, they would be cursed by the prophecy of Isaiah:

> Wherefore hear the word of the Lord, ye scornful men, that rule this people which is in Jerusalem. Because ye have said, we have made a covenant with death, and with hell are we at agreement. Your covenant with death shall not be disannulled, and your agreement with hell shall not stand; when the over-flowing scourge shall pass through, then ye shall be trodden down by it.

Outside of abolitionists, there were few whites who placed any stock in the prophecy until expediency and moral concerns led to the formation of the nation's first antislavery political parties.

With a passion born of denial, blacks struggled consistently to obtain the right to hold office as a means of gaining freedom and equality in American society. Whites just as consistently denied blacks the right to vote or to hold office in order to guarantee the economic and social subordination of Afro-Americans. Free Negroes before the Civil War and blacks after emancipation believed, however, that the franchise held the key to gaining true citizenship. Blacks wanted political power because they believed it would end racial discrimination and ultimately result in improved economic and social conditions in the black community. Beyond the usual rewards of political action in a democratic system—patronage, influence on domestic and foreign policy, and access to decision makers—they expected better jobs, better education, and ultimately equal status with whites in the society. They believed political participation would free white Americans from bondage to the practices of racism and inequality and would liberate blacks from their oppression.

Throughout most of American history the efforts to gain some of the traditional rewards from political participation failed, with some major exceptions—Reconstruction after the Civil War, machine politics in Chicago in the twentieth century, the post-1965 period in the South, and the election of Jimmy Carter to the presidency in 1976. But when the exceptions arose, blacks saw that the rewards of political participation had limits. They saw that voting and holding office alone could lead to the end of overt racial discrimination but did not solve the social and economic problems facing the black community.

The legacy of slavery and racism required more radical solutions than the normal business of politics. Protest was perceived as an essential element. But before this truth became evident, blacks had to win the battle to participate in politics.

POLITICAL PARTICIPATION BEFORE THE CIVIL WAR

The masses of black people were slaves who were not permitted to participate in American politics in the period before slavery's abolition, the enactment of the Reconstruction Act of March 1867, and the Fifteenth Amendment. Free Negroes before the Civil War believed political participation would provide the leverage for ending their unequal status. But by 1830, free Negroes had been excluded from voting, state by state. They had little political influence.

The political powerlessness of the free blacks led to numerous systematic attempts to win or regain the franchise. Despite overwhelming and repeated rejections of their claims by white voters, judges, and legislators, the free blacks persisted. Elaborating their political philosophy in petitions, periodicals, and state and national conventions, the free Negroes demonstrated their deeply held belief in the redemptive power of the ballot. In Rhode Island, free Negroes petitioned in 1831 for full voting rights or an exemption from taxes, and the 1834 Negro National Convention proposed a committee to investigate voting rights in the various states. In August 1840, the New York State Convention of Colored Men met in Albany and resolved that the absence of respect for Negroes stemmed "from the want of the elective franchise." The New York *Colored American* of October 10 that same year insisted that the "possession of political rights," was the essential power needed to destroy caste. "The reason the colored population of this country are not socially and morally elevated is because they are almost universally, as they ever have been, disarmed of this power for their own, and the good of others. . . . "

The Pennsylvania decision to disfranchise blacks in 1838 stirred new efforts on the part of free Negroes to gain the vote. In the fall elections of 1837, Bucks County Democrats had been defeated, they claimed, by black votes. The Democrats obtained a county court decision that blacks were not "freemen" as defined by the 1790 Constitution and therefore could no longer vote. The second session of the state constitutional convention incorporated this ruling into the state constitution. Blacks responded by campaigning unsuccessfully against ratification of the new constitution through "an appeal of forty thousand citizens threatened with disfranchisement to the people of Pennsylvania." The Pennsylvania developments alarmed New York blacks, who expanded the suffrage campaign started earlier by Henry Highland Garnet and Charles Reason. The target of the campaign was the provision in New York's constitution permitting blacks to vote only if they could prove they held at least $250 worth of property. Since white voters did not have to meet a property requirement, blacks appealed to the legislature to repeal the discriminatory constitutional provisions. In county and state meetings blacks passed condemnatory resolutions, wrote addresses to white voters and state officials, and drafted petitions demanding an unrestricted ballot.

After the Albany convention, Garnet and others repeatedly pressed their petitions for suffrage before the New York legislature. They failed each time. The repeated defeats when the issue was put to a vote, according to Frederick Douglass, resulted from "unmitigated pride and prejudice"; whites intended to continue to "depress and degrade" blacks. In Pennsylvania and Connecticut repeated efforts to obtain the vote could not overcome white prejudice. Rhode Island blacks, however, took advantage of the revolt by Thomas Dorr and his followers in 1841 to gain the vote. The Dorrites demanded universal manhood suffrage, but for whites only. Blacks openly supported the conservative government and volunteered to fight when violence was threatened. The anti-Dorrite constitutional convention eliminated all restrictions on the franchise in 1842.

Blacks lost the right to vote in most northern states in the years prior to the Civil War. In New Jersey they were disfranchised in 1844. In the Northwest Territory states, black laws denied them the vote. As new western states came into the Union, black suffrage was prohibited. By the time of the Civil War, except in five New England states, blacks either could not vote or, as in New York, had to meet special qualifications. Despite their struggles, nowhere had blacks gained the vote, except in Rhode Island. In New York and northern and central New England, where some blacks could vote, their numbers were too small to be politically significant.

Although their small numbers reduced the political influence they had at the polls, free Negroes clearly recognized that they had to establish their right to vote if they were ever to improve their unequal status. They were left out of a political process which was of enormous interest to the general public. Unlike the twentieth century, mass participation in politics was pronounced in the antebellum period. Voter turnouts ran as high as 84 percent for the North in 1860, for example. Local political rallies in 1856 easily mobilized from 20,000 to 50,000 persons. Politics was, in part, mass entertainment, and leading politicians served as a focus for popular interests, aspirations, and values. Politics was both fun and a serious business from which blacks were largely excluded.

In pressing for suffrage in the 1840s, blacks were caught up in the general debate in abolitionist circles over whether slavery should be attacked by organizing an antislavery party, by moral suasion, or by noninvolvement in politics. Most blacks supported the political action group among the abolitionists.

Denied their natural, God-given rights, and perceiving themselves as descendants of men who had fought and died in the American Revolution, blacks held firmly to the view that the Declaration of Independence and the Constitution guaranteed their citizenship. Any laws denying them the right to vote were negated by God's laws. Disfranchisement, blacks contended, was immoral, undemocratic, and tyrannical. It subjected blacks to taxation without representation. Believing with the abolitionists that "politics rightly conducted are properly a branch of morals," blacks tried to convince American whites to vote for men of principles, free the slaves, enfranchise blacks, and to see clearly the distinction between political and social equality.

White politicians and voters were not convinced by the appeals of blacks. When, for example, the Liberty Party ran on a platform calling for the abolition of slavery in 1840, its presidential candidate James G. Birney only received a total of 7,000 votes out of the 2,500,000 cast. Running on the Free Soil ticket in 1848, former President Martin Van Buren received only 14 percent of the votes cast in the North. Given a choice between an antislavery or a proslavery presidential candidate, whites consistently voted for the proslavery one. In fact, between 1789 and 1852, southern slaveholders held a virtual monopoly on the White House.

The bleakness of the antebellum political horizon was relieved for blacks with the rise of the Republican party, the nomination of John C. Frémont as its first presidential candidate in 1856, and the adoption of its heavily symbolic slogan, "Free Speech, Free Press, Free Men, Free Labor, Free Territory, and Frémont." Despite its large reservoir of antislavery sentiment, the Republican party initially had a very limited conception of the citizenship rights of blacks. Even so, the Republicans were considerably more sympathetic to Afro-Americans than were the Democrats. Their differences appear in sharp relief in the words of two Illinois politicians, Democrat Stephen A. Douglas and Republican Abraham Lincoln.

Basing his assessment partially on the Declaration of Independence, Lincoln opposed the Dred Scott decision in 1857 and urged his fellow Republicans to preach "with whatever ability they can, that the negro is a man; that his bondage is cruelly wrong, and that the field of his oppression ought not to be enlarged." Unlike Lincoln, Stephen Douglas did not believe slavery was a moral issue. Supporting the Dred Scott decision and insisting repeatedly that the Negro was an "inferior being," Senator Douglas asserted in 1858 that

> I believe this government of ours was founded, and wisely founded, upon the white basis. It was made by white men, for the benefit of white men and their posterity, to be executed and managed by white men. . . . I am utterly opposed to any amalgamation on this contingent. . . . The Negro is not a citizen, cannot be a citizen, and ought not to be a citizen.

CIVIL WAR DEVELOPMENTS

On the eve of the Civil War, blacks confronted a Democratic party that denied rights of any kind to Negroes, slave or free, and a Republican party that denied them all political rights. Republican leaders asserted that free Negroes were human beings with civil rights to life, liberty, and property, but without the right to participate in politics. Women, children, unnaturalized foreigners, and Negroes had natural rights but not political rights. Even the Republican position was unacceptable to H. Ford Douglass, a runaway slave and an abolitionist orator, who told a Massachusetts audience in July 1860, that no party deserved their votes "unless that party is willing to extend to the black man all the rights of a citizen." But other blacks, like Frederick Douglass and John Rock, supported the Republicans, and black conventions throughout the North endorsed Republican candidates. When choosing between Republicans and Democrats, the Republicans were the only logical alternative.

When the Civil War started, free blacks believed that general abolition would be one step on the road to political and civil rights. They also knew that enlisting blacks into the military service was the fastest route to abolition. They encouraged the enlistment of blacks in the service and exerted every effort to convert what began as a war to save the Union into a war to free the slaves. They urged the War Department to accept black troops and organized volunteer black regiments in their own states. As the war continued and a great movement of slaves away from their masters ensued, they opposed any effort to solve the black problem short of abolition.

Free Negroes disagreed with most of Lincoln's early plans for the disposition of blacks, including his plan for compensated emancipation and colonization elsewhere. A joint resolution of April 10, 1862, provided that the United States would cooperate with any state adopting a plan of gradual emancipation together with satisfactory compensation for the owners. A law passed in April 1862, provided for the emancipation of slaves in the District of Columbia, with compensation not in excess of $300 paid to the owner of each slave. The law provided $100,000 to support voluntary emigration of freedmen to Haiti and Liberia. Lincoln called a prominent group of free blacks to the White House in August 1862, and urged them to support colonization, and he instructed the State Department to inquire if various South American and African governments would be willing to accept blacks. Two places were regarded favorably by Lincoln: Panama and the Isle à Vache in the Caribbean. But most blacks knew that the Civil War offered the best opportunity for gaining equality in America. They continued to oppose colonization and, in fact, denounced such suggestions as stridently as they had earlier proposals. As Isaiah Wears, a prominent black Philadelphian, asserted, "To be asked, after so many years of oppression and wrong have been inflicted in a land and by a people who have been so largely enriched by the black man's toil, to pull up stakes in a civilized and Christian nation, and to go to an uncivilized and barbarous nation, simply to gratify an unnatural wicked prejudice emanating from slavery, is unreasonable and anti-Christian in the extreme."

Free blacks encouraged and supported Lincoln, however, in the antislavery aspects of his policy. They were thrilled when on June 19, 1862, he signed a bill abolishing slavery in the territories and on July 17 signed the Confiscation Act, setting free all slaves of disloyal masters who were found or fled into Union-held territory. As he prepared an Emancipation Proclamation to free all slaves in states in rebellion on January 1, 1863, antislavery delegations including blacks encouraged him to issue it. When Lincoln issued the proclamation on September 22, 1862, with a reminder of the availability of compensated emancipation and of the benefits of voluntary colonization, there was jubilation. The document was not all it could be, but it was a stride toward freedom and was eagerly embraced by blacks. As the *Christian Recorder,* official organ of the AME Church, announced, "It will be said that the President only makes provision for the emancipation of a *part* of an injured race, and that the Border states and certain parts of the rebel states are exempted from the relief offered to others by this most important document. We believe those who are not immediately liberated will be ultimately benefitted by this act, and that Congress will do something for those poor souls who will still remain in degradation. But we thank God and President Lincoln for what has been done, and take courage." The proclamation provided that "all persons held as slaves within any state, or designated part of the state, the people whereof shall be in rebellion against the United States, shall be then, thenceforward, and forever free." On December 31, 1862, blacks held watch meetings to see in not only the New Year but also emancipation. Emancipation, as Lincoln said, was "a fit and necessary war measure"; it helped to save the Union but it also had political consequences.

Black politicians worked to shape the politics of black people in the new atmosphere of freedom. They focused on general abolition and the enactment of measures giving some recognition of black citizenship during the war as a precondition for black political participation. The State Department issued a passport to Henry Highland Garnet in August 1861, which stated that he was a "citizen of the United States." In response to a request as to whether a black could legitimately command a ship flying an American flag, since only citizens were permitted such commands, Attorney General Edward Bates advised Secretary of the Treasury Salmon P. Chase in 1862 that every free person born in the United States was "at the moment of birth prima facie a citizen." A measure providing for the acceptance of the testimony of black witnesses in federal courts was passed in 1864, and in March 1865, a bill permitting blacks to carry the mails became national law. Congress admitted blacks to its visitors' galleries during the Civil War, public lectures at the Smithsonian Institution were opened to blacks for the first time, blacks were invited to public receptions at the White House, and in February 1865, John Rock was admitted to the bar of the U.S. Supreme Court. But as Frederick Douglass said in December 1863, "Our work will not be done until the colored man is admitted as a full member in good and regular standing in the American body politic."

In Louisiana, where Union victories came early, the suffrage question did not wait until the end of the war. Free men of color in New Orleans insisted on obtaining the right to vote as a condition of the restoration of Louisiana to the Union. They submitted a petition to President Lincoln in March 1864, reminding the nation of their service in the War of 1812 and the Civil War and asking that "the right of suffrage may be extended not only to natives of Louisiana of African descent, but also to all others, whether born slave or free, especially those who have vindicated their right to vote by bearing arms, subject only to such qualifications as shall equally affect the white and colored citizens." In response, Lincoln wrote to Louisiana Governor Michael Hahn, "I barely suggest for your private consideration whether some of the colored people may not be let in as, for instance the very intelligent, and especially those who have fought gallantly in our ranks."

Northern free Negroes also actively pushed the suffrage issue. In October 1864, 144 blacks from eighteen states, meeting in Syracuse, New York, in a National Convention of Colored Citizens of the United States, issued an address to the people of the United States, written by Frederick Douglass, which asserted, "We want the elective franchise in all the states now in the union, and the same in all such states as may come into the union hereafter. . . . The position of that right is the keystone to the arch of human liberty; and without that the whole may at any moment fall to the ground; while, with it, that liberty may stand forever. . . . "

POLITICAL POWER DURING RECONSTRUCTION

The leadership for blacks in their struggle for political power would come, at first, largely from that articulate class of leaders before the war led by Frederick Douglass, the most prominent black political leader until his death in 1895. These leaders understood that the true meaning of freedom was not automatically encompassed by the Thirteenth Amendment's declaration that neither slavery nor involuntary servitude shall exist in the United States. Slavery could be defined narrowly, and merely lifting the shackles could be enough; slavery could be defined broadly, and political enfranchisement might be one result of the amendment. But as the Nashville *Colored Tennessean* asserted in August 1865, blacks expected whites to

> Deal with us justly. Tell us not that we will not work, when it was our toil that enriched the South. Talk not to us of a war of races, for that is to say you intend commencing to butcher us, whenever you can do so with impunity. All we want is the rights of men. Give us that and we shall not molest you. We do not intend leaving this country. No land can be fairer in our eyes, than the sunny one beneath whose skies we have lived. We were born here. Most of us will die here. We are Americans and prouder of the fact than ever. Deal justly with us. That's all we want. That we mean to have, come what may!

Despite the views of blacks, abolition was narrowly defined by southern whites, who enacted legislation designed to insure the continued exploitation of blacks as a permanent underclass. No southern state provided for black suffrage or office holding, and many of the same whites who were bulwarks of the Confederacy were picked to lead this new Old South. The Lincoln and Johnson plans of Reconstruction did not require black suffrage. The only national concession to the needs of blacks seemed to be a relief agency, the Freedmen's Bureau.

Douglass and other black leaders objected strongly to what they regarded as the reestablishment of slavery. Practical Republicans became concerned that their party could never grow and hold power with an unreconstructed Democratic party in control in the South. Northern industrialists were eager to exploit the cheap labor and markets of the South—to modernize the southern economy—and were not interested in the mere reestablishment of the old plantation system. By the time Congress met in December 1865, it was ready to create a Joint Committee on Reconstruction to inquire into the condition of the southern states and to make recommendations for a new policy.

Two major pieces of legislation, the Freedmen's Bureau Extension Bill and the Civil Rights Act of 1866, were vetoed by President Andrew Johnson, who also condemned a proposed Fourteenth Amendment which provided for civil equality. The resulting fight between Johnson and Congress, including the overriding of his vetoes and the enactment of the Fourteenth Amendment, paved the way for congressional control of Reconstruction. Congress passed its own Reconstruction Act in 1867, disfranchising participants in the rebellion and enfranchising blacks, with elections held under the supervision of the Union Army. The beginning of congressional Reconstruction presented the opportunity for blacks to become elected political officials.

Congressional Reconstruction established martial law in the South and provided that, on the basis of universal male suffrage, a convention in each state was to draw up a new constitution acceptable to Congress. No state would be readmitted to the Union unless it ratified the Fourteenth Amendment. Former rebels who could not take the iron-clad oath of allegiance were disfranchised after Congress overrode Johnson's veto of the legislation.

Each of the constitutional conventions called in the southern states had black members, but blacks were in a majority only in South Carolina and Louisiana. In most states, blacks constituted a small minority. In six states, native whites were in the majority. Some black members were slaves and others free, some were emigrants from the North, and many were veterans of the Union Army. The blacks who spoke in the conventions took a moderate conciliatory position toward white Confederates, even supporting their enfranchisement.

In South Carolina's constitutional convention the subject of political rights of former Confederates stimulated heated debate. True to their affection for the principles of the Declaration of Independence, blacks refused to vote to disfranchise whites. Black delegate R. C. DeLarge offered a resolution to petition Congress to remove all political disabilities from citizens of the state. Francis Cardozo thought this was an opportunity for blacks to show that "although our people have been oppressed and have every inducement to seek revenge, although deprived of education and learning," they could rise above "all selfishness and exhibit a Christian universality of spirit." The Charleston *Advocate* explained in May 1867, that "in the great work of reconstruction we should scorn the idea of the white or black man's party. . . . All should be admitted to equal rights and privileges in church and state whatever may be their race or color. . . . we should all live together in peace and harmony. . . ."

The state constitutions approved by the Reconstruction conventions were much more progressive than the constitutions of antebellum days. They abolished property qualifications for voting and holding office; some abolished imprisonment for debt. Slavery was abolished formally in all constitutions, and some eliminated race distinctions in real property law. In every constitution universal male suffrage was enacted, except for certain classes of former Confederates. Public school systems and modernized local government administrative machinery were also included. These constitutions were apparently so highly regarded that even when Reconstruction was overthrown by white supremacists, their basic provisions were maintained.

During congressional Reconstruction, blacks obtained the traditional fruits of political participation. They held public office and wielded some political power and influence in each state, although they were never in control in any, even where they constituted a majority of the population. In South Carolina whites always had a majority in the senate and there was always a white governor, but there were eighty-seven blacks and forty whites in the first legislature. There were two black lieutenant governors, Alonzo J. Ransier in 1870 and Richard Gleaves in 1872, and two black speakers of the house, Samuel J. Lee in 1872 and Robert B. Elliott in 1874. Francis L. Cardozo, who had been educated at the University of Glasgow, was secretary of state from 1868 to 1872 and treasurer from 1872 to 1876.

In Louisiana between 1868 and 1896, there were 133 black members of the legislature, 38 senators, and 95 representatives. Most who served between 1868 and 1877 were veterans of the Union Army and educated free men of color before the war. But some were former slaves. John W. Menard was elected to Congress but denied a seat. Oscar Dunn, P. B. S. Pinchback, and C. C. Antoine served as lieutenant governors. Pinchback was acting governor for forty-three days in 1873 when Governor Henry C. Warmoth was impeached.

In national politics between 1869 and 1901, two blacks served in the U.S. Senate and twenty in the House of Representatives. The two senators were Hiram R. Revels and Blanche K. Bruce, both of whom represented Mississippi. Revels was born free in North Carolina in 1822. He migrated to Indiana, Ohio, and Illinois, receiving his education at a Quaker seminary in Indiana, a black seminary in Ohio, and Knox College in Illinois. While living in Illinois, he was ordained a minister in the AME Church in Baltimore in 1845. Revels was in Baltimore when the Civil War began and assisted in organizing the first two Maryland black regiments. In 1863 he moved to St. Louis, founded a school for freedmen, and helped recruit a black regiment there. He went to Vicksburg, Mississippi, in 1864 to work with the Freedmen's Bureau provost marshal in managing the affairs of freedmen. Revels also served as pastor of the Bethel AME Church in Vicksburg. He was elected as a compromise candidate to the state senate in 1869 and was elected by the state senate to fill the seat previously occupied by Jefferson Davis in the U.S. Senate. He served one year in the Senate in 1870, during which he supported the removal of all political disabilities from former Confederates, appointed a black to West Point, and obtained the admission of black mechanics to work in the U.S. Navy Yard. At the end of his term, Revels became president of Alcorn A & M University, established as a segregated institution of higher education for blacks.

Blanche K. Bruce, elected to the U.S. Senate in 1874, was the only black who served a full term in the Senate until the election of Edward Brooke from Massachusetts in 1966. Unlike Revels, Bruce was born a slave in Virginia. He escaped from his master in St. Louis when the Civil War came. He studied for several years and in 1869 went to Mississippi, where he entered politics. He served as tax collector, sheriff, and superintendent of schools. In the Senate he took an interest in both race-related matters and matters of general interest. He spoke in support of P. B. S. Pinchback when Pinchback was denied a seat in the Senate in a contest over irregularities in his election. He worked diligently with the Manufactures, Education, and Labor Committee and the Pensions Committee and chaired a committee that conducted a careful investigation into the causes for failure of the Freedmen's Bank.

The first of the twenty blacks to serve in the U.S. House of Representatives were seated in 1869. There were eight from South Carolina, four from North Carolina, three from Alabama, and one each from Georgia, Mississippi, Florida, Louisiana, and Virginia. James H. Rainey and Robert Smalls, both of South Carolina, each served five consecutive terms. John R. Lynch of Mississippi and J. T. Walls of Florida both served three terms. Their activities in Congress did not differ substantially from those of white congressmen. Most of them had served in some state political capacity before being elected to the House. They fought for such local issues as rivers and harbors legislation, as well as civil rights and education measures. Overall, ten of the blacks who served in Congress between 1869 and 1900 were drawn from the old free Negro caste. On the local level, 43 of the 102 who held office in Virginia between 1867 and 1890 had been free before the war. Of the 59 black delegates in the 1868 South Carolina constitutional convention, at least 18 were former free Negroes; another 14 had been born free in other parts of the nation. All but 20 of the 111 black delegates to the Louisiana Republican Convention in 1865 were freeborn. But the most influential and successful black Reconstruction politician in South Carolina, Robert Smalls, was born and lived out his antebellum life as a slave, and Oscar Dunn, a former Louisiana slave, was as significant a figure in politics as P. B. S. Pinchback.

Most blacks who were influential during Reconstruction had been urban slaves, blacksmiths, carpenters, clerks, or waiters in hotels and boarding houses. A few of them had been favored body servants of influential whites. Some had been preachers, lawyers, or teachers in the free states or in Canada. Others were self-educated free men like Robert Carlos DeLarge, the tailor from Charleston who was the best parliamentarian in the South Carolina convention. P. B. S. Pinchback had only a common school education, and Oscar James Dunn was a plasterer.

Black politicians learned a very significant lesson during Reconstruction: the limits of coalition politics and the limits of the officeholders they elected. Northern politicians who enacted Reconstruction measures wanted black participation in the state governments but not black control. They wanted reform but not an economic revolution. They were not prepared to sanction the expropriation of white-owned property in order to give property to blacks. Northerners wanted middle-class, white-dominated governments operated on business principles, not an overthrow of capitalism and white control. Generally, black politicians were in accord with these views. Some, such as James T. Rapier of Alabama, were separated from the black masses by their own interests. Others, such as Francis Cardozo, who kept reminding his colleagues of the necessity of not "impairing the obligations of contracts," were prisoners of their own education. Men such as Beverly Nash of South Carolina spoke eloquently in the defense of voting and officeholding privileges for the very Confederates who were at that moment preparing for the destruction of blacks who dared participate in the political process.

There were dissenters from the black political strategy of coalition politics. The Pure Radicals in Louisiana urged blacks to take power into their own hands. But forty-six-year-old Oscar James Dunn, a former slave who managed to manipulate power for the Pure Radicals for three years as lieutenant governor, died a month before a crucial effort to impeach the incumbent governor in November 1871.

THE OVERTHROW OF RECONSTRUCTION

By the time Reconstruction was overthrown completely in 1877, blacks had voted, held office, and wielded some influence in the political system. In addition, the Fourteenth and Fifteenth Amendments gave permanent legal recognition to black citizenship and outlawed denial of the right to vote for racial reasons. But the continued enfranchisement of whites meant that if they could by force or fraud prevent blacks from voting in opposition to them, they would regain power. The Republican party discovered that it could maintain power in national affairs even while letting the Democrats regain power in the South. Through duplicity, bloodshed, riot, and murder, whites forced blacks out of the political arena while the national government acquiesced. Reconstruction unraveled even as it began; by 1877 it was at an end.

The three enforcement acts passed by Congress in 1870–71, under the authority of the Fifteenth Amendment, seemed to ensure protection for blacks in the enjoyment of their political rights. The laws provided for extensive enforcement machinery, including authority for the president to call out the Army and Navy and to suspend the writ of habeas corpus if necessary. The acts permitted states to restrict suffrage on any basis except race or color. But between 1870 and 1896, when the bulk of this legislation was repealed, 7,372 cases were tried and hundreds of offenders, who were never brought to trial, were arrested. Despite this pre-1896 activity, the disfranchisement of blacks proceeded successfully. After 1874, enforcement efforts gradually declined altogether. The white South remained opposed, the white North was not interested, and the Supreme Court soon decided that most of the federal efforts to punish individual violations of voting rights were unconstitutional. Local officials arrested and punished blacks, who complained to harassed federal officials. The new federal troops who were stationed in the South were not used to enforce the law. Additionally, Congress failed to provide adequate funds to finance the federal courts and officials refused to undertake serious enforcement. Many federal officials disagreed with the effort and were not willing to attempt enforcement. The protection of black voting rights in the South was not a national priority.

As the federal government continued to ignore white terrorism in the South, blacks spoke out against the perfidy of the Republican party. The *Col-*

ored Citizen of Fort Scott, Kansas, in October 1878, said, "The Democrats of the South are determined that the colored voters shall either be Democrats or not vote at all." T. Thomas Fortune in the New York *Globe* in October 1883, expressed the view that "we have the ballot without any law to protect us in the enjoyment of it. . . . The Democratic Party is a fraud—a narrowminded, corrupt, bloody fraud; the Republican Party has grown to be little better."

Political participation by blacks became increasingly fraught with dangerous consequences. A variety of so-called legal measures, including gerrymandering, poll tax requirements, and elaborate election procedures, applied in fact only to blacks, were instituted to keep most blacks permanently disfranchised. By 1889, blacks had been practically eliminated from Southern politics. Rather than a temporary setback, the overthrow of Reconstruction marked a long-term withdrawal from political power.

BLACK RECONSTRUCTION FAILS IN SOUTH CAROLINA

A closer look at the Reconstruction experiences of blacks and their political leadership in South Carolina provides an example of the successes and failures of political participation. If black political participation during Reconstruction could succeed at all in improving social and economic conditions for blacks, it should have succeeded in South Carolina. Blacks were a distinct majority of the population and their political leadership was stronger in both numbers and influence than in any other state, but they were not able to maintain political power. As Thomas Holt explains in his *Black Over White, Negro Political Leadership in South Carolina During the Reconstruction,* one reason for the failure lay in the origins of black leadership. Divisions between the freeborn mulatto *petit bourgeoisie* and slave-born blacks and mulattoes emerged quickly in the leadership group. Out of a total of 255 Negroes elected to state and federal offices between 1868 and 1876, one in four had been free before the war and one of every three was a mulatto. Almost one in three owned some real estate, and 46 percent possessed some form of wealth, real or personal. One fifth had combined property holdings in excess of $1,000; 11 percent had more than $1,000 in real property alone. Only 15 percent had no property at all. Sixty-five percent were literate, and 10 percent were professionally or college trained. Ministers and teachers predominated among the professionals, but ten of these lawmakers were or became lawyers during their terms of office. Those engaged in agriculture were the next largest group, and more of these appear to have been landowners than field hands.

Although it might appear that intraracial color prejudices between mulattoes and blacks were the basis for the divisions which inhibited political power, the divisions were in fact due to class differences. The free Negro class before the war, although hedged about with restrictions, was in a better economic position than was the slave class. Free Negroes were wealthier, better educated, and in many ways better prepared for political competition than were slaves. Slaves manumitted before the war were often provided with cattle, land, or other property, and many of them were the mulatto products of unions between white planters and slave women. Therefore, those with greater resources happened to be mulattoes, and some of the hostility between blacks and mulattoes resulted from their different class positions. Many of the black leaders freed during the war had served in the Army and had acquired enough financial resources to gain economic ground on the old free Negro class. In any event, all black legislators of whatever color had a constituency consisting largely of illiterate ex-slaves, upon whom they relied for continued power and who expected some improvement in their condition in return for bestowing that power.

Another significant factor which prevented the exercise of black power was the way in which blacks became politicians. The new politicians, black and white, were novices, but blacks had absolutely no experience in partisan politics. Most of the antebellum history of blacks had been spent trying to gain access to politics. The Freedmen's Bureau, the Army, and the missionary societies and churches provided whatever political experience they had gained in establishing a constituency. What these three institutions provided was a job, an opportunity for developing leadership qualities, and a pattern of public contacts, but these opportunities fell far short of the kind of local experience required for quick, effective action as a state or national political official.

These particular black officials were not able to convert a base of 60 percent of the population into political control in South Carolina. The population base was quickly converted into a majority in the legislature and control of the offices of secretary of state, lieutenant governor, adjutant general, secretary of the treasury, speaker of the house, and president pro tem of the state senate. But blacks never held the offices of governor, U.S. senator, comptroller general, attorney general, and superintendent of education, or more than one of the three positions on the state supreme court. In the legislature blacks were very successful in controlling some of the key committees in the general assembly until 1874. When it came to executive branch appointments, however, blacks early adopted the policy of supporting whites, because they had real or presumed contacts in the North and because of the urgings of their northern white supporters. This was one reason why black leaders never even considered pushing a black for governor, a position that required contacts with northern centers of power. "We don't want a colored Governor," Martin Delany insisted in the June 25, 1870, *Daily Republican*. "Our good sense tells us differently."

Not until the spring of 1870 did blacks in South Carolina fully realize that they had to have a larger portion of the appointed positions and of those elected by the legislature before they could develop a strong political organization. The *Daily Republican* reported on June 24, 1870, that Robert DeLarge had announced at a celebration in Charleston that blacks were thankful to the Republican party, but "some impudent scoundrels in the party now say, 'You want too much; you want everything.' We placed them in position, we elected them and by our votes we made them our masters. We now propose to change this thing a little, and let them vote for us." He was followed by Alonzo Ransier and Martin Delany, who expressed their support for this new approach. The result was an increase in political offices for blacks.

The failure to control the governorship was a significant problem for blacks. The governor appointed most local officeholders, including county treasurer, auditor, jury commissioner, and trial justices. The economic insecurity of many Republicans, which led even professional men to need part-time political appointments, increased the power of the governor. Even local newspapers, dependent on contracts to publish laws and governmental announcements, could be manipulated by the governor.

Although blacks normally dominated the apparatus for running the election campaigns, their control was tenuous. The largely black state central committee, the party convention, the county chairmen, and the union leagues organized the freedmen. The party central committee was responsible for raising and distributing campaign funds. But when black leaders ignored the policy of not electing blacks to conspicuously high offices and elected a black chairman to the state central committee, an agent of the Republican National Committee who was in South Carolina in 1868 simply advised the national party to bypass the central committee. The funds should instead be sent directly to the four congressional district campaign committees.

Federal patronage for local offices was controlled by the senior U.S. Senator and the local Congressman. The collector of the port of Charleston was the most important post, because the collector could hire a number of workers. Blacks were never able to gain control of the custom house patronage, because no black was ever elected Senator. Overall, blacks failed to control another avenue for developing a political machine and lost one of the most important traditional fruits of political participation.

On issues that could have crippled their white opponents, black members of the legislature showed a lack of resolve. They rejected confiscation of land and redistribution to the freedmen. They also withheld support from a measure that would have used tax collection as a measure for ending white control of land, even though Richard H. Cain explained that if the large landowners "are obliged to sell their lands the poor man will have a chance to buy."

The weaknesses of origins, interests, experience, and reliance on northern Republicans created conditions in which the Republicans and blacks lost power to the Democrats in South Carolina in 1876. President Rutherford P. Hayes' decision to withdraw federal troops in April 1877, merely ratified a result that had already taken place. The Democrats had, through violence, intimidation, and the aid of certain Republicans including the governor, undermined the Reconstruction regime and taken control of the state. The Republicans' division over legislative policy and patronage was the very ingredient needed to consolidate political power. Daniel Chamberlain, elected Republican governor in 1874, consciously adopted a policy of destroying existing Republican alliances and forming a Democratic-Republican coalition which he could control. Chamberlain asserted that he was merely bent on decreasing corruption in government. Even so, the cuts in programs and budgets made by Chamberlain undermined Republican political support and his insistence on appointing Democrats to many local offices further destroyed the party. Chamberlain became the darling of the Democrats.

In July 1876, the Hamburg massacre of a black militia company during an attack by whites on a barracks in which the militia was barricaded ushered in more violence and marked the end of Republican rule in South Carolina. Wade Hampton was the Democratic gubernatorial candidate and his militia, called the "Red Shirts," forced Republican officials to resign their offices and took over effective control of local government. In a similar situation in 1870, Governor Robert K. Scott had mobilized the black militia long enough to carry the election. But under Chamberlain's policies, the militia, a constant irritant to whites, had been unused and practically disarmed. Indeed, there is some evidence that the white clubs obtained arms from the state arsenal. By the time the disputed election was settled in favor of Hampton and federal troops were removed, the result was a foregone conclusion.

It can be argued that greater unity among the Republicans would have prevented the overthrow of Reconstruction. The preconditions for such unity at that time, however, are difficult to find. To expect more experienced black politicians is a self-evident contradiction, and to expect stronger northern white support of black control of politics is to expect more radical views than even the most radical Republicans then espoused. Not only did black politicians fail significantly to improve the conditions of their black constituency, they did not even receive all of the patronage and influence that are the usual concomitants of political power. However, given the general inexperience of black politicians, the perfidy of white Republicans like Chamberlain in the South, and the unwillingness of northern Republicans to support black control, it is phenomenal that blacks were as successful as they were.

QUESTIONS FOR DISCUSSION

1. What was the basis for the political divisions among blacks?
2. Why did Reconstruction fail in South Carolina?

Chapter Three

A Changing Social Order

JAMES TURNER

Understanding the Populists

In 1892, the People's party polled over one million votes for president and elected three governors and twenty-two congressmen. In 1894, Populist candidates polled nearly one and one half million votes—a 50 percent increase over 1892. By 1896, the party had disappeared as a political force in American life.

For more than a half-century, historians have tried to understand the reasons behind the rise and fall of Populism as a political and social movement. In the following selection, James Turner first reviews the efforts of earlier historians and then outlines his own schema for "understanding the Populists." He begins by trying to determine, first, who the Populists were, and second, how they differed from their neighbors who were not Populists. Why, he wants to know, did economically depressed farmers in some regions support the Populists, while their just-as-depressed neighbors continued to vote for Democrats? What was it that distinguished the Populist regions and Populist voters from the non-Populist?

What Turner discovers is that the localities that voted Populist were those that were most "isolated" from the "social and economic mainstream." Populists lived further from towns, from railroads, and in more sparsely populated regions than other rural folk. They remained on the "fringe of the metropolitan culture," "fearful and uncertain of the new order" as the "United States underwent what time may demonstrate to have been the most fundamental transformation in its history: the change from a basically rural nation to an urban society."

Pushing on toward a century after Populism burned its course across the American horizon, we have yet to puzzle out what impelled that brief meteor. This is not for lack of trying. Even the historian's infinite capacity for disagree-

---

James Turner is a member of the history department at the University of Michigan. The following article was first published in *The Journal of American History* in September 1980.

Reprinted from *The Journal of American History,* Volume 67, No. 2 (September 1980), pp. 354–373, by permission of the Organization of American Historians and the author.

ment has barely accommodated the quarrels over the Populists. Were they racists? Where they anti-Semites? Were they victims of capitalism? Or of their own agrarian mythology? Radicals? Reactionaries? Conceivably liberals? Possibly Marxists without Marx? The reason for this confusion is simple. No one yet has plausibly explained why people voted Populist. But without understanding the motivation of ordinary Populists, it is impossible to get to the heart of their ideology or their politics.

This is not to say that historians have never offered explanations of Populism's appeal. John D. Hicks thought that he had told the story back in 1931, and he did tell it convincingly. Hicks, who studied at Wisconsin under the lingering spirit of Frederick Jackson Turner, saw Populism as a frontier movement. When railroads opened the Great Plains, settlers poured in, mortgaging themselves to the hilt to purchase and stake their farms. In 1887 drought broke the boom and choked the flow of eastern capital. The arid, westernmost areas simply collapsed, as settlers streamed back east; the better-watered easterly regions suffered but held their own. It was in the central counties, with marginal rainfall, that "the grinding burden of debt," made intolerable by falling crop prices and an appreciating dollar, finally provoked "open revolt."

The other hotbed of Populism, the South, lacked a frontier, except in Texas. Hicks evaded this difficulty by arguing that military defeat had produced "a return to the primitive" and recreated frontier circumstances. In Dixie the crop lien played the role of the mortgage. But it also helped to trap farmers in disastrous reliance on a single crop, cotton. When cotton prices plummeted, southern farmers found themselves in the same sinking boat with Kansans and Nebraskans; "then the weight of debt was keenly felt and frenzied agitation began." In the West and South, the economic structures generated by frontier conditions could not bear the weight of depression. The resulting economic hardship explained Populism.

Hicks's book was enormously influential, for it established the axiom that succeeding historians invoked to account for the origins of Populism. Even Chester McArthur Destler, who claimed in 1946 that the People's party owed its ideology to urban radicals, never challenged Hicks's claim that the party owed its existence to rural hard times. This was not surprising. In one sense Hicks's argument was almost self-evident; only under the stress of the agricultural depression did Populism in fact emerge. Yet in stating the obvious he glossed over what was crucial to understanding the movement. Not every hard-pressed farmer turned to Populism; in fact, a majority stuck by the old parties. Even in the strongholds of Populism, like Kansas, only fusion with one of the major parties permitted Populist victories. Did this mean that only the most distressed farmers embraced Populism? Or did it mean something else? Hicks's evidence did not permit an answer.

The next landmark in the literature of Populism was Richard Hofstadter's *The Age of Reform*. Hofstadter placed greater emphasis than Hicks on the role of international commodity markets in creating the agrarian crisis of the 1880s and 1890s and on the farmer's psychological difficulties in coming to terms with these "commercial realities." But he, too, was fundamentally arguing that economic hardship bred Populism, even if via a different route. And he, too, tripped over Hicks's fallacy: most farmers "caught in the toils of cash-crop commercial farming" did *not* become Populists.

Hofstadter, however, was mainly interested in Populist ideology. His depiction of struggling petty-capitalist farmers bedeviled by an "agrarian myth" into xenophobia and anti-Semitism sparked an historical debate that lasted well into the 1960s. Reactionary Populists chased socialist Populists through the learned journals in a quarrel that generated considerably more heat than light. The meagerness of the results was understandable. It is difficult to know what a Populist's attack on Jewish bankers or the foreign Money Power signified, unless one understands the Populist's ideology; the Populist's ideology, in turn, is bound to remain foggy until one understands why he turned to Populism in the first place. And this question had still not received a satisfactory answer.

The Hofstadter imbroglio therefore dragged a red herring across the trail that historians ought to have followed first, if they wished to track down the meaning of Populism. But the fracas issued in one considerable achievement. It inspired a number of younger historians to look very closely at the grass-roots realities of Populism. The first was Walter T. K. Nugent, whose *Tolerant Populists,* a study of Kansas, helped to scotch the stereotype of Populist as bigot. But the most celebrated apostle of grass-roots Populism so far has been Lawrence Goodwyn. His *Democratic Promise,* a work of both synthesis and original research, was the first full-dress history of Populism since Hicks's.

If you want to understand Populism, Goodwyn sensibly observed, you must attend to the "voiceless members of American society" who *were* the Populists. He then went on to explain Populism as a "cooperative crusade" emerging from the experience of the farmers' co-ops formed under the aegis of the Texas Farmers' Alliance. From this seedbed grew the ideology of a "cooperative commonwealth" opposed to "the coercive potential of the emerging corporate state." This cooperative ideal, embodied in the Populist platform and, more importantly, in a "movement culture," *was* Populism. The collapse of the People's party thus accelerated the decline of freedom in America.

More, perhaps, than any previous historian of Populism, Goodwyn poignantly combined scholarship with sympathy for the human meaning of the movement. But some crucial weaknesses debilitated his argument. First was a tendency to tailor his Populists to his hypothesis. Members of the People's party who did not fit his schema—such as the silverites who dominated Populism in the northern prairies—Goodwyn simply excommunicated as pseudo-Populists, followers of a "shadow movement." He also exaggerated the "cooperative" element in Populism. Certainly the Alliance exchanges brought many farmers into the movement. But, after the exchanges collapsed and the People's party replaced the Alliance at the movement's center, what these farmers had on their minds was less a cooperative ideal than a bitter, vituperative suspicion of a vaguely defined Money Power. A reading of the Populist county weeklies in Texas (the closest thing to a grass-roots literature in what Goodwyn considered the heartland of Populism) makes this clear. Moreover, these local Populists, editors and letter writers alike, typically advocated only some foggy reform, varying from farmer to farmer, of the monetary or taxation system in order to put "plutocracy" in its place. They did not talk of a cooperative commonwealth and seldom mentioned even the subtreasury.

Goodwyn's difficulties may have stemmed from two problems. The first was the failure to follow his own injunction to listen to ordinary Populists. Instead, he substituted for the voiceless millions "the men and women who came to speak in their name." True, the voiceless are hard to hear, but the business of consecrating spokesmen for them, though common among historians, is highly problematical. William Jennings Bryan, no friend of Goodwyn's heroes, also spoke in the name of the voiceless millions. As far as that goes, so did William McKinley. McKinley certainly did not represent many Populists, but the People's party did endorse Bryan. Goodwyn insisted that those Populists were not real Populists, and perhaps he was right. But what warrant is there for claiming Cyclone Davis and Stump Ashby as *voces populi?* One needs first to look more carefully at the *populus.*

In considering why people became Populists in the first place, Goodwyn followed the historiographic tradition and implicitly assumed that economic hardship made Populists. Paying little attention to the issue of motivation, he, like historians before him, glossed over the awkward fact that most distressed farmers never joined the Populists. But without understanding the conditions of life that separated some farmers from their fellows and led them into the People's party, how will any historians penetrate to the meaning of Populism?

Fortunately, several younger scholars—what might be called a post-Hofstadter generation of Populist historians—have begun to examine in some detail the local and regional parameters of Populism. The results are still patchy, but a few pieces of a hazy pattern are emerging. Stanley B. Parsons, Peter H. Argersinger, and Sheldon Hackney have analyzed statistically factors influencing the Populist vote in, respectively, Nebraska, Kansas, and Alabama. Relative poverty seemed important in Kansas and Alabama, though this was not clear for Nebraska. In any case, other factors were considerably more significant in all three states. These included variations in types of farming, percentage of farms mortgaged, and a combination of geographic mobility and downward social mobility. But, oddly, each of these circumstances seems to have been associated with Populism in only one of the three states. The one significant influence common to all three was geographic isolation from towns and villages. Parsons and Argersinger found that Populists tended to live in wholly rural areas, that proximity even to villages significantly lowered the Populist vote. In Alabama, where Populism in industrial cities added an important cross-influence, Populists came not only from "areas experiencing extraordinary influxes of population," but also from isolated regions.

Gerald B. Gaither [studied patterns of] voting in all the old Confederate states during the Populist era. Though he analyzed fewer variables than Parsons, Hackney, and Argersinger, his work leaves one with the same impression as theirs. The tables show no consistent pattern across state lines for the more purely economic indicators: percentage of farms operated by owner and value of farmland per acre. But—with the exception of Alabama, where industrial

Populism confused the statewide statistics—there is a persistent negative correlation between the Populist vote and the percentage of population in towns over 2,500.

When one combines all this statistical evidence with gleanings from more impressionistic descriptions of Populism in recent works on Kansas by O. Gene Clanton and Louisiana by William Ivy Hair, two tentative conclusions emerge. The first is that narrowly economic conditions do not suffice to explain Populism. Indices of income and wealth, and even patterns of mortgages and tenancy, do not consistently show that the agricultural crisis meant more hardship for Populists than other farmers. The second is that Populists tended to live out of the social and economic mainstream. Populist farmers seem to have been, not merely rural folk, but rural folk outside of the orbit of towns. Hackney, writing about both Populist farmers and industrial workers in Alabama, goes so far as to generalize about a sort of social rootlessness:

> Populists were only tenuously connected to society by economic function, by personal relationships, by stable community membership, by political participation, or by psychological identification with the South's distinctive myths. . . . they were vulnerable to feelings of powerlessness. . . . their opportunity for the sort of psychological integration with the state's social system that developed from long-term personal interaction was limited.

This may go too far, especially in the unspoken assumption that the state had only one social system, with those outside the mainstream thus being more or less "unconnected" with any society. But Hackney touches on a reality. Populists do seem commonly to have lived on the fringe of the dominant society.

Yet what did this mean? What, more precisely, was this isolation like? How, beyond vague "feelings of powerlessness," did it influence how Populists thought? Did it, under the stress of economic disaster, impel people into Populism? If so, how and why? Definitive answers to these questions must await extensive new research, directed to answer them. But it is not too early to propose some speculative answers—indeed, just such tentative hypotheses are now very much needed to orient new research.

Texas offers a particularly good basis for informed speculation, not only because of its active role in the genesis of Populism, but because of its geographic location. Lying at the juncture of the two major Populist regions, the Great Plains and the South, Texas Populism combined characteristics of both the farmer's frontier and the sharecropping South. The experience of grassroots Texas Populists in fact suggests a new understanding of the social basis of Populism that, taken in conjunction with writings on other periods of American history, may be of wider significance in comprehending the origins of American political dissent.

Well over two million people lived in Texas in the 1890s, most of them in a wide central belt running roughly north and south from the Red River to the Gulf of Mexico. Here black loam and (closer to the coast) rich alluvial soil provided fertile ground for the cotton that dominated the region's agriculture;

here the cities and industries were found; here railroads proliferated. The business and commerce of Texas flourished within this middle region, but Populism did not.

It was in the peripheral, less populated regions of East and West Texas that Populism sank its deepest roots. Fifteen Texas counties voted for a Populist governor in at least three of the four elections between 1892 and 1898. Three or four of these hugged the less developed edges of the central belt; the rest lay well beyond it. Moreover, both within and without this Populist heartland, cities and towns gave the People's party a cool reception; the rural countryside accounted for its potency on the ballot. One suspects that, in Texas as elsewhere, Populism prospered outside of the social and economic mainstream. Other evidence heightens the impression. Not only were railroads thicker in the central portions of the state, but in every section Populist counties received service inferior to that in neighboring Democratic counties. This meant limited, even irregular commerce with the rest of the state. And the Populist regions were not fully integrated with the cotton economy. The leading cotton-producing counties shied away from Populism, while Populist counties tended toward agricultural self-sufficiency. This did not necessarily mean that Populists were poorer—in fact, throughout the state, Populist counties compared favorably with Democratic counties in farm income—but it did suggest that Populists lived "on the outskirts" of Texas.

Yet this impression is too vague. One needs to probe more deeply into the circumstances in which ordinary Populists lived, and this is not easy. The anonymity of the Populist masses makes the only practical approach indirect: to ask how life in areas that consistently voted Populist differed from life elsewhere. And even this roundabout inquiry can only achieve crude approximations, for the loss of many precinct voting records prevents any survey of the state from penetrating below the county level. At best, then, this technique yields only a secondhand and schematic sense of Populist experience. But, lacking a series of detailed local studies, there seems no way of going deeper without trading representativeness for idiosyncrasy.

Since a cursory view makes clear that Populism flourished especially in certain regions of Texas, what is needed is a closer examination of these general areas. They were not uniformly Populist; some counties stood by the Democracy as staunchly as any in the state. To try to determine what impelled some people into Populism, while others remained Democrats, the fifteen strongly Populist counties were paired with neighboring counties which consistently voted for the Democratic gubernatorial candidate. This permitted a comparison of farmers in roughly the same area, who engaged in pretty much the same types of farming, but who ended on different sides of the political fence. . . .

The comparison of Populist and Democratic strongholds immediately scotches any lingering notion that Populism attracted particularly those farmers who suffered most from the agricultural depression. Farm tenancy rates, often taken as evidence of economic conditions, fluctuated so peculiarly in Texas that one questions their usefulness. In any case, the difference between

Populist and Democratic counties in both average tenancy rate and average increase in tenancy was marginal—only two percentage points—and hardly suggests unusual problems for Populists. Mortgages are even less helpful, for only a tiny fraction of farms in any of these counties were mortgaged, and the average difference between Populist and Democratic counties in both proportion of farms mortgaged and mortgage interest rates was miniscule. The two counties with the largest proportion of farm families on mortgaged farms–5 and 7 percent—always enjoyed unusually low interest rates.

Probably the best indicator of relative prosperity, though hardly ideal, is the average value of products per farm: the closest approach in available statistics to the individual farmer's annual income. Here the Populist counties actually outperformed their Democratic neighbors. "Farm income" in Populist strongholds averaged $432, compared to $403 in the Democratic counties. Morever, Populist counties showed a larger increase between 1880 and 1890: 111 percent to 78 percent. This does not prove, though it certainly suggests, that Populists were better off than Democrats in these counties. But the important point is that no reliable evidence indicates the reverse. Economic problems were a necessary condition for the Populist revolt. But they alone did not determine who became a Populist.

Other indices, however, do point to significant differences between Populist and Democratic areas. None of these counties had large towns, but the county seats in Populist counties averaged fewer than 1,000 people, while the Democratic seats averaged over 1,600. No county had major industry, but the Populist counties numbered fewer than a fifth of the manufacturing workers of Democratic counties. Railroad lines less frequently crossed the Populist counties, and the Democratic counties had all but one of the six important railroad depots. Slightly less of the farmland in Populist areas had been improved. Formal church membership was somewhat less common in Populist counties, and fewer religious denominations were represented there. Populist counties also included fewer than a third as many inhabitants of foreign birth.

Individually, none of these circumstances amounted to much. But they linked together with remarkable persistence. If one point is awarded for having a higher figure in each category [of "social development": i.e., population, number of manufacturing employees, number of railroad lines, proportion of farmland improved, percentage of church members in population, number of sects/denominations, and number of foreign born] the Democratic counties "outscore" their Populist neighbors by an average ratio of three to one. In twelve of the fifteen pairings, the Democratic county outscores the Populist, in nine cases by a wide margin of three or more points. In only two pairings does the Populist county have a higher score, and the difference is only one or two points.

A pattern certainly exists here, but what do the statistics mean? Taken together, they substantiate in some detail what recent writings on Populism have begun to hint at and what the general geography of Texas Populism suggests: that Populists lived in relative isolation from the larger society of their state and nation.

Consider the opportunities that a farmer had for contact with the "outside" world. For the typical farmer in the 1890s—in Texas as in most of the South and Midwest—market day highlighted the week. The farmer hitched his horses or mules to the wagon, loaded his family, and drove to the county seat (or some other fair-sized nearby town). There he purchased the week's supplies. He sold his produce or consigned it to the local agent. He picked up the week's mail—maybe a letter or two and the county's weekly newspaper. His wife bought material for a new dress or clothes for the children. The youngsters tasted the fascination of "town life." For most rural Texans, these trips to town every several days provided their only regular exposure to life beyond their immediate neighborhood.

The farther a farmer lived from town, the fewer trips. Elias Sanders was a typical Texas Populist, unusual only in that he left a diary. A farmer near the village of Grandview, Sanders tilled the mediocre Johnson County soil. About once a week he rode into Grandview for supplies. Only very seldom did he venture as far as Cleburne, the county seat. Church on Sundays, visits with neighboring farmers, and political rallies provided his only other contact with the world beyond his farm. Populism was his chief enthusiasm and one of his few diversions. A more extreme case was the farmer in Blanco County (one of the most strongly Populist counties) who chalked on his door: "250 miles to the nearest post office: 100 miles to wood; 20 miles to water; 6 inches to hell"; and then debarked.

Trips to town mattered very much. But all market centers were not the same. The county seats in Populist counties, averaging only a little more than half the size of their Democratic counterparts, had fewer shops, fewer places to encounter strangers. Being smaller, they were less likely to attract traveling salesmen, itinerant evangelists, or campaigning politicians. The Democratic towns were hardly metropolises. But, as the figures on manufacturing employment suggest, they offered a wider diversity of economic activities and social roles. More likely to have a rail line passing through, still more likely to have a railroad junction in town, and even more likely to be an important rail depot, they became more important trading centers than Populist towns. Trains stopped more frequently; more strangers passed through; commercial links with the rest of Texas and the nation were stronger. A broader range of economic activities and occupations brought Democratic county towns into more frequent contact with outside markets, as well as with outside businessmen and banks. One should not exaggerate the differences. Most Democrats shared the rural existence of third-party men; the line between them was not the border between city and country. But the typical Democrat lived physically and psychologically closer to the city than his Populist cousin.

Other circumstances reinforced the Populists' relative isolation. That Populist counties had a slightly higher proportion of unimproved farmland hints at a less developed economy and society; although not large, the difference appeared in ten of the fifteen pairings. The data on organized religion points in the same direction. The main southern evangelical denominations—Methodists, Baptists, Disciples of Christ—dominated the Populist and Democratic counties. But in eleven of the fifteen pairings a smaller proportion of the citizens in the Populist county belonged formally to any church, although most Texas Populists exhibited a shouting and singing enthusiasm for old-time religion not usually matched by Democrats. The anomaly suggests weaker Populist ties with the organized life of their society. That Populist counties contained fewer denominations not only seconds this impression, but also implies less exposure to the diversity and controversies of the larger society.

The smaller number of foreign-born in Populist counties is open to two interpretations. Most of the foreigners in Democratic counties were German. Several active prohibitionists were leaders of the People's party, and this may have discouraged German voters. On the other hand, the party took care to dissociate itself from prohibitionism and assiduously courted Germans. If these maneuvers succeeded in erasing the taint of prohibitionism, then the incompatibility of Populism and foreigners requires another explanation. That Populism had little success in counties with large Mexican populations has the same effect. Possibly the paucity of foreigners was simply a further instance of the Populists' insularity. Knowing almost entirely Texans of his own ethnic background limited still more the Populist's contact with outside ideas and attitudes.

The members of the new third party were many, various, and complex. Like all humans beings, they resist easy pigeonholing. But a common theme appears to weave through their diverse worlds: relative isolation from the society surrounding them. This conclusion will eventually be confirmed or controverted by detailed studies of individual counties. In the interim, one can only say that the sparse surviving precinct-level voting statistics indicate the same pattern of relative isolation for Populists within individual counties as existed between Populist and Democratic counties. In Brown County, for example, most of the consistently Populist voting boxes do not even appear on detailed railroad maps of the period. Those which do—Cross Cut, Byrd's Store, and May—were tiny hamlets far off the beaten track and well away from Brownwood, the "urban" center of the county.

One would like to know a great deal more about the background of rank-and-file Populists. How many were active in the old parties before the rise of Populism? How many came out of the Greenback movement? How many had recently immigrated to Texas, and where did they come from? Had many experienced unusual difficulties with banks or merchants? What were their personal histories of economic success or failure? How many had dealt with the Alliance co-ops? Some of these questions may never find answers; answering any will require prodigious research.

Yet there is already enough evidence to broach a tentative conclusion: the primary cause of Populism was the impact of economic distress on socially isolated farmers. But to say that relative isolation fostered Populism really explains nothing. The problem is understanding the relationship between the two. What did isolation mean in human terms? How did it push farmers toward Populism?

Isolation meant, among other things, rather limited contact with other human beings. Populism appealed to farm families starved for social life—thus the camp-meeting political rallies, the picnics, the incessant fraternizing that characterized it. Here Goodwyn's concept of a "movement culture" touches on an important truth about Populism. The camaraderie it offered probably helps to explain how it mushroomed in a few short years. But its even more rapid collapse shows the limits of sociability, nor can the fraternal side of Populism account for its politics or world view. Isolation had a deeper impact.

At the level of practical politics, isolation probably meant inexperience, and inexperience often resulted in exclusion. Consider the vicissitudes of the founders of Comanche County's Human party, one of the several local precursors of the People's party. Severe drought and agricultural depression had brought Comanche County, later to become a West Texas Populist bastion, to the edge of famine by the summer of 1886. The hard-pressed farmers sought action through the local Democratic party, traditionally dominated the "mostly town folks with a few countrymen mixed in." Farmer efforts to win representation through the precinct nominating conventions were frustrated by the maneuvering of the old leadership. One observer (who remained a loyal Democrat) commented "that if all men have equal political rights under the law, this equality is certainly not always preserved in a convention where men skilled in debate and parliamentary practice are enlisted on one side and farmers who are unskilled in such matters are on the other." The desperate dissidents were forced to organize a new party. They did not lack a majority—their Human party swept the boards at the general election—but they lacked the political sophistication to translate their majority into control of existing political machinery.

This story was repeated elsewhere. J. W. H. Davis, a Populist from Grimes Country in East Texas, described his own experience: "When the primary convention was called and rules read, we found all who was not willing to obey the dictation of political trixters and town rings were read out of the democratic party." Hard-pressed farmers less politically isolated than the Populists could work for relief within existing party organizations. And, in fact, the Texas Democracy featured an active reform wing under Governor James Hogg. But less sophisticated sufferers seem to have found themselves effectively excluded by town-oriented political operators, and Populism became the refuge of the shutout. Much of the rage and alienation that powered Populism may originally have surged up in battles between backwoods farmers and courthouse elites, like that in Comanche County, and then found another target in other dominating elites. How much of the deceit, greed, and megalomania that Populists attributed to Wall Street and Lombard Street had they first discovered in the courthouse ring?

Isolation may also have shaped Populism in deeper, more personal, and more important strata. Here the historian treads on slippery ground, for ordinary Populists left little evidence of their interior selves. The shreds that survive consist mostly of scattered copies of county weeklies—important for not only the locally produced editorial content but especially the letters to the editor—and a rare letter or diary. These fragmentary remains often impart a sense of people bewildered by the complexities of the world around them. Populists struggling with practical political realities commonly wrote in real perplexity. One local "Investigator" could not fathom why the general economic discontent did not immediately produce a political remedy: "Why not change our statu[t]es so they will be in accordance with the will of the majority? It appears strange to me that the only obstacle that prevents it is a lack of agreement upon the best policy or methods by which it can be accomplished."

Perhaps this sense of confusion encouraged the Populist tendency to rely on scapegoats and panaceas. The "plutocracy," the "pirates" of the Money Power, lay behind all the farmer's troubles. And some simple, single reform— though just which one was never agreed upon—would transform his condition almost overnight; it would, as the *Lampasas People's Journal* assured its readers, "cause a revolution in less than two years." But these miraculous remedies remained frustratingly vague. Local third-party men enthusiastically endorsed the concrete provisions of state and national platforms, but before these were promulgated, during the birth of the movement, grass-roots Populists could come up with embarrassingly few specific proposals. W. M. Robinson of Comanche defended this fuzziness: "The declaration of independence does not tell how to guarantee to every man life, liberty, and the pursuit of happiness. Its authors only declared the truth." But he conceded that Populists floundered in trying to conceive an effective reform program. "We go a step further and declare against monopolies, bonds, and other evils that we don't know exactly how to remedy, but being convinced that the principles are just, we must carry them forward."

Much of Populist rhetoric, like these samples, suggests that third-party men felt themselves at sea in the society in which they lived. Bewilderment appears to have bred an incessant worry that more sophisticated men preyed on their naïveté. Populists saw themselves as cruelly hoodwinked for years, until the third party had opened their eyes. A greedy plutocracy controlled the government and economy of Texas and the nation, and the money kings remained secure in their high places through their success in duping the citizenry. "The brigand has his headquarters in legislative halls, and the pirate fees a lawyer and goes into business. Of course, the masses must be kept in ignorance and deceived, and nothing gives deception and error such power over men as to be clothed in the garb of law." "The trouble with us," one Populist sighed, "is that we have too many men who are too easily fooled."

Not surprisingly, suggestions that sophisticated economic problems were beyond the ken of ignorant farmers seem to have touched a sensitive nerve among Populists. The ordinary Populist tended to hide his naïveté behind a mask of cocky certitude whenever Democrats reminded him of the limitations of his political education. In the past, third-party members agreed, the masses had been lamentably ill informed. But recently, owing to the efforts of the Alliance and the People's party, Texans had opened their eyes to the skullduggery around them. "The people now are reading and thinking for themselves as never before," claimed the *Lampasas People's Journal*. In fact, "we find our farmers better posted on the great questions now agitating the country than any other class of men."

The very brashness of Populist protestations seemed a defense against their own uncertainty. The self-image of the typical Texas Populist contrasted sharply with his vocal confidence. Populists depicted themselves as gullible people— "poor deluded, hard working farmers"—deceived before by cleverer men and readily susceptible again to the tricks of the worldly-wise. People's party men themselves confessed that what went on in their society was often foreign to their understanding. They admitted their fears that the more sophisticated members of society were "out to get them." Psychologizing on such slender evidence as remains is a risky business. But the evidence suggests that Populist perplexity and fear spawned self-doubt.

It does not seem altogether improbable that this cast of mind resulted from the sort of social isolation described earlier. A foggy and partial understanding of the political system, vague and uncertain gropings toward reform, a nagging fear of being hoodwinked, and a prickly defensiveness about their own naïveté all suggest a people cut off from full participation in their own society, a people, in consequence, retreating in confusion and distrust, apt on occasion to stray into irrationality.

At the same time, this isolation may also have been the Populists' greatest strength. As strangers in their own land, Populist farmers would more easily have probed and questioned accepted political and economic verities. They could more comfortably desert the Democratic party, the party of the fathers, treason to which was betrayal of the South. The could even break the united front of white supremacy and breach the color line. Above all, they could support (though not necessarily generate or fully understand) the wildest, the most improbable—perhaps the most penetrating and hopeful—schemes for remodeling an industrializing America. Their relative isolation gave Populists enough independence from the dominant political culture to allow the growth of an original politics and ideology. Yet isolation was perhaps also the reason why Populism, so powerful, was so easily undercut, divided, and defeated.

John D. Hicks may not have been far from the mark, after all, when he explained Populism as a product of the frontier. Yet the "frontier" characteristics that spawned Populism were not the qualities that Turner attributed to the frontier: an enforced self-reliance breeding individualism and democracy. Rather, Populism grew from the tenuousness of connections with the larger society, the distance between the centers of American political culture and farmers living on the periphery of this culture.

A puzzling question remains. If, as proposed here, social isolation is a key to understanding Populism, why did no farmers' revolt explode earlier? Tillers of the soil had lived in rural insularity before; they had suffered severe economic depression before. Yet never before had they responded with the intensity and power of the 1890s. Why was isolation especially galling at this particular moment of American history?

Between the end of the Civil War and the turn of the twentieth century, the United States underwent what time may demonstrate to have been the most fundamental transformation in its history: the change from a basically rural nation to an urban society. The cultural impact was radical. Especially with the advent of national chain stores, smaller towns grew more closely linked with the great metropolises. The huge mail-order houses brought home even to rural folk the new city-oriented civilization. The ideal of a single national pattern of life and set of values, reinforced by the proliferation of national-circulation magazines, came much closer to realization. Even the county weeklies commonly read by Populists, though unconnected with the new wire services, usually filled half their space with nationally produced boiler plate. Ways of living in New York and Chicago were becoming the standard to which the rest of the nation wished to conform. The central culture was swallowing more and more of the diverse local cultures.

However, some citizens—very few in most of the country, but many in the recently settled Midwest and the war-retarded South—remained on the fringe of the metropolitan culture. Tantalizing tastes of the wider culture they certainly had; real participation they did not. Rural free delivery and decent roads, with automobiles to travel them, still lay in the future. Although the offerings of Montgomery Ward tempted them along with other farmers, nevertheless, on the whole, these "backward" people remained the last outpost of the old America.

Their isolation made them, perhaps, fearful and uncertain of the new order. Being snickered at as hicks and soaptails (a term of abuse specific to Populist hicks) did not encourage them. The tensions between the new America and their familiar world appeared in the most unexpected places. The *Lampasas People's Journal* recounted with ill-concealed fury a joke printed in the town's Democratic paper:

> Will you please tell me how I may recognize a soaptail when I call at his home? I am an agent and am anxious for information on this point.
>
> Answer:—You can always tell a soaptail by shaking hands with his wife. If her hands are covered with corns and have the appearance of having wielded the ax and held the plow, you may rest assured her husband is a genuine soaptail.

The Populists' rage was all the greater because, undeniably, the work-roughened hands of their women did clash embarrassingly with the soft feminine hands now demanded by the city. The felt differences between backwoods farmers and other Americans were growing sharper, isolation becoming more awkward, even painful, the sense of being left out deepening. This could push men close to tears of anger and hurt, as it did the Grimes County Populist, J. W. H. Davis:

> the chairman of our great state democratic executive comeety, call us all skunks, anything that has the sent of the plowhandle smells like a polecat to them. (I want you to tell me how in the dickens these God forsakin money mongers know how anything would smell in the norstal of an honest man.)

And Judge Terrell went out of his way in his speech at Georgetown to call our wives and little children in their cabbins over the country, spoonds by the wayside, a reglar fish pond off of which nabobs feed.

Populists were not so much pulling away from their society as their society was from them. The distress that this induced may well have generated much of the angry energy in Populism. It certainly made isolation more deeply felt.

This interpretation places Populism firmly in the broadest context of American historical development. The movement cannot be understood as simply a farmers' revolt against penury and oppression, a rebellion that could have flared up, given the right conditions, at any time in American history. Instead, Populism resulted specifically from the "ending of the frontier"—not in Turner's sense of the drying up of free land, but in a wider sense of the curtailment of social isolation.

Yet implicit in this view of Populism is a notion that applies, not only to a specific historical moment, but to much of American political history: that isolation breeds a political culture at odds with the mainstream of political habits and attitudes. It follows that the tensions thereby generated ought to have been a continuing feature of the politics of an expanding nation with a frontier that pulled many citizens into a relatively isolated life.

The limited evidence available points to precisely this conclusion. The most striking case is Jackson Turner Main's analysis of *Political Parties before the Constitution*. Main argues that a division between "Localists" and "Cosmopolitans" dominated politics in all the states during the 1770s and 1780s, foreshadowing the Antifederalists and Federalists in the struggle over ratification of the Constitution. The well-populated, long-established economic and cultural centers were the strongholds of the Cosmopolitans. But away from the towns, away from the major rivers, in the inland villages and on the frontiers, where commercial agriculture gave way to subsistence farming, in regions "culturally backward" and cut off from "short, cheap access to markets," the Localists dominated. *Mutatis mutandis,* Main could almost have been describing the Populist heartlands. One cannot help wondering whether the politics of the Antifederalists—their suspicion of central government, their persistence in the "outmoded" whig radicalism of the early Revolution—owed much to the political culture of the relatively isolated areas in which many of them apparently dwelt.

Yet this was neither the first nor last conflict between established centers of political and cultural influence and people living on the periphery of the dominant society. Before the Revolution the Regulator movements of Carolina pitted up-country frontiersmen against low-country planters. Much of antebellum—and indeed postbellum—southern politics centered on tensions between Piedmont dirt farmers and lowland elites. The Great Awakening split New England along lines roughly corresponding to the division between established sociocultural centers and culturally and commercially peripheral areas. The American Revolution itself was a conflict between the sociocultural center of the empire and a provincial region three thousand miles away.

To point to these examples is to raise questions rather than to suggest answers. Historians have seldom pursued the kinds of research that might reveal in these cases similarities of the Populist milieu such as Main's book indicates. But the possible inferences are intriguing. Do we need a richer, more complex interpretation of these persistent conflicts in American politics, an explanation in terms of clashing political cultures as well as inequalities of political and economic power? Does all of this hint at a much broader, more flexible, more subtle remodeling of the Turner thesis? Perhaps we should try to understand Populism, not only as a response to the economic modernization of America, but as a manifestation of one of the most central and venerable characteristics of the American political tradition.

QUESTIONS FOR DISCUSSION

1. If, as Turner proposes, "social isolation is a key to undersanding Populism," why did no farmers' revolt explode prior to the 1890s?
2. How does Turner's "understanding of the social basis of Populism" contribute to our understanding of the "origins of American political dissent"?

PAUL BOYER

The Progressives and the City

*In the preceding chapter, James Turner locates the rise of Populism within
the context of what he calls "the most fundamental transformation in [United
States] history: the change from a basically rural nation to an urban society."
The Populists, Turner argues, were distressed and angered that "their society
was [pulling away] from them." They were, as we shall see, not the only Americans to feel this way.*

*Between 1870 and 1900, the population of the United States doubled. The
new Americans were not, however, evenly spread across the face of the nation.
More than two thirds settled in the cities, many of them recent emigrants from
eastern and southern Europe.*

*Americans have, from the first days of the Republic, expressed an ambivalent
attitude toward their cities. American cities have been portrayed as centers of
culture, industry, and productivity, but also as dens of sin from which few
innocents escape unscathed. The rapid growth of the turn-of-the-century cities—and of the proportion of southern and eastern European immigrants
within them—exacerbated the fears of those who saw the cities as the devil's
workshop in America.*

*In the decades surrounding the turn of the century, the "progressives," a
broad reform coalition, took on the task of rescuing the city, its people, and,
they believed, the larger society, from the evils spawned by the urban environment. In the following selection, Paul Boyer describes the common concerns
and the strategies of the progressive reformers.*

COMMON CONCERNS, DIVERGENT STRATEGIES

One century yielded to another, and the flow of humanity cityward continued. In the census of 1920, with sixty-eight cities exceeding the 100,000 figure,

Paul Boyer is a professor of history at the University of Wisconsin. He is the author of
several books including *By the Bomb's Early Light: American Thought and Culture at the Dawn
of the Atomic Age* and *Urban Masses and Moral Order in America: 1820–1920* from which the
following selection has been excerpted.

Excerpted by permission of the publishers from *Urban Masses and Moral Order in America,* pp. 189–202, 205–211, 220–224, by Paul Boyer, Cambridge, Mass.: Harvard University Press,
©1978 by the President and Fellows of Harvard College.

America's urban population for the first time surpassed the symbolic 50 per-cent mark. In the first two decades of the new century, New York City grew by 2.2 million, Chicago by 1 million, Detroit by 425,000—and so on down the roster of established urban giants and fast-growing contenders. Even in the South (historically a laggard in urbanization), though the great surge still lay ahead, the early twentieth century saw a quickened pace of city growth. For-eign immigration continued to account for a large share of this expansion. After a dip in the 1890s, immigration soared to unprecedented levels in these years—over 17 million from 1900 to 1917, with the single-year total exceeding 1 million for the first time in 1905—and most of these millions remained in the cities. By 1920, over 80 percent of all Russian, Irish, Italian, and Polish-born people in the United States were urban residents. Only war and the Immigra-tion Act of 1924 would finally stem the tide.

With such statistics as a backdrop, the familiar warnings persisted. Josiah Strong returned to the fray with the *The Challenge of the City* (1907), giving his chapters such lugubrious titles as "The Modern City as Menace to State and Nation," and quoting Shelley's epigram: "Hell is a city much like London." Even those who took a less alarmist view agreed that urban growth was a looming social reality whose full implications America had not yet begun to grasp. The problem of the city, declared the Boston sociologist Frank Parsons, in 1899, was "the problem of civilization." William B. Munro, professor of government at Harvard, agreed that cities were becoming the "controlling factor" in Amer-ican life. "The modern city marks an epoch in our civilization," wrote Frederic Howe, adviser to Mayor Tom Johnson of Cleveland, in 1906; "Through it, a new society has been created."

As this conviction deepened, the urban social-control impulse, its roots lying deep in the past, assumed fresh urgency. "How to reach the heart of the city and to change its life is, indeed, the question of questions," declared the Amer-ican Methodist bishops as the new century dawned. William Munro quoted with approval Henry Drummond's challenging aphorism, "He who makes the city makes the world."

Influenced by such battle cries, a large and diverse company of men and women sought a role in shaping the urban moral order. . . .

Whereas the earlier [nineteenth century] voluntarist movements had con-centrated on influencing individuals or families, those of the Progressive era were based on the conviction that the moral destiny of the city would be most decisively influenced through broad programs utilizing a full panoply of gov-ernmental power and aimed at a fundamental restructuring of the urban environment.

This central environmentalist assumption, however, led in two radically dif-ferent directions. . . . On one hand, some reformers—"negative environmen-talists," we might call them—pursued a coercive and moralistic approach, concentrating on eradicating two institutions that for them had come to epito-mize urban moral and social breakdown: the brothel and the saloon. The other category of reformers—the "positive environmentalists"—took their cue from the more hopeful and visionary side of late-nineteenth century urban reformism. Their goal was to create in the city the kind of physical environment that would gently but irresistibly mold a population of cultivated, moral, and socially responsible city dwellers.

Despite profound differences, however, these two approaches shared certain fundamental moral-control purposes: the elevation of character, the inculcation of a "higher" standard of individual behavior, the placing of social duty above private desire, the re-creation of the urban masses in the reformers' own image. At this basic level, both remained firmly linked to an urban social-control tradition extending back to the Jacksonian period.

BATTLING THE SALOON AND THE BROTHEL

The Great Coercive Crusades

On June 25, 1910, President William Howard Taft signed into law a bill introduced by Congressman James Mann of Illinois making it a federal offense to transport a woman across a state line for "immoral purposes." A death blow had been struck, so the framers of the Mann Act claimed, against prostitution, the brothel, and the dread "white-slave traffic."

Seven and a half years later, on December 22, 1917, in the midst of a world war, Congress submitted to the states a constitutional amendment barring the manufacture, sale, or importation of intoxicating liquor within the United States. In January 1919, the necessary thirty-six states having ratified, prohibition became the law of the land. (By the terms of the Eighteenth Amendment, actual enforcement began a year later: a final crumb tossed to the liquor interests by the triumphant prohibitionists.)

These two measures were among the crowning achievements of the great Progressive-era crusades against the "liquor evil" and the "prostitution evil." Although these crusades hardly represent unexplored historical terrain, they are central to the present study, for the brothel and the saloon were widely perceived as the great bastions of urban vice. So long as they stood, the dream of an urban moral awakening would be no more than that; if they could be subdued, the purified, morally homogeneous city might at last become a reality.

Intemperance and prostitution were not, of course, discoveries of the Progressives. Both had been the object of reformist attention since the days of Lyman Beecher and John R. McDowall. In the Gilded Age, the Woman's Christian Temperance Union (1874) had revived the temperance cause, and the antiprostitution banner had been upheld by "social purity" leaders like Abby Hopper Gibbons of New York and the Philadelphia Quaker Aaron Macy Powell, as well as by local civic organizations campaigning against municipal regulation (and hence tacit acceptance) of prostitution. The decade of the 1890s saw an intensification of both antialcohol and antiprostitution effort, including state campaigns to raise the legal age of consent, national temperance conventions and "purity" congresses, the formation of the Anti-Saloon League (1895) and the American Purity Alliance, and the organization of rescue work aimed at prostitutes and unwed mothers.

For all this, the dawning century found both vices still deeply entrenched. In 1900 only three states had prohibition laws on the books; saloons, liquor stores, and the infamous "bucket shops" flourished in every major city; and per capita alcohol consumption—augmented by the new national favorite, German lager beer—stood at nearly twice the 1860 figure. As for prostitution, every city had its red-light district, including some now bathed in a nostalgic glow: Gayosa Street in Memphis; the Levee in Chicago; San Francisco's Barbary Coast; New Orleans' Storyville (named for the alderman who drafted the statute establishing its boundaries); "Hooker's Division" in Washington, an appellation immortalizing the Civil War general who had confined prostitutes to that section. In 1900, two Omaha madams, Ada and Minna Everleigh, felt confident enough of their prospects to invest thousands of dollars in a luxurious Chicago brothel, the Everleigh Club, which soon became the showplace of the Levee.

In focusing attention on these evils—indeed, in making them stand symbolically for much that was unsettling about city life—urban moral reformers of the Progressive era succeeded in channeling the urban uplift enthusiasm of the 1890s into highly organized efforts involving specific goals and carefully planned strategies. In the prohibition drive, the Anti-Saloon League—supported by innumerable small contributors and a few very large ones like John D. Rockefeller, Jr., and dime-store baron S. S. Kresge—played the crucial organizational role. From the first, the ASL's single-minded goal was legal prohibition, and its major target, the cities. In counties and townships where prohibitionist sentiment was strong, the league organized local-option campaigns and worked for the election of sympathetic state legislators. The local groundwork laid, it moved to the state level, exhibiting the same skill in legislative lobbying that it displayed in marshaling public opinion. By concentrating on state legislatures (where the cities were underrepresented), the Anti-Saloon League gradually isolated urban America. In the campaign's final stages, thousands of ASL speakers promoted the cause in the nation's Protestant pulpits, and oceans of propaganda (including the League's principal organ, the *American Issue*) poured from ASL presses in Westerville, Ohio. The triumph of 1919 was thus the culmination of more than two decades of grass roots effort, reinforced by wartime moral fervor, grain-conservation enthusiasm, and anti-German-brewer sentiment.

While the ASL was orchestrating the prohibition campaign, a more complex organizational effort was focusing diffuse sexual-purity impulses on a specific issue: urban prostitution. The issue first surfaced in New York City, where the number of saloons harboring prostitutes had increased sharply after 1896, when a revision of the state licensing code–dubbed the Raines Law after its sponsor—had inadvertently made it advantageous for them to add bedrooms and transform themselves into "hotels." The spread of these "Raines Law hotels" into well-to-do neighborhoods aroused a storm of indignation, and in November 1900 Episcopal Bishop Henry C. Potter penned a stinging protest to

Tammany mayor Robert Van Wyck. (Unruffled, Van Wyck declared that New York had "the highest standard of morality in the world"; Tammany boss Richard Croker, taking a rather contradictory tack, argued that in any city there were "bound to be some unusually vile places.")

A few days after Potter's letter, the New York Committee of Fifteen was formed. This organization of businessmen, publishers, academics, and other elite figures—the prototype of antiprostitution commissions that would soon emerge in scores of cities—set out quietly to investigate vice conditions and develop legislative remedies. It soon became involved in more stirring matters, however, through its support for a flamboyant young special-sessions judge, William T. Jerome—the "second Theodore Roosevelt," his admirers claimed— who had won celebrity for his dramatic raids on brothels and other vice dens. In the municipal elections of 1901, thanks in part to the support of the Committee of Fifteen and the Reverend Charles Parkhurst's City Vigilance League, Jerome was elected district attorney, while Seth Low, a "fusion" candidate backed by the reformers, defeated Tammany's man in the mayoral race.

Meanwhile, a team of prostitution investigators had been recruited by the Committee of Fifteen, and in 1902 its findings were published as *The Social Evil, with Special Reference to Conditions Existing in the City of New York.* A 1909 *McClure's* exposé, "The Daughters of the Poor: A Plain Story of the Development of New York City as a Leading Center of the White Slave Trade of the World, under Tammany Hall," helped sustain the cause, as did the 1910 investigations of a special grand jury under John D. Rockefeller, Jr.

At the same time, Chicago was emerging as a second major center of the antiprostitution campaign. In a 1907 *McClure's* article, "The City of Chicago: A Study of the Great Immoralities," muckraker George Kibbe Turner accorded prostitution a prominent place in his catalog of evils. ("As in the stock-yards, not one shred of flesh is wasted.") Soon an ambitious assistant state's attorney named Clifford G. Roe was organizing a series of white-slave prosecutions. Thwarted by his superiors, Roe resigned, secretly arranged financial backing from a group of sympathetic Chicagoans, and proceeded with his investigations as a private citizen. In 1911 Roe organized the National Vigilance Society (with himself as director, secretary, and general counsel) and over the next few years published several lurid books on prostitution.

Meanwhile, in January 1910, under pressure from the Chicago church federation, Mayor Fred Busse had appointed a thirty-member vice commission (twenty-eight men, two women), under the chairmanship of Walter T. Sumner, dean of the Cathedral of Saints Peter and Paul (Episcopal), to investigate prostitution in the city. Given a $5,000 appropriation, the Commission in 1911 produced *The Social Evil in Chicago,* a 394-page report ending with a set of recommendations aimed at implementing its motto: "Constant and Persistent Repression of Prostitution the Immediate Method; Absolute Annihilation the Ultimate Ideal." The report was based on data compiled by a research team under George J. Kneeland, a Yale Divinity School dropout who had worked as an editor with several New York magazines before becoming director of investigations for New York's Committee of Fifteen in 1908.

Also involved in the antiprostitution crusade were the American Society of Sanitary and Moral Prophylaxis (founded 1905), a medical group headed by the prominent dermatologist Prince A. Morrow, whose influential *Social Diseases and Marriage* had appeared in 1904, and the Bureau of Social Hygiene (1910), a small, New York-based agency financed with Rockefeller money. Among the latter's publications was *Commercialized Prostitution in New York* (1913), a somewhat popularized version of the various vice reports already in circulation.

Some order emerged in this organizational thicket in 1913 when the Rockefeller and Morrow groups, together with several other societies (including the old American Purity Alliance), merged to form the American Social Hygiene Association. While no single group ever dominated the antiprostitution movement as the Anti-Saloon League did the prohibition crusade, the ASHA and its magazine *Social Hygiene* played a central role.

Sparked by all this organizational activity, the antiprostitution drive had assumed the characteristics of a national crusade. "No movement devoted to the betterment and uplift of humanity has advanced more rapidly within recent years," reported the *New Encyclopedia of Social Reform* in 1909. From 1902 to 1916, 102 cities and three states conducted vice investigations modeled on those of New York and Chicago. By 1920 practically every state had outlawed soliciting, and more than 30 had passed Injunction and Abatement laws empowering the courts to close brothels upon the filing of citizens' complaints. At the federal level, the reform found expression not only in the Mann Act but also in President Roosevelt's 1908 announcement of America's adherence to an international white-slave convention recently adopted in Paris, as well as a series of reports on prostitution—"the most accursed business ever devised by man"—by the United States Immigration Commission.

"White slavery" proved a gold mine to journalists, editors, moviemakers, and publishers. George Kibbe Turner's exposés are merely the best remembered of many in the periodicals of the day. *Traffic in Souls,* a film purporting to document the nationwide prostitution business, appeared in 1913. As for books, the scores of vice commission reports simply added to a torrent of works including such diverse titles as Clifford Roe's *Horrors of the White Slave Trade* (1911), with its 448 pages and thirty-two illustrations; Jane Addams's thoughtful *A New Conscience and an Ancient Evil* (1912); and David Graham Phillips's novel *Susan Lenox; Her Fall and Rise* (1917).

Just as it provided the final impetus for prohibition, the wartime mood of 1917–18 also intensified the antiprostitution crusade. With the support of Secretary of War Newton D. Baker (who as mayor of Cleveland had taken a strong antiprostitution stand), the wartime Commission on Training Camp Activities closed a number of red-light districts hitherto resisting purification—an achievement perhaps praised more heartily in *Social Hygiene* than in the barracks.

MORALISM AND EXPERTISE: THE LINKS BETWEEN THE GREAT COERCIVE CRUSADES AND PROGRESSIVISM

Historians have engaged in a lively debate over whether prohibition—and, by implication, the antiprostitution crusade—should be included within the canon of legitimate Progressive reforms. Writing in 1955, Richard Hofstadter said no. Prohibition, he contended, was "a ludicrous caricature of the reforming impulse"—a "pinched, parochial substitute" for genuine reform, imposed by spiteful rural folk upon the more tolerant and urbane cities. In the same vein, Egal Feldman in 1967 described the coercive aspects of the antiprostitution crusade as "irrational, evangelical, uncompromising, and completely divorced from the humanitarianism of the early twentieth century." Other historians have challenged this thesis. Demonstrating the close connections—in terms of personnel, mutual affirmations of support, and overlapping organizational commitments—that can be established between the moral-control crusades and other strands of progressivism, they argue that the former must be considered an authentic expression of the broader Progressive impulse.

Interestingly, the Progressives themselves had trouble reaching a consensus on this question. Although some reformers and ideologues welcomed the prohibition and antiprostitution campaigns, others denied any kinship between what *they* stood for and the coercive moral-control crusades. Walter Lippmann, for example, ridiculed the "raucous purity" of some antivice campaigners, and Charles A. Beard in 1912 criticized the "moral enthusiasts" who were "pushing through legislation which they are not willing to uphold by concentrated and persistent action." Herbert Croly in *The Promise of American Life* declared that reformers who functioned merely as "moral protestants and purifiers" were engaged in a fundamentally "misdirected effort." Only "personal self-stultification," he insisted, could result from such an "illiberal puritanism." True reform, Croly characteristically added, involved "an intellectual as well as a moral challenge."

The answer depends in large part, of course, on where one looks on the Progressive spectrum and, indeed, on how one defines progressivism, and that, as Peter Filene has reminded us, can be a very difficult task. But one trait common to most reformers of these years—and one which helped establish a bond between the coercive reformers and other Progressives—was an infinite capacity for moral indignation. For Progressives of all stripes, as for their predecessors in the 1890s, questions of social injustice, corporate wrongdoing, governmental corruption, and personal morality were inextricably linked. Almost every Progressive cause had its moral dimension; almost every condition Progressives set out to change was seen as contributing to a debilitating social environment that made it easier for people to go wrong and harder for them to go right. Child labor and the exploitation of women workers were evil not only because they were physically harmful, but also because they stunted the moral and spiritual development of their victims. (Society had the right to limit the hours of women in industry, Louis D. Brandeis argued before the United

States Supreme court in 1908, because the fatigue of long hours was undermining their moral fiber and driving them to "alcoholic stimulants and other excesses.") Urban graft and misgovernment were evil not only because they wasted taxpayers' money but also because they debased the moral climate of the city. ("The influence and example of bad municipal government . . . , of public servants dishonest with impunity and profit," cried an officer of the National Municipal League in 1904, echoing his reform predecessors of the Gilded Age, "constitutes a disease against which we have greater need of a quarantine than we ever had against yellow fever.") As Stanley K. Schultz has written of progressivism's journalistic advance guard the muckrakers, their writings often "assumed the nature of a moral crusade, . . . because ultimately their search was a moral endeavor."

The moral substratum of progressivism is heavily underscored in the autobiography of Frederic C. Howe, in many respects a prototypical Progressive, in which he describes his intensely evangelical upbringing and its shaping influence on his later reform career: "Physical escape from the embraces of evangelical religion did not mean moral escape. From that religion my reason was never emancipated. By it I was conformed to my generation and made to share its moral standards and ideals. . . . Early assumptions as to virtue and vice, goodness and evil remained in my mind long after I had tried to discard them. This is, I think, the most characteristic influence of my generation."

Some historians have drawn sharp distinctions between progressivism's various facets, opposing the economic and political reforms to those that were explicitly moralistic. Such an approach, if too literally applied, does violence to the powerful moral thrust underlying *all* these reforms. For the Progressives, society had the right—indeed the duty!—to intervene at *any* point where the well-being of its members was threatened, since every such threat had its moral aspect. A 1914 article in a reform journal edited by Josiah Strong and W. D. P. Bliss put the matter plainly: "We are no longer frightened by that ancient bogy—'paternalism in government.' We affirm boldly, it is the business of government to be just that—paternal. . . *Nothing human can be foreign to a true government.*"

Within this intensely moralistic ambience, it was easy to see the coercive social-control crusades as simply one piece in the larger reform mosaic. In *The Shame of the Cities* (1904), for example, muckraker Lincoln Steffens frequently called attention to organized gambling and prostitution as by-products of municipal political corruption. Similarly, a leading San Francisco Progressive, newspaper editor Fremont Older, in fighting boss Abraham Ruef in 1907–1909, revealed many seamy details of Ruef's involvement with organized vice.

Those who were seeking to rid urban America of these vices, for their part, never doubted that they were in the mainstream of the era's broader reform current. "We are tired of poverty, of squalor, of ignorance . . . , of the wretchedness of women and the degradation of men," wrote a prohibition leader in 1908. "Our hearts bleed when we look upon the misery of child life." Convinced that intolerable conditions of work and habitation were driving men into the saloons and women into the streets, they supported such Progressive reforms as wage-and-hour laws, tenement codes, and factory-safety legislation. "Is it any wonder," asked the Chicago Vice Commission rhetorically, "that a tempted girl who receives only six dollars per week working with her hands sells her body for twenty-five dollars per week when she learns there is a demand for it and men are willing to pay the price?"

A second important respect in which the coercive moral reformers were closely attuned to the broader Progressive impulse was in their reliance on statistics, sociological investigation, and "objective" social analysis to buttress their cause—a strategy characteristic of many otherwise quite disparate Progressive reforms. For the antisaloon and antiprostitution forces, this represented a significant shift from earlier approaches. Through much of the Gilded Age, the temperance and social purity enthusiasts had concentrated on moral appeals to the individual, assuming that they and the objects of their benevolent attention shared, at some level, a common body of values and standards. (There were exceptions to this personalistic approach—the state drives to raise the legal age of consent, the quadrennial electoral campaigns of the Prohibition party—but in general the personal moral appeal was the preferred strategy.)

By the end of the century, as the old assumptions faded, overtly moralistic personal appeals were being supplanted by a more generalized emphasis on the reformers' technical expertise and superior factual grasp of urban issues. Moral reform must be rooted in careful investigation and social analysis, insisted Benjamin Flower in *Civilization's Inferno.* "Mere sentimentality will not answer. We must have incontrovertible data upon which to base our arguments." The first step of a prestigious Committee of Fifty for the Investigation of the Liquor Problem formed in New York City in 1893 was to "secure a body of facts which may serve as a basis for intelligent public and private actions." Even the WCTU established a Department of Scientific Temperance Instruction that lobbied for alcohol-education programs in the public schools.

In the Progressive years this shift accelerated, and the personalistic approach was largely abandoned. Now, by contrast, intemperance and sexual deviation came to be viewed less as personal failings than as products of an urban environment that needed to be purified—by force of law if necessary. The Chicago Vice Commission expressed the prevailing view when it dismissed as "naive" those who looked for the sources of prostitution in the individual prostitute's flaws of character. The emphasis was now on eliminating from the urban environment those *institutions* that undermined individual moral resistance—especially the saloon and the brothel.

With this development, the "scientific" aura of urban moral reform intensified. A *Scientific Temperance Journal* was established in Boston in 1906 by Cora Frances Stoddard. Muckraking journalists like George Kibbe Turner marshaled facts, statistics, dates, and names to buttress their indictment of the saloon, and the antiprostitution crusaders similarly strove for a tone of objective expertise as remote as possible from the thundering moral denunciations of earlier years. Indeed, in a number of cities the antiprostitution groups called themselves "Morals Efficiency Commissions." The 1902 report of New York's

Committee of Fifteen exuded the scholarly aura appropriate to what its secretary called in the preface "a valuable scientific contribution," and *The Social Evil in Chicago,* a forbiddingly dry compendium of charts, statistics, appendixes, medical data, and analysis of interviews with 2,420 prostitutes, was similarly described by its sponsors as a "scientific study" based on the findings of "experts and trained investigators."

The fetish of scientific objectivity took many forms. One national group concentrated on assigning exact numerical ratings to various cities' success in eradicating prostitution: Chicago, 37 percent; New York, 41 percent; Houston, 86 percent; and so on. In many vice commission reports, the antiseptic aura was heightened by the substitution of numbers and letters for actual names: "One woman, Mollie (X61), lives near Oak Park and solicits in (X62). Her husband is dying in (X62a)." The point of view underlying all this was summed up by the chairman of the Moral Survey Committee of Syracuse, New York. "It is a waste of time and energy to begin dealing with commercialized vice with talk, talk, talk," he wrote. "What we need is facts, facts, facts." The ASL's *National Issue* and its hefty annual *Yearbook* fairly bristled with charts, tables, and graphs purporting to establish positive or negative correlations between the saloon and death rates, arrest rates, tax rates, divorce rates, wages, insanity, pauperism, bank deposits, industrial efficiency, housing investment, and public-school enrollment. Drawing upon data compiled by Cora Frances Stoddard, the ASL in 1917 reported—with the usual flourish of graphs—that studies undertaken in Germany and Finland had proved conclusively a link between drinking, sloppy typing, and the inability to thread needles.

This obsession with technical expertise and factual data completed the secularization of the urban moral-control movement. To be sure, these reforms ultimately depended on the moral energy of Protestant America, and denominational agencies like the Methodist Board of Temperance and Morals played an important role in rallying support. Yet appeals to the evangelical moral code do not figure strongly in either the prohibition or the antiprostitution movements, and the organizations promoting these reforms were not by any means overweighed with clergymen. The top ASL men were ministers, to be sure, but during the prohibition struggle they functioned almost entirely as secularized managers, lobbyists, and propagandists rather than as latter-day Jeremiahs pronouncing God's judgment on the saloon. The lower echelons of ASL administration were even more completely secular. The organization's general superintendent, Purley A. Baker, set the tone. "The narrow, acrimonious and emotional appeal is giving way," he declared in 1915, "to a rational, determined conviction that the [liquor] traffic . . . has no rightful place in our modern civilization."

The antiprostitution movement, despite the prominence of an occasional cleric like Chicago's Dean Sumner, was even more completely divorced from the Protestant establishment. Indeed, by around 1910, antivice zealots among the clergy had become a distinct embarrassment. The Chicago Vice Commission roundly condemned an evangelist who was conducting prayer meetings in front of the city's leading brothels. An *Arena* writer in 1909 urged that the cause be pursued "sanely and scientifically" and not through " 'moral' rant from the pulpits." The local vice commissions usually had only token ministerial representation, and many delegated the actual investigative work to the team of New York-based researchers originally put together by George Kneeland for the Committee of Fifteen. As an older generation of urban moral reformers passed from the scene, the movement came to exude more of the aura of the laboratory, law library, and university lecture hall than the pulpit.

Indeed, the very shift in terminology in the antiprostitution movement, from "social *purity*" to "social *hygiene*," is significant. The entire urban moral-control effort in these years was suffused with public-health terminology and rhetoric. A writer in *Social Hygiene* in 1917 predicted that New Orleans would soon conquer prostitution just as she had eradicated yellow fever, and in *The Challenge of the City*, Josiah Strong suggested that the polluters of the city's "moral atmosphere" should be considered as deadly as the "vermin of an Egyptian plague." In Boston, the Watch and Ward Society won praise in these years from Harvard Professor Francis G. Peabody for "unobtrusively working underground, guarding us from the pestiferous evil which at any time may come up into our faces, into our homes, into our children's lives." Picking up on these cues, the Watch and Ward, like similar moral-control agencies elsewhere, increasingly defined its mission in public-health terms. "The old idea of 'charity' . . . has gradually given way to a larger conception," it declared in 1915, "to prevent . . . the moral diseases which lead to misery and crime."

The fullest elaboration of the public-health analogy in this period was probably that offered by the Massachusetts prohibitionist Newton M. Hall in *Civic Righteousness and Civic Pride* (1914). "The moral evil of the community does not remain in the foul pools in which it is bred," he wrote. "A moral miasma arises from those pools, and . . . enters not the poorest homes of the city alone, but the most carefully guarded, and leaves its trail of sorrow and despair. . . . Why should the community have any more sympathy for the saloon . . . than . . . for a typhoid-breeding pool of filthy water, . . . a swarm of deadly mosquitoes, or . . . a nest of rats infected with the bubonic plague?" For Hall, the logic of the analogy was irresistible: "Cut off the impure water and the typhoid epidemic is conquered"; destroy the saloon and the urban "moral epidemic" would vanish.

The ubiquitous medical terminology in the utterances of these reformers had more than rhetorical significance, because recent advances in venereal disease research had made clear the ravages of the disease's advanced stages, the process of transmission, and the clear link with sexual promiscuity. For the antiprostitution reformers, the moral implications of these findings were no less important than the medical. "In all previous efforts to safeguard the morality of youth," wrote one reformer in *Social Hygiene*, "the ethical barrier was alone available," and "the situation seemed . . . hopeless"; now, happily, the "ethical ideal" could be "grounded upon the most convincing facts." Jane Addams welcomed these findings as a powerful force in the emergence of a "new conscience" on prostitution, and Dr. Prince A. Morrow expressed his pleasure that "punishment for sexual sin" no longer need be "reserved for the hereafter."

Through lectures, tracts, posters, exhibits, and graphic films, the antiprostitution reformers warned of promiscuity's grim consequences—for the wrongdoer and his innocent progeny alike. The Chicago Vice Commission vividly spelled out VD's long-range effects—"the blinded eyes of little babes, the twisted limbs of deformed children, degradation, physical rot, and mental decay"—and demanded that every brothel be quarantined forthwith as a "house of contagious disease." The control of sexual expression, in short, was simply another of the social constraints essential to modern urban life. Just as "the storage of gasoline and other combustibles is controlled by the city," argued the Louisville Vice Commission, so dance halls and other "vice combustibles" had to be "carefully watched and controlled." . . .

ONE LAST, DECISIVE STRUGGLE

The Symbolic Component of the Great Coercive Crusades

For all their scientific aura and trappings of objectivity, the prohibition and antiprostitution crusades touched countless Americans at a deep emotional level—a level where flourished profound apprehensions about the long-range implications of massive, unremitting urban growth. Though obviously shaped by the prevailing ethos of the Progressive era, these crusades were rooted in the long-standing impulse to subject the cities to a greater degree of conscious social control.

Repeatedly, almost obsessively, the prohibition and antiprostitution reformers emphasized that these were crusades against urban evil. True to its name, the Anti-Saloon League directed its propaganda less against alcohol per se than against that quintessentially urban institution: the saloon. ASL lecturers made shrewd use of large maps of the United States that showed in white the vast rural areas where prohibition had triumphed, and in sinister black the urban centers where the saloon still held sway. "The Gibraltar of the American liquor traffic," declared the ASL in 1914, "is the American city." The ASL *Yearbook* repeatedly called attention to dry strength in rural regions and the fact that half the nation's saloons were to be found in her six largest cities. It also noted the high correlation between urban liquor consumption and the large numbers of immigrants settling in the cities, especially New York, where the most "ignorant and vicious" of the newcomers were concentrating. "If there is a liquor problem in America—which every one seems to concede," wrote the ASL's strongest friend among the muckrakers, George Kibbe Turner, in 1909, "it is obviously of the city."

Similarly, the Progressive sex reformers displayed less interest in the nation's general level of sexual morality than in a single limited phase of the subject: large-scale commercial prostitution—by its very nature a phenomenon of the city. Some vice commission investigators did call attention to the many urban prostitutes first "ruined" by farm boys back home and to the role of male visitors from the hinterlands in sustaining the big-city red-light districts, but in general these matters were played down. Prostitution was an evil of the city, and this connection was extremely important to those who fought it so vehemently. "The City—from scarlet Babylon to smoky Chicago—" declared George Kibbe Turner, "has always been the great marketplace of dissipation."

Time and again in the literature of these reforms, the discussion "spills over" from the immediate issue to a broader consideration of urbanization's impact on personal behavior. The prototypical vice report, that of New York's Committee of Fifteen in 1902, set the tone. The problem of prostitution, it declared, was "intimately connected" with the rise of the city. In urban centers, young men who earned enough to maintain themselves but not enough to support a wife or family all too often turned to illicit sexual outlets—a practice made possible by that aspect of city life that had vexed urban moralists for a century: its anonymity. In the city, declared the committee:

> the main external check upon a man's conduct, the opinion of his neighbours, which has such a powerful influence in the country or small town, tends to disappear. In a great city one has no neighbours. No man knows the doings of even his close friends; few men care what the secret life of their friends may be. Thus, with his moral sensibilities blunted, the young man is left free to follow his own inclinations.

For young women, too, the report added, the impersonality of city life made it possible "to experiment with immorality without losing such social standing as they may have, and thus many of them drift gradually into professional prostitution."

This generalized concern over urban moral breakdown crops up repeatedly in the vice reports of various cities. Prostitution, declared the Louisville Vice Commission, was merely symptomatic of city dwellers' "craze for pleasure" and their "modern, careless way of upbringing the young." The reports discuss all kinds of social behavior only peripherally related to commercialized prostitution, but which their authors clearly found dismaying: the New York dance hall where intoxicated young people were observed "hugging and kissing"; the girl on the Hudson River excursion boat who "became friendly" with an investigator and "offered to make a 'date' "; the Hartford hotel bar where a patient investigator one afternoon observed a "veritable 'carnival of fornication.' . . . Eight men and five women were smoking, singing, and indulging in very suggestive dances. Couples frequently left the room and returned in about half an hour, and the remarks made . . . plainly indicated the nature of their occupation while they were away."

This tendency to use the prostitution issue as a jumping-off point for a broader attack on moral decay in the city is especially evident in *The Social Evil in Chicago*. In listing prostitution's "contributing factors," the Chicago Vice Commissioners simply drew up a catalog of everything about the city that disturbed them: "immoral" movies; the high divorce rate; dance halls where short-skirted girls competed "in being 'tough' " as they whirled through the

Turkey Trot and the Grizzly Bear; "coarse and . . . vulgar" vaudeville shows with their "suggestive and indecent songs"; ostensibly respectable theaters where scantily clad actresses displayed themselves "under the guise of art"; the "nauseous and repulsive" homosexual subculture (including "people of a good deal of talent"); the very streets, with their suggestive billboards, magazine stands, and countless other allurements to "vice and immorality."

Still worse, the Chicago vice report went on, this same urban environment with its overcharged sexual atmosphere afforded endless opportunities for the gratification of artificially heightened desire. Pinpointing the particular danger spots, the commission listed not only the obvious places—brothels, dance halls, saloons with curtained booths and back rooms—but also lake excursion boats; amusement parks; darkened movie theaters in which "boys and men slyly embrace the girls near them"; and public parks, where girls "sit around on the grass with boys, or go with them into . . . the shrubbery."

On and on goes the list: Turkish baths, state fairs, cheap hotels, massage and manicure establishments, even ice-cream parlors with their moveable screens. (Behind one such screen a keen-eyed investigator observed a youth fondling a girl's breast and taking "other liberties" with her as well.) The entire city, it seemed, was one vast place of concealment where men and women could pursue their pleasure safe from prying eyes. With so many opportunities for sexual gratification in the modern city, concluded another vice report presciently, the brothel would soon hardly be necessary.

The Syracuse vice commission, describing a well-known "secluded spot" popular with the city's youth, summed up the frustration of the Progressive moral reformers as they tried to reduce their fears to a manageable shape: "It is so dark there that you can scarcely see your hand before your face. As you go slowly along you can *see* nothing, but you can *hear* whisperings all about."

In answer to such diffuse fears, the prohibition and antiprostitution leaders offered a deceptively simple answer: the saloon and the brothel lay at the heart of urban immorality and social disorder. If they could only be rooted out, the entire character of the city could be transformed. Syracuse, reported the chairman of that city's vice committee, picking up a theme found everywhere in the antiprostitution crusade, was being "corrupted and rotted" by her brothels. The central refrain of the Anti-Saloon League's propaganda—that prohibition would remove at a single stroke most of the political, social, and moral problems associated with the city—emerges starkly in this 1914 pronouncement by the league's general superintendent:

> The vices of the cities have been the undoing of past empires and civilizations. It has been at the point where the urban population outnumbers the rural people that wrecked Republics have gone down. . . . The peril of this Republic likewise is now clearly seen to be in her cities. There is no greater menace to democratic institutions than the great segregation of an element which gathers its ideas of patriotism and citizenship from the low grogshop. . . . Already some of our cities are well-nigh submerged with this unpatriotic element, which is manipulated by the still baser element engaged in the un-

American drink traffic and by the kind of politician the saloon creates. . . . If our Republic is to be saved the liquor traffic must be destroyed.

The task, of course, was a monumental one. Endlessly, the leaders of these purification crusades emphasized the enormous and sinister power of the men controlling these fountainheads of evil in the cities. While the individual prostitute or saloon keeper might be treated sympathetically as victims of the system, the higher-ups—the brewers, distillers, brothel owners, and shadowy "white slavers"—were portrayed as men of almost boundless malignant influence. An "invisible government," warned vice crusader Clifford Roe, was scheming to enlarge the sway of organized vice in urban America. Josiah Strong made the same point from the perspective of the prohibition cause. "What if the saloon controls the city," he asked rhetorically in 1911, "when the city controls state and nation?" Jane Addams painted a disturbing picture of the "multiplied ramifications" of the urban vice network. "Prostitution has become a business," declared George Kneeland, "the promoters of which continually scan the field for a location favorable to their operations. . . . No legitimate enterprise is more shrewdly managed . . . , no variety of trade adjusts itself more promptly to conditions, transferring its activities from one place to another, as opportunities contract here and expand there."

These magnates of vice were typically painted in loathsome colors. "A large diamond ring sparkled on his fat hand," begins Kneeland's description of a New York brothel owner; "a diamond horse shoe pin flashed in his tie, and a charm set with precious stones hung from a heavy gold watch chain." Clifford Roe pulled out all the stops in describing the "low and degenerate, grasping and avaricious" character of the leaders of the "great, hideous business" of commercialized prostitution. Ethnic stereotypes were employed to good effect. George Kibbe Turner informed *McClure's* readers that "the acute and often unscrupulous Jewish type of mind" was behind the liquor business, and that "the Jewish dealer in women" had done more than any other instrumentality to erode "the moral life of the great cities of America in the past ten years."

By such means the conviction was subtly fostered that the social disruptions of urbanization were the work of alien and sinister men who collectively formed, in George Kneeland's words, a "whole network of relations . . . , elaborated below the surface of society." The most fundamental of these subterranean links was seen to be the one between the liquor interests and the prostitution interests. Readers of ASL literature or the vice commission reports might justifiably have concluded that most saloons were little more than fronts for illicit sex. The two were intimately related, contended settlement-house leader Robert Woods in 1919, predicting that the triumph of prohibition would deal a death blow to prostitution.

The link between prostitution and the saloon was not wholly a product of reformers' overheated imaginations. New developments in brewing, transportation, and refrigeration squeezed out many local brewers in the late nineteenth century and concentrated beer production in the hands of a few major companies, all competing to open as many saloons as possible featuring their brand. Constantly pressured to increase sales, with the threat of franchise removal ever present, the local tavernkeeper occupied somewhat the position of the modern gas-station owner vis à vis the oil companies. In the early twentieth century, the annual turnover of ownership in Chicago's more than 7,000 saloons was about 50 percent. Obviously, the more marginal saloon keepers had compelling economic reasons to stimulate sales by tolerating the presence of prostitutes. Some even provided bedrooms or curtained compartments with couches. As we saw [earlier] such practices were inadvertently fostered in New York State by the Raines Law of 1896. This measure outlawed Sunday liquor sales except when the beverage was served with a meal in a hotel—defined as an establishment with at least ten bedrooms. The unanticipated consequences were the "free lunch" that magically transformed many a saloon into a restaurant (one magistrate held that seventeen beers and a pretzel constituted a meal, complained police commissioner Theodore Roosevelt) and the emergence of over 1,200 "Raines law hotels": saloons with the addition of ten tiny, shabby bedrooms. With no economic reason for existence, these "hotels" quickly became the haunts of prostitutes and their customers.

But while there was *some* factual basis for this specter of a shadowy urban vice network masterminded by brewers, distillers, and "white slavers," the way the reformers wove these sinister themes together, and the melodramatic imagery in which they presented them, revealed more about their own frame of mind than it did about the urban reality. Earlier urban moral-reform rhetoric had to a degree been moderated by the self-corrective encounter with flesh-and-blood city dwellers. The Progressive-era struggles to purify the city were under no such constraints. Drained of much of their concrete meaning and specificity, terms like "the saloon" and "the brothel" became, at times, simply code words for the larger menace of urban social change.

Investigative reports, statistical analyses, and public-health analogies may have lent these crusades a scientific aura, but their central import was psychological and symbolic. They reduced the manifold threats of urbanization to manageable proportions. Robert Wiebe has noted how the complicated issues of the late nineteenth century were gathered into "rhetorical clusters" as "antagonists confronted each other behind sets of stereotypes [and] frozen images," and a similar process was at work in the great moral crusades of the Progressive era. The disturbing aspects of the urban reality were the work of sinister but identifiable evil forces. If those forces could be exterminated, the larger threat would subside. Many members of this generation of Americans very much wished to believe the Anti-Saloon League promises that a constitutional amendment would purify the cities overnight, and the assurances of the antiprostitution reformers that urban sexual morality could be transformed with equal ease. They must have exulted when they read in *Social Hygiene* that organized prostitution in notorious Kansas City had been "abolished after a sharp campaign of one week in October 1913." This was urban purification at lightning speed, achieving at a single stroke the elusive objectives to which earlier movements had devoted decades of frustrating effort!

As we grasp the symbolic component of these crusades, we begin to understand their strident and coercive quality. Mesmerized by their own rhetoric, these moral purifiers became increasingly vituperative in their charges and absolutist in their goals. In 1902, New York's Committee of Fifteen had taken a moderate line, concluding that since "the present state of . . . moral and social evolution" made the elimination of prostitution impossible, only its "public, obtrusive" manifestations were a proper object of reform effort and criminal prosecution. As the white-slave crusade gained momentum, however, caution gave way to full-scale attack. Anything less than all-out war on vice, declared the Minneapolis Vice Commission in 1911, was "foreign to the sentiment and feeling of the American people, and repugnant to their high moral sense." Former President Theodore Roosevelt in 1913 described those who recruited women into prostitution as "far worse criminals than any ordinary murderers," and advocated public whipping as the proper punishment for such monsters; the only way to reach "brutes so low, so infamous, so degraded and bestial," he declared "is through their skins." The leader of the San Antonio, Texas, antiprostitution campaign (a "lean, gray-haired Yankee type of lawyer," according to *Social Hygiene*) announced at the organizational meeting, "I understand that we propose to fight vice and its allies with the cold steel of the law, and to drive in the steel from point to hilt until the law's supremacy is acknowledged." Clearly, the *Social Hygiene* account noted approvingly, the moral forces of San Antonio were "beginning to speak like 75 mm. guns."

The leader of a 1914 prohibition campaign in Washington State, a Savonarola-like Seattle Presbyterian minister described as "six feet five inches tall, white-faced, red-lipped, angular and lean," blasted the saloon as "the most fiendish, corrupt and hell-soaked institution that ever crawled out of the slime of the eternal pit." Perhaps the pinnacle of such bloodthirsty rhetoric was reached at the 1913 ASL convention, when a speaker declared: "Day and night we will pursue [the saloon]. And when it lies dying among its bags of bloody gold and looks up into our faces with its gasp and whispers, 'Another million of revenue for just one breath of life,' we will put the heel of open-eyed national honor on its throat and say, 'NO! Down to hell and say we sent thee thither!' " . . .

POSITIVE ENVIRONMENTALISM

The Ideological Underpinnings

It was 1914, and Newton D. Baker had a problem. He had been mayor of Cleveland for two years, and among such reform objectives as lower transit fares, municipal ownership of utilities and the other familiar goals of municipal progressivism was the desire to achieve in this great industrial city, with its diverse immigrant population, at least an approximation of the moral order he remembered from his own West Virginia boyhood.

Focusing his attention on Cleveland's numerous dance halls with their drunkenness, sexual laxity, and general ribaldry, he had first tried the familiar approach: denunciation and repression. But police surveillance, arrests, and padlocking all proved ineffective. The dance halls seemed only to grow more popular and more brazen.

In desperation, Baker tried a different tack. Instead of fighting the dance halls head-on, he opened several municipal dance pavilions in the city parks, seeing to it that they were attractive, well lit, alcohol-free, and "chaperoned by carefully selected men and women." Soon the disreputable private establishments were standing practically empty, outdistanced by the more wholesome publicly sponsored alternative. Early in 1918, Baker took time from his massive duties as secretary of war to recover this instructive experience for the American Social Hygiene Association.

For Baker, as for many of his generation, the lesson was clear: the most promising long-range strategy of urban moral control was not repression but a more subtle and complex process of influencing behavior and molding character through a transformed, consciously planned urban environment. Growing from the positive-environmentalist initiatives of the 1890s, this conviction found expression not only in municipally sponsored amusements like Baker's dance pavilions but also in tenement reform, in park and playground development, in civic pageants and municipal art, and ultimately in the city-planning movement. While the crusades against the saloon and the brothel have traditionally shaped our image of urban moral reform in the Progressive era, these other efforts had an important moral-control dimension as well.

The positive environmentalists often shared the underlying moral assumptions of the coercive crusaders, but they differed fundamentally on basic strategy. Their aim (as they constantly stressed), was not to destroy urban vice through denunciatory rhetoric or legal repression, but by creating the kind of city where objectionable patterns of behavior, finding no nurture, would gradually wither away. In an influential 1904 work, *The American City,* Delos F. Wilcox yielded to no one in portraying urban immorality and vice as dire social threats "preying upon the vitals of municipal democracy," but with equal firmness he rejected coercive solutions to the problem. Instead of "repression" and "puritanic legislation," he called for "other and more effective weapons of warfare" to create in city dwellers "a wider social consciousness, a heartier spirit of cooperation, [and] a keener sense of responsibility to the future."

Even the coercive moral reformers, implicitly conceding the drawbacks of their approach, occasionally endorsed positive environmentalist strategies. In *Substitutes for the Saloon,* for example, Raymond Calkins insisted that the answer to the saloon and other urban vices did not lie in forcing the masses into a rigid moral straitjacket. Instead, he argued, reformers must study the social needs met by the saloon, the dance hall, and so forth, and develop alternatives to meet those needs without the evil side effects. Among Calkins's "substitutes" were parks, playgrounds, municipal theaters, and "temperance saloons" offering camaraderie but not alcohol. (In one experimental temperance saloon, Calkins reported hopefully in 1919, the patrons were as convivial as ever, but instead of beer mugs at their tables, one now saw "milk chocolate, a peanut candy bar, or perhaps a soda or iced drink.") As such changes were effected in the city, Calkins concluded, "the coarser elements of the environment" would "exert a gradually diminishing influence."

Among the antiprostitution crusaders, the Louisville Vice Commission contended that one way to produce "vice-proof or vice-resisting young people" was to encourage "the wholesome use of their leisure hours." Similarly, Hartford's vice investigators, noting that one thoroughfare had been "cleansed of prostitutes in 1908 when it was broadened [and] paved," urged further environmental improvements as a means toward their city's moral purification. From its founding in 1914, the American Social Hygiene Association insisted that "remedial and constructive measures" were as important in the antiprostitution struggle as legal repression. "Legislation is essential . . . , but we must go deeper," argued on ASHA spokesman. "The ideal is to so mould the interests, activities, and organized volitions of youth, that it will put the brothel out of business through lack of patronage."

The conviction that the most enduring moral advance would come through a gradual reshaping and enrichment of the urban environment found strong support among Social Gospel spokesmen in these years. In the ethical realm, argued Walter Rauschenbusch in *Christianity and the Social Crisis* (1907), "physical compulsion" was "impotent" unless it rested upon a "diffused, spontaneous moral impulse in the community." The law might represent the "stiff skeleton of public morality," but the "finer tissues . . . must be deposited by other forces." Even Josiah Strong, who continued to paint the urban menace in lurid colors now concluded that the challenge was not to engage urban vice in frontal combat through "Draconian law," but to nurture the "awakening social conscience" of the urban masses and thereby "overcome evil with good."

Among settlement leaders, Jane Addams emerged as a persuasive champion of the environmentalist outlook—an outlook which grew naturally from the settlements' emphasis on the role of environmental factors in shaping the lives of the immigrant masses. Although in *The Spirit of Youth and the City Streets* (1909) and other writings of the period Addams made no effort to conceal her distaste for the moral ambience of the modern city with its "vicious excitements and trivial amusements," she rejected preurban modes of social control as "totally unsuited to modern city conditions." If public authorities were to "intelligently foster social morality," they must offer municipally sponsored alternatives to the exploitative and debasing commercial amusements. Warming to her theme, Addams described a transformed city in which publicly supported recreational and leisure activities would become the social cement of a cohesive urban community. "We are only beginning to understand," she wrote, "what might be done through the festival, the street procession, the band of marching musicians, orchestral music in public squares or parks." In the urban future she envisioned, the stroller in the city would encounter not the jangling distraction of raucous commercialized entertainment, but "spontaneous laughter, snatches of lyric song, the recovered forms of old dances, and the traditional rondels of merry games." The "delicious sensation to be found in a swimming pool" would surely outweigh the temptation "to play craps in a foul and stuffy alley, even with the unnatural excitement which gambling offers."

In her 1912 work on prostitution, *A New Conscience and an Ancient Evil,* despite a fleeting nostalgia for the days when the village gossip kept people in line, Addams conceded that the new social reality demanded a rethinking of the entire question of urban morality. The "new conscience" she envisioned was rooted not in the coercive enforcement of a rigid moral code but in a gradually maturing popular awareness that the imperatives of urban life required the subordination of individual gratification to the larger social good. "Fortunately . . . for our moral progress . . . , a new form of social control is slowly establishing itself . . . This new and more vigorous development . . . , while reflecting something of that wholesome fear of public opinion which the intimacies of a small community maintain, is much more closely allied to the old communal restraints and mutual protections to which the human will first yielded." This new urban moral consciousness could not be artificially imposed, Addams insisted; it would emerge only slowly, through careful nurture, from sources within individual city dwellers. In contrast to "the forced submission that characterized the older forms of social restraint," the "new control" would be "based upon the voluntary cooperation of self-directed individuals."

Other settlement leaders picked up the theme. The role of the settlement house, wrote Chicago's Graham Taylor, was to help create neighborhoods where it would be "easier to live right and harder to go wrong." The way to deal with the "debasing" amusements and general ethical breakdown of the laboring masses, agreed Mary Kingsbury Simkhovitch of New York's Greenwich House in 1917, was not by plunging into repressive crusades but by working to change the fundamental conditions of urban-industrial life.

In charity-organization circles, too, the earlier tentative interest in environmentalist strategies intensified after 1900. As in the 1890s, a crucial figure in articulating the new viewpoint was Edward T. Devine, secretary of the New York COS from 1896 to 1912, editor of the influential social-work periodical *Survey,* and professor of "social economy" at Columbia University. In a stream of books, articles, and speeches, Devine chipped away at the COS's still deeply rooted preoccupation with personal moral defects and its family-by-family approach. Devine's fullest exposition of his ideas came in *Misery and Its Causes* (1909). Conceding that the belief in a direct causal connection between personal immorality and poverty was "thoroughly interwoven into a vast quantity of literature and into almost the whole of our charitable tradition," he nevertheless dismissed it as a "halfway explanation." The causes of destitution, he declared, were "economic, social, transitional, measurable, [and] manageable"; the urban vice and immorality that so distressed middle-class social workers were "more largely the results of social environment than of defective character." Charity organizations, he concluded firmly, should shift from "arbitrary and artificial" efforts at individual uplift to a broader program of environmental change.

Clearly, this was an idea whose time had come. "Bad physical environment means bad moral environment," intoned an official of the General Federation of Women's Clubs that same year, as though reciting a self-evident truth. Chicago juvenile-court judge Julian W. Mack was another who added his voice to the chorus. Antivice laws were not enough, he declared. "Constructive help is the real thing." Give youth innocent pleasures to replace immoral ones, Mack urged, and "they will not go to their downfall."

In a 1915 *Atlantic Monthly* article on his campaign to drive Cleveland's dance halls out of business by offering a wholesome municipal alternative, Newton D. Baker tried to sum up the new mode of thinking. In urban moral reform, he declared, both the "emotional excitability" of the "sensational pulpit" and the "rigid regimentation" of the coercive crusade were being supplanted by positive efforts to strengthen the city dwellers' innate preference for order and "social self-control." As this new outlook gradually spread through urban America, he concluded confidently, the chronic problem of moral breakdown in the cities would at last be solved.

QUESTIONS FOR DISCUSSION

1. Why did the Progressives, like the Populists, feel that the new urban society was "pulling away from them"?

2. Compare and contrast "negative environmentalism" and "positive environmentalism" as reform strategies.

3. Why did the progressive reformers focus so much of their energy and attention on the saloon and the brothel?

4. What, according to Boyer, was the "Symbolic Component" of the great coercive crusades?

This photograph of the young Jane Addams was probably taken around 1896. The dress Addams is wearing was known among her friends and family as her "Tolstoy dress." She had worn it when she visited Leo Tolstoy at his Russian home. Tolstoy had reportedly pulled a sleeve out and remarked that there was enough cloth wasted in it to make a whole dress for a child. *(Sophia Smith Collection, Smith College)*

The Subjective Necessity for Social Settlements

Commentary by Kathryn Kish Sklar

In her autobiography, *Twenty Years at Hull House* (1909), Jane Addams described the circumstances under which she first presented "The Subjective Necessity for Social Settlements." The essay was delivered as a lecture at a summer school organized in 1892 at Plymouth, Massachusetts, by the Ethical Culture Societies. Leaders in the new settlement movement were invited to discuss with members of Ethical Culture Societies and others the theme of "Philanthropy and Social Progress."

Within the group assembled that "one golden summer afternoon . . . on the shores of a pond in a pine wood a few miles from Plymouth" were Robert A. Woods, a graduate of Andover Theological Seminary, who had briefly resided in Toynbee Hall, London, the original social settlement, and whose first book, *English Social Movements,* had just been published; Vida Scudder and Helena Dudley from the College Settlement Association in Boston; and Julia Lathrop, Addams' colleague at Hull House.

Looking back on that group from the perspective of 1909, Addams doubted "if anywhere on the continent that summer could have been found a group of people more genuinely interested in social development or more sincerely convinced that they had found a clew by which the conditions in crowded cities might be understood and the agencies for social betterment developed." Though they were at the time "all careful to avoid saying that we had found a 'life work,' perhaps with an instinctive dread of expending all our energy in vows of constancy, as so often happens," eighteen years later every one of them was still associated with the settlement movement.

Addams' memories point to three remarkable features of the social settlement leadership that can help us understand its contemporary impact. First, she and her colleagues were as knowledgeable as anyone about the new social forces shaping American cities. Second, their dedication to social reform was not a passing phase, but was lifelong. Finally, the settlements offered them the physical and spiritual space wherein they could link their talents with other like-minded reformers.

Hull House typified these aspects of the settlement movement. Inspired by the example of Toynbee Hall, which she visited in 1888, Addams and her friend, Ellen Gates Starr, founded Hull House the next year. During the first decade of its existence the settlement attracted a group of gifted reformers whose writings broke new ground in the analysis of urban America. For example, their 1895 publication, *Hull House Maps and Papers,* contained the most systematic data ever collected on American urban life by a nongovernmental agency. This data was collected by Florence Kelley, who joined the settlement in 1892, and in 1893 completed a study of Chicago sweatshops for the U.S. Bureau of Labor Statistics. Focusing on the Nineteenth Ward in which the settlement was located, one of the two pathbreaking maps in the book depicted the Ward's eighteen nationalities; the other revealed the weekly family income of each household. The book's range was as impressive as its analytic depth, for in addition to analyses of the maps and Chicago's sweatshops, it included articles on the city's Jewish, Bohemian, and Italian communities, on Cook County charities, and on "The Settlement as a Factor in the Labor Movement"—all written by the settlement's residents.

A concluding article, written by Jane Addams on Hull House itself, enumerated the wide range of activities regularly scheduled at the settlement in 1894. Most of these reflected her view of the settlement as "an intellectual and social centre about which a neighborhood of working-people may group their various organizations and enterprises." The settlement's educational and social services provided practical means by which Addams and her colleagues could come to grips with "the social problem" and justify the presence of middle-class reformers in working class neighborhoods—not as social superiors who were seeking to improve inferior cultures, but as socially privileged persons who sought to help working people express their own social impulses under the trying conditions of tenement house life.

In this spirit Hull House offered college extension courses in literature, languages, art, history, mathematics, and drawing, and maintained a reading room with foreign as well as American magazines, newspapers, and books. The settlement encouraged debate across various ethnic groups through the Working People's Social Science Club, the Arnold Toynbee Club, the Chicago Question Club, a club room with billiard and card tables, and the Hull House Women's Club. Solidarity within ethnic groups was fostered by weekly receptions for Germans and for Italians. A wide variety of young people's activities included debates, literary programs, social occasions, and classes designed to develop practical skills, such as those in sewing that by 1894 were in such demand that they required fifteen teachers. Through theatrical pageants the settlement supported the expression of immigrants' native cultures; the "labor museum" displayed spinning wheels and other tools once used in Europe but discarded in the New World.

Use of the new tools of political democracy was encouraged by the Nineteenth Ward Improvement Club, which opened a cooperative coal yard and promoted better representation of the neighborhood's interests in the State legislature at Springfield. Links with the labor movement were strong, especially with the garment workers union, the Typographical Union, and the Bindery Girls' Union. The example of cooperative, nonprofit effort was advanced through a public coffee and lunch room, which at noon delivered nourishing lunches for ten cents to hundreds of workers in neighboring factories.

A free kindergarten and day nursery was provided for mothers who needed to work. A lodging house was organized for young women. Hull House also provided the services of a physician who lived at the settlement, a nurse from the Visiting Nurses' Association, a public pharmacy, a savings bank branch (with six hundred depositors by 1894), and a labor bureau that cooperated with Cook County in providing relief work for destitute men or women.

By 1894, Addams estimated that two thousand people came to Hull House each week, one hundred of these as teachers, lecturers, or directors of clubs. The style of settlement reform was eclectic and pluralistic. While it encouraged the assimilation of immigrants into American life, it also tried to preserve immigrant cultures from the obliterating influences of factory and tenement life.

In her 1895 article Addams also explained how residents were admitted to the settlement. Meant to assist working people but not to lodge them, Hull House accepted residents who were mostly middle-class college graduates. New buildings were quickly constructed next to the original house to accommodate the settlement's burgeoning activities and its growing number of residents. In 1894 a limit of twenty was placed on the number of residents, and men were admitted to a nearby annex. Residents paid cooperatively the portion of their room and board expenses that were not covered by philanthropic contributions to the settlement. They were admitted on a conditional basis for six weeks, and "if they have proved valuable to the work of the House," they were invited to remain, provided they could expect to continue in residence for six months. A limited number of fellowships were established to defray the expenses of residents, including one provided by the Chicago branch of the Inter-Collegiate Alumnae Association, a predecessor of the American Association of University Women.

Like those at other settlements, the great majority of Hull House residents remained for two years or less. Typically, they were exploring urban-related career options, or, as was the case with many women, alternatives to marriage. Most moved on to marriage or careers outside of settlement work, but a few remained committed to the settlement movement for the rest of their lives, creating a formidable group of experts in social reform.

"The Subjective Necessity for Social Settlements" was addressed to both groups of young people—those seeking a hiatus from the life course that their parents had planned for them, and those exploring the possibility of a lifelong commitment to the settlement movement. After the essay's presentation at Plymouth in the summer of 1892, it was published that year as "A New Impulse to an Old Gospel" in *Forum* magazine and reprinted in 1893, along with others from the 1892 Plymouth conference, in *Philanthropy and Social Progress,* edited by Henry C. Adams. This exposure placed it in the hands of thousands of middle-class readers, especially college students.

Appealing directly to the restless idealism of youth, Addams emphasized the outlet that settlements provided for their energies. Her three themes of (1) social democracy, (2) shared humanity, and (3) the Social Gospel opened wide avenues of access to the sympathies of her readers. Insisting that democracy embraced more than political formulas, that the destinies of social elites were closely tied to those of the "poorest and most crowded wards of the city," and that true Christianity was best expressed in social service, Addams showed that each of these motivations justified a decision to join the settlement movement.

Her appeal captured the new spirit of the 1890s. In many respects the decade marked a turning away from the belief in Social Darwinism that had characterized the 1870s and 80s. Many of the leading thinkers of the 1890s abandoned systems of thought that centered around "the survival of the fittest," in favor of views that emphasized the ability of humans to shape their own society. Lester Ward, for example, the first sociologist to challenge Social Darwinism on scientific grounds, lectured in 1891 on "Subjective Psychology or the Philosophy of Feelings," and argued in his most popular book, *The Psychic Factors of Civilization* (1893), that civilization was a collective moral effort through which it was possible for people to control their destinies. On a more popular level, the "Social Gospel" influenced the lives of average churchgoers through such writings as William Stead's 1894 book, *If Christ Came to Chicago: A Plea for the Union of All Who Love in the Service of All Who Suffer,* which urged a return to the simple humanitarianism of early Christianity. "The Subjective Necessity for Social Settlements" brought these contemporary ideas to bear on one specific social movement and one plan of action. The results were extremely persuasive.

Adding to the effectiveness of the essay's ideas was its tone of compassionate understanding for the distress of middle-class youths who "feel a fatal lack of harmony between their theory and their lives." This disharmony was especially evident in the lives of women, Addams maintained, because they were "taught to be self-forgetting and self-sacrificing, to consider the good of the Whole before the good of the Ego," but when they turned to social service beyond their families and apart from missionary activity, "the family claim is strenuously asserted."

Addams' special defense of the entry of college-educated women into the social settlement mirrored the movement's strong appeal to young women. For her and other women at Hull House in the 1890s, the settlement offered a lifelong alternative to married family life, as well as a basis for the development of an innovative career in public service. This was true for Addams herself, as well as for Julia Lathrop, a Vassar graduate who joined Hull House in 1890 after working nearly a decade in her father's law office and later became head of the U.S. Children's Bureau; for Florence Kelley, a Cornell graduate who arrived in 1892 after a decade's search for a meaningful career in social reform and later became the nation's chief voice in advocating protective labor legislation for women and children; and for Alice Hamilton, a young physician who joined the settlement in 1898 and later originated the field of industrial medicine. Sophonisba Breckinridge from Kentucky and Grace and Edith Abbott, sisters from Nebraska, did pioneering work in the field of social welfare after affiliating with Hull House. What was true for these women was multiplied hundreds of times throughout urban America as middle-class women discovered in social settlements the emotional companionship that could substitute for traditional family life and an institutional context that could nourish their individual career goals.

A higher proportion of American women than ever before or since remained unmarried in the 1890s and 1900s. College-educated women were especially likely to remain single. These demographic factors, combined with the tremendous expansion of college opportunities for women, the links between women's colleges and women's settlements, and the dearth of other career opportunities, channeled into the social settlement movement many able women who later in the twentieth century might have entered other professions, especially law, politics, or academics. These women tended to dominate the leadership of the settlement movement.

This was not the case in England, where women were more limited in their educational opportunities and were deliberately excluded from major social settlements such as Toynbee Hall. In the United States, as in England, male leaders within the social settlement movement were seeking alternatives to more orthodox careers of religious service; they were usually ministers linked with the Social Gospel. Women reformers who dominated the movement in the United States were more secular, however. They sought in settlements not an alternative to religious careers, but a substitute for the political careers from which they were excluded by reason of their gender.

A multitude of contemporary missionary societies and semireligious organizations such as the Women's Christian Temperance Union provided ample opportunities for women seeking religious careers; such women did not need to turn to the settlement movement. For women from politically active families such as Jane Addams, however, the settlements offered an ideal opportunity to engage in political activity without seeming to violate popular preconceptions about women's sphere being limited to the home. They simply expanded the definition of "home" to include social settlements. Unlike England, where major women reformers such as Beatrice Webb, Margaret McDonald, and Emilia Dilke were married to leading politicians, a significant number of the most powerful women reformers in the United States were concentrated in the social settlement movement. This greatly increased their social and political impact.

In an era when women were still excluded from the professions of law, politics, and academics, the settlements provided a meaningful alternative to those careers, since it permitted residents to explore legislative, political, and sociological solutions to America's urban problems. Addams' speech on the "subjective necessity of social settlements" legitimized the discontent her first generation of college-educated women felt with parental homes that tried to deny them work commensurate with their skills and training. "After college, what?" was, for young women, a question that reverberated throughout the 1890s. Addams' essay provided a resounding answer.

In its tone her essay reflected the diversity of individual styles that was welcomed at Hull House. Embracing the analytic insight of the sociologist, the penetrating concern of the psychologist, the lofty vision of the minister, and the practicality of the politician, Addams' overall tone of assurance reflected her own successful combination of these roles as the presiding genius of one of Chicago's most important institutions. Through frequent use of the pronoun *we,* she often included herself in her social criticisms, affiliating with, rather than condemning, her reader in such phrases as "we are all uncomfortable in regard to the insincerity of our best phrases." To lend authority to some of her assertions, she cited well known experts such as Locke or Pestalozzi. Much of the authority in her essay, however, derived from reliance on her own experience and her use of the pronoun, *I.* Her colorful and inventive language engaged the reader through such phrases as "besotted with innocent little ambitions." Her use of metaphor was equally effective, as in her notion that "the good we secure for ourselves is precarious and uncertain, is floating in mid-air, until it is secured for all of us and incorporated into our common life." Above all, the rhetorical success of her essay arose from the coherence and consistency with which she built her central idea—"social democracy."

The Subjective Necessity for Social Settlements

Hull House, which was Chicago's first Settlement, was established in September 1889. It represented no association, but was opened by two women, backed by many friends, in the belief that the mere foothold of a house, easily accessible, ample in space, hospitable and tolerant in spirit, situated in the midst of the large foreign colonies which so easily isolate themselves in American cities, would be in itself a serviceable thing for Chicago. It was opened on general Settlement lines, in the conviction that along those lines many educated young people could find the best outlet for a certain sort of unexpressed activity. Hull House is neither a University Settlement nor a College Settlement: it calls itself a Social Settlement, an attempt to make social intercourse express the growing sense of the economic unity of society.[1] It is an attempt to add the social function to democracy. It was opened on the theory that the dependence of classes on each other is reciprocal; and that as the social relation is essentially a reciprocal relation, it gave a form of expression that has peculiar value.

I attempt in this paper to treat the subjective necessity for a Social Settlement, to analyze, as nearly as I can, the motives that underlie a movement which I believe to be based not only on conviction, but on genuine emotion. I have divided the motives which constitute the subjective pressure toward Social Settlements into three great lines: the first contains the desire to make the entire social organism democratic, to extend democracy beyond its political expression; the second is the impulse to share the race life, to bring as much as possible of social energy and the accumulation of civilization to those portions of the race which have little; the third springs from a certain renaissance of Christianity, a movement toward its early humanitarian aspects.

It is not difficult to see that although America is pledged to the democratic ideal, the view of democracy has been partial and that its best achievement thus far has been pushed along the line of the franchise. Democracy has made

Note: Edited by K. K. Sklar.

[1]Most settlements were supported by funds raised by college or university students, and hence were called college or university settlements.

thus far has been pushed along the line of the franchise. Democracy has made little attempt to assert itself in social affairs. We have refused to move beyond the position of its eighteenth-century leaders, who believed that political equality alone would secure all good to all men. We conscientiously followed the gift of the ballot hard upon the gift of freedom to the Negro, but we are quite unmoved by the fact that he lives among us in a practical social ostracism. We hasten to give the franchise to the immigrant from a sense of justice, from a tradition that he ought to have it, while we dub him with epithets deriding his past life or present occupation and feel no duty to invite him to our houses. . . .

In politics "bossism" arouses a scandal.[2] It goes on in society constantly and is only beginning to be challenged. Our consciences are becoming tender in regard to the lack of democracy in social affairs. We are perhaps entering upon the second phase of democracy, as the French philosophers entered upon the first, somewhat bewildered by its logical conclusions. The social organism has broken down through large districts of our great cities. Many of the people living there are very poor, the majority of them without leisure or energy for anything but the gain of subsistence. They move often from one wretched lodging to another. They live for the moment side by side, many of them without knowledge of each other, without fellowship, without local tradition or public spirit, without social organization of any kind. Practically nothing is done to remedy this. The people who might do it, who have the social tact and training, the large houses, and the traditions and customs of hospitality, live in other parts of the city. The clubhouses, libraries, galleries, and semi-public conveniences for social life are also blocks away. We find workingmen organized into armies of producers because men of executive ability and business sagacity have found it to their interests thus to organize them. But these workingmen are not organized socially; although living in crowded tenement houses, they are living without a corresponding social contact. The chaos is as great as it would be were they working in huge factories without foreman or superintendent. Their ideas and resources are cramped. The desire for higher social pleasure is extinct. They have no share in the traditions and social energy which make for progress. Too often their only place of meeting is a saloon, their only host a bartender; a local demagogue forms their public opinion. Men of ability and refinement, of social power and university cultivation, stay away from them. Personally, I believe the men who lose most are those who thus stay away. But the paradox is here: when cultivated people do stay away from a certain portion of the population, when all social advantages are persistently withheld, it may be for years, the result itself is pointed at as a reason, is used as an argument, for the continued withholding.

It is constantly said that because the masses have never had social advantages they do not want them, that they are heavy and dull, and that it will take

---

[2]Municipal politics in the late nineteenth century were often controlled by leaders, called *bosses,* and groups called *machines,* whose main goals were to retain access to the rewards of political patronage rather than to represent interests of those who elected them.

political or philanthropic machinery to change them. This divides a city into rich and poor; into the favored, who express their sense of the social obligation by gifts of money, and into the unfavored, who express it by clamoring for a "share"—both of them actuated by a vague sense of justice. This division of the city would be the more justifiable, however, if the people who thus isolated themselves on certain streets and used their social ability for each other gained enough thereby and added sufficient to the sum total of social progress to justify the withholding of the pleasures and results of that progress from so many people who ought to have them. But they cannot accomplish this. The social spirit discharges itself in many forms, and no one form is adequate to its total expression. We are all uncomfortable in regard to the insincerity of our best phrases, because we hesitate to translate our philosophy into the deed.

It is inevitable that those who feel most keenly this insincerity and partial living should be our young people, our so-called educated young people who accomplish little toward the solution of this social problem, and who bear the brunt of being cultivated into unnourished, oversensitive lives. They have been shut off from the common labor by which they live and which is a great source of moral and physical health. They feel a fatal want of harmony between their theory and their lives, a lack of co-ordination between thought and action. I think it is hard for us to realize how seriously many of them are taking to the notion of human brotherhood, how eagerly they long to give tangible expression to the democratic ideal. These young men and women, longing to socialize their democracy, are animated by certain hopes. These hopes may be loosely formulated thus: that if in a democratic country nothing can be permanently achieved save through the masses of the people, it will be impossible to establish a higher political life than the people themselves crave; that it is difficult to see how the notion of a higher civic life can be fostered save through common intercourse.

The blessings which we associate with a life of refinement and cultivation can be made universal and must be made universal if they are to be permanent. The good we secure for ourselves is precarious and uncertain, is floating in midair, until it is secured for all of us and incorporated into our common life. These hopes are responsible for results in various directions, preeminently in the extension of educational advantages. We find that all educational matters are more democratic in their political than in their social aspects. The public schools in the poorest and most crowded wards of the city are inadequate to the number of children, and many of the teachers are ill-prepared and overworked; but in each ward there is an effort to secure public education. The schoolhouse itself stands as a pledge that the city recognizes and endeavors to fulfill the duty of educating its children. But what becomes of these children when they are no longer in public schools? Many of them never come under the influence of a professional teacher after they are twelve. Society at large does little for their intellectual development. The dream of transcendentalists that each New England village would be a university, that every child taken from the common school would be put into definite lines of study and mental development, had its unfulfilled beginning in the village lyceum and lecture courses, and has its feeble representative now in the multitude of clubs for study which are so sadly restricted to educators, to the leisure class, or only to the advanced and progressive workers.

The University Extension movement—certainly when it is closely identified with Settlements—would not confine learning to those who already want it, or to those who, by making an effort, can gain it, or to those among whom professional educators are already at work, but would take it to the tailors of East London and the dock-laborers of the Thames. It requires tact and training, love of learning, and the conviction of the justice of its diffusion to give it to people whose intellectual faculties are untrained and disused. But men in England are found who do it successfully, and it is believed there are men and women in America who can do it. I also believe that the best work in University Extension can be done in Settlements, where the teaching will be further socialized, where the teacher will grapple his students, not only by formal lectures, but by every hook possible to the fuller intellectual life which he represents. This teaching requires distinct methods, for it is true of people who have been allowed to remain undeveloped and whose faculties are inert and sterile, that they cannot take their learning heavily. It has to be diffused in a social atmosphere. Information held in solution, a medium of fellowship and goodwill can be assimilated by the dullest.

If education is, as Froebel defined it, "deliverance," deliverance of the forces of the body and mind, then the untrained must first be delivered from all constraint and rigidity before their faculties can be used.[3] Possibly one of the most pitiful periods in the drama of the much-praised young American who attempts to rise in life is the time when his educational requirements seem to have locked him up and made him rigid. He fancies himself shut off from his uneducated family and misunderstood by his friends. He is bowed down by his mental accumulations and often gets no farther than to carry them through life as a great burden. Not once has he had a glimpse of the delights of knowledge. Intellectual life requires for its expansion and manifestation the influence and assimilation of the interests and affections of others. Mazzini, that greatest of all democrats, who broke his heart over the condition of the South European peasantry, said: "Education is not merely a necessity of true life by which the individual renews his vital force in the vital force of humanity; it is a Holy Communion with generations dead and living, by which he fecundates all his faculties. When he is withheld from this Communion for generations, as the Italian peasant has been, we point our finger at him and say, 'He is like a beast of the field; he must be controlled by force.'"[4] Even to this it is sometimes added that it is absurd to educate him, immoral to disturb his content. We stupidly use again the effect as an argument for a continuance of the cause.

---

[3]German-born Friedrich Froebel (1782–1852) contributed to educational theory the notion that early play and toys were important parts of education.

[4]Giuseppe Mazzini (1805–1872) was a leading advocate of Italian nationalism and a central figure in insurrections against French rule and Austrian rule in Italy in the 1840s and 50s.

It is needless to say that a Settlement is a protest against a restricted view of education, and makes it possible for every educated man or woman with a teaching faculty out find out those who are ready to be taught. The social and educational activities of a Settlement are but differing manifestations of the attempt to socialize democracy, as is the existence of the Settlement itself.

I find it somewhat difficult to formulate the second line of motives which I believe to constitute the trend of the subjective pressure toward the Settlement. There is something primordial about these motives, but I am perhaps overbold in designating them as a great desire to share the race life. We all bear traces of the starvation struggle which for so long made up the life of the race. Our very organism holds memories and glimpses of that long life of our ancestors which still goes on among so many of our contemporaries. Nothing so deadens the sympathies and shrivels the power of enjoyment as the persistent keeping away from the great opportunities for helpfulness and a continual ignoring of the starvation struggle which makes up the life of at least half the race. To shut one's self away from that half of the race life is to shut one's self away from the most vital part of it; it is to live out but half the humanity which we have been born heir to and to use but half our faculties. We have all had longings for a fuller life which should include the use of these faculties. These longings are the physical complement of the "Intimations of Immortality" on which no ode has yet been written. To portray these would be the work of a poet, and it is hazardous for any but a poet to attempt it. . . .

There is nothing after disease, indigence, and a sense of guilt so fatal to health and to life itself as the want of a proper outlet for active faculties. I have seen young girls suffer and grow sensibly lowered in vitality in the first years after they leave school. In our attempt then to give a girl pleasure and freedom from care we succeed, for the most part, in making her pitifully miserable. She finds "life" so different from what she expected it to be. She is besotted with innocent little ambitions and does not understand this apparent waste of herself, this elaborate preparation, if no work is provided for her. There is a heritage of noble obligation which young people accept and long to perpetuate. The desire for action, the wish to right wrong and alleviate suffering, haunts them daily. Society smiles at it indulgently instead of making it of value to itself. The wrong to them begins even farther back when we restrain the first childish desires for "doing good" and tell them that they must wait until they are older and better fitted. We intimate that social obligation begins at a fixed date, forgetting that it begins with birth itself. We treat them as we would children, who, with strong-growing limbs, are allowed to use their legs but not their arms, or whose legs are daily carefully exercised that after awhile their arms may be put to high use. We do this in spite of the protest of the best educators, Locke and Pestalozzi.[5] We are fortunate in the meantime if their unused

---

[5] John Locke (1632–1704), an English philosopher, rejected the notion of innate ideas and emphasized that knowledge was gained through experience. Johann Pestalozzi (1746–1827) a Swiss educator, emphasized experiential learning and the relationship of thought to concrete objects.

members do not weaken and disappear. They do sometimes. There are a few girls who, by the time they are "educated," forget their old childish desires to help the world and to play with poor little girls "who haven't playthings." Parents are often curious about this. They deliberately expose their daughters to the knowledge of the distress in the world. They send them to hear missionary addresses on famines in India and China; they accompany them to lectures on the suffering in Siberia; they agitate together over the forgotten region of East London. In addition to this, from babyhood the altruistic tendencies of these daughters are persistently cultivated. They are taught to be self-forgetting and self-sacrificing, to consider the good of the Whole before the good of the Ego. But when all this information and culture begins to show results, when the daughter comes back from college and begins to recognize her social claim to the "submerged tenth" and to evince a disposition to fulfill it, the family claim is strenuously asserted; she is told that she is unjustified, ill-advised in her efforts. If she persists the family too often are injured and unhappy, unless the efforts are called missionary, and the religious zeal of the family carry them over their sense of abuse.

We have in America a fast-growing number of cultivated young people who have no recognized outlet for their active faculties. They hear constantly of the great social maladjustment, but no way is provided for them to change it, and their uselessness hangs about them heavily. Huxley declares that the sense of uselessness is the severest shock which the human system can sustain, and, if persistently sustained, it results in atrophy of function. These young people have had advantages of college, of European travel and economic study, but they are sustaining this shock of inaction. They have pet phrases, and they tell you that the things that make us all alike are stronger than the things that make us different. They say that all men are united by needs and sympathies far more permanent and radical than anything that temporarily divides them and sets them in opposition to each other. If they affect art, they say that the decay in artistic expression is due to the decay in ethics, that art when shut away from the human interests and from the great mass of humanity is self-destructive. They tell their elders with all the bitterness of youth whatever lines their ambition for them has run, they must let them consult all of humanity; that they must let them find out what the people want and how they want it. It is only the stronger young people, however, who formulate this. Many of them dissipate their energies in so-called enjoyment. Others, not content with that, go on studying and come back to college for their second degrees, not that they are especially fond of study, but they want something definite to do, and their powers have been trained in that direction of mental accumulation. Many are buried beneath mere mental accumulation with lowered vitality and discontent. Walter Besant . . . calls it the sense of humanity.[6] It is not philanthropy nor benevolence. It is a thing fuller and wider than either of these. This young life, so sincere in its emotion and good phrases and yet so undirected, seems to me as pitiful as the other great mass of destitute lives. One is supplementary

---

[6]Walter Besant (1836–1901) was an English novelist and philanthropist.

to the other, and some method of communication can surely be devised. Mr. Barnett, who urged the first Settlement—Toynbee Hall in East London—recognized this need of outlet for the young men of Oxford and Cambridge and hoped that the Settlement would supply the communication. It is easy to see why the Settlement movement originated in England, where the years of education are more constrained and definite than they are here, where class distinctions are more rigid. The necessity of it was greater there, but we are fast feeling the pressure of the need and reaching the necessity for Settlements in America. Our young people feel nervously the need of putting theory into action and respond quickly to the settlement form of activity.

The third division of motives which I believe make toward the Settlement is the result of a certain renaissance going forward in Christianity. The impulse to share the lives of the poor, the desire to make social service, irrespective of propaganda, express the spirit of Christ, is as old as Christianity itself. . . . Jesus had imposed no cult nor rites. He had no set of truths labeled "Religious." On the contrary, his doctrine was that all truth was one, that the appropriation of it was freedom. His teaching had no dogma of its own to mark it off from truth and action in general. The very universality of it precluded its being a religion. He himself called it a revelation—a life. . . . the Christians looked for the continuous revelation, but believed what Jesus said, that this revelation to be held and made manifest must be put into terms of action; that action is the only organ man has for receiving and appropriating truth. "If any man will do His will, he shall know of the doctrine." . . .

I believe that there is a distinct turning among many young men and women toward this simple acceptance of Christ's message. They resent the assumption that Christianity is a set of ideas which belong to the religious consciousness, whatever that may be, that it is a thing to be proclaimed and instituted apart from the social life of the community. They insist that it shall seek a simple and natural expression in the social organism itself. The Settlement movement is only one manifestation of that wider humanitarian movement which throughout Christendom, but preeminently in England, is endeavoring to embody itself, not in sect, but in society itself. . . . If love is the creative force of the universe, the principle which binds men together, and by their interdependence on each other makes them human, just so surely is anger the destructive principle of the universe, that which tears down, thrusts men apart, and makes them isolated and brutal.

I cannot of course speak for other Settlements, but it would, I think, be unfair to Hull House not to emphasize the conviction with which the first residents went there, that it would simply be a foolish and an unwarrantable expenditure of force to oppose and to antagonize any individual or set of people in the neighborhood; that whatever of good the House had to offer should be put into positive terms; that its residents should live with opposition to no man, with recognition of the good in every man, even the meanest. I believe that this turning, this renaissance of the early Christian humanitarianism, is going on in America, in Chicago, if you please, without leaders who write or philosophize, without much speaking, but with a bent to express in social service, in terms of action, the spirit of Christ. Certain it is that spiritual force is found in the Settlement movement, and it is also true that this force must be evoked and must be called into play before the success of any Settlement is assured. There must be the overmastering belief that all that is noblest in life is common to men as men, in order to accentuate the likenesses and ignore the differences which are found among the people the Settlement constantly brings into juxtaposition. . . .

It is quite impossible for me to say in what proportion or degree the subjective necessity which led to the opening of Hull House combined the three trends: first, the desire to interpret democracy in social terms; secondly, the impulse beating at the very source of our lives urging us to aid in the race progress; and thirdly, the Christian movement toward Humanitarianism. It is difficult to analyze a living thing; the analysis is at best imperfect. Many more motives may blend with the three trends; possibly the desire for a new form of social success due to the nicety of imagination, which refuses worldy pleasures unmixed with the joys of self-sacrifice; possibly a love of approbation so vast that it is not content with the treble clapping of delicate hands but wishes also to hear the bass notes from toughened palms, may mingle with these.

The Settlement, then, is an experimental effort to aid in the solution of the social and industrial problems which are engendered by the modern conditions of life in a great city. It insists that these problems are not confined to any one portion of a city. It is an attempt to relieve, at the same time, the overaccumulation at one end of society and the destitution at the other; but it assumes that this overaccumulation and destitution is most sorely felt in the things that pertain to social and educational advantage. From its very nature it can stand for no political or social propaganda. It must, in a sense, give the warm welcome of an inn to all such propaganda, if perchance one of them be found an angel. The one thing to be dreaded in Settlement is that it lose its flexibility, its power of quick adaptation, its readiness to change its methods as its environment may demand. It must be open to conviction and must have a deep and abiding sense of tolerance. It must be hospitable and ready for experiment. It should demand from its residents a scientific patience in the accumulation of facts and the steady holding of their sympathies as one of the best instruments for that accumulation. It must be grounded in a philosophy whose foundation is on the solidarity of the human race, a philosophy which will not waver when the race happens to be represented by a drunken woman or an idiot boy. Its residents must be emptied of all conceit of opinion and all self-assertion, and ready to arouse and interpret the public opinion of their neighborhood. They must be content to live quietly side by side with their neighbors until they grow into a sense of relationship and mutual interests. Their neighbors are held apart by differences of race and language which the residents can more easily overcome. They are bound to see the needs of their neighborhood as a whole, to furnish data for legislation, and use their influence to secure it. In short, residents are pledged to devote themselves to the duties of good citizenship and to the arousing of the social energies which too largely lie dormant in every neighborhood given over to industrialism. They are bound to regard the entire life of their city as organic, to make an effort to unify it and to protest against its overdifferentiation.

Our philanthropies of all sorts are growing so expensive and institutional that it is to be hoped the Settlement movement will keep itself facile and unencumbered. From its very nature it needs no endowment, no roll of salaried officials. Many residents must always come in the attitude of students, assuming that the best teacher of life is life itself and regarding the Settlement as a classroom. Hull House from the outside may appear to be a cumbrous plant of manifold industries, with its round of clubs and classes, its day nursery, diet kitchen, library, art exhibits, lectures, statistical work, and polyglot demands for information, a thousand people coming and going in an average week. But viewed as a business enterprise it is not costly, for from this industry are eliminated two great items of expense—the cost of superintendence and the cost of distribution. All the management and teaching are voluntary and unpaid, and the consumers—to continue the commercial phraseology—are at the door and deliver the goods themselves. In the instance of Hull House, rent is also largely eliminated through the courtesy of Miss Culver, the owner. Life is manifold and Hull House attempts to respond to as many sides as possible. It does this fearlessly, feeling sure that among the able people of Chicago are those who will come to do the work when once the outline is indicated. It pursues much the same policy in regard to money. It seems to me an advantage—this obligation to appeal to businessmen for their judgment and their money, to the educated for their effort and enthusiasm, to the neighborhood for their response and cooperation. It tests the sanity of an idea, and we enter upon a new line of activity with a feeling of support and confidence. We have always been perfectly frank with our neighbors. I have never tried so earnestly to set forth the gist of the Settlement movement, to make clear its reciprocity, as I have to them. At first we were often asked why we came to live there when we could afford to live somewhere else. I remember one man who used to shake his head and say it was "the strangest thing he had met in his experience," but who was finally convinced that it was not strange but natural. There was another who was quite sure that the "prayer-meeting snap" would come in somewhere, that it was "only a question of time." I trust that now it seems natural to all of us that the Settlement should be there. If it is natural to feed the hungry and care for the sick, it is certainly natural to give pleasure to the young and to minister to the deep-seated craving for social intercourse all men feel. . . .

The Settlement movement is from its nature a provisional one. It is easy in writing a paper to make all philosophy point one particular moral and all history adorn one particular tale; but I hope you forgive me for reminding you that the best speculative philosophy sets forth the solidarity of the human race, that the highest moralists have taught that without the advance and improvement of the whole, no man can hope for any lasting improvement in his own moral or material individual condition. The subjective necessity for Social Settlements is identical with that necessity which urges us on toward social and individual salvation.

Commentary: Part II

The legacy of the social settlement movement was twofold. From the subjective perspective of its middle-class residents it provided a unique opportunity for college-educated women and men to encounter the chaotic reality of life as it was lived among the urban poor. For those who made a lifelong commitment to the movement it provided a supportive context for their personal and professional lives. In this sense nothing before or since, with the possible exception of the Peace Corps, could equal what it offered to college-trained youth.

At the Plymouth conference in 1892 Jane Addams presented two lectures. One addressed subjective motivations for settlement work, the other focused on "The Objective Necessity for Social Settlements." Thus, important as subjective motivations were to settlement residents, the objective conditions of poverty, exploitation, and other forms of human misery and injustice were also obvious ingredients in the advancement of the settlement movement. Settlements were a response to the social transformations engendered by three interrelated changes in American life—the rapid expansion of American industry, the arrival of unprecedented numbers of European immigrants to fuel that expansion, and the tremendous urban growth that embraced both industry and immigrants.

The geometric increase in the number of settlements reflected their success in confronting, if not solving, a wide variety of urban problems. By 1891 only six settlements had been founded in the United States, but by 1897 there were seventy-four, by 1900 over one hundred, by 1905 over two hundred, and by 1910 more than four hundred.

Objectively considered, the settlement movement had a wide-ranging impact on other social movements and institutions. Individuals within the movement significantly affected public policy related to their own expertise. Jane Addams, for example, participated in many political activities, including the development of the Progressive Party of 1912. Settlement reformers initiated many activities that later were adopted by municipal, state, and federal governments. Grace Abbott and an organization she founded, the Immigrants' Protective League, provided basic services for European immigrants, reducing their exploitation through positive governmental programs as well as the IPL's efforts. Edith Abbott developed social welfare policies in Chicago's School of Civics and Philanthropy that were later adopted by governmental agencies. Based in the Henry Street Settlement in New York, Lillian Wald pioneered the development of the field of public health nursing—an activity that was quickly integrated into educational policy.

In addition to these individual achievements in public policy by the movements' leaders, the settlements provided a forum where supporters of diverse branches of social reform could meet. For example, at Hull House in the 1890s Abraham Bisno, a leading labor organizer in the garment industry, met with prominent attorneys to draft antisweatshop legislation. As was the case histori-cally in American politics, Progressive reform was advanced by shifting coali-tions of groups and individuals. The settlements contributed significantly to the formation of many such coalitions by providing a setting where middle-class and working-class constituencies could converge.

A good example of the settlement's impact on other social movements was its effect on the woman suffrage movement. Since its beginning in 1848, the suffrage movement had developed two rationales for women's political partic-ipation—one based on their equal rights as human beings, one on the special qualities that women would bring to politics, particularly their bias against corruption and their concern for social welfare issues. The consolidated ener-gies of women reformers within the settlement movement provided weighty support for this second argument, and carried much of the suffrage movement into pragmatic rather than theoretical justifications for women's voting rights.

The impact of the social settlements crested in the two decades before World War I. Thereafter the reform spirit that animated much of American life between 1890 and 1914 dramatically diminished, and so too did the moral authority of the social settlements. After 1920 they ceased to attract the "best and the brightest," and after 1930 many were run by governmental or quasi-governmental agencies—an ironic measure of their ongoing importance. Jane Addams herself focused almost exclusively on world peace during her two decades of life remaining after 1914, depriving the settlement movement of the diversity of interests that had characterized her earlier leadership.

Partly due to their affiliation with peace movements, partly because of their advocacy of protective governmental actions, partly as a result of the shift in political climate, settlement leaders were attacked in the 1920s by right wing political groups who tried to discredit their achievements by branding them as socialistic and un-American. Actually, however, they represented the best in the American tradition of middle-class initiatives and activism on behalf of the larger social good. They helped mold the social conscience of their generation and in so doing left a legacy of concern that remains valid a century later.

Jane Addams' most original contribution to the Progressive Era was the ideal of social democracy set forth in this essay. To this vision she successfully at-tracted wealthy businessmen who contributed to the settlement's support; col-lege graduates who formed its volunteer force of reformers; and immigrants who sought new opportunities for themselves and their children in the United States. Her notion that modern democracy needed to go beyond its eighteenth-century political origins and become a more organic part of society and human relationships identified her as one of the more radical leaders of social reform in the Progressive Era, dedicated not merely to efficiency in government, or a curbing of vice, but to a transformation in social relations. In that sense she deserves to be remembered as one of the greatest apostles of American de-mocracy, who, with Abraham Lincoln and Martin Luther King, greatly extended the possibilities for a better way of life in the United States.

Chapter Four

A New World Power

EMILY S. ROSENBERG

Capitalists, Christians, Cowboys

When Frederick Jackson Turner presented his "frontier thesis" at Chicago's Columbian Exposition in 1893, the American overseas empire consisted of a handful of tiny islands in the Pacific Ocean. Within a decade that empire would be expanded to include the Hawaiian Islands, Guam, Puerto Rico, the Philippine Islands, and a protectorate over Cuba.

The capitalists, missionaries, private citizens, and government officials who spearheaded the construction of an American empire in the years surrounding the turn of the century were, as Emily Rosenberg shows us in the following selection, motivated by both self-interest and humanitarian concerns.

The expansion of American power and influence would, they were convinced, benefit both Americans and the peoples of the world. The American economy—and those who stood atop it—would of course gain from increased overseas trade, but so too would those in foreign lands who were brought into contact with American culture, values, and the free enterprise system. "American traders would bring better products to greater numbers of people; American investors would assist in the development of native potentialities; American reformers—missionaries and philanthropists—would eradicate barbarous cultures and generate international understanding. . . . A world open to the benevolence of American influences seemed a world on the path of progress."

INTRODUCTION: THE AMERICAN DREAM

The Columbian Exposition of 1893

A spectacular World's Fair, the Columbian Exposition, opened in Chicago in 1893. Acres of classical buildings, constructed especially for the fair, created an urban wonderland; it glittered with artistic splendor and burgeoned with America's latest technological achievements. After a visit to this White City, the

Emily Rosenberg teaches history at Macalester College. She is the author of *Spreading the American Dream: American Economic and Cultural Expansion, 1890–1945* from which the following selection has been excerpted.

Excerpts from *Spreading the American Dream* by Emily S. Rosenberg, pp. 3–4, 14–25, 27–28, edited by David Nasaw. Copyright © 1982 by Emily S. Rosenberg. Reprinted by permission of Farrar, Straus and Giroux, Inc.

French novelist and critic Paul Bourget wrote: "Chicago, the enormous town we see expanding, the gigantic plant which grows before our eyes seems now in this wonderfully new country to be in advance of the age. But is not this more or less true of all America?"

Bourget's comment was the kind Americans liked to quote; the exposition's exhibitors displayed their hopes for their country and for the world. Contrived and temporary, this Dream City flaunted America's faiths and glossed over its contradictions. Glamour triumphed over decay; time seemed suspended near the peak of perfection. From John Winthrop to Ralph Waldo Emerson to Josiah Strong, many Americans had thought, or hoped, that their country had escaped from history, that America was not just another power that would rise and then decline but that it was the quintessential civilization that would permanently culminate some long progression toward human betterment. Here, in rhetoric, iron, and stone, were the ideas and products that Americans prized and believed others would gratefully accept. In the Dream City, America's most significant gifts to the twentieth-century world were already apparent: advanced technology and mass culture. . . .

CAPITALISTS, CHRISTIANS, COWBOYS: 1890–1912

One of the speakers who lectured at the Columbian Exposition's so-called World Congress was Frederick Jackson Turner, a young historian from the University of Wisconsin. Turner presented his famous "frontier thesis," a historical interpretation suggesting that westward expansion had been the formative influence on American life. Although Turner was primarily concerned with the past—the westward movement across the continent into territories once claimed by Native Americans, Mexicans, and various European nations—his message had implications for the future. Would Americans—thoroughly accustomed to seizing new lands, justifying their actions as inevitable or ordained, and having a frontier safety valve for social and economic problems—continue to seek new frontiers overseas? In "The Problem of the West" (*The Atlantic Monthly,* 1896) Turner himself suggested the answer: "For nearly three centuries the dominant fact in American life has been expansion . . . and the demands for a vigorous foreign policy . . . and for extension of American influence to outlying islands and adjoining countries, are indications that the movement will continue."

Expansion did continue. The outpouring of American economic and cultural influence, spearheaded by the efforts of private citizens and accelerating rapidly after 1890, provided the basis for America's global preeminence—a role dependent on advanced technology, surplus capital, and mass culture. And as Americans looked beyond their shores, they also refined their basic liberal beliefs to fit a global context. Traders, investors, missionaries, philanthropists, and entertainers: all contributed both to expansion and to the [ideology] that accompanied it.

Traders

Frank Norris, in "The Frontier Gone at Last" (*World's Work,* 1902), wrote that the close of the American frontier brought new ways of expending "our overplus energy":

> We are now come into a changed time and the great word of our century is no longer War but Trade. . . . Had the Lion-Hearted Richard lived today he would have become a "leading representative of the Amalgamated Steel Companies" and doubt not for one moment that he would have underbid his Manchester, England, rivals in the matter of bridge girders.

The year before, an Englishman, William T. Stead, described what he termed the "Americanization of the World":

> In the English domestic life we have got to this: The average man rises in the morning from his New England sheets, he shaves with "Williams" soap and a Yankee safety razor, pulls on his Boston boots over his socks from North Carolina, fastens his Connecticut braces, slips his Waltham or Waterbury watch in his pocket, and sits down to breakfast. There he congratulates his wife on the way her Illinois straight-front corset sets off her Massachusetts Blouse, and he tackles his breakfast, where he eats bread made from prairie flour . . . tinned oysters from Baltimore, and a little Kansas City bacon, while his wife plays with a slice of Chicago ox-tongue. The children are given "Quaker" oats. At the same time he reads his morning paper, printed by American machines, on American paper, with American ink, and probably edited by a smart journalist from New York City.

Such observations reflected a statistical reality: the value of American exports surged from $800 million in 1895 to $2.3 billion in 1914, an increase of nearly 240 percent. The growth rate for manufactured goods alone was nearly 500 percent during that twenty-year period.

What lay behind the growth of American exports in the pre–World War I era? Although a definitive answer would include analysis of world demand and of the economies of leading competitors, the strengths of America's own domestic economy provided the foundation for its exportable surplus. These strengths included an efficient internal transportation system, a high degree of specialization and mechanization, rapid scientific advance, and innovative marketing techniques.

The activities of railroad baron James J. Hill nicely illustrate the link between the continental transportation revolution and the outreach overseas. In 1893, while the World's Fair attracted crowds to Chicago, St. Paul, Minnesota, held a three-day celebration to mark the completion of Hill's Great Northern railroad to the West Coast port of Tacoma, on Puget Sound. More important, Minnesotans and Hill celebrated because they realized the international possibilities of their venture. Hill had built his railroad empire on one cardinal rule—that lower rates and higher profits depended on two-way traffic. But Hill faced a problem, although the Great Northern carried large quantities of timber from the Pacific Northwest to the Midwest, most westward-bound box-cars were empty. Filling them with exports from the American interior bound for the Orient offered a solution. Hill printed and distributed wheat cookbooks written in various Asian languages, and he energetically tried to sign up customers, especially in Japan. Wheat was not all that Hill hoped to ship west. To encourage American rather than European steel exports, he obtained quotations on steel prices from European countries to Japan, compared them with American prices, and then adjusted his transportation charges so that the total cost of American steel would be less than the European. The wheat and steel sales he negotiated, Hill hoped, would be the first of many. In these activities, Hill reflected the mid-nineties optimism about trade with the Orient.

Hill's fascination with trade across the Pacific proved misplaced. American exports to the Orient never comprised more than a small fraction of total export trade; neither Hill nor most other traders found much profit in Asia. Nevertheless, Hill's efforts did highlight the connection between internal transportation and expansionist impulses. American transportation tycoons helped spread the idea of international destiny, just as they had once championed transcontinental expansion. They were accustomed to thinking of distance not as a barrier to commerce but as a problem amenable to technological solution. Distance merely enhanced the possibility for profit, if problems were solved. Furthermore, the transportation barons' outspoken advocacy of foreign commerce helped popularize the liberal economic tenet that increased trade brought greater wealth for all. In order to dangle the prospect of huge profits before American agricultural and industrial exporters, Hill used the fanciful arithmetic so commonly employed by those fascinated with the China market. "If the Chinese should spend only one cent per day per capita," Hill wrote, "it would amount to $4,000,000 a day . . . " Railroad builders such as Hill, Edward H. Harriman, Collis P. Huntington, and Jay Gould were the advance agents and the propagandists for America's new commercial might.

In their efforts to crisscross the American continent and then to connect America to the rest of the world, railroad entrepreneurs believed that a benign providence supported their cause. The title of Hill's book, *Highways to Progress,* epitomized his message. One speaker at the World's Fair's Railway Conference further embellished the theme, hailing railroad-building around the globe as

> the largest human calling. . . . We blow the whistle that's heard round the world, and all peoples stop to heed and welcome it. Its resonance is the diplomacy of peace. The locomotive bell is the true Liberty bell, proclaiming commercial freedom. Its boilers and the reservoirs are the forces of civilization. Its wheels are the wheels of progress, and its headlight is the illumination of dark countries.

Thus, the same railway entrepreneurs who had helped to provoke a populist revolt and a host of governmental regulations at home proclaimed that, if given access to the world, they would usher in an era of peace, freedom, civilization, and development abroad. Railroad profits, world trade, and global progress were to go hand in hand. The practical experience and liberal-developmental vision of late-nineteenth-century moguls eased America's transition from continentalism to globalism.

The promotional activities of railroad builders also illustrated that private, rather than governmental, initiatives provided the basic force behind turn-of-the-century economic expansion. President Grover Cleveland, after a discussion with Hill, said that the railroad baron knew more about Oriental needs than any other person he had met, a fact he found less surprising when he discovered that Hill "had spent more money than the government in sending competent men to Japan and China to study the need of those countries."

The growth of American exports also rested upon technological sophistication and specialization. The productivity of the agricultural sector, which until 1914 generated over half of America's total exports, leaped ahead throughout the late nineteenth century, as farmers used improved machinery to cultivate more extensively than ever before. Human ingenuity and governmental encouragement through the Morrill Act of 1862 promoted scientific advances in irrigation, farm mechanization, crop management, seed variety, and food processing. Scarcity of labor, aridity of land, barriers of distance were all overcome, and land once thought to be a Great American Desert was transformed into the Great American Breadbasket, spilling out its plenty to the world. Cotton production doubled between the early 1880s and about 1900, and America's wheat crop increased by about one third.

Because nearly 20 percent of America's total agricultural production was exported, farmers depended heavily on foreign markets. In 1900, two thirds of America's cotton crop was exported, and in some years 40 percent of its wheat went abroad. Europe, especially Great Britain, was the primary purchaser of those two major exports. But as production increased and oversupply depressed prices, farmers clamored for the opening of other markets. . . . Although the farmer and the railroad baron often clashed over domestic issues, both agreed that America's great productivity could supply large new markets. And they both identified expanding exports with world progress.

American agriculture was so productive that the world studied and borrowed its methods. As early as 1875, for example, experts from Massachusetts Agricultural College established, at the request of the Japanese government, an agricultural college and experimental farm at Sapporo. In addition to agricultural science, the school promoted American-style Christianity, field sports, military drill, white frame houses, and the Yankee slogan "Be Ambitious." . . .

Advanced technology also contributed to what some Europeans called the American export invasion. Though exports were not as great as the word "invasion" implied, the impact came from the sudden appearance of American products abroad and their surprisingly low cost and high quality. In addition to its great agricultural capacity, America had created—overnight, it seemed—a formidable industrial plant so modern its products could often undersell European-made goods despite higher transportation costs. The growth of the farming and food-processing sectors continued, but exports of manufactured goods increased even faster, overtaking those of agriculture in 1914.

American industrialists pioneered mass-production techniques. The lowering of unit costs by using interchangeable parts, mechanization, and specialization at each stage of production promised greater availability of goods for all. Mass production, first applied in making firearms, spread after the Civil War into other industries. The same man who developed Remington's breech-loading rifle, for example, perfected the company's new mass-produced typewriter, and Remington's products for both war and peace found ready overseas markets in the late nineteenth century. The boot and shoe industry provided another conspicuous example of mechanization and specialization. Relying on machines rather than individual craftsmen, American firms lowered labor costs until their products competed well even in European markets. Ready-made into standardized sizes, high-quality footwear became available to large numbers of people, not simply to the upper class. . . .

Products that sold well overseas were also often scientifically advanced. Thomas Edison's electrical inventions and Alexander Graham Bell's telephone patents made America a pioneer in communications and electrification. Establishment of national telephone systems abroad, some even initially owned by American companies, provided ready markets for telephone parts manufactured by American Bell, Edison Electric, and Western Electric. In electrical equipment, General Electric (formed in 1892) and Westinghouse (1886) were the giants, supplying many areas of the world. Other pathbreaking American exports included National Cash Registers, Otis Elevators, Columbia Gramophones, Kodak cameras, Heinz ketchup, Colgate tooth powder, Borden condensed milk, Ford and General Motors cars, New York Life Insurance policies, McCormick reapers, and business machines sold by forerunners of IBM and Burroughs. These innovative products, largely aimed at middle-class consumers, contributed to America's international image as the nation on the cutting edge of the future. In 1901 an Englishman, Fred A. McKenzie—in his book *The American Invaders*—claimed that "these newcomers have acquired control of almost every new industry created during the past fifteen years . . ."

The major characteristics of American exports, then, were established by 1900. American trade advantages were based on an extensive transportation network, technological advances, aggressive marketing, and scientific innovation. Americans enlarged existing markets by making products (such as sewing machines) available on a mass basis, and they created new markets by developing new products (such as electrical equipment).

As traders cultivated markets, they also developed a rationale for rapid overseas expansion and for the benevolent impact of their goods. Foreign critics might charge that an American export invasion could harm native industries, cause unemployment, or force the spread of . . . harsh industrial discipline, stirring labor violence; but American exporters saw their activities as inevitable, efficient, and highly moral.

Most trade expansionists viewed American commercial supremacy as an evolutionary necessity. They saw export expansion as simply an inexorable part of America's economic development. Albert Beveridge bragged in 1898 that "American factories are making more than the American people can use;

American soil is producing more than they can consume. Fate has written our policy for us; the trade of the world must and shall be ours." Similarly, J. G. Kitchell's book *American Supremacy* (1901) predicted: "Commercially we are breaking into every market in the world. It is a part of our economic development. We are marching fast to the economic supremacy of the world." The State Department's primary economic adviser, Charles Conant, described overseas commercial expansion as "a natural law of economic and race development."

The very nature of America's exports—food grains, agricultural machinery, manufactured goods aimed at a mass market, and public improvements such as electricity—suggested the moral justification. Because they did not grow or manufacture for a small, elite market, American traders claimed that their impact uplifted their customers; they linked mass production, mass marketing, and technological improvement to an enlightened democratic spirit. According to the historian Robert Davies, for example, "Singer management concluded that poverty could be removed from society by self-help, and that the company was placing in the hands of hundreds of thousands a technological device by which the masses could improve their station in life as well as their material rewards."

By enlarging the world marketplace, American producers believed they leveled barriers of country and class; by lowering costs, they moved the world closer to an age without scarcity. To its celebrants, liberal capitalism would bring a rising level of abundance, and the means of consumption, not the means of production, would govern feelings of status and social contentment. In the emerging litany of the American dream, what the historian Daniel Boorstin later termed a "democracy of things" would disprove both Malthus's predictions of scarcity and Marx's of class conflict.

Farm and industrial exporters linked this vision of global social progress with their own freedom to penetrate any market. Increasing America's exports would presumably contribute to a general increase in living standards, to greater equality, and to personal freedom. If government barriers or monopolies closed access to America's products, class privilege and scarcity would remain unassaulted. Free enterprise, free trade, free men: these liberal tenets, embedded in mid-nineteenth-century domestic politics, matured and ripened in the service of overseas commercial expansion and bolstered the myth of American exceptionalism. America's economic extension abroad was unique; it was not exploitative or restrictive (as was the economic expansion of other powers) but liberating and democratic. International advancement, expansion of American trade, and personal freedom became indistinguishable.

Investors

The export invasion paralleled an outflow of investment capital. Some of this money went for the purchase of foreign government bonds or foreign-owned corporations, but most of the capital that Americans sent overseas took the form of "direct investment," a situation in which the investor holds managerial control (usually a branch business). The acceleration of American direct investment during the 1890s formed the basis of many of today's huge international corporations. . . .

To reap the benefits of vertical integration, large traders often became direct investors in the goods they traded. W. R. Grace and Company, which had become important as a shipping company in the Peruvian guano trade of the 1870s, later acquired sugar estates as payment for a debt, and finally formed the Cartavio Sugar Company in 1891. . . . United Fruit Company, organized in 1899, expanded its banana plantations in Central America with the encouragement of a railroad builder, Minor C. Keith, who hoped to augment his company's cargoes. The interlocking interests of Keith and United Fruit—which ultimately included railroads, shipping lines, plantations, and livestock—gave them enormous leverage in Central America, especially in Costa Rica.

Some firms dealing in raw materials also began to integrate foreign sources into their corporate domains. Before the nineties, most American companies simply exported American minerals; they traded, distributed, and perhaps maintained sales outlets in foreign lands, but they controlled few foreign supplies. The American continent, after all, produced enormous quantities of raw materials. . . . But as American firms consolidated and moved into the world, foreign sources of supply became increasingly attractive. Many of the major primary producers of the 1920s—firms such as Amalgamated Copper, Guggenheim Brothers, Alcoa Aluminum, Du Pont, Standard Oil, Doheny Oil, United Fruit, Atlantic and Pacific Tea, and the Havemeyer sugar interests—invested in some foreign raw materials before World War I; these small prewar holdings foreshadowed the great influx of American investment during the 1920s.

Market-oriented manufacturers were the most important of the early American investors abroad. High tariffs imposed in many countries in the late nineteenth century, or the threat of imperial restrictions, forced American exporters either to produce their goods within the restricted market or to face exclusion. Even when tariffs posed no barriers, the decision to manufacture near an overseas market, especially the lucrative ones in Europe, reduced shipping costs. Singer established a huge plant in Scotland, producing machines there for Europe, and set up smaller branches in Canada and Australia. American Tobacco moved into Australia, Japan, and Germany to avoid being shut out by tariffs. . . . Westinghouse built huge plants in Russia and Western Europe. Food companies and meat-packers such as J. F. Heinz, Armour, Swift, and American Tobacco increasingly processed aboard—closer to potential markets—thereby avoiding spoilage, breakage, and shipping costs. After America's Pure Food and Drug Act, which required labeling of the contents of patent medicines, Parke Davis and other drug companies established plants abroad in order to supply foreign markets unhampered by domestic regulation.

Before World War I, then, many American businesses expanded into foreign lands; from 1897 to 1914, American direct investments abroad more than quadrupled, rising from a estimated $634 million to $2.6 billion. . . .

To develop the world's industrial enterprises, investors from the United States offered not only capital but the gospel of technology as well. The benevolence of technology and the transferability of technological solutions formed a major part of the new credo. Some critics warned that machines might degrade labor, produce unemployment, induce social distress or wreak environmental havoc, but these views had few adherents among overseas investors. . . . The majority of those American publicists and promoters who reached the outside world projected a faith that technology, introduced by American investors, would elevate anyone that embraced it.

Missionaries

As American traders and investors of the 1890s developed a world view that linked their own expansionist interests to the general improvement of mankind, other private groups also sought to provide uplift to the world. The conspicuous outpouring of American Protestant missionary activity during the 1890s provided a cultural counterpart to the American economic invasion, although missionaries, unlike businessmen, tended to concentrate primarily on Asia, Africa, and the Middle East. . . .

Protestant missionaries of the 1890s mixed the Christian concept of stewardship and a faith in the new social sciences with the evangelical impulses of popular preachers such as Dwight Moody. Notions of racial destiny and Anglo-Saxon superiority saturated missionary writings, but these coexisted with buoyant optimism that racial and cultural virtues were transferable. Often challenging the grim racial determinism that denied the possibility of reforming "backward" people, missionaries argued that transforming foreign cultures was not only possible but was the duty of any true Christian. . . . The symbolism of a parent-child relationship recurred in missionaries' arguments: it connoted utter dependence and domination at present, but promised eventual self-sufficiency if the "parents" performed their Christian duty and if the "children" learned their lessons.

The Student Volunteer Movement (SVM) of the YMCA epitomized the crusading spirit of the 1890s. The SVM, formed . . . in the late 1880s by students from two hundred colleges, enthusiastically extended American cultural influence. . . . In 1891, six thousand students signed pledge cards to become foreign missionaries, and in the next decade the movement became larger and larger. Although other missionary groups existed, the SVM was probably the most important missionary arm of American Protestantism.

The SVM made the Far East, particularly China, a major target. Yet despite the volunteers' numbers and dedication, conversion progressed slowly. The first groups of young missionaries felt that a thorough knowledge of the Gospel would bring success, and they entered China with little sensitivity toward its language or culture. Why learn the values of a heathen civilization that would shortly be transformed? Inevitably, there was confusion of cultural symbols. Did a serpent represent evil, as it did to missionaries, or wisdom, as it did to the Chinese? Cultural chauvinism and racial superiority obstructed communication, and most Chinese considered missionaries eccentric rather than inspired. Moreover, the SVM's early emphasis on individual salvation as a solution to China's problems was much too simplistic. China's social disintegration, after all, had less to do with the heathen state of individual souls than with rigid class structure, appalling poverty, and the deleterious influence of foreign businessmen, especially those in the opium trade. . . .

Missionary activities had broad and often unexpected results. In the 1890s and later, those who had advocated extending American culture abroad generally assumed that what they called cultural exchange (really a one-way process) gained friends, promoted understanding, and shaped the world in America's image. Some foreigners gained an enduring affection for things American, but others reacted against Americanization by turning—sometimes violently—to traditional ways and religions, as in the Boxer Uprising in China. Despite missionaries' efforts at the grass-roots level, they seldom became part of the host country, but remained an external force acting upon it, often creating social dislocation. . . . Contrary to the expectation of late-nineteenth-century missionaries, their activities did not necessarily promote goodwill toward the United States. . . .

Finally, the results of the early missionary movements illustrated another trend: the tendency of cultural expansionists to become involved with economic expansionists and, ultimately, to link both causes together. Although some missionaries had initially disdained the "godless materialism" that traders sometimes brought overseas, most believed that America's commercial presence could assist their efforts. Missionaries, after all, flourished in port cities and had their greatest success in converting foreigners employed by, or trading with, American businesses. In appealing for business support, missionaries claimed that their work would open potential markets. Samuel Capen, for example, wrote: "When a heathen man becomes a child of God and is changed within he wants his external life and surroundings to correspond: he wants the Christian dress and the Christian home and a Christian plow and all the other things which distinguish Christian civilization from the narrow and degraded life of the heathen." Self-interest, Capen argued, demanded that businessmen contribute to the missionary effort. Under Capen's influence, large donations from wealthy businessmen, rather than solicitations from congregations, increasingly became the mainstay of missionary finance. From a fund raiser's point of view, it was easier to concentrate on collecting a few big contributions than to coax small change out of individual churchgoers. Eventually this growing dependence on the country's financial elite helped shape the missionaries' social and political policies.

Philanthropists

Like the missionary movement, organized philanthropy also began to reach overseas during the 1890s. The Russian famine of 1891 produced America's first large-scale effort to send philanthropic relief to a foreign country. An enterprising Minnesota newspaper, seeking shocking stories to build circulation, mounted a crusade to alleviate the famine. As a public-relations gesture, Minnesota millers, whose elevators were glutted by overproduction, donated excess grain. Finally, Minnesota's governor sponsored a fund-raising commission to publicize the problem. From these beginnings in the farm belt, which reflected both humanitarianism and an aggressive strategy to develop foreign grain markets, the campaign to alleviate Russia's famine took on national proportions. Philanthropists marshaled the new promotional and organizational techniques to stir up public enthusiasm, and humanitarian groups and commercial interests around the country donated their products and their time. (Iowa not only sent large quantities of corn to wheat-eating Russia but also dispatched housewives to demonstrate how to prepare and cook it.) . . .

After 1891, Americans seemed never to be without a foreign crisis to relieve: attention turned quickly to the massacres of Armenians, to famine in India, and then to the Spanish suppression of Cuba's independence movement. With these crises, the limits of private philanthropy became clear. The country could be marshaled to support only one emergency at a time. In a world full of disasters, the question of which would get the most attention turned more on who controlled the organizational and propaganda networks in the United States than on the objective need. The Russian famines of 1893 and 1897 were probably more severe than that of 1891, yet Americans were by then concentrating on other parts of the world and hardly heard about them. In the late nineties, the Hearst papers and other "yellow journals" were directing public attention to atrocities in Cuba.

More important, there was no effective supervision of overseas relief. How could people distinguish a legitimate philanthropist from an opportunist? And even had there been only bona-fide relief committees, which surely was not the case, duplication of effort and organizational feuding confounded humanitarian intentions.

The problems of fund raising also caught philanthropists in the same traps as missionaries. They accentuated the helplessness and deprivation of foreign people, while inflating American egos, and they cemented ties to the business community in order to ensure large donations. The connection between benevolence and business made fund raising easier but undercut the myth of apolitical assistance. During the Mexican Revolution of 1910, for example, efforts to relieve suffering were spearheaded by Joseph Cudahy, the Guggenheims, and other large investors friendly to the old, prerevolutionary order; their philanthropy was neither politically neutral nor purely humanitarian.

Mass Culture

Initially, missionaries and philanthropists were the most active groups involved in America's cultural expansion. But, by the turn of the century, purveyors of mass culture began to employ the techniques they would soon use to flood the world. Buffalo Bill's Wild West Show was one of the first examples of the export of popular culture.

Building its appeal on a mixture of nostalgia and promotional hype, Buffalo Bill's show displayed little of the originality and technical accomplishment associated with "elite" art. Instead, it repetitively presented archetypal themes that later analysts of popular culture would call "formula." Buffalo Bill's successful formula consisted of a simplified presentation of conflict between good and evil, between the forces of civilization and barbarism. The cowboy-hero of the American frontier became a mythic creature of extraordinary virtue and skill with whom the audience identified. (Buffalo Bill never missed a shot; in fact, he really could not miss, since he used buckshot.) The cowboy exemplified popular values: he stood above man-made law, but always followed a higher law; he was close to nature, yet a foe of savagery; he was civilized and gentlemanly, yet an enemy of contrivance or corruption. The inevitable triumph of nature's nobleman, after a series of predictable trials, provided ritualistic catharsis.

In the early 1890s, Buffalo Bill's show circled the world, introduced huge crowds of foreigners to American popular entertainment, and demonstrated that the American Western formula had universal appeal. In some countries the protagonists and villains changed to fit the locality (Indians cued their hair to become the Chinese Boxers, who were then defeated by civilized forces), but the formula remained the same: the skill and heroism of the forces of progress pushed back the legions of darkness. And crowds throughout the world identified with the victors and loved it. The Wild West Show revealed a virtually insatiable worldwide demand for mass-produced formula art—art based on ritual and value confirmation.

Although the Wild West Show's nostalgia and structural predictability offered a conservative message, its production techniques were revolutionary. Nate Salsbury, Buffalo Bill's promoter, advanced the arts of nineteenth-century advertising and public relations by building larger-than-life images, arranging publicity stunts, and pandering to popular stereotypes. Moreover, to reach widely scattered audiences, the show adopted the latest technology. Specially equipped trains efficiently transported the troupe from destination to destination. So quickly could the Wild West Show set up and break camp that German military officials, who followed the show in Europe, used it as a model for their armies, the most mobile in the world.

American journalism of the late nineteenth century also wedded advanced techniques to formulas for mass appeal. In the 1890s, American journalistic trends became popular, especially in Europe. The export of the Hoe rotary presses, which produced 20,000 impressions an hour, lowered the cost of newspapers and spread America's graphic revolution abroad. Trying to expand circulation to match the new possibilities of production, a few European newspapers moved toward sensational formats modeled on the American yellow press. American editors were themselves sometimes imported to apply the methods and energy of mass journalism. For example, the halfpenny morning *Daily Mail,* established in London in 1896, hired one of William Randolph Hearst's editors to Americanize the paper. Some Europeans decried the inroads of American-style journalism, then a pejorative term for sloppy sensationalism; they saw popularized features and flashy headlines as a threat to truth and even to social stability. But the profits from mass-circulation papers could not be ignored, and the graphic revolution spread. American news services were not yet internationally prominent, but American newspaper technology and mass-circulation methods preceded them.

The Wild West Show and mass journalism pointed the way toward the American-dominated, globalized mass culture of the twentieth century. America's mass culture, like its mass-produced exports, was democratic in that it appealed to a broad social spectrum, but oligarchic in that it was carefully contrived and narrowly controlled. Appealing to the masses, it could appear revolutionary, yet by its ritualistic, escapist, and standardized nature, it could also prove profoundly conservative.

The nature of American expansion and its ideological justification crystallized during the 1890s. American traders would bring better products to greater numbers of people; American investors would assist in the development of native potentialities; American reformers—missionaries and philanthropists—would eradicate barbarous cultures and generate international understanding; American mass culture, bringing entertainment and information to the masses, would homogenize tastes and break down class and geographical barriers. A world open to the benevolence of American influences seemed a world on the path of progress. The three liberal pillars—unrestricted trade and investment, free enterprise, and free flow of cultural exchange—become the intellectual rationale for American expansion.

THE PROMOTIONAL STATE: 1890–1912

Private impulses, more than government policies, laid the basis for America's enormous global influence in the twentieth century, an influence based on advanced technology, surplus capital, and mass culture. Yet from the 1890s on, as Americans sought wider and easier access to foreign lands, the government had necessarily to define its relationship to these overseas activities. Operating on the assumption that the growing influence of private groups abroad would enhance the nation's strategic and economic position, the government gradually erected a promotional state; it developed techniques to assist citizens who operated abroad and mechanisms to reduce foreign restrictions against American penetration.

Expansionism—National Interest and International Mission

For a number of reasons, the government began to take an active interest in overseas expansion during the 1890s. As American traders and investors enlarged their international stakes, many people argued that the national welfare depended, in part, on continued access to global opportunities. It would, of course, be a mistake to exaggerate the extent of American overseas economic expansion prior to World War I. Compared to Britain's foreign activity, America's efforts seemed slight (except in Mexico and Cuba); by today's standards, the absolute value of exports and investment seems minuscule—export trade and foreign investment comprised only a fraction of domestic economic activity. Yet overseas trade and investment comprised about the same percentages of the United States' GNP at the turn of the century as in recent years, a time when foreign economic activity has certainly been a major governmental concern.

For a variety of reasons, most policymakers of the late nineteenth century, like their more recent counterparts, *did* believe that free participation in international trade and open access to investment opportunities were vital to the nation's well-being. Early multinational companies and the many American firms with international aspirations pressed for greater governmental assistance. Certain important industries, then as later, derived a substantial portion of their profits abroad. By the early twentieth century, Standard Oil, International Harvester, and New York Life—to name only three giant firms—already depended heavily on foreign earnings.

The expansive outlook of these new and powerful international companies gained additional strength from the formation of trade associations. In the late nineteenth and early twentieth centuries most industries developed associations designed to transcend intraindustry rivalry and operate on behalf of the group as a whole. The National Association of Manufacturers (formed in 1895), the American Asiatic Association (1898), the United States Chamber of Commerce (1912), and the American Manufacturers' Export Association (1913) were just a few of the influential offspring of the trade-association movement that urged more governmental support and promoted the identification between foreign commerce and national interest.

But government's new interest in commercial promotion did not stem simply from special pleading. Especially during and after the severe depression that began in 1893, business leaders and policymakers alike became convinced that expansion was needed to avoid overproduction and to maintain prosperity and social cohesion at home.

The reality of overproduction in the 1890s—that is, the validity of any particular ratio placing production higher than consumption—is of little historical importance in assessing the motives behind government's new commercial activism. The so-called crisis of overproduction of the 1890s was rooted less in empirical data than in contemporary attitudes. Twentieth-century Americans have witnessed a process that nineteenth-century analysts could not have imagined: the expansion of domestic demand through techniques such as planned obsolescence, mass advertising, and annual model change. To most American businessmen and policymakers of the 1890s, however, it was domestic production, rather than consumption, that seemed almost infinitely expandable.

Foreign commercial expansion and national prosperity seemed intertwined. The National Association of Manufacturers resolved in 1903: "If, as is claimed, the capacity of our mills and factories is one-third greater than is necessary to supply the home demand, it is obvious that the time is near at hand when we must obtain a broader foreign market, in order to keep the wheels of the factories moving." The *Forum* was more direct: "It is the duty of our government in order to supply remunerative employment to the greatest number of our citizens to take every step possible towards the extension of foreign trade." And farmers also echoed the call for greater governmental assistance. In 1899, the National Grange argued that government had begun to spend "very large sums of money . . . to widen the market for our manufacturing industries in foreign countries" and demanded that it devote "the same energies and efforts" to agricultural marketing. Thus, the overproduction thesis (which mistakenly presumed a fairly inelastic domestic demand) did provoke a reassessment of government's role. Accepting the proposition that government had new responsibilities to enlarge foreign markets, a State Department memo of 1898 stated that the "enlargement of foreign consumption of the products of our mills and workshops has, therefore, become a serious problem of statesmanship as well as of commerce . . . and we can no longer afford to disregard international rivalries now that we ourselves have become a competitor in the world-wide struggle for trade."

Policymakers' social attitudes were also easily compatible with a new role for government. Drawing support from the ideas of Social Darwinism and "scientific" racism, America's dominant groups felt confident of their own superiority. Moreover, they had grown accustomed in domestic affairs to calling upon government to enforce and maintain their prerogatives. In the late nineteenth century, governmental power crushed those ethnic groups that were perceived as threats to social stability. On the frontier, federal troops quashed the last great Indian resistance at Wounded Knee in 1890; in the South, state governments enforced Jim Crow apartheid against blacks, and the Supreme Court buttressed the system with the separate-but-equal doctrine of *Plessy v. Ferguson;* in Northern cities, governmental power clashed with strikers branded as radical "new immigrants"; in the Far West, immigrant restriction laws were enforced against the Chinese.

Concepts of racial mission, so well rehearsed at home, were easily transferred overseas. Editor Theodore Marburg argued: "We have brushed aside 275,000 Indians, and in place of them have this population of 70,000,000 of what we regard as the highest type of modern man . . . [W]e hold to the opinion that we have done more than any other race to conquer the world for civilization in the past few centuries, and we will probably go on holding to this opinion and go on with our conquests." And because governmental power had consistently supported Anglo-Saxon dominance at home in the name of advancing republicanism and progress, so it seemed natural for policymakers to adopt a similar activist role and rationale abroad. Senator Albert Beveridge urged President William McKinley not to shirk the white man's burden. God, he declaimed, "has made us adept in government that we may administer government among savage and senile peoples . . . He has marked the American people as His chosen nation to finally lead in the regeneration of the world." Theodore Roosevelt, who became President in 1901, agreed. Drawing on America's own history, he argued in 1901 that when the United States government fought "wars with barbarous or semi-barbarous peoples" it was not violating the peace but merely exercising "a most regrettable but necessary international police duty which must be performed for the sake of the welfare of mankind."

Crusades to dominate those who were not Anglo-Saxon also found support from the burgeoning Progressive movement, of which Roosevelt, Beveridge, and other imperialists considered themselves a part. Progressivism, a reform impulse that profoundly reshaped American domestic life and foreign relations from the 1890s through World War I, comprised a loose and often contradictory coalition of clean-government crusaders, conservationists, Anglo-Saxon supremacists, muckraking journalists, social-welfare workers, efficiency experts, middle-class professionals, and advocates of business regulation. Although people who adopted the "progressive" label could champion causes as diverse as prohibition, juvenile courts, national parks, and antitrust laws, almost all shared a fundamental faith in professional expertise. Progressives sought to guide the nation and the world away from the social disorders of the late nineteenth century by the scientific application of the problem-solving technique: define the problem, search out relevant facts, deduce a solution, carry it out. Progressives enshrined bureaucratic method and expertise, opening the way for greater governmental action while excluding "irresponsible elements" from decisionmaking. If only they could take charge and attack social problems in a scientific way, the new professionals believed, they would bring order and progress at home and abroad. Such elevation of expertise easily became paternalistic: "expert" and "efficient" people had to dominate lesser breeds in order to uplift them, and, as at home, the force of government might be needed to support, indeed to institutionalize, this effort.

Thus, the entire rationale for overseas expansion was shaped in a domestic crucible. Economic need, Anglo-Saxon mission, and the progressive impulse joined together nicely to justify a more active role for government in promoting foreign expansion.

To say that perceived economic conditions and dominant values supported greater governmental involvement in expansion is not to argue that all, or even most, people favored militant colonialism. Americans differed profoundly over *how* to spread civilization. At home, "undercivilized" peoples were made to conform to Anglo-Saxon standards by many means, ranging from violence to educational persuasion. So, in dealing with foreigners, some believed that "backward nations" could be brought into civilization only by means of force, while others sought to conquer the world peacefully, armed with sewing machines, Bibles, schools, or insights from the new social sciences. Whether the government would promote expansion by brutal domination or peaceful reform (or a mixture of the two) presented a tactical question within a broader consensus that accepted the necessity and ultimate benevolence of American expansion.

Colonialism

Cuban rebellion against Spanish rule stirred Americans into a crusade to free Cuba and, ultimately, to seize an empire at Spain's expense. In 1898, the Republican Administration of William McKinley annexed Hawaii, defeated Spain in a quick war, and acquired Puerto Rico, the Philippines, and Guam as fruits of victory. (Cuba could not be annexed, because Congress had passed the Teller Amendment promising the island independence, but American military occupation dragged on after the war until Cuba agreed to accept protectorate status.) To some people, acquisition of these overseas colonies seemed to offer a way in which the government could both advance its economic interests and fulfill its mission of improving mankind.

The debate over colonialism centered on the issue of acquiring the Philippines. The economic arguments in support of keeping those islands as a possession stressed their importance as a stepping-stone to China. Both farmers and industrialists hoped to open Oriental markets and yet, after China's defeat in the Sino-Japanese War in 1895, China seemed in imminent danger of being closed off to Americans. A military and political presence in the Philippines, trade expansionists hoped, would give the United States more leverage in dealing with the big-power scramble for concessions and spheres of influence in China. By serving as a coaling station and base for America's newly strengthened navy and as a relay point for an infant communications system, the Philippines would become, one business publication predicted, America's Hong Kong—its gateway to the Orient. McKinley's Assistant Secretary to the Treasury, the prominent banker Frank Vanderlip, stated that the islands would be "pickets of the Pacific, standing guard at the entrances to trade with the millions of China and Korea, French Indo-China, the Malay Peninsula, and the islands of Indonesia."

Possession of the Philippines would also advance American Protestant missionary efforts, both in those Catholic islands and on the Asian mainland. "The Christian view of politics," explained one missionary in 1901, "emphasizes the burden of Government and the responsibility of dominion, and thereby transforms empire from an ambition to an opportunity. Blindly and unworthily, yet, under God, surely and steadily, the Christian nations are subduing the world, in order to make mankind free." . . .

After the seizure of the Philippines, however, the taste for imposing colonial status on an alien people turned sour for most Americans. The costs of colonialism seemed to outstrip potential advantages. The Filipino independence movement, led by Emilio Aguinaldo, allied itself with the United States in the victory over Spain, but when McKinley's imperial policy became clear, Aguinaldo resumed warfare against the United States. By the time American troops had quelled the nationalist resistance, one of every five Filipinos was dead from war or disease, and America's own casualties reached 4,300 men. The American commander in southern Luzon admitted, "it has been necessary to adopt what in other countries would probably be thought harsh measures." Such slaughter in the name of "freedom" fueled the anti-imperialist movement by making humanitarian arguments for colonialism appear ridiculous. Even Dr. Jacob Gould Schurman, president of the Philippine Commission that had so strongly defended American subjugation of the Philippines, publicly confessed his error after touring the battlefields and seeing the horrors there. By 1902, Schurman had become outspoken in denouncing the brutality of the war and in calling for a government based on Filipino consent.

The anti-imperialists also turned concepts of national mission and economic advantage against colonialism. John W. Burgess, the widely read advocate of Anglo-Saxon supremacy, opposed colonialism on the grounds that it incorporated "inferior" people into the American system. Upper-class reformer Carl Schurz and others suggested that the militarism that would inevitably accompany the seizure of colonies would undermine America's best traditions of representative government and equality under the law. Joining the imperial game would tarnish, not spread, the American dream. Even staunch expansionists such as Theodore Roosevelt and Alfred Thayer Mahan supported acquisition of naval bases but felt grave reservations about annexing large populations of alien peoples. And the prominent anti-imperialist businessman Edward Atkinson attacked the economic argument: "We may not compute the cost of our military control over the Philippine Islands at anything less than 75,000 dollars a day . . . I leave to the advocates . . . to compute how much our export trade must be increased from last year's amount, to cover even the cost of occupation." The expense of empire, Atkinson argued, would always outweigh the benefits.

As the Philippine insurrection demonstrated the moral ambiguity and expense of colonialism, domestic divisions over the issue doomed any further attempts to accumulate an empire. Although most Americans continued to favor expansion, a national consensus never formed to support more acquisition of territory.

The new relationship developed with Cuba—the protectorate—presented fewer problems. After the defeat of Spain, American military officials set up an occupation government in Cuba; in late 1899, General Leonard Wood became military commander and vowed to create a polity "modeled closely upon lines of our great Republic." Wood brought in a host of experts to reshape Cuba. Americans assumed direction of the customhouses (the major source of government revenue), controlled the country's finances, organized a postal service, established telephone and telegraph lines, encouraged railroad and shipping facilities, built roads, carried out sanitation projects (Wood even included "before and after" photos of public toilets in his reports to Washington), established schools (the new Cuban school law closely resembled Ohio's), and invited New York City police to organize their counterparts in Havana. Mark Twain's Connecticut Yankee could not have done more. These measures superficially Americanized and "developed" the island, but Wood bowed to the pressure of the native elite and American landowners and avoided basic changes in land tenure or tax structure—important changes that would have accorded with a liberal, Americanized model. Wood's program further entrenched Cuba's foreign-dominated, export-oriented monoculture of sugar.

America refused to terminate its occupation of Cuba until Cubans accepted the Platt Amendment, which made their country a protectorate. Reluctantly voted by Cubans into their constitution in 1901, the Platt Amendment and its economic counterpart— the Reciprocity Treaty of 1902—gave the United States the right to establish a naval base in Cuba, to intervene against internal or external threats to the country's stability, and to maintain a privileged trading relationship. Under the Platt Amendment, Cuba was independent, but only nominally so.

The protectorate relationship seemed to work economic magic. Trade boomed; American investment in sugar and tobacco shot up; manufacturing sales outlets opened by the score. Integration into America's economy was labeled "development." In 1918, the head of the Latin American Division in the State Department drew this happy conclusion:

> The total trade of Cuba with the United States just prior to the end of the Spanish rule over the island (1897) amounted to about twenty-seven million dollars per annum. During the decade following the termination of our war with Spain the island of Cuba, guided by American influence, increased her trade with us over four hundred and thirty million dollars. This unprecedented *development* of Cuba may serve as an illustration of what probably would take place in the Central American countries provided this government extended to them aid of a practical character as it did to Cuba. [My emphasis.]

Cuba thus became a laboratory for methods of influence that fell short of outright colonialism. Using the Platt Amendment as a model, American Presidents negotiated protectorate treaties with other nations in the strategically and economically important canal area: Panama (1903), Dominican Republic (1905), Nicaragua (1916), Haiti (1916). These protectorates also received a dose of military-directed Americanization. Moreover, the American military and many of the technical advisors who worked to "develop" and Americanize protectorates continued to offer their skills to other foreigners, seldom doubting the universal applicability of their expertise. After a great earthquake in Messina, Italy, in 1909, for example, the navy supervised construction of three thousand new cottages (unfortunately, choosing building materials and styles totally inappropriate to the region). And a great number of American technical and financial missions during the 1920s were staffed by personnel who received their initial foreign experience in Cuba.

With outright colonialism out of fashion, the expansionist debate revolved around other means of control: tutelage under theoretically independent protectorates, or more important, governmental encouragement of private connections, especially economic ones. Increasingly, Americans understood that the extension of American know-how and the expansion of trade and investment could best proceed without formal colonialism. William Graham Sumner, for example, wrote: "What private individuals want is free access, under order and security, to any part of the earth's surface, in order that they may avail themselves of its natural resources for their use, either by investment or commerce." Colonialism was not necessary, or even desirable, to Sumner's ends. If Americans, Sumner added, could have open access to foreign countries but let others actually run the foreign governments, "we should gain all the advantages and escape all the burdens" of colonialism. One exporter, ridiculing the notion that American political control was vital to commercial expansion, confidently proclaimed: "Trade follows the flag is the slogan of laziness!"

QUESTIONS FOR DISCUSSION

1. What was the role of the railroad and the railroad entrepreneurs in the establishment of the American Empire?

2. What was the religious rationale for American imperial expansion? What was the economic rationale? Discuss the ways in which these rationales were combined into a coherent ideology.

This photograph of Henry Cabot Lodge was taken in 1896. It expresses the fierce self-confidence of the Senator from Massachusetts who so strenuously advocated an imperial policy for the United States. *(The Bettmann Archive)*

Henry Cabot Lodge: Speech to the U.S. Senate on the Philippine Islands, March 7, 1900

Commentary by Lloyd Gardner

In April 1898, the United States went to war with Spain. The immediate cause was the mysterious sinking of the USS *Maine,* anchored in Havana harbor. Years later investigations cast serious doubt on the contemporary belief that the warship had been sunk on Spanish authority. But for nearly a century Americans, in and out of government, had been waiting for an opportune moment to "liberate" Cuba. And this was it.

From Jefferson's time American statesmen had talked of Cuba as a ripening apple that must fall in the North American orchard. When a new Cuban insurrection erupted in the last decade of the nineteenth century, Americans happily added considerations of political freedom and its own "need" to the Newtonian argument. The United States needed a secure Caribbean area to protect its burgeoning interests in world affairs.

At the end of the war, the United States gained possession of Cuba and nearby Puerto Rico. But the Teller Amendment, a self-denying ordinance Congress passed at the time it agreed to President William McKinley's request for a declaration of war, forbade outright annexation. Teller's Amendment said nothing about the Philippines, on the other hand, but it was a harbinger of the debate over "imperialism" that would call forth Henry Cabot Lodge's oratorical skills to defend acquisition of these Pacific outposts.

Determined not to leave Cuba under Spanish rule—nor Cubans to their own devices—the administration maneuvered to fashion a "protectorate" for the island that would endure for five decades and longer. By the terms of the peace treaty with Spain, Madrid was required to cede also the Philippine Islands and Guam. Added to the recently acquired Hawaiian Islands, these possessions constituted a genuine "empire" in the European sense, in structure and purpose if not in size.

Thus arose a full-scale debate in the United States over imperialism and the spirit of democracy. Not everyone agreed that President McKinley had acted wisely, or even that America's new role in world affairs required a less squeamish attitude about the finer points of democratic self-determination. This debate would cut across party lines and geographical sections of the country and would stimulate much thought about America's origins and destiny.

The acquisitions of 1898 were counted a result of the fortunes of "a splendid little war." But what to do with them now? Advocates of a "large policy" (also known as "imperialists") asserted their firm belief that America's national interests demanded strategic strongpoints overseas to support a steadily expanding role in world affairs. Did America require a modern navy? Yes, of course, and that meant refueling stations dotted across the Pacific. Were America's rivals ready to see the lion and lamb lie down together for the commercial benefit of all? No, of course not, so imperialism was only self-defense.

These rhetorical questions were also part of a general fascination of this era with "Social Darwinism," a widely held view that attempted to explain international behavior in biological terms: survival of the fittest. Colonial responsibilities were, in this view, proof of a nation's adaptability to industrial conditions (at home and abroad) and a stern test of its moral fiber. In some ways it was not unlike what President John Kennedy had in mind when he called for Americans to be first to land on the moon.

The expansionists of 1898 were not indiscriminate land grabbers, however, and they certainly did not see themselves as mere imitators of European empire builders. Americans had watched the partition of Africa with a growing concern about what would happen in Asia and Latin America. The United States desired no great tracts of land to add to its national domain (or new millions of different races to add to what many already feared was an intractable social dilemma). Expansionists argued that a limited territorial empire was the only alternative for a nation in America's particular place and time.

To put it in modern terms, ethics allowed for acquisition of Cuba and the Philippines, as long as Americans did what they could to improve the lot of the people. Besides, could anyone argue that Spanish rule was better for the "natives" than what America promised?

This last point needs an additional word. Large-policy advocates were not land grabbers, nor were they standpatters on domestic issues. Theodore Roosevelt is the obvious example of these imperialists, but he was not alone. Many of the leading reformers of the Progressive Era were among their number. Most liberal, or perhaps "radical," reformers in the era, however, were anti-imperialists. There were also conservative anti-imperialists who, from John C. Calhoun's day, feared the extension of federal power in any area. Once established overseas, these men would argue, the power of the government could not but be enlarged at home, if only because of the increased taxes needed to pay for the "empire."

To both liberal and conservative anti-imperialists, the acquisition of overseas territories was at odds with everything the nation had stood for since 1776. Did not the Declaration of Independence forever discredit the concept of empire, let alone an *American empire?* Would these fervid admirers of Europe's grasping partition of Africa cast aside a priceless political heritage of self-government for what, at most, would yield a temporary advantage?

When the peace treaty with Spain came before the Senate in 1898, the sides had been drawn. Given the ratification requirements of the Constitution, opponents of the treaty needed only one third plus one to defeat the treaty with all its projected burdens and implications. Outside the Senate chambers, moreover, anti-imperialist leagues were being formed to influence the decision makers. It promised to be a dramatic confrontation.

And it was. A resolution to bar annexation of the Philippines was defeated by one vote, with the vice president casting the tiebreaker. The peace treaty itself came within two votes of defeat. "The line of opposition stood absolutely firm," reported treaty advocate Senator Henry Cabot Lodge to his friend Theodore Roosevelt in grudging admiration of the anti-imperialist determination. It had been the "hardest fight I have ever known, and probably we shall not see another in our time where there was so much at stake." That prediction proved premature.

McKinley's opponent in the presidential campaign of 1900 was William Jennings Bryan, the Nebraska hero of the Free Silver crusade of 1896. Bryan wanted to make this contest a referendum on imperialism. The focus had shifted, however, from the strategy and tactics of expansion to the methods being used to pacify a Philippine insurgency. Word of this unexpected complication reached the Senate at the time of the final vote on the treaty, and it became the central issue.

American troops occupying the islands to ensure peace and tranquility had been attacked, according to official reports, by Filipino forces under Emilio Aguinaldo. Aguinaldo charged that he had been misled and betrayed by American promises of full partnership in the fight with Spain and assurances of early independence for the Philippines. Before this "insurrection" finally came to an end in 1902, over 5,000 American troops and an estimated 200,000 Filipinos would die.

To be sure, most of the Philippine deaths were only an indirect result of this "war" when the conflict produced a famine. Still, it would take 125,000 American soldiers and $160 million to accomplish Washington's orders that Aguinaldo's army be put down. Mark Twain, among other leading citizens, vehemently denounced the campaign, suggesting bitterly that the new American flag have "the white stripes painted black and the stars replaced by a skull and crossbones."

No one foresaw how long it would take to defeat the Filipinos, but the situation was bad enough for Bryan to see it as a new crusade in 1900. Republican leaders did not shy at the challenge. They had beaten Bryan four years earlier on the Free Silver issue, his chosen ground, and now they would do the same on imperialism. A spellbinding orator, William Jennings Bryan thought it would be possible to unseat his era's "Eastern establishment" by employing single-issue politics. His verbal shafts at Republican "plutocrats" often struck home, but he could not be in enough places enough times to ensure the kill.

At least that is why he thought he lost. Republicans, on the other hand, were more than ready to answer his charges that they were seeking to undermine the system the Founding Fathers had conceived, and the next generations had nurtured through troubled times and civil war. Bryan's dire predictions were pooh-poohed, and his reading of American history faulted, especially his insistence on the purity of the tradition from Jefferson and Jackson in the Democratic Party.

Republicans were also happy to accommodate Mr. Bryan because they were sure that the nation approved President McKinley's foreign policy, associated it with the return of prosperity after the serious depression of the 1890s, and would show their gratitude by returning him to office. The issue in the campaign, Bryan maintained, nevertheless, was perfectly plain for all to see: "A republic can have no subjects. The doctrine that a people can be kept in a state of perpetual vassalage, owning allegiance to the flag, but having no voice in the government, is entirely at variance with the principles upon which this government has been founded. An imperial policy nullifies every principle set forth in the Declaration of Independence."

Nailing that banner—"A republic can have no subjects"—to the Democratic platform, Bryan marched forth to slay the Republicans. Lying in wait was Henry Cabot Lodge, himself no mean orator, fully armed with historical allusions to sling back in Bryan's face.

The speech that Senator Henry Cabot Lodge delivered on March 7, 1900, filled the Senate chambers with echoes from the nation's past. Picking out the weak spot in the Democrat's armor, Lodge put Bryan's adherents in the uncomfortable position of being nay-sayers at a time of widening economic horizons and promised future greatness. To understand how easily he accomplished this feat, it is necessary to keep in mind several things about Lodge and his times.

The senator was, to begin with, not only a skilled politician, but a respected historian who knew how to marshal individual facts into a compelling phalanx of arguments. He depended on racist interpretations to make his case, which were not shocking in his day, and were believed by many (indeed, probably most) who listened to him or read excerpts in the press. Lodge did not bellow out his words, but paced himself through three hours, so that he left no argument unanswered and demonstrated he had anticipated all the possible replies. Only a part of the speech is printed below, but its main argument is easily understood. Even an opposing newspaper, the *New York Times,* found his remarks free from jingoism and the main argument both moderate and temperate.

Commentators generally agreed that Lodge had succeeded in his goal of establishing a historical connection between continental expansion in the nation's first century and the current situation. Focusing on Thomas Jefferson, the presumed father of the modern Democratic Party, Lodge dissected the Declaration of Independence and skewered Bryan with its slivers. Jefferson, said Lodge, talked about the consent of the governed, but he never intended to overturn white, male dominance.

With that beginning, the senator went on to tell listeners some other things about the author of the Declaration of Independence. The men who penned those immortal words, he said, had also devised the plan for ruling the newly acquired territories in the Louisiana Purchase. If Jefferson is to be faulted, then, "our whole past record of expansion is a crime," and all of our presidents are "traitors to the cause of liberty and to the Declaration of Independence."

Now look at the Philippines, he went on, peopled by disparate groups and mixed races: it was impossible either to set them free (incapable as they were of self-government) or to incorporate them into the union. What would Jefferson have done about them, he implied, that was different from what McKinley was doing? Tradition and duty required that the nation accept its responsibilities.

Having walked with the Founding Fathers, Lodge turned to the future. He saw America reaching its destined greatness out there, in the Pacific. But it did not stop with the Philippines; beyond those stepping-stones was China. At that time, desire for trade with the great China market captivated many a statesman's heart and inspired flights of oratory that soared far above anything Lodge said on this particular afternoon.

Whatever happened in China, the down-to-earth reality was that nations were in sharp competition for world trade and raw materials. Strategic points, coaling stations, and *entrepôts* were in demand for navies of all countries. Lodge's assignment was to put the Philippines into their proper perspective historically from an American imperialist viewpoint.

The lines from William Ernest Henley's popular poem "Invictus," quoted by Lodge at the conclusion of his speech perfectly captured the mood he hoped to create, that of a nation casting aside doubt and seeing itself succeeding in overcoming all obstacles to greatness. And so Lodge began:

HENRY CABOT LODGE

Speech to the U.S. Senate on the Philippine Islands

MR. LODGE: I ask the Secretary to read Senate bill 2355, reported from the Committee on the Philippines.

The PRESIDENT pro tempore: The bill will be read.

The Secretary read the bill (S. 2355) in relation to the suppression of insurrection and to the government of the Philippine Islands, ceded by Spain to the United States by the treaty concluded at Paris on the 10th day of December, 1898, reported from the Committee on the Philippines, as follows:

> *Be it enacted, etc.,* That when all insurrection against the sovereignty and authority of the United States in the Philippine Islands, acquired from Spain by the treaty concluded at Paris on the 10th day of December, 1898, shall have been completely suppressed by the military and naval forces of the United States, all military, civil, and judicial powers necessary to govern the said islands, shall, until otherwise provided by Congress, be vested in such person and persons, and shall be exercised in such manner as the President of the United States shall direct for maintaining and protecting the inhabitants of said islands in the free enjoyment of their liberty, property, and religion.

Mr. LODGE: This bill, Mr. President, is simple but all sufficient. It makes no declarations and offers no promises as to a future we can not yet predict. It meets the need of the present and stops there. The President, under the military power, which still controls and must for some time control the islands, could do all that this bill provides. But it is well that he should have the direct authorization of Congress and be enabled to meet any emergency that may arise with the sanction of the lawmaking power, until that power shall decree otherwise. . . . I believe it will be of great importance to define our position, so that it may be perfectly understood by the inhabitants of the Philippines, as well as by our own people.

Negotiations, concessions, promises, and hesitations are to the Asiatic mind merely proofs of weakness, and tend only to encourage useless outbreaks, crimes, and disorders. A firm attitude, at once just and fearless, impresses such

From *The Congressional Record,* March 7, 1900, pp. 2616–2630.

people with a sense of strength and will calm them, give them a feeling of
security, and tend strongly to bring about peace and good order. This bill con-
veys this impression, states the present position of the United States, and does
nothing more. The operative and essential part of it is in the very words of the
act by which Congress authorized Jefferson to govern Louisiana, and which
received his approbation and signature. It was also used by Congress and by
President Monroe in 1819 in regard to Florida. I think that in such a case we
may safely tread in the footsteps of the author of the Declaration of Independence. He saw no contradiction between that great instrument and the treaty
with Napoleon, or the act to govern Louisiana. Some modern commentators
take a different view and are unable to reconcile the acquisition of territory
without what they call the consent of the governed with the principles of the
Declaration. Jefferson found no such difficulty, and I cannot but think that he
understood the meaning of the Declaration as well as its latest champions and
defenders. At all events, I am content to follow him, content to vote for his
bill, content to accept his interpretation of what he himself wrote. . . .

One of the great political parties of the country has seen fit to make what is
called "an issue" of the Philippines. They have no alternative policy to propose
which does not fall to pieces as soon as it is stated. A large and important part
of their membership, North and South, is heartily in favor of expansion, because they are Americans, and have not only patriotism, but an intelligent perception of their own interests. They are the traditional party of expansion, the
party which first went beyond the seas and tried to annex Hawaii, which plotted for years to annex Cuba, which have in our past acquisitions of territory
their one great and enduring monument. In their new wanderings they have
developed a highly commendable, if somewhat hysterical, tenderness for the
rights of men with dark skins dwelling in the islands of the Pacific, in pleasing
contrast to the harsh indifference which they have always manifested toward
those American citizens who "wear the shadowed livery of the burnished sun"
within the boundaries of the United States. The Democratic party has for years
been the advocate of free trade and increased exports, but they now shudder
at our gaining control of the Pacific and developing our commerce with the
East. Ready in their opposition to protection, to open our markets to the free
competition of all the tropical, all the cheapest, labor of the world, they are
now filled with horror at the thought of admitting to our markets that small
fragment of the world's cheap labor contained in the Philippine Islands, something which neither Republicans nor anyone else think for one moment of
doing. Heedless of their past and of their best traditions, careless of their in-
consistencies, utterly regardless of the obvious commercial interests of the
South, which they control; totally indifferent to the wishes and beliefs of a large
portion of their membership, and to the advice and example of some of their
most patriotic, most loyal, and most courageous leaders, to whom all honor is
due, the managers of the Democratic organization have decided to oppose the
retention of the Philippines and our policy of trade expansion in the East, for
which those islands supply the corner stone. Their reason appears to be the
highly sagacious one that it is always wise to oppose whatever Republicans

advocate, without regard to the merits of the policy or to the circumstances which gave it birth. I will make no comment upon this theory of political action, except to say that it has seemed for a long time exceedingly congenial to the intelligence of the Democratic party, and that it may perhaps account for the fact that since 1860 they have only held for eight years a brief and ineffective power. As an American I regret that our opponents should insist on making a party question of this new and far-reaching problem, so fraught with great promise of good both to ourselves and to others. As a party man and as a Republican I can only rejoice. Once more our opponents insist that we shall be the only political party devoted to American policies. As the standard of expansion once so strongly held by their great predecessors drops from their nerveless hands we take it up and invite the American people to march with it. We offer our policy to the American people, to Democrats and to Republicans, as an American policy, alike in duty and honor, in morals and in interest, as one not of skepticism and doubt, but of hope and faith in ourselves and in the future, as becomes a great young nation which has not yet learned to use the art of retreat or to speak with the accents of despair. In 1804 the party which opposed expansion went down in utter wreck before the man who, interpreting aright the instincts, the hopes, and the spirit of the American people, made the Louisiana purchase. We make the same appeal in behalf of our American policies. We have made the appeal before, and won, as we deserved to win. We shall not fail now. . . .

Our opponents put forward as their chief objection that we have robbed these people of their liberty and have taken them and hold them in defiance of the doctrine of the Declaration of Independence in regard to the consent of the governed. As to liberty, they have never had it, and have none now, except when we give it to them protected by the flag and the armies of the United States. Their insurrection against Spain, confined to one island, had been utterly abortive and could have never revived or been successful while Spain controlled the sea. We have given them all the liberty they ever had. We could not have robbed them of it, for they had none to lose. . . .

It has been stated over and over again that we have done great wrong in taking these islands without the consent of the governed, from which, according to American principles, all just government derives its powers. The consent of the governed! It is a fair phrase and runs trippingly upon the tongue, but I have observed a great lack of definite meaning in those who use it most. I have always thought it well in discussing any subject to know, as a preliminary precisely what we mean by a word or a phrase. What do we mean by the "consent of the governed?" We quote it from the Declaration of Independence. What did Jefferson mean by the phrase? Some persons say that he meant the consent of all the governed. Others that he meant the consent of some of the governed. Sentiment seems to be with the former amendment to Jefferson's language; the facts appear to be with the latter. But neither "all" nor "some" are in Jefferson's famous sentence. Nor is there any indication of how the consent is to be obtained or expressed, although the present especial guardians of the Declaration seem to assume that it must be by a vote.

In order to interpret Jefferson's language aright let us see what kind of a government he was himself engaged in setting up, for there alone can we get light as to his meaning. The Declaration of Independence was the announcement of the existence of a new revolutionary government upon American soil. Upon whose consent did it rest? Was it upon that of all the people of the colonies duly expressed? Most assuredly not. In the first place we must throw out all negroes and persons of African descent, who formed about one quarter of the population, and who were not consulted at all as to the proposed change of government. So we must immediately insert the word "white" in Jefferson's sentence. Let us go a step further. Were women included in the word "governed"? They certainly were not permitted by voice or vote to express an opinion on this momentous question. They must, therefore, be excluded, and we must add to the word "white" the word "male" as a further limitation upon the governed whom Jefferson had in mind. Did the revolutionary government rest on the consent of all the white males in the colonies? Most assuredly not. There was the usual age limitation which shut out all male persons under twenty-one, and manhood suffrage, as we understand it, did not exist in a single colony. Everywhere the suffrage was limited, generally by property qualifications, sometimes by other restrictions. So another amendment becomes necessary to Jefferson's phrase if we are going to make it fit the government which he was actually engaged in setting up. Conforming to the facts the sentence then would read something like this: "Deriving their just powers from the consent of the white male governed who have the right to vote according to the laws of the various colonies." This is not all. The white male population of voting and military age in the colonies was divided upon the question of the Revolution. In some States the Loyalists were in a majority; in others the Patriots were in a majority, and in still others the two parties appear to have been pretty evenly balanced. Taking the colonies as a whole, a very large minority, if not half, of the people whom the Continental Congress proposed to govern were utterly opposed to the Revolution. Did we ask their consent? Not at all. We crowded the revolutionary government on the Loyalists at the point of a bayonet, and when the Revolution was over they had to accept the government thus forced upon them or go into exile, which many of them did. Therefore, if we test Jefferson's phrase by the facts of the government which we see he was engaged in setting up himself we find that it does not in the least meet the fantastic extensions which it has been sought to put upon it in the interests of the Filipinos. . . .

Thus, Mr. President, I have reviewed our former acquisitions of territory. The record of American expansions which closed with Alaska has been a long one, and to-day we do but continue the same movement. The same policy runs through them all—the same general acceptance of the laws of nations, in regard to the transfer of territory, the same absence of any reference to the consent of the governed. It has not only been the American policy, it is the only policy practicable in such transactions. Why should we now be suddenly confronted with the objection that it is a crime to acquire the territories ceded to us by Spain in 1898, when we cheerfully accept all the previous cessions, which do not differ one whit in principle from the last? If the arguments which have been offered against our taking the Philippine Islands because we have not the consent of the inhabitants be just, then our whole past record of expansion is a crime, and Thomas Jefferson, and John Quincy Adams, and James Monroe, and all the rest of our Presidents and statesmen who have added to our national domain are traitors to the cause of liberty and to the Declaration of Independence. Does anyone really believe it? I think not. Then let us be honest and look at this whole question as it really is. I am not ashamed of that long record of American expansion. I am proud of it. I do not think that we violated in that record the principles of the Declaration of Independence. On the contrary, I think we spread them over regions where they were unknown. Guided by the principles of that record, I am proud of the treaty of Paris, which is but a continuance of our American policy. The taking of the Philippines does not violate the principles of the Declaration of Independence, but will spread them among a people who have never known liberty and who in a few years will be as unwilling to leave the shelter of the American flag as those of any other territory we ever brought beneath its folds.

The next argument of the opponents of the Republican policy is that we are denying self-government to the Filipinos. Our reply is that to give independent self-government at once, as we understand it, to a people who have no just conception of it and no fitness for it, is to dower them with a curse instead of a blessing. To do this would be to entirely arrest their progress instead of advancing them on the road to liberty and free government which we wish them to achieve and enjoy. This contention rests, of course, on the proposition that the Filipinos are not to-day in the least fitted for self-government, as we understand it. The argument on this point is, I will admit, much simplified by the admissions of our opponents. The past, present, and prospective leader and Presidential candidate of the Democratic party said at Minneapolis, on January 10:

> I am a firm believer in the enlargement and extension of the limits of the republic. I don't mean by that the extension by the addition of contiguous territory, nor to limit myself to that.
>
> Wherever there is a people intelligent enough to form a part of this republic, it is my belief that they should be taken in. Wherever there is a people who are capable of having a voice and a representation in this government, there the limits of the republic may be extended.
>
> The Filipinos are not such a people. The Democratic party has ever favored the extension of the limits of this republic: but it has never advocated the acquisition of subject territory to be held under colonial government.

I do not assert that this is his view to-day, for Mr. Bryan gives forth a great variety of opinions on a great variety of topics. I have not, unfortunately, either time or opportunity to indulge in the delight of reading all he says, for even if he does not from night to night show knowledge, he certainly from day to day uttereth speech. The passage that I have quoted seems, however, to be the last authentic deliverance on the subject, and in it Mr. Bryan distinctly admits that the Filipinos are unfit for self-government, as we understand it. What is far more important and to the purpose, the Senator from Washington, in the able and interesting speech which he delivered on this subject, has made the same admission. Thus our differences narrow. They think that we should abandon the Philippines because they are not fit for self-government. I believe that for that very reason we should retain them and lead them along the path of freedom until they are able to be self-governing, so far, at least, as all their own affairs are concerned. I should be glad to let the matter rest here and confine myself to this very narrow ground of difference, but, unfortunately, there are people who do not recognize facts so frankly as the Senator to whom I have referred, and who contend either that the Filipinos are fit for self-government in the highest acceptation of the term, or that it is our duty to withdraw and leave them to set up such a government as they can evolve for themselves. . . .

Is it to be supposed that a people whose every instinct, every mode of thought, and every prejudice is hostile to what we consider the commonplaces of political existence are going to take up in the twinkling of an eye and work successfully the most intricate forms of self-government ever devised by man? To make such an assumption is not only to betray an utter ignorance of history, but is to give the lie to all human experience. We must not confuse names with things. It does not follow because a government is called a republic that it is therefore a free government, as we understand it; or because it is called a monarchy that it is therefore a tyranny or a despotism. To the south of us lie many governments called republics. Are they free governments, as we understand the term? He would be a bold man who would undertake to answer that question in the affirmative. Haiti and Santo Domingo are called republics, and yet they are bloody tyrannies. The condition they create is anarchy. Neither life, liberty, nor property is safe, and as the island slides downward in the scale of civilization the controlling power shifts from the hands of one military adventurer to those of another. Because they are called republics, will anyone say that they are freer, more representative, better for individual liberty and for civilization than the Government of Holland, which is called a monarchy? Again, I say, let us not confuse names with things. The problem we have before us is to give to people who have no conception of free government, as we understand it and carry it on, the opportunity to learn that lesson. What better proof could there be of their present unfitness for self-government than their senseless attacks upon us before anything had been done? Could anything demonstrate more fully the need of time and opportunity to learn the principles of self-government than this assault upon liberators and friends at the bidding of a self-seeking, self-appointed, unscrupulous autocrat and dictator? Some of the inhabitants of the Philippines, who have had the benefit of Christianity and of a measure of education, will, I have no doubt, under our fostering care and with peace and order, assume at once a degree of self-government and advance constantly, with our aid, toward a still larger exercise of that inestimable privilege, but to abandon those islands is to leave them to anarchy, to short-lived military dictatorships, to the struggle of factions, and, in a very brief time, to their seizure by some great Western power who will not be at all desirous to train them in the principles of freedom, as we are, but who will take them because the world is no longer large enough to permit some of its most valuable portions to lie barren and ruined, the miserable results of foolish political experiments.

Now, Mr. President, before discussing the advantages to the United States which will accrue from our possession of these islands, I desire to state briefly the course of our action there since the outbreak of the insurrection. I can do that best by dealing directly with an assertion that has been reiterated here to the effect that in some way we recognized the government which Aguinaldo[1] set up, a government representing all the Filipinos and founded on their assent, and that therefore we have been doing those people a great wrong and have been engaged in a war of conquest, or, in the cant phrase, of "criminal aggression." . . .

It is not necessary to follow in detail the events of the war which . . . began on February 4, 1899. The insurgents, repulsed with heavy loss in their attack on Manila, were afterwards forced back from the immediate neighborhood of the city. An expedition under General MacArthur captured Malolos, which Aguinaldo had selected as his capital, and various other expeditions were equally successful; but we had not enough troops to hold and garrison the points thus taken. A large force was required in Manila, our army was small, it was necessary to send home the volunteers and replace them by regular regiments, while the rainy season made all military operations for a time impracticable. General Otis, therefore, contented himself with holding Manila and its immediate neighborhood, and with carrying through the return of one army to the United States and the organization of a new one which was sent out. All this difficult and trying work was successfully accomplished. The various insurgent attempts to burn the city, and thus create panic and disturbance, were successfully repressed. The insurgents were held at a safe distance, and when the dry season came again the old army had gone, the new army had come, and we were able to take the field effectively. . . .

There is no longer any semblance of a government there to be recognized. The government which Aguinaldo personally established, and which some people in this country were so anxious to recognize, has ceased to exist. There never was anything really to be recognized except Aguinaldo himself and the adventurers who surrounded him, and now his counselors are in prison and he can not be found. He, with his government concealed about his person, is lost somewhere in the jungle.

But although Aguinaldo and his government have melted away, there are some facts in regard to him and his followers which should be noted, because they throw light upon the leader himself and his purposes, and disclose at once the utter absence of any ground for recognition and at the same time the most conclusive reasons against it. Aguinaldo himself is what is known in the islands as a Chinese Mestizo. In his first cabinet he had some representatives

---

[1]Emilio Aguinaldo, the insurgent leader.

of the Spanish Mestizos, but they are not energetic and are naturally a quiet people, who were opposed to the wild scheme of independence. In his second cabinet, therefore, he got rid of them, and his advisers were almost all Chinese halfbreeds, like himself. These Chinese Mestizos are the most active, energetic, restless, and unscrupulous class in the islands. Although relatively but a very small element in the population, there are many thousands of them, and they are almost altogether in the neighborhood of Manila, where the Chinese are chiefly gathered, and the intermixture has taken place with the Tagalos because that is the tribe nearest to the capital city. It was to people of mixed blood like himself and to the Tagalos that Aguinaldo naturally made his appeal, and it was from these sources almost exclusively that he drew his followers and soldiers. The first government he set up was a pure dictatorial government, created by himself. The revolutionary government, of which he made himself president, differed from the first only in name, and the constitutional government which succeeded that was still the same, with the addition of certain forms imitated from American and European constitutions. There is no proof that any election was held which indicated in any way a general popular acceptance of this government, even by the Tagals, and it is known that many members of the congress which he assembled were appointed by Aguinaldo himself as representing outlying provinces. They were all liable to removal by him, and this gave him absolute control of the body whose powers, in any event, were more nominal than real. . . .

Thus we see that under Aguinaldo's government, which represented only the leaders who set it up, and never had the support of anything but a very small proportion of the Filipino population, warfare of the most barbarous sort was carried on, and every kind of crime was committed, not only against every open enemy, but against helpless prisoners, and against the inhabitants of the islands, of whose freedom they were loudly proclaiming themselves the champions for the benefit of their sympathizers in the United States. We have no need to say that if we had left the Filipinos alone anarchy would have come. Anarchy came, and existed in full force wherever Aguinaldo held sway, coupled with bloodshed, pillage, and corruption. . . .

Such were the men to whom it is seriously proposed that we should intrust the control of all the other millions of human beings, some half civilized, some wholly wild, who live in these other islands. Such is the government, stained with assassination, with the burning and pillage of the villages of their own people, with plans for the massacre of all foreigners, and for murder and looting in Manila, cruel, arbitrary, despotic, treacherous; such, I say, is the government which we are gravely asked to assist in forcing upon the innocent population of those islands, and are denounced because we have not done so. To have recognized Aguinaldo's government and helped him to thrust it upon the other natives, or to have drawn aside and allowed him to try to wade "through slaughter to a throne" by himself would have been a crime against humanity. Those who have urged, or who now urge, such a policy should study with care and with thoroughness the government of Aguinaldo. They never do so. They never take the trouble to learn the facts about the despotism which

Aguinaldo and his friends tried to set up. They laugh at facts, deride all who are in a position to bear witness, sneer at history and experience, and declaim against the ʻGovernment for not giving recognition and support to something which never existed, which is the mere creature of their fancy.

How different their attitude when they come to considering the actions of their own countrymen. Men who will take the lightest word of a half-bred adventurer, of whose existence they had never heard two years ago, impugn the actions and doubt the statements of the highest officers of our Government, of the commanders of our fleets and armies, of men who have gone in and out before the American people for years, and whose courage, patriotism, and honor have never been questioned or assailed. It must be a weak and bad cause indeed which rests its support upon accusations of falsehood and prevarication directed against the President and his advisers, and against the gallant and honorable men who wear our uniform and lead our Army and our Navy in the day of battle. . . .

There are many duties imposed upon a President in which it is easy to imagine a personal or selfish motive, in which such motives might exist even if they do not. But here even the most malignant must be at a loss to find the existence of a bad motive possible. Suddenly at the end of the Spanish war we were confronted with the question of what should be done with the Philippines. Their fate was in our hands. We were all able to discuss them and to speculate as to what that fate should be. No responsibility rested upon us. But one man had to act. While the rest of the world was talking he had to be doing. The iron hand of necessity was upon his shoulder, and upon his alone. Act he must. No man in that high office seeks new burdens and fresh responsibilities or longs to enter on new policies with the unforeseen dangers which lie thick along untried paths. Every selfish motive, every personal interest, cried out against it. Every selfish motive, every personal interest, urged the President to let the Philippines go, and, like Gallio, to care for none of these things. It was so easy to pass by on the other side. But he faced the new conditions which surged up around him. When others then knew little he knew much. Thus he came to see what duty demanded, duty to ourselves and to others. Thus he came to see what the interests of the American people required. Guided by this sense of duty, by the spirit of the American people in the past, by a wise statesmanship, which looked deeply into the future, he boldly took the islands. Since this great decision his policy has been firm and consistent. He has sought only what was best for the people of those islands and for his own people. It is all there in the record. Yet although he fought in his youth for liberty and union, he is now coarsely accused of infatuation for a vulgar Cæsarism. He who is known to everybody as one of the kindest of men, eager to do kindly acts to everyone, is denounced as brutal and inhuman to a distant race whom he has sought in every way to benefit. When every selfish interest drew him in the other direction he has been charged with self-seeking for following the hard and thorny path of duty. . . .

I come now to a consideration of the advantages to the United States involved in our acquisition and retention of the Philippine Islands. . . . When these arguments are offered in behalf of our Philippine policy the opponents of that policy stigmatize them as sordid. . . . I do not myself consider them sordid, for anything which involves the material interests and the general welfare of the people of the United States seems to me of the highest merit and the greatest importance. Whatever duties to others might seem to demand, I should pause long before supporting any policy if there were the slightest suspicion that it was not for the benefit of the people of the United States. I conceive my first duty to be always to the American people, and I have ever considered it the cardinal principle of American statesmanship to advocate policies which would operate for the benefit of the people of the United States, and most particularly for the advantage of our farmers and our workmen, upon whose well-being, and upon whose full employment at the highest wages, our entire fabric of society and government rests. In a policy which gives us a foothold in the East, which will open a new market in the Philippines, and enable us to increase our commerce with China, I see great advantages to all our people, and more especially to our farmers and our workingmen.

The disadvantages which are put forward seem to me unreal or at best trivial. Dark pictures are drawn of the enormously increased expense of the Navy and of the Army which will be necessitated by these new possessions. So far as the Navy goes, our present fleet is now entirely inadequate for our own needs. We require many more ships and many more men for the sure defense of the United States against foreign aggression, and our guarantee of peace rests primarily upon our Navy. Neither the possession nor the abandonment of the Philippines would have the slightest effect upon the size of the Navy of the United States. If, as I hope, we shall build up a Navy adequate to our needs, we shall have an abundant force to take care of the Philippines and find employment there in times of peace without the addition of a man or a gun on account of our ownership of those islands. . . .

So much for the objections commonly made to our Philippine policy, which have as little foundation, in my opinion, as those which proceed on the theory that we are engaged in the perpetration of a great wrong. Let us now look at the other side, and there, I believe, we shall find arguments in favor of the retention of the Philippines as possessions of great value and a source of great profit to the people of the United States which can not be overthrown. First, as to the islands themselves. They are over a hundred thousand square miles in extent, and are of the greatest richness and fertility. From these islands comes now the best hemp in the world, and there is no tropical product which can not be raised there in abundance. Their forests are untouched, of great extent, and with a variety of hard woods of almost unexampled value. Gold is found throughout all the islands, but not in large quantities, and there is no indication that the production of gold could ever reach a very great amount. There appears to be little or no silver. There are regions in Luzon containing great and valuable deposits of copper which have never been developed. But the chief mineral value of the islands is in their undeveloped coal beds, which are known to exist in certain parts and are believed to exist everywhere, and which are certainly very extensive and rich. The coal is said to be lignite, and, although 20 to 30 percent inferior to our coals or to those of Cardiff, is practically as good as the Australian coal and better than that of Japan, both of which are largely used in the East today. To a naval and commercial power the coal measures of the Philippines will be a source of great strength and of equally great value. It is sufficient for me to indicate these few elements of natural wealth in the islands which only await development.

A much more important point is to be found in the markets which they furnish. The total value of exports and imports for 1896 amounted in round numbers to $29,000,000, and this was below the average. The exports were nearly $20,000,000, the imports a little over $9,000,000. We took from the Philippines exports to the value of $4,308,000, next in amount to the exports to Great Britain, but the Philippine Islands took from us imports to the value of only $94,000. There can be no doubt that the islands in our peaceful possession would take from us a very large proportion of their imports. Even as the islands are to-day there is opportunity for a large absorption of products of the United States, but it must not be forgotten that the islands are entirely undeveloped. The people consume foreign imports at the rate of only a trifle more than $1 per capita. With the development of the islands and the increase of commerce and of business activity the consumption of foreign imports would rapidly advance, and of this increase we should reap the chief benefit. We shall also find great profit in the work of developing the islands. They require railroads everywhere. Those railroads would be planned by American engineers, the rails and the bridges would come from American mills, the locomotives and cars from American workshops. The same would hold true in regard to electric railways, electric lighting, telegraphs, telephones, and steamships for the local business. . . .

But the value of the Philippine Islands, both natural and acquired, and as a market for our products, great as it undoubtedly is, and greater as it unquestionably will be, is trifling compared to the indirect results which will flow from our possession of them. . . . The struggle for the world's trade, which has for many years been shaping ever more strongly the politics and history of mankind, has its richest prize set before it in the vast markets of China. Every great nation has recognized the importance of this prize, either by the acquisition of Chinese territory or by obtaining certain rights and privileges through treaty. But after the war between China and Japan this movement rapidly assumed an acute form. It grew daily more apparent that Russia was closing in upon the Chinese Empire, and that her policy, at once slow and persistent, aimed at nothing less than the exclusion of other nations from the greatest market of the world. To us, with our increasing population, and an agricultural and industrial production which was advancing by leaps and bounds, the need of new markets in the very near future, if we hoped to maintain full employment and ample returns to our farmers and our workingmen, was very clear. More than ready to take our chance in a fair field against all rivals, and with full faith in the indomitable ingenuity and enterprise of our people, it was more than ever important that we should not be shut out from any market by unjust or peculiar discriminations if by any methods such a misfortune could be avoided. The great danger to our interests in China became clearer and clearer as the months went by to those who watched the progress of great economic and political forces outside our own boundaries. . . .

That Hawaii was necessary as the first and essential step toward our obtaining that share to which we were entitled in the trade of the Pacific, the ocean of the future, was obvious enough, but beyond that all was doubt and darkness. Then came the Spanish war, and the smoke of Dewey's guns had hardly cleared away when it was seen by those who were watching that he had not only destroyed the Spanish fleet, but had given to his countrymen the means of solving their problem in the far East. He had made us an Eastern power. He had given us not only the right to speak, but the place to speak from.

Let me now try to show the importance and meaning of the Eastern question, with regard to which Dewey's victory has given us such a commanding position. The Empire of China has a population of which we have no accurate statistics, but which is certainly over four hundred millions. The rate of consumption among the Chinese per capita is at present low, but even as it stands it affords a great market for foreign imports. The work of opening up the country by railroads and of developing its still untouched natural resources has begun and is advancing with giant strides. There is the greatest opportunity in China for trade expansion which exists anywhere in the world. I desire to call the attention of the Senate to the value of the Chinese trade to us now despite our neglect of it, and to the enormous advance which that trade has made in the last four years, and more especially since the Spanish war carried our flag into the East and turned the attention of our people more sharply to the unlimited opportunities for commerce which there exist.

In our commerce with China during 1889–1899 there was a gain of $13,293,168. The increase occurred almost entirely in the export trade, which advanced from $2,791,128 in 1889 to $14,493,440 in 1899. Our imports for 1899, amounting to $18,619,268, were only slightly larger than in 1889, when a value of $17,028,412 was reported. The exports to China, like those to Japan, showed an exceptional growth in 1897, 1898, and 1899, the records for these years being $11,924,433, $9,992,894, and $14,493,440, respectively. Our trade with the port of Hongkong, although less important than that credited directly with China, was nearly doubled during 1898–1899, making a gain of $5,045,149. The exports for 1899 had a value of $7,732,525 as compared with only $3,686,384 for 1889. The imports were considerably smaller and showed marked fluctuations. In 1889 they were valued at $1,480,266, but these figures were not equaled again until 1899, when a value of $2,479,274 was recorded. From these figures it will be seen that our exports to China and Hongkong in 1899 were over $22,000,000, and that the growth in the last three years had been phenomenal. The gain in exports to China, Hongkong, and Japan in 1899 over 1889 was 256 percent and it almost all came in the last years of the decade. . . . The loss of that market and of its prospects and possibilities I should regard as one of the greatest calamities which could befall the farmers and the workingmen of the United States. How, then, are we to hold and develop it? Look at your tables of statistics and note the increases which have occurred since the capture of Manila. The mere fact that we hold the Philippine Islands increases our trade with all the East—with China and Japan alike. Trade certainly has followed the flag, and its appearance at Manila has been the signal for this marked growth in our commerce with the neighboring states and empires.

But we must go a step further. Having this opportunity to obtain a large and increasing share in the trade of China, how shall we make sure that it is not taken from us? We know well that China is threatened by Russia, and that Russian dominion, if unrestrained would mean discrimination and exclusion in the Chinese market. Sooner than anyone dreamed it has been shown how far the Philippines have solved this pressing problem for us. The possession of the Philippines made us an Eastern power, with the right and, what was equally important, the force behind the right to speak. Mr. Hay, as Secretary of State, has obtained from all the great powers of Europe their assent to our demand for the guaranty of all our treaty rights in China and for the maintenance of the policy of the open door. I do not belittle one of the most important and most brilliant diplomatic achievements in our hundred years of national existence when I say that the assent of these other powers to the propositions of the United States was given to the master of Manila. They might have turned us aside three years ago with a shrug and a smile, but to the power which held Manila Bay, and whose fleet floated upon its waters, they were obliged to give a gracious answer. Manila, with its magnificent bay, is the prize and the pearl of the East. In our hands it will become one of the greatest distributing points, one of the richest emporiums of the world's commerce. Rich in itself, with all its fertile islands behind it, it will keep open to us the markets of China and enable American enterprise and intelligence to take a master share in all the trade of the Orient. We have been told that arguments like these are sordid. Sordid indeed! Then what arguments are worthy of consideration? A policy which proposes to open wider markets to the people of the United States, to add to their employment, and to increase their wages, and which in its pursuit requires that we should save the teeming millions of China from the darkness of the Russian winter, and keep them free, not merely for the incoming of commerce, but for the entrance of the light of Western civilization, seems to me a great and noble policy, if there ever was such, and one which may well engage the best aspirations and the highest abilities of American statesmanship. . . .

Like every great nation, we have come more than once in our history to where the road of fate divided. Thus far we have never failed to take the right path. Again we are come to the parting of the ways. Again a momentous choice is offered to us. Shall we hesitate and make, in coward fashion, what Dante calls "the great refusal"? Even now we can abandon the Monroe doctrine, we can reject the Pacific, we can shut ourselves up between our oceans, as Switzerland is inclosed among her hills, and then it would be inevitable that we should sink out from among the great powers of the world and heap up riches that some stronger and bolder people, who do not fear their fate, might gather them. Or we may follow the true laws of our being, the laws in obedience to which we have come to be what we are, and then we shall stretch out into the Pacific; we shall stand in the front rank of the world powers; we shall give to our labor and our industry new and larger and better opportunities; we shall prosper ourselves; we shall benefit mankind. What we have done was inevitable because it was in accordance with the laws of our being as a nation, in the defiance and disregard of which lie ruin and retreat. . . .

I do not believe that this nation was raised up for nothing, I do not believe that it is the creation of blind chance. I have faith that it has a great mission in the world—a mission of good, a mission of freedom. I believe that it can live up to that mission, therefore I want to see it step forward boldly and take its place at the head of the nations. I wish to see it master of the Pacific. I would have it fulfill what I think is its manifest destiny if it is not false to the laws which govern it. I am not dreaming of a primrose path. I know well that in the past we have committed grievous mistakes and paid for them, done wrong and made heavy compensation for it, stumbled and fallen and suffered. But we have always risen, bruised and grimed sometimes, yet still we have risen stronger and more erect than ever, and the march has always been forward and onward. Onward and forward it will still be, despite stumblings and mistakes as before, while we are true to ourselves and obedient to the laws which have ruled our past and will still govern our future. But when we begin to distrust ourselves, to shrink from our own greatness, to shiver before the responsibilities which come to us, to retreat in the face of doubts and difficulties, then indeed peril will be near at hand. I would have our great nation always able to say:

> It matters not how strait the gate,
>   How charged with punishments the scroll,
> I am the master of my fate,
>   I am the captain of my soul.

Commentary: Part II

In the final weeks of the 1900 campaign, Bryan largely abandoned the imperialist issue. It was not Lodge's speech, by itself or in company with the Republican rhetoric generally, that forced this decision. They took their toll. But the Republicans had succeeded in staking out a middle road between mindless land grabbing and total forbearance. Despite continuing reports of violence from the Philippines, the moral imperative, the framework for these scenes, became a new chapter in the winning of the West.

Publisher William Randolph Hearst, whose newspaper had sounded a clarion call for war with Spain, had warned Bryan not to pursue the imperialist beast to its lair, for it would turn on him with devastating force. The American people were not the "give-up" kind, he sent word to the Democratic candidate; and, besides, "There are seventy millions of dissatisfied people in America.

They are all anxious for someone who shall suggest measures as useful to them as McKinley is useful to the trusts and millionaires."

With the outbreak of the Boxer Rebellion in China Lodge's predictions, and Hearst's, were put to an early test. Possession of the Philippines did, in fact, give the United States a forward jumping-off place, and American soldiers from the islands were among those in the international brigades that lifted the siege of foreign embassies in the Chinese capital. Because of its role in lifting the Boxer siege, moreover, Washington determined for itself that it should be consulted about China's future. That kind of self-determination was more suitable, the imperialists had argued, than the idealized or mistaken notions about Jefferson propagated by the likes of William Jennings Bryan.

Yet as the years passed concerns arose causing America to question the wisdom in undertaking its share of the "White Man's Burden" in the Pacific. Throughout the imperial era legislation had been introduced pointing toward a decision to grant independence to the islands, but as Japan's naval power increased in the post World War I era and the depression, it also became necessary to wonder whether the strong forward point had not become an Achilles heel.

The return of the Democrats to national power raised all these issues. Added to the list of worries was a bipartisan concern about the impact of Philippine products on domestic agricultural producers. What was to have been a springboard to the Asian market now became a slingshot aiming at depression-weakened American farmers. In 1916 Congress had passed the first bill pointing toward eventual independence for the Philippines. The promise was reconfirmed in the early New Deal years. Postponed by World War II, Philippine independence became a reality in 1946.

Lodge's arguments reflected a particular moment in this nation's history. His contemporaries applauded his logic while overlooking its flaws. Critics and historians questioned his dubious assertion that taking the Philippines was nothing more than adding a new Florida or Texas. And Lodge himself never wanted statehood for the islands. Students of the "new" imperialism, exemplified by America's acquisition of the Philippines, point out that the partition of Africa and Asia differed from earlier colonialism which had been characterized by the colonizing of overseas territories and the search for new land. Now the quest was for new markets and raw materials.

Lodge's speech illuminates the imperialists' argument, as it developed in the United States, and how they saw America's future role as leader among nations. Lodge's defense of retaining the Philippines, based on Social Darwinism, reflected the contemporary consensus about the limitations of "native peoples" and provided sufficient moral justification for doing what the McKinley administration perceived as its duty in the struggle for survival among nations.

After World War I, however, popular opinion shifted. Imperialism was on the defensive. The hypocrisy of the League of Nations mandate system notwithstanding, the industrial nations could now claim only a temporary role in "guiding" the colonial areas to freedom. World War II only speeded up the process by fatally weakening the European empires. With less at stake in formal empire, it was easiest for the United States to fulfill its promise to the Philippines.

Today Lodge's speech seems filled with oddities associated with now-abandoned pretension. The world he knew is gone forever. in one sense, it never existed. The assertions of racial superiority were only the illusions of a culture temporarily endowed with superior technology that was misidentified as a natural order. But international rivalries remain a dominant reality in the late twentieth century. If imperialism no longer has any defenders, other names, such as "spheres of influence," enable the superpowers to continue to claim the right to intervene in Third World crises.

In the debates over defense budgets and "covert" activities, these claims are put forth by Lodge's successors. Debates over foreign policy, by their nature, still center on themes of "fitness" and "preparedness" against prospective enemy nations. Appeals to "history" are as common today as in his times. In Lodge's day, America was aspiring to world leadership, so his arguments featured a futuristic projection of an optimistic past that had prepared the nation for its responsibilities. Today, America defends its place in a world far more complex and dangerous, so arguments carry dire warnings about the wisdom of abandoning outposts and about the consequences of military inferiority.

BARRY D. KARL

Managing the War

When war broke out in Europe in August 1914, "few serious observers would have predicted that in less than two and a half years American soldiers, drafted by an aroused and angry citizenry, would be crossing the Atlantic to fight on European soil."

Like the Civil War—and other modern wars—the Great War was fought on the battlefields and on the home front. It was at home that a war machine had to be built—and quickly—to oversee the production and transportation of the matériel needed by American soldiers overseas. It was at home that public opinion had to be converted from "neutrality" to a commitment to fight "a war to make the world safe for democracy." And it was at home that Americans had to be prepared to accept a new role for their nation in international affairs.

In everything it touched, from the management of the railroads to the re-definition of our role in international affairs, the "war was a disruptive experience that swept across the American landscape like a firestorm." The changes it wrought, though widespread, were not widely accepted. The Americans who elected Warren Harding president in 1920 may, in so doing, have been ex-pressing their wish to take a giant step back "not only from the war experience itself but from the whole reform mood that had been part of it." Unfortunately for those who wished to put the entire episode behind them, the war had re-vealed, once and for all, the interdependence of American interests with those of Europe and the world.

Barry Karl is the Norman and Edna Freehling Professor of History at the University of Chicago. The following selection is taken from a chapter of his most recent book, *The Uneasy State: The United States from 1915 to 1945.*

Reprinted from *The Uneasy State: The United States from 1915 to 1945* by Barry D. Karl (University of Chicago Press, 1983), pp. 34–49. Copyright ©1983 by The University of Chicago. All rights reserved. Published 1983. Reprinted by permission of the University of Chicago Press and the author.

The outbreak of war in Europe in August 1914 was not looked on by most Americans as an event that urgently affected the interests of the United States. Businessmen involved in international trade of course wondered what the consequences of so widespread a conflict might be, and when they saw foreign trade come to a virtual halt in the first few months of the war, they became intensely concerned. The general public followed the war in the newspapers, but it was probably more troubled by disturbances immediately to our southwest, where Mexican revolutions seemed threatening. Few serious observers would have predicted that in less than two and a half years American soldiers, drafted by an aroused and angry citizenry, would be crossing the Atlantic to fight on European soil. The transformation of popular attitudes in so brief a period of time was as remarkable as the experience of the war itself. American interest in international affairs entered a new phase as public opinion shifted from its familiar focus on protection of "our" hemisphere to salvation of the world.

Foreign trade and world salvation seem distinctly different issues, but their persistent entanglement as reflections of reality and idealism had been part of American history from its beginnings. As a major producer of such world-market crops as cotton, tobacco, and wheat, the United States had long played a significant role in international trade. And as a country committed to its own industrialization, it had had the experience of debating tariffs and their effects on American consumers of foreign goods. By 1914, certainly, the arguments were familiar, however heated they may have tended to become from time to time. Duties on sugar, for example, had helped provoke the successive crises in Cuba and Puerto Rico that resulted in the Spanish-American War. A battle over duties on Canadian wheat and its effect on American wheat producers had split the Progressives and Republicans in 1911. Americans wanted the freedom to compete on international markets at the same time that they wanted government protection from competition of cheaper goods from abroad.

When the outbreak of war in Europe threatened to bring trade to a halt, it introduced a set of factors that American policymakers had not had to deal with on such a scale for years—indeed, not since the Napoleonic era. Ever since the early nineteenth century, international law had provided codes of procedure for enabling trade to continue during wartime and for protecting the status of nonbelligerent nations. Rules defining "contraband" and governing "search and seizure" had all been methods of controlling that trade in ways that would limit the shipment of armaments to countries at war without destroying international shipment of nonwar items.

The breakdown of that system under the peculiar demands of World War I and its new technologies was what actually drew the United States in, although that was not foreseen at the beginning. The "neutrality" Wilson proclaimed in August 1914 accurately reflected American attitudes. The term not only meant that Americans felt no consensus on the causes of the war, on the rights or wrongs being committed on either side; it also meant that they wanted to continue to deal as openly as possible with all the participants. American philanthropists organized shipments of food and clothing to supply the homes and families in need, wherever they might be. The Wilson government offered its services as mediator; and, gradually, American suppliers of materials of all kinds seized the opportunity to expand their markets abroad. Banks facilitated loans while the Wilson government stood nervously by, fearful of the outcome of such involvement but inexperienced at managing it. After the initial period of paralysis, international trade took off. Americans were benefiting from the war, no matter how much they deplored it.

Within a year it was clear that a shift was taking place. Americans were still following journalistic descriptions of the battle scenes of Europe, the horrors of trench warfare and poison gas, and the terror wrought by new weapons like "Big Bertha," a huge German cannon that hurled its missiles over previously unheard-of distances; but on the sea lanes of the North Atlantic a new war and a new weapon were now perceived by the European belligerents as the key influences on the outcome. The submarine had become a crucial weapon in determining what would ultimately happen in the land battles in Europe.

Thus, while Americans were reading accounts of village invasions like Gertrude Abernathy's *House on the Marne* and speculating on the damage being done to the great continental cathedrals, it was becoming clear to the belligerent governments that the outcome of the war depended as much on the power to blockade shipments of supplies as on any other single factor. Americans considered their shipments of food and clothing to the starving children of France and Belgium as acts of mercy, despite the fact that this relief, by weakening the blockade, had the effect of prolonging the war. Great Britain's island isolation made them in some respects vulnerable, but the British navy's control of the North Atlantic and the success of its blockade of Germany at first were serious irritants to American policymakers, who persisted in refusing to consider the consequences of their "charity."

Germany, unable to compete with the British navy, countered with the submarine, a weapon that effectively destroyed the nineteenth-century tradition of naval warfare. The submarine's power depended on secrecy and surprise. "Search and seizure" and other methods of humanizing military encounters were simply ignored by the new attack vessel. On the surface it had relatively little power and virtually no defenses. Underwater it was a monster, a hidden beast of prey against which there was seemingly no defense. Like the Continental troops of the colonial era, arrayed in colors, accompanied by fifes and drums, and organized in neat lines, the ships of the traditional navies faced an enemy not unlike the Indians, hidden behind trees and aware of the utility of silence and surprise. The equation of the submarine with barbarism was thus not difficult to make. Indeed, the notion of surprise attack as somehow immoral, a violation of the legal practices and moral commitments by which international-law theorists had been attempting to civilize modern warfare, would remain a problem for American public opinion for many years to come.

On 7 May 1915 a German submarine sank the British ship *Lusitania*. Among the 1,198 passengers and crew who died were 128 Americans. The fact that the vessel was British and hence, by German definition, an "enemy" did not mollify American feelings, which ran high. It was, moreover, a passenger vessel, not a purely merchant ship, a fact that occasioned much argument, not only in the United States but within the German General Staff, where it was clear that the novelty of the submarine as a weapon had reduced many of the formal definitions to rubble. The ship had been sunk without warning, despite the fact that it was unarmed. No effort had been made to find out what, in fact, it might have been carrying.

For Americans the event could be distinguished even from the sinking of vessels known to be carrying goods and supplies. The *Lusitania,* whatever its cargo, was loaded with passengers; and the freedom of Americans to travel the seas, even on the ships of nations at war, became the issue that galvanized popular response and began the crucial shift in the official position, which was no longer to be based on the freedom of neutral states to engage in trade in wartime but on the freedom of American citizens to travel as they chose. The first was a legal issue, already badly disturbed by the novel method of attack but amenable, at least, to some redefinition of the older rules. The second became an emotional issue of such intensity that its legal status rapidly lost meaning. The American secretary of state, William Jennings Bryan, could still see the distinction, and he argued against Woodrow Wilson's taking a strong stand; but Wilson, pressed by public opinion and perhaps by his own sense of outrage, insisted on a harsh and threatening response. Bryan resigned.

The debate that raged from May 1915 to the American declaration of war on 6 April 1917 reveals the gradual escalation of emotions on all sides. Great Britain was growing increasingly dependent on American supplies. Germany could not continue to allow its enemies to be supported by a supposed neutral. German strategy, dependent as it was on speed and surprise, could not be maintained indefinitely. The stalemated war in the trenches of Europe had developed into a ghastly inferno, where soldiers crawled in the mud and darkness, lit only by the rocket flares, to achieve little but mutual destruction. The German decision to engage in unrestricted submarine warfare was based on an acceptance of the fact that the United States would probably intervene; but the Germans also calculated that internal divisions in the United States and the disorganized state of American industry, already revealed by Wilson's efforts at "preparedness," would render America's entry irrelevant. The benefits of halting American shipping, they reasoned, would outweigh any direct American involvement.

The Germans should have been right. The fact that they were not—and the reasons why they were not—reveals important aspects both of America's experience in the war and of the ways that experience affected postwar American thought. The sinking of the *Lusitania* had shown the inherent weaknesses of "neutrality," but Wilson's attempts to persuade Americans to prepare themselves by adopting even a limited form of military conscription, like his

attempts to get American industry to organize itself voluntarily for war production, had demonstrated the profound limits of presidential power over the
nation's industrial system. What is more, it revealed that there was no national
system capable of centralized management.

Readers of American newspapers and journals of various political persuasions and ethnic identifications would also have noted deep divisions in public
opinion. It was, initially at least, not easy to hate the Germans. After all, they
were Anglo-Saxons, like the English. Their contributions to American intellectual development were clear, not only to Americans of German origin but to
the generation of American scientists and social scientists who had gone to
Germany to work for higher degrees. Moreover, the American Irish sympa-
thized with the Irish revolutionaries, who were seeking to win independence
from Great Britain; they were contributing money as well as young fighters to
what had become a bloody battle for the kind of freedom Americans of older
English stock felt they had won from the mother country. Their concern for
British interests on the continent of Europe were obviously very limited. Pro-
British enthusiasts like Henry James and, ultimately, Theodore Roosevelt reflected a WASP America in decline, particularly to young intellectuals like Walter Lippmann and the editors of the *New Republic,* who opposed involvement
on a variety of grounds. Popular political leaders associated with midwestern
and western progressivism—men like Robert M. LaFollette, William E. Borah,
and Hiram Johnson—were part of an older antiinternationalism that would
ultimately be defined as isolationist. Some, like Borah, favored an American
imperial stance but resisted the notion that America should defend any interest
but its own. All in all, observers of the American scene from abroad would
have had difficulty in detecting a national consensus on the war.

The American war machine gradually took shape, but it did so like a lumbering leviathan, willing to respond to the demand the new age was making
upon it but slow and clumsy in its efforts to do so. The assumption that so vast
a national program could be built on a voluntary basis, that Americans, from
the top industrial managers down to the lowliest factory laborers, would organize themselves to serve the national war purpose, required the creation of
a national will far more purposeful and far more self-sacrificing than Americans had ever before been asked to sustain. The insistence, too, that a significant portion of the cost of the war be borne by public subscription through
the sale of bonds also required a national consciousness different from that
demanded by any previous crisis. The belief that all such things could be done
with the minimum of legal coercion rested on a willingness to use the maximum of rhetorical persuasion and popular pressure to being them about. Yet,
long before the American decision to intervene, the tone had been irrevocably
set. The war that no one could justify in 1914 had become a national crusade
for aims no one could define in 1917; but everyone knew they were right, that
they reflected a justice to which all Americans would have to subscribe. The
Great War had been transformed. A puzzle in international power relationships
had become a new democratic revolution; for the world, as Wilson put it, was
going to be made "safe for democracy."

The American declaration of war against Germany on 7 April 1917 could be viewed as the culmination of one process of development and its transformation into something else. "Freedom of the seas" and the assertion of neutral rights had been the key concepts in the early years of the war, when America's interests in international trade had been, for better or worse, transformed by the unprecedented expansion of American trade with Great Britain and France. The crusade to "make the world safe for democracy," however, was another matter. By asserting its rights not only to protect its own interests but to change the basic international structures that had presumably placed those interests under threat in the first place, the United States was seeking a new role for itself in international affairs, a role much closer to that of the sympathetic revolutionary state it had so often tried to be in nineteenth-century international politics. Whether Wilson and the military-industrial state he assembled reflected a national consensus was, as we have seen, highly questionable, but it was absolutely necessary that such a state be created, consensus or not. In fact, it became necessary that the consensus itself be created. Wilson's speeches were all calculated to produce a fervent national agreement, to call upon all Americans to help him fight not only the war but internal opposition to it. The Allied victory was produced by the power of an American industrial system created specifically for that purpose and placed under the command of a national administration with powers the United States had never before granted to its federal government. While the process of getting the system in place was slow and awkward, at the peak of its power, from December 1917 to November 1918, it exercised extraordinary control over American industrial life.

Wilson's decision to staff the war administration with volunteers recruited from the nation's industries was crucial not only to the way the war effort was ultimately organized but to the American approach to the war itself. Selecting leaders from the nation's railroad industry and its clothing and manufacturing concerns, as well as key figures in banking and finance, meant that Wilson would have an experienced cadre of industrial managers to work with. Given the fact that there was no alternative group in the federal government itself, the decision was less a matter of choice than a quickness to take advantage of the options open to him. These leaders in turn brought a younger group of executives with them. The top echelon consisted of men who, wealthy in their own right, could work for the government for "a dollar a year," the phrase used to characterize their patriotism.

Equally important, the private managerial system was inspired by a nationalism just as intense in its control of the life of the nation as the patriotism that justified wartime service. The need to "win the war" produced a sense of urgency that veiled a fear, not simply that the war might be lost or that the consequences of losing it would be dire, but that the cause of failure would be the internal divisions that the years from 1914 to 1917 had revealed so clearly. The war aboard had to be won; but that victory seemed to many to depend on winning the other war—the war at home.

On 14 April 1917, a week after his address requesting a declaration of war, President Wilson issued an executive order creating the Committee on Public

Information. Headed by a newspaperman and magazine writer, George Creel, the committee was intended to organize the distribution of information required to keep the public properly informed on the course of the war. While part of the initial intention, at least on the part of Wilson, was to provide Americans with alternatives to the propaganda with which they were being bombarded from all sides, the committee in fact became a propaganda agency itself; that is, it assumed responsibility not only for informing the public opinion but for controlling it. Members of the new advertising industry joined with journalists and academicians to promote the war effort. The public schools were provided with pamphlets to distribute to schoolchildren, explaining America's role in the war and the need for loyalty to the American cause. Local committees tapped citizen volunteers to speak on behalf of the war effort to schoolchildren, clubs, and other organized citizen groups and in movie theaters between the end of the film and the beginning of the vaudeville acts. Such "four-minute men," as they were called (partly because they promised to speak for only four minutes and partly to recall the volunteer fighters of Revolutionary days), exhorted audiences to all forms of engagement in the war, from military service to volunteer activity, like rolling bandages for the Red Cross, knitting sweaters and scarves for servicemen, serving in the coffee and cookie canteens that sprang up in cities and towns near military camps and railroad transfer points, and, ultimately, purchasing the bonds with which the war was financed.

The promotion of Americanism and a spirit of wartime loyalty inevitably focused on the dissenters, the un-American and the disloyal, who opposed the war for whatever reason. The line between promotion and coercion dimmed as the effort to define loyalty intensified. A failure to volunteer for service, even an inability to do so for legally acceptable reasons, became tantamount to opposition in the eyes of a community aroused to furor against the enemy. Freedom of the seas, rights of neutrals, competition of national empires for world markets—all of the issues that had been central to the debates of the previous three years—were pushed aside in the turmoil of the war effort, replaced now by a rage against Germans and things German. The German language was removed from school curricula, German operas and symphonies were cut from repertoires, German street names were changed, often being replaced with some form of the term "Liberty," and "von" vanished from family names, where it had once signified some proudly remembered identification with nobility. The British royal family of Saxe-Coburg-Gothas became Windsors, the Battenbergs became Mountbattens, and Americans with German names followed suit.

The actual organization of the war effort itself brought many of the progressives' arguments to the fore. The financing of the war had played no role as an issue in any of the preparedness debates. A tacit understanding that American industry and American agriculture would benefit from expanded war trade rested on the assumption that the Allies were customers with funds of their own to pay for what they bought or with borrowing capacities attractive to American bankers willing to lend. The possibility that the war would become dependent on the American public for funding was not seriously considered in advance. The income tax was still a novelty, and the initial rates were still set by the compromises made by the progressives. Thus it did not weigh heavily on the wealthy, and it bypassed all Americans with incomes of less than $4,000—the vast majority. By 1916, increases in military expenditures had begun to produce a national deficit, but Congress was unwilling to increase taxes.

The War Revenue Act of 4 October 1917 was in some respects a progressive triumph. It authorized a graduated income tax beginning at 4 percent on personal incomes of more than $1,000, raised the corporation tax, and placed an excess-profits tax on corporate and personal income. Excise taxes on alcohol and tobacco were increased, and new excise taxes were levied on luxuries, amusements, and transportation. This triumph was short-lived, but the progressive principle was nonetheless established; almost three-quarters of the cost of the war was to be borne by corporations and those with large incomes, not by the consumption taxes conservatives had tried to promote. The costs skyrocketed far beyond what was envisaged at the beginning. Ultimately, a third of the money came from war-bond subscriptions; the rest was charged to future generations of Americans. War-financing was a mixed experience, and few on either the progressive or the conservative side of the debate were satisfied. The issue was destined to return in the aftermath of the war as critics reexamined the experience and tried to assess its meaning.

The effective management of the war was again a subject of dispute. It was clear by the winter of 1917 that volunteerism was not working. The collapse of the nation's railroad system was the most threatening sign. It was also the oldest and most familiar example of American industrial inefficiency. The railroads had led in the creation of virtually every aspect of national American industry, but they had done so like Hannibal's elephants lumbering over Alpine passes they would never have chosen to traverse, not like the innovational industries their supporters claimed them to be. Reluctant pioneers, they had been forced to face the development of a national labor force, the pressures of regional customer demand, the puzzles of technological innovation in materials and equipment, and, above all, the impact of federal regulation well ahead of their companions in the American technological revolution. They had also served as the most logical target of those who called for government ownership of public utilities. Even William Jennings Bryan had returned from Europe convinced that public ownership of the railroads was a national need, and, by the eve of the war, that conviction was shared by a sizable segment of informed public opinion.

By 1917, the American railroads had experienced almost thirty years of federal regulation, but this had been administered, by and large, with their advice and consent. As critics had been pointing out for more than two decades, railroad ownership had become centralized to a degree that had disturbed trust-busters without eliciting clear judicial decisions on what the government's response ought to be. The American railroad system was not a "system" in any serious sense. The lack of standardization in such obvious mechanisms as the couplings that attached one car to another made it impossible to ship a loaded car across the country without several reloadings into cars of different lines. Shippers complained about rates, while local railyards maintained platoons of workers whose job it was to reload cars. Gossip about wage differentials was carried along the same lines that carried cargo. Railroad managers rejected innovations and safety features as too costly and insisted that they could not raise wages or rationalize rates. Centralization in fact had produced few of the efficiencies the proponents of centralization claimed. The United States had a national railroad system in one sense only: the rail lines spanned the nation.

The war effort compelled the adoption of a national system. Shipments of troops and materials had to be organized for one basic purpose: support of the war effort. The demands of war exposed the inner workings of the rail system as they had never been seen before, and the strain on the system was already very great when the weather—December 1917 was an unusually snowy month—produced the straw that broke the camel's back. The federal government took over the running of the railroads the day after Christmas. Secretary of the Treasury William Gibbs McAdoo became director-general of the Railroad Administration, which controlled almost 400,000 miles of track operated by 3,000 companies. The progressives cheered. Innovative managers moved in. They introduced technical improvements, modernized the system, rationalized rates, and raised wages, not only to keep the system going but to keep it going well. But again the progressives, who had seen all this as a needed revolution, turned out to be wrong; for the government did not choose to go on managing the reformed system after the war. The Transportation Act of 1920, against President Wilson's advice, returned the system to its private owners, much improved, more efficient, and more profitable. The war, and the public, had bailed out the railroads. They had also created the necessary transportation system for making the war effort work, and that, when all was said and done, was all they had intended to do.

The War Industries Board, established in July 1917, is another example of a centralized administrative control replacing a failed volunteer effort. In March 1918, President Wilson authorized a sweeping reorganization that placed financier Bernard M. Baruch in charge of the group that controlled war industry, set priorities, and fixed prices. Congress had already authorized strict presidential control over food production and fuel, and it moved now to take over patents and other property of enemy aliens and to control all trade with enemy nations. The creation of a War Finance Corporation to lend money to financial institutions, who would in turn lend money to industries engaged in war work, was another dramatic step in the process of government intervention, while the National War Labor Board and the War Labor Policies Board were presidential efforts to resolve labor disputes in war industries.

Progressives pressed all of the industrial boards and committees to follow progressive principles and to use their power to institute reforms that progressives had long been advocating. Economists on the War Industries Board had their first opportunity to acquire systematic information on the economics of national industrial production and to push for standardized reporting. The Labor Board, under the joint chairmanship of Frank P. Walsh and former president William Howard Taft, committed itself to the ideal of a living wage, carrying a significant step further the argument against the treatment of labor as a commodity in the production system whose compensation was determined only by the law of supply and demand. The Labor Policies Board under Felix Frankfurter made important strides by requiring accurate and realistic reports on labor conditions and gave great impetus to the idea of justifiable grievance. Presidential threats to use war power to take over industries whose management refused to negotiate with labor were effective in forcing bargaining and in gaining support from the leaders of the labor movement. Yet, as the experience of the twenties was to demonstrate, the balance between wartime fervor and commitment to progressive ideals was considerably more uneven than even the most knowledgeable of the progressives were inclined to believe in the heat of what some preferred to see as a wartime revolution. At the same time, the experience was there. It was intense, and it was available for later use in the New Deal decades. Even so, it was the sense of emergency, one could argue, that could be appealed to, not any commitment to reform.

Federal support of farm prices, to encourage expanded production, posed a similar problem for those who would later look back on the war years. It answered an immediate wartime purpose in a nation responsible for supplying not only its own needs but those of its allies; and price was no object. But when price became an object, as world production returned to normal, the experience of price supports was there to be appealed to, not necessarily in recollection of the emergency but certainly in recollection of the prosperity it had produced. No one would have argued for a return to war emergency, but the mechanism, many thought, could be reshaped for peacetime use if only one could figure out how.

All in all, the war was a disruptive experience that swept across the American landscape like a firestorm feeding on every source of energy it touched. Prohibition had been an issue for more generations than anyone could remember. Wartime morality, plus the belief that most American manufacturers of alcohol were German, gave the Eighteenth Amendment movement the edge it needed. The intensity of the need to create and sustain a national sentiment in favor of the war was based on a fear that failure to do so would make victory impossible; but it led to repressive legislation that severely limited any criticism of the war or of the nation's conduct of it. The Espionage Act of June 1917 was intended to control treasonable or disloyal activities, and the coupling of treason and loyalty is the key to the difficulties that were encountered in interpreting and administering the law. Treason could be defined by forms of behavior determinable by law as treasonous. The same standard could not be applied to loyalty, a concept that depended on beliefs and on statements in speech or writing. The act empowered the postmaster general to exclude from the mails anything he deemed treasonable or seditious. Its constitutionality was upheld by the Supreme Court, even though Oliver Wendell Holmes's ringing dissent became the standard, ultimately, by which the Court would defend free speech. Before the war was over, the act was amended to make it even more severe, particularly in its penalties against socialists and pacifists.

Faced with congressional pressures to create a national war cabinet to build a more effective war machine, Wilson himself wrote the legislation that became the Overman Act of 1918, which granted the president greater administrative authority than any previous president ever had. Passed in May 1918, the Overman Act gave Wilson enormous powers of reorganization and concentration of government where war activities were concerned. The American war machine had reached its peak. It could now win the war, but it would do so at a price that many were beginning to consider much more costly than anyone had anticipated. Americans had nationalized themselves to face threats that had gradually become more internal than external, although it grew increasingly difficult to see the distinction. Even the Zimmerman Note—Germany's effort in March 1917 to enlist Mexico against the United States in the event that America entered the war against Germany—paled as a threat when Americans faced the thought that they might lose the war through failure to achieve a national consensus on the effort required to win it. The enemy at home became the most visible enemy to attack.

Part of the problem lay in the initial inability of any of the combatants to explain the reasons for the war in the first place. Wilson had pointed to the problem in his earliest efforts to negotiate a settlement, long before America's entry. Neither side would define its war aims. Wilson's attempt to promote what he called "peace without victory" had failed to stimulate even a rudimentary list of the demands each side would make as the price of settlement. After America entered the war, Wilson sought to establish a list—the famous Fourteen Points—but by then it was clear that, at least as far as America was concerned, the list was no longer negotiable. The Fourteen Points were, he asserted, "the only possible program." Basic attitudes toward war in general and this war in particular had undergone changes, and these had begun to differentiate this war from previous wars. To the extent that previous wars had reflected a nineteenth-century view of war as an extension of diplomatic policy, designed to bring about specific aims with regard to borders and territorial authority, they had been managed by governments as policymaking activities. From such a perspective, the proponents of perpetual world peace were characterized as dreamers, out of touch with the realities of world politics.

The transformation of Wilson's attitude toward the war from "peace without victory" to "the war to end war" and then to a "war to make the world safe for democracy" was a transformation from the instrumental realism of much of the nineteenth century to a dramatic idealism that became much more of a religious crusade. Nor was this simply an American aberration, traceable to a unique American idealism or to Wilson's personal naïveté. Russia's withdrawal from the war, following the November 1917 revolution, led to the enunciation of similar criticisms of the aims of the war. Couched in Marxist terms, they held little appeal for Americans, even though they spoke to some of the same issues of international politics and to the ultimate uselessness of war as a policy instrument. Instead of arousing American sympathies, the Bolshevik position exacerbated American fears; for Russia's withdrawal liberated German troops for service on the Western front and underscored the growing fear that the antiwar movement, led by socialist and pacifist groups in other countries, would lead other allies to withdraw. The Committee on Public Information opened an office in Rome for the precise purpose of influencing Italian public opinion and countering the antiwar literature being circulated there. In the United States the hostility to socialism and to immigrant groups who were identified, rightly or wrongly, with leftist ideological positions came to be tied directly to the commitment to winning the war. It appeared to be a simple step in logic to argue that socialism and communism alike were pro-German.

The entry of the United States determined the outcome of the war; but the United States did not win the war. The victory went to the Allies, who dictated the terms of the peace. Germany had agreed to an armistice on the understanding that the United States would dictate the terms of the peace and that Wilson's Fourteen Points would serve as the basis of the terms. But Wilson joined the Versailles Conference as only one of the four heads of state who drafted the terms, and his influence was limited, especially given his inexperience and given the fact that the election in November 1918 had turned control of Congress over to the Republicans. Those who considered the election results a repudiation of Wilson seemed to forget that none of Wilson's political victories had been clear-cut. The Democrats had not been a majority party in 1912 and they were not one in 1918. The factors that had given them their slender margins had quite possibly been balanced by the experience of the war. The return to normal politics was on the way, and normal politics meant Republican majorities at the polls.

For so brief an experience, even if one dates it from 1914 rather than 1917, the American involvement in World War I was as intense and as significant as any since the Civil War. The regular army in 1917 consisted of about two hundred thousand men. By 1919 that number had reached more than four million, over two million of whom had gone to France.

For the first time since the Civil War Americans had been drafted to serve in the armed services. Fearing riots like those that had attended the Civil War draft, particularly in cities with large German populations, Wilson had distributed registration forms through the sheriffs' offices, but there was no need for concern. The patriotic mood held. Public hostility to "slackers" and "draft-dodgers" had its effects, while management and selection by local boards helped smooth the transition from the old nineteenth-century system of locally recruited units to the establishment of a national army.

That Americans were fighting on the battlefields of Europe was something new and shocking, both for those who went and for those who joined the labor force to serve the nation's industrial needs. American industry responded, too, to its first major taste of government intervention; but even that was an experience of gradual escalation of control. One could remember the voluntary beginnings or the coercive last months and be remembering something quite different. The new industrial efficiency, developed along lines recommended by Frederick Winslow Taylor, gave some an opportunity to see what might come of scientific management; but the tests were too sporadic and too incomplete for anyone to draw clear conclusions.

The introduction of psychological testing brought professionals from a new academic field into consulting positions where industrial managers could see the possible effects of their methods. An experimental field hospital funded by the Rockefeller Foundation advanced medical knowledge of burn and wound treatment. Modernization in the teaching of foreign languages was hastily adopted to meet the needs of those who had to learn quickly to communicate by word of mouth rather than to read the literature or comprehend the subtleties of the grammar. Historical and cultural knowledge of Europe was necessary to guide policymakers faced with the responsibility of advising the first president to engage in face-to-face negotiation with the leaders of the victorious powers of the wartime alliance. Yet, in virtually every field, the lesson was always the same. From the economists who worked for the War Industries Board to the historians and political scientists who advised the president at Versailles, the issue boiled down to one basic problem: American specialization in such fields was essentially in its infancy. American energy was great. The creation of the industrial machine that won the war had supplied an undeniable demonstration of that energy. But efficient management of the machine had depended entirely on the emergency of the war, on the fear of losing it, and on the support of a popular fervor the government worked desperately to sustain. The speed with which Congress dismantled the machine at the war's end, to the point of leaving Washington office workers to find money for their passage home when federal funds were abruptly cut off, suggests that national management was basically viewed as something temporary, even dangerous.

Yet progressives had argued, long before the war emergency gave them what they took to be their opportunity, that American society was seriously threatened by its inability to organize its resources and rationalize its industrial system. From the conservationists to the scientific industrial managers, the depth of concern was profound. The war had revealed the precarious condition of the American industrial system. Concerned Americans who lamented the closing of the frontier, the disorganization of the industrial labor force, the weaknesses of the transportation system, the pointless duplications and inefficiencies in agricultural and industrial production methods, the pockets of illiteracy and substandard health among the young, and the lack of technical information on national finance and industry found that they had indeed been correct in their assessment of conditions. They looked to the war to make their point for them, to prove to public opinion and even the most backward congressmen that their prescriptions would have to be followed. Nothing could have been further off the mark. All down the line, from their conviction that the new wave of American internationalism could not now be turned back to their belief that the war had put industrial management on a new course, with government firmly in command, the progressives simply turned out to be wrong.

The war had become a reform movement of its own, sweeping up all of the reform interests in one way or another but turning them to the one central purpose, winning the war. Still, what really destroyed the reform movement was not just the excesses generated by that purpose but the exhaustion produced by the war effort itself. Trench warfare had been a nightmare. As if to be certain that civilian populations would share the nightmare, an influenza pandemic, which originated on the Western front, spread to the United States with extraordinarily devastating effect in the winter of 1918–19. The high mortality rate from the disease accounted for more than half of the 112,432 American war fatalities and for thousands more at home.

The failure to consolidate, let alone to extend, wartime gains was nowhere more apparent than in the American labor movement. Spurred by an immediate postwar inflation, which by 1919 had driven the cost of living 77 percent above its prewar level, labor unions began to organize strikes. The most dramatic were the strike in the steel industry, where workers had for years suffered conditions among the worst in American industry, and the strike of the Boston police. Public reaction to both was colored by the antiradical hysteria of the period. Violence in the steel strike and the threat of violence in the police strike touched old nerves in the American public's general suspicion of unionization and its association with radical ideas. Yet these two were among 2,665 strikes involving more than four million workers, while the cost of living rose to 105 percent above prewar levels by 1920. Faced with the opposition first of state officials and ultimately of the United States attorney general, labor backed down. That it was forced to do so during the immediate period of postwar prosperity suggests something markedly antilabor in the public response. The Boston police strike became the symbol. Public protectors had no right to strike; they must have been led to do so by insidious forces.

The war effort demanded and enforced a national unity unlike anything Americans had ever known. The Civil War had been fought to define the Union. No one who looked honestly at the aftermath of that divisive explosion wanted to reexamine the nation's queasy unity. Foreign observers like James Bryce were forever trying to explain to their countrymen the sensitivity Americans felt about the rights of their state governments—"*these* United States" they persisted in reminding anyone who wanted to describe the American nation. The creation of a unity sufficient for the successful prosecution of World War I revealed the costly divisions that still existed in the form of regional differences, ethnic and racial hostilities, and urban and agrarian competitions.

Former wartime managers, when writing of their part in the war effort, continued to extol the voluntarism with which Americans had joined together to forget their differences and win the war; but even many of those who praised that victory still insisted that the national industrial system should not be required to undertake such a burden again. Businessmen and labor leaders had not found government intervention in their interest, and neither side thought that the government had been even-handed. Even the language used to urge cooperation, like the repeated exhortations to make "sacrifices," suggested that wars were temporary emergencies that required the violation of some basic principles, chiefly the primacy of self-interest. The progressives' use of the war as an occasion for achieving the reforms they had failed to achieve in peacetime was more than a failure; for by linking the war with a fearful centralization, they proved the point about reformers that their critics had so often made: they were seen as oppressive zealots seeking to impress a national unity on an inherently free people. In the years to come, Prohibition would be taken as another proof to this point. And when the crisis of the thirties began, the reluctance to go back to wartime measures of national control was based in part on recollection of what had happened before. The fear that leaders used emergencies to justify the imposition of state controls was part of a historical experience with war that had nothing to do with voluntarism. Like children whistling past a cemetery, postwar memoirists praised voluntarism, but there was always a gnawing fear that it had not really worked. The truth of the matter was that it hadn't.

Americans were willing to assert their national commitments when they celebrated the Fourth of July; but there were many who still mourned the dead of the Confederacy. Now there would be Armistice Day to celebrate on November 11th and a monument to an Unknown Soldier to visit in the nation's national cemetery at Arlington. But behind occasions and monuments there was a multitude of commitments to local needs, regional prejudices, and ethnic practices and attitudes, and there were widely differing points of view that were not capable of resolution in the melting pot. In the rural and urban landscape alike there were sheltered enclaves of citizens who looked to one another for identity first, and who gathered together to sustain one another in their daily lives.

The war to end all wars had ended. The brief sense of triumph gave way to bickering as Wilson and the supporters of the League of Nations attempted to revive the wartime fervor, now for an international agency to preserve peace. But they failed. Like a rubber band stretched beyond its breaking point, the idea snapped back to injure both those who fought the League and those who defended it, while the majority of Americans looked on in puzzlement and waited for the future to begin. Throughout the 1920s and '30s the response to the war resonated like a distant sound in a literature that talked about something other than the war. *The Enormous Room* (1922), a novel by e. e. cummings, described the war as an experience in a French prison among the outcasts of Europe, a kind of pilgrim's progress for an American who went to France to drive an ambulance and wound up in jail as the result of a bureaucratic and legal goof. Ernest Hemingway's stories published as *In Our Time* (1924) and William Faulkner's *Soldier's Pay* (1926) deal with the war as an experience suffered by those who return home, are unable to manage the world to which they have returned, and are wounded far more deeply than anyone understands. Katherine Anne Porter's novella *Pale Horse, Pale Rider* (1936) is perhaps the most recollective work of the war as a domestic experience, in which enforced patriotism, the ravages of war, and the flu epidemic are all tangled together in one feverish nightmare.

Many of those who backed Warren Harding for the presidency in 1920 did so in the belief that he would support the League; but his assertion in his inaugural address that Americans wanted "not nostrums but normalcy" suggested a stepping-back not only from the war experience itself but from the whole reform mood that had been part of it. And when the stimulus to general economic conditions, supplied by Europe's reconstruction needs, ended in 1921, the depression that followed, while brief, seemed to prove that the costs of international adventure might be higher than Americans could afford. The fact that Americans had afforded it, that they had invested heavily in the economic future of Europe through loans and investments, was brought home to them now by the remaining war debts. The war-debts issue would remain beyond resolution. The responsibilities the United States had assumed by involving itself in the war were beyond popular understanding. Americans still preferred to consider themselves independent of the fortunes of Europe, but they were not. Wartime America had not been a familiar America, in a sense, but was undeniably American. Efforts to blame Europe and Europeans would continue to override the possibility that something in American society itself had generated the hostilities and threats revealed by the war.

QUESTIONS FOR DISCUSSION

1. Describe the shift in public opinion from "neutrality" to "intervention" to support for a crusade "to make the world safe for democracy." What do you think were the sources of this shift in opinion? Was the American public "manipulated"? Or was it responding responsibly to the press of events?

2. How did the war "become a reform movement of its own"?

Chapter Five

Between the Wars

WARREN SUSMAN

Piety, Profits, and Play: The 1920s: Bruce Barton; Henry Ford; Babe Ruth

"The Roaring Twenties": the phrase brings to mind an image of easy living and prosperity. The image is not entirely false, but we must look beyond it if we want to understand the truly fundamental changes in American culture and society that occurred in the brief period that began with the conclusion of the Great War and ended with the coming of the Great Depression.

In the following essay, Warren Susman explores these changes by focusing our attention on three central institutions in twentieth-century American life that were transformed in the 1920s: advertising, the automobile, and spectator sports. Using a biographical approach to history, he describes the "significant and lasting developments" in these areas by looking at the lives and legends of three exemplary Americans: "Bruce Barton in advertising, Henry Ford in automobile production, and George Herman 'Babe' Ruth in baseball."

As Susman demonstrates, each of these men, in his own unique way, encapsulated some aspect of the new era, the new lifestyle, and the new value structures that emerged in the course of this decade.

$\mathbf{F}$ew decades in American history have been so little analyzed and so thoroughly caricatured as the 1920s. With the mere mention of these years, who among us does not think back, almost as if by reflex, on "Scarface" Al Capone

Warren Susman was until his death in 1985 a member of the history department at Rutgers University. A collection of his articles was published in 1985 under the title, *Culture as History: The Transformation of American Society in the Twentieth Century.* The following essay first appeared in *Men, Women, and Issues in American History.*

Reprinted from *Men, Women, and Issues in American History,* revised edition (Dorsey Press, 1980), pp. 202–227. © The Dorsey Press, 1974 and 1980. Reprinted by permission of The Dorsey Press and Beatrice Susman.

and his mobsters, John Held's shapeless flappers, Warren G. Harding's lives, loves, and scandals; Calvin Coolidge's notorious propensity for silence, Hiram Evan's legions of hooded Ku Klux Klanners, and Flo Ziegfeld's gorgeous and leggy follies girls? Those were the days, it seems, when life was still in tune with the rhythms of small-town America, when one could shoot off a week's salary (and sometimes one's fingers) on Fourth of July fireworks or feel slightly wicked meeting the local bootlegger under the cloak of night to purchase a bottle of forbidden booze.

But to approach the '20s in this essentially superficial vein is to ignore the really fundamental changes that were occurring simultaneously in American life. For it was in the '20s that the art of advertising was perfected as an indispensable component of the country's industrial economy and as a dictator of the public taste. It was in the '20s that the United States went through the automobile revolution which was to change the very nature of the American's society as well as its landscape. And it was in the '20s that the American infatuation with professional athletics began, giving a virtual coup de grace to religion as the non-economic and non-sexual preoccupation of millions of middle-class Americans. A convenient way of looking at these significant and lasting developments is to consider the careers of Bruce Barton in advertising, Henry Ford in automobile production, and George Herman "Babe" Ruth in baseball.

BRUCE BARTON

When Bruce Barton died at the age of 80 in 1967 it seemed almost inevitably and perfectly logical that at least one writer of his obituary should refer to his own life story as "legendary in the best Horatio Alger sense." Among the most prominent men of his time, Barton had come out of a small Tennessee town to become one of the most widely read and respected authors of his day. He would serve in the Congress of the United States, run for the Senate, and even be considered as a possible presidential candidate. He was to found one of the most important advertising agencies and to shape the development of the advertising business—so crucial itself in shaping the new mass society of the period—in significant ways. Barton's success in managing his agency can in part be measured by the fact that when he retired in 1961 the company could boast of billings in excess of $230 million. While Barton himself was known to millions of Americans through his writings and public service, his company could, in a special memorandum on the occasion of his death, point to the special meaning of his vast "contacts." "It meant contact with presidents of the United States, with senators, with cabinet members, with leaders of industry. . . . Bruce could call anyone in the United States and time would be found for him." But perhaps most significant, Barton's life recalls Horatio Alger because, in a sense, he rewrote the American primer on success in a special way that most effectively served the middle class of the 1920s. This revision provided a necessary kind of secular religion, a special vision of piety essential to the nation's transformation into a modern industrial mass society. His version of the success story helped ease the transition from an older, more producer-centered system with its traditional value structure to the newer, more consumer-centered system with its changed value structure. Barton's inspirational writings (and in a sense this includes his brilliant advertising copy) found a way of bridging the gap between the demands of a Calvinistic producer ethic with its emphasis on hard work, self-denial, savings and the new, increasing demands of a hedonistic consumer ethic: spend, enjoy, use up.

Barton once explained his own success in a tongue-in-cheek article he published in 1919:

> We preachers' sons have an unfair advantage over the rest of the world. Out of about 12,000 names in one of the editions of *Who's Who,* more than 1,000 were names of us. In England's *Dictionary of National Biography* we appear 1,270 times; while the sons of lawyers are there only to the number of 510, and the sons of doctors score only 350 times. In fact, we show up so well that any unprejudiced man will agree that all the money given to the church would have been well invested had it done nothing more than enable preachers to raise sons. . . . Not all of us make good, of course. A third of us go to the devil; another third float around in between; but another third rule the world.

A well-known authority on the American idea of success has provided a shrewd generalization: "Whenever Calvinism's stern demands bit deep, as in Woodrow Wilson, Henry Luce, Norman Thomas, Robert Hutchins, Adolf A. Berle, Jr., DeWitt Wallace, or John Foster Dulles [all sons of preachers], there was a moral earnestness, a mission—and often a destiny." William Eleazer Barton instilled this evangelical sense and moral purpose in his son. Bruce Barton, in his writings as in his life, provided convincing evidence of his deep dedication to and the profound influence of his Congregational minister-father.

William Barton, a descendant of a soldier in the American Revolution, was at the time of his son's birth in 1886, a circuit rider working out of a small church in Robbins, Tennessee. Bruce Barton was the eldest of five children. His father's missionary zeal led him to seek further education even after he had started his family. Moving on to Oberlin Theological Seminary, William Barton graduated at the top of his class when he was almost 30 years old. That same zeal plus a special flair for writing and preaching enabled him to move from one important church to another. At the same time, he lectured at seminaries, edited a magazine, wrote a series of books (significant among them detailed and scholarly studies of Abraham Lincoln and a biography of Clara Barton, no relative, the founder of the Red Cross). Eventually he became a famous preacher and at one time was Moderator of the National Council of Congregational Churches. In speaking of his childhood it pleased Bruce Barton to insist: "We were not poor; we just didn't have any money." The family's wealth included a library, with books coming before cakes in this intensely intellectual household. His mother, who was a school teacher, helped establish such priorities. Barton delighted in the memories of that environment of books, simple living, and countryside trips with the father he worshipped and whom he held onto as they both rode on the back of the family's white mare.

Meanwhile, he was also being prepared for a more sophisticated life in commerce and journalism.

In the hallowed Alger tradition, Bruce Barton had a paper route by the time he was nine. The family eventually settled in a fairly comfortable middle-class professional life with a ministry in the Chicago suburb of Oak Park, Illinois. He went to high school there, and received his initiation into the business world. Arranging with an Ohio uncle to sell maple syrup tapped from trees on his uncle's farm, young Barton netted some $600 a year. Simultaneously, he was also developing his skills as a journalist, serving as writer, editor, proofreader, and copy-runner on the high school newspaper. Barton also found work as a part-time reporter (at three dollars a week) on a community newspaper. His intellectual interests did not slacken; and as graduation approached, he determined to go to Amherst College.

While William Barton had no objections, he induced his son to take at least one year at Berea College in Kentucky where all students worked part-time to pay for tuition. Bruce Barton's own accounts make clear that his father's desire was not prompted by financial necessities or by loyalty to Berea, which had been his own alma mater. Reverend Barton's object was simple: to guarantee that his son remain sympathetic toward those who must work for what they want. At Berea, Barton chose the printing office, where he learned to set type, read proof, and handle a press—for eight cents an hour.

After his freshman year, Bruce Barton did transfer to Amherst. There he was elected to Phi Beta Kappa, headed the Student Council, served on the debating team in outstanding fashion, and even managed to play some football as a substitute lineman. Predictably, he worked his way through college (by selling pots and pans) and was elected the member of his class "most likely to succeed"—the whole pattern of his biography demands such things. Bruce Barton's post-graduation plans, however, were not consonant with this formula for worldly success. He had decided that being a professor of history would be a sufficient goal and was delighted at the prospect of a fellowship from the exciting department at the University of Wisconsin. But 1907 was a depression year and Bruce Barton felt the need to work. After weeks of job hunting in Chicago, one of his father's parishioners found a position for him—as timekeeper in a western Montana construction camp. Working ten hours a day, he earned $65 a month; he valued the experience because it taught him to get along with tough men in a tough job.

Bruce Barton returned to Chicago at the age of 21 to sell advertising space for three magazines. He was soon working as a public relations counselor and as editor of a small religious paper. His paper was nearing bankruptcy, but the crisis, Barton's biographers love to recall, led not to personal failure; rather it only served to heighten his "enterprising spirit." It also gave him his first opportunity to write an advertisement. He asked for, and received, permission to take back salary in advertising space and made arrangements with a friend who operated a travel agency. He would drum up customers for a Bavarian tour, this being the year of the Oberammergau Passion Play, and would receive a fee for every customer he secured. "Just a few dollars will take you to Europe to see the Passion Play" was typical ad copy, as salesmanship and religion united. The result: enough money to take Barton to New York City where he settled in at the YMCA, first to work at *Vogue* magazine and then as managing editor of another religious weekly that soon folded. P. J. Collier and Son soon hired him as assistant sales manager. His flair for promotion and sales led to increased self-confidence and a firm belief in the value of salesmanship. His copy for Collier's Five-Foot Shelf of Harvard Classics (sometimes known as Dr. Eliot's Five-Foot Shelf of Books) helped lift that work to fame and played a significant role in the popularization of knowledge and culture so characteristic of this age. It was Bruce Barton who successfully urged countless readers to "let Dr. Eliot of Harvard give you the essentials of a liberal education in only 15 minutes a day."

From 1914 to 1918 Barton served with the Collier company as editor of *Every Week,* a Sunday supplement with a format that presaged the modern picture magazine. His editorials and articles brought him a flourishing literary career, and one article in particular, about Billy Sunday, the evangelist, attracted the attention of an editor of the *American Magazine.* Invited to contribute to this journal, his articles, especially his interviews with famous people, stressed the inspirational and up-lift aspects of life and long remained popular. Indeed, these articles were so admired that they were reproduced in a series of volumes during the 1920s; their titles suggest the over-all theme: *More Power to You, It's a Good Old World, Better Days, On the Up and Up.*

During World War I, the federal government asked Barton to coordinate fund drives of the YWCA and YMCA, Knights of Columbus, Salvation Army, and Jewish Welfare Board. Out of this experience two significant developments emerged. First, Barton's effort to help publicize the Salvation Army inspired one of his most famous slogans—indeed one of the most famous in an era of sloganeering—"A man may be down but he is never out." Second, the fund-raising campaign itself led him to enlist the aid of two advertising men, Alex Osborn of Buffalo and Roy Durstine of New York. That this campaign did not start until Armistice Day, failed to discourage the trio, since funds were still needed. Their determination was justified: They topped their goal of $150,000,000 by some $50,000,000 more. Out of their successful team effort came the creation of a new advertising agency, Barton, Durstine, and Osborn, in January 1919. In 1928 this company merged with another agency, the George Batten Company, to become the highly publicized BBD&O. Its fame was hardly limited to professional advertising men. The agency was well known to the general public and was very much the product of a transformed America, of a new era of the consumer-oriented mass society. Jokes, cartoons, and other popular references to its kind of activities made the agency's name a commonplace. By the time of Barton's retirement, it was the nation's fourth largest advertising firm. Its clients included many of the industrial giants— General Electric, General Motors, United States Steel. Founded on a $10,000 loan the company had become a multi-million dollar enterprise. Barton, who never seemed to seek money, attracted it with extraordinary ease. At the beginning, legend has it, he took a salary of only $5,000 a year from the agency, claiming that it was all anybody needed. He and his family obviously lived well (although never extravagantly) in later years, but it is probably true, as Barton delightedly used to insist, that "it would be a scandal if people knew how little I make as chairman of BBD&O. I think it's almost a disgrace for a man to die rich." He was always equally generous with his contributions to charity and his time to public service work.

Barton's original fame rested on his prolific and unsubtle contributions to inspirational literature. Some found his work sentimental, even cloying but there seemed to be a ceaseless public demand for it. Many of these qualities appeared in his most famous advertising copy. What Bruce Barton possessed was a special insight into human nature, especially into the character of the American middle-class in a period of transformation. He had a special sensitivity to its fears and hopes, yearnings and ideals. Richard M. Huber rightly finds him a man, "with a knack for retailing simple homilies"—very much like the poet Edgar Guest. It seemed both easy and natural when "this leading retailer of values poured most of his energies into retailing products." But perhaps Alistair Cooke was most perceptive of all in seeing the special meaning of Barton's career in advertising. Writing in his column for the *Manchester Guardian* on the occasion of Barton's death, Cooke stated: "He came as close as any one will to achieving a philosophy of advertising, because he saw the whole of human history as an exercise in persuasion."

Bruce Barton understood the power of communication in an era when new techniques of communications were remaking the social order. In a memorable piece immediately after World War I, "They Shall Beat Their Swords Into Electrotypes," he pleaded for a new effort in the cause of international understanding. Each nation, he said, should pledge itself to spend at least one percent of its war costs in international advertising, "explaining to the rest of the world its own achievements and ideals; and seeking to eradicate from the character of its own people those characteristics which are a source of irritation to their neighbors." In the same article he urged the international exchange of newspapermen, clergymen, professors—of every group that had "in its power the shaping of public opinion." And, he continued, "In all these ways—plus the regular use of the printed word and motion picture—I would make the people of the world know each other, knowing that ultimately they would come to like each other." These are ideas very much in harmony with so-called advanced thinking in an era fascinated by the power of new agencies of communication and mass culture. In the early 1930s, Barton's article "Let's Advertise This Hell," proposed an entirely new series of ads that would be offered to any publication that could be persuaded to print them as a way of keeping the United States out of another war. Late in 1923 he was busy proposing to Calvin Coolidge's political advisors a publicity campaign for the President's 1924 bid.

Barton's famous "Creed of an Advertising Man," first delivered as an address in 1927, is even more characteristic of his thinking and greatly contributed to an understanding of his 1920s vision of the importance of advertising in the social order. He writes:

I am in advertising because I believe in business and advertising is the voice of business. I recognize the waste and inefficiencies of business. I recognize the cruelties of competition, and the dishonesty that still stains too many business operations. Yet I believe that in the larger development of business and the gradual evolution of its ideals lies the best hope of the world.

I am in advertising because advertising is the power which keeps business out in the open, which compels it to set up for itself public ideals of quality and service and to measure up to those ideals. Advertising is a creative force that has generated jobs, new ideas, has expanded our economy and has helped give us the highest standard of living in the world. Advertising is the spark plug on the cylinder of mass production, and essential to the continuance of the democratic process. Advertising sustains a system that has made us leaders of the free world: The American Way of Life.

If advertising sometimes encourages men and women to live beyond their means, so sometimes does matrimony. If advertising is too often tedious, garrulous and redundant, so is the U.S. Senate.

Advertising, then, was persuasion and persuasion could and would change the world; but advertising at the moment was doing its greatest and most necessary service in its special relationship to business—by publicizing products and urging consumers to buy them. (His method of dealing with Communism, stated later in life, is characteristic: "Give every Russian a copy of the latest Sears-Roebuck Catalogue and the address of the nearest Sears-Roebuck outlet.") The special genius of Barton's own advertising copy was based on the assumption that the use of products advertised effectively contributed to growth and progress, sometimes of the nation but more often of the individual himself. The most successful ads would seek to employ the products of a business in the service of the sanctity or betterment of human life. Witness, for instance, one General Electric ad: "Any woman who is doing any household task that a little electric motor can do is working for three cents an hour. Human life is too precious to be sold at the price of three cents an hour." Or that ad for the Alexander Hamilton Institute (a two-year correspondence course): "A wonderful two years' trip at full pay. But only men with imagination can take it. Only one man in ten has imagination, and imagination rules the world." Or that for General Foods: the creation of Betty Crocker as "the kitchen familiar of every lonely American housewife." The ad shaped for each situation sought to provide everyone with a simple way to understand a rapidly standardizing and mechanizing way of life. In a world of increased complexities, mass technology, and fearful changes, such advertisements offered a chance to retain human dignity as well as individual meaning and development. Bruce Barton, the great master of the uplift essay, without doubt had put uplift at the service of American business enterprise; without doubt he did so largely because of that learning he had received as a young boy at his father's table.

Bruce Barton, it is clear, had been fascinated by ideas about salesmanship and religion many years before writing his 1925 best seller, *The Man Nobody*

Knows. He had often commented, in writing and conversation, what a great textbook the Bible could be for an advertising man. Barton's own writings delighted in Biblical-like parables and even his advertising copy had a Biblical quality to its prose. But it was only in 1925, the year of the Scopes Trial and William Jennings Bryan's fundamentalist interpretation of the Old Testament, that the Republican business-oriented Barton finally provided his important and widely read interpretation of the New Testament, which especially emphasized the life of Jesus.

Ever since the nineteenth century had sought and found an historical Christ, it had become increasingly popular to see Him in ways that suited the historical needs of a given moment. Jesus had been recreated as a fairly respectable Christian Socialist or a not-so-respectable proletarian revolutionary. Now in the 1920s Barton claimed Him for yet another historical role. He set out specifically, we might argue today, to give Christ a new image. In the process he provided a new vision of Christianity. Such a vision was consistent both with the tough demands of a more difficult and rigorously ordered mass society and with a new religious glow destined, not as a simple justification of capitalism and the virtues necessary to sustain it, but as a means of sanctifying the new order of modern business—one organized through the instrumentality of salesmanship to service the newly emerging consumer-based mass society. In a society where the older ideal of the stewardship of wealth could no longer serve, a new idea evolved: business—all business—as service to others and something fundamental to the development of self. Barton, Richard Huber observed, "soaked the idea of success in the sanctity of the New Testament." He moved American Puritanism, in a profound sense, from a more traditional dependence on the God of the Old Testament, to a greater reliance on a carefully reexamined and reconstructed vision of the New Testament.

The initial task at hand was to develop a necessary new view of the personality of Jesus and the basic values that went with it. Barton took special aim at the Sunday School image of Jesus: a weakling, a kill-joy, a failure, a sissy, meek and full of grief. In its place there was a new Jesus: the physically strong carpenter, a healthy and vigorous outdoors man, a sociable companion, a strong and effective leader. "A kill-joy! He was the most popular dinner guest in Jerusalem! . . . A failure! He picked up twelve men from the bottom ranks of business and forged them into an organization that conquered the world." Barton insisted on Jesus' masculinity, suggesting his attractiveness to women and stressing his role as father figure and even emphasizing the role of Jesus' own "historical" father, Joseph. Jesus emerges, as it were, a consumer himself, enjoying life and parties, turning water into wine. His methods are those of advertising; He is the founder of "modern business" and modern entrepreneurial tactics. Barton's understanding of what Jesus meant by his "Father's business" is the key to his own analysis. God seeks, Barton tells us,

> to develop perfect human beings, superior to circumstance, victorious over Fate. No single kind of human talent or effort can be spared if the experiment is to succeed. The race must be fed and clothed and housed and transported,

as well as preached to, and taught and healed. Thus *all* business is his Father's business. All work is worship; all useful service prayer. And whoever works wholeheartedly at any worthy calling is a co-worker with the Almighty in the great enterprise which He has initiated but which he can never finish without the help of men.

The Man Nobody Knows first appeared in serial form in the *Woman's Home Companion* and then for several years in the late 1920s continued to ride high on the best seller lists. Barton followed it in 1927 with *The Book Nobody Knows,* a study of the Bible. These works have never been without an audience since they were first published but they remain peculiarly documents of the 1920s and in a sense the high points of Barton's career.

Barton, of course, continued with his agency and his writing. He was elected to Congress from Manhattan's East Side "silk-stocking" district in 1937 and easily re-elected in 1938. Earning a considerable reputation, among reporters at least, for his ability and service in the House, he was a vigorous opponent of Franklin Roosevelt's New Deal. He lost a bid for the Senate in 1940 and retired from politics—only after the President borrowed something from Barton's book with a little sloganeering of his own. His jocular condemnation of three outstanding GOP House critics with the repeated phrase "Martin, Barton, and Fish" delighted his audience and gave Bruce Barton still another claim to national fame.

But it is fair to say that the major impact of Barton's life and ideas rests in the 1920s. Somehow his special vision of the world served these pre-Depression years in a special way. Barton's optimism, his defense of business, and especially his profound sense of the importance of communications, of techniques of persuasion, of the significant role played by salesmanship and advertising in the new order of things served this period most particularly. Of no less service to the '20s was his basic and old-fashioned evangelicalism, which he carried with him from the 19th century and which was transformed in a way that coincided with the needs of millions of middle-class Americans living in a time of clashing values and sharp institutional change. Much of Barton, of course, today seems camp, unsophisticated, self-serving, unreal. We know that most of his ardent beliefs were being attacked or mocked even during the period in which he wrote. Yet Barton tried to accept the new order as well as redefine older values without abandoning what he deemed best in the latter— ideals of self-development and individual human dignity in an era of mass technology, mass organization, mass society. He tried to redefine Christianity and make it again a potent moral force.

Barton's salesman as hero replaced William Graham Sumner's savings-bank depositor as hero for the conservative sons of American puritan ministers— much like one age of social order was in effect replacing another. At a time in which the values of a producer society dominated, Sumner, the Yale sociologist, could claim that the man who saved his money and practiced self-denial was the hero of civilization; in an age of increasing consumer orientation stressing sales and spending and joy rather than self-denial, Barton, the advertising man, glorified the salesman-businessman. The type, of course, was subject to Sinclair Lewis' bitter satire at almost the instant Barton was creating him. Later, by 1935, novelist Thornton Wilder would present his extraordinary study of both modern salesmanship and modern Protestantism in *Heaven's My Destination*. And during the 1940s and 1950s the images of the salesman that emerged from works like Eugene O'Neill's *The Iceman Cometh* and Arthur Miller's *Death of a Salesman* have the appearance of tragedy and perhaps even symbolize the whole tragedy of American life. Only in the mid-60s, with the Maysles brothers' documentary film *Salesman,* does the salesman image evoke neither heroism nor tragedy; rather pathos and perhaps a touch of comedy. But these are other times.

To return to the 1920s, however, it is apparent that we will not understand this decade until we understand Bruce Barton's life and contribution to it—or better yet, why so many Americans responded to Barton's message in quite the way they did. A successful salesman best served the world, Barton firmly believed, and in the 1920s he was perhaps the best salesman of all. A secular piety and a new priesthood. Preacher's sons might indeed rule the world.

HENRY FORD

By the time of Henry Ford's death in 1947, at least one of the crucial ideas in Bruce Barton's life and work—the proposition that business was service— was firmly fixed in American thought. Notwithstanding depression and world war, the idea of business success had also become sharply identified with the business of being American. Maybe Calvin Coolidge had said it crudely in the 1920s, but the overwhelming majority of the public opinion makers in 1947 seemed to agree: the business of America *was* business. This identification was so complete that Ford himself as well as his achievements seemed, as the *New York Times* declared, the very "embodiment of America in an era of industrial revolution." Yet Ford's career had been made possible *because* of the American system itself; he was the product of our "free enterprise" way while also serving as the living symbol of its achievement and success.

This account of the relationship between Ford and America produced a series of complex intellectual problems. First, the portrait of Ford was that of a simple man who sought neither a vast fortune nor luxuries, whose constant concern was for "the great multitude," for the "common man." Second, his great accomplishments, possible "only in America," were ultimately based on a "single-minded devotion to fundamentals as he saw them: hard work, the simple virtues, self-reliance, the good earth. He profited by providing what was new, but he also treasured that which was bygone." None of this enables us to come to grips with the essentially radical if not revolutionary consequences of Ford's achievement. Nor do we necessarily understand why, even outside America and indeed in the very heart of socialist Europe, Ford and his system—*fordismus,* the Europeans often called it—was hailed in the 1920s as a major contribution to the twentieth-century revolution by Marxists as imposing as Vladimir Lenin. Indeed, it was not at all unusual to find Ford's portrait hanging alongside that of Lenin in Soviet factories. (Nor was Ford himself unappreciative of the achievement of Soviet engineers and factories.) Ford's favorite authors may have been Horatio Alger and Ralph Waldo Emerson; he may have repeatedly quoted homilies from the McGuffy *Readers,* which appear to be his only source of formal education, but he was nonetheless considered a major architect of the new social order that came into being during the first two decades of the twentieth century and must be understood if we are to grasp the nature of the 1920s.

Biography, then, includes both the subject's achievements and the way these provide for continuity and/or change in society. It also tells us, by the use some elements in society make of a man's life, something about that society as well. The Ford as Horatio Alger hero—simple mechanic to industrial giant; the Ford as living evidence of the success and meaning of the American way; the Ford as villainous autocrat, brutally exemplifying the worst features of class warfare; the Ford as genius whose wisdom gives him the right if not the responsibility to speak with authority on all human and social problems; the Ford as revolutionary who remade the modern world in his own vision—the "legends" of Henry Ford are in many ways as significant to an understanding of history as is any study of the "true" achievements of a life's work, properly assessed.

Ford was 57 years old in 1920 (Bruce Barton was 34, and Babe Ruth 25). The decade saw the culmination of his major work and witnessed even the beginning of the decline of the system he had dreamed and schemed to create. Like Barton, he was a man with a mission and the story of that mission and what happened to it in the 1920s dominates this discussion. Roger Burlingame has insisted "It is hard to deny that Henry Ford was ridden by two obsessions: mechanical perfection and the 'common man.'" Those obsessions, the way they often conflicted and the attempts to achieve some kind of effective balance between them, is important here. They are explored not only because such an approach helps us to understand more fully the life of Ford himself but because in a profound sense their story is the central theme of our century, a theme that reached a peak of sorts in the 1920s.

Henry Ford did not worship his father. William Ford was a prosperous farmer of pioneer Scots-Irish stock, well established on a largely self-sufficient and profitable farm near Dearborn, Michigan, when Henry was born in July 1863. The farm had its own saw mill and grist mill and machinery for making homespun of wool that was sheared from William Ford's own sheep. There were, of course, many chores for a farm boy, but Henry from earliest childhood seemed to loathe such work. From the outset however, he seemed attracted to and useful in dealing with the machinery on the place. By all local accounts, he had a special mechanical aptitude and a kind of intuitive mechanical logic. At an early age, for instance, he developed a passion for timepieces and spent considerable time fixing things; that is, "tinkering"— a fine old Yankee tradition. Mechanization even in the years of Henry's boyhood, had become important to midwest farm life especially in more prosperous regions.

Significant, too, was the increasing industrialization occurring around the Ford farm in Wayne County. But the boy's fascination with the machine and with mechanics did not please his father who not only disliked the new industrial and urbanized world growing up around him but also had other needs for the boy's labor. At 16 arguments between the two proved too much: Ford's dislike of farming, his disagreements with his father, and the positive attraction of work in a machine shop led him to Detroit. It was around this time, Ford himself tells us, that his dream of making something in quantity without reduction in quality began to take hold of his imagination.

Evidence indicates not only little formal education in Henry Ford's life, but also almost no use at all of books; further, there seems to be no sense of any religious training or commitment. Even before Ford left home for the first time in 1879, and though he was unaware of it, George Selden had already applied for his celebrated patent for a gasoline-motored car. (It would later play a significant role in the development of Ford's company.) Clearly, then, people— both in the United States and abroad—were responding to the possibilities inherent in new sources of energy. Ford himself experimented with steam engines, before he began to study the internal-combustion engine. But from a very early age his commitment was to engines and to production in quantity, not to the manufacture of luxury items for the few.

Ford did return to the farm for a period. His father, hoping to give him a worthwhile occupation that would provide independence and livelihood, bequeathed 40 acres of timberland to Henry. Ford used the opportunity to get married, to build himself a house, as well as a machine shop—and to avoid any farming whatsoever! By 1891 he had left the rural homestead for good— for a position as an engineer with the Edison Illuminating Company. He advanced rapidly and became chief engineer. In his spare time he worked at home on a small motor-driven vehicle of his own design. By 1893 the Duryea brothers successfully had demonstrated the first American gasoline automobile. Two years later, a meeting with Thomas A. Edison, perhaps Ford's only hero, encouraged him to continue work on his engine. By 1896 he had demonstrated his own first car; by 1899 the Company asked him to choose between his hobby and his job. Ford made his decision: a full dedication of his future to the automobile.

Detroit was taking young Ford seriously as a builder of automobiles and the nation as a whole was increasingly fascinated by the possibilities of the "horseless carriage." Yet Ford's first corporate venture, the Detroit Automobile Company was short-lived; within a year a new firm had been formed, the Henry Ford Automobile Company. But it, too, did not survive. Such detail is significant only because it documents Ford's intense difficulties in working under conditions in which he lacked complete control, and he vowed never again to be in a position where others could give him orders. Meanwhile, between 1899 and 1902, Ford had used his time well. He was becoming famous. He knew that one of the central propositions of the new age was self-advertisement and publicity, and that car speed was the way to it in the automobile business. Ford himself did not believe that high speed added to a car's value, but he was aware that breaking speed records made one a celebrity in the social world at large. Furthermore, such records cornered the attention of the rich and, notwithstanding his growing dream, they alone could afford this new toy—expensive as such handmade objects inevitably had to be. And when Ford began to win races at fashionable tracks such as that at Grosse Pointe, Michigan—at one event he reached the speed of 70 miles an hour—international publicity came to him. Finally, the famous driver Barney Oldfield broke all records at the Grosse Pointe course in the "999," a car Ford had built.

By 1903 the Ford Motor Company was a reality. Incorporated with basic capital investment of only $28,000 provided by a Detroit coal dealer (most of that in the form of shop, machinery, patents, contracts), the company managed to assemble an extraordinary group of businessmen, engineers, etc. Within five years it had become one of the leading automobile manufacturers. There was little to distinguish the company's product. Ransome E. Olds had already pioneered in producing inexpensive cars. "Mass production" methods were available to all manufacturers. But, as Roger Burlingame tells us, the automobile of 1903 was still in an early experimental stage:

> no detail of engine or transmission was settled, no design of any part frozen; there was no standardization of tools or processes, and it was not until four years later that true interchangeability of parts even among supposedly identical cars made in a single factory was demonstrated. . . . In 1903 there were more than 25 American manufacturers of passenger cars and, with the exception of Olds, no manufacturer sold more than a few hundred cars each year. The automobile, therefore, was for the most part a strictly handmade article.

Meanwhile, the famous public fancy was increasingly captured by the possibilities of the automobile. There was clearly a rising demand although obviously most cars remained too expensive for the wide and hungering middle-class market. Woodrow Wilson in fact feared the motorcar mania because, he suggested in 1906, the automobile might very well bring socialism to America by inciting the poor to envy the rich!

In 1907, against "sound" advice, Ford announced his mission and his dream:

> I will build a motor car for the great multitude. It will be large enough for the family but small enough for the individual to run and care for. It will be constructed of the best materials, by the best men to be hired, after the simplest designs that modern engineering can devise. But it will be so low in price that no man making a good salary will be unable to own one—and enjoy with his family the blessing of hours of pleasure in God's great open spaces.

From the vantage point of the time it was issued, this extraordinarily simple statement was breathtaking in its implications. It is, in fact, a prediction of a new social order, an introduction to the world that was to be in the 1920s. It had enormous significance for the individual, the family, the mass society—and perhaps even in a sense proposed a serious redefinition of each. It hinted at a new definition of work and of production. It projected the likelihood of a new lifestyle. It implied a new kind of possible egalitarianism unheard of in the

world's history—and it did all of this not in the name of needs, basic requirements of life, but in terms of possible pleasure: here, indeed, was a consumer
vision of the world.

The creation of the Model T—the Tin Lizzie or the flivver as "she" was also
called—is the climax of the story, the final convergence of Ford and history. It
called for a series of key decisions, each Ford's fundamental responsibility no
matter where the original idea came from. First, there was the matter of the
huge new plant covering over 65 acres at Highland Park and the start of a
major effort to cut back on dividends to stockholders, to plow some of the
profits into new production. Second, there was the decision to make one car
and only one car: "The way to make automobiles is to make one automobile
like another automobile, to make them all alike, to make them come from the
factory just alike—just like one pin is like another pin when it comes from
the pin factory." In this decision, of course, Ford simply followed the well-
established tradition of mass production as developed in the United States but
never applied to the automobile industry. It meant the search for a car design
suitable for mass use rather than one simply for cheap manufacture. Third,
there was a need for low-cost production techniques. It resulted in the introduction of the famous moving assembly line, which involved an enormous
financial commitment in terms of tools. The idea of continuous movement
seemed simple enough and it rested on two seemingly simple principles:
(1) the work must be brought to the worker and not the worker to the work,
and (2) the work must be brought waist high so no worker would have to
stoop. Taking almost *seven* years to perfect, the system at Highland Park was an
established fact by 1914 and the production revolution had been wrought.
Men and machine, through the central conveyor belt, had been in effect
merged into one gigantic machine. It made possible a dramatic reduction in
the time required to produce a car. By 1920 one completed Model T rolled
off the line every minute; by 1925 one every ten seconds. Production rose
from 39,640 in 1911 to 740,770 in 1917. In 1920 every other car in the world
was a Model T Ford.

By the early 1920s Ford commanded over 60 percent of the American output. Never before had such a complex mechanical process been devised or
such production been possible. The achievement required a spectacular degree of synchronization, precision and specialization. Yet this in itself created
newer problems that led to still further revolutionary consequences. For instance, such mechanization meant that little real skill was required by any particular worker. Only the top engineers and designers had to know anything
about the total process. It suggested the possibility of an easily obtainable work
force, but it had inherent drawbacks—in the form of the sheer monotony of
the work, which led to an alarming turnover in the labor force.

With production methods already radically altered by 1914, Ford announced
yet another daring step. He proposed a new wage scheme, a kind of profit-
sharing (in advance of actual profits) in which the minimum for any class of
work would be (under certain conditions) five dollars a day. At the same time,
he reduced the working day from nine to eight hours. The key fact here was

that in *no* sense was pay tied into productivity. There were conditions attached to the minimum-pay stipulation: certain minimum standards of conduct and behavior as outlined by the company; that is, standards by which the company judged men to be "good workers." Ford, in effect, doubled the wages of those "who could pass his sociology examination on the clean and wholesome life," stated John R. Commons, who reported on the operation of Ford's plan with considerable enthusiasm. Not only did the resultant stable work force please Ford, but he was able to show an increase in profits as well. And, as he was well aware, he had also made every workman a potential customer.

There was still one more remaining piece in the mosaic of a new order of work and life, production and consumption. Ford established a "Sociological Department" (later called the "Education Department") initially under the direction of an Episcopal minister. Its aim was paternalistic: to teach Ford's workers how to live the exemplary life, how to budget their new-found high wages, to encourage them to refrain from liquor or tobacco, to provide elemental lessons in hygiene and home management, to suggest steps helpful in the "Americanization" of the huge numbers of foreign-born in the company's work force. Under pressure from those who opposed such paternalism and charged Ford with spying or a special kind of tyranny, the scheme was eventually given up. But it was in effect replaced by the company's extraordinary trade school with perhaps more lasting effects. Nonetheless, it is important to see the social aspects of Ford's thinking about his world and to see how the whole dream finally produced a totally new order, the object of Ford's mission and dream, whether or not he fully realized it.

By the 1920s, then, Ford and his new system were being widely hailed as the American System. The miracles he had wrought in production and consumption made his name synonymous with American success. A national figure, his advice sought on all kinds of issues, Ford began to yield to pressures to go beyond the world of automobile manufacture. With war raging in Europe, he sailed off in 1915 on his famous and much maligned "peace ship," a venture in personal diplomacy by which he hoped to dramatize the crusade for peace. In 1918, at the urging of Woodrow Wilson, he ran for the Senate in Michigan and lost in a close contest in which voter fraud was later established. Ford's writings grew more voluminous on many subjects; he owned his own newspaper, the *Dearborn Independent* in which he conducted "his own" column (it was obvious that he increasingly relied on ghost-writers for much of his published work, although this dependence, of course, did not relieve him of responsibility for what was said in his name). The blatant anti-Semitic material published in the paper, for example, was one of the worst mistakes of his career. It cost him countless followers, and threatened him with court action as well.

Ford's national dreams in the 1920s led him to propose the development of Muscle Shoals (site of the later T.V.A.) under his own auspices. It was a grand scheme to bring industry to the countryside, and to decentralize industrial concentration while at the same time offering the advantages of industrial life to isolated rural areas. George Norris and others in the Senate blocked this private takeover. Ford continued to remain a much sought-after man politically. There was even talk of his running for the presidency in 1924, but he finally decided against encouraging such a move.

Meanwhile, in Ford's immediate world, potential disaster turned almost literally to gold. He had lost a stockholders' suit to compel the payment of special dividends. Company stockholders were more and more frightened by his apparent lack of interest in profits; the "socialism" of his Five-Dollar-a-Day wage scheme and the Sociology Department; the idea of profit-sharing; and the projected society of the common man. Ford was now determined to obtain complete control to carry out his plans. Taking a daring chance, he bought out all the stockholders. But he hated banks and bankers, and refused to borrow from them to achieve his goal of complete family ownership (something unique for an industrial corporation of that size and wealth). To obtain increased operating capital, he put a squeeze play on Ford dealerships. He pushed through a production speed-up, forced cars on unwilling dealers, threatened franchise losses if they didn't pay for cars, ordered or not, and forced them to go to *their* banks, leaving Ford free and clear and, finally in the 1920s, his own master.

The 1920s initially seemed to bring increased growth; Ford's organization weathered the 1921 depression better than any other company in the industry. Meanwhile, he continued his struggle for full integration in production. He sought to make his enterprise completely self-sufficient, acquiring raw materials and methods of transportation to achieve an even flow of raw materials into the processes of production and then an even flow of finished goods coming off the production line—a kind of universal and unceasing procession of the universal car, the Model T.

Ford was unable to create the final realization of his vision either on the technological side (with the system of complete integration) or the social or human side (with the reshaping of human lives by means of the Sociological Department) any more than he had been able to transcend Highland Park and later River Rouge. The wider regional or national dreams remained unfulfilled. But the impact of Ford's revolutionary mission continued to unfold in the United States and through the rest of the world. *Fordismus* had in fact created a 1920s different from what the decade would have been without it. Nevertheless, other forces had begun to threaten the basic assumptions on which Ford's radical revision of things had been partly based.

In 1927 the Ford Motor Company made its crucial decision to end production of the great Tin Lizzie, the Model T, and begin work on the replacement Model A. Ford had perhaps belatedly learned a fundamental fact about the new and affluent mass society he had done so much to shape if not to create: price and efficiency alone would not dictate consumer choice. Many of his competitors already knew as much. This new world of mass consumption was also a new world of mass communications in which national advertising and newer forms of national media (radio, film, the new journalism) helped play upon human needs and desires, hopes and fears. Ford was not familiar with the world of Bruce Barton; he did not sense the need for individual and even private fulfillment; he had not perceived that the common man did not want to *feel* common; mechanical perfection, although often desirable, was not enough.

Ironically, of course, it was profits (or the lack of them) that forced Ford's move. He himself was clearly uninterested in simply making money for its own sake; his whole career is a testament to that observation; his own simple and sometimes austere way of life are sufficient evidence. But the Company did exist as part of a capitalist order and survival meant coming to grips with competition—no matter how much Ford might wish to rely on internal strengths and isolate himself from external dangers, and no matter how "false" for him were the values that led to rejection of the cheap, ugly, durable, efficient, simple, and black Model T. Having in a sense created the 1920s, he failed to see what else had also been created.

The retreat of 1927—with the decision to end the Model T—was a fateful one. Except for some of the production miracles he contributed to during World War II, Ford's life was increasingly given over to a bitter series of struggles—within management and with labor, the latter often being bloody affairs. The seemingly progressive Henry Ford of 1907 to 1927 seemed unable to understand the world of the 1930s. The Ford of the Five-Dollar-a-Day and the Sociological Department could not believe that workers really wanted unions and that strikes could ever achieve a real purpose.

Even in terms of the day-to-day operation of the business Ford could admit in 1933 that the new plant at River Rouge "is so big that it isn't any fun any more." Increasingly (again, ironically for the man who "made" the twentieth century) he continued to turn to the past; new interest in rediscovered folk dancing; republication of McGuffy *Readers;* historical collecting for his special museum or for Greenfield Village, which was a kind of sentimental reconstruction of his own past, that past that he had run away from so many years ago. We face a strange portrait: the man who invented the future now carefully rediscovering the past.

Was there an answer to the fundamental problem his life so startlingly posed? Could the ideals projected by the phrases "mechanical perfection" and "common man" ever really be reconciled? Would even a totalitarian regime be able to achieve the perfect reconciliation? Ford tried and we have seen the outcome in the America of the 1920s. Yet the question continues to haunt us—partly because of how far Ford went, because we are still feeling the consequences of that accomplishment, because we still respond to the experiences of the 1920s with a continued sense of hope and fear.

BABE RUTH

When George Herman Ruth, Jr., died in 1947, the *New York Times* devoted more than two of its large eight-column pages to him. While each column clearly supplemented the other, they were vastly different in tone and method of presentation. The headline on the first read:

> Ruth, Baseball's Great Star and Idol of Children, Had a Career Both Dramatic and Bizarre/World-Wide Fame Won on Diamond/Even in Lands Where Game is Unknown, Baseball's Star Player Was Admired

There followed a traditional and detailed obituary, rich in sentiment of recalled moments of sorrow and joy as well as prosaic biographical fact, with strenuous effort to recount both significant achievements and recapture an extraordinary personality. The second headline presented something else:

> Ruth Set Fifty-Four Major League Records and Ten Additional Marks in American Circuit/Slugger Starred in 10 World Series/Ruth Set Major League Homer Mark on Total of 714—Hit over 40 Eleven Seasons/Had Most Walks in 1923/All-Time Batting Great also Struck Out Most Times in Career Lasting 22 Years

The page itself had no prose story. It was simply a serial listing of all kinds of records, a careful selection of complete box scores of games important in Ruth's career, a carefully outlined and specially-headed box that listed his yearly salary from the first days in Baltimore ($600) in 1914 to the final year at Brooklyn ($15,000), for a lifetime total of $925,900.

In these two descriptions of the career of one of the great sports heroes of the 1920s (so often called "The Golden Age of American Sports"), it is perhaps possible to see two aspects of the enormous appeal spectator sports held for this decade. The mechanization of life generally, when combined with the mounting effort to rationalize all aspects of man's activities produced a particular middle-class delight in what could be measured and counted. (How fitting, then, were statistics on the "home run," with both numbers hit and distances travelled by the ball.) Americans could delight in the data that Ruth and other players provided. Athletic records provided a means of measuring achievement—success—in sport as such statistics did in other aspects of the mechanized and rationalized life. Salary figures most especially also assisted in judging success.

But no matter how fascinated a society may be with this mechanized aspect of the life that its athletes lead (and naturally transfer to the games they play and watch), it apparently was not enough. "Star," "Idol," "Dramatic," "Bizarre," were words featured in Ruth's official obituary, suggesting the public demands something more. Perhaps in an increasingly mechanized world more was called for. Grantland Rice, the sports writer, once wrote this about the great sports figures like Ruth:

> they had something more than mere skill or competitive ability. They also had in record quality and quantity that indescribable asset known as color, personality, crowd appeal, or whatever you may care to call it.

And if our sports mirror other aspects of our lives in a significant way, it might not be inappropriate to propose that what Rice suggests about sports figures was the lesson Ford had bitterly learned by 1927 when he discovered that his "common man" was no longer willing to settle for record-book cheapness, mechanical efficiency, and the like. People, he discovered, also wanted "style" (a favorite subject of Henry's son Edsel with whom old Henry constantly fought) in their cars; that is, "color, personality, crowd appeal."

Also in 1927, another major American corporation was enjoying huge success. Col. Jacob Ruppert's New York Yankees was the best baseball team in the world; there are those who claim it was the greatest baseball team of all time. Ruth hit 60 home runs that season, Lou Gehrig drove in 175 runs, the Yankees won the pennant by 19 games and swept the World Series against the Pittsburgh Pirates in four straight games. Babe Ruth earned $70,000 in 1927 for simply playing under contract with the Colonel. And Ruth was worth every penny of it to Ruppert's corporation that owned a gigantic stadium (often known as "The House that Ruth Built") with 70,000 seats to fill. This was big business for the Colonel and the Yankee organization—and seeing the Babe perform and produce was something big and special for the fans. It was more than a question of team loyalties, more than winning or losing the game. The *New York Times* account of one 1927 World Series game perhaps captures a little of this sentiment:

> his majesty the Babe had sent 64,000 folks in a paroxysm of glee by clubbing a screaming liner into the right field bleachers. . . . The big time came in the seventh. The Yanks had the game safely stowed away and the suspense was over . . . but the fans still stood up and demanded that Mr. Ruth get busy and do something for home and country. . . . "A homer, Babe! Give us a homer!" ran the burden of the plea, and the big fellow pulled his cap on tighter, took a reef in his belt, dug spikes into the ground and grimly faced [the pitcher]. . . . Upward and onward, gaining speed and height with every foot, the little white ball winged with terrific speed until it dashed itself against the seat of the right-field bleachers, more than a quarter of the way up the peopled slope. And now the populace had its homer and it stood up and gave the glad joyous howl that must have rang out in the Roman arena of old. . . .

This description is itself revealing evidence of another pertinent aspect of the world of George Herman Ruth, Jr., perhaps an aspect helping to "make" him into the heroic Babe he would become. The new mechanized era of mass society was also one of mass communications as well, and the media demanded suitable material for copy. A new group of reporters and writers— Ring Lardner, Grantland Rice, Haywood Broun, John Kiernan among them— were ready exploiters of achievement and personalities, anxious to expand the traditional meaning of "news" for a whole series of publications, radio broadcasts, sometimes even films, which constantly demanded copy to feed a growing number of hungry consumers of this kind of news. They invented along the way an often brilliantly different and always special kind of rhetoric and style. Their unique prose delighted readers, sold more copies, appealed to more advertising agencies with products to sell—which was done through buying space in publications or time on the radio. "The Ruth is mighty and shall prevail," Haywood Broun wrote in 1923. It is still quoted by enthusiasts of the special sports' writing prose of this golden age of sports and of sports promotion.

The "mighty Ruth" of 1923 was born among the most lowly in a poor, third-floor apartment over a saloon in the waterfront section of Baltimore, Maryland in 1895. His parents, both children of immigrants, constantly struggled with poverty in a home described as an "angry, violent, desperately poor place, tense with all the frustrations of extreme poverty and shabbiness." Ruth confessed that he hardly knew them, and the major recollections of his father seem to be those of repeated and brutal beatings. "I was a bad kid," Ruth tells us in his autobiography. Unable to take care of their seven-year-old son and describing him as "incorrigible," his parents put Ruth in St. Mary's Industrial School in Baltimore. He would remain there—with occasional returns to the parental home—until he was 19.

The story of Ruth's upbringing reads like a stereotype of Victorian childhood among the lowliest urban poor, a kind of Dickensian horror tale without any cheerful relief, without any sentimental moments of escape from nightmare. The school stressed order and discipline; it tried to educate but clearly did little in the case of Ruth: he could barely read and write. There was no privacy. And there were few if any friends for Ruth who was the object of unkind verbal abuse because of his size and shape. After leaving school, he continued to have—and to retain almost until the end of his life—the most primitive of personal habits and the crudest of manners. There is little evidence that the strict Catholicism administered at St. Mary's had any significant effect on him. Ruth's excessive and obsessive interest in gambling, sex, and drinking appear to be schoolboy products he carried throughout his life. When at home, he lived near the harsh waterfront, mixing with rough sailors and bums. In effect he was an abandoned child. "I had a rotten start," he tells us, "and it took me a long time to get my bearings." But St. Mary's appears to have been of little help in getting those "bearings" and Ruth's life story leads one to wonder whether he ever really got them. Perhaps this upbringing accounts for what appears to be his genuine fondness for the countless number of children who idolized him during his great career and for his willingness to visit children in hospitals and homes throughout these later years.

St. Mary's did try to give Ruth a vocation. He was assigned to the shirt factory to learn the tailor's trade and the assignment itself indicates that the brothers noted no special potential or skills during his many years with them. But two positive things do emerge from his life at St. Mary's. First, he appeared to learn (as Ken Sobol, his ablest biographer tells us) that his "personal crudities" became "uproarious crowd-pleasers" in the presence of an audience. This was certainly important preparation for the "colorful" personality and always willing performer Ruth was to become. He would be eager to provide "good copy" and to delight fans off the field as well as on. (The shy, educated, craftsmanlike Lou Gehrig, for example, never learned to be a showman and never earned the kind of vast following or the money that Ruth did.) But St. Mary's most important gift was not any special training but a special opportunity. Baseball was about the only recreational outlet given to the boys at St. Mary's. So it was here that Ruth learned to play the game and to develop the enormous native skills, the coordination and power, that would make him the most spectacular ball player of his time.

Baseball had been a successful professional activity since the 1870s, and by 1903 it had become sufficiently developed and well organized to create the beginnings of a mass audience and the source of significant careers for many young men. For Ruth—a man without learning, traditional skills, or alternate route—it offered a miraculous escape from the treadmill of poverty. Baseball could provide him with effective social mobility. Ruth was certainly not the first nor the last of the children of fairly recent immigration and urban poverty to find their way to national status and success. But in many ways his career was among the most spectacular. One of St. Mary's Brothers recommended Ruth to the owner of the Baltimore club and he signed his first professional contract in 1914. That same year his contract was sold for $2,900 to the *Boston Red Sox* and with that organization he soon matured into a pitcher of rare ability.

While at Boston, Ruth also began to show remarkable prowess as a hitter. Baseball fans started to talk of his home runs and by 1919 he was more often in the outfield than on the pitching mound. The following year was a turning point in both Ruth's career and in the game itself. The Yankees purchased his contract for $100,000 and also guaranteed the $350,000 mortgage in the financially shaky Red Sox stadium. It was a record sum—but the Babe delivered with a record number of home runs and enthusiastic fan response. The winter of 1920–21, however, produced a scandal that rocked the entire structure of professional baseball. Gamblers had managed to buy the services of several members of the Chicago White Sox (subsequently labeled "Black Sox") to "throw" the 1919 World Series. The owners then reorganized baseball's business structure and appointed a stern federal judge, James Kenesaw Mountain Landis, as new high commissioner with unlimited power to assure the sanctity of the sport, though they still worried whether this reform would be enough, whether the fans would return. Many historians of the game attribute Ruth's brilliant performance during the following season´as the most important factor in reviving spectator enthusiasm. Nine to ten million fans in the 1920s annually paid to see major league baseball.

By the end of the 1921 season (again to quote Sobol) more words were written about Ruth "than had ever been devoted to any other athlete in any single year. More people had watched him play than any other player. And more citizens of America, young and old, knew his name and could even recognize his homely round face than ever heard of Ty Cobb or John J. McGraw." Sports writers vied with one another to provide him with appropriate nicknames ("Sultan of Swat") but somehow he always remained "Babe" or "Bambino" (a change from "Nigger-Lips" he was often called at St. Mary's). He was the nation's great boy-child and Americans loved their big boy who often did so many childish things.

Whatever his achievements on the field, his growing contributions to the record books, the Babe also delighted millions of his countrymen by the sheer bigness of his affable personality and even by his awesome inability to curb his overwhelming appetites. Most Americans seemed to tolerate at least some of the indulgences of their big boy. No Ford or Barton, Ruth enjoyed spending money as well as earning it. An incorrigible gambler, and for large sums, he never seemed concerned about winning or losing. He loved expensive and fancy clothes. His interest in sex seemed limitless, and he frequented the better brothels even while in training or on tour with the ball club. His gluttony became equally legendary; he often overate and overdrank to the point of actual and severe physical illness. Like so many celebrities in our modern mechanized age, Ruth's frequent illness, physical collapse, even hospitalization became almost routine. The Babe's most publicized collapse and hospitalization occurred during spring training in 1925, and the public apparently accepted the official explanation that his illness was the result of influenza and indigestion; the real cause, it appears, was a serious case of syphilis. A much concerned public watched intensely for reports of Ruth's condition. One well-known sports writer called it "the stomach ache heard round the world."

Ruth was a heroic producer in the mechanized world of play. He was also an ideal hero for the world of consumption. Americans enjoyed the Babe's excess; they took comfort in the life of apparently enormous pleasures that Ruth enjoyed. Seldom if ever (even in this age of the rising popularity of Freudian thought) did they seem aware of what might exist behind this pattern of excess and illness. "Babe Ruth," Bill McGeehan said in 1925, "is our national exaggeration. . . . He has lightened the cares of the world and kept us from becoming overserious by his sheer exuberance."

Ruth found a way of making all of this pay; he made himself into a marketable product. In 1921 he hired an agent—or perhaps Christy Walsh snared Ruth. Walsh saw the vast possibilities in this extraordinary era of communications. He originally developed a ghostwriting syndicate especially in the sports field: writers who would sell articles and books under the name of a contracted sports figure. Increasingly the ghostwriter was becoming important in the public relations field. More and more distinguished Americans who wished to be heard or read (like Henry Ford), or whom the public would like hearing from (like Babe Ruth), contracted with professional writers to do the job. Soon there was no field without such literary talent and the number and range of such ventures increased markedly in the 1920s. Walsh provided Ruth with a great deal more than ghostwriting: as agent he worked out product endorsements for advertising; he solicited special assignments in movies (Ruth made a few but was never very successful in this field); he arranged and booked barnstorming tours during the off-season or even tours on the vaudeville circuits. In 1926, for example, Ruth played 12 weeks in vaudeville—in effect just appearing on stage so that fans in dozens of small towns could see their hero close up—for over $8,000 a week. This sum was considerably more than many notable show business people with special talents for entertaining were earning. Barnstorming around the country in 1927 and playing with hastily arranged teams of local citizens, Ruth added over $30,000 to his already sizeable income. Press agent activity was hardly new; neither was Walsh's. He served as a kind of business manager arranging investments, bank accounts, and the like in an effort to keep Ruth from squandering all his money. But what he did for Ruth added in a special 1920s way to the ballyhoo that promoted a professional athlete into a celebrity of ever exaggerated proportions.

The year 1925 marked a low point in Babe Ruth's career and few believed he would recover. His "stomach ache heard round the world" was followed later the same season by failures to maintain training and to perform effectively. Manager Miller Huggins, in exasperation, fined him $5,000 for "misconduct off the ball field," and his decision was upheld by Col. Jacob Ruppert, the Yankee owner. Ruth, with his own special arrogance, had originally taken the whole thing as a joke but now began to pay greater attention to his work, the management of his affairs, and possibly even to his image. His exceptional comeback in the 1926 season became, according to Sobol, a "symbol of continuity." Ruth was 30 and no longer a boy; he had suffered a kind of depression and the fact that he could recover gave the whole country a sense of hope. Increasingly, the writers waxed sentimental over him and his generosity to the kids. (Ruth himself may have begun to believe the new image the writers had projected of him; he even began to color his days at St. Mary's in terms of kindnesses done him by some of the Brothers.) Increasingly, the press transformed him into an older, less boyish "idol of the American boy." They began to forget the excesses and the crudities. His relationship with Mrs. Claire Hodgson many have also contributed to the change in his life. He married her in 1929 after the death of his estranged first wife. He paid greater attention to training, developing a shrewder interest in investments. The new Mrs. Ruth provided structure and order in his life; a tighter rein and necessary stability. It is difficult to avoid speculating on whether she was not providing as well the kind of love that Ruth never received from his mother so long ago in Baltimore.

But the Bambino of the 1930s and 1940s—the sentimentalized and reformed "idol" of American youth—is not the hero of the 1920s. Historian William E. Leuchtenberg may be somewhat unkind in describing him in 1934 as "a pathetic figure, tightly corseted, a cruel lampoon of his former greatness" when he took off his Yankee uniform for the last time. But Ruth by now was out of place and out of time. He might be transformed into a sentimental figure by sentimental writers. Perhaps the times called for that kind of hero. But for the 1920s he was the perfect creation for an increasingly mechanized world that still hungered as well for the extraordinary personality, that tired merely of the Model T automobiles and yet was also appreciative of their virtues—wanting only something more, something bigger than life.

What kind of personality did Ruth bring to the era he so aptly characterized? And what was the price to himself and to the kind of society that enjoyed and admired "our national exaggeration?" What does it say about our values and his values, about the tragic set of conditions and circumstances that may lurk beneath the surface of his life and as well as of the life of his nation in the 1920s?

One series of probing questions, at least, is suggested in a passage from the work of a great Dutch historian who made a significant effort to come to an understanding of American history and especially the current American culture during the First World War. He is writing, in effect, about the onset of the 1920s and is considering what will follow. I do not know whether or not he saw Ruth during his own visit to this country during the Babe's comeback year (1926) but he most certainly must have heard about him. It would be interesting to listen to him discuss this view with special reference to Ruth's career. Perhaps we can do it for him:

> One of the preeminent elements of modern civilization is sport, in which intellectual and physical culture meet. In it too mechanization seems to attain the opposite of its purposes. Gregarious modern man tries to save his individualism, as it were, in sport. But sport is not just the strictly physical development of skills and strength; it is also the giving of form, the stylizing of the very feeling of youth, strength, and life, a spiritual value of enormous weight. Play is culture. Play can pass over into art and rite, as in the dance and in sacred stage presentations. Play is rhythm and struggle. The competitive ideal itself is a cultural value of high importance. Play also means organization. But now, as a result of the modern capacity for very far-reaching organization and the possibilities created by modern transportation, an element of mechanization enters sport. In the immense sport organizations like those of football and baseball, we see free youthful forces and courage reduced to normality and uniformity in the service of the machinery of rules of play and the competitive system. If we compare the tense athlete in his competitive harness with the pioneer hunter and the Indian fighter, then the loss of true personality is obvious.
>
> Johan Huizinga
> *America*

QUESTIONS FOR DISCUSSION

1. What was Bruce Barton's message to Americans of the 1920s? Why did they respond so positively?

2. In what ways was Henry Ford a man of the future? In what ways did he remain wedded to the past?

3. "What kind of personality did Ruth bring to the era he so aptly characterized?"

4. In what ways do the lives of these three men highlight the transformative developments in American social, economic, and cultural life that were occurring in the 1920s?

CAROLINE BIRD

The Superfluous People of the Great Depression

More than a half century has passed since this nation was hurled into the Great Depression of the 1930s. Time, as the saying goes, heals all wounds, but not—as Caroline Bird shows us in the following selection—without leaving scars.

While the underlying causes stretched back much further, the Depression began in the fall of 1929 with a steady and rapid decline in stock prices. Following quickly on the collapse of the market came the overall economic depression. By 1932, when Franklin Delano Roosevelt began his campaign for the presidency, the median income was one-half what it had been, construction spending one-sixth, and one out of every four Americans was unemployed.

The Great Depression of the 1930s was the source of countless human tragedies. Unemployment can be measured in statistics, but statistics alone cannot describe the suffering that accompanies it. In this selection from her book, The Invisible Scar, *Caroline Bird shows us precisely how and why the massive, prolonged unemployment of the 1930s robbed individuals not only of their jobs, but of their self-respect, their dignity, their identity, and, in some cases, their lives.*

A few years ago a well-paid staff specialist retired early from a corporation famous for its lush fringe benefits so that he and his wife could paint, travel, and enjoy their country home. Almost at once, his wife began worrying about money. Within six months, she recognized the irrationality of her distress and consulted a psychiatrist. With his help she discovered that as a little girl she

Caroline Bird, a journalist and historian, is the author of a number of books on twentieth century American life. The following selection has been excerpted from her social history of the Depression years, *The Invisible Scar.*

Reprinted from *The Invisible Scar* by Caroline Bird (David McKay Company, 1966), pp. 41–69. Copyright © 1966 by Caroline Bird. Reprinted by permission of Caroline Bird.

had learned that whenever her adored father stayed at home to play with her during the day, it meant that he was out of work, and disaster quickly followed. The psychiatrist suggested that the husband offer his services to a nonprofit organization. As soon as he began leaving the house at the same time every morning, the wife rapidly recovered.

This could have happened only in America. Americans not only say they would continue working if sudden riches struck them, they really do it. One of the reasons is that most American men and women over 50 spent their youth running away from a fate that, but for the grace of God, could have happened to almost anyone.

The image was specific and graphic: a bent, graying man turning away from a factory gate that bore the sign "No Help Wanted Today."

Cartoonists used the figure so often that all the misery of unemployment came to be symbolized in the sagging shoulder line of a man shuffling aimlessly away from the reader, carrying the bad news back to his wife and children.

As conservatives repeated all through the Depression, the poor we have always had with us. But all along there had been more of them than we realized. After the Crash we discovered how many, and how poor they were, because for the first time the poor were also idle and they became conspicuous. They were poor, not because they did the lowest-paid and hardest work, but because they were of no use. In non-Catholic America they did not even provide the rich with an opportunity to practice the Christian virtue of charity. They were superfluous people.

What happens to people when they are not needed? What happens to a society loaded with superfluous people? Any serious study of the impact of mass unemployment must begin with the Depression. Men who remember the Depression personally look back to it for their answers. . . .

It is hard to realize now that so many were idle for so long. . . . In 1931, 16 percent of the people who wanted to work could not find jobs, and the rate kept straight on up to 25 percent in 1933. In 1937, there was "prosperity" because real income per capita had climbed back almost to 1929 levels and unemployment had broken a few decimal places below 15 percent. In 1938, however, unemployment was up again to 19 percent. In 1941, when we thought we were rearming at full blast, we rejoiced because unemployment was down to 10 percent. . . .

The Depression unemployed were not the hard-core poor alone. They were a good fat sample of people of all kinds. During the 1930s, one in every four or five persons of working age was unable to find work for long enough periods to learn how it feels to be unwanted.

It was as if the law of supply and demand was being applied to human beings. The unemployed treated themselves as a glut on the market and tried to get rid of themselves. There was something "dead" about them. There were so many superfluous people around during the Depression that it did not seem quite decent for the others to act fully alive. Careful studies showed that the unemployed moved more slowly than the employed poor, were sicker more often, more unhappy, more suicidal, more distrustful, and less self-confident. The decade in which American society was visibly loaded with superfluous people was a time of life-denying morals and manners. During the 1930s we played down sexual passion, regarded pregnancy as a disaster, treated children as burdens, and thought of food as an exercise in nutrition.

The economic waste was easy enough to see, and it was, of course, astronomical in terms of the value of goods and services the unemployed could have produced. Less calculable but more tragic was the waste of human skills. People took any kind of job they could get, regardless of training or aptitude. When the Government needed skilled war workers, a test survey in Kokomo, Indiana, disclosed that, as a result of the Depression emergency, almost half the workers in town were in the wrong jobs: a sheet-metal worker was a shipping clerk; a diemaker was running a sewage plant; a drill-press operator was a janitor, a molder was a policeman, and a barrel reamer was digging ditches.

Skilled workers laid off by factories clerked in stores, slung food across lunch counters, washed dishes, tended gas stations, wrapped packages, delivered groceries, swept out beauty parlors. So few people were able to pay for medical care that airlines were able to hire registered nurses to serve as stewardesses. At $4 a day, jury duty was a break. Construction was so hard hit that you could have an architect for an office boy if you wanted one. Many employers did not. The personnel problems of hiring people who "thought they were too good for the job" were indignantly discussed. Meanwhile, skills rusted with disuse. Unemployed stenographers hired on work relief were known to break down and cry, out of sheer nervousness, the first time they tried to take dictation on their new jobs. . . .

At a time when established farmers were being foreclosed and wheat growers talked of lighting out to the sub-Arctic brush country with a hog and a cow and a gun to kill moose, urban workers were drifting back to the country looking for something to eat. Between 1930 and 1935, a million acres went into cultivation in farms of ten acres and less. While a few may have been high-powered cash truck farms, most yielded only enough vegetables and chickens to feed a single family. Many were on land so poor that it never had been seriously farmed.

Some of the unemployed were pathetically enterprising. One relief client concealed from social workers the little income he made on the side from selling cast-off corsets salvaged from garbage dumps. People on relief actually starved themselves to save up enough money to start a little business. Five million people bought a book entitled *Think and Grow Rich,* which Dr. Napoleon Hill said he wrote while advising Franklin D. Roosevelt in the White House.

We have no way of knowing how many people borrowed on life insurance or shot their last few hundred dollars to go into business and fail, but there must have been millions. . . . At the end of the war a survey in Oakland, California, indicated that probably one man out of three had been in business for himself at some time. Turnover was high among the two million or more "firms" employing one to three people. They failed quietly and looked for jobs.

Ways were found to exploit these eager entrepreneurs. Certain oil companies encouraged the unemployed to open gas stations that boosted sales slightly for the refinery, but returned less than relief subsistence to the "owner." Millions of painfully saved dollars were wasted on gas stations that never had a chance. Beauty "schools" flourished on the unpaid labor of students. Manufacturers set women up in little front-parlor shops and got rich selling them beauty equipment for $250 down and $25 a month. Giving a wash, set, and manicure for a dollar, these amateurs could return a handsome rate of interest to the supplier who was bankrolling them. Like nurses, professional beauticians began to lobby for state licensing to limit entry into their field.

People invested their savings in "parlor" grocery stores. Between 1929 and 1939, while retail sales dropped $6 billion, nearly 400,000 *more* people were trying to make a living from little stores. Suppliers flourished meeting the demand for cash registers, but some of the little grocery-store proprietors barely sold enough to be able to replenish the stock they ate off the shelves. At a time when people were cutting their own hair, washing their own clothes, and resoling their own shoes to save money, thousands hopefully started one-chair barber shops, diaper laundries, shoeshine stands, cleaning and pressing shops, antiques shops, tearooms, and catering services. At a time when money was scarce, thousands plodded from door to door peddling books, magazines, vacuum cleaners, pressure cookers, and other nonessential consumer articles—no more efficiently than household goods were purveyed in Homer's day.

Companies increased sales at little expense by inducing the unemployed to sell on a commission basis. The harder the times, the better the talent that sales managers were able to enlist. Alfred C. Fuller reports that sales of his Fuller Brush Company "suddenly upended, like a tired freighter, and headed toward the bottom" during the prosperous closing years of the boom, but jumped from $15,000 to $50,000 in the doldrum month of August 1932 alone, and grew at the rate of a million dollars a year all through the Depression. . . .

Door-to-door salesmen of all kinds swarmed from town to town competing with local merchants for any loose change the lady of the house might have on hand. Cities tried to stop them by instituting licensing and fingerprinting. Green River, Wyoming, originated a widely adopted ordinance forbidding anyone to solicit a home without invitation. Fuller Brush fought back by offering the housewife a gift if she invited the salesman inside. Empty hotels, straining to meet boom-time mortgage payments, posted signs saying, "Patronize firms that keep salesmen on the road!"

Most of all, the unemployed eagerly exploited themselves. They took on piecework at ruinous rates. In Connecticut, a family of six worked at stringing safety pins on wires late into the night for less than $5 a week. Unemployed textile workers set up looms in their homes, reviving the evils of the early industrial revolution in England. At a time when oil and gas were forcing coal-mine operators to mechanize mines for greater efficiency or abandon them, unemployed coal miners were bootlegging coal by the most primitive and dangerous hand methods and selling it cut-rate in cities.

Bootleg coal became a big industry. In some years it accounted for 10 percent of the anthracite consumed in New York City. More than 6,500 miners made a living of sorts out of it, some hiring others for as little as 50 cents a day. Bootlegging hastened the bankruptcy of the Philadelphia & Reading Coal Company, which estimated that four million tons of coal a year were diverted from legal channels by the individual enterprisers of the mountains. The bootleggers organized an Independent Anthracite Miners Association for mutual defense and to keep each other from such dangerous practices as digging under highways. The preamble of this extraordinary organization was frank:

We must dig coal out of these mountains as a means of supplementing our measly income that we receive in the form of relief, in order to keep the wolf from our doorsteps. Knowing that the coal which is in these mountains was put there by our Creator and that this mineral wealth was stolen away from us by the greedy rich class, the coal operators and the bankers . . .

What the unemployed really wanted was a job, in spite of the clichés to the contrary, and some went to heroic lengths to find work. Job-hunting stories became Depression folklore. A persistent one was about a man in the Northwest who set a fire in order to get a job putting it out. Another was about the employment-agency head whose business was so bad that he took the first job he was asked to fill. Still another reports that a man whose "Situation Wanted" ad was put in the "Help Wanted" column by mistake drew 45 "applicants." A girl is supposed to have landed a job as a secretary by offering to cope with the flood of replies received by a man who had advertised for one.

In Detroit, men stood outside automobile plants all night to be at the head of the line when the office opened. They built bonfires to keep warm. They wrapped their feet in gunnysacks to keep them from freezing while they waited.

Untold foot-pounds of energy were spent just looking for work. In 1931, commercial employment agencies reported 5,000 applicants for every 100 job openings. The unsuccessful 4,900 simply wasted their shoe leather. This was no joke. The unemployed worried about their shoes. Jack Conroy, a miner's son, described what a hole in a shoe could mean to a man walking the streets for a job:

Maybe it starts with a little hole in the sole; and then the slush of the pavements oozes in, gumming sox and balling between your toes. Concrete whets Woolworth sox like a file, and if you turn the heel on top and tear a pasteboard innersole, it won't help much. There are the tacks too. You get to avoiding high places and curbstones because that jabs the point right into the heel. Soon the tack has calloused a furrowed hole, and you don't notice it unless you strike something unusually high or solid, or forget and walk flat-footed.

You pass a thousand shoe-shops where a tack might be bent down, but you can't pull off a shoe and ask to have *that* done—for nothing.

The picture of the retreating father, with his sagging back, goaded the un-employed to seek work as relentlessly as the starving picked over garbage dumps for food, but it really spoke to everybody. The cartoonist's national emblem of unemployment conveyed a profound uneasiness, a malaise that getting a job could not cure. The image haunted millions who lived in fear that momentarily they might lose their jobs. It told millions of others not even to try to find work: until World War II, we never realized how many employa-ble people had never worked for pay because they had taken it for granted that the nation's economy did not want them.

"Get lost," the silent figure seemed to say, and it gave different reasons to different people. "You are too black or too Jewish or too old or the wrong sex to work here."

"Move on," it said to the newcomers. "Why don't you go back where you came from?" So many country boys got the message that there were years when more people went back to the farms than came to the cities.

"Stay home," it said to women. "Don't take a job from a man. And you'd better not have a baby, either."

And to men it said, "Keep away from women. Don't get hooked. If you can do it, keep away from your wife. You don't need children."

"Be careful," it said to everybody. "Save your money. Don't spend. Don't get your hopes up. Keep clean and sober. Don't ask for anything. Don't take any chances."

"Light out," it seemed to say to some fathers. "You're just a mouth around the house. They'll be better off without you. Drop dead." . . .

Unemployed heads of families were the certified superfluous. They . . . felt that there was something unseemly about being alive at all. They crept around the house trying to act as if they were not there. They made as few demands as possible, sexually and otherwise. They did not think they had the right to beget children. And they thought a great deal about suicide.

Men who killed themselves rather than go on relief, or so that their families could collect their insurance, were classified by sociologist Emil Durkheim as "altruistic" suicides. One of the most dramatic was Albert R. Erskine, president of the Studebaker Company, who kept announcing that the Depression was over, and paid out five times the net profit of his company in dividends in the attempt to prove that he was right. When Studebaker went bankrupt in 1933, Erskine invited his wife's family to their house so she would not be alone when he was found, wrapped a bath towel around his middle, and shot himself to death in the bathroom. Erskine's estate collected his $900,000 life insurance and paid his debts. . . .

Harvard epidemiologists Brian MacMahon and Thomas Pugh find that sui-cides go up with unemployment. Suicides rose gently all through the Twenties and passed October 1929 without a visible hump, but they rose faster in 1930,

1931, and 1932. They peaked in 1933, the year of deepest unemployment, and then fell jaggedly down. They dropped sharply in the war years, when everyone who could work was in the armed forces or on a defense job. . . .

The birthrate reflects unemployment, too. The decline was dramatic in the Depression. In some years we did not produce enough girl babies to be sure of reproducing ourselves. We came out of the Depression with nearly three million fewer babies than would have been born at 1929 rates, and if the birth rate had continued as low as it was in 1933, nearly 30 million people alive in 1965 would never have been born at all. . . .

Feminists and liberals worried . . . about getting means of birth control to the poor. . . . They pointed out that half of the births were in families on relief, or with less than $1,000 a year, and that families on relief accounted for more than their share of children. When Catholic Monsignor Ryan objected that the country really needed more consumers, liberal journalist Dorothy Dunbar Bromley retorted that it really needed fewer unemployed.

The earnest public discussions did more than help overcome scruples against using birth control. It taught people how to ask for it. Gas stations began to sell contraceptives, and soon they were offered in the Sears, Roebuck catalog. Although rich white women had a head start in adopting birth control, the poor caught up rapidly. Opinion polls reported overwhelming public sentiment for making birth control widely available.

Moralists blamed women for "selfishness" in preferring consumer goods to babies, but selfishness was not the reason for limiting families. The cliché of the times states the real reason straightforwardly: "I don't want to bring children into a world that has no use for them."

The world had less use for some, of course, than for others. This is always true, but the tragedy of a world full of superfluous people was that it could afford the irrational preferences we now outlaw as "discrimination in employment." Not only could it afford them, it actually needed them, in order to choose among the hordes who were equally qualified. Consider, for instance, what happened when a "Secretary Wanted" ad drew scores of crackerjack applicants. An employer could interview the first ten, but when he discovered that all were competent, he still had to find some reason for preferring one over the others.

Some of the reasons for discrimination were bizarre. A hospital rejected an applicant for nursing school on the ground that her crooked teeth might disturb patients. Women who hoped to teach did not dare to smoke, drink, or dress too fashionably, at least in public. One Rose Freistater was refused a permanent job teaching in New York City, for instance, because she weighed 182 pounds—too fat, the examiners said, to move quickly in a fire drill. Rose was a spunky girl. She protested to the newspapers, and the examiners gave her six months to get down to 150 pounds. When Major General John F. O'Ryan became police chief of New York City in 1934, he looked over 75 patrolmen qualified to serve as his chauffeur and decided to make his decision on the basis of height. "Some of the men who drive the cars now are too tall," he explained to reporters. "They have to bend down when they get into the cars. That does not look so good. A man should be able to get in without lowering his head."

It was more impersonal, of course, to rule out whole classes of applicants on the basis of age, sex, color, or marital status. These exclusions were so generally accepted that most people did not stop to think that they were purely arbitrary, or at least archaic, criteria for organizing industrial work, and it was not until the war brought full employment that people saw how unreasonable they really were. When people were superfluous, everyone, including the victims, tended to take the mythical disqualifications for real. In the effort to get jobs, men dyed their hair, women took off their wedding rings, Jews changed their names and their noses, and Negroes enriched the lotion manufacturers who promised to straighten their hair.

Before the full employment of World War II, there were no black faces in department stores. There were no black faces in offices. There were not even very many in that outpost of equal opportunity, the Post Office. There were "nigger jobs" and "white men's jobs," but during the Depression the distinction broke down. White men wanted the "nigger jobs," and in any case the "nigger jobs" were so vulnerable that the Negro job market was what we would now call an "early economic indicator" of downturn. The Negro newspaper in Chicago, *The Defender,* noticed the slowdown before the Crash, and for the first time in its history warned Southern Negroes to stay in the South.

The Negroes took more than their share of the Depression damage. They got it from all sides. Unions hated them because many of the Negroes in Chicago and East St. Louis had come originally as strikebreakers, but when under Communist influence unions began to admit them and force them to charge union rates, they could not get jobs at all. Low relief standards were tolerated in part at least because welfare clients were predominantly Negroes who had "never known anything better." In Chicago, for instance, four out of ten relief clients in 1939 were Negro.

White relief clients felt that equal treatment was an injustice. "It makes me boil," an unemployed white relief client told a reporter. "Where do I come in to be compared with the colored people? They have always lived like animals." In Baltimore, in 1935, *The Sun* reported it as a scandal that the Federal Government was running a work relief camp where "colored women live in screened-in cabins, possess a beautifully furnished main room for recreation and study, and have tennis courts, swings, and a croquet ground for sports." Worse yet, the women were given chicken and ice cream for Sunday dinner.

The Negroes were the most superfluous of the superfluous people and they adjusted, as did the white unemployed, by lying low. Like the rest of the unemployed, they clung desperately to anything that passed for a "place" in the world, no matter how humble. . . . Once a Negro woman quietly removed a hat she had bought at a rummage sale when she discovered that Eleanor Roosevelt was wearing one like it. The Negro professional people who should have led protests against discrimination were so scared by the Depression that even as late as 1954 they still were unable to stand up and demand compliance with the Supreme Court decision integrating the public schools. The Negro protests of the 1960s were led by Negroes who had grown up during the war when people were needed so badly that war plants and the armed forces could not afford discrimination.

Jews fared better than Negroes, but we forget how openly they were barred thirty years ago. Big law firms excluded them, or relegated them to the back room. Medical schools had a Jewish quota, which meant that a Jewish boy had to be brighter than a Christian boy to get in, reason enough for the recognized superiority of medicine as practiced in Jewish hospitals compared to that in Catholic hospitals. When the *New York Times* refused ads specifying "Christian," Jews were warned away by such phrases as "out-of-towner preferred," or "near churches." Hitler's persecution of the Jews seems to have struck a responsive cord in people looking for a scapegoat for their business troubles, particularly small retailers who complained that the Jews were unfair competition because they stayed open on Sundays.

During the Depression, a surprising number of otherwise decent people commented (in lowered voice betraying their moral uneasiness) that maybe Hitler "had something"—Jews were getting pretty aggressive in this country, too. Anti-Semitic jokes flowed freely, and many newspapers identified Jews in their columns as Jews, whether this was pertinent to the rest of the story or not, much as Southern newspapers carefully identified Negroes. Few saw the unconscious bias in the protest that "some of my best friends are Jews." Many other clichés that the ear [today] detects as bias were not identified as such when Hitler was in power. It was not until we had full employment that Jewish organizations were able to press effectively for an end to "gentlemen's agreements" and to real-estate covenants excluding Jews from clubs and summer resorts. The war and postwar demand for talent helped break down discrimination against Jewish professional and staff specialists everywhere but in the most stately executive suites.

Married women workers suffered from discrimination as much as Negroes and Jews. A surprising number of people thought the Depression could be cured if married women were sent back home and their jobs were given to men. In 1931, a majority of cities had laws against hiring married women as civil servants, and for a while even the Federal Government would not let both a husband and a wife draw Federal paychecks. The laws were repealed later on in the decade, when it turned out that sending the women home did not open up jobs for men, but deprived some households of their only means of support.

Most school systems forced a teacher to give up her job when she married. The rule had no foundation in merit or mercy. People thought men teachers would be better than women for schoolboys more than 13 years old, but there was no move to employ men. A teacher no sooner got to know her job than she was forced to choose between her job and marrying the man she loved. When he did not have a job, which was frequently the case, she was tempted to marry in secret or live with him out of wedlock. The National Association of Women Lawyers reported that teachers were marrying, then heading for

Reno to get a quickie divorce during the summer months, before they could be fired. Most of them, said the Association, intended to remarry their husbands when the men found work.

It is hard to escape the conclusion that the rule against married teachers was intended to benefit the *husband* of the teacher rather than the children or the teaching staff itself. It seems to have been one of those backhanded reasons of the heart rather than of the head, but it was based on emotional realities everyone understood. The plain truth was that unemployment hurt men much harder than women.

The hourly-paid factory and construction work most men did was more subject to layoff than the lower-paid but steadier clerical and service work performed by women. The result was that more households than would admit it were in fact supported by women. Most families simply could not—or it was thought that they could not—survive this radical reversal of roles. Then, too, wives of unemployed men fared much better than their husbands. Even when there was not a cent in the house they had an occupation. They were still in command of "their" homes. Men were displaced persons, moping around the house, interfering with the routine. Relief investigators reported more quarreling among families of the unemployed.

"Have you anybody you can send around to tell my wife you have no job to give me?" a husband asked a social worker.

"Certainly I lost my love for him," a wife told another social worker matter-of-factly. "How can you love a husband who causes you so much suffering?"

Unemployment is less damaging in Latin America, where men do not have to support a family to prove their masculinity. In the United States the threat to male pride was sensed as a threat to civilization itself. Because women were so much less vulnerable, it was easy to blame them for undermining the confidence of their men. The contemporary folklore of the sexes pictured women as aggressive. A popular notion of the time was that women were getting control of all the money and property in the country. Another notion was that women were ruining men by egging them on to make money and then withholding from them sexually, like the "Bitch Goddess" movie heroines, or castrating them emotionally, like Philip Wylie's "Mom." . . .

The Depression hurt people and maimed them permanently because it literally depressed mind and spirit. . . . During the first half of the decade the spending of recreational groups dropped to half, a third of the Grange and rural women's clubs disappeared, and millions of telephones were taken out. Even the mails were lighter. Travel dwindled. Meetings and church services were poorly attended. Restaurants lost business.

When a man lost his job, he shunned his former friends and refused invitations. One reason was that it took money to see people, and often there was not money enough to offer a visitor so much as a cup of coffee. Children had to have at least a penny to put on the collection plate at Sunday School, and they needed shoes for school. A great many children stayed at home because they lacked clothes to go out. It took carfare—at least a dime, a nickel going and a nickel coming back—to get almost anywhere. Housewives rarely got a

chance to leave the house. Hard times isolated women in the city as traumati-
cally as the farms had tethered an earlier generation of mothers who taught
their daughters to look for jobs in town.

People intuitively know that human contact heals and isolation deranges.
. . . Isolation made the unemployed suspicious, or at least more fearful of
being snubbed than it is possible for anyone who has never lacked for carfare
to imagine.

"As soon as you are out of the dough, your friends don't want to know you
any more," they said gloomily, whether it was true or not. When Robert and
Helen Lynd returned to their "Middletown" during the Depression, they de-
tected a streak of meanness and suspicion that was out of character with the
Middletown they had studied before the Crash. Men who had lost money said
their old friends cut them on the street for fear of being "touched" for a loan.
Everywhere the unemployed were excluded. Children whose parents were on
relief hung back from the others at school. High-school girls needed clothes
for dates, and without them they avoided beaux. Older people tried to keep
out of sight when they lost their teeth and could not afford bridgework.

Like prisoners in solitary confinement, the superfluous people got up every
morning as late as they could and fought time as if it were an enemy. Some of
them went to the public library and read, or simply sat for hours on end.
Communist demonstrators, or anyone else offering a free show, could always
be sure of an audience. People came for the animal presence of other people.
The message did not matter. And it was not the unemployed alone who had
time on their hands. Factories spread work so that in factory towns most of
the "employed" were working only two or three days a week, often taking
home little more than the totally unemployed could get on relief. Many offices
gave up the traditional half day's work on Saturday so that salaried people had
an extra day, a day uncommitted by the traditional churchgoing and visiting of
Sunday.

There was more time for everybody, and less to do in it. It had to be "killed"
at home, either alone or with people who were fellow prisoners at home.
According to a National Recreation Association survey of 1934, people were
killing time in sedentary, solitary, and spectatorial activities, when what they
really wanted was to go somewhere, do something, or make something. People told the investigators they had given up outside group activities because
they had "no money for carfare" and "no proper clothes" or were "too discouraged or worried because of loss of job to concentrate on anything." The
most commonly mentioned leisure-time activities were reading newspapers
and magazines, listening to the radio, and going to the movies, in that order.
. . . Stamp collectors quadrupled during the Depression. Double-feature movies were a dark hole into which a superfluous person could crawl when he
was supposed to be looking for a job. There were fads for knitting, games, and
jigsaw puzzles. . . .

The radio was a Depression success, and it addicted millions. People who
yearned to be out and doing consumed activity vicariously, like the retired
farmers who watched the world go by from their front porches. Amateur

photography, the spectatorial sport *par excellence,* gained almost as dramatically as the radio.

Spectacle loomed bigger to people living a limited life, and it seemed to be more prized, like the fiestas that break the monotony of peasant routine. The movie palladium with its ornate lobby where the lonely crowd could see and be seen is no longer in taste for those who do go to movies. . . . The burlesque show, the splashy big-name band, the musical movie with a cast of thousands, the extravaganza double length for good measure (*Gone With the Wind* was a four-hour sensation)—all these routine-breakers attracted people. . . .

Idleness did not precipitate a gross crime wave, although comparisons are inexact because police were so shorthanded that they could not afford to notice any crime that did not attract immediate attention. The best observers think that crimes of violence did not increase, but petty offenses against property did. If the "bezzle" (to use J. K. Galbraith's word for the amount of money misappropriated by employees) rose with stricter checkups when times were hard, the "pilfer" in grocery stores was harder to control when people put their wits to scrounging food.

Crimes that seemed like games against the rich multiplied. The idle constructed false claims against insurance companies. In some New York City neighborhoods, small-business people resorted to arson to bail themselves out of failing stores so frequently that no one really believed any fire to be accidental. One fantastic plot against an insurance company is notable because it delayed noncancelable health insurance for thirty years.

In December 1933, a lawyer and a salesman for the Maccabees, an old-line insurance company experimenting with health insurance, cooked up an extraordinary scheme for milking the company by simulating heart-attack symptoms by the use of digitalis. Extended to insured persons whose names were abstracted from the company files, the scheme eventually involved hundreds of people and millions of dollars. When the racket was uncovered, insurance companies were so disillusioned with health insurance that many of them bought back the few policies they had issued and discontinued the coverage.

Box-top contests were ideal pastimes—cheap, solitary, and time-consuming, with the hope of something for nothing to cherish, however remotely. Two million people entered the Old Gold contest offering $100,000 to the winner of a series of rebus riddles. Tip-sheets to the answers were sold, and Post Office inspectors coped with a flood of real and fake contests in the mails. Some became professional prize winners. Actress Thelma Ritter's husband, Joe Moran, won so many radio slogan contests that Young & Rubicam, the advertising agency that ran many of them, hired him as a copywriter.

The great chain-letter craze of 1935 swept millions into passing along a dime to the top name on a list of six mailed to him, adding his own to the bottom, and writing a letter to the other five asking them to do likewise. Nearly every adult in Colorado was involved. The scheme burned itself out when no new prospects remained, but it left three million dead letters in the post office and required special mintings of dimes. Even people who disapproved could not bring themselves to break the chain.

When pari-mutuel betting on horse racing was legalized in the dark year 1933, enough money mysteriously appeared to triple the receipts. But the really big boom was in the low end of gambling—the bingo games, the bank nights of movie houses desperately seeking to attract trade, and above all the "one-armed bandits" installed in beer parlors to sedate the restless.

The slot machine was simply an automatic vending machine designed to give back the nickels, dimes, or quarters put into it at a rate that favored the machine over many turns. Its fatal attraction was that it might or might not belch forth a jackpot of change at each crank. The appeal was hypnotic. You put in your quarter and pulled the lever. The symbols whirled. They might be plums, apples, cherries. If all three windows showed the same fruit, a jingle of coins notified you that you were in luck. It didn't matter that the machine was rigged to keep from 20 to 70 percent of all coins put into it. It didn't matter that half the take went into organized crime, which had moved in on the slots after Prohibition was repealed. What mattered was the anesthetic of the whir, punctuated by the momentary thrill of getting something for nothing. By the time Pearl Harbor produced some real excitement, the slots were gobbling up more than ten times as much change as they had taken at the time of the 1929 Crash.

Dance marathons took the country by storm in 1933. June Havoc recalls them as a "tiny pocket of the human struggle during the Great Depression." They were held in armories and usually started with 60 couples dancing or moving in dance positions 45 minutes of every hour, 24 hours a day, eating Army-style food from a board on sawhorses while the audience came and went, sometimes bringing picnic-style meals, throwing money, and sometimes offering food to the contestants or buying little postcard pictures of them. After 1,000 hours, partners took turns sleeping while leaning on each other and lapsed into a shadowy, subconscious state called "squirrelly," which June Havoc says provided amusement for the other marathoners, if not the audience. "Horses" were professional marathoners with thick, carefully tended calluses who went from contest to contest for the prize money. "Endurance shows" were so popular that the show-biz magazine *Billboard* devoted a special column to them. Six-day bicycle races staged a comeback, putting audience and contestants alike into a trance induced by the monotonous, whirring motion of the wheels around the track. . . . For people trying to endure, to make money last, to hold out for a break, they were a ritual murdering of the enemy—time.

The mood of the marathon was very similar to the aimless, endless movement of superfluous people around and around the country in rickety cars or on freight trains. Like the marathoners, the wanderers were impelled by a vague hope that something might break for them, although they were not surprised when it did not. In 1933, between one and two million people were on the road, "Address Unknown." A reporter asked a girl in a crowded jalopy headed south from Seattle where her party was going. "Going?" she echoed. "Just going."

There were all kinds. Some were Okies blown off their farmlands in the Dust Bowl by a dry spell that coincided with the Depression to create the conditions John Steinbeck immortalized in his novel *The Grapes of Wrath*. There were occupational wanderers, the stoop-crop pickers, the gandy dancers and construction stiffs and lumberjacks and many other seasonal semi-skilled workers of a simpler technology. Many of them were hoboes who, in good times or bad, took to the wandering life from choice, or as modern psychiatry would put it, from inner compulsions to escape from authority in general and the home authority of women in particular.

Their numbers increased with unemployment. Boys could not face parents who expected then to get out and work. One frank woman wrote a magazine article to complain that she had to share her home, her friends, and the family car with a grown daughter and son who wouldn't "face life on their own." A high-school graduate thanked a newspaper columnist for writing a column that convinced her father that it was not his fault that he could not find work. "Dad keeps throwing up to me all he has done for me, and it is a lot," the boy wrote. "But I am not going to be dependent upon him a minute longer than I can get away with it even if I have to take to the road." . . .

Sadder even than the boys were the grown men, the unemployed fathers who, one night, simply could not bear going home and headed for a freight train instead. Sometimes they acted on a rumor that there was work in another city, only to find that there was none. Once footloose, it did not matter much where they went. Hope of warm weather, word of a friend, memory of relatives perhaps never actually known, was excuse for a jaunt across the continent. It is hard for people who have jobs and careers, who sleep in beds, and have neighbors, to appreciate how planless a man cut loose can be.

President Herbert Hoover simply could not understand the Bonus Army. He could not grasp that 20,000 war veterans could pick each other up and roll—like a red tide, some thought—into Washington. All he could see was a great plot. But it was not that way.

The Bonus March started in Portland, Oregon, early in 1932 with 300 veterans led by ex-Sergeant Walter W. Waters. Their aim was to march across the country and ask Congress to pass the Patman Bill for immediate payment of a bonus that World War I soldiers were scheduled to get in 1945. Because they were all veterans, they fell into military discipline. They caught freight trains and camped. As word of their mission spread, thousands of unemployed veterans drifted along to join them. It was better than staying at home, and the idea of being in an "Army" again was appealing. The numbers grew. On June 8, 1932, 8,000 veterans paraded down Pennsylvania Avenue. Neither Waters nor the Communists, who were accused of starting the March, nor the Washington police had expected so many, but there was no violence, no disorder. Crime actually declined in the District of Columbia while they were there. . . .

Once they arrived in Washington they did not seem to know what to do. When news of the defeat of the Patman Bill was announced to them, Hearst columnist Elsie Robinson whispered to Waters that he should tell his men to sing "America." They did. Hoover flatly refused to talk to them. Instead, he ordered regular Army troops to disperse the men. General Douglas MacArthur burned their shacks and routed them out with gas. Stunned, they broke and fled.

Local authorities passed along the routed Bonus Marchers like so many hot potatoes. Virginia and Maryland stationed troopers along their boundaries to turn the men back. Maryland provided trucks to take them to Johnstown, Pennsylvania, where the mayor offered asylum, but the Pennsylvania trucks were misdirected to take them out of the state. A Washington Negro who happened to be in the veterans' camp when MacArthur attacked could not escape, and was trucked all the way to Indianapolis. The nimble made their way back to friendly Johnstown. The president of the Baltimore & Ohio Railroad finally offered to haul them home free on B. & O. trains. Cities of destination plotted to get rid of them. Kansas City scraped together $1,500 to keep the train from stopping. Discovering that they were objects of pity, many of those "passed along" turned to begging for a living.

Hoover thought that the Bonus Army was a mixture of hoodlums, ex-convicts, Communists, and a few veterans, and he stuck to this view even after careful investigation by the Veterans Bureau and the Pennsylvania State Department of Welfare failed to substantiate it. Most people who read about the Bonus March in the newspapers though the Marchers intended to start a revolution.

The truth was more frightening. The unemployed veterans of the war to save democracy were superfluous people—thousands and thousands of them marching, camping, and huddling together for sheer human warmth.

QUESTIONS FOR DISCUSSION

1. What was the effect of unemployment on family life?

2. How did the unemployed "exploit themselves"?

3. Interview a member of your family, a neighbor, or a friend who lived through the Depression. Did he or she experience the sense of being "superfluous" that Bird describes in this selection?

4. Is unemployment today as destructive of human lives and as socially disruptive as it was in the 1930s?

President Franklin Roosevelt delivers his first inaugural address on March 4, 1933. Roosevelt's three other inaugurations produced some memorable phrases—such as his 1937 declaration that he saw "one-third of a nation ill-housed, ill-clad, ill-nourished"—but none of the speeches moved the country the way his assurance that "the only thing we have to fear is fear itself" had that grey and somber March day at the nadir of the Great Depression. *(The Bettmann Archive)*

Franklin Delano Roosevelt: First Inaugural Address March 4, 1933

Commentary by Susan Ware

"The only thing we have to fear is fear itself" is perhaps the most famous phrase from Depression-era America. These words, from President Franklin Delano Roosevelt's first inaugural address, were uttered at a time when the United States had endured almost four years of the gravest economic contraction in its history; and there was no end in sight.

At the moment Roosevelt took the oath of office, more than one quarter of the nation's work force was unemployed, industrial production had fallen to half its 1929 level, and thirty-eight states had closed their banks. Yet the new president refused to give in to despair and defeatism. He rallied the country by instilling faith in the American people that they could weather the crisis. Roosevelt's restoration of hope and confidence, a process begun with this first inaugural speech, was perhaps his greatest contribution to American life during the Great Depression of the 1930s.

Franklin Roosevelt took over the presidency from Herbert Hoover, who was by 1932 a thoroughly discredited leader. Hoover's political fortunes had changed quickly. He had won an easy victory in 1928 over Democratic challenger Alfred E. Smith. Just one year into his term, however, the prosperity of the 1920s collapsed with the dramatic crash of the stock market in October 1929. The downturn became self-feeding, with business failures causing more layoffs, which in turn reduced the consumer spending necessary to pull the economy out of the tailspin. The economic contraction was especially damaging to the country's fragile banking structure.

Herbert Hoover responded along lines dictated by his conservative Republican philosophy. He stressed voluntary efforts to meet the crisis, asserting that successful recovery was mainly a matter of restoring business confidence. Yet as unemployment continued to rise and production fall, many Americans began to demand more action from the federal government. In 1932, Hoover took bolder steps, such as the authorization of the Reconstruction Finance Corporation whose loans to railroads, banks, and other financial institutions represented the first direct peacetime intervention of the federal government into the economy. He also supported a major public works program. Unfortunately, his steps were too little, too late. His refusal to provide federal work relief for the unemployed caused special bitterness, as did his ill-considered statements that nobody was starving and that hoboes were better fed than ever before. Soon shanty towns—pointedly referred to as *Hoovervilles*—sprung up in the nation's cities.

The 1932 election pitted the unpopular Hoover against New York Governor Franklin Roosevelt. The product of a privileged upbringing on his family's Hudson River estate at Hyde Park, Roosevelt had entered politics in 1910, in part out of admiration for his distant cousin Theodore Roosevelt, whose niece Eleanor he had married in 1905. After a stint as assistant secretary of the navy under Woodrow Wilson, Franklin Roosevelt had run as the vice-presidential candidate on the unsuccessful Democratic ticket in 1920. His political ambitions were temporarily sidetracked in 1921 by an attack of polio, which left him paralyzed from the waist down. Teaching himself to walk with heavy braces and crutches, he plotted his political comeback. He narrowly won election as governor of New York in 1928 while Democratic presidential candidate Al Smith went down to defeat. But Roosevelt easily won reelection in 1930, capitalizing on his administration's innovative record of state relief during the early years of the Depression. Overnight he became a frontrunner for the upcoming presidential campaign.

When Roosevelt won the Democratic presidential nomination in 1932, he was practically assured election over the unpopular Republican incumbent, who had become the scapegoat for the Depression in the public mind. Roosevelt's campaign foreshadowed little of the New Deal. "The country needs and, unless I mistake its temper, the country demands bold, persistent experimentation," he proclaimed in one campaign speech. At the same time, he promised to cut federal expenditures by 25 percent in order to balance the budget. In the end, Roosevelt won 22.8 million votes to Hoover's 15.7 million, with many people voting against Hoover as much as for Roosevelt. Candidates of the Socialist and Communist parties polled less than a million votes, showing that Americans remained firmly committed to the two-party system despite the economic upheaval of the Great Depression.

Then came a cruel irony. Under the Constitution, Roosevelt could not be inaugurated until March, a full four months after the election. (This long interregnum was never again repeated. The Twentieth Amendment, ratified in 1933, moved the inauguration to the 20th of January.) Those months, the winter of 1932–1933, were the worst of the depression. Private charity had been exhausted, and state and local governments had run out of funds to feed the hungry and house the homeless. In Midwestern industrial centers such as Akron and Toledo, unemployment ran as high as 80 percent. New York City hospitals reported ninety-five deaths from starvation.

During this long wait to take office, President-elect Roosevelt remained cheerful and confident. As Eleanor Roosevelt observed, "I have never known a man who gave one a greater sense of security. I have never heard him say there was a problem that he thought it was impossible for human beings to solve. He recognized the difficulties and often said that, while he did not know the answer, he was completely confident that there was an answer and that one had to try until one either found it for himself or got it from someone else." This confidence that problems, no matter how difficult, could be overcome was a spirit that Roosevelt soon communicated to the American people.

In February 1933, the president-elect began to work on his inaugural address. While on a train to Florida, he dictated ideas and suggestions to his chief speechwriter, Columbia political science professor Raymond Moley, who shaped them into a first draft. On Monday evening, February 27th, Roosevelt sat down at a card table in the living room of his Hyde Park estate and wrote out his own version of the speech in longhand on a yellow legal pad. By 1:30 A.M. he had finished. Moley burned his original draft in the Hyde Park fireplace. Thus only Roosevelt's handwritten version remained.

The crowd of 100,000 that gathered at the Capitol on March 4, 1933, to watch the inauguration was in a somber mood. Although the Democrats were returning to power for the first time in twelve years, it was hardly a festive occasion. The weather was raw and dreary, a typical March day. All the flags on Capitol hill flew at half mast in deference to a recently deceased senator. Army machine guns were mounted ominously in case of trouble from the crowd.

Franklin Roosevelt began the day by attending Episcopal church services led by Reverend Endicott Peabody, the Groton headmaster who had influenced the young Franklin in prep school. At 11 A.M., dressed in formal attire of striped trousers and a silk top hat and walking slowly with a cane on the arm of his eldest son James, Roosevelt paid a courtesy call on outgoing President Hoover. Conversation between the two men was strained, and they rode in an uneasy silence to the capitol. After the ceremony, the two men never saw each other again.

While the new president waited in the anteroom for the ceremonies to begin, he reviewed the address he had written out in longhand in his Hyde Park living room the Monday before and added a new opening line. "This is a day of consecration," he penciled in. Soon he changed it to the even more effective opening, "This is a day of national consecration." Then, proceeding carefully along specially constructed ramps, he emerged on the platform where he would officially become the thirty-second president of the United States.

The chief justice of the Supreme Court, Charles Evans Hughes, administered the oath of office using an old Dutch bible that had been in the Roosevelt family for three hundred years. Instead of merely affirming "I do" to the presidential oath, Roosevelt repeated the entire pledge in a clear, calm voice. Then he maneuvered to the podium where, standing bareheaded in the cold March wind and clutching the sides of the stand for support, he began to read the speech that set the tone for one of the most successful presidential administrations in United States history.

Franklin Roosevelt, his demeanor grim and purposeful, preached his first inaugural address like a sermon. Evocatively using religious imagery throughout the speech, he asked the blessing and protection of God in the days ahead. Such Christian values found a ready reception in his audience, both the thousands gathered on the Capitol grounds and the millions who listened on the radio. In fact, the whole speech was laced with the ethical and moral values widely shared in the America of the 1930s. By tapping this common set of ideals and beliefs, Roosevelt added greatly to the effectiveness of his message.

If his listeners were looking for a blueprint of the New Deal (a phrase first coined by Roosevelt in his acceptance speech to the Democratic National Convention in 1932), they were probably disappointed. Roosevelt identified the issues and their possible solutions only in the most general terms. Putting people to work was the top priority, but the imbalance in urban and rural population, the crisis in agriculture, and the need to balance the budget were also identified as pressing problems. He cited reform of banking and investment practices and the need for an adequate but sound currency as "two safeguards against the return of the evils of the old order." In foreign affairs, he pledged the United States to a policy based on the "good neighbor" principle, but made it clear that domestic concerns would take priority over international issues until the Depression was licked. But he deliberately passed up the opportunity to describe specific programs, only saying that he would soon submit appropriate measures to a special session of Congress.

Roosevelt's inaugural speech was not really concerned with legislation and public policy, however, but with values and ethics. He did not deny what he called "the dark realities" afflicting America, but he reminded the country's citizens that they still had much to be thankful for. It was in this context that he used the resonant phrase that Americans had nothing to fear but fear itself. The exact origin of this quotation remains obscure. Presidential adviser Louis Howe, who first suggested it, later claimed he saw it in a New York newspaper advertisement in January 1932, but this source has eluded historians. Eleanor Roosevelt believed the phrase drew on nineteenth-century American writer Henry David Thoreau, who had written "Nothing is so much to be feared as fear." In any case, the idea was hardly new to the 1930s, being part of a philosophical tradition that dated back at least as far as Sir Francis Bacon in the seventeenth century.

In the speech, Roosevelt minced no words about where he thought the responsibility for the current crisis lay. Using hard-hitting words such as "stubbornness" and "incompetence," he indicted a "generation of self-seekers," the nation's business and financial leaders, for their failure of vision. The Depression had finally forced these leaders "of an outworn tradition" to abdicate their power, a process Roosevelt described in the powerful image that "the money changers have fled from their high seats in the temple of our civilization." Americans could now "restore that temple to the ancient truths." Roosevelt decisively aligned himself on the side of the people against the "false leadership" of the "unscrupulous money changers," promising that his administration would provide a new "leadership of frankness and vigor" which these business leaders had lacked.

Roosevelt also used his inaugural speech as a spiritual, almost religious, indictment of material wealth as a standard of success. When he intoned that the difficulties Americans faced concerned "only material things," he was not trying to deny the terrible suffering that Americans had endured since 1929, but to remind his audience that there was more to life than financial success. "Happiness lies not in the mere possession of money," he lectured the assembled audience; "it lies in the joy of achievement, in the thrill of creative effort." Now that the money changers had been driven from the temple and the ancient truths restored, "The measure of the restoration lies in the extent to which we apply social values more noble than mere monetary profit."

Another predominant theme of the speech, indeed of the whole New Deal, was a rejection of individualism for an ideal of interdependence and mutual cooperation. American lives were bound together by common action, a sense of belonging—what Roosevelt called "our interdependence on each other." It was no longer appropriate for every member of society to go his or her own way; individual actions had to be weighed against broader social needs. The new president proposed that the ethics of cooperation and mutuality replace the aggressive selfishness and material acquisitiveness that many believed were poisoning national life—in his words, Americans must realize "that we cannot merely take but we must give as well." Such values were not only the way to recovery, but the best guarantee that recovery would endure.

With Roosevelt's emphasis on interdependence came an important corollary: a commitment to strong national leadership on the part of the federal government. In order to balance competing economic interests and to work for the common good, the federal government had to take a more active role. Such a stance was essential to combat the Great Depression. Throughout the speech, Roosevelt issued ringing declarations of this vision of governmental activism: "This Nation asks for action, and action now." "We must act and act quickly." "The people of the United States . . . have registered a mandate that they want direct, vigorous action." Such a conception of presidential leadership was well suited to Roosevelt's self-confident and pragmatic personality.

As Roosevelt rallied the country, he often employed the analogy of fighting a war. Military and war imagery rivaled religious images as the dominant rhetorical devices of the speech. Roosevelt called for the American people to become a "trained and loyal army willing to sacrifice for the good of a common discipline"; he called for a unity of duty usually found only in times of "armed strife." The most explicit parallel was his willingness to ask Congress for broad executive powers "to wage war against the emergency, as great as the power that would be given to me if we were in fact invaded by a foreign foe." Such declarations received the greatest applause during his speech, although onlookers such as First Lady Eleanor Roosevelt found them "a little terrifying": "The crowds were so tremendous and you felt that they would do anything— if only someone would tell them what to do." Given the enormity of the crisis facing the country, however, Franklin Roosevelt believed it was totally appropriate to employ war imagery to galvanize the country into realizing how serious the situation was and how drastic the remedies might have to be.

In the end, however, Roosevelt intended not to scare the American people, but to reassure them. The American democratic system was basically sound, he told the American people. He confidently believed that hard times could be overcome, but only if a dispirited nation chose not to wallow in lethargy. He urged his fellow citizens to return to the values and ethics that had made the country great in the past. Then he humbly yet self-confidently asked their help, and God's, as he prepared to lead the country through the arduous days ahead.

FRANKLIN DELANO ROOSEVELT

Inaugural Address, March 4, 1933

This is a day of national consecration.[1] I am certain that my fellow Americans expect that on my induction into the Presidency I will address them with a candor and a decision which the present situation of our Nation impels. This is preeminently the time to speak the truth, the whole truth, frankly and boldly. Nor need we shrink from honestly facing conditions in our country today. This great Nation will endure as it has endured, will revive and will prosper. So, first of all, let me assert my firm belief that the only thing we have to fear is fear itself—nameless, unreasoning, unjustified terror which paralyzes needed efforts to convert retreat into advance. In every dark hour of our national life a leadership of frankness and vigor has met with that understanding and support of the people themselves which is essential to victory. I am convinced that you will give that support to leadership in these critical days.

In such a spirit on my part and on yours we face our common difficulties. They concern, thank God, only material things. Values have shrunken to fantastic levels; taxes have risen; our ability to pay has fallen; government of all kinds is faced by serious curtailment of income; the means of exchange are frozen in the currents of trade;[2] the withered leaves of industrial enterprise lie on every side; farmers find no markets for their produce; the savings of many years in thousands of families are gone.

More important, a host of unemployed citizens face the grim problem of existence, and an equally great number toil with little return. Only a foolish optimist can deny the dark realities of the moment.

Yet our distress comes from no failure of substance. We are stricken by no plague of locusts. Compared with the perils which our forefathers conquered

---

Source: Samuel I. Rosenman, ed. *The Public Papers and Addresses of Franklin D. Roosevelt,* Vol. Two (New York: Random House, 1938), pp. 11–16.

[1]The *New York Times,* March 5, 1933, carried the full text, which included the opening line that Roosevelt added just before the ceremony, "This is a day of national consecration."

[2]On inauguration day, the United States effectively lacked a banking system, the result of actions by governors and legislatures to avoid further runs on deposits in their individual states. Thirty-eight states had closed their banks entirely, and the rest allowed banks to operate only on a severely restricted basis.

because they believed and were not afraid, we have still much to be thankful for. Nature still offers her bounty and human efforts have multiplied it. Plenty is at our doorstep, but a generous use of it languishes in the very sight of the supply. Primarily this is because rulers of the exchange of mankind's goods have failed through their own stubbornness and their own incompetence, have admitted their failure, and have abdicated. Practices of the unscrupulous money changers stand indicted in the court of public opinion, rejected by the hearts and minds of men.

True they have tried, but their efforts have been cast in the pattern of an outworn tradition. Faced by failure of credit they have proposed only the lending of more money. Stripped of the lure of profit by which to induce our people to follow their false leadership, they have resorted to exhortations, pleading tearfully for restored confidence. They know only the rules of a generation of self-seekers. They have no vision, and when there is no vision the people perish.

The money changers have fled from their high seats in the temple of our civilization. We may now restore that temple to the ancient truths. The measure of the restoration lies in the extent to which we apply social values more noble than mere monetary profit.

Happiness lies not in the mere possession of money; it lies in the joy of achievement, in the thrill of creative effort. The joy and moral stimulation of work no longer must be forgotten in the mad chase of evanescent profits. These dark days will be worth all they cost us if they teach us that our true destiny is not to be ministered unto but to minister to ourselves and to our fellow men.

Recognition of the falsity of material wealth as the standard of success goes hand in hand with the abandonment of the false belief that public office and high political position are to be valued only by the standards of pride of place and personal profit; and there must be an end to a conduct in banking and in business which too often has given to a sacred trust the likeness of callous and selfish wrongdoing. Small wonder that confidence languishes, for it thrives only on honesty, on honor, on the sacredness of obligations, on faithful protection, on unselfish performance; without them, it cannot live.

Restoration calls, however, not for changes in ethics alone. This Nation asks for action, and action now.

Our greatest primary task is to put people to work. This is no unsolvable problem if we face it wisely and courageously. It can be accomplished in part by direct recruiting by the Government itself, treating the task as we would treat the emergency of a war, but at the same time, through this employment, accomplishing greatly needed projects to stimulate and reorganize the use of our natural resources.

Hand in hand with this we must frankly recognize the over-balance of population in our industrial centers and, by engaging on a national scale in a redistribution, endeavor to provide a better use of the land for those best fitted for the land.[3] The task can be helped by definite efforts to raise the values of agricultural products and with this the power to purchase the output of our cities. It can be helped by preventing realistically the tragedy of the growing loss through foreclosure of our small homes and our farms. It can be helped by insistence that the Federal, State, and local governments act forthwith on the demand that their cost be drastically reduced. It can be helped by the unifying of relief activities which today are often scattered, uneconomical, and unequal. It can be helped by national planning for and supervision of all forms of transportation and of communications and other utilities which have a definitely public character. There are many ways in which it can be helped, but it can never be helped merely by talking about it. We must act and act quickly.

Finally, in our progress toward a resumption of work we require two safeguards against a return of the evils of the old order: there must be a strict supervision of all banking and credits and investments, so that there will be an end to speculation with other people's money; and there must be provision for an adequate but sound currency.

These are the lines of attack. I shall presently urge upon a new Congress, in special session, detailed measures for their fulfillment, and I shall seek the immediate assistance of the several States.

Through this program of action we address ourselves to putting our own national house in order and making income balance outgo. Our international trade relations, though vastly important, are in point of time and necessity secondary to the establishment of a sound national economy. I favor as a practical policy the putting of first things first. I shall spare no effort to restore world trade by international economic readjustment, but the emergency at home cannot wait on that accomplishment.

The basic thought that guides these specific means of national recovery is not narrowly nationalistic. It is the insistence, as a first consideration, upon the interdependence of the various elements in and parts of the United States—a recognition of the old and permanently important manifestation of the American spirit of the pioneer. It is the way to recovery. It is the immediate way. It is the strongest assurance that the recovery will endure.

In the field of world policy I would dedicate this Nation to the policy of the good neighbor[4]—the neighbor who resolutely respects himself and, because he does so, respects the rights of others—the neighbor who respects his obligations and respects the sanctity of his agreements in and with a world of neighbors.

---

[3]Roosevelt sincerely believed in the superiority of rural to urban life, and hoped to convince some of the nation's unemployed industrial workers to leave the cities and return to farming as a way of life.

[4]This term, coined by Raymond Moley, usually refers to Roosevelt's policy of nonintervention in the internal affairs of Latin American nations. More broadly, it represents the New Deal's commitment to hemispheric solidarity against the forces of fascism and totalitarianism.

If I read the temper of our people correctly, we now realize as we have never realized before our interdependence on each other; that we cannot merely take but we must give as well; that if we are to go forward, we must move as a trained and loyal army willing to sacrifice for the good of the common discipline, because without such discipline no progress is made, no leadership becomes effective. We are, I know, ready and willing to submit our lives and property to such discipline, because it makes possible a leadership which aims at a larger good. This I propose to offer, pledging that the larger purposes will bind upon us all as a sacred obligation with a unity of duty hitherto evoked only in time of armed strife.

With this pledge taken, I assume unhesitatingly the leadership of this great army of our people dedicated to a disciplined attack upon our common problems.

Action in this image and to this end is feasible under the form of government which we have inherited from our ancestors. Our Constitution is so simple and practical that it is possible always to meet extraordinary needs by changes in emphasis and arrangement without loss of essential form. That is why our constitutional system has proved itself the most superbly enduring political mechanism the modern world has produced. It has met every stress of vast expansion of territory, of foreign wars, of bitter internal strife, of world relations.

It is to be hoped that the normal balance of Executive and legislative authority may be wholly adequate to meet the unprecedented task before us. But it may be that an unprecedented demand and need for undelayed action may call for temporary departure from that normal balance of public procedure.

I am prepared under my constitutional duty to recommend the measures that a stricken Nation in the midst of a stricken world may require. These measures, or such other measures as the Congress may build out of its experience and wisdom, I shall seek, within my constitutional authority, to bring to speedy adoption.

But in the event that the Congress shall fail to take one of these two courses, and in the event that the national emergency is still critical, I shall not evade the clear course of duty that will then confront me. I shall ask the Congress for the one remaining instrument to meet the crisis—broad Executive power to wage a war against the emergency, as great as the power that would be given to me if we were in fact invaded by a foreign foe.

For the trust reposed in me I will return the courage and the devotion that befit the time. I can do no less.

We face the arduous days that lie before us in the warm courage of national unity; with the clear consciousness of seeking old and precious moral values; with the clean satisfaction that comes from the stern performance of duty by old and young alike. We aim at the assurance of a rounded and permanent national life.

We do not distrust the future of essential democracy. The people of the United States have not failed. In their need they have registered a mandate that they want direct, vigorous action. They have asked for discipline and direction under leadership. They have made me the present instrument of their wishes. In the spirit of the gift I take it.

In this dedication of a Nation we humbly ask the blessing of God. May He protect each and every one of us. May He guide me in the days to come.

Commentary: Part II

The immediate response to Roosevelt's inaugural address was overwhelmingly positive. Members of Congress from both parties hailed its pledge of decisive leadership, and editorials from Democratic and Republican newspapers alike endorsed its call for action. The *Chicago Tribune* said that it "strikes the dominant note of courageous confidence," while the *Nashville Banner* saw it as proof "that, as every great epoch has called for a great leader, so never has the nation lacked the citizen to measure to the demands." The *New York Herald Tribune* headlined its coverage "A Call to Arms." The editors at the *Nation* intoned, "Never in our national history has there been so dramatic a coincidence as this simultaneous transfer of power and the complete collapse of a system and a philosophy. At that zero hour Roosevelt's words had something of the challenge, the symbolism, and the simplicity of a trumpet blast." While many newspapers would later turn against the New Deal, most initially greeted Roosevelt's ascent to power with approbation.

President Roosevelt's inaugural address also struck a personal chord for many of the nation's citizens. In the next few days, more than 450,000 Americans wrote letters to the White House, letting the president know that they supported his efforts. Humorist Will Rogers summed up the public mood in the wake of the inauguration. "The whole country is with him. Just so he does something. If he burned down the Capitol, we would cheer and say, 'Well, we at least got a fire started.' "

Franklin Roosevelt quickly delivered on his inaugural promise of "action, and action now." His first step as president was to declare a "bank holiday," closing the nation's banks to prevent further runs on the already gravely weakened banking system. Within five days of his inauguration, Congress had passed a banking bill which mandated federal investigations into each bank's financial situation before it could reopen and which made federal money available to back up bank deposits. The weekend after he took office, Roosevelt went on the radio to give the first of his "fireside chats." To an audience estimated at sixty million listeners, he reassured the American people in careful and simple terms that the banks were now safe. So effective was Roosevelt's speech that deposits exceeded withdrawals when the banks reopened the following Monday.

The warm reaction that greeted Roosevelt's inaugural address and his first fireside chat foreshadowed his successful use of the mass media throughout his presidency. Roosevelt was a master of the radio. He intuitively grasped radio's potential to allow him to enter directly into households across the country and to establish a close rapport with millions of ordinary Americans. Rather than a distant figure in Washington who occasionally made dry public pronouncements, this president was a warm and intimate part of daily life. Many Americans came to think of him as their close personal friend—for the rest of the decade, the White House received between 5,000 and 8,000 letters from ordinary citizens every day. Roosevelt's ability to communicate directly with the American people was one of the major accomplishments of the New Deal.

Confirming the promise of presidential activism which Franklin Roosevelt had outlined in his first inaugural address, the federal government became a factor in everyday life in the 1930s. The Banking Act was the first of the approximately fifteen pieces of major legislation passed by Congress in the first hundred days of the Roosevelt administration. This outpouring of legislation from the nation's capital—what became known as the New Deal's "alphabet agencies" because of their acronyms—gave the American people hope that the end of hard times was just around the corner. By the end of the decade, more than one third of the population had received direct help from the federal government, whether in the form of a relief job on the Works Progress Administration, a mortgage guarantee from the Home Owners Loan Corporation, a check from the Social Security Administration, a farm subsidy from the Agricultural Adjustment Administration, or a stipend from the National Youth Administration. Decisions made in Washington now affected ordinary citizens throughout the country; in turn, Americans increasingly looked to Washington, specifically the federal government and the president, for leadership. This increased federal presence, which soon became a permanent aspect of modern American life, was one of the most far-reaching changes of the 1930s.

Ironically, the New Deal never ended the depression. Unemployment remained high throughout the 1930s, even topping 20 percent once again during the 1937–1938 recession when Roosevelt made an ill-conceived attempt to balance the budget by cutting back on relief spending. Roosevelt spent his way out of that downturn, but it was defense mobilization for World War II that finally pulled the country out of the depression, not any of the New Deal measures.

Despite its failure to end the depression, the New Deal stands as one of the most creative periods in American political history. The United States survived the worst extended economic downturn in its history with its political system intact, indeed strengthened, at a time when democracy was under siege throughout the world. The federal government accepted the responsibility for intervening in economic life when private initiatives faltered and for protecting and promoting key elements of the welfare of its citizens. America's welfare state was born during the Great Depression of the 1930s.

The New Deal's accomplishments, while substantial, went only so far. Federal programs remained small, benefits limited, and agencies temporary. Not everyone benefited equally from New Deal programs, but the majority of Americans in the 1930s were simply too grateful for the federal aid to complain that it did not go further. Such federal assistance, coming at a time when many citizens had few, if any, personal resources to fall back on to deal with unemployment, illness, and old age, was often the difference between survival and going under.

Franklin Roosevelt played a central role in shaping these institutional changes in the 1930s. In the process begun as soon as he stepped to the podium to deliver his first inaugural address, Roosevelt provided the presidential leadership to survive one of the gravest challenges the United States had ever faced. His special gift to the nation during this crisis was his ability to inspire hope that things indeed would get better, that hard times would be overcome. The American people responded in part by electing him to the presidency an unprecedented four times, and by cementing the New Deal Democratic coalition of farmers, urban dwellers, black voters, ethnic groups, and a broad spectrum of the middle class. This coalition would dominate national political life through the 1960s. When Franklin Roosevelt stated so forcefully at his first inauguration that there was nothing to fear but fear itself, he was calling on the country to follow his own deeply felt conviction that the crisis of the Great Depression could indeed be overcome. He did not betray this trust.

HARVARD SITKOFF

Black Americans and the New Deal

Was the New Deal an attempt by a left-leaning president to collectivize the American economy and bring about revolutionary changes in American society? Or was it a last-ditch effort by a conservative president to rescue drowning capitalism and preserve the social status quo? This, baldly stated, is the question that lies at the heart of any analysis of Franklin Delano Roosevelt and the New Deal.

In the following article, Harvard Sitkoff asks a variation of this central question. How did Franklin Delano Roosevelt approach the plight of black people in Depression America? Did the New Deal effect a significant change in race relations and civil rights for blacks? Or did it simply paper over the problems with public relations gestures?

According to Professor Sitkoff, these questions cannot be answered if we focus our attention only on legislation sponsored and passed. To understand the true impact of the New Deal for American blacks, we must also consider the tone and spirit of the Roosevelt administration as established by Franklin and Eleanor in their official and unofficial dealings with black Americans.

Perhaps no aspect of the New Deal appears more anomalous or paradoxical than the relationship of Afro-Americans and the administration of President Franklin Roosevelt. On the one hand are the facts of pervasive racial discrimination and inequity in the recovery and relief programs, coupled with the evasiveness of New Dealers on civil rights issues. On the other hand, there is

Harvard Sitkoff teaches history at the University of New Hampshire. He is the author of *A New Deal for Blacks* and *The Struggle for Black Equality*. The essay that follows was originally written for a conference held to commemorate the golden anniversary of President Roosevelt's first inauguration. The papers presented at this conference, edited by Professor Sitkoff, have been published under the title, *Fifty Years Later: The New Deal Evaluated*.

From *Fifty Years Later: The New Deal Evaluated,* edited by Harvard Sitkoff, pp. 93–111. Copyright © 1985 by Alfred A. Knopf, Inc. Reprinted by permission of the publisher.

the adoration of FDR by blacks and the huge voting switch of Afro-Americans from the party of Lincoln to the Roosevelt coalition between 1932 and 1940. Faced with this enigma, some historians have concluded that Roosevelt gulled blacks in the 1930s, seduced them with rhetoric and gestures that left untouched the actual harm perpetuated by New Deal neglect and political cowardice. Others conjecture that the blacks' positive opinion of Roosevelt in the thirties had little to do with any effort the New Deal made to improve race relations and everything to do with the desperate need of Afro-Americans for the New Deal programs designed to aid the unemployed and the poor, regardless of color. As Congressman Jack Kemp of New York recently surmised: "Hoover offered a balanced budget, and FDR offered buttered bread." Both interpretations have greatly enriched our historical understanding of blacks and the New Deal. Together they give us a more accurate assessment of Roosevelt's shortcomings and his image as a savior. But, both interpretations omit the impact of the New Deal on civil rights in the context of the prevailing racial conservatism of the period. However limited and tentative they may seem in retrospect, the New Deal's steps toward racial justice and equality were unprecedented and were judged most favorably by blacks at the time. Their significance is the theme of this essay.

A RAW DEAL

Certainly no racial issue or matter had greater priority for blacks in the 1930s than the opportunity to earn a living or to receive adequate relief. The Great Depression devastated Afro-Americans, who were disproportionately mired in farm tenancy or who were the "last hired and first fired" in industry. At the bottommost rungs of the economic ladder, no group was in greater need of governmental assistance simply to survive. Accordingly, every civil rights organization and Afro-American leader scrutinized the various New Deal programs for their material effect on blacks. They found much to condemn. Blacks were never aided to the full extent of their need. New Deal legislation and local administration often resulted in discrimination against blacks or their exclusion from benefits. And, at times, the New Deal augmented the educational, occupational, and residential segregation of Afro-Americans.

However much blacks hoped for a new deal of the cards from Roosevelt, they found the deck stacked against them. The heritage of black poverty and powerlessness brought them into the Depression decade without the wherewithal to overcome at the local level those insisting that they remain the lowest social class or to prevail over their opponents at the national level in a political system granting benefits mostly on the power of the groups demanding them. Largely due to the measures taken by Southern state legislatures at the turn of the century to disenfranchise blacks, they could do little to lessen the President's dependence for New Deal legislation and appropriations on the white southerners who held over half the committee chairmanships and a majority of the leadership positions in every congressional session during the thirties. The very ubiquity of the worst depression in American history, moreover, limited the possibility of a major New Deal effort to remedy the plight of blacks. Hard times defined Roosevelt's mandate and kept the pressure on the New Deal to promote the economic recovery of middle-class America rather than to undertake either the long-range reform of the structural bases of poverty or to engage in a protracted effort to vanquish Jim Crow. In addition, the traditions of decentralization and states' rights further undermined the effort of blacks to gain equitable treatment from the New Deal. Despite the laudable intent of many Roosevelt appointees in Washington, those who administered the New Deal at the state and local levels, especially in the South, saw to it that blacks never shared fully or fairly in the relief and recovery projects.

Thus the National Recovery Administration (NRA) quickly earned such epithets as "Negroes Ruined Again," "Negro Run Around," and "Negro Rights Abused." The NRA wage codes excluded those who toiled in agriculture and domestic service—three out of every four employed blacks—and the administrators in Washington connived to accept spurious occupational classifications for black workers, or their displacement by white employees. Denied the benefits of the NRA's effort to raise labor standards, blacks nevertheless felt the impact of the NRA as consumers by having to pay higher prices for most goods. Similarly, the Agricultural Adjustment Administration (AAA) cotton program achieved about as much for the mass of the nearly 3 million black farm tenants as a plague of boll weevils. The AAA eschewed safeguards to protect the exploited landless black peasantry and acquiesced in the widespread cheating of croppers out of their share of the subsidy to planters, or the wholesale eviction of tenants whose labor was no longer needed. Those who had traditionally oppressed blacks in the South also controlled the local administration of the Tennessee Valley Authority (TVA), and the consequences were the same. Blacks were initially excluded from clerical employment and from living in the TVA's new model town of Norris, Tennessee. Local officials segregated work crews and relegated blacks to the least-skilled, lowest-paying jobs. They refused to admit blacks to TVA vocational schools or to training sessions in foremanship. And, everywhere in the Tennessee Valley, white southern administrators insisted upon Jim Crow housing and recreational facilities, and on segregated drinking fountains and employment offices in the TVA.

The early relief and welfare operations of the New Deal proved to be only marginally more beneficial to blacks. The Civilian Conservation Corps (CCC) allowed local officials to choose the enrollees, and, not surprisingly, young black men were woefully underrepresented. They were also, in the main, confined to segregated CCC units and kept out of the training programs that would lead to their advancement. Moreover, despite the laudable intentions of Harry Hopkins, the Federal Emergency Relief Administration and the Civil Works Administration succumbed to the pressure brought by angry whites who thought that blacks were being spoiled by direct relief or were earning more on work-relief than white laborers in private enterprise. New regulations lowered the minimum wages on work-relief and prohibited relief payments from exceeding prevailing wages in a region. They also gave greater discretion to state and local relief officials in the administration of their programs. Consequently, blacks saw both their chances for obtaining relief and the amount of relief drop. Especially in 1933 and 1934, discrimination was rife and blacks depended on the mercy of the lily-white personnel in local relief offices. Similarly, the New Deal's capitulation to racial prejudice became manifest in the refusal to admit blacks in the subsistence homestead program; the failure to prohibit racial discrimination in unions protected by the National Labor Relations Act; the passage of a Social Security Act with enough loopholes to exclude two-thirds of all Afro-American workers in 1935; and the encouragement of residential segregation by the Federal Housing Administration.

PRESSURE FOR CHANGE

Gradually, however, counterforces pushed the New Deal toward a more equitable treatment of blacks. A clear demonstration by blacks of their determination to achieve full, first-class citizenship seemed foremost among the interrelated reasons for that transformation. On a scale, and with an intensity, unknown in any previous decade, a host of black advancement and protest organizations campaigned for racial justice and equality. More blacks than ever before marched, picketed, rallied, and lobbied against racial discrimination. They boycotted businesses with unjust racial practices. The National Association for the Advancement of Colored People (NAACP) and the National Urban League adapted to the mood of militance. They forged additional weapons of struggle, developed greater skills and sophistication, and acquired powerful allies and sources of support. New militant organizations such as the National Negro Congress and Southern Negro Youth Congress prodded the more moderate black groups to greater aggressiveness and amplified the volume of the growing movement for black rights. Simultaneously, the Negro vote in the 1930s developed into a relatively sizable and volatile bloc that politicians of both major parties in the North could no longer ignore. A marked upsurge in the number of blacks who registered and voted resulted from the continuing migration of Afro-Americans from the South to cities above the Mason-Dixon line, and from the new immediacy of government to the life of the common people during the New Deal. Concentrated in the states richest in electoral votes, the black vote began to be ballyhooed as a balance of power in national elections, a swing bloc that would go to whichever party most benefited blacks. Northern big-city Democrats became especially attentive and displayed unprecedented solicitude for black needs. At the same time, the power of the South within the Democratic party declined; Dixie Democrats prominently joined in the conservative criticism of the New Deal; and racism became identified with fascism. One result was that northern Democrats ceased to support their southern brethren in opposing black rights.

Augmenting these developments, members of the radical left and the labor movement in the thirties preached the egalitarian gospel to millions of white Americans. Communists and the Congress of Industrial Organizations, in particular, advocated an end to racial discrimination and insisted on the necessity for interracial harmony. Their desire for strong labor unions or class unity, unhampered by racial divisions, propelled them into the forefront of mainly white organizations pressing for civil rights. White southern race liberals, although few in number, joined the fray, stressing the connections between economic democracy in the South and the cause of black rights. What George Washington Cable once called the "Silent South" grew vocal, shattering the image of a white South that was solidly united on racial matters. These trends, in turn, gained from the changes in the 1930s in the academic and intellectual communities. Biologists refuted the doctrines of inherent and irremediable racial differences. Social scientists started to undermine white racism by emphasizing environment rather than innate characteristics; by stressing the damage done to individuals by prejudice; and by eroding the stereotype of the Afro-American as a contented buffoon. A new ideological consensus began to emerge, an American creed of treating all people alike, of judging each person as an individual.

Roosevelt could neither ignore what these occurrences portended, nor disregard the strength of the forces arrayed against racial reform. He understood that however much black powerlessness had decreased and white hostility to blacks had begun to diminish, the majority of white Americans still opposed desegregation and equal opportunities for blacks. He knew that to combat the worst depression in the nation's history he needed the backing of the southern Democrats who wanted no modification of traditional racial practices. Roosevelt, the consummate politician and humanitarian, therefore, husbanded his political capital on racial matters, doing what he thought was right, if it would not cost him dearly. Above all, he avoided an all-out confrontation with those whose support he deemed necessary. Always the fox and never the lion on civil rights issues, Roosevelt nevertheless acted in ways that had the unintended consequence of laying the groundwork for the Second Reconstruction.

A BETTER DEAL FOR BLACKS

After 1934, although Jim Crow remained largely intact, blacks gained a much fairer, but still far from fully adequate, share of New Deal benefits and services. In the CCC the percentage of black enrollees rose from 3 percent in 1933 to 6 percent in 1936, to nearly 10 percent in 1937, and to over 11 percent in 1938. In that same year about 40,000 young blacks were sending $700,000 a month home to their parents and dependents. By the start of 1939, some 200,000 blacks had served in the Civilian Conservation Corps, and when the CCC ended in 1942 the number stood at 350,000. In addition, over 40,000 blacks who had entered the Corps as illiterates had learned to read and write.

The National Youth Administration (NYA) directly aided another 300,000 black youths. Like other New Deal agencies, the NYA accepted segregated projects in the South, employed a disproportionate number of blacks in servile work, and lacked the resources to assist Afro-Americans to the extent their privation required. Yet the fervor of Aubrey Williams, head of the NYA until it ended in 1943, led that agency to hire black administrative assistants to supervise black work in every southern state, to forbid either racial or geographic differentials in wages, and to an insistence that black secondary and college students in every state receive aid at least in proportion to their numbers in the population. The NYA also employed more blacks in administrative posts then any other New Deal program, and Afro-Americans annually received between 10 and 20 percent of NYA's appropriations.

With a zeal similar to that of Williams, Dr. Will Alexander, the chief of the Farm Security Administration (FSA) managed to insure benefits for black farmers that were roughly proportionate to their percentage of farm operators. Overall, blacks received about 23 percent of the New Deal's farm security assistance. This was achieved only because FSA officials in Washington kept constant pressure on local authorities to prevent racial discrimination. But the FSA could never convince Congress to appropriate the funds needed to make more than the slightest dent in the problem of the needy and displaced tenant farmers. By 1940, despite its egalitarianism, the FSA had placed a mere 1,393 black families on its resettlement communities and had provided tenant purchase loans to only 3,400 blacks. Even this minimal effort, however, earned the FSA a reputation as a "disturber of the peace," and the top place on the southern conservative's "death list" of New Deal programs.

Equally vigilant on matters of race, Secretary of Interior Harold Ickes, who ran the Public Works Administration (PWA), employed a quota system on government construction projects to root out discrimination against black laborers. Beginning in 1934, the PWA included a clause in all its construction contracts stipulating that the number of blacks hired and their percentage of the project payroll be equal to the proportion of blacks in either the local labor force or in the 1930 occupational census. The quota was effective in diminishing discrimination. It led to the admission of hundreds of skilled blacks into previously lily-white southern construction trade unions, and resulted in over $2 million, nearly 6 percent of the total payroll to skilled workers, being paid to blacks—a portion considerably greater than that warranted by the occupational census. Similar quota systems would later be adopted by the U.S. Housing Authority, the Federal Works Agency, and the President's Committee on Fair Employment Practices.

Ickes' concern for racial fairness also led to the PWA expenditure of over $45 million for the construction and renovation of Afro-American schools, hospitals, and recreational facilities. The nearly $5 million granted for new buildings at black colleges increased their total plant value by more than 25 percent. In addition, the PWA loaned municipalities and states more than $20 million to build and repair scores of schools, dormitories, auditoriums, and gymnasiums for blacks. Of the 48 PWA housing projects completed by 1938, 14 were solely for Afro-Americans and 15 for joint black-white occupancy. Blacks occupied one-third of all PWA housing units and 41,000 of the 122,000 dwelling units built by the U.S. Housing Authority (USHA). The determination of the PWA and USHA to be racially fair and to meet the black demand for public housing also led them to charge blacks a lower monthly average rent than they did whites, and to set a higher maximum family income for blacks than whites as the cut-off for admission to the housing projects.

Likewise, the concern for black welfare of Harry Hopkins was manifest in the constant efforts in the Works Progress Administration (WPA) to forbid racial discrimination by local relief authorities in assigning jobs to the unemployed and in establishing wage rates. Hopkins did not succeed in ending such practices in the South, but as the Urban League proclaimed: "It is to the eternal credit of the administrative offices of the WPA that discrimination on various projects because of race has been kept to a minimum and that in almost every community Negroes have been given a chance to participate in the work program." Indeed, during Roosevelt's second term, roughly 350,000 blacks were employed by the WPA annually, about 15 percent of the total in the work relief program. For the most part, blacks received their proper job classifications from the WPA, gained the equal wages promised them, and were included in all special projects. Over 5,000 blacks were employed as teachers and supervisors in the WPA Education Program, where nearly 250,000 Afro-Americans learned to read and write. Tens of thousands of blacks were trained for skilled jobs in WPA vocational classes. The Federal Music Project performed the works of contemporary Afro-American composers; featured all-black casts in several of its operas; made a special effort to preserve, record, and publish Negro folk music; and conducted music instruction classes for blacks in more than a score of cities. The Federal Art Project, the Federal Theatre Project, and the Federal Writers' Project also employed hundreds of blacks and made special efforts to highlight the artistic contributions of Afro-Americans.

Blacks, long accustomed to receiving little more than crumbs, largely accepted the New Deal's half a loaf. The continuance of discrimination and segregation appeared secondary to the vital importance of work-relief, public housing, government-sponsored health clinics and infant care programs, NYA employment to keep a child in school, a FSA loan to purchase a farm, or new educational facilities in the neighborhood. Primarily because of the PWA and WPA, the gap between both black unemployment rates and black median family income relative to whites diminished during the 1930s, and the percentage of black workers in skilled and semiskilled occupations rose from 23 to 29 percent.

In no small part because of the myriad of New Deal programs that improved the nutrition, housing, and health care available to Afro-Americans, black infant and maternal mortality significantly decreased, and black life expectancy climbed from 48 to 53 years in the 1930s. Over 1 million blacks learned to read and write in New Deal-sponsored literacy classes. Federal funds and New Deal guidelines for the expenditure of those funds also resulted in a lengthening of the school term for blacks, and a significant growth in the number of schools for blacks. The percentage of Afro-Americans, aged 5 to 18, attending school jumped from 60 to 65 percent, and the gap in expenditures per black pupil narrowed from 29 percent of the average for white students in 1930 to 44 percent in 1940. In addition, the average salary paid to black teachers, only one-third of that paid to white teachers in 1930, increased to about one-half in 1940.

Summing up the prevailing Afro-American response to the New Deal efforts to relieve black distress, the *Pittsburgh Courier* editorialized that "armies of unemployed Negro workers have been kept from the near-starvation level on which they lived under President Hoover" by the work provided by the WPA, CCC, PWA, and other federal projects. It acknowledged the unfortunate continuation of racial discrimination and the New Deal's failure to end such practices. "But what administration within the memory of man," the *Courier* concluded, "has done a better job in that direction considering the very imperfect human material with which it had to work? The answer, of course, is none."

DIMINISHING RACISM

Blacks expressed their thankfulness for the uncommon concern the Roosevelt Administration showed for their well-being, and for the direct material assistance that enabled them to endure the Depression. The very novelty of simply being included—of being considered and planned for—elicited praise in hundreds of letters written to the White House and to New Deal agencies. As a group of black social workers visiting Hyde Park proclaimed: "For the first time Negro men and women have reason to believe that their government does care." That sentiment was bolstered time and again by the battles that Alexander, Ickes, Williams, and other New Dealers waged in pursuit of a more equitable deal for blacks, by their overt disdain for racist attitudes and practices, and by their public championing, in articles and speeches, of the cause of racial justice and equality. Blacks viewed their actions with hope as symbolic of a new high-level governmental disposition to oppose racial discrimination.

Blacks in the 1930s also applauded the success of these New Dealers in enlarging the roster of Afro-Americans working for the government. The number of blacks on the federal payroll more than tripled during the Depression decade. The proportion of black government employees in 1940 was twice what it had been in 1930. In addition, the Roosevelt Administration unprecedentedly hired thousands of blacks as architects, engineers, lawyers, librarians, office managers, and statisticians. This was viewed at the time as "the first significant step toward the participation of Negroes in federal government activity," and as "representing something new in the administration of our national affairs." To insure further steps, the Administration also abolished the Civil Service regulations that had required job seekers to designate their race and to attach a photograph to their application forms. Some New Deal officials desegregated the cafeterias, restrooms, and secretarial pools in their agencies and departments; others highlighted their abhorrence of Jim Crow by having blacks and whites work at adjoining desks.

Roosevelt also reversed two decades of diminishing black patronage. He appointed over one hundred blacks to administrative posts in the New Deal. Previous administrations had, at best, reserved a handful of honorific and innocuous positions for loyal Negro party leaders. Roosevelt selected a large number of nonpartisan black professionals and veterans of the civil rights movement and placed them in formal positions of public importance so that both government officers and the Afro-American community regarded their presence as significant. Popularly referred to as the Black Cabinet or Black Brain Trust, these black officials had considerably more symbolic value than actual power. They rarely succeeded in pushing the New Deal further along the road to racial equality than it wished to go. Most of their efforts to win greater equity for blacks were defeated by interest groups that were better able to bring pressure to bear on Roosevelt. But their very being and prominence, Roy Wilkins of the NAACP noted, "had never existed before." This fact alone elicited howls from white southerners that "Negroes were taking over the White House," which was hardly the case. Still, the presence of the Black Cabinet, like Roosevelt's selection of William Hastie as the first Afro-American federal judge in American history, hinted at a New Deal determination to break, however timorously, with prevailing customs of racial prejudice. As Mary McLeod Bethune, director of the NYA's Division of Negro Affairs, emphasized during the thirties, such appointments were not "tokenism" but the essential first steps in making the government aware of black needs and in planning policies that would help the race.

The Black Cabinet certainly did raise the level of national awareness of racial issues. The race advisers appointed by Roosevelt articulated the problems of blacks, the ultimate goal of integration, and the specific responsibility of the federal government in the area of civil rights, both within the corridors of the various agencies in which they worked and in the public conferences and reports they generated. "At no time since the curtain had dropped on the Reconstruction drama," wrote Henry Lee Moon of the NAACP, "had government focused so much attention upon the Negro's basic needs as did the New Deal." For example, the NYA convened a three-day National Conference on the Problems of the Negro and Negro Youth in 1937, for the purpose of increasing support for greater governmental assistance to blacks. It was addressed by four Cabinet members, half-a-dozen agency chiefs, and Eleanor Roosevelt. Such a conference would have been inconceivable before the New Deal. As Mary Bethune noted in her opening remarks: "This is the first time in the history of our race that the Negroes of America have felt free to reduce to writing their problems and plans for meeting them with the expectancy of sympathetic understanding and interpretation." Even Ralph Bunche, who was perhaps the New Deal's severest black critic, admitted at the end of the 1930s that the New Deal was without precedent in the manner in which it granted "broad recognition to the existence of the Negro as a national problem and undertook to give specific consideration to this fact in many ways."

A NEW HOPE

Roosevelt appointees also stirred the hopes of Afro-Americans by establishing precedents that challenged local white control over blacks. The National Advisory Committee on Education, which was appointed by Roosevelt, called in 1938 for specific guarantees that federal grants to states for education would be spent equitably for black as well as white schooling. No governmental body had said that before. Less than a decade earlier, in fact, that exact proposition had been overwhelmingly rejected by President Hoover's National Advisory Committee on Education. In fact, only the blacks on the Hoover committee supported it. But, during the New Deal, the earlier all-black minority opinion became a part of the official proposal, and the committee's recommendation appeared verbatim with Roosevelt's support in the Harrison-Fletcher-Thomas federal aid to education bill submitted to Congress.

The New Deal, indeed, substantially expanded the scope of the federal government's authority and constricted traditional states' rights. The states' failures to cope with the economic crisis enlarged the responsibilities of the national government, and the New Deal involved the states in joint programs in which the federal government increasingly imposed the standards and goals. This alteration in the system of federalism augured well for black hopes of future federal civil rights actions, as did the emergence of a new conception of positive government, the "powerful promoter of society's welfare," which guaranteed every American a minimally decent economic existence as a matter of right, not charity, and which assumed the role of the protector of weak interests that could not contend successfully on their own.

Roosevelt's appointments to the Supreme Court immediately sanctioned the expansion of federal power over matters of race and strengthened the rights of blacks. After FDR's abortive attempt at "court packing" in 1937, the personnel on the Supreme Court changed swiftly and power passed into the hands of New Dealers, who articulated a new judicial philosophy which championed the rights of racial and religious minorities and formulated new constitutional guarantees to protect civil rights. As a result, both the number of cases involving black rights brought before the federal courts and the percentage of decisions favorable to black plaintiffs leaped dramatically. What would culminate in the Warren Court clearly began in the Roosevelt Court. With the exception of James Byrnes, Roosevelt's eight appointees to the Court were truly partisans of the cause of civil rights. Together, men who had long been associated with the NAACP and issues of racial justice, such as Felix Frankfurter, Wiley Rutledge, and Frank Murphy, joined with new converts like Hugo Black and William O. Douglas to begin dismantling a century of legal discrimination against blacks. Their decisions in cases involving the exclusion of blacks from juries, the right to picket against discrimination in employment, racially restrictive covenants, inequality in interstate transportation, peonage, disfranchisement, and discrimination in the payment of black teachers and in graduate education signaled the demise of the separate-but-equal doctrine established by *Plessy v. Ferguson* (1896).

Such decisions, according to legal scholar Loren Miller, made the Negro less a *freedman* and more a *free man*. The federalizing of the Bill of Rights left blacks less at the mercy of states' rights. The inquiry into the facts of segregation, rather than just the theory, diminished the possibility of anything racially separate meeting the test of constitutionality. And, the expansion of the concept of state action severely circumscribed the boundaries of private discrimination. Perhaps most importantly, the decisions of the Roosevelt Court had a multiplier effect. They stimulated scores of additional challenges to Jim Crow, both in court and out. Fittingly, in 1944, when the Supreme Court struck down the white primary, the only dissenter was Owen Roberts, the sole justice then sitting whom Roosevelt had not appointed.

ELEANOR ROOSEVELT

Although not a presidential appointee, Eleanor Roosevelt certainly made the most of her position as First Lady to link the civil rights cause with the New Deal. Working quietly within the administration, at first, Mrs. Roosevelt influenced her husband and numerous agency heads to be more concerned with the special needs of blacks. Gradually her commitment became more open and visible. Functioning as an unofficial ombudsman for blacks, she goaded bureaucrats and congressmen into lessening racial discrimination in federal programs, and acted as the main conduit between the civil rights leadership and the higher circles of the New Deal and the Democratic party. Repeatedly breaking with tradition, Eleanor Roosevelt openly entertained Afro-American leaders at the White House, posed for photographs with blacks, and publicly associated herself with most of the major civil rights organizations and issues. The peripatetic Mrs. Roosevelt spoke out for National Sharecroppers Week, addressed conventions of the Brotherhood of Sleeping Car Porters and National Council of Negro Women, candidly backed the civil rights activities of the American Youth Congress, and frequently pleaded for racial tolerance and fairness in her syndicated newspaper column, published articles, and radio broadcasts.

"Nigger Lover Eleanor," as some whites derided her, squarely placed her authority and prestige behind the drive for civil rights legislation in President Roosevelt's second term. Delivering the keynote address at the first meeting of the Southern Electoral Reform League, she emphasized the necessity for a federal act to end all poll tax requirements for voting. Mrs. Roosevelt also publicly endorsed the quest for anti-lynching legislation, and sat prominently in the Senate gallery during the efforts of northern liberals to invoke cloture and shut off the southern filibuster of the 1938 Wagner-Van Nuys-Gavagan antilynching bill. In the same year Eleanor Roosevelt also helped to organize the Southern Conference for Human Welfare. At its opening session in Birmingham, Alabama, she defied the local segregation ordinance, conspicuously taking a seat on the "Colored" side of the auditorium. White supremacists immediately condemned the First Lady's act as "an insult to every white man and woman in the South." But in the Negro press, Eleanor Roosevelt's disdain for Jim Crow was a "rare and precious moment in the social history of America." Further stirring the wrath of white supremacists and gaining the admiration of blacks, Mrs. Roosevelt began to denounce racial discrimination in the defense program. In 1939, she publicly decried the bigotry of the Daughters of the American Revolution when that organization refused to rent its Constitution Hall for a concert by the famous black contralto, Marian Anderson. Mrs. Roosevelt then used her "My Day" newspaper column to explain why she could no longer remain a member of a group practicing such discrimination and, working with her husband and the NAACP, she arranged for Marian Anderson to sing her concert in front of the Lincoln Memorial. Two months later, on behalf of the NAACP, Eleanor Roosevelt officially presented the Spingarn Medal for Freedom to Marian Anderson.

PROGRESS, NOT PERFECTION

Such highly publicized actions of Mrs. Roosevelt, as well as the President's increasingly more egalitarian gestures and rhetoric, had a vital impact on blacks in the 1930s. Although Franklin Roosevelt shied away from any direct challenges to white supremacy, the very fact that he frequently invited blacks to the White House, held conferences with civil rights leaders, and appeared before Afro-American organizations indicated to blacks that they mattered. It was a start. Mindful of political realities, blacks sought progress, not perfection. They understood that no president would act boldly and unyieldingly on black rights until a majority constituency for dramatic change had emerged. Until then, symbolic actions would count, for they played an important role in educating and persuading, in inspiring hope and commitment.

Accordingly, the civil rights leadership and their allies in the 1930s utilized the President's association with the campaigns for antilynching and antipoll tax legislation to mobilize future support. Their public complaints to the contrary, these black rights spokesmen recognized the insurmountable barriers to cloture being voted in the Senate and the necessity for Roosevelt to maintain the backing of the southern leadership in Congress. They knew he would not jeopardize his relief and defense programs for a futile attempt at civil rights legislation. Accordingly, blacks extracted the greatest possible advantages from what the President said and did, however lukewarm and timorous.

On the poll tax, Roosevelt publicly supported the legislative efforts for its abolition. "The right to vote," he declared, "must be open to all our citizens irrespective of race, color, or creed—without tax or artificial restriction of any kind. The sooner we get to that basis of political equality, the better it will be for the country as a whole." In a public letter Roosevelt vigorously endorsed the antipoll tax movement in Arkansas. At a press conference in 1938 he opposed the use of poll taxes: "They are inevitably contrary to the fundamental democracy and its representative form of government in which we believe." No legislator or informed citizen doubted where the President stood on this matter. In part, this helps to explain why the House of Representatives in 1941 voted to pass an antipoll tax bill by a better than three-to-one margin.

Similarly, the President aided the civil rights movement on antilynching, both with public statements to influence mass opinion and private pressures on the Senate to get it to consider legislation, but Roosevelt would neither place the antilynching bills on his list of "must" legislation, nor intervene with the Senate leadership to end the filibusters that doomed the proposals from even coming to a vote. Over a coast-to-coast radio hook-up, early in his administration, Roosevelt denounced lynching as "a vile form of collective murder." Lynch law, he continued, "is murder, a deliberate and definite disobedience of the high command, 'Thou shalt not kill.' We do not excuse those in high places or low who condone lynch law." No president had ever spoken like that before. W. E. B. DuBois, writing immediately afterward in *The Crisis,* observed: "It took war, riot and upheaval to make Wilson say one small word. Nothing ever induced Herbert Hoover to say anything on the subject worth the saying. Even Harding was virtually dumb." Only Roosevelt, DuBois concluded, "has declared frankly that lynching is murder. We all knew it, but it is unusual to have a President of the United States admit it. These things give us hope."

More ambiguously, Roosevelt in 1934 authorized Senators Edward Costigan and Robert Wagner to inform the Majority Leader "that the President will be glad to see the anti-lynching bill pass and wishes it passed." And, in 1935, he requested that the Majority Leader permit the Senate to consider the bill. The half-heartedness of Roosevelt's support did nothing to avert the inevitable southern filibuster that killed the measure in 1935. Meanwhile, Roosevelt's private encouragement of others to keep up the fight led to a protracted and bitter wrangle over antilynching legislation in 1938. A far cry from the charade of 1935 in which both sides went through the motions, the two-month-long talkathon of 1938 smacked of fratricide. The southern senators overwhelmingly blamed the New Deal for provoking the civil rights issues that alienated the South from the Democratic party. They pledged to talk as long as necessary to "preserve the white supremacy of America." And, they held Roosevelt responsible for having the Senate rules enforced "in a technical manner," for holding night sessions in an attempt to break the filibuster, and for trying to invoke cloture twice.

The result in Congress notwithstanding, black leaders gained significantly from the struggle against lynching and from the President's involvement in the cause. Lynchings declined from a high for the decade of twenty-eight in 1933 to eighteen in 1935, six in 1938, and two in 1939. To ward off federal legislation, most southern states made greater efforts to prevent lynchings and enacted their own bills to stop the crime. At the end of the decade, Roosevelt established a special Civil Rights Section of the Justice Department and empowered it to investigate all lynchings that might involve some denial of a federal right. And, in no small part because the public identified the crusade against lynching with the First Family, the campaign for federal legislation attracted new supporters and allies to the black cause who would stay to fight against discrimination in the defense program, segregation in education, and the disfranchisement of Afro-Americans. In this limited regard, the President's pronouncements meant much to blacks. In political language, at least, they were yet another manifestation of Roosevelt's desire to win the allegiance of blacks and to take the steps necessary to retain their loyalty, even at the risk of gradual southern disenchantment with the New Deal.

Roosevelt's overtures in this direction also showed in the series of precedent-shattering "firsts" that he orchestrated in the 1936 campaign. Never before had the Democrats accredited an Afro-American as a convention delegate; in 1936 they accorded thirty blacks that distinction. For the first time, additionally, the national party in 1936 invited black reporters to the regular press box; chose a black minister to offer the convention invocation; selected blacks to deliver the welcome address and one of the speeches seconding Roosevelt's renomination; and placed a black on the delegation to notify the Vice President of his renomination. Yet another significant event at the convention occurred when liberals and New Dealers wiped out the century-old rule, utilized by the South as a political veto, which required the Democratic nominee to win two-thirds of the delegates' votes in order to obtain the nomination. The white South recognized the threat and resented the intrusion. And its fears of a future attempt by the New Deal to alter race relations were heightened when Roosevelt pointedly campaigned before black audiences and promised that in his administration there would be "no forgotten races" as well as no forgotten men. Then in the 1940 presidential race, Roosevelt affirmed his desire to include blacks evenhandedly in defense training and employment, promoted the first black to the rank of Army Brigadier General, and insisted that, for the first time, the Democrats include a specific Negro plank in the party platform, pledging "to strive for complete legislative safeguards against discrimination in government services and benefits."

A NEW DEAL FOR BLACKS: AN ASSESSMENT

However circumspect this New Deal record seems today, for blacks in the thirties it meant change for the better. The mixture of symbolic and substantive assistance, of rhetoric and recognition, led blacks to cast their ballots overwhelmingly for Roosevelt once the New Deal began. After voting more than 70 percent for Herbert Hoover in 1932, a majority of black voters deserted the Republican party for the first time in history in 1934, about two-thirds of the Afro-Americans registered in 1936 entered the Roosevelt coalition, and nearly 68 percent of all black voters in 1940 went for FDR. This startling shift in the black vote, more pronounced than that of any other ethnic, racial, or religious group, according to the NAACP came not only because of black "concern for immediate relief, either in jobs or direct assistance," but because of "a feeling that Mr. Roosevelt represented a kind of philosophy of government which will mean much to their cause."

Virtually every civil rights spokesman stressed both the value of new government precedents favorable to blacks and the manner in which the New Deal made explicit the federal government's responsibility in the field of civil rights. Editorials in the black press and journals frequently reiterated that the New Deal had ended the "invisibility" of the race problem and had made civil rights a part of the liberal agenda. Perhaps most importantly, blacks in the thirties lauded the manifold ways in which the New Deal reform spirit ushered in a new political climate in which Afro-Americans and their allies could begin to struggle with some expectation of success. They took heart from the expanding authority of the federal government and the changing balance of power in the Democratic party, as well as from the overt sympathy for the underprivileged shown by the Roosevelt Administration; and they made common cause with fellow-sufferers in pressing the New Deal to become even more of an instrument for humane, liberal reform.

These developments did little to change the concrete aspects of life for most blacks in the 1930s. The New Deal failed to end the rampant discrimination against blacks in the North, who were living in ghettos that had turned to slums and who were twice as likely to be unemployed as whites. The Roosevelt Administration also failed to enfranchise black southerners, to eradicate segregation, or to elevate the great mass of blacks who remained a submerged caste of menials, sharecroppers, unskilled laborers, and domestics. These facts cannot be gainsaid. The New Deal record on race is replete with failures and timidity, unfulfilled promises, and insufficient effort. The New Deal did not fundamentally transform the economic, legal, or social status of Afro-Americans.

But for the millions of blacks who hung FDR's picture on their walls, who kept voting for Roosevelt, and naming their children after him, something vital did begin in the New Deal, breaking the crust of quiescence that had long stifled even the dream of equal opportunity and full participation in American life. The New Deal gave blacks hope. A black newspaper called it "the emergence of a new type of faith." The pervasive despondency that had led several generations of Americans, black and white, to regard the racial status quo as immutable gradually gave way to a conviction that racial reform was possible. The dream that would prove indispensable in the continuing struggle for black equality could at last be dreamt. The barely visible flicker of black hope at the start of the New Deal would shine brightly as the United States mobilized for World War II.

QUESTIONS FOR DISCUSSION

1. What were the political constraints that might have deterred President Roosevelt from more actively supporting the struggle of black Americans for racial justice and equality?

2. Why did black Americans so dramatically shift their votes from the Republican to the Democratic parties between 1932 and 1936?

Chapter Six

War and Postwar

THOMAS G. PATERSON

From World War to Cold War

The writing of history would be so much simpler if events ordered themselves as neatly as the chapters of a book, with one ending before the next one began. Unfortunately, it doesn't often happen that way. No one, for example, can say with any degree of certainty when World War II ended and the Cold War began. What we do know, however, is that the domestic and international dislocations of the World War laid the groundwork for the Cold War.

Americans, fortunately, have not had to fight a war on their soil for well over a century. For that reason alone, it is difficult for us to understand the enormity of the devastation wrought by the Second World War on the nations and peoples of the world. "Europe lost more than 30 million people in the Second World War." Well over 100,000 Japanese were killed in the few seconds it took to explode atomic bombs over Hiroshima and Nagasaki. The living suffered from the dislocations of war as well. Millions were left homeless or stateless, nations and economies devastated, the international order pulled apart. The war, in short, as Thomas Paterson shows us in the following selection, "had overturned a world. . . ."

World War II gave way to the Cold War, and the United States and the Soviet Union, allies in the first, became enemies in the second as each "intervened" beyond its borders "to exploit the political opportunities created by the destructive scythe of World War II."

Winston S. Churchill wore his usual bulldog visage. The ever-present cigar and hunched gait, other familiar trademarks of the British prime minister, also drew the crowd's attention on that very hot day of July 16, 1945. He was surveying the dusty remains of the Nazi capital—"that rubble heap near Potsdam,"

Thomas Paterson teaches history at the University of Connecticut. He is the author of a number of books on diplomatic history and the Cold War, including *On Every Front: The Making of a Cold War,* from which the following selection has been taken.

Adapted from *On Every Front: The Making of the Cold War,* by Thomas G. Paterson, pp. 1–3, 9–32, footnotes deleted, by permission of the author and W. W. Norton & Company, Inc. Copyright © 1979 by W. W. Norton & Company, Inc.

murmured one Berliner. This time a preoccupied Churchill evinced little interest in his curious onlookers. What captured Churchill's regard was the grisly aftermath in Berlin of heavy Allied bombing and artillery fire and stout German resistance. He and the passengers in his motorcade grew sick, utterly stunned by the stark display of carnage in the German city.

"There is nothing to do here," sighed a dispirited Berliner. Old men, women, and children trudged along, aimlessly pushing wheelbarrows. Over a million people lived in cellars, ruins, and makeshift suburban shacks, trading what they could for precious scraps of food to support their meager diet. Sixty-five to 75 percent of the city was leveled or damaged. The once-prized chariot of victory on the Brandenberg Gate had been reduced to a gnarled mass of molten metal. The Reichstag was a hollow shell. Some "*Nicht fur juden*" signs were still posted, ugly reminders of the German extermination of European Jews. Industrial equipment which survived the bombings had been torn from its foundations by the Russians as war booty, leaving stripped, hull-like factories. Partially buried corpses lay rotting in the sun. Visitors and citizens alike recoiled from the stench of death that hung everywhere. Lord Moran, who accompanied Churchill in Berlin, "felt a sense of nausea." Worse, "it was like the first time I saw a surgeon open a belly and the intestines gushed out."

The curious prime minister entered what was left of Adolf Hitler's Chancellery. The Führer's marble-topped desk lay in a thousand pieces. Iron Crosses, military ribbons, and papers littered the floor. Uncharacteristically, Churchill said little as the descent into Hitler's damp hideaway apparently induced quiet reflection. Members of the prime minister's party picked up souvenirs; one pocketed a fragment of Hitler's world map. Depressed by what he saw, General H. L. Ismay hurried away to his villa to take a hot bath and a strong drink. That night Churchill finally talked about his visit to the Chancellery. "It was from there that Hitler planned to govern the world," he mused. "A good many have tried that; all failed." Savoring the Allied victory, the prime minister smiled contentedly and went to bed.

The president of the United States, Harry S. Truman, surveyed Berlin that same day. After reviewing the American 2nd Armored Division, the president led his entourage down the Wilhemstrasse to the Chancellery of the Third Reich, all the while growing more awestruck by the destruction of the city. "That's what happens," he remarked, "when a man overreaches himself." For two hours Truman rode through Berlin streets. "I was thankful," he noted later, "that the United States had been spared the unbelievable devastation of this war." Berlin had actually appeared worse a month earlier, before Berliners, under the stern guidance of Russian and other Allied soldiers, began to stack bricks and shovel ashes. American diplomat Robert Murphy found that "the odor of death was everywhere." Indeed, "the canals were choked with bodies and refuse." General Lucius Clay, who would soon become the military governor of the American zone, was also stunned. "The streets were piled high with debris which left in many places only a narrow one-way passage between mounds of rubble, and frequent detours had to be made where bridges and viaducts were destroyed. . . . It was like a city of the dead."

From urban center to rural village, Germany looked charred and ravaged. Bomb-gutted Cologne and Nuremberg were hardly recognizable. Ninety-three percent of the houses of Düsseldorf were totally destroyed. Hamburg, Stuttgart, and Dresden had been laid waste by firebombs and firestorms. In Dresden mounds of bodies had to be bulldozed into mass graves or burned on huge makeshift grills, so great was the toll and the fear of epidemic disease. An American Army Air Corpsman flying low over the country at the end of the war could not spot streets or houses in Mannheim—only tossed dirt. "Aachen," he observed, "lay bleaching in the sun like bones on a desert." A disbelieving companion gazed at the pulverized land below and asked, "Where do the people live?" . . .

Europe lost more than 30 million people in the Second World War. The grisly statistical gallery ranked Russia an uncontested first. Then came Poland with 5.8 million dead; Germany, with 4.5 million; Yugoslavia, 1.5 million; France, 600,000; Rumania, 460,000; Hungary, 430,000; Czechoslovakia, 415,000; Italy, 410,000; Britain, 400,000; and the Netherlands, 210,000. C. Day Lewis's "War Poem" read:

> They lie in the Sunday Street
> Like effigies thrown down after a fête
> Among the bare-faced houses frankly yawning revulsion,
> Fag ends of fires, litter of rubble, stale
> Confetti sprinkle of blood. . . .

*   *   *   *   *

As for the living, they had to endure food shortages, closed factories, idle fields, cold stoves, currency inflation, festering wounds. In West Germany alone, two million cripples hobbled about. Thirty-four percent of Germans born in 1924 were badly mutilated in some way by 1945. The sad photographs of ill-clad, skeletal bodies struggling for life in Germany's concentration camps provided evidence enough of the human depredation. Displaced persons (DPs) provided another picture. "The wind will tell you what has come to us; /It rolls our brittle bones from pole to pole," went "The Refugees' Testament." Many dazed refugees wandered helplessly through Europe, searching for relatives, for friends, for a livelihood, for a ride home. The words of British writer Richard Mayne have poignantly depicted the lives of Europe's survivors:

> To many of the troops who first encountered them, the people in parts of Europe seemed a population of cripples, of women and children and the very old. Some were starving; some were sick with typhus or dysentery. . . . The survivors, gray-faced ghosts in parodies of clothing, trundled their salvaged belongings in homemade handcarts—rugs, threadbare overcoats, a kettle, an alarm clock, a battered toy. They waited at stand-pipes for a dribble of brown water; they queued for bread and potatoes; they rummaged for sticks and scraps. For them, this waste land of rubble, rags, and hunger was a prison without privacy or dignity; and like all prisons, it smelled. It smelled of dust, oil, gunpowder, and greasy metal; of drains and vermin; of decay and burning and the unburied dead.

*   *   *   *   *

For defeated Japan, the bitter results of imperial dreams could be measured in the loss of 2 million lives. Tokyo's population was reduced from 6.5 million to 3 million by war's end, and 700,000 of the city's buildings were destroyed. American planes had dropped napalm-filled bombs, engulfing the city in chemically induced firestorms which generated temperatures of up to 1,800°F. The odor of burning flesh drifted upwards, sickening the pilots who delivered the horrible punishment. In one savage attack alone, on May 23, 1945, 83,000 people died in what observers described as a mass burning. The fifteen-mile stretch between Yokohama and Tokyo, said an American officer who accompanied American general Douglas MacArthur to Japan, had become a "wilderness of rubble." A light dust hung in the air, staining visitor's clothing. Wood-and-paper houses had been reduced to powdered ashes, factories to twisted metal. A shanty town of rusted, corrugated sheets and other junk ringed the capital city, its inhabitants reminding some observers of the Okies who trekked to California during the Great Depression—except that the Japanese scene was more emotionally debilitating. Only the downtown commercial district was free from the mounds of debris. One of the first American naval officers to arrive in the humbled Japanese city wrote to a friend that "I feel like a tramp who has become used to sleeping in a graveyard." A British visitor, Lord Alan-brooke, also visited Tokyo: "Everywhere the same desolation; it must be seen to be believed."

Hiroshima and Nagasaki were special cases, sharing and suffering a special fate. Hiroshima had been Japan's eighth largest city. A residential, commercial center of 250,000 people, it was singled out by American officials because it also housed regional military headquarters. Until August 6, 1945, a cloudless, warm day, Hiroshima had not had to endure large-scale American bombing raids. But at 8:15 A.M. the crew of the *Enola Gay,* a specially outfitted B–29, unleashed "Little Boy," an atomic device packing the power of 20,000 tons of TNT. The bomb fell for fifty seconds and exploded about 2,000 feet above ground. A blinding streak of light raced across the sky; a tremendous boom punctuated the air. A huge, purplish cloud of dust, smoke, and debris shot 40,000 feet into the atmosphere. At ground level the heat became suffocating, the winds violent. Buildings instantly disintegrated. Shadows were etched in stone. Trees were stripped of their leaves. Fires erupted everywhere, and the sky grew dark. Survivors staggered toward water to quench their intense thirst. Skin peeled from burned bodies. A maimed resident, Dr. Michihiko Hachiya, noted that "no one talked, and the ominous silence was relieved only by a subdued rustle among so many people, restless, in pain, anxious, and afraid, waiting for something else to happen." The toll: seventy to eighty thousand dead, an equal number wounded, and 81 percent of the city's buildings destroyed. Three days later the nightmare was repeated in Nagasaki, where at least 35,000 died. Upon hearing of the success of the world's first nuclear destruction of a city, President Truman remarked, "this is the greatest thing in history."

Whether this historical judgment was accurate or not, the tragedy at Hiroshima was but one chapter in the story of massive, war-induced destruction.

This story, with all its horrid details, must be catalogued not for its shock value but for its illustration of how large were the problems of the postwar world, how shaky the scaffolding of the international order. Hitler once said about his warmongering pursuits that "we may be destroyed, but if we are, we shall drag a world with us—a world in flames." He partially succeeded, and World War II, like any war of substantial duration, served as an agent of conspicuous change, of revolution. The conflagration of 1939–45 was so wrenching, so total, so profound, that a world was overturned—not simply a material world of crops, buildings, and rails, not simply a human world of healthy and productive laborers, farmers, businessmen, and intellectuals, not simply a secure world of close-knit families and communities, not simply a military world of Nazi stormtroopers and Japanese kamikazis, but all that and more. The war also unhinged the world of stable politics, inherited wisdom, traditions, institutions, alliances, loyalties, commerce, and classes. When Acting Secretary of State Dean Acheson surveyed the problems facing American foreign policy in the postwar era, he saw as uppermost "social *disintegration,* political *disintegration,* the loss of faith by people in leaders who have led them in the past, and a great deal of economic *disintegration.*"

Leaders of all political persuasions, as they witnessed the immensity of the destruction, spoke of a new age without knowing its dimensions. The normal way of doing things now seemed inappropriate, although as creatures of the past, the survivors remained attached to ideas and institutions which seemed to provide security through familiarity. They sensed the seriousness and the enormity of the tasks of cleaning up the rubble, of putting the broken world back together again, of shaping an orderly international system. Yet it was evident, too, that few nations or individuals had the material resources, talent, and desire—the sheer energy, guts, and money—to mold a brave new world out of the discredited and crumbled old. If the reconstruction tasks seemed herculean, however, the opportunities appeared boundless for the ambitious, the hearty, and the caring. One vigorous, optimistic, well-intentioned, competitive voice sounded above the rubble that constituted London, Berlin, Warsaw, Minsk, and Tokyo. That voice echoed with power from the United States, the wartime "arsenal of democracy."

At war's end President Truman declared a two-day national holiday. Horns, bells, and makeshift noisemakers sounded across the nation. Paraders in Los Angeles played leapfrog on Hollywood Boulevard; further north, jubilant sailors broke windows along San Francisco's Market Street. In New York City tons of litter were tossed from the windows of skyscrapers on cheering crowds below. Stock market prices shot up. A five-year-old boy recorded the August 1945 moment: "This is the best year. The war is over. Two wars are over. Everyone is happy. Tin cans are rolling. Everything is confused. And little pieces of paper." It was truly a happy time. Not only was the dying over, but the United States had emerged from the global conflict in the unique position of an unscathed belligerent. No bombs fell on American cities. No armies ravaged the countryside. No American boundaries were redrawn. Factories stood in place, producing goods at an impressive rate. In August, at the General Motors plant in Moraine, Ohio, shiny new Frigidaire refrigerators and airplane propeller blades moved along parallel assembly lines. Farms were rich with crops, and full employment during the war years had buoyed family savings. "The American people," remarked the director of the Office of War Mobilization and Reconversion, "are in the pleasant predicament of having to learn to live 50 percent better than they have ever lived before."

Whereas much of Europe and Asia faced the massive task of "reconstruction," the United States faced "reconversion"—adjusting the huge war machine to peacetime purposes. Automobile plants had to convert production from tanks to cars, a delightful prospect for auto manufacturers, who knew that Americans were eager to spend their wartime earnings on consumer goods once again. With great pride Americans applauded their good fortune. They were different. They had no rubble to clear. The Russians knew, said Josef Stalin in a grand understatement, that "things are not bad in the United States."

Americans had worries. Some feared that the sparkling prosperity of the war years would dissipate in a postwar economic disaster. They remembered that military production, not Roosevelt's New Deal reform program, had pulled the United States out of the Great Depression of the 1930s. Would there be enough jobs for the returning GIs? They also suffered temporary shortages of many goods, sugar and gasoline among them, and resented the rationing which limited their economic freedom. "Hey, don'tche know there's a war on?" said clerks to anxious consumers. There were not enough houses to meet the needs of an expanding and mobile American population, which grew from 131 million to 140 million during the war years. The national debt skyrocketed from $37 billion to $269 billion. The war cost the federal government $664 billion. Inflation threatened economic stability. At least 10 million American families lived in poverty. Still, these national pains, although arousing grumbles, seemed bearable or were played down. As *Fortune* magazine commented two months after V-J Day: "August 14, 1945, marked not only the war's end but the beginning of the greatest peacetime industrial boom in the world's history."

Cold data justified *Fortune's* enthusiasm. The Gross National Product of the United States expanded from $90.5 billion (1939) to $211.9 billion (1945). Steel production jumped from 53 million tons in 1939 to 80 million tons at the close of the war. American businessmen, cut off from rubber imports from the Dutch East Indies during the war, developed synthetic rubber, launching a new industry. New aluminum plants went up, and the aircraft industry, in infancy when Germany attacked Poland, became a major new business as well. In 1939 only 5,856 military and civil airplanes were turned out; but in 1945 the figure reached 48,912, a decline from the peak of over 95,000 in 1944. All told, over 300,000 aircraft rolled from American factories during the war—a figure far surpassing that of any other nation, including Germany and Japan combined. Employment in the aircraft industry swelled 1,600 percent. With its numerous aircraft factories, Southern California bustled, becoming a mecca for dreamers of wealth and adventure. Four hundred forty-four thousand people moved to Los Angeles during the war.

Workers' wages kept up with inflation during the war years. Women took jobs once held by men who were called to military duty. Unable to spend their abundant incomes on the shrinking supply of consumer items during the war, many Americans visited their banks. Total personal savings increased from $6.85 billion to $36.41 billion. Americans continued to spend for pleasure as well. The World Series of baseball played on, and films whirred at local theaters. Beaches beckoned vacationers. In the summer of 1944, as Europe and Asia reeled from the blasts of war, Americans flocked to resorts and racetracks. Betting in horse racing totalled a record-breaking $1.4 billion in 1945, even though the tracks were closed from January to May. Farmers enjoyed some of their best years of the twentieth century. Whereas in 1939 they counted 66 million head of cattle, by 1945 that figure reached 83 million. Agricultural output increased 15 percent. American universities also enjoyed improvements. Government contracts for scientific research went to the California Institute for Technology for rocket studies; Princeton received grants for ballistics research. In mid-1945 the Massachusetts Institute for Technology held government contracts worth $117 million. The GI Bill, which offered money to veterans for their college educations, promised higher enrollments. Despite uncertainties about the future, life looked good to Americans, and after the hardships and setbacks of the depression decade, "the old self-confident America was coming into its stride again." Wartime musicals like *Carousel* and *Oklahoma* caught the optimistic mood, and sluggers Joe DiMaggio and Ted Williams were heading home to reclaim their baseball fame.

When foreign delegates journeyed to San Francisco for the United Nations Conference in April of 1945, many crossed the territorial United States and could not help but notice the stark contrast with war-torn Europe and Asia. Soviet Foreign Minister V. M. Molotov once referred to statistics in the *World Almanac* to remind Americans about their uniqueness as prosperous survivors of the Second World War. During a conversation with Stalin in 1944, the President of the United States Chamber of Commerce, Eric A. Johnston, citing the American example, lectured the Soviet leader about the need for better distribution of goods in Russia. Stalin replied, ". . . but in order to distribute, there must be something to distribute." Months before, at the Teheran Conference, Stalin had toasted the United States as a "country of machines," applauding its great productive capacity for delivering victory to the Allies. Truman's words also bear repeating: "I was thankful that the United States had been spared the unbelievable devastation of this war." Even the death count for American servicemen, about 400,000, appeared merciful when compared to staggering figures elsewhere. Indeed, the *Saturday Evening Post* editorialized in 1945 that "we Americans can boast that we are not as other men are." The war had overturned a world, and many Americans believed that they were now on top of it. A new international system for the postwar era was in the making.

*   *   *   *   *

In the rubble-strewn postwar world, international relations changed markedly from prewar interactions. Any historical period, such as the Cold War, is identified by a particular structure of relationships among the world's leading nations—by, in short, the international "system." . . .

Higher degrees of conflict are reached when the international system undergoes significant change, when it metamorphoses into a new or revised system. Such was the case after World War II. Change, by definition, is destabilizing. Some postwar leaders, even though immersed in day-to-day decision-making, pondered the general characteristics of the international system. They knew that significant changes had altered the configuration of power. As participants in and shapers of a new age, they were "present at the creation." But the outline of the new system was only vaguely evident. With the historian's advantage of hindsight, however, we can delineate the peculiar properties of the postwar world and suggest that the process of creating a new system out of the ashes of the discredited prewar system intensified the conflict inherent in any international structure.

Yet this view of systemic conflict cannot serve as a comprehensive explanation for the origins of the Cold War. For if the Soviet-American confrontation was simply the inevitable product of the conflict-ridden international system, there would be little purpose in studying the leaders, ideas, policies, or needs of individual nations, because events would be largely beyond their control. Under this interpretation the system would dictate antagonistic relations. It would not matter whether different personalities or different national policies existed. Few scholars, however, subscribe to this restricted analysis of history. We know that leaders made choices, even if they only dimly understood their consequences. Harry S. Truman, Winston Churchill, and Josef Stalin helped to create the international system to which they had to react. A complete history of the beginnings of the Cold War, then, must include not only the traits of the international system but also the dynamics of particular nations and individuals. . . . [A] macroanalytic view will enable us to identify the opportunities and constraints which faced the major actors. Or, as Professor Bruce M. Russett has suggested, this level of analysis outlines the "menu" of world affairs—the choices available, as well as the limits of choice. It sketches the "big picture," so that the disparate components of the postwar system can be examined in proper relationship. It helps us to determine which nations held real or potential power and why, ultimately, they moved toward restrictive spheres of influence and away from a community of interest and international cooperation.

Conflict in the postwar years was accentuated by wrenching changes in the international system—a redistribution of power and a departure from a Europe-centered world. Two nations emerged from the rubble of World War II to claim first rank. The competitive interaction between the United States and the Soviet Union—"like two big dogs chewing on a bone," said Senator J. William Fulbright—contributed to the bipolarism of the immediate postwar years. "Not since Rome and Carthage," Dean Acheson observed, "had there been such a polarization of power on this earth." This new bipolar structure replaced the multipolar system of the 1930s, wherein at least six nations were active, influential participants. By the late 1940s, decisions made in Washington, D.C. and Moscow often determined whether people in other nations voted, where they lived, and how much they ate. The nations which had tried to wield such authority in the 1930s had fallen from their elevated status. Japan, Italy, and Germany were defeated and occupied; England, nearly bankrupt, dependent, and unable to police its empire, was reduced to a resentful second-rate power; France, much of whose territory had been held by the Germans during the war, was still suffering from unstable politics and no longer mustered international respect.

The abrupt removal of Germany and Japan from positions of high authority in international relations created power vacuums in Europe and Asia. The United States and Soviet Russia, eager to fulfill their visions of the postwar world and to seize opportunities for extending their respective influence, were attracted to these vacuums. With the old barriers to American and Soviet expansion gone, Russia and America clashed over occupation policies in Germany, Italy, Japan, Austria, and Korea. They squabbled over which political groups should replace the Nazi regimes in Eastern Europe. The filling of gaps or vacuums in any system is a natural process. In the postwar period the gaps were huge and worldwide, inviting a high degree of competition and conflict.

Another change wrought by World War II was the destruction of the economic world. The war cut an ugly scar across Europe and Asia, but bypassed one major nation, the United States. "If Hitler succeeds in nothing else," mused OSS officer Allen Dulles, "like Samson, he may pull down the pillars of the temple and leave a long and hard road of reconstruction." The postwar task was forbidding. Not only did cities have to be rebuilt, factories opened, people put back to work, rails repaired, rivers and roads made passable, and crop yields increased, but the flow of international commerce and finance had to be reestablished if nations were to raise through exports the revenue needed to buy the imports required for recovery. Many old commercial and financial patterns had been broken and, given the obstacle of economic wreckage, new exchanges were difficult to establish. Where would Germany's vital coal and steel go? Would industrial Western Europe and agricultural Eastern Europe recreate old commercial ties? Would the restrictive trade practices of the 1930s, especially the trade barriers, continue into the 1940s? Would subservient colonies continue to serve as sources of rich raw materials? Could international agreements and organizations curb economic nationalism? Would trade be conducted on a multilateral, "open door" basis, as the United States preferred, or by bilateral or preferential methods, as many others, such as Britain and Russia, practiced? The answers helped to define the international system of the post-1945 era. These issues held more importance than simple economics, for leaders recognized that the economic disorders of the 1930s and the far-reaching impact of the Great Depression contributed to political chaos, aggression, and war. The new international system, it was hoped, would create stable economic conditions which would facilitate the development of pacific international relations. Yet the very efforts to realize these hopes engendered conflict.

World War II also bequeathed domestic political turmoil to its survivors. The regimes of the 1930s, now discredited, vied with insurgent groups for the governing power in many states. Socialists, Communists, and other varieties of the political left, many of whom had fought in the underground resistance movements and had thus earned some popular respect, challenged the more entrenched, conservative elites, many of whom had escaped into exile when the German armies rolled into their countries. In Poland, the Communist, Soviet-endorsed Lublin Poles challenged the political standing of the Poles who had fled to London. The conservative Dutch government-in-exile watched warily as leftist resistance groups gradually built a popular following. Political confusion in the Netherlands was heightened by the wartime loss of voting lists. In Greece a coalition of leftists in the National Liberation Front (EAM) vigorously resisted the return to power of a British-created government and the unpopular Greek monarchy of King George. In France Charles de Gaulle vied for power with the Communists. In China the civil war, which had raged for years between the Communists of Mao Tse-tung and the Nationalists of Chiang Kai-shek, flared up again at the close of the war. Yugoslavia was the scene of political battle between Josip Broz Tito's Partisans and a group headed by Dr. Ivan Subasic of the London emigré government, which in turn suffered strained ties with King Peter. Moreover, in the occupied nations of Germany, Austria, and Korea, the victors created competitive zones, postponing the creation of central governments. In the defeated countries of Japan and Italy, American officials decided who would rule, whereas in parts of Eastern Europe, Soviet officials placed Communists in positions of authority.

The major powers, in short, intervened abroad to exploit the political opportunities created by the destructive scythe of World War II. The stakes seemed high. A change in a nation's political orientation might presage a change in its international alignment. The great powers tended to ignore local conditions which might mitigate against alignment with an outside power. Americans feared that a leftist or Communist Greece would look to the East and permit menacing Soviet bases on Greek territory or open the door to a Soviet naval presence in the Mediterranean. The Russians dreaded a conservative anti-Soviet Polish government led by the London faction, for it might prove so weak and so hostile to Moscow as to permit a revived Germany to send stormtroopers once again through the Polish corridor into the heart of Russia. A Communist China, thought Americans, might align with Russia; a Nationalist China would remain in the American camp. All in all, the rearranging of political structures *within* nations drew the major powers into competition, accentuating the conflict inherent in the postwar international system.

If the war threw politics into chaos, it also hastened the disintegration of colonial and informal empires. The Japanese movement into French Indochina and their drive for Dutch East Indies oil led to Pearl Harbor in 1941. The initially successful Japanese expansion had the effect of demonstrating to many Asian nationalists that their white imperial masters could be defeated. Some nationalists collaborated during the war with their Asian brethren from Tokyo, and the Japanese, in need of administrators to manage occupied areas, trained and armed some native leaders. Japan granted Burma considerable autonomy in 1942, for example, and after the war the Burmese were determined not to return to a position of subservience to Great Britain. At the end of the war, the European powers, exhausted and financially hobbled, had to struggle to reestablish mastery over rebellious colonies. The appeal of the principle of self-determination, still echoing from the days of Woodrow Wilson and given new emphasis by the Atlantic Charter of 1941, was far-reaching.

No empire seemed immune to disintegration. The United States granted the Philippines independence in 1946. The British, worn low by the war and by the challenges of nationalist groups demanding independence, retreated from India (and Pakistan) in 1947 and from Burma and Ceylon in 1948. Israel, carved out of British-governed Palestine, became a new independent state in 1948. The British also found it difficult to maintain their sphere of influence in Iran, Greece, and Egypt and began retreats from those politically unsteady states. The French attempted to hold on to Indochina, where nationalist forces led by Ho Chi Minh had declared an independent Vietnam. Bloody battle ensued, leading ultimately to French withdrawal in 1954. The Dutch also decided to fight, but after four debilitating years of combat, they pulled out of Indonesia in 1949. The defeated Japanese were forced to give up their claims to Formosa and Korea, as well as Pacific island groups. Italy departed from Ethiopia and lost its African colonies of Tripolitania (Libya) and Eritrea. Lebanon, Syria, and Jordan, areas once managed by Europeans, gained independence in 1943, 1944, and 1946, respectively.

The world map, as after World War I, was redrawn. The emergence of so many new states, and the instability associated with the transfer of authority, shook the very foundations of the international system. Power was being redistributed. In varying degrees, Russia and America competed for the allegiance of the new governments, meddled in colonial rebellions, and generally sought to exploit opportunities for an extension of their influence. Again, the stakes seemed high. The new nations could serve as strategic bases, markets for exports, sources of vital raw materials, sites for investments, and votes in international organizations. States such as India, which chose nonalignment in the developing Cold War, were wooed with foreign aid and ideological appeals. In the case of Indochina, the powers supported different sides: Washington backed the ruling French, and Moscow endorsed Ho and his insurgents.

As one United States government study noted, the disintegration of empires, especially the withdrawal of the British from their once vast domain, created an "over-all situation of near chaos" in the international system. In some areas, such as Southeast Asia, it meant a "new balance of power." The upheaval was fundamental: "Old values are being changed and new ones sought. New friendships are being formed." The international system creaked and swayed under this unsettled burden.

Conflict also sprang from efforts to launch a new international organization to replace the defunct League of Nations. At the Dumbarton Oaks Conference in 1944, the Allies initiated plans for a United Nations Organization. The United States, Britain, and Russia were its chief architects, and the institution they created at the San Francisco Conference from April to June of 1945 reflected their insistence on big-power domination. They agreed upon a veto power for the five "permanent members" of the Security Council (Britain, Russia, United States, France, and China) and assigned the General Assembly, the forum for smaller nations, a subordinate status. Nevertheless, because each of the Allies recognized that the new international body was potentially an instrument, through bloc voting, of one nation's foreign policy, they argued. Churchill crudely complained that China, hardly a "great" power, would be a "faggot vote on the side of the United States," and Russia protested that France would simply represent a British vote. "China was a joke," remarked State Department veteran John Hickerson, "a FDR joke." Because Great Britain could marshall the votes of several of its Commonwealth countries and the United States could count on most of the Latin American nations in the General Assembly, the conferees at the Yalta Conference of early 1945 granted Russia three votes, in order to alter somewhat the glaring imbalance.

Such compromise, however, broke down at the San Francisco Conference. Membership applications from Argentina and Poland produced heated differences. Against vehement Soviet objections Argentina, which had declared war against Germany at the last minute and which some critics considered a "fascist" nation, gained membership after the United States backed its application and the nations of the Western Hemisphere voted "yes" as a bloc. Yet when Lublin-led Poland, not yet reorganized according to the American interpretation of the Yalta accords, applied for entry, the United States voted "no," and the conference denied Poland a seat. Moscow railed at this, charging a double standard. The United Nations Organization, which held its first session in January of 1946, thus began amidst controversy. Rather than serving as a stabilizing force in the postwar international system, the United Nations early became a source of conflict, a verbal battleground for the allegiance of world opinion, a vehicle for condemnatory resolutions, a largely United States-dominated institution, and a graveyard for idealistic hopes—in short, part of a "masquerade peace."

The postwar international system suffered, too, from the destabilizing effect of the new atomic bomb. The "most terrible weapon ever known in human history," Secretary of War Henry L. Stimson quietly told the President, unsettled the world community, for it was an agent of massive human destruction, and "in a world atmosphere already extremely sensitive to power, the introduction of this weapon has profoundly affected political considerations in all sections of the globe." Nations which possessed "the bomb" seemed to hold an advantage in international politics, for it could serve as a deterrent against an adversary as well as a means to annihilate an enemy. When combined with air power and a long-range delivery capability, it also hurdled geographical boundaries, rendering them useless as protective elements in a nation's security shield. With the perfecting of air war in World War II, "the roof blew off the territorial state." As General Douglas MacArthur remarked after the atomic explosions: "Well, this changes warfare!" The prospect of nuclear annihilation bothered everybody, but the United States was especially concerned about nuclear proliferation, which meant the loss of its atomic monopoly.

A question dogged the peacemakers: How were they to control the development, spread, and use of atomic energy? There had been arms races before, and ineffective disarmament conferences in the 1920s and 1930s, but the postwar nuclear race was conducted at a far different and more dangerous level. The atomic bomb was the "absolute weapon," not only more violent but also capable of speedy delivery, rapid retaliation, and immediate cataclysm. Challenging the American monopoly, the Soviet Union successfully produced its own bomb in 1949. As the two bickering major powers groped for ways in which to deal with "the bomb" and undertook their atomic development programs, others held their breath. One observer suggested that a Soviet-American war "might not end with *one* Rome but with *two* Carthages." The atomic bomb, uncontrolled, envied, copied, and brandished, became a major obstacle to a peaceful, orderly postwar international system.

The shrinkage of the world and the growth of a global outlook must be included in any estimation of the impact of World War II on the international system. Geography had not changed, but ways of moving across it and of thinking about it had. Improvements in transportation, especially in aviation, brought nations closer to one another. The world seemed more compact and accessible. People had to think now not only in traditional land miles but also in flying hours. In a popularization for school children, N. L. Englehardt, Jr., urged his young readers to think "air thoughts" and titled one of his chapters "How the World Has Shrunk." Because the Atlantic Ocean could be traversed easily and quickly, that once-prominent barrier between the Old and New Worlds disappeared. As America was brought closer to Europe and the world, American strategic thinking expanded as well. In the world contracted by science, events in Greece or Iran or China held greater significance than ever before for American security. The Japanese attack upon Pearl Harbor, accomplished after crossing 3,500 miles of Pacific Ocean, had proved that great distances no longer served as protectors of security. "If you imagine two or three hundred Pearl Harbors occurring all over the United States," prophesied Assistant Secretary of State A. A. Berle, "you will have a rough picture of what the next war might look like. . . ." Observers began to speak not only of an "atomic age," but of an "air age" and a "global age." The global war of 1939–45 had helped spawn a postwar globalism—an international interdependence. "The entire relations of the United States with the world," declared Dean Acheson, "are a seamless web. . . ." Geographical isolation was gone with the past. Stimson perceived that the United States could never again "be an island to herself. No private program and no public policy, in any sector of our national life can now escape from the compelling fact that if it is not framed with reference to the world, it is framed with perfect futility."

United States Chief of Staff General George C. Marshall typified strategic reconsiderations. "For probably the last time in the history of warfare those ocean distances were a vital factor in our defense. We may elect again to depend on others and the whim and error of potential enemies, but if we do we will be carrying the treasure and freedom of this great Nation in a paper bag." Because frontiers had been extended, because nations were brought nearer one another, and because the world had shrunk, the major powers coveted bases far from home, much as the United States had sought and acquired bases in the Caribbean in the early twentieth century to protect the Panama Canal. "We are now concerned with the peace of the entire world," said Marshall. Two years later President Truman described a "much smaller earth—an earth whose broad oceans have shrunk and whose national protections have been taken away by new weapons of destruction." In a similar vein, a Joint Chiefs of Staff report of late 1947 looked ten years into the future and predicted a "continuing shrinkage of the world from the accelerated pace of technological progress." In short, a new aspect of the postwar international system was the interdependence or intertwining of events in all parts of the world, thereby drawing great powers into confrontations as never before. Globalism insured conflict.

Such was the postwar international system—with its opportunities and constraints, with its characteristics insuring conflict. The makers of the peace sought to reduce the conflict, but their decisions exacerbated it.

QUESTIONS FOR DISCUSSION

1. What does Paterson mean when he says of World War II that it "served as an agent . . . of revolution"?

2. In the conclusion of this selection, Paterson states that "globalism insured conflict." What does he mean by this? Do you agree with him?

This cartoon by Talburt from the now defunct New York *World Journal Tribune* perfectly portrays the vise that Truman put Congressional "isolationists" into with his "Truman Doctrine" message. If they didn't help bail out the other end of the boat (in Europe), they were soon going to drown in their end (in the United States). With the help of such cartoons, the American people were able to grasp Truman's point quickly.

Address on Foreign Economic Policy, Delivered at Baylor University, March 6, 1947, and Special Message to the Congress on Greece and Turkey: The Truman Doctrine, March 12, 1947

Commentary by Walter LaFeber

Seldom has a single United States policy declaration changed the course of world affairs. President Harry S Truman's speech to a joint session of the U.S. Congress on March 12, 1947, however, did just that. In this speech, Truman formulated the arguments that he and his successors in the White House used in later decades to obtain support from the American people for a vast, costly, and often dangerous policy of containing communism wherever the president determined a Communist threat existed. Remarkable as the March 12 speech was, however, a full understanding of the new U.S. foreign policy is possible only if another, lesser known speech of Truman's is also studied. At Baylor University in Texas on March 6, the president discussed the political, social, and—especially—economic assumptions that shaped the "Truman Doctrine" speech he would deliver six days later. As the president declared at Baylor, economic and political problems were "indivisible." Taken together, the two speeches provide a unique, comprehensive statement of American ideals and the foreign policy required to realize those ideals at a pivotal point in United States history.

The March 6 and 12 addresses climaxed three of the most intense weeks in U.S. diplomacy. On the early morning of February 21, Undersecretary of State Dean Acheson was one of the few top officials on weekend duty in the brand new State Department building when a messenger from the British Embassy arrived with two diplomatic notes. The first declared that the British economy, crippled by six years of war, was so weak that it no longer could supply military aid to the conservative Greek government that was fighting Communist and other left-wing rebels. The second stated that England could no longer afford to help Turkey's military forces. A historic turning point had been reached. After acting as the world's greatest power for nearly 150 years, the British begged the Americans to take over responsibility for such corners of the globe as Greece and Turkey.

Acheson and his boss, Secretary of State George Marshall, were not surprised by the British notes. During the previous eighteen months the United States had assisted the British by providing over $200 million to keep the Greek government afloat. Indeed, the very morning the notes arrived Marshall had ordered Acheson to draw up legislation for Congress to authorize a new loan and military equipment for Athens. The problem for the Truman administration was not that the British request arrived as a lightning bolt from the blue. The problem was more complex.

Truman could have dealt with the Greek situation without making a dramatic appearance before Congress. He could simply have called the conflict a civil war, asked Congress for some economic aid, sent the Greeks surplus military equipment out of the large U.S. stockpiles, and ignored the problem of Turkey (a problem that was by no means pressing anyway). Truman, however, decided to play for much larger stakes by asking Congress to support a costly foreign policy that could be applied to regions beyond Greece and Turkey.

The president was most worried about conditions in Western Europe. The horrors and destruction of World War II hung over that region like a dark, sulphurous cloud. People in Austria, Italy, and neighboring countries faced starvation. Half of all British industry lay idle. In Western Europe money was in such short supply that people could not buy food and other necessities that only the United States could provide. This shortage of hard currency not only caused hardship for the Europeans, it also threatened Americans with the loss of their most profitable overseas markets. If Western Europe did not recover quickly, the United States could return to the terrors of the 1930s economic depression. Saving the region, however, would cost billions of dollars in U.S. aid.

Truman had to find a way to convince Americans to send huge amounts of their hard-earned tax dollars overseas. He could not simply argue that Europeans were endangered by Soviet military aggression. Americans would have rallied quickly to fight such a threat, but the Soviet dictator, Josef Stalin, was deeply involved in rebuilding war-devastated Russia and consolidating power in the Eastern European nations his Red Army had occupied in 1944–45. No one in the U.S. Department of State believed that either Western Europe or Greece and Turkey were endangered by a direct Soviet attack. A confidential State Department analysis of informed U.S. public opinion even concluded in January 1947: "reviewing international developments during the past year, commentators are most encouraged by the 'easing of tension between Russia and the West.' " *Newsweek* magazine forecast "at least five years of real peace." In Greece, moreover, Stalin's direct involvement was minor. He had given diplomatic recognition to the conservative Greek government that Americans were helping. Soviet aid to the Greek Communists was slight. Truman could not blame the Greek civil war on Stalin.

The Communists in Greece were strong and popular. During World War II they had led the resistance against the German occupation. Communist-led forces pinned down as many as 300,000 Nazis and liberated sections of the country before Allied armies arrived. British Prime Minister Winston Churchill, however, was determined to prevent the Communists from taking power in a country that had long been vital to the British Empire and controlled strategic routes in the eastern Mediterranean. Over strong U.S. objections, Churchill launched attacks against the left-wing in 1944–45. Through 1946–47 the civil war continued, but two new actors appeared onstage. One was the United States, which switched its position in late 1945 to help the British struggle against the leftist forces. The other was Josip Broz Tito, leader of the Communist government in Yugoslavia. Attempting to realize his dream of incorporating parts of Greece into an eastern Mediterranean confederation under his rule, Tito had begun to supply the left-wing rebels. Stalin opposed Tito's policy, as he did anything that might make another Communist leader stronger and more independent of Stalin himself. Given this background, Truman could not mobilize support in the United States by crying "the Russians are coming." The problems in Greece and Western Europe were much more complicated.

Truman faced another, more immediate problem. He had to beg the money needed to save Western Europe and the Greek regime from a Congress that was deeply conservative and stingy with its funds. The Republicans had won a stunning victory in the 1946 congressional elections. The triumph ended sixteen years of Democratic power and gave the Republicans a margin of 127 members in the House and a majority of six in the Senate. The newly elected Republicans were bitterly anti-Communist, but they had run on platforms that promised to cut the government budget, cut taxes, and cut (if not destroy) foreign aid programs.

As the Republicans' strength increased, Truman's declined. The nation's most important newspaper columnist, Walter Lippmann, put it bluntly: the president had "lost the support of his party" and was "not in command of his own administration." One opinion poll showed that in mid-1945 87 percent of the electorate had supported Truman. By late 1946 the figure plummeted to 32 percent. Some Democratic party leaders even believed that Truman should resign. With weakening support, the president had to go head-to-head with a Republican Congress and try to obtain millions of dollars for Greece and Turkey, and billions for the rebuilding of Western Europe.

During the weeks before the March 6 and 12 speeches, Truman and Acheson arrived at a solution for their problems. Because they could not go to Congress and ask for money to protect the British Empire in Greece (to "pull British chestnuts out of the fire," as a popular Midwestern phrase went), they asked the Greek government itself to request aid and personnel to oversee the spending of the aid. To ensure that the Greek request was properly phrased, Acheson and a few other U.S. officials wrote the request and then sent it to themselves. As one of those officials (Loy Henderson) put it, the note had to be drafted carefully "with a view to the mentality of Congress. . . . It would also serve to protect the U.S. government against internal and external charges that it was taking the initiative of intervening in a foreign state or that it had been persuaded by the British to take over a bad legacy from them. The note would also serve as a basis for the cultivation of [U.S.] public opinion."

With the invitation simultaneously written and received, Truman turned to his most important task: persuading Congress to appropriate large sums of money. He and Acheson knew that if properly phrased, a message on the Greek crisis could be used to pry a major, perhaps worldwide, commitment out of Congress. The key moment for extracting such a commitment came in late February when Truman invited the Senate and House leaders to the White House. Acheson told the legislators that the world was at a historic point. "No time," he warned, "was left for measured appraisal." For some eighteen months, he accurately reported, the Soviets had put great pressure on Iran and Turkey. Now the pressure had spread to Greece. He said nothing about Tito's involvement, but instead hinted that Stalin was the villain. When no one challenged this point, Acheson went on to lay out the argument that later became famous as the "domino theory." In Acheson's hands, however, it was known as the "rotten apple theory." He declared that "like apples in a barrel infected by one rotten one, the corruption of Greece would infect Iran and all to the east." The "infection" could spread through Africa, Egypt, and finally Europe, which was "already threatened" by Communist parties. "The Soviet Union," Acheson continued, "was playing one of the greatest gambles in history at minimal cost. . . . We and we alone are in a position to break up the play."

Silence followed until Senator Arthur Vandenberg, a Republican from Michigan and the new chairman of the Senate Foreign Relations Committee, solemnly declared, "Mr. President, if you will say that to Congress and to the country, I will support you and I believe that most of its members will do the same." His statement has been transformed in some textbooks into a warning to Truman to "scare hell out of the American people." Whatever Vandenberg said, however, Acheson had obviously found the lever for prying dollars out of a tightfisted Congress. That lever was strengthened by a threat Acheson never directly mentioned, but left implied: should Congress not go along, it, not Truman, would have to answer to the American people if Greece and perhaps even parts of Western Europe turned Communist.

Acheson supervised the drafting of Truman's speeches in early March. He worked closely with Clark Clifford, a top presidential adviser in the White House. Clifford, like Acheson, believed the crisis was political and global. The Greek problem was important because it provided the opportunity to form a consensus for standing up to Communism in other parts of the world as well. As Clifford remarked, the president's March 12 speech was to be "the opening gun in a campaign to bring people up to [the] realization that the war isn't over by any means."

In deciding how to present their case to Americans, Acheson and Clifford were determined not only to downplay the British role, but also the possibility that the United Nations might help resolve the Greek problem. UN debates could consume precious time. More important, UN actions could be vetoed by the Soviet Union. It was obviously better to keep the policy entirely in American hands. The two men also glossed over the complexities of internal politics in Greece and Turkey. To explain such complexities as Greek nationalism or Tito's role might only bore and confuse Americans. Moreover, the conservative government supported by the United States was weak, reactionary, and had become known for using torture and massive violations of human rights. As U.S. Ambassador to Greece Lincoln MacVeagh privately told a congressional committee, "the best men," among Greek leaders were the Communists. They were "the most vital fellows in the country. That is the sad part of it." Nevertheless, MacVeagh concluded, "you have to go ahead" and support the right-wing forces "or you are going to lose the country."

Truman, Acheson, and Clifford wanted the speech to be both general and outspoken. But their approach ran into strong opposition within the State Department. Secretary of State Marshall and his personal adviser on Soviet affairs, Charles Bohlen, were attending a conference in the Soviet Union when they saw the March 12 speech draft. Bohlen believed "there was a little too much flamboyant anticommunism in the speech." Marshall also wanted it toned down. They were joined in their protest by George Kennan, probably the most respected U.S. expert on Soviet affairs.

In 1946, while on assignment in Moscow, Kennan had written a secret telegram that soon became the basis for the tough U.S. "containment" policy towards Russia after 1947. But when he saw the draft of the March 12 speech, Kennan objected that the phrases "were more grandiose and more sweeping than anything that I, at least, had ever envisaged." He feared that such a "universal policy" would distort and corrupt U.S. foreign policy. Kennan urged a more specific and limited policy. While not opposing economic aid to Greece, he argued that aid should not be given to Turkey. That country was not a democracy, and no serious Communist influence existed there. Sending military aid to Turkey, a nation that sat on the sensitive borders of the Soviet Union, could dangerously heighten tension between the two superpowers, Kennan warned. Finally, he questioned the central assumption of the speech. Kennan doubted that the "infection" would spread as Acheson feared. Not only did the Moslems in the Middle East hate Soviet ideology, but the Russians "were just not that good"—that is, they were neither clever nor strong enough to make the infection spread.

Truman and Acheson overruled Kennan, Bohlen, and Marshall. The president cared less about the historical accuracy of his argument than its political impact on the American people. But then another objection to the speech appeared. Top officials, notably Secretary of the Navy James Forrestal, insisted that the message spell out the need to protect U.S. economic interests (especially vast oil holdings) in the Middle East. Acheson flatly refused. He did not want this historic debate over whether the United States should confront communism to deteriorate into an argument over whether Americans should protect oil wells in the Middle East.

Acheson nevertheless realized that a critical economic situation did exist. The most powerful U.S. officials fervently believed that world markets had to be open to free trade and the dealings of private business. The disasters of the 1930s had dramatically taught this lesson. During the Depression, countries had tried to survive by erecting tariff walls around their markets and directly injecting the government into the marketplace. U.S. leaders concluded that such actions had helped produce fascism, revolution, and finally World War II itself. Bitter economic competition inevitably led to political and military clashes. The United States had to make certain that the globe would be an open marketplace in which individual trade could flourish. No more territory could be allowed to fall to Communist regimes.

Congress, moreover, had to understand its responsibility for keeping world trade open and, more directly, appropriating billions of dollars to rebuild the destroyed markets of Europe. A secret administration analysis concluded that the Western Europeans were some $8 billion short of the amount they needed to buy U.S. goods for reconstruction, not to mention survival. If Congress did not send the $8 billion to the Europeans, both Europe and U.S. producers faced stark alternatives. It was this economic component of U.S. foreign policy that Truman discussed at Baylor University on March 6.

The speech was one of several economic initiatives taken in early March. The day before the Baylor address Acheson ordered that State Department officials expand the Greek-Turkish aid program into a plan for all of Western Europe. Within months, this directive led to the $12 billion Marshall Plan that rebuilt friendly nations in Europe between 1948 and 1952. As the president later observed, the Truman Doctrine and the Marshall Plan were "two halves of the same walnut"—that is, they formed a coherent package of security, political, and economic policies.

On March 6, Truman appeared at Baylor to give his speech on U.S. economic interests in the world. The president explained exactly what Americans had at stake in the world marketplace: nothing less than their personal freedom. In an argument that merits close attention and extensive discussion, Truman declared that without freedom of trade people would lose their other freedoms as well. Without mentioning the Soviet Union by name, he pointed to government-controlled economies (such as the Communists') as the great danger. The speech, which Acheson helped draft, was a brilliantly written argument that was driven home by the history lesson that Truman taught about the 1930s.

With these economic points made, on March 12 the president told Congress that it had to commit itself to a cause beyond the specific problems of Greece and Turkey if American freedom was to survive. Again, he did not directly mention the Soviet Union. Truman instead referred to the more general threat of communism and thus blurred the relationship between communism (for example, the nationalistic communism outside the Soviet Union, as in Tito's Yugoslavia or Mao Tse-tung's movement in China) and the Soviet threat itself.

He did not ask Americans to prepare for a fight against the Red Army, but to mobilize themselves for perhaps an unlimited political, ideological, and economic struggle to "support free peoples who are resisting attempted subjugation by armed minorities or by outside pressures." The appeal was thus highly general, and it glossed over the complexities in Greece and Turkey that raised questions about how "free" the peoples of those nations were.

Truman and Acheson had achieved their objective. They issued a call to action for Americans to make a general commitment to fight "armed minorities or . . . outside pressures" anywhere the president believed such dangers existed. The Baylor speech explained what was at stake for every American. The Truman Doctrine explained what was at stake globally, and then it demanded the commitment the president thought necessary to win the struggle.

HARRY S. TRUMAN

Address on Foreign Economic Policy, Delivered at Baylor University, March 6, 1947

. . . **A**t this particular time, the whole world is concentrating much of its thought and energy on attaining the objectives of peace and freedom. These objectives are bound up completely with a third objective—reestablishment of world trade. In fact these three—peace, freedom, and world trade—are inseparable. The grave lessons of the past have proved it.

Many of our people, here in America, used to think that we could escape the troubles of the world by simply staying within our own borders. Two wars have shown how wrong they were. We know today that we cannot find security in isolation. If we are to live at peace, we must join with other nations in a continuing effort to organize the world for peace. Science and invention have left us no other alternative. . . .

Our foreign relations, political and economic, are indivisible. We cannot say that we are willing to cooperate in the one field and are unwilling to cooperate in the other. I am glad to note that the leaders in both parties have recognized that fact. . . .

Economic conflict is not spectacular—at least in the early stages. But it is always serious. One nation may take action in behalf of its own producers, without notifying other nations, or consulting them, or even considering how they may be affected. It may cut down its purchases of another country's goods, by raising its tariffs or imposing an embargo or a system of quotas on imports. And when it does this, some producer, in another country, will find the door to his market suddenly slammed and bolted in his face.

Or a nation may subsidize its exports, selling its goods abroad below their cost. When this is done, a producer in some other country will find his market flooded with goods that have been dumped.

In either case, the producer gets angry, just as you and I would get angry if such a thing were done to us. Profits disappear; workers are dismissed. The producer feels that he has been wronged, without warning and without reason.

He appeals to his government for action. His government retaliates, and another round of tariff boosts, embargoes, quotas, and subsidies is under way. This is economic war. In such a war nobody wins.

Certainly, nobody won the last economic war. As each battle of the economic war of the thirties was fought, the inevitable tragic result became more and more apparent. From the tariff policy of Hawley and Smoot,[1] the world went on to Ottawa and the system of imperial preferences,[2] from Ottawa to the kind of elaborate and detailed restrictions adopted by Nazi Germany. Nations strangled normal trade and discriminated against their neighbors, all around the world.

Who among their peoples were the gainers? Not the depositors who lost their savings in the failure of the banks. Not the farmers who lost their farms. Not the millions who walked the streets looking for work. I do not mean to say that economic conflict was the *sole* cause of the depression. But I do say that it was a *major* cause.

Now, as in the year 1920, we have reached a turning point in history. National economies have been disrupted by the war. The future is uncertain everywhere. Economic policies are in a state of flux. In this atmosphere of doubt and hesitation, the decisive factor will be the type of leadership that the United States gives the world.

We are the giant of the economic world. Whether we like it or not, the future pattern of economic relations depends upon us. The world is waiting and watching to see what we shall do. The choice is ours. We can lead the nations to economic peace or we can plunge them into economic war.

There must be no question as to our course. We must not go through the thirties again. . . .

If the nations can agree to observe a code of good conduct in international trade, they will cooperate more readily in other international affairs. Such agreement will prevent the bitterness that is engendered by an economic war. It will provide an atmosphere congenial to the preservation of peace.

As a part of this program we have asked the other nations of the world to join with us in reducing barriers to trade. We have not asked them to remove all barriers. Nor have we ourselves offered to do so. But we *have* proposed negotiations directed toward the reduction of tariffs, here and abroad, toward the elimination of other restrictive measures and the abandonment of discrimination. These negotiations are to be undertaken at the meeting which opens in Geneva next month. The success of this program is essential to the establishment of the International Trade Organization,[3] to the effective operation of

---

[1]The Smoot-Hawley tariff, passed by Congress in 1930, raised U.S. tariffs to their highest levels in the twentieth century. Other nations saw this tariff as a U.S. declaration of economic war on them.

[2]At Ottawa, Canada, in 1932, the British organized their Commonwealth (which included such key U.S. customers as Canada and India) into an Imperial Preference System that erected an economic wall around the Commonwealth and kept out many U.S. goods.

[3]The International Trade Organization was created at the end of the war by the United States and other leading trading nations to work for the reduction of trade barriers (such as tariffs).

the International Bank and the Monetary Fund,[4] and to the strength of the whole United Nations structure of cooperation in economic and political affairs.

The negotiations at Geneva must not fail.

There is one thing that Americans value even more than peace. It is freedom. Freedom of worship—freedom of speech—freedom of enterprise. It must be true that the first two of these freedoms are related to the third. For, throughout history, freedom of worship and freedom of speech have been most frequently enjoyed in those societies that have accorded a considerable measure of freedom to individual enterprise. Freedom has flourished where power has been dispersed. It has languished where power has been too highly centralized. So our devotion to freedom of enterprise, in the United States, has deeper roots than a desire to protect the profits of ownership. It is part and parcel of what we call American.

The pattern of international trade that is most conducive to freedom of enterprise is one in which the major decisions are made, not by governments, but by private buyers and sellers, under conditions of active competition, and with proper safeguards against the establishment of monopolies and cartels. Under such a system, buyers make their purchases, and sellers make their sales, at whatever time and place and in whatever quantities they choose, relying for guidance on whatever prices the market may afford. Goods move from country to country in response to economic opportunities. Governments may impose tariffs, but they do not dictate the quantity of trade, the sources of imports, or the destination of exports. Individual transactions are a matter of private choice.

This is the essence of free enterprise.

The pattern of trade that is *least* conducive to freedom of enterprise is one in which decisions are made by governments. Under such a system, the quantity of purchases and sales, the sources of imports, and the destination of exports are dictated by public officials. In some cases, trade may be conducted by the state. In others, part or all of it may be left in private hands. But, even so, the trader is not free. Governments make all the important choices and he adjusts himself to them as best he can.

This was the pattern of the seventeenth and eighteenth centuries.[5] Unless we act, and act decisively, it will be the pattern of the next century.

Everywhere on earth, nations are under economic pressure. Countries that were devastated by the war are seeking to reconstruct their industries. Their

---

[4]The International Bank (or World Bank) and Monetary Fund (or International Monetary Fund, the IMF) were set up in 1944 by the United States and other leading trading powers to prevent the kind of economic conflicts that had tormented the 1930s. The World Bank provides funds for roads and other infrastructure needed by private traders. The IMF helps nations suffering from severe trade imbalances so those nations will not erect trade barriers to protect themselves.

[5]Truman here refers to the "mercantilistic systems" of the 1600s and 1700s in which governments played a large role in directing private enterprise. Americans believed that their revolution in 1776 was a revolt against the restraints of the British mercantilistic system.

need to import, in the months that lie ahead, will exceed their capacity to export. And so they feel that imports must be rigidly controlled.

Countries that have lagged in their development are seeking to industrialize. In order that new industries may be established, they, too, feel that competing imports must be rigidly controlled.

Nor is this all. The products of some countries are in great demand. But buyers outside their borders do not hold the money of these countries in quantities large enough to enable them to pay for the goods they want. And they find these moneys difficult to earn. Importing countries, when they make their purchases, therefore seek to discriminate against countries whose currencies they do not possess. Here, again, they feel that imports must be rigidly controlled. . . .

If this trend is not reversed, the government of the United States will be under pressure, sooner or later, to use these same devices to fight for markets and for raw materials. And if the government were to yield to this pressure, it would shortly find itself in the business of allocating foreign goods among importers and foreign markets among exporters and telling every trader what he could buy or sell, and how much, and when, and where. This is precisely what we have been trying to get away from, as rapidly as possible, ever since the war. It is not the American way. It is not the way to peace. . . .

Peace and freedom are not easily achieved. They cannot be attained by force. They come from mutual understanding and cooperation, from a willingness to deal fairly with every friendly nation in all matters—political and economic. Let us resolve to continue to do just that, now and in the future. If other nations of the world will do the same, we can reach the goals of permanent peace and world freedom.

Special Message to the Congress on Greece and Turkey: The Truman Doctrine, March 12, 1947 (Delivered before a joint session of the U.S. Congress.)

The gravity of the situation which confronts the world today necessitates my appearance before a joint session of the Congress.

The foreign policy and the national security of this country are involved.

One aspect of the present situation, which I present to you at this time for your consideration and decision, concerns Greece and Turkey.

The United States has received from the Greek Government an urgent appeal for financial and economic assistance. Preliminary reports from the American Economic Mission now in Greece and reports from the American Ambassador in Greece corroborate the statement of the Greek Government that assistance is imperative if Greece is to survive as a free nation.

I do not believe that the American people and the Congress wish to turn a deaf ear to the appeal of the Greek Government.

Greece is not a rich country. Lack of sufficient natural resources has always forced the Greek people to work hard to make both ends meet. Since 1940, this industrious, peace loving country has suffered invasion, four years of cruel enemy occupation, and bitter internal strife.

When forces of liberation entered Greece they found that the retreating Germans had destroyed virtually all the railways, roads, port facilities, communications, and merchant marine. More than a thousand villages had been burned. Eighty-five percent of the children were tubercular. Livestock, poultry, and draft animals had almost disappeared. Inflation had wiped out practically all savings.

As a result of these tragic conditions, a militant minority, exploiting human want and misery, was able to create political chaos which, until now, has made economic recovery impossible.

Greece is today without funds to finance the importation of those goods which are essential to bare subsistence. Under these circumstances the people of Greece cannot make progress in solving their problems of reconstruction. Greece is in desperate need of financial and economic assistance to enable it to resume purchases of food, clothing, fuel and seeds. These are indispensable for the subsistence of its people and are obtainable only from abroad. Greece must have help to import the goods necessary to restore internal order and security so essential for economic and political recovery.

The Greek Government has also asked for the assistance of experienced American administrators, economists and technicians to insure that the financial and other aid given to Greece shall be used effectively in creating a stable and self-sustaining economy and in improving its public administration.

The very existence of the Greek state is today threatened by the terrorist activities of several thousand armed men, led by Communists, who defy the government's authority at a number of points, particularly along the northern boundaries. A Commission appointed by the United Nations Security Council is at present investigating disturbed conditions in northern Greece and alleged border violations along the frontier between Greece on the one hand and Albania, Bulgaria, and Yugoslavia on the other.

Meanwhile, the Greek Government is unable to cope with the situation. The Greek army is small and poorly equipped. It needs supplies and equipment if it is to restore authority to the government throughout Greek territory.

Greece must have assistance if it is to become a self-supporting and self-respecting democracy.

The United States must supply this assistance. We have already extended to Greece certain types of relief and economic aid but these are inadequate.

There is no other country to which democratic Greece can turn.

No other nation is willing and able to provide the necessary support for a democratic Greek government.

The British Government, which has been helping Greece, can give no further financial or economic aid after March 31. Great Britain finds itself under the necessity of reducing or liquidating its commitments in several parts of the world, including Greece.

We have considered how the United Nations might assist in this crisis. But the situation is an urgent one requiring immediate action, and the United Nations and its related organizations are not in a position to extend help of the kind that is required.[1]

---

[1]In 1947 many Americans had great faith in the United Nations. The Truman administration and Congress, however, increasingly mistrusted the UN because the Soviet veto could tie up the organization. This paragraph was Truman's way of recognizing, then dismissing, a possible UN role.

It is important to note that the Greek Government has asked for our aid in utilizing effectively the financial and other assistance we may give to Greece, and in improving its public administration. It is of the utmost importance that we supervise the use of any funds made available to Greece, in such a manner that each dollar spent will count toward making Greece self-supporting, and will help to build an economy in which a healthy democracy can flourish.

No government is perfect. One of the chief virtues of a democracy, however, is that its defects are always visible and under democratic processes can be pointed out and corrected. The government of Greece is not perfect. Nevertheless it represents 85 percent of the members of the Greek Parliament who were chosen in an election last year. Foreign observers, including 692 Americans, considered this election to be a fair expression of the views of the Greek people.[2]

The Greek Government has been operating in an atmosphere of chaos and extremism. It has made mistakes. The extension of aid by this country does not mean that the United States condones everything that the Greek Government has done or will do. We have condemned in the past, and we condemn now, extremist measures of the right or the left. We have in the past advised tolerance, and we advise tolerance now.

Greece's neighbor, Turkey, also deserves our attention.

The future of Turkey as an independent and economically sound state is clearly no less important to the freedom-loving peoples of the world than the future of Greece. The circumstances in which Turkey finds itself today are considerably different from those of Greece. Turkey has been spared the disasters that have beset Greece. And during the war, the United States and Great Britain furnished Turkey with material aid.

Nevertheless, Turkey now needs our support.

Since the war Turkey has sought additional financial assistance from Great Britain and the United States for the purpose of effecting that modernization necessary for the maintenance of its national integrity.

That integrity is essential to the preservation of order in the Middle East.

The British Government has informed us that, owing to its own difficulties, it can no longer extend financial or economic aid to Turkey.

As in the case of Greece, if Turkey is to have the assistance it needs, the United States must supply it. We are the only country able to provide that help.

I am fully aware of the broad implications involved if the United States extends assistance to Greece and Turkey, and I shall discuss these implications with you at this time.

One of the primary objectives of the foreign policy of the United States is the creation of conditions in which we and other nations will be able to work out a way of life free from coercion. This was a fundamental issue in the war

---

[2]Many scholars disagree with Truman on this point. They note that left-wing parties boycotted the election (because the election process was controlled by rightist groups and police), and only 49 percent of the registered Greek voters went to the polls. For the best critical analysis, see Lawrence S. Wittner, *American Intervention in Greece, 1943–1949* (New York: Columbia University Press, 1982), pp. 38–41.

with Germany and Japan. Our victory was won over countries which sought to impose their will, and their way of life, upon other nations.

To ensure the peaceful development of nations, free from coercion, the United States has taken a leading part in establishing the United Nations. The United Nations is designed to make possible lasting freedom and independence for all its members. We shall not realize our objectives, however, unless we are willing to help free peoples to maintain their free institutions and their national integrity against aggressive movements that seek to impose upon them totalitarian regimes. This is no more than a frank recognition that totalitarian regimes imposed upon free peoples, by direct or indirect aggression, undermine the foundations of international peace and hence the security of the United States.

The peoples of a number of countries of the world have recently had totalitarian regimes forced upon them against their will. The Government of the United States has made frequent protests against coercion and intimidation, in violation of the Yalta agreement, in Poland, Rumania, and Bulgaria. I must also state that in a number of other countries there have been similar developments.[3]

At the present moment in world history nearly every nation must choose between alternative ways of life. The choice is too often not a free one.

One way of life is based upon the will of the majority, and is distinguished by free institutions, representative government, free elections, guarantees of individual liberty, freedom of speech and religion, and freedom from political oppression.

The second way of life is based upon the will of a minority forcibly imposed upon the majority. It relies upon terror and oppression, a controlled press and radio, fixed elections, and the suppression of personal freedoms.

I believe that it must be the policy of the United States to support free peoples who are resisting attempted subjugation by armed minorities or by outside pressures.

I believe that we must assist free peoples to work out their own destinies in their own way.

I believe that our help should be primarily through economic and financial aid which is essential to economic stability and orderly political processes.

The world is not static, and the *status quo* is not sacred. But we cannot allow changes in the *status quo* in violation of the Charter of the United Nations by such methods as coercion, or by such subterfuges as political infiltration. In helping free and independent nations to maintain their freedom, the

---

[3]Truman came closest to mentioning the Soviets directly in this paragraph. His use of "totalitarian" and his reference to Poland, Rumania, and Bulgaria—all of which had fallen under Stalin's control—did not have to be translated further for the president's audience. Truman did not want to focus on the Soviets directly; their responsibility for the grave problems in Greece and Western Europe was small. He instead focused on the role of leftist ("totalitarian") ideology, and by the way he phrased this paragraph allowed his listeners to make the link between that ideological threat and the Soviet danger. Thus without mentioning the Soviets he played on the growing anti-Soviet fears of Congress and the American people.

United States will be giving effect to the principles of the Charter of the United Nations.

It is necessary only to glance at a map to realize that the survival and integrity of the Greek nation are of grave importance in a much wider situation. If Greece should fall under the control of an armed minority, the effect upon its neighbor, Turkey, would be immediate and serious. Confusion and disorder might well spread throughout the entire Middle East.

Moreover, the disappearance of Greece as an independent state would have a profound effect upon those countries in Europe whose peoples are struggling against great difficulties to maintain their freedoms and their independence while they repair the damages of war.[4]

It would be an unspeakable tragedy if these countries, which have struggled so long against overwhelming odds, should lose that victory for which they sacrificed so much. Collapse of free institutions and loss of independence would be disastrous not only for them but for the world. Discouragement and possibly failure would quickly be the lot of neighboring peoples striving to maintain their freedom and independence.

Should we fail to aid Greece and Turkey in this fateful hour, the effect will be far reaching to the West as well as to the East.

We must take immediate and resolute action.

I therefore ask the Congress to provide authority for assistance to Greece and Turkey in the amount of $400,000,000 for the period ending June 30, 1948. . . .

In addition to funds, I ask Congress to authorize the detail of American civilian and military personnel to Greece and Turkey, at the request of those countries, to assist in the tasks of reconstruction, and for the purpose of supervising the use of such financial and material assistance as may be furnished. I recommend that authority also be provided for the instruction and training of selected Greek and Turkish personnel.

Finally, I ask that the Congress provide authority which will permit the speediest and most effective use, in terms of needed commodities, supplies, and equipment, of such funds as may be authorized.

If further funds, or further authority, should be needed for the purposes indicated in this message, I shall not hesitate to bring the situation before the Congress. On this subject the Executive and Legislative branches of the Government must work together.

This is a serious course upon which we embark.

I would not recommend it except that the alternative is much more serious.

The United States contributed $341,000,000,000 toward winning World War II. This is an investment in world freedom and world peace.

---

[4]In this paragraph and the one preceding it, Truman alludes to what was later called the "domino effect," or, as Acheson called it at the time, the "rotten apple" effect. The best accounts of how U.S. officials viewed the development of this effect and other parts of the Truman Doctrine are Dean G. Acheson, *Present at the Creation* (New York: W. W. Norton, 1969), especially pp. 292–93; and Joseph M. Jones, *The Fifteen Weeks* (New York: Harcourt Brace Jovanovich, 1955).

The assistance that I am recommending for Greece and Turkey amounts to little more than ¹⁄₁₀ of 1 percent of this investment. It is only common sense that we should safeguard this investment and make sure that it was not in vain.

The seeds of totalitarian regimes are nurtured by misery and want. They spread and grow in the evil soil of poverty and strife. They reach their full growth when the hope of a people for a better life has died.

We must keep that hope alive.

The free peoples of the world look to us for support in maintaining their freedoms.

If we falter in our leadership, we may endanger the peace of the world— and we shall surely endanger the welfare of this Nation.

Great responsibilities have been placed upon us by the swift movement of events.

I am confident that the Congress will face these responsibilities squarely.

========= Commentary: Part II =========

Immediately after Truman finished his message before a joint session of Congress, an impassioned public debate erupted. Observers quickly understood that the doctrine marked "a reversal of the traditional American policy to avoid involvement in the political difficulties of European states," as one of Truman's closest military advisers, Admiral William Leahy, remarked. The Republican leader of the Senate, Robert Taft of Ohio, expressed the fears of many when he told a reporter that sending military advisers to the eastern Mediterranean could mean "war with Russia" and, at the least, divide the world into permanent "Communist and anti-Communist" zones. Many leading newspapers, which headlined the speech, shared Taft's concerns. A San Francisco editor wrote that the message reminded him of sights and smells from World War II—the trenches, the "brackish water" in canteens, the bloodshed. Walter Lippmann wrote in his widely read column that the doctrine was too general. Instead of being a "workable policy," it would instead become "a vague global policy . . . , the tocsin of an ideological crusade" that "has no limits. It cannot be controlled." Nor did Lippmann believe the United States was "rich enough to subsidize reaction [that is, right-wing regimes] all over the world or strong enough to maintain it in power."

Truman and Acheson won the argument. In secret congressional hearings Acheson emphasized the need to move quickly to save Greece and Turkey. At the same time, he refused to be pinned down on any limits to the global application of the doctrine. Truman had turned the tables on the Republicans. He had forced them to "put up or shut up" about their opposition to communism. He did this by redefining a highly complex world into a simple world divided between "totalitarian regimes" and "free peoples." That kind of simpler world busy Americans could easily understand. Once his definition of the world was accepted, Truman forced his listeners to accept his conclusion:

"every nation must choose" between the two "ways of life." By the way he framed the problem, Truman determined the choice. Americans, fortunate in having such wealth and freedom, must assist the "free peoples." Once Congress accepted Truman's argument, it was difficult to make money much of an issue. One did not pinch pennies if the freedom of the world was at stake.

The president made his argument in simple, easy-to-understand prose. His sentences, for the most part, were short and direct. Indeed, the simplicity of the style helped hide realities Truman did not want to discuss—for example, how Greece was involved in a civil war rather than being threatened by a "totalitarian" Soviet Union, or how the Turks did not qualify in most experts' minds as "freedom-loving peoples."

Truman successfully created a new political environment. He reinforced his success when, nine days after the March 12 speech, the President ordered a "loyalty program" to discover and remove suspected Communists or their "fellow travelers" from government service. Truman's order followed the uncovering of a large spy ring in Canada and growing allegations that pro-Communists occupied important positions in Washington. Several hundred supposed "security risks" did leave the government, but no important spies or spy rings were found under the president's program. Over the next seven years, Truman's loyalty plan was commandeered, over his bitter opposition, by congressional zealots led by Senator Joe McCarthy (R-Wis.). The ensuing witchhunt became a nightmare in American politics. In the short run, however, Truman's security program—the first search in peacetime for "un-Americans" ever conducted by the government in 160 years of its history—demonstrated the president's anticommunism, increased the sense of danger in Washington itself, and helped pass the money bills required by the Truman Doctrine and Marshall Plan.

Congress appropriated the $400 million for Greece and Turkey, then began the legislative process that produced $12 billion to rebuild Western Europe. The legislators moved in step with U.S. public opinion that had just weeks before deeply mistrusted Truman. The president's 32 percent public approval rating of late 1946 shot up to 60 percent in March 1947. A majority of Americans had been convinced by the chief executive that foreign policy, not his bothersome domestic problems, comprised the most important national issue. Truman had redefined the national agenda.

The president not only sent the money to the eastern Mediterranean. He also dispatched 350 U.S. military officers to work closely with the Greek army. Some 74,000 tons of U.S. equipment rolled into Greece during the last half of 1947, but the situation continued to deteriorate until the State Department considered sending two U.S. divisions to save Greece. The number of Greek left-wing guerrillas rose from 18,000 in 1947 to between 22,000 and 25,000 in 1948. Fortunately the president was spared having to make the agonizing decision to send large numbers of U.S. troops to Greece (the kind of decision that led Presidents John Kennedy and Lyndon Johnson into war in Vietnam during the 1960s). In the spring of 1948 the growing division between Tito and Stalin became a violent, open break. The Greek left split between pro-Tito and pro-Stalin factions. Preoccupied with fending off Stalin's threats against Yugoslavia, Tito gave up his ambitious plans for Greece. By the end of 1949 the U.S.-supported regime controlled the country.

The Truman Doctrine had passed its first test. It succeeded not because it had singlehandedly defeated left-wing armies in a civil war, but because the outside aid on which those armies depended had suddenly dried up. The United States had little to do with the ending of that aid, but the belief grew that the Americans had unilaterally determined the outcome of the civil war. That belief indeed grew until Americans came to believe that they could exert nearly godlike powers over most revolutions, whether those outbreaks were as close as Guatemala between 1950 and 1954, or as far away as Iran in 1951 to 1953. In both of those countries the United States intervened to lead conservative forces to triumph. Even as Truman moved into Greece in 1947, he made historic commitments to help the French control their rebellious colony in Vietnam. In 1958 when President Dwight D. Eisenhower sent 22,000 U.S. Marines into Lebanon to damp down left-wing nationalism in the Middle East, he referred to Greece and the Truman Doctrine as precedents. In 1967, Lyndon Johnson publicly justified his policy in Vietnam by celebrating the twentieth anniversary of the Truman Doctrine. In 1980, as President Jimmy Carter threatened to use force unilaterally to protect U.S. interests in the Persian Gulf region, he modeled his declaration on the Truman Doctrine speech. In 1983, when President Ronald Reagan asked Congress for large amounts of military aid to defeat leftist guerrillas in Central America, he quoted from the Truman speech of March 12, 1947.

And with good reason. Truman had discovered the key that unlocked the great mystery facing every president: how to define a foreign policy crisis that the president believes he sees—but about which most Americans refuse to become excited—so that he can obtain not only those Americans' consent, but their dollars and perhaps, as in Vietnam and Central America, even their lives. A leading critic of the Doctrine, Senator J. William Fulbright (D-Ark.) admitted in 1972 that from the Korean War of 1950 to the Vietnam conflict "the Truman Doctrine governed America's response to the Communist world. . . . Sustained by an inert Congress, the policymakers of the forties, fifties, and early sixties were never compelled to reexamine the premises of the Truman Doctrine or even to defend them in constructive adversary proceedings."

Truman performed a political miracle with his two speeches of March 1947. His successors only had to repeat the themes of those messages to obtain the American people's agreement to fight communism around the globe, regardless of whether the threat actually came from the Soviet Union—or was even Communist.

JAMES GILBERT

Postwar Families

From the present vantage point, the immediate postwar period appears to have been one of peace, prosperity, and stability for the American family. The Depression had passed into memory, the boys were home from the war, and "Rosie the Riveter" had become a suburban housewife—with two children in the backyard and two cars in the garage. If we look closely at the popular culture of the period, however, we see a series of images of family life, each of which contradicts the others.

"Americans," as James Gilbert tells us in the following essay, "have long lived with contradictory attitudes about the success of the family as a social institution." But seldom have those attitudes been as strongly held, as widely represented, or as sharply contradictory as they were in the postwar period. "From the 1940s to the 1960s, Americans looked at the family with double vision: with optimism and despair." While they celebrated the family as the central institution of American life, they feared for its future, worried about its wayward youth, and wondered why the divorce rate was so high.

The American family was not, as Gilbert shows us in the following essay, a dying institution, but it was a changing one, pushed and pulled into the future by economic and social forces it could neither control nor, at the time, comprehend.

In the last scene of the epochal film *Giant* (1956), an elderly Texas couple, played by Elizabeth Taylor and Rock Hudson, relax for the first time in 201 minutes. Recalling their good life together, they look approvingly at the baby

James Gilbert is a professor of history at the University of Maryland. He is the author of several books, including *A Cycle of Outrage: Juvenile Delinquency and Mass Media in the 1950s*. The following selection is excerpted from *Another Chance: Postwar America, 1945–1985*.

Reprinted from *Another Chance: Postwar America, 1945–1985,* Second Edition (The Dorsey Press, 1986), pp. 54–75. © Alfred A. Knopf, Inc., 1981; © The Dorsey Press, 1986. Reprinted by permission of The Dorsey Press.

crib at the end of the room. Here, two grandchildren, one obviously Anglo-Saxon, the other Mexican, smile into the camera. And, behind them, through the open window, the camera brings into focus another symbol of integration, a white sheep and a black Angus calf standing side by side. Thus, George Stevens's remarkably successful film ends in a vision of marriage and the perpetuation of the family as the solution to immense social problems.

This family ideology figured in a thousand ways in Hollywood movies in the 1940s and 1950s. Countless films ended in the same fashion, as if to say that romance, marriage, and children were sufficient goals for Americans: If only Americans strengthened the bonds of kinship, then the frightening transformations of modern life could be comprehended. Thus, in *Giant,* the struggle over racial integration becomes an episode in the renewal of family ties. In that film, East merges with West, civilization is united to the frontier, and two races join in marriage in a visual hymn to the American family.

During the same years, however, Hollywood made as many films that focused on the unraveling of the American family structure, in which divorce, extramarital love, alcoholism, and juvenile delinquency shattered the ideal of bliss and turned American men, women, and children into hostile, warring generations. James Dean, who played a grown-up delinquent in *Giant,* had only one year earlier achieved his first acting triumph in *East of Eden.* In that movie, the message was simple, but reversed: The American family was deeply troubled; parents lacked understanding. The result was tormented youth and generational conflict.

Americans have long lived with contradictory attitudes about the success of the family as a social institution. This immense subject has been a staple of modern culture in novels, films, and popular psychology and sociology. Yet the period after World War II owes some of its special character to unique developments in the social and cultural history of the family.

From the 1940s to the 1960s, Americans looked at the family with double vision: with optimism and despair. In one of the most popular novels of the period, J. D. Salinger's *Catcher in the Rye,* published in 1951, both visions exist. The contradictory attitudes of his society toward the family confuse the adolescent hero, Holden Caulfield. In his search for authenticity, he discovers only "phoniness"; instead of fathers, he finds betrayers. Yet Salinger's much-censored book ends affirmatively. After scrambling down the rungs of his private hell, Holden returns home with a larger, more tolerant view of society. He decides to live with contradiction.

A sense of the importance—and a tone of worry about—the family and of the changing roles of parents and children was pervasive, even tingeing child-rearing and baby-care books. The remarkable sales of Dr. Benjamin Spock's *Baby and Child Care* book reveal a deep popular concern for family health in the decades following 1945. Between 1946, when it was published, and 1976, the pocket edition of this work sold over 23 million copies. Only the Bible and the combined works of Mickey Spillane and of Dr. Seuss sold significantly more copies. Spock's work was not entirely new, for it built upon previous child-rearing advice books, but the author was one of the first to popularize the theories of Sigmund Freud and of the American philosopher John Dewey. From these thinkers, Spock drew a theory of child-rearing designed to create well-adjusted individuals—a generation of guiltless, happy adults who could move easily into a modern world of large, socialized institutions. As he put it: "How happily a person gets along as an adult in his job, in his family and social life, depends a great deal on how he got along with other children when he was young." Early behavior depended upon mothers and fathers. In most cases, Spock advised, parents should follow their instincts with their children: "Trust your own instincts, and follow the directions that your doctor gives you." In many cases, a child could indicate what was best for him. As for parenting roles, the bulk of the obligation should fall to the mother, although a father might change diapers or make formula on Sundays.

It is difficult to measure the influence of Spock's advice on the parents who read the baby book. Many, if not most, probably got no further in the index than "measles symptoms" or "diaper rash." Yet Spock fully intended to help liberate the modern family from the long, repressive reach of tradition. Publication of his book signaled the important ideal of a child-centered, family-centered America on the verge of unprecedented prosperity and optimism. The fact that he updated and changed it frequently underscores his serious interest in affecting the family by writing about the baby.

Although the most popular, Benjamin Spock was not the only child-rearing expert in this era. The psychologist B. F. Skinner offered a remarkably different notion of the American family and of child-rearing for those who carefully read his utopian novel *Walden Two* (1948). In his books following World War II, Skinner proved himself to be one of the most inventive and controversial of modern behaviorist psychologists. In this period, he developed two significant inventions: the teaching machine and the "air crib." These instruments, intended to replace or aid teachers and parents, suggest the implicit direction of his thinking about child-rearing. The hopes of rationality and traditional religion had been dashed in Fascism, depression, and world war. Skinner proposed to raise a new generation of Americans, unaffected by guilt or misguided by false beliefs in religion and reason, which had been wrongly distilled by indulgent parents.

Walden Two, named after Henry David Thoreau's famous nineteenth-century book, described a perfected society incorporating management practices, equality, elimination of the family, and behavioral conditioning of children. Skinner suggested that the community, not the biological parents, assume the risks and rewards of child-rearing. He implied that excessive parental love was a key to the failure of Americans to adjust to modern society.

Both Spock and Skinner, in their own ways, responded to strong forces reshaping the American family. Some of these encouraged the view that family stability was increasing. Other trends appeared to threaten the very existence of the institution. As the economy changed, as more women sought full-time employment, as trends in marriage, birth, and divorce rates and in family size shifted rapidly, the shape of the family seemed to be evolving in several directions at once. No wonder, then, that American culture reflected contradictory attitudes toward this institution.

After the war, the American family experienced the inconveniences and stresses of reconversion to peacetime living. Millions of women with absent husbands and children with absent fathers suddenly confronted returning GIs. Readjustment often proved difficult for both men and women. Demobilized soldiers had jobs or careers to resume or possibly several years of school under the generous provisions of the GI bill. In industry, returning GIs resumed seniority in unions and took up jobs on the production lines or in offices. This was not always an easy readjustment, as William Wyler's sympathetic film *The Best Years of Our Lives* depicted in 1946. Yet the problems faced by women were probably as disruptive. Returning soldiers and closed munitions plants spelled fewer jobs for women. While many of these workers intended to stay on the job, millions were forced out of the factory and into the home.

An enormous surge in divorce rates in 1946 suggests that these problems sometimes became too serious to settle. The year 1946 was an extraordinary year: 18.2 percent of existing marriages were dissolved, a rate significantly higher than the years on either side of this date. Although the divorce rate rose during the war to around 14 percent, 1946 represented the peak year, for the rate gradually dropped back to about 10 percent in 1950, where it remained stable for several years. . . . The divorce rate rose sharply after the war, declined to a plane fifteen years in length, and then rose abruptly after 1968. Only post-1973 divorce rates equaled the high percentage that prevailed briefly in 1945 and 1946.

The impact of the war on family life also registered in marriage rates. Most countries fighting in World War II had significant increases in postwar marriage rates, but the United States showed a particularly striking percentage of persons over fifteen who married. From 1944 to 1948, the United States had the highest marriage rate of any reporting country in the world, except Egypt. This statistic means that a higher percentage of Americans married than before or since that interval. Almost 70 percent of males and 67 percent of females over fifteen were married in 1950. Compared to figures collected during the Depression, this statistic represents a large increase. In 1946, the number of eligible persons who married during that year was almost twice the proportion joined in wedlock during 1932.

The consequence of the marriage boom and of lower average marriage ages was a baby boom: More marriages meant more children. The number of live births also increased because of other factors. The illegitimacy rate rose much faster than in previous periods, although this increase occurred in tandem with the higher rates for legitimate births from 1940 to 1957. The infant mortality rate (fetal death ratio) dropped significantly after World War II, reflecting major advances in obstetrics and also a rapid increase in the percentage of births in hospitals.

The American desire for larger families also pushed the baby boom. Translated into statistics, this desire of parents for more children showed up in an exceptional upward curve in the generally downward trend toward fewer children and smaller families typical of most of the twentieth century. Birthrate figures illustrate this trend.

The war-induced postponements of marriage and children partly account for the precipitate rise in family formation and births. Another factor was the undoubted prosperity that many Americans experienced. (The gross national product doubled between 1945 and 1962.) Because of the postwar employment boom and few new immigrants, many Americans increased the size of their families in anticipation of continued economic stability. Although unmeasurable, the widespread emphasis on family values, plus federal economic stimulation in areas like home ownership, undoubtedly registered in these statistics. After the Depression, the years following the war seemed to fulfill a middle-class dream of prosperity and security.

More intensely involved than ever before in marital arrangements, Americans also talked, thought, and debated about the stability and future of this institution, sometimes as if the future of society or even victory in the Cold War depended upon it. New institutions to deal with family problems, developed by psychologists, indicated widespread concern for the continued health of the family.

Although the profession of marriage counseling appeared in the 1930s, it expanded enormously after the war in concert with a general increased interest in psychology. Up to the Depression, the mental health movement concerned itself primarily with individual adjustment and therapy. After the war, interest began to shift to the context of the family. In the 1950s, this attention became an organized movement. Beginning in 1950, with the formation of the Committee on the Family as part of the Group for the Advancement of Psychiatry headed by the noted psychologist William C. Menninger, the practice of family therapists spread in psychological circles. By 1956, this approach had become respectable and established.

Public opinion also reflected keen interest in the health of the family unit. Just after the war, the Gallup poll published a survey indicating that about 35 percent of Americans desired stricter divorce laws, 31 percent felt they should be unchanged, and only 9 percent thought they should be relaxed. Although some differences of opinion reflected age groups, with older people supporting a stricter marriage code, other surveys uncovered majoritarian conservative attitudes that disapproved of women wearing slacks or shorts in public or occupying public office.

Conservative attitudes toward the family, particularly enunciated by the Catholic Church, made legislators and health officials reluctant to legalize or disseminate information about birth-control devices. For the first two decades following the war, federal and state laws generally prohibited easy access to methods of family planning and limitation. This prohibition did not prevent widespread recourse to contraceptives and illegal abortions, but it did express and uphold an older, religiously sanctioned view of the family.

Nonetheless, during the 1950s, rapid progress marked the technology of birth control: The intrauterine device was reinvented, and researchers developed oral contraceptives for women. Although opposed by the official hierarchy of the Catholic Church, contraception by birth-control devices was promoted by Protestants. In 1961, for example, the National Council of Churches reported favorably on family planning schemes. Those states, such as Connecticut and New York, with legislative bans on the sale of contraceptives gradually eased their restrictions. The result was a franker and more open discussion of birth control and sexuality, increased activities by planned parenthood associations, and the legal use of contraceptives. By the middle 1960s, a number of population experts could realistically envision a drastic cut in the birthrate to effect zero growth in population.

As a method of birth control, abortion remained illegal throughout the United States until well into the 1970s. The problem of widespread illegal abortions, however, received widespread attention as early as 1955 at a conference on abortions sponsored by the Planned Parenthood Federation of America. Four years later, the American Law Institute, in its Model Penal Code, proposed revision of state bans on abortions for reasons of health, for risk of deformity, and for conception resulting from rape or incest. Although some states, such as Maryland, enacted such legislation, not until January 1973, when the United States Supreme Court in *Roe* v. *Wade* struck down the abortion laws on the grounds of invasion of privacy, did therapeutic termination become universally legal.

With so much attention given to child-rearing, the role of women in marriage attracted a great deal of discussion. Many American women held jobs after the war—over 2 million more in 1946 than in 1940—but others were forced out of work or voluntarily returned to the family. They were encouraged to do so by a popular culture that pictured domesticity as the most rewarding goal in life. From the nostalgic view of child-rearing in the best-selling family biography *Cheaper by the Dozen* to the pages of ladies' magazines, the message remained the same: House and garden were the ideal environment for American women. A good example of this ideology appeared in *McCall's Complete Book of Bazaars,* an advice book for holding a successful charity gathering. Obviously aimed at the middle-class suburban housewife, the book promised that a successful bazaar would create a feeling of "identification" in the community, as well as uncover hidden talent of neighbors. "A bazaar," the tract solemnly proclaimed, "can be a miniature world of its own, for the potentialities and challenges it offers are manifold."

The middle-class ideal for the family required prosperous suburban living. Success rested upon the ingenuity of the wife, who had to master different and conflicting roles. As mother, she guided the socialization of her children; as family manager, she directed the consumption of new household products; as sexual partner and seductress, she cemented the loyalty and attention of her husband. While certainly a stereotype, this view of women's roles existed in countless popular women's magazines that filled their pages with cooking tips, household cleaning advice, and short, romantic stories stressing the rewards of female sacrifice. Dubbed "the feminine mystique" by writer Betty Friedan in 1963, this ideology operated as a powerful justification for believing that the family was the most important institution in society. Because being a housewife was the most rewarding career, those women who worked or remained single risked guilt and neurosis.

Friedan's negative description of the miniature world of suburban house-wifery probably exaggerated the pervasiveness and the uniqueness of the feminine mystique, but it did accurately reflect the picture of women in popular culture. While the idealized family was obviously a middle-class institution, even those few explicit portrayals of the working class, such as Jackie Gleason's *The Honeymooners,* expressed variations on the same theme. The majority of television programs indulged America's love affair with family life. By the mid-1950s, television had replaced the movies as the basic medium of family entertainment. As film companies in desperation began to aim their product toward specialized audiences, such as teenagers, television captured the family and adopted a conservative model of the institution.

Early television's most perfect family was the Andersons of *Father Knows Best,* a series that ran for eight years after 1954 on CBS and NBC and then survived in reruns on ABC. Although exhibiting a timeless quality, *Father Knows Best* mirrored postwar America. As if to signal the end of the Depression and the war era and the beginning of a hopeful and secure age, the producers of the show chose a title song, "Just Around the Corner There's a Rainbow in the Sky."

Initially a radio program begun in 1949, the series explored the troubles and triumphs of an American middle-class family, presided over by a wise and kindly father played by Robert Young. The town and characters were as typical and idealized as a Norman Rockwell cover for the *Saturday Evening Post:* Maple Street, Springfield, was an address with countless resonances in the collective memory and literary imagination. As manager of the General Insurance Company, Jim Anderson exercised his patient and benign rule over his wife, Margaret, and three children. So seriously did Robert Young take his role as paternal protector of the American family, that he sometimes stepped across the fictional frontier into real life. Thus, in 1950, he began an extensive campaign for safe driving, using his show to convince teenagers to modify their driving habits.

A comic variation on the ideal family and television's most popular production of the 1950s was the *I Love Lucy Show.* From its beginning in 1951, the show enjoyed an enormous success. The setting was apartment life in New York City; the two main characters were Lucy and her Cuban-born (and real-life) husband, Ricky Ricardo. Although the couple had no children initially, an upstairs couple, Fred and Ethel Mertz, acted sometimes as friends, sometimes as grandparents. When Lucille Ball became pregnant, the pregnancy and birth were written into the show. On Monday, January 19, 1953, one of the largest television audiences ever assembled heard the announcement of the birth of a son.

The premises of the show were comic, and the situations Lucy found herself in varied considerably, but each episode renewed the battle of the sexes. Ricardo was a popular bandleader. And whatever she did, Lucy could never achieve her greatest goal: to be an actor, a singer, a dancer, a star equal to her husband. Her aspirations always ended in chaos and comic hopelessness. The "situation" always resolved itself, however, as she resigned herself to being a housewife and helpmate.

The show ended in real-life divorce in 1960 (since 1957, the series had been replaced by hourly specials). In 1962, however, Lucille Ball returned with Vivian Vance on the *Lucy Show* in a situation without husbands. Their new series also proved to be enormously popular, and its success suggested that the television comedy format could do far more than reflect the traditional boundaries of home life. Its success indicated that the paternal, nuclear family was not the only living arrangement acceptable to Americans. The reality of American family life had become far broader, looser, and diverse than an ideal mother, father, and children living in pleasant harmony. Americans were well aware of this fact in the early 1960s. By the end of the 1960s, the broken family appeared as a staple in popular culture.

Contrary to the postwar hopes of a great many Americans, the family also sustained changes that threatened to alter its traditional form. These changes appeared in two varieties: some threatened the traditional nuclear family, while others fundamentally altered relationships within the institution. Divorce, long the most ominous threat to the family, began to increase after 1958, rising rapidly in the late 1960s and 1970s. Pressure on relationships inside the family mounted with the steady increase in the number and percentage of married working women. By the end of the 1960s, the American family began to assume the characteristics of a dual nuclear family, with two centers: a husband and wife sharing both the task of breadwinner and the prerogatives of the role.

Although, from one perspective, the statistical profile of the family revealed stability and continuity in the period after 1945, a number of disruptive trends also emerged shortly after 1945. Early marriages and births out of wedlock increased rapidly. In 1940, the median age at the time of a first marriage for men was 24.3 years; for women, it was 21.5. By 1968, this figure fell to 23.1 and 20.8 years, respectively. In real terms, this meant many marriages with one or both partners who were still teenagers.

The rapid rise in illegitimacy rates—quadrupling between 1940 and 1970—enormously increased the number of single-parent family arrangements, most of them headed by women. While the number of households headed by women by no means approached the number headed by men, their growth was approximately twice the rate of two-parent families after 1940. These changes were especially striking in the black population. By 1974, about 29 percent of all households headed by women were black, even though the percentage of black households in the population was only about 11. Such disproportionate figures gave rise to a sociology of broken families and cultural deprivation affirming that single-parent families breed delinquency and criminality. As the 1955 report of the Congressional Joint Committee on the Economic Report said: "Broken families are more common in the low-income group. One seventh of the low-income urban families included one adult and one or more children but only one-twentieth of the middle income families were of similar structure." To some sociologists, this set of facts explained higher incidences of crime, unemployment, and other social ills among poorer populations.

If the feminine mystique aimed at creating competent, happy women devoted to child-rearing, then rising juvenile delinquency figures, especially in the suburbs, suggested their failure. After 1948, official juvenile court case records and FBI arrest tallies for children under eighteen years old recorded a sharp increase in apprehensions and trials of young people. Almost every year, police arrested more children for crimes ranging from breaking curfews and smashing windows to criminal theft and murder. Crime rates for adults increased as rapidly, but teenage delinquency particularly worried social workers, sociologists, criminologists, and psychologists, all of whom agreed that the broken family breeds delinquency. For all the beneficial influences of suburban living—the idealized family, "togetherness," and permissive upbringing—children appeared to suffer acute alienation from their parents that they expressed in antisocial acts. And, as the average age of the American population plunged in the late 1950s and early 1960s, this trend threatened to persist.

Working women changed the family most significantly in this period. Over a ninety-year period, the percentage of women working rose from about 19 in 1890 to 43 in 1970. Most of this increase came from the entry of married women into the labor market. This group rose from a mere 5 percent in 1890 to around 41 percent in 1970. Significantly, one of the largest increases in women's employment occurred during the 1950s, a fact that may help explain the prosperity felt by many American families. (Increased employment did not necessarily mean increased career opportunity. This fact can be illustrated by changing percentages of women receiving master's and doctoral degrees. In the mid-1930s, women received 13 percent of Ph.D. and 37 percent of M.A. degrees. By the mid-1950s, this portion had shrunk to 9 percent of Ph.D. and only 33 percent of M.A. degrees.) The effects of this change in women's employment, of course, were experienced differently by different classes and in different regions of the United States. Nonetheless, rising employment provided a major key in the development of a strong women's movement in the 1960s.

A final large demographic shift that altered the basis of the traditional nuclear family was increased longevity. The average age expectancy increased by about five years between 1945 and 1970. This was a change of some significance. It meant that many more people could hope to live several years beyond retirement. Looked at comparatively, it also meant that women outlived men by an average of seven years in 1970 as opposed to four years in 1945. Another comparison indicates that blacks increased their longevity by a much higher percentage than whites, so that by 1970, this segment of the population lived, on the average, to sixty-five years.

Altogether, these figures point to an increasing part of the population that was either childless or characterized by the absence of one spouse through death or divorce. This extended period of later life, referred to by the French as the "third age," became increasingly important after the war, although its effects were temporarily masked by the marriage boom and baby boom. Despite the focus on youth in the 1950s and 1960s, the American population grew steadily older. The percentage of married persons living beyond sixty-five years of age increased after 1940, and the absolute numbers of single, elderly people increased. Among elderly Americans, widowed women constituted by far the largest group, with almost 30 percent surviving beyond sixty-five.

Political power of aged Americans first emerged during the 1930s in the Townsendites, a grass-roots movement that promised to end poverty among the retired. The passage of the Social Security Act in 1935 and its subsequent modifications, however, established policy for dealing with America's elderly. Primarily a strategy to convince workers to retire by providing income security, the program succeeded, but not without controversy. Millions of workers retired with some steady income; at the same time, inadequate funds for medical care, unemployment, boredom, and alienation plagued older Americans. The Golden Age movement, beginning in 1940, tried to confront these problems, as did the *Senior Citizen,* a journal first published in January 1955. Despite these efforts, the addition of large numbers of citizens in the third age created a group whose primary interests were neither marriage nor children. Many of them felt out of place in a family-oriented society, living a precarious existence in the retirement or nursing homes that spread rapidly after the war.

Modifications in laws concerning the status of families reflected the changing structure of American family life. Sociologists and anthropologists called the resulting legal institution a "companionship family," or sometimes a "democratic family." In essence, this language implied increased freedom—sanctioned by law—ensuring individuals more latitude in choosing a marriage partner or in deciding to break off a relationship. Where the community and parents once severely curbed individual freedom, the state established liberal guidelines for divorce, inheritance, legitimacy, and the selection of marriage partners. At the same time, society more readily invaded family privacy. For example, in 1971, the United States Supreme Court, in *Wyman* v. *James,* ruled that social workers could enter the home in the interests of a child member, against the wishes of the parents. In this case, the rights of one member of the family were ajudged superior to the interests of the whole: Rights of individuals increased at the expense of the family unit.

Many Americans sensed doom in such postwar modifications of American family life. "Declining" moral standards and juvenile delinquency symbolized this danger, and a vast sociological literature sprang up to explain changes in behavior and morals. Alfred Kinsey's bestselling *Sexual Behavior in the*

Human Male, published in January 1948, proved to be one of the most sensational of these works. Undertaken in 1940, Kinsey's questionnaire research into the sexual habits of American men attracted wide attention and comment in the press. It elicited stern jeremiads from conservative religious leaders, but celebrations from liberal psychologists, who delighted in Kinsey's frank approach. The report became the subject of intellectual round-table discussions, cocktail party witticisms, *New Yorker* cartoons, and a great deal of uninformed speculation. From 12,000 individual case histories, Kinsey and his fellow researchers concluded that sexual practices could be explained best by linking them to socioeconomic factors, race, age, occupation, and region. They found, for example, that upper-level economic groups tended to encourage kissing and masturbation but frowned on nonmarital intercourse. Lower-level economic groups were more prudish about kissing but did not worry terribly about nonmarital intercourse. Differences occurred in other groups with different taboos.

Most important, this relativistic approach to sexual practice challenged the notion of a single, prevailing moral standard for all Americans. Kinsey discussed every variety of sexual activity dispassionately. He categorized behavior by types of sexual outlets: self-stimulation, heterosexual petting or intercourse—including marital, premarital, and extramarital—and homosexual activities. Making no moral distinction between types, Kinsey seemed to define normality as a combination of normal and "abnormal" acts. He wrote, for example, that one-third of all American males had participated in serious homosexual activities at one time or another, but affirmed that this cast no doubt on their identity as heterosexuals. Also, simply by reporting widespread extramarital practices, Kinsey appeared to be legitimizing them.

His second publication, *Sexual Behavior in the Human Female* (1953), again a best-seller, continued his exploration of the same rich but controversial vein. Widely discussed in the media and made the explicit subject of several Hollywood films, including *Two Plus Two,* these books invoked a wide debate about American sexual practices. They became the starting place for an attack on older standards of morality. Liberals cited Kinsey's works when challenging film and book censorship or when pushing for revocation of city and state blue laws. Actual sexual practices, they claimed, differed enormously from the unrealistic laws that were meant to control them.

Sexual liberalism aimed not just at debunking normality and accepted standards; it also pursued public sensuousness for profit. In October 1953, a young Chicago writer and cartoonist, Hugh Hefner, on a shoestring budget and the fortuitous acquisition of the rights to publish a nude photograph of movie star Marilyn Monroe, launched *Playboy,* a new men's magazine. An immediate success, the magazine combined carefully circumscribed pornography with sophisticated articles and stories. Hefner made a bunny in a tuxedo and the monthly centerfold nude, complete with rouged and powdered breasts, the symbols of a new public sensuality.

By the 1960s, Hefner presided over a commercial empire of sex. *Playboy* reached a circulation of over 800,000 in 1959. By this time a celebrity, Hefner turned his private life into further entrepreneurial ventures. His renowned parties were telecast in 1959 as the *Playboy Penthouse Show*. In 1960, he opened his first Playboy Club in Chicago. And, from 1963 to 1966, he published the "Playboy Philosophy," attacking repression and Puritanism in American culture, in his magazine. Greeted initially with considerable outrage, *Playboy* had become so accepted by 1976 that the future president, Jimmy Carter, confessed his private sexual fantasies in its pages without any permanent damage to his candidacy.

When critics began to reflect on American expectations about family life, they often questioned the glorification of the housewife. Philip Wylie's 1942 diatribe, *Generation of Vipers*, anticipated later views of "Momism." Wylie blamed every social ill he could imagine on the frustrations of women trapped in the home. This misogynist handbook of epithets described women as raging, quarreling, murdering Cinderellas, responsible for civic corruption, smuggling, bribery, theft, and murder. Dr. Vincent A. Strecker repeated these charges in a more moderate guise in two books, *Their Mother's Sons*, published in 1951, and *Their Mother's Daughters*, published in 1956 with Vincent T. Lathbury. Here, too, the authors blamed a variety of ills on the "life-wrecking crew of wives."

These pictures of enraged women trapped in unrewarding marriages constituted a small part of the criticism of the family. Throughout the 1950s and into the 1960s, there were countless other bleak portrayals of the American family. Perhaps the finest writer to test the brittle metal of the postwar marriage ideal was John Updike. Almost all of Updike's novels dwelt upon sexual satisfaction, or lack of it, in marriage. *Couples*, a heralded novel published in 1968, explores the loveless marriages and casual sexual encounters of couples who possess children but have no family life. Husbands and wives are pretty much interchangeable. While they can find no real existence outside marriages, they find no salvation within their relationships either. Marriage appears as a customary but hollow institution, an impermanent interlude in the eternal struggle to achieve sexual conquest.

The literature of the shattered family in the 1950s and 1960s was extensive, frank, and sometimes brutal. Its counterpart in describing the younger generation is almost as wide and foreboding. In fact, popular culture seemed to be obsessed with the problems of youth. From the film *The Bad Seed*, in which innocence and youth disguise a brutal murderer, to *Rebel Without a Cause*, to the ominous *Wild One*, starring Marlon Brando, Hollywood repeatedly examined the angry and destructive lives of young people.

Of all the teenage juvenile delinquency films, perhaps the most interesting is *Rebel Without a Cause*. In this enormously successful movie, James Dean portrays a middle-class boy whose arrival at a new high school triggers events that end in tragedy and death. The three main characters, all fated to participate in the final destruction, live in broken or misshapen families. In Dean's family, the mother dominates a passive father; in the second, the father is overbearing; in the third, the family scarcely exists, and the young man runs wild in search of love and security. These stereotyped broken families became the standard explanation for every variety of juvenile misbehavior. Not only were these truisms repeated just in popular culture, but they also became a staple of politics.

Many of the witnesses who appeared before the special Senate Judiciary Subcommittee set up to investigate juvenile delinquency in 1953 repeated the charge that the American family had bred a generation of young criminals. Under the leadership of Senator Robert C. Hendrickson, of New Jersey, and Senator Estes Kefauver, of Tennessee, the committee held extensive and widely publicized hearings during 1955 and 1956 exploring the causes of delinquency. The committee even subpoenaed the publishers of crime comic books and leading film and television producers to answer charges about the influence of media on young people. Although the committee generally supported the position of academics and social workers, who stressed the complexity of the issue, its hearings helped popularize the notion that the United States suffered from a tidal wave of delinquency. Sensationalized news reports of violent and brutal incidents involving teenage delinquents underscored this national concern.

Kefauver's own feelings about the cause of delinquency probably paralleled the reaction of most Americans: He blamed the American family. But recriminations did not end at the fireside. Parents tended to blame schools; the media portrayed parents as weak and vacillating and child-care institutions as callous and brutalizing. The Gallup poll, however, repeatedly found that most Americans blamed declining discipline and loose family ties for youthful misbehavior.

The misbehavior that shocked some observers expressed freedom to others. Jack Kerouac, whose novel *On the Road* appeared in 1957, portrayed the juvenile delinquent as a cultural hero. In a breathless, Whitmanesque style, Kerouac penned a *roman à clef*—a thinly disguised autobiographical description of the lives of his friends in New York and San Francisco. As the author sped back and forth across the country, he encountered the cultures of down-and-out Americans, the music of urban blacks, and the macho masculinity of the American working class. And, as Walt Whitman had done before him, Kerouac celebrated the vitality and energy of these people.

Writing in a more academic mode, Edgar Friedenberg, in his book *The Vanishing Adolescent* (1959), described young people as scapegoats for social institutions that had malfunctioned. The adolescent, he wrote, was an individual in conflict with society: No wonder his contempt for a "society which has *no purposes* [his italics] of its own, other than to insure domestic tranquility by suitable medication." Delinquent behavior, he continued, was the understandable response of people treated as a class with few rights or responsibilities. As for crusaders against delinquency, he noted, their lurid overreaction to the behavior of teenagers displayed unhealthy aggression.

By 1961, it was no longer fashionable to worry about wayward youth. Since the publication of Friedenberg's book, much had happened: John Kennedy was elected in a campaign stressing youth and activity, and children born of the baby boom had entered their teens. Exploited by burgeoning media and consumer industry and no longer feared so much as courted and solicited, young people, merely in terms of numbers, came of age socially. As sociologist Kenneth Keniston told a conference assembled in 1961 to discuss the challenge of youth culture: "The Rock'n'roller, the Joe College student, the juvenile delinquent, the beatnik, whatever their important differences, all form part of this general youth culture." By the early 1960s, seventeen-year-olds emerged as the largest single age group in the American population, and their weight and special interests helped to shape society for several years.

Of all the works to explore the demographic and cultural changes in the family—to slit the seamless web of successful marriage—none was so sharp or ruthless in its implications as the nonfiction best-seller *In Cold Blood,* written by Truman Capote in 1966. Stylistically, Capote's work made a significant contribution to the "New Journalism," a new technique pioneered by other writers, such as Norman Mailer and Tom Wolfe, stressing their own participation in the events they experienced or fictionalized. But notice came to Capote because he focused on a brutal and pointless murder. To the author, the Clutter family was the perfect American family—loving, happy, successful, and healthily dependent upon each other. Their murder by two desperate thieves, therefore, became all the more senseless and tragic. Yet, the author's exploration of his own undisguised tenderness and sympathy for the murderers implied values that deeply compromised the traditional family and heterosexual love. For all the tragedy of the situation, Capote seemed to repeat what other contemporary authors were saying: The American family was disappearing. If perhaps not murdered by society, it was doomed by the extreme pressures of modern life and changes in values.

Obviously, the American family changed after World War II. It was pulled in several directions simultaneously, and it responded by changing in contradictory ways. As early as 1929, President Hoover's Committee on Recent Social Trends reported trouble: the American family was losing its functions; division was increasing. Yet, immediately after World War II, the family reflected new optimism, and marriage and birthrates rose sharply. Then, just as abruptly, the bottom fell out of the marriage boom in 1957 and 1958, and the index of instability began a rapid increase.

Those who predicted the death of the American family or lamented the passing of the paternal, nuclear family based their judgments upon nostalgia for what had been. That the structure and internal relations of families altered after the war is certain. Divorce by the 1960s rapidly increased, but so did remarriage. Various experimental relationships and living arrangements became commonplace by the 1960s. While many of these contradicted traditional moral axioms, they retained family characteristics. That these alternatives might become permanent was suggested at the American Psychological Association's annual meeting in 1967. Papers presented to the conference formed a symposium on "Alternative Models for the American Family Structure." As the editor of the series remarked, America was still committed to the family, but within this broad allegiance, room existed for experimentation and change, from group marriages to Margaret Mead's suggested "two-step marriage," new living arrangements for elderly people, and serial marriages. The future form of family life would be determined in large measure by the economic and cultural forces that influenced this institution. And none of these was permanent.

QUESTIONS FOR DISCUSSION

1. Describe the changes that occurred in the structure and internal relations of American families in the immediate postwar period.

2. What caused the postwar "baby boom"?

3. Why, according to Gilbert, did the popular culture of this period appear to be "obsessed with the problems of youth"?

Chapter Seven

American Dreams, American Nightmares

PAULA GIDDINGS

Black Women and the Civil Rights Movement

The Confederacy was defeated in 1865. Yet ninety years later, in the middle of the twentieth century, black citizens of our southern states could not vote or send their children to the same schools, eat at the same lunch counters, drink at the same water fountains, or swim in the same public pools as Whites.

The civil rights movement of the 1950s and 1960s was born of anger and of hope: anger that blacks were still denied their basic civil rights and hope that these rights could be secured without violence, bloodshed, or inordinate delay.

Many of us know something about the role played by Martin Luther King, Jr., in this campaign. But King, no matter how significant his role in representing and articulating the hopes and dreams of the black people before the nation and the world, did not act alone.

In the following selection, Paula Giddings shows us the crucial role played by black women in the civil rights movement. From Montgomery through the Freedom Rides to the voter registration campaigns in the Mississippi delta, it was women who provided much of the inspiration, organization, and daily leadership of the movement. Rosa Parks, Ella Baker, Fannie Lou Hamer, and thousands of black women whose names will never find their way into history books changed the course of U.S. history by refusing to remain seated at the back of the bus.

Ironically, it was the *Brown* v. *Topeka* Supreme Court decision of 1954 that brought a simmering discontent to an angry boil. The court's desegregation mandate had prescribed no timetable for compliance with its ruling. It was the

Paula Giddings is a journalist. This selection is taken from her book, *When and Where I Enter: The Impact of Black Women on Race and Sex in America.*

From pp. 261–275, 277–280, 287–290 in *When and Where I Enter: The Impact of Black Women on Race and Sex in America* by Paula Giddings. Copyright © 1984 by Paula Giddings. Abridged by permission of William Morrow & Company.

first time, as historian Milton Viorst pointed out, that the Court had vindicated a constitutional right and then "deferred its exercise for a more convenient time." There was no "more convenient time" for southern racists, who dug in their heels. On Capitol Hill the loophole was gleefully welcomed by such senators as Harry Byrd of Virginia, who issued a "Southern Manifesto"—a call for massive resistance—and nineteen senators and twenty-seven House members signed it.

In the South it became clear that the struggle would be a bloody one. Within a year there were the deaths of Reverend George Lee, killed for helping Blacks to vote in Belzoni, Mississippi, and Emmett Till, a fourteen-year-old, lynched for allegedly whistling at a Mississippi White woman. Ruby Hurley was dispatched by the NAACP to investigate the deaths—at great personal risk—and to attempt to gather evidence against the killers.

There was no one more anxious to translate the Court's words into action than E. D. Nixon, president of the Montgomery branch of the NAACP and regional director of the Brotherhood of Sleeping Car Porters. In the wake of the Court decision he attempted to enroll some Black youngsters in a local White school, only to see them turned out by the police. Nixon contacted the NAACP national office—but the racial logjam wasn't going to be broken that way. He was told not to take any direct action, and his frustration lingered—until Friday, December 1, 1955. On that date, Rosa Parks, secretary to E. D. Nixon, boarded the Cleveland Avenue bus in Montgomery. And on that day a movement began. "The Negro revolt is properly dated from the moment Mrs. Rosa Parks said 'No' to the bus driver's demand that she get up and let a White man have her seat," wrote the late Black journalist Louis Lomax.

It was only appropriate that the modern civil rights movement was sparked in just that way. The refusal of Rosa Parks had been spontaneous on her part, but not uncharacteristic. The middle-aged, bespectacled Parks had long been a member of the Montgomery chapter of the NAACP and had served as the organization's elected secretary. For the last twelve years, she had run the office headquarters for E. D. Nixon. Rosa Parks had had similiar confrontations with bus drivers before. She was previously evicted from a bus and sometimes drivers refused to pick her up. And her refusal to be humiliated reflected a historical pattern.

There had always been a tinderbox quality to the ill-treatment of Black women on public conveyances. As early as 1866 the millionaire activist Mary Ellen Pleasant sued the San Francisco Trolley Company after she was prevented from riding on one of its cars. A few years later Sojourner Truth successfully subdued a conductor in Washington, D.C., who tried to physically evict her from a trolley. The abolitionist and newspaper publisher Mary Ann Shadd Cary glared at a trolley driver determined to pass her by with such a "fire-like" gaze that he found himself mysteriously compelled to stop and pick her up. Treatment on the Jim Crow cars had been a catalyst in Ida B. Wells's activist career, had fired up Charlotte Hawkins Brown, and had been an issue Black women had put on the agendas of NAWSA and CIC and NACW. Yes, there was an old and special relationship between Black women and public transportation.

Their treatment on public transportation was probably the most vivid reminder of how they were perceived in a society that was moving forward while most of them were being left behind. Black women needed public vehicles to get to the White part of town to perform the numbing and exploitative work that had been their lot for centuries. They needed the vehicles to return home for precious and fleeting moments with their children before morning, when they had to ride them to work again. Ill-treatment on public transport represented the final insult and humiliation to Black women in a society run by White men.

Riding the buses in Montgomery was especially humiliating. Blacks, who made up the vast majority of riders, were forced to pay their fares at the front of the bus, disembark, and then reenter through the back door. To be required also to give up a seat in the segregated back section of the bus was asking a lot—too much for some. Years before the 1954 decision, a Black woman by the name of Viola White had refused to get up when a bus driver ordered her to. When he attempted to remove her, she "had nearly beaten him to death," according to E. D. Nixon. Viola White was arrested and later sentenced to a term in jail. And though her conviction was appealed, the case languished in the courts for over a decade. White died before she could get a hearing.

Just weeks before Rosa Parks's fateful bus ride, a young Black teenager had refused a bus driver's demand to move to the back of the bus. "Nigger," the driver had commanded, "I told you to move back." The girl replied, "I done paid my dime. I ain't got no right to move." The driver repeated his order; the young girl repeated her answer. Finally the driver stopped the bus in the middle of Dexter Avenue, called the police, and the teenager was taken away in handcuffs. When the girl was jailed, E. D. Nixon believed that this could be the test case he was looking for. Rosa Parks called a meeting of the NAACP youth group to discuss plans for a campaign. But there was an unforeseen hitch. The girl's mother forbade the young girl to appear in court, for her daughter was visibly pregnant—and unmarried.

Rosa Parks was both disappointed and deeply disturbed by the turn of events—not only by the failure of the test case, but also by the personal circumstances of the young girl. She "took [the case] very hard," recalled Virginia Durr, a White activist who had been prominent in the southern interracial movement since the forties. "She felt that the child had been extremely brave and that she had suffered for it; and also that for a fifteen-year-old to get pregnant in that kind of inconsequential way . . . was also a curse of Negro women. . . . She felt that this was the kind of burden that Negro women had to bear for so many generations—you know, of being used." Rosa Parks lived with the consequences of being used. Her husband, according to Durr, was a fair-skinned man whose father had been White. His mother later married a Black man, but she died when Parks was a teenager, and the stepfather turned Parks and his sister out of the house. "Go to the big house and tell your own daddy to feed you," Mr. Parks was told. "I have fed you long enough." Rosa Parks's husband seemed never to recover from the cruelty of his early life. He worked only intermittently, as a barber, and was, said Durr, an alcoholic.

On that December day there was probably a lot on Rosa Parks's mind. There was the frustrating situation in the South; there was the indelible image of the defiant teenager. There were the upcoming Christmas holidays, which meant that she had a heavier load of work than usual. In addition to her duties at Nixon's office, Rosa Parks was employed in a tailor's shop as a seamstress. With her paltry salary of $23 a week, she often did extra work to make ends meet. In fact, she had been doing some sewing for Virginia Durr. On this day, Rosa Parks also had a full bag of groceries. As was her custom, she had done the food shopping, and was undoubtedly looking forward to a quiet weekend at home.

She got on the bus with her groceries and sat down. When the bus filled up, leaving a White man without a seat, the driver demanded that she and three other Blacks get up and stand in the back. The three other passengers reluctantly arose; Rosa Parks remained seated. The bus driver became abusive. "Nigger, move back," he barked. As Rosa Parks subsequently told inquirers, she was tired. But it wasn't just her feet that ached for relief.

Although Rosa Parks's refusal was a spontaneous act, the response of Black women community leaders to her arrest was not. The Women's Political Council, led by Joanne Robinson, had long prepared to transform a singular act of defiance into a citywide demonstration. The council—formed in 1946 by Mary Burke, an instructor at Alabama State College, to provide youths with greater educational opportunities—had been reorganized in 1950, when Robinson became president. The group had adopted a more protest-oriented direction. "It wasn't that we were so militant," said Robinson, "but we felt that the Council should direct itself more toward bringing decency to Black people in Montgomery." The treatment of Blacks on the buses, especially of Black women who utilized them to go to work, was a natural starting point. "Not a week went by where someone wasn't fined or insulted," Robinson recalled.

Well before Parks's arrest, the Women's Political Council had decided a bus boycott would be an effective tactic, "not to just teach a lesson but to break the system," said Robinson. "We knew if the women supported it, the men would go along." Flyers had already been printed to distribute throughout the community: ". . . don't ride the bus to work, to town, to school, or anyplace. . . . Another Negro woman has been arrested and put in jail because she refused to give up her seat," the flyers read. Added to the preprinted leaflets were the date and time for the mass meeting and the boycott. A network had also been put in place for the distribution of the flyers. Key people, mostly students, knew to pick up the packets containing the flyers and post or distribute them in strategic places around the city. At 5:00 P.M. Joanne Robinson heard of the Parks arrest, and within two hours, she said, some fifty thousand leaflets calling for a bus boycott had blanketed the city.

About six o'clock the same evening, E. D. Nixon telephoned Clifford Durr, a White liberal civil rights lawyer and husband of Virginia Durr. Nixon told him that Rosa Parks had been arrested and was in jail, and the Durrs and Nixon went to the police station to post Parks's bond. They knew that the moment had come, that the arrest of Parks would by the rallying point for challenge of the stubborn South. In the first place, Rosa Parks was the perfect symbol for the campaign. "She was morally clean," said Nixon, "and she had a fairly good academic training. . . . She wasn't afraid and she didn't get excited about anything." In addition, the circumstances surrounding the arrest worked in their favor. The Montgomery authorities prosecuted Parks under a segregation ordinance—whose constitutionality could now be challenged—instead of charging her with something like disobeying an officer. This meant the case could be litigated directly through the federal courts instead of having to wind its way through the lethargic and unpredictable state judicial system. Indeed, the civil rights activists now had their test case.

As for Parks, the decision to be the symbol of the challenge to southern segregation must have been difficult—despite her activist background. The road ahead was a dangerous one, and her husband pleaded with her not to take it. "He had a perfect terror of White people," Virginia Durr recalled. "The night we went to get Mrs. Parks from the jail, we went back to her apartment and he was drunk and he kept saying, 'Oh, Rosa, Rosa, don't do it, don't do it. . . . The White folks will kill you.' "

But Parks would go through with it. The movement was on.

E. D. Nixon pulled together a number of community leaders, including prominent ministers like Ralph Abernathy, H. H. Hubbard, and a twenty-six-year-old Ph.D. who had recently come to Montgomery from Atlanta as pastor of the Dexter Avenue Baptist Church: Martin Luther King, Jr. The ministers agreed to support a boycott—anonymously. Their idea was to pass around the leaflets but not to let the White authorities know of their active participation.

Nixon was furious at the suggestion, and accused them of acting like "little boys." "What the hell you talkin' about?" he demanded. "How you gonna have a mass meeting, gonna boycott a city bus line without the White folks knowing it?" Nixon was merciless. He told them: "You guys have went around here and lived off these poor washerwomen all your lives and ain't never done nothing for 'em. And now you got a chance to do something for 'em, you talkin' about you don't want the White folks to know it." He then threatened to tell the community that the boycott would be called off because the ministers were "too scared."

Faced with a choice of confronting either the wrath of White racists or those Black women, they chose the safer course. The Montgomery Improvement Association (MIA) was formed, and the young pastor from Atlanta was nominated as president. That seemed to be Nixon's idea. He had been impressed by a speech of King's and perhaps saw some advantage in having a relative outsider lead the boycott. But Martin Luther King, Jr., was not at all sure he wanted the responsibility. Someone suggested in the meeting that perhaps he was scared. King accepted the post.

On Monday, the Montgomery buses, symbols of an age-old indignity, drove along the streets with no Black passengers in them. The one-day boycott was an eloquent testimony of courage and determination. Now the question was, should it continue? The plan was for it to last only for that Monday. But as

Robinson said, "It was so wonderful to feel free, no one wanted to go back. We were willing to fight or die for what we believed." But could a boycott be sustained?

The answer was yes, largely because the tactic was an effective way to engage the entire community. Men organized a car pool and alternate transport system. Women, who made up a large part of the Black passengers who rode the city's buses (about three quarters of all passengers who used them were Black), proved to be a firm spine for the boycott. Yancey Martin, a college student who was a car-pool driver, remarked, "We saw the transportation end really kinda being the backbone of the movement. . . . We didn't mind them getting to work late to keep Miss Ann from getting to her job on time, and of course, they was just tellin' Miss Ann, 'We not ridin' the bus, and you can come pick me up, or you can find somebody else to get the job done, or you can quit *yo'* job and stay at home and keep your house and baby yourself.' "

But participation wasn't just at the grass-roots level in the Montgomery movement. The same student spoke of Montgomery's "Mrs. Middle-Class Black America" who threw in her lot with the others. "She was like the chairman of the board, see. And, when Mrs. West got involved, even the ladies who were not directly involved and directly participating in meetings were supportive."

As the boycott continued (it would last over a year), White authorities stepped up the pressure. People were harassed, threatened, beaten. Attempts were made to disrupt the legal process after the NAACP had persuaded four women to join a complaint in the federal courts. At the last minute, one changed her mind and dropped out—inciting the Montgomery authorities to bar the NAACP attorney on the grounds that he had sought to represent her without permission. Fortunately, E. D. Nixon had tape-recorded the MIA's negotiations with the women, and so had proof of the original intent. The woman who had dropped out of the proceedings, a municipal worker, subsequently told Bayard Rustin: "I had to do what I did, or I wouldn't be alive today."

The bus boycott attracted national attention. Financial support and other kinds of assistance came pouring in from civic groups, civil rights organizations, Black churches, organized labor. One of the Montgomery Improvement Association's staunchest supporters was an organization called In Friendship. Organized in 1955 or 1956 in New York, In Friendship provided financial assistance to southern Blacks who were suffering reprisals for their political activity. In 1956 the organization sponsored a rally in New York's Madison Square Garden to salute the activists, and a large percentage of the funds raised went to the MIA. Three prominent members of In Friendship were the civil rights activist Bayard Rustin (who was one of the first outsiders to offer voluntary assistance to Martin Luther King, Jr., in the early weeks of the boycott), Stanley Levison, and Ella Baker.

In the meantime, the case was making its way through the courts. On June 4, 1956, the federal court ruled in favor of the MIA, and the case headed to the Supreme Court. At that time, Montgomery Whites made a last desperate effort to harass Blacks by attempting to break up the car pools. But the movement had grown too strong, and fifty thousand Black people still refused to ride the buses. On November 13 the Supreme Court confirmed the lower court's ruling, and by December 20, 1956, the court order reached Montgomery, Alabama.

But then everything just stopped. There were no plans for any follow-up and the movement was on the verge of withering away. There was almost "a complete letdown," recalled Ella Baker. "Nothing was happening." There was no "organizational machinery" to continue the fight. The situation was of deep concern to Baker and the other leaders of In Friendship. Even before the Montgomery boycott, she, Levison, and Rustin had been discussing, as Baker put it, "the need for developing in the South a mass force that would . . . become a counterbalance . . . to the NAACP, which was based largely, in terms of leadership, in the North." They had followed the events in Montgomery with keen interest. All the elements were there for a mass movement: a community politicized by a common issue, an active clergy, and a strong coherent base— the Black church. Nevertheless the momentum had been braked.

Baker met with Martin Luther King, Jr., and asked him why he had permitted that to happen. "I irritated [him] with the question," she recalled. "His rationale was that after a big demonstration, there was natural letdown and a need for people to sort of catch their breath. I didn't quite agree," Baker said in understatement. "I don't think that the leadership in Montgomery was prepared to capitalize . . . on [what] . . . had come out of the Montgomery situation. Certainly they had reached the point of developing an organizational format for the expansion of it."

The In Friendship activists *were* prepared to capitalize on it. By January of 1957 the Southern Christian Leadership Conference (SCLC) was founded on the theory that clergymen in various southern cities were ready to assume civil rights leadership in their communities, according to Louis Lomax. With headquarters in Atlanta, SCLC was a loosely structured organization with sixty-five affiliates in various southern cities. The head of SCLC was Martin Luther King, Jr., but the person designated to run its office and do the groundwork of developing the organization was Ella Baker. It would have been difficult to find a better coordinator.

There was probably a great deal of steely will in Ella Baker's genes. Her grandparents were former slaves, and her grandmother had once refused to marry a light-skinned man of her master's choice, preferring a less refined man of darker hue. As a consequence her grandmother, a house slave, was banished to the life of a field hand. The woman's grandchild, Ella Baker, was born in Virginia in 1905, and was brought up in North Carolina, where she attended Shaw University. Like Mary McLeod Bethune, she had ambitions to be a missionary, and like Bethune never had the finances to realize her dream. So Baker settled for sociology and domestic radicalism.

She came to New York City just before the Depression; the times and the suffering made a great impression on her: "With the Depression, I began to see that there were certain social forces over which the individual had very little control," Baker recalled. "It wasn't an easy lesson to learn. . . . I began to identify . . . with the unemployed." She became involved with workers' education, consumer, and community groups, and joined the Young Negroes' Co-operative League before coming to the NAACP. But Baker eventually became dissatisfied with that civil rights organization. When her efforts to bring it "back to the people," as she put it, seemed utterly futile, she went her own way. She had become more and more interested in exploring the area of "ideology and the theory of social change," and so became associated with In Friendship.

By the time she became SCLC's coordinator, Baker was fifty-two years old and a seasoned activist. She had planned to work with the organization for six weeks, but its lack of funds made it difficult to find a replacement who had the skills and willingness to perform the unglamorous spadework so sorely needed. Baker ended up as SCLC's coordinator for two and a half years.

From that vantage point she watched the movement gain momentum. In May 1957 the largest civil rights demonstration ever staged by Black Americans, "The Prayer Pilgrimage," was held in Washington, D.C. Three months later a civil rights bill was enacted which, though relatively weak, was the first legislation of its kind to be passed since Reconstruction. When the school year began, the school systems in the South, still unintegrated, became the rallying point, and the front lines were largely staffed by Black women. In that year Autherine Lucy became the first Black student to be admitted to the University of Alabama at Tuscaloosa—the first, in fact, in any public school in the state. By her side when she confronted thousands of mob-angry Whites was Ruby Hurley of the NAACP. The challenge, by some accounts, caused some forty thousand new members to join the White Citizens Council. Under similarly violent circumstances, Hamilton Holmes and Charlayne Hunter integrated the University of Georgia, and Vivian Malone, the University of Alabama. The two women became the first Black students to receive degrees from those schools.

But the most savage reactions would come in Little Rock, Arkansas, where Daisy Bates, president of the NAACP chapter, led the integration of Central High School. From the time that the plans to enroll nine Black children were known, Bates and the children were threatened with violence. In August 1957, before school opened, a rock was hurled through Bates's window with a note tied to it: "Stone this time, dynamite next." The note proved prophetic. Daisy Bates's home was subsequently bombed, and the newspaper that she and her husband published, the *State Press,* was shut down.

As the struggle proceeded, the brutality in Little Rock escalated. Two Black women, not directly connected with the integration effort, were dragged from their cars and beaten. Reporters who came down to cover the event were not exempt from the hysteria either; some were beaten and kicked, their cameras smashed. Most tragically, the young students themselves were surrounded by venomous hatred. Daily they were met by armed and screaming mobs. Inside the school, one child had acid thrown in her face. The National Guard was called in. The governor of Arkansas ordered them to *bar* the children from the school, not protect them. After that, the violence swelled so alarmingly that for the first time in eighty-one years an American President sent troops to protect Blacks in the South. In the end, enough soldiers were dispatched to subdue a small nation: 11,500 men, including 1,000 paratroopers from the 101st Airborne Division, were called upon to safeguard nine schoolchildren in Little Rock.

As leader of the integration effort, Bates was constantly faced with the decision whether to continue or desist. After all, her own life was only one of those threatened, and many supporters had questioned her determination to go on in the face of such peril. But Bates had unshakable faith that the time had come "to decide if it's going to be this generation or never," as she wrote in her autobiography. "Events in history occur when the time has ripened for them, but they need a spark. Little Rock was the spark at that stage of the struggle of the American Negro for justice."

Montgomery and Little Rock in turn would ignite the next spark in the struggle three years later, when four students from North Carolina Agricultural and Technical State University staged a sit-in at a Woolworth lunch counter in Greensboro.

REVOLT WITHIN THE REVOLT: THE STUDENT MOVEMENT

The events of the late fifties were especially riveting for the children of the Black Bourgeoisie. Most had grown up in material comfort that their parents could scarcely have envisioned in their own adolescence. No wonder that many had come to have a firm faith in the American dream. If Black parents had doubts that the dream was as attainable for *their* children they rarely expressed them for fear of passing on too bitter a cup. "She did not want me to think of guns hidden in drawers or the weeping Black women who had come screaming to our door for help," recalled activist Angela Davis of her mother, who well knew the racial reality of Birmingham, Alabama, "but of a future world of harmony and equality." Along with this knowing silence, the increasing isolation in middle-class enclaves would make some of the younger generation's awakening all the more startling. As they came of age, the shock of realizing that not all Blacks had been lifted upon the wave of postwar affluence was a rude one. Angela Davis, whose mother was a schoolteacher and whose father managed a gas station, recalled such an experience when she became conscious of class differences within her school. "We were the not-so-poor," she observed of her family:

> Until my experiences at school, I believed that everyone else lived the way we did. We always had three meals a day. I had summer clothes and winter clothes, everyday dresses and a few "Sunday" dresses. When holes began to wear through the soles of my shoes, although I may have worn them with pasteboard for a short time, we eventually went downtown to select a new pair.

Jean Smith, who was born in Detroit and who became a field worker for the Student Nonviolent Coordinating Committee (SNCC) in Georgia and Mississippi, spoke of a similar kind of revelation. Her mother, a widow, had managed to send Jean and her sisters through school, and had herself graduated from college at the age of forty. Although the family, in Smith's words, was "upper lower class," she and her sisters grew up feeling that they had or could get anything they really wanted, such as a house, a car, or a trip to Europe. "Thus my personal experiences suggested that there was room for everybody. After all," she said, "I was nobody special and yet I was doing quite well." When such young women did realize that not everyone was doing well, they felt compelled to do something about it. "My job," Smith commented, "was simply to develop the skills I possessed . . . to create for every person a place of comfort and freedom." Angela Davis's earliest experiences involved stealing change from the kitchen cabinet for her schoolmates who couldn't afford school lunches. "Like my mother," she said, "what I did, I did quietly, without fanfare. It seemed to me that if there were hungry children, something was wrong and if I did nothing about it, I would be wrong too."

In the writings of several of the activists, it is apparent that the value of equality, so vital a part of the traditional American dream, was taken to heart. Chicago-born Diane Nash, a Nashville student leader, saw the desegregation battle as bringing "about a climate in which every individual is free to grow and produce to his fullest capacity." The emergence of the Black Bourgeoisie, despite its apolitical notions, created—at least in some—a keen awareness of the have-nots, a need to do something about them, even a sense of guilt. What the war years had set in motion was the dynamic of a discontented middle class, the stuff of which reform and even revolutions are made.

There was also a more negative, if no less significant, side to this discontent. Many children of the Black Bourgeoisie had paid a heavy price for their physical comfort. The energy expended on materialism and the striving for social position had left emotional scars. In 1963 the Black social scientist Hylan Lewis revealed some of the consequences in a study of three Black mothers who felt they had been victimized by their parents' materialism. The women believed they had been "sacrificed" for material things, like a car or a house, new furniture, or moving into a higher-status neighborhood. In another study, interviews with forty-four unmarried Black mothers revealed that twenty-nine had been rejected by their families, not so much for morality's sake as because of the feeling that their out-of-wedlock children "had broken the family's stride toward social mobility."

Preoccupation with social mobility was not confined to Blacks, of course, but some studies suggest that it was more intense with them than among Whites. An analysis of forty-six Black families and twenty-two White families revealed that "getting ahead" meant an improved or new home for almost twice as many Black families (40 percent) as White (22 percent), though both valued security above upward mobility.

As Frazier suggested in *The Black Bourgeoisie,* many Black colleges bred in their students the same values of social mobility that had been so integral to the postwar experience. Many students saw a future of emotional bankruptcy and great frustration. As Frazier implied in a preface to the 1962 edition of his book, the motives of some young leaders of the sit-ins could be attributed to their reluctance to become the kind of people described in *The Black Bourgeoisie.*

Yet as a result of the migration of the forties and fifties and the upward mobility of their parents, more young Blacks shared the life experiences of their White peers. But at the same time they were frustrated by racism in the North and traditionally Black colleges and universities in the South where there were unaccustomed restrictions and conservative—even reactionary—administrators.

Political awareness was also sharpened by the independence movement in Africa, whose most articulate spokesman, Kwame Nkrumah, president of Ghana, had been educated at Lincoln University in Pennsylvania. Finally, the election of John F. Kennedy further stimulated the racial atmosphere. More fundamental than his gesture of phoning Coretta Scott King when her husband was in jail was that the idea of change was given a positive value in his administration.

But to the Black students, at least in the beginning, *change* carried no radical implications. As Carson observed, the activist students were dissatisfied with the *pace* of change (by 1960 only 6 percent of public schools were integrated, and those mostly in Washington, D.C.), not with its assimilationist direction. Southern prejudice was "slowing the region's progress in industrial, political, and other areas," stressed Diane Nash. Except for their willingness to take on the private sector, the perspective of the students was little different from that of the interracialists of the past.

So when four well-dressed students from North Carolina A & T State University almost casually decided to sit in at a Woolworth lunch counter in Greensboro on February 1, 1960, the act was far from revolutionary. Yet the sit-ins not only detonated a movement within a movement but hurled an entire generation onto a radical path. In less than a decade, students would become the catalysts of a movement that forced a nation to examine its most fundamental values.

Few, not even the A & T students themselves, would have predicted the spontaneous reaction to the Greensboro sit-in. Two critical decisions fanned the spark of protest into a flame that would engulf the nation. First, the students immediately realized that outside assistance was needed, and called upon Dr. George Simkins, a dentist, who was president of the local chapter of the NAACP. Yet Simkins bypassed the national office, knowing that the organization was embroiled in a policy debate over the support of mass demonstrations. Instead he called in the Congress of Racial Equality (CORE)—which had been leading nonviolent demonstrations since the forties—as well as SCLC and the NAACP youth group.

Within a week, sit-ins had spread to 15 southern cities in 5 states. By March, San Antonio had become the first southern city to integrate its lunch counters, and soon after, 4 national chains representing 150 stores in 112 cities announced that they were integrating *their* lunch counters. White students also joined the movement. In less than 2 months, 1,000 demonstrators were arrested. The sit-in movement not only spread through the South but touched northern states as well. All told, the action involved more people than any other civil rights movement in history. Within 18 months, some 70,000 people participated in sit-ins. After more than 3,600 arrests, 101 southern communities desegregated their eating places.

Amid all the excitement, one person grasped the significance of what was happening and moved to do something about it. "The sit-ins had started, and I was able to get the SCLC to sponsor the conference," recalled Ella Baker. Baker realized that the tremendous potential of the student movement was weakened by its lack of coordination. For the first three months of the sit-ins, each campus group was acting autonomously. It was Baker's idea to pull the students together into one organization. She persuaded the SCLC to contribute $800 to underwrite a student conference toward that end. So, in April 1960, more than three hundred students from fifty-six colleges in the South, nineteen northern colleges, fifty-eight southern communities, twelve southern states, and thirteen observer organizations met at Shaw University in Raleigh, North Carolina.

The energy and latent power of the students was not lost on the established civil rights organizations, which were also in Raleigh for the meeting. "The SCLC, the NAACP and CORE wanted us all to become youth wings of their organizations," recalled Julian Bond, who was present at the conference. Undoubtedly the SCLC, because of its role in the conference and because of Baker's influence with the students, believed they had the inside track. Ella Baker suggested, however, that the students form their own independent organization. She was concerned that they maintain not only their zeal, idealism, and independence, but also their inclination "toward group-centeredness, rather than toward a leader-centered group pattern of organization." Their approach, she said, "was refreshing indeed to those of the older group who bear the scars of battle, the frustrations and the disillusionment that come when the prophetic leader turns out to have heavy feet of clay." Thus the Student Nonviolent Coordinating Committee was born, and Ella Baker had become midwife to the two organizations that would have the most far-reaching impact on the civil rights movement: SCLC and SNCC.

The decision of the students to form an independent organization added a new dimension to the civil rights movement. SNCC's autonomy meant they could—and would—move beyond the operational methods and perspectives of older civil rights groups. Their emphasis on voter registration and the "freedom school" idea took them into the deep, rural South, an area ordinarily bypassed by the other Black organizations. Their "group-centeredness" and lack of a rigid hierarchy allowed individuals to take independent actions. "Everyone was their own leader to some extent," observed SNCC staffer Jean Wiley. "Whoever took it upon themselves to do something, generally did it." Both the structural nature and the goals of SNCC propelled women into the forefront of the struggle in a way that was not possible in more hierarchical male-led organizations.

In a group that depended on individual initiative and doers it was natural that women would play a major part. Whatever the political orientation of their families, most of the young women in SNCC had female doers as role models. At the least their mothers worked, and were usually capable of coping with *any* situation that could affect their children's lives. Additionally, some had politically active mothers and most had seen other Black women in activist roles. Jean Wiley recalled that many of the political activities in her hometown of Baltimore were led by Black women. Angela Davis, who grew up on Birmingham's Dynamite Hill—so named because of the number of Black homes bombed there—had politically involved parents. Her mother had participated in antiracist movements in college in the campaign to free the Scottsboro Boys, and had remained actively associated with the Birmingham NAACP even after it was banned by authorities in the mid-fifties. Despite her mother's conscious decision to downplay racial antipathies, Davis knew she could always count on her parents' moral support. And like many of the young activists, Davis was influenced by a strong-willed grandmother who made a point of talking about slavery so that her grandchildren "did not forget about that." Davis wrote of her, "She had always been a symbol of strength, age, wisdom and suffering."

Many of the Black women coming of age in the sixties not only had such women as models but were encouraged to be independent, to do what had to be done, regardless of prescribed gender roles. "My mother always told me that I could do anything I was big enough to do," recalled Jean Smith. Gloria Richardson, who led one of the most violent SNCC campaigns in Cambridge, Maryland, came from a politically active family, and had also seen her parents casually exchange gender roles. Her mother worked; sometimes her father cooked and performed other domestic duties within the family.

These young Black women activists not only had role models, but also strong convictions, self-confidence, and at least implicit sanction for what they were doing. Few thought themselves incapable of doing anything men could do, including facing physical danger. That Black women were such an integral part of SNCC helped make the organization the most dynamic and progressive in the history of civil rights. In SNCC's most critical moments, women were there.

One important aspect of SNCC's evolution was the "jail, no bail" strategy. During the first year of the sit-ins, demonstrators who were arrested looked toward other organizations, notably the NAACP, or friends and family to pay the bail or fines to get them out of jail. With all the arrests, financial resources were becoming strained and continuing dependence on outside help was compromising SNCC's position. So almost exactly a year after the first sit-in, a new tactic was tried with students from the NAACP and CORE in Rock Hill, South Carolina. After attending a CORE workshop, arrested demonstrators refused to be bailed out of jail.

After the first round of arrests CORE asked for help, and four students from SNCC, including Diane Nash and Ruby Doris Smith, answered the call. Nash, a leader of the Nashville students, was attending Fisk University at the time. Smith, just seventeen years old, was a student at Spelman College in Atlanta. The women, along with SNCC students Charles Sherrod and Charles Jones, served thirty days: a month of hard labor, fragile health, and racial indignities. The "Rock Hill Four," as they came to be known, were among the earliest students willing to spend long periods of time away from school and to subject themselves to such treatment. Ruby Doris Smith contracted a stomach ailment from which she never fully recovered. All had difficult emotional experiences at Rock Hill, and obviously their schoolwork suffered as well. But their tenacity showed the potential effectiveness of the "jail, no bail" strategy. It was less costly, it could put authorities in an awkward position when jails overflowed, and it was inherently dramatic—a strategy to catch the eye and the hearts of the public. The most important lesson of Rock Hill, however, was the personal effect it had on the students. It forged a strong bond among them and made them more determined than ever to devote their lives to the movement. Both Smith and Nash would eventually leave school to work full time for SNCC. Nash became SNCC's first paid field staff member, and in five years Smith would be elected executive secretary of the organization and become, in James Foreman's words, "one of the few genuine revolutionaries in the Black liberation movement."

The "jail, no bail" tactic also fit in with the posture of moral superiority that characterized the early years of the movement. Nash most poignantly illustrated this attitude when she was arrested and jailed in Mississippi. Although pregnant at the time, she refused to appeal her conviction, opting to remain in jail. For despite her circumstances, Nash would not cooperate with the state's "evil" court system. "We in the nonviolent movement have been talking about jail without bail for two years or more," Nash said, explaining her decision. "The time has come for us to mean what we say and stop posting bond. . . . This will be a Black baby born in Mississippi and thus, wherever he is born, he will be born in prison. I believe that if I go to jail now it may help hasten that day when my child and all children will be free—not only on the day of their birth but for all their lives." Initiated by CORE, used and developed by SNCC, and utilized most effectively by Martin Luther King, Jr., the "jail, no bail" stratagem revolutionized the southern movement.

Smith, Nash, and several other young women in SNCC were also crucial to the success of another important innovation: the Freedom Rides. Conceived by James Farmer, head and founder of CORE, the rides challenged the continued segregation of interstate transportation facilities throughout the South. Departing from Washington, D.C., demonstrators would ride buses scheduled to stop in Virginia, South Carolina, North Carolina, Georgia, Alabama, and finally New Orleans, Louisiana. On May 4 the buses were boarded. Many were relieved when the buses proceeded with little incident through the first four states. But then came news of the demonstrators' arrival in Anniston, Alabama.

When the first bus arrived there, a waiting mob broke windows, slashed tires, and hurled a smoke bomb, forcing the demonstrators to evacuate the vehicle. Heavily armed Whites met them as they got out. When the second bus arrived in Anniston, the mob stopped it and several of them boarded the vehicle. They forced the passengers toward the back, savagely beating anyone who resisted. The Freedom Riders managed somehow to pull themselves together and continued to Birmingham. But if Alabama was one of the meanest states in the country, it was largely because Birmingham was one of its meanest cities. From 1957 to 1963 the city had had no less than fifty cross burnings and eighteen racially motivated bombings. Not surprisingly, angry mobs awaited the demonstrators there, assaulting them so viciously that one rider required fifty stitches.

Obviously, federal assistance was needed if the rides were to continue. But though President Kennedy supported the goal of the rides, he was reluctant to intervene. Kennedy didn't like such confrontations, and anyway, he was much more interested in protecting Black voting rights than in integrating public facilities. Blacks agreed, of course, that the vote was important, but at that stage of the struggle, so was ending the indignity of being denied the use of public facilities that Whites took for granted. Yet the violence, undeterred by lukewarm federal support, was just too much. Many of the demonstrators decided to fly to New Orleans, and CORE was talking about calling the rides off.

When Nashville student activists Diane Nash, Lucretia Collins, and Katherine Burke heard that the rides might be discontinued, they were disturbed. They believed, as Daisy Bates had some years earlier, that the moment was critical. If the segregationists stopped them now, it would be a shattering blow to the future of the movement. "We felt that even if we had to do it ourselves [the Freedom Rides] had to continue," explained Collins, who would leave Tennessee State University to join the rides just weeks before her graduation. "We knew we were subject to being killed," she said. "This did not matter to us. There was so much at stake, we could not allow the segregationists to stop us." Several of the prospective riders made out wills, Nash recalled; others gave her sealed letters to be mailed in the event of their death.

With other demonstrators, the students boarded a bus in Nashville and headed for Birmingham, where they would face some of the most harrowing experiences in the history of the movement. The policemen who stopped the bus in Birmingham must have been shaken by Collins's cool questions: "Are you a Christian?" "Do you believe that Jesus Christ died for all people?" She recalled that one of the exasperated officers said, "Look, this is my job." He didn't want to make trouble. He was hungry. And Katherine Burke replied that she was hungry too; why didn't they all go to the bus station and have dinner? All the policemen seemed to be nervous, she remembered: "One was shaking." Finally the decision was made to arrest the demonstrators.

The following evening Sheriff Bull Connor, who had harassed Mary McLeod Bethune thirty years earlier, visited their cell. They would have to return to Nashville, he said. The women resisted, but were forcibly carried out of the jail and driven to a dark, deserted train station. Though they had no idea if they were being watched, or what would happen to them if they didn't board the train, they decided, defiantly: "If we went home . . . it would be exactly what they wanted us to do," said Burke. The riders called Nashville and waited for a coordinator to pick them up by car and take them to the Reverend Fred Shuttlesworth's house in Birmingham, where they prepared for the next leg of the journey to Montgomery.

In Montgomery a small crowd of Whites was waiting, and after they attacked the reporters and cameramen there, all hell broke loose. Lucretia Collins and some of the others were rescued by a black cabdriver, who with some difficulty was able to pull away from the scene. Collins looked back to see a White protestor, James Zweig, being held by the thugs so White women could dig their fingernails into his face. The women even got their children into the act, holding the toddlers up so they could maul him too.

But the Freedom Riders weren't finished yet, and neither were the racists. Later that day the First Baptist Church, where they held a rally, was surrounded by a mob. They were forced to spend the night until federal authorities came to protect them. Astonishingly, their determination had not been broken. The Freedom Riders next boarded a bus for Jackson, Mississippi, where they were relieved this time to be simply arrested and jailed. The Freedom Rides had continued. On September 22, 1961, the Interstate Commerce Commission banned racial discrimination in interstate buses and facilities. And the riders? Lucretia Collins, for one, would have been "willing to do it all over again because I know a new world is opening up". . . .

The best known of the women who both transformed the movement and were transformed by it was Fannie Lou Hamer. She was forty-four years old when, in 1962, she first saw SNCC workers and heard about a voter registration campaign in Ruleville, Mississippi, the home district of Senator James Eastland. Hamer had spent all her years in Sunflower County, Mississippi, not knowing that Black people had the right to register to vote. But when she heard the young civil rights workers, it was as if a whole new vision of the world opened up to her. "Just listenin' at 'em," she recalled, "I could see myself votin' people out of office I know was wrong and didn't do nothin' to help the poor. I said, you know, that's sumin' I wanna be involved in." "Involved" was an understatement. Hamer showed a tenacity and determination few thought possible, given the limits of human suffering.

The idea that Blacks had the right to vote may have been new to Hamer, but courage wasn't. She was one of twenty children of a sharecropping family, and among the lessons her mother had instilled in her were pride and the determination that went along with it. "There weren't many weeks passed that she wouldn't tell me . . . you respect yourself as a Black child, and when you get grown, if I'm dead and gone, you respect yourself as a Black woman; and other people will respect you."

To respect oneself and be a Mississippi sharecropper added up to another emotion: anger. "So as I got older—I got madder," Hamer said. "It's been times that I've been called 'Mississippi's angriest woman' and I have a right to be angry." In her earlier years, much of that anger, and sadness as well, was forged into determination by the life her mother was forced to lead.

By the forties, farming machines that could do the work of field hands were all over the South. Industrialization had forced many farm workers to leave in search of a better life in the cities. For those left behind, work seemed all the more painful and ironic. "I used to watch my mother with tears in my eyes," Hamer recalled, "how she would have to go out where you see all of these big machines clearing up new grounds. . . . I used to see my mother cut those same trees with an axe just like a man . . . she would carry us out . . . in these areas . . . and we would have to rake up the brush . . . and burn it. . . . The same land that's in cultivation now, that they got closed to us that we can't own, my parents helped to make this ground what it is." Their poverty literally weighed down on them. "As she got older," Hamer said, she saw how her mother's clothes "would be heavy with patches, just mended over and over, where she would mend it and that mend would break, and she would mend it with something else. Her clothes would become very heavy. So, I promised myself if I ever got grown, I would never see her wear a patched-up piece. . . . I began to see the suffering she had gone through."

But when Hamer "got grown," her life was much the same as her mother's. She did manage to be the "time-keeper" of the plantation—and even got a few rebellious licks in. One time she told the proprietor: "I said, you know the thing that shocked me, our people go to the army just like your white people go . . . and then when they come back home, if they say anything, they killed, they lynched, they murdered. . . . I just don't see no reason they should fight." Hamer went on: "You know they would look at me real funny but I was rebelling in the only way I knew how to rebel. I just steady hoped for a chance that I could really lash out, and say what I had to say about what was going on in Mississippi."

When the SNCC people came to town, she got that chance, and she would take advantage of it by the act of "simply" casting a ballot. "The only thing they could do to me was kill me, and it seemed like they'd been trying to do that a little bit at a time ever since I could remember."

In August, 1962, she and seventeen others took a bus to the county seat in Indianola and registered to vote. When Hamer returned, the proprietor told her she must withdraw her name from the voter rolls or leave the plantation. She had worked there eighteen years; her husband, thirty. Still, the choice wasn't hard. "I didn't go down there to register for you," she told him. "I went down to register there for myself." In no time she was gone, and stayed with a friend nearby. That evening, marauding Whites shot into the friend's house sixteen times, forcing Hamer to leave the county for several months.

Hamer eventually returned to Ruleville, found a house for herself and her family, and by December was registered to vote. She subsequently became an instructor of a voter-education program run by SNCC. Her determination was partly due to what she termed "just sick and tired of being sick and tired. We just got to stand up as Negroes for ourselves and our freedom," she said, "and if it don't do me any good, I do know the young people it will do good."

The year that Hamer registered, 1963, was the most violent of the civil rights movement. By that spring and summer the protests had intensified, and so had the reaction. The Southern Regional Council estimated that before the year was over, 930 public protest demonstrations had been held on civil rights issues in at least 115 cities within 11 southern states. Voter registration was going on in Greenwood, Mississippi, where Mary Booth was a field secretary, and where one of the SNCC organizers was shot in the head by Whites. Fortunately, he survived. Medgar Evers, the courageous head of that state's NAACP, did not. He was assassinated in front of his home in Jackson. Fannie Lou Hamer and Annelle Ponder were arrested in Winona and viciously beaten with leaded leather straps. Hamer was permanently debilitated by the assault and disfigured so badly that she wouldn't let her family see her for a month. Ponder, one of two SCLC voter-education teachers stationed permanently in Mississippi, was also brutally beaten. Hamer had overheard Ponder's guard in the adjacent cell:

"Cain't you say *yessir,* nigger? Cain't you say *yessir,* bitch?"

Then Ponder's voice: "Yes, I can say *yessir.*"

"Well, say it," the guard said.

"I don't know you well enough," Ponder retorted.

And then Hamer heard the strokes. "She kept screamin', and they kept beatin' her," said Hamer, "and finally she started prayin' for 'em, and she asked God to have mercy on 'em because they didn't know what they was doin'."

Some days later, a SNCC worker went to see Annelle Ponder in jail. Her face was so swollen that she could scarcely talk, the worker reported. "She looked at me and was able to whisper one word: Freedom."

QUESTIONS FOR DISCUSSION

1. Why do you think the story of the civil rights movement is so often told in terms of Martin Luther King, Jr.?

2. Why were the black women natural leaders and participants in the struggle for civil rights?

Many of the leaders of the August 28, 1963, March on Washington link arms during the walk to the Lincoln Memorial for the major afternoon rally. Those in the front rank include National Catholic Interracial Council executive director Mathew Ahmann (in bow tie), CORE's Floyd McKissick, Martin Luther King, Jr., trade union leader Cleveland Robinson, Rabbi Joachim Prinz of the American Jewish Congress, civil rights lawyer Joseph Rauh (in bow tie), Whitney Young, executive director of the National Urban League, NAACP executive secretary Roy Wilkins, and Brotherhood of Sleeping Car Porters president A. Philip Randolph, the moving force behind the 1963 March. The participants' placards reflect how the explicit goals of the March gave jobs and employment as high a priority as the passage of federal civil rights legislation. *(Bettmann Newsphotos)*

"I Have a Dream" Speech

Commentary by David J. Garrow

Martin Luther King, Jr.'s, "I Have a Dream" speech at the August 28, 1963, March on Washington was one of the greatest orations in American history and one of the most notable highlights of the civil rights movement of the 1950s and 1960s. Heard by over 200,000 people gathered near the Lincoln Memorial that warm summer day and by millions more on television and radio, King's speech conveyed the moral power of the movement's cause to an international audience and confronted white America with the undeniable justice of black citizens' demands for an end to racial segregation and discrimination.

King was only thirty-four years old when he gave that address, a still youthful Baptist minister who, as the eldest son of a well-to-do Atlanta clergyman, had grown up in the black Southern Baptist tradition. King had graduated from a trio of notable schools: Atlanta's Morehouse College, one of America's best-regarded black institutions, Crozer Theological Seminary, and Boston University, where he received a doctorate in systematic theology. Long before he had finished his education, King knew that he wanted to serve as a pastor in the South. In 1954 he became minister of the Dexter Avenue Baptist Church in Montgomery, Alabama, a well-to-do church in the rigidly segregated city that proudly styled itself "the cradle of the Confederacy."

New to town, new to his job, and with his wife Coretta expecting their first child, King took only a modest role in black civic affairs until December 1955, when Mrs. Rosa Parks was arrested for refusing to surrender her seat to a white man on a segregated city bus. King's colleagues drafted him as spokesman for the Montgomery Improvement Association, the new organization set up to oversee the black boycott of Montgomery's segregated bus line. King's gift for powerful Biblical oratory made him a public figure as the black community's year-long protest became a national and international news story.

Between 1957 and 1963, Martin Luther King, Jr., emerged as the foremost spokesman for black Americans in their renewed struggle to obtain their full constitutional rights. King's 1960 arrest for sitting-in at a segregated Atlanta lunchroom, his prominent role in sustaining the 1961 Freedom Rides, and his involvement in the 1961–62 demonstrations in Albany, Georgia, placed him in the nation's headlines and reinforced his role as the most visible representative of black southerners' increasing civil rights activism.

Early in 1963 King and the Southern Christian Leadership Conference (SCLC), the region-wide organization he had founded in 1957, launched a major protest campaign in Birmingham, Alabama, where public safety commissioner Eugene "Bull" Connor had already become famous for his rough tactics against black demonstrators. Together with long-time Birmingham activist Reverend Fred Shuttlesworth, King's SCLC staff organized a month-long series of sit-ins and protest marches. Graphic news photos of Connor's men using police dogs and high-powered fire hoses against peaceful demonstrators created a national outrage and stimulated even hesitant supporters of civil rights, like President John Kennedy and Attorney General Robert Kennedy, to call for white concessions to SCLC's demands for desegregation.

The Birmingham protests made civil rights a prominent national issue. Sympathy demonstrations took place in cities across the country as civil rights activists promised to intensify. their nonviolent attack on segregation. Several of King's aides talked of staging a major demonstration in the nation's capital, an idea already proposed by A. Philip Randolph, president of the Brotherhood of Sleeping Car Porters and the Negro American Labor Council. The dean of America's black leaders, Randolph in 1941 had successfully used the threat of a massive march on Washington to pressure President Franklin D. Roosevelt into issuing an executive order banning racial discrimination by government defense contractors. Randolph's purpose in calling for a 1963 march on Washington was to highlight pervasive black unemployment and call attention to the need for greater economic justice in American life. Before the protests in Birmingham, black leaders had shown little interest in his proposal. In early June, however, as King and others began to articulate the need for comprehensive federal legislation to eliminate racial discrimination, Randolph's plans for a march and SCLC's idea of a massive civil rights demonstration were combined. A "March on Washington for Jobs and Freedom" was scheduled for late August.

The violence in Birmingham and the national indignation it aroused also had a powerful effect on John and Robert Kennedy. Although they had, in the first two years of the Kennedy administration, been reluctant to propose any meaningful civil rights legislation to a disinterested Congress, they now recognized that Birmingham had changed the political climate. They also realized, for the first time, that racial discrimination was a moral issue that America had to confront and resolve. In mid-June President Kennedy went on national television to announce his intention to ask Congress for a far-reaching civil rights bill. Kennedy and his aides worried, however, that the upcoming march on Washington would hinder rather than help congressional passage of that bill. King, Randolph, and others were summoned to the White House and asked to cancel the demonstration. They refused. Popular support for the march increased throughout the summer as a talented team of movement organizers, headed by long-time Randolph aide Bayard Rustin, made plans for the nationwide move on Washington. They anticipated more than 100,000 participants.

By mid-July the Kennedy administration, faced with the fact that the march was going to take place whether it wanted it to or not, endorsed the demonstration. Still hoping to avoid any damage to the civil rights bill's uncertain congressional fate, the Kennedys shifted to a strategy of trying to moderate the march's political tone. Middle-of-the-road civil rights leaders such as Roy Wilkins, executive secretary of the National Association for the Advancement of Colored People (NAACP), and Whitney Young, executive director of the National Urban League, stressed that the primary purpose of the march was to rally support for Kennedy's civil rights bill, not Randolph's economic agenda. The addition of four white cosponsors—United Auto Workers President Walter Reuther, Protestant notable Reverend Eugene Carson Blake, Jewish leader Rabbi Joachim Prinz, and Catholic layman Mathew Ahmann—to the six-man black leadership also gave the march a more moderate and legislative orientation. What had started out as a protest against federal government inaction on civil rights was looking more and more like a celebration of the movement's growth and Kennedy's congressional initiative.

In the weeks leading up to the August 28 event, the march leaders decided to focus their efforts on a mass rally and program at the Lincoln Memorial rather than on any Capitol Hill protests. Each of the ten leaders would address the crowd. Popular entertainers and other celebrities would also appear on the podium. Some female activists complained privately about the absence of any woman from the list of speakers, but a more serious dispute broke out when Kennedy aides and supporters got a look at the advance text of Student Nonviolent Coordinating Committee (SNCC) chairman John Lewis's speech, which blasted the Kennedy administration for its tardy and incomplete support of the civil rights movement. Throughout the night of August 27 and into the morning of the 28th, as other plans fell into place, the march leaders argued with Lewis and his SNCC colleagues about toning down the speech. Only moments before the actual program began was a final accord reached.

Martin Luther King, Jr., did not finish preparing his advance text until the early morning hours of August 28. What he wanted, King told a friend, was something short and straightforward, "sort of a Gettysburg address." When typed up double-spaced on legal-size paper for mimeographing and distribution to reporters, it came to only three pages. (With ten speakers, everyone had been instructed to keep his remarks brief.) King's speech was scheduled last, at the climax of the program. Long before he moved forward with his prepared text in hand, it had become clear that the massive rally was a powerful and joyous success. Official estimates numbered the crowd at over 200,000, the largest single gathering in American history.

Master of ceremonies A. Philip Randolph introduced King as "the moral leader of our nation." King began with his untitled, advance text, following it closely as he made reference to Abraham Lincoln's Emancipation Proclamation and to the promises of the Declaration of Independence and the Constitution, all of which, he noted, remained unfulfilled for black Americans. Speaking metaphorically, King compared those promises to a "bad check" which the United States now had to make good on. Using one of his favorite rhetorical devices, King reiterated that "Now is the time" for America to live up to those commitments. Linking the goal of racial equality to the language of traditional American patriotism, King underlined the necessity of nonviolence and biracial cooperation in the civil rights struggle and cited some of the discriminatory evils that federal legislation could eliminate. Then, after quoting the prophet Amos on justice and righteousness and emphasizing his own conviction that unmerited suffering was redemptive, King was close to the end of his prepared text. He recalled that moment in an unpublished interview several months later. "Just all of a sudden—the audience response was wonderful that day— and all of a sudden this thing came to me that I have used—I'd used it many time before, that thing about 'I have a dream'—and I just felt that I wanted to use it here. I don't know why, I hadn't thought about it before the speech." King believed he had used the phrase at a rally in Albany eighteen months earlier and at a Birmingham mass meeting that spring. He had also employed it at a huge civil rights rally in Detroit on June 23. But on none of those occasions had it had anywhere near the impact that it did at the March on Washington.

"I have a dream," King declared, introducing a strong, repetitive cadence often used in the oratorical tradition of black Baptist preaching. He quoted from the Declaration of Independence, alluded to the segregationist legal doctrines of interposition and nullification that Alabama Governor George C. Wallace had cited in his unsuccessful effort to block court-ordered desegregation of the University of Alabama, and then repeated his "dream" that one day even Alabama would achieve a state of interracial harmony. He ended his "I Have a Dream" passage by quoting from the Bible's Book of Isaiah, and then, in his concluding lines, returned in large part to the closing that appeared in his prepared text. He added a passage of several lines from a traditional American patriotic song, and expanded on its call to "let freedom ring" from every mountainside by appending the names of some notable southern mountains to the list of American peaks. He ended the speech with a line he had often used as his closing. "Free at last, free at last. Thank God Almighty, we are free at last." Dripping with sweat, King stepped back as the audience gave him a thundering ovation.

DR. MARTIN LUTHER KING, JR.

"I Have a Dream"

I am happy to join with you today in what will go down in history as the greatest demonstration for freedom in the history of our nation.

Five score years ago, a great American, in whose symbolic shadow we stand today, signed the Emancipation Proclamation. This momentous decree came as a great beacon light of hope to millions of Negro slaves who had been seared in the flames of withering injustice. It came as a joyous daybreak to end the long night of their captivity.

But one hundred years later, the Negro still is not free; one hundred years later, the life of the Negro is still sadly crippled by the manacles of segregation and the chains of discrimination; one hundred years later, the Negro lives on a lonely island of poverty in the midst of a vast ocean of material prosperity; one hundred years later, the Negro is still languished in the corners of American society and finds himself in exile in his own land.

So we've come here today to dramatize a shameful condition. In a sense we've come to our nation's capital to cash a check. When the architects of our republic wrote the magnificent words of the Constitution and the Declaration of Independence, they were signing a promissory note to which every American was to fall heir. This note was the promise that all men, yes, black men as well as white men, would be guaranteed the unalienable rights of life, liberty, and the pursuit of happiness.

It is obvious today that America has defaulted on this promissory note in so far as her citizens of color are concerned. Instead of honoring this sacred obligation, America has given the Negro people a bad check, a check which has come back marked "insufficient funds." But we refuse to believe that the bank of justice is bankrupt. We refuse to believe that there are insufficient funds in the great vaults of opportunity of this nation. And so we've come to cash this check, a check that will give us upon demand the riches of freedom and the security of justice.

We have also come to this hallowed spot to remind America of the fierce urgency of now. This is no time to engage in the luxury of cooling off or to take the tranquilizing drug of gradualism. Now is the time to make real the promises of democracy; now is the time to rise from the dark and desolate valley of segregation to the sunlit path of racial justice; now is the time to lift our nation from the quicksands of racial injustice to the solid rock of brotherhood; now is the time to make justice a reality for all of God's children. It would be fatal for the nation to overlook the urgency of the moment. This sweltering summer of the Negro's legitimate discontent will not pass until there is an invigorating autumn of freedom and equality.

Nineteen sixty-three is not an end, but a beginning. And those who hope that the Negro needed to blow off steam and will now be content, will have a rude awakening if the nation returns to business as usual. There will be neither rest nor tranquility in America until the Negro is granted his citizenship rights. The whirlwinds of revolt will continue to shake the foundations of our nation until the bright day of justice emerges.

But there is something that I must say to my people, who stand on the worn threshold which leads into the palace of justice. In the process of gaining our rightful place, we must not be guilty of wrongful deeds. Let us not seek to satisfy our thirst for freedom by drinking from the cup of bitterness and hatred. We must forever conduct our struggle on the high plain of dignity and discipline. We must not allow our creative protests to degenerate into physical violence. Again and again we must rise to the majestic heights of meeting physical force with soul force. The marvelous new militancy, which has engulfed the Negro community, must not lead us to a distrust of all white people. For many of our white brothers, as evidenced by their presence here today, have come to realize that their destiny is tied up with our destiny. And they have come to realize that their freedom is inextricably bound to our freedom. We cannot walk alone. And as we walk, we must make the pledge that we shall always march ahead. We cannot turn back.

There are those who are asking the devotees of Civil Rights, "When will you be satisfied?" We can never be satisfied as long as the Negro is the victim of the unspeakable horrors of police brutality; we can never be satisfied as long as our bodies, heavy with the fatigue of travel, cannot gain lodging in the motels of the highways and the hotels of the cities; we cannot be satisfied as long as the Negro's basic mobility is from a smaller ghetto to a larger one; we can never be satisfied as long as our children are stripped of their selfhood and robbed of their dignity by signs stating "For Whites Only"; we cannot be satisfied as long as the Negro in Mississippi cannot vote and a Negro in New York believes he has nothing for which to vote. No! No, we are not satisfied, and we will not be satisfied until "justice rolls down like waters and righteousness like a mighty stream."

I am not unmindful that some of you have come here out of great trials and tribulations. Some of you have come fresh from narrow jail cells. Some of you have come from areas where your quest for freedom left you battered by the storms of persecution and staggered by the winds of police brutality. You have been the veterans of creative suffering. Continue to work with the faith that unearned suffering is redemptive. Go back to Mississippi. Go back to Alabama. Go back to South Carolina. Go back to Georgia. Go back to Louisiana. Go back to the slums and ghettos of our Northern cities, knowing that somehow this situation can and will be changed. Let us not wallow in the valley of despair.

I say to you today, my friends, so even though we face the difficulties of today and tomorrow, I still have a dream. It is a dream deeply rooted in the American dream. I have a dream that one day this nation will rise up and live out the true meaning of its creed, "We hold these truths to be self-evident, that all men are created equal." I have a dream that one day on the red hills of Georgia, sons of former slaves and the sons of former slave owners will be able to sit down together at the table of brotherhood. I have a dream that one day even the state of Mississippi, a state sweltering with the heat of injustice, sweltering with the heat of oppression, will be transformed into an oasis of freedom and justice. I have a dream that my four little children will one day live in a nation where they will not be judged by the color of their skin, but by the content of their character.

I have a dream today! I have a dream that one day down in Alabama—with its vicious racists, with its Governor having his lips dripping with the words of interposition and nullification—one day right there in Alabama, little black boys and black girls will be able to join hands with little white boys and white girls as sisters and brothers.

I have a dream today! I have a dream that one day every valley shall be exalted, and every hill and mountain shall be made low. The rough places will be plain and the crooked places will be made straight, "and the glory of the Lord shall be revealed, and all flesh shall see it together."

This is our hope. This is the faith that I go back to the South with. With this faith we will be able to hew out of the mountain of despair a stone of hope. With this faith we will be able to transform the jangling discords of our nation into a beautiful symphony of brotherhood. With this faith we will be able to work together, to pray together, to struggle together, to go to jail together, to stand up for freedom together, knowing that we will be free one day. And this will be the day. This will be the day when all of God's children will be able to sing with new meaning, "My country 'tis of thee, sweet land of liberty, of thee I sing. Land where my father died, land of the pilgrims' pride, from every mountainside, let freedom ring." And if America is to be a great nation, this must become true.

So let freedom ring from the prodigious hilltops of New Hampshire; let freedom ring from the mighty mountains of New York; let freedom ring from the heightening Alleghenies of Pennsylvania; let freedom ring from the snow-capped Rockies of Colorado; let freedom ring from the curvaceous slopes of California. But not only that. Let freedom ring from Stone Mountain of Georgia; let freedom ring from Lookout Mountain of Tennessee; let freedom ring from every hill and mole hill of Mississippi. "From every mountainside, let freedom ring."

And when this happens, and when we allow freedom to ring, when we let it ring from every village and every hamlet, from every state and every city, we will be able to speed up that day when all of God's children, black men and white men, Jews and Gentiles, Protestants and Catholics, will be able to join hands and sing in the words of the old Negro spiritual: "Free at last. Free at last. Thank God Almighty, we are free at last."

=========== **Commentary: Part II** ===========

▓ ▓ ▓

Although King did not then know it, the speech had been the rhetorical achievement of a lifetime, a clarion call that had communicated the moral justice and spiritual fervor of the civil rights movement to an audience of millions. Now, more than ever before, America and the world were faced with the powerful truth about black people's unavoidable demand for justice and equality.

As the crowd quieted, Bayard Rustin stepped to the podium and presented to the audience the specific goals of the March on Washington: passage of Kennedy's civil rights bill, a two dollar minimum wage, desegregation of schools, a federal public works job program, and federal action to bar racial discrimination in employment practices. The crowd roared its approval as each demand was read. As the last act of an incredible drama, Morehouse College President Benjamin E. Mays, King's mentor from his college years, came forward and gave the benediction. While the crowd slowly dispersed, the march's leaders headed to the White House for an appointment with President Kennedy.

The president was in a jovial mood when King and his colleagues arrived. He was especially pleased that no disruptive incidents had marred an event that had begun as a demonstration against him but had ended as a public relations bonanza for both the civil rights movement and Kennedy's new legislative effort. When Roy Wilkins mentioned that the leaders had all missed lunch, Kennedy ordered sandwiches for them from the White House kitchen.

The leadership group briefed the president on the success of the day's events, pressed him to strengthen certain provisions in the civil rights bill, and then posed with smiles as photographers snapped pictures of them with the president. From the White House they went to a television studio to tape a special hour-long interview on the march. Randolph stressed that "the mood of the Negro today is one of impatience and anger, frustration if not desperation." Wilkins and King emphasized the importance of obtaining congressional passage of the landmark civil rights bill. "This is a revolution to get in," King said of the civil rights movement, "a quest to get into the mainstream of American society."

After the taping, King returned to his hotel in a particularly buoyant mood. It had been a memorable day, one of the two or three most gratifying moments in his civil rights career. He and the movement's small group of full-time activists were no longer alone; hundreds of thousands of people were now willing to actively support their cause.

It was a moment of supreme pleasure, but one that Martin King knew would be short-lived. His faith that the movement could "redeem the soul of America," as SCLC's official slogan put it, had been reinvigorated. But he knew that the dream was still far from fruition, and that the task at hand, as he had indicated that afternoon, was to "go back to the South" and resume a struggle that now, for the first time in its history, appeared to have truly massive support among the American people.

The March on Washington generated an emotional and political glow in which the civil rights movement could bask for weeks. It culminated a summer during which the race issue finally had moved to the front of the American political agenda. Although most press coverage focused on the impressive turnout and tone of the march rather than on the leaders' speeches, King's address had had an impact unlike any previous articulation of the movement's cause. Some activists took the opportunity to catch their breath. The principal leaders, however, were afraid of a letdown and hopeful that the march could inaugurate a period of renewed activism. Bayard Rustin stressed that it ought to be viewed as "not a climax but a new beginning." He worried that an atmosphere of stagnant self-satisfaction would result from the march and he feared, as did many march organizers, that the economic goals of the pilgrimage had made no impact at all on the wider public. King shared those concerns, and told reporters that he would soon launch new demonstrations in the South.

King and Rustin also appreciated how the march had succeeded in drawing new white allies to the movement's side. The potential political influence of such a broadened interracial coalition seemed enormous, and Rustin busily sketched out the possibilities while King pondered how to initiate new protests across the South.

The pleasant afterglow of the march and King's speech was suddenly and completely wiped away on Sunday morning, September 15, when white terrorists bombed Birmingham's Sixteenth Street Baptist Church, one of the movement's major churches, killing four young girls who were attending Sunday school. The rage and desperation felt by black Birmingham exploded on the city's streets. Hundreds of furious citizens pelted police with rocks, two black youths were killed in shooting incidents, and a half dozen other people were injured.

King flew to Birmingham where he called for U.S. army intervention, warning that the city faced an "emergency situation." President Kennedy decried the bombing but decided against any federal military action. He met with King and black Birmingham leaders to discuss other possibilities. "The Negro community is about to reach a breaking point," King cautioned the president while asking for clear federal action to reassure black Birmingham and black America. Kennedy agreed to send two presidential mediators to the city. King welcomed the decision as evidence of "the kind of federal concern needed." Nonetheless, in the weeks to follow, King would argue again and again that only quick congressional passage of an undiluted civil rights bill could meaningfully stem the deep anger and frustration that the Birmingham killings had awakened in black America and the civil rights movement.

The fatal bombing, hardly two weeks after the march, substantially circumscribed the ongoing short-term impact of the Washington pilgrimage and

King's "I Have a Dream" oration. Indeed, the conjunction of those two events later loomed large in the retrospective memories of both King and other movement activists.

In historical perspective, the march on Washington appears as one of the two emotional high-water marks of the 1960s civil rights crusade. The other, the dramatic Selma-to-Montgomery voting rights march in early 1965, brought an even greater outpouring of white support for the movement and helped secure congressional passage of the civil rights movement's second great legislative milestone, the Voting Rights Act of 1965. The first milestone had been reached a year earlier when President Lyndon Johnson successfully steered Kennedy's 1963 civil rights bill through Congress.

In the three years between the Selma march and King's April 1968 assassination in Memphis, Tennessee, the character of the black freedom struggle and the content of King's own thinking changed significantly. Following the triumphant Selma campaign, King and SCLC's attention turned to a year-long effort in the urban ghettos of Chicago that ended without notable success, while in the South, the real shock troops of the movement, the young field workers of SNCC, became increasingly disillusioned with the ideals of nonviolence and integration as white harassment and terror took their emotional and physical toll. When James Meredith, who in 1962 had become the first black student at the University of Mississippi, was shot and wounded during a one-man "March Against Fear" across the state in June 1966, SNCC joined with other groups to take up his trek and introduced the call for "Black Power" to America's civil rights vocabulary. Martin King had mixed reactions to the phrase, but NAACP and Urban League chiefs Roy Wilkins and Whitney Young openly condemned both the slogan and the racially separatist ideas that activists in both SNCC and CORE were beginning to articulate. The movement increasingly split into two opposing wings, with King struggling unsuccessfully to preserve an undergirding of unity.

King too changed substantially in the years after his "I Have a Dream" speech. In particular, he came to see that antidiscrimination legislation like the 1964 Civil Rights and 1965 Voting Rights Acts could have only a modest impact in alleviating the actual day-to-day burdens of many black Americans. Economic deprivation and inequalities, King realized, played an even larger role than racial discrimination in keeping black citizens at the bottom of American society. More and more King focused his complaints on those concerns—on inadequate housing, insufficient jobs, and inferior schools—and on the need for the federal government to undertake a massive program of economic redistribution. King also became an extremely outspoken critic of America's involvement in the Vietnam War and of U.S. policies that he considered militaristic and imperialistic.

In the final eight months of his life King laid plans for a massive "Poor Peoples Campaign" that would involve a descent on Washington quite unlike the one of 1963. This time, King warned, the movement's supporters would go to the nation's capital not to beseech the federal government to approve reform legislation, but to nonviolently disrupt the day-to-day functioning of

Washington until the Congress and President Johnson implemented programs to eliminate poverty and suffering in America. King spoke in strong language about America's need for "a radical redistribution of economic and political power." The movement, he claimed, needed to address "class issues . . . the problem of the gulf between the haves and the have nots." In the relative privacy of SCLC staff meetings, King now talked of how America would have to move toward some type of democratic socialism.

Throughout those last three years of his life King repeatedly told his audiences that "the dream I had in Washington back in 1963 has too often turned into a nightmare." Indeed, King in those later years had little of the optimism about American society and its chances for extensive racial progress that he manifested in his 1963 address. His understanding that the roots of black oppression were deeply economic was coupled with a growing sadness that much of white America seemed largely disinterested in achieving a more racially just society. The upbeat comments King had offered in earlier years about white people's support for black freedom were more and more replaced by an angry, sometimes bitter condemnation of the white disinterest that greeted black initiatives as the years passed and graphic pictures of southern lawmen with police dogs and fire hoses no longer filled American television screens.

In recent years, some commentators and political figures have cited King's "Dream" as an example of what King and the movement were about. King's "dream that my four little children will one day live in a nation where they will not be judged by the color of their skin, but by the content of their character," is sometimes quoted as proof that King and the mid-60s movement favored a "color blind" approach to public policy questions and opposed any programs involving "affirmative action." In fact, however, King openly and explicitly supported special remedial plans designed to redress the ongoing effects of past, widespread deprivations suffered by millions of Americans simply because of the color of their skin.

Thus it would be misleading for anyone to draw their image of either Martin Luther King, Jr., or the civil rights struggle of the 1950s and 1960s entirely from King's magnificent "I Have a Dream" oration. At the time of his death, King explicitly believed that his dream had *not* come true, and that the political direction of American society offered little hope that it would. The years since 1968 have done little to challenge King's expectation.

In short, while "I Have a Dream" represents one of the emotional peaks of the civil rights era, it is simply one snapshot—an upbeat and uplifting snapshot—from the history of a movement that so far has achieved only a part of its agenda and only a part of Martin Luther King, Jr.'s, "dream."

WALTER LAFEBER

The War in Vietnam

Though Lyndon Johnson was not the first American president to send troops to Vietnam, it is with him that we associate the longest war in American history. When he inherited the presidency—and the war—from John Fitzgerald Kennedy, there were 16,000 American military "advisers" in Vietnam. When he left office there were well over half a million troops there.

Richard Nixon succeeded Johnson with a "secret plan" to end the war in Vietnam. But the war did not end until another four years had passed and 26,000 more Americans had lost their lives.

The war had to be fought not only in Asia but, as Lyndon Johnson and Richard Nixon were to discover, at home as well. As the years passed without victory, more and more Americans asked why? Why were we there in the first place? Why weren't we winning? Why couldn't we get out?

The war in Vietnam cost the nation much more than the 56,000 American lives that were lost there. President Johnson was forced to cut back, then to scuttle his Great Society program. As war costs mounted, "the world's greatest economy stumbled" and inflation and budget deficits began an upward spiral that would continue long after the war itself was concluded.

Why, we are left wondering, when the costs were so high, did we ever get involved in a land war in Asia and why, having gotten involved, did we lose that war? It is these questions that Walter LaFeber attempts to answer in the following selection.

Walter LaFeber teaches history at Cornell University. He is the author of *America, Russia, and the Cold War, Inevitable Revolutions,* and several other books on U.S. foreign policy. This essay is from *America in Vietnam: A Documentary History,* edited by William Appleman Williams, Thomas McCormick, Lloyd Gardner, and Walter LaFeber.

Within hours after taking control of the earth's greatest military and economic power, President Lyndon Johnson uttered his first words on the war: "I am not going to lose Vietnam. I am not going to be the President who saw Southeast Asia go the way China went." With that historical memory (that is, that the United States truly has a manifest destiny in Asia), and political lesson (Americans do not reelect those who lose territory to Communists), Johnson set out with incredible military might and the overwhelming support of Congress and the American people to climax 130 years of U.S. involvement in the distant Pacific region.

He seemed the perfect leader to cap the era. Few could match his ability to sway audiences, especially with off-the-cuff, colorful remarks. In nearly two centuries of American history, none surpassed his ability to lead Congress. As Senate Majority Leader in the 1950s, Johnson had mastered governmental processes and exerted a personal force that was "elemental," in the word of his shrewd, long-time associate George Reedy. "He may have been a son-of-a-bitch but he was a colossal son-of-a-bitch," Reedy recalled. Johnson's "elemental" force controlled another kind of force: a nuclear superiority so great that the Soviets had first tried to blunt and then bowed to it in the 1962 Cuban Missile Crisis, and a powerful conventional force so mobile that by merely picking up the phone, Johnson could station 100,000 of those troops in South Vietnam in a matter of weeks.

This enormous power worked, as always, at the pleasure of history—or, more accurately, the history as understood by Americans and their President. In this sense, Johnson believed he had inherited from Presidents Eisenhower and Kennedy (indeed, from McKinley and Truman), a commitment to prevent Southeast Asia from being closed off. From Truman, whom Johnson idolized, he also inherited the doctrine of Containment. In this case, Chinese communism and its supposed surrogates in North Vietnam had to be contained. Otherwise China would rule supreme in Southeast Asia and U.S. credibility would be ruined worldwide. Few Americans questioned this view of Containment in 1965 or later. If Chinese power was not contained, the theory continued, non-Communist areas would fall like dominoes. The domino theory made little distinction between Asian nations, their histories, or their nationalisms. In the words of one U.S. official of the mid-1960s, this theory perhaps "resulted from a subconscious sense that, since 'all Asians look alike,' all Asian nations will act alike." The domino theory rested on a view of history that was totally ahistorical, but Lyndon Johnson never questioned it.

He did not do so because to him history was to be manipulated, not studied. As Reedy observed, "His whole life was lived in the present and he was tenacious in his conviction that history always conformed to current necessities." Johnson's political needs dictated his view of historical reality. He interpreted Vietnam within two historical contexts. The first was the 1930s, the years when as a young congressman he used the New Deal to help the poor of Texas, but also watched European powers "appease" Hitler's territorial demands at the 1938 Munich conference. Johnson believed ever after that the New Deal could work anywhere, but only if appeasement was tolerated nowhere.

His determination to stop disorder also arose out of a second, more general, historical framework: his view of the American frontier and himself as an actor in that ongoing drama. Asia, he declared in 1967, was "the outer frontier of disorder." It had to be civilized as the pioneers had civilized his home region of Texas: with "a rifle in one hand and an axe in the other." One of his close friends, Congressman Wright Patman of Texas, called Johnson "the last Frontiersman." Acting the cowboy in the late twentieth century could create problems. Ronnie Dugger, a distinguished Texas journalist who knew Johnson, observed that "the one great trouble with a foreign policy for pioneers is that you need savages for it. For Communists the savages may be capitalists; for Americans, Communists." There was also another problem with Johnson's approach. He attempted to bring order to Vietnam not with sailing ships and Gatling guns, but with B-52 bombers that carpet-bombed miles of territory in an instant, defoliants that destroyed jungles and humans alike, and ground firepower unequaled in the history of warfare. In 1907 the great historian Henry Adams watched another "cowboy in the White House," Theodore Roosevelt, and quietly warned that it is a dangerous thing to put unlimited power in the hands of limited minds. Vietnam became a test of Adams's insight.

Johnson focused this unparalleled power on a situation that, as his Secretary of Defense Robert McNamara told him in early 1964, was disintegrating rapidly in the wake of Diem's assassination. By late summer both civilian and military advisers believed that only a full-scale conventional bombing campaign could save a South Vietnamese government that displayed little effectiveness and less stability. Few questioned whether such a bombing attack could work in a bitter civil war that had lasted for decades. When one lower-level official suggested to his superior that "in some ways, of course, it *is* a civil war," an Assistant Secretary of State angrily retorted, "Don't play word games with me!" It was more Johnson's consuming desire to win a landslide victory in the 1964 election that a realistic view of Vietnam's history that prevented him from triggering a major escalation during midyear.

He was opposed in the race by the Republican senator from Arizona, Barry Goldwater. The Republican nominee so vigorously demanded applying military force (he even mentioned how satisfying it would be to lob a nuclear-tipped missile "down into the gent's room in the Kremlin,") that Americans turned away from him in droves. Johnson gathered up these voters by keeping his voice low: "Sometimes our folks get a little impatient. Sometimes they rattle their rockets some. . . . But we are not about to send American boys nine or ten thousand miles away from home to do what Asian boys ought to be doing for themselves." The President, however, had it both ways. Promising no U.S. troop involvement, he seized upon two incidents—North Vietnamese torpedo boats supposedly attacking U.S. warships in the Gulf of Tonkin—that allowed him to obtain congressional approval for escalating the war. Later investigations revealed that the alleged second attack that led Johnson to submit his Tonkin Gulf Resolution to Congress probably never occurred. It also turned out, contrary to his assertions that the attacks were "unprovoked," that U.S. warships were actually monitoring Communist positions while South Vietnam commandos carried out raids in North Vietnam. The revelations appeared several years later, too late to save either Goldwater (who went down to a landslide defeat), Congress's reputation as an easy mark for Presidents who justified any foreign policy with "anticommunism," or, finally, Lyndon Johnson himself.

By the autumn of 1964 the President actively considered escalating the U.S. involvement. Not any limit of American power but the weakness of the South Vietnam Government and the fear of possible Chinese intervention prevented escalation at that time. In February 1965, however, Johnson believed he had no alternative. He launched Operation Rolling Thunder, a massive bombing of North Vietnam. The President's motives were complex. He had concluded that only a greater application of U.S. power could save the shattered South Vietnam regime. But at home he wanted to be the President who, through his so-called Great Society programs, fulfilled the New Deal's promises to the minorities, poor, elderly, and ill in America. Johnson believed his programs stood little chance of passing Congress and taking effect if he lost South Vietnam to Communists. The Goldwater right wing would destroy his administration, he feared, as the right wing had destroyed Truman after China fell to communism and the Korean War stalemated. Johnson's Vietnam and Great Society plans became linked, first for mutual protection, then—by 1967—as a sharklike struggle in which each tried to survive by killing the other.

In early 1965 another danger also appeared. A year earlier the United States had helped install General Nguyen Khanh in power. But Khanh had proved ineffective militarily and politically in the eyes of Washington officials, and they now moved to oust him. Khanh struck back by obtaining support from powerful Buddhist leaders and then making contact with the National Liberation Front (the South Vietnamese Communists) for the purpose of finding a neutral solution. That solution would have required a U.S. withdrawal from Vietnam. Johnson countered Khanh's plans by launching the bombing raids, then claiming they were in retaliation for Communist attacks on U.S. quarters at Pleiku that had killed 7 and wounded 109 Americans. But as Johnson's National Security Adviser, McGeorge Bundy, observed, "Pleikus are like streetcars—such an opportunity for retaliation arose regularly." The President seized this "streetcar" in the hope the bombing would strengthen the Saigon regime's will to continue fighting, stop South Vietnamese neutralization initiatives, and demonstrate his determination to doubters in Congress.

Shortly before the bombing raids began, Khanh's regime fell to a U.S.-supported coup led by right-wing army officers. Many of those officers were Roman Catholic, a religion that represented only about 10 percent of the population. Most important to the White House, the new government willingly went along with Johnson's plans. Not surprisingly, within two months the situation worsened. The President ordered U.S. Marines to protect the air bases and, when the bombing failed to be effective, gave the troops an actual combat role. By April 1965 he had ordered U.S. forces into battle, but did so secretly so the American people would not think it was a desperate throw of the dice.

Johnson did not believe these momentous steps would win the war, but only prevent him and his South Vietnamese allies from losing it. His advisers assumed, wrongly, that bombing would severely reduce Communist supplies moving into the South and improve Saigon's morale, thus making possible a negotiated settlement on Washington's terms. Johnson thus announced his commitment to "unconditional discussions" in a major speech at Johns Hopkins University in April 1965. The address was largely for American public opinion. U.S. officials privately believed that no discussions (the term "negotiate" was carefully not used) were possible at the time because the Saigon regime was too weak to make deals. The Communists then issued their own program. It little resembled Johnson's.

U.S. officials began to understand they were locked in a battle that, as Secretary of Defense Robert McNamara privately remarked, might require the use of nuclear weapons to prevent a "Red Asia." Faced with that terrible alternative, Johnson followed the logic of the policy he had accepted in late 1963: he began a massive buildup of U.S. ground forces. . . . Johnson understood, as he put it, he was jumping "off the diving board." He could believe, however, that he was aiming for the middle of the pool—neither "turning tail and running," nor fighting a fully declared, perhaps nuclear, war that would bring China and maybe even the Soviet Union into the conflict. The Great Society could also be shielded from political attack. The United States, Johnson assumed in the language of the day, was so rich that it could produce "both guns and butter."

The President, indeed most Americans, also assumed U.S. power to be so great that North Vietnam had to reach an early breaking point and settle on Johnson's terms. At a Washington dinner party a guest suggested to an administration official that it might take as long to rid Vietnam of Communists as the decade it took the British to banish them in Malaya. The official arched an eyebrow and retorted, "We are *not* the British." He meant that Americans did not bear the horrible onus of being colonialists in Asia, and their military power was infinitely greater than the British. The colonial issue, however, blurred as the number of U.S. troops reached the 200,000 level and Americans virtually took over the responsibility for running South Vietnam. This policy now less resembled the traditional U.S. open-door approach than British rule in India. Unlike the British in the nineteenth century, however, the United States was immersed in a mass, antiforeign revolution. No matter how large the scale of the U.S. buildup, it could not solve the complex political deterioration in the South. Indeed, the buildup actually worsened the deterioration, for it gave nationalists in North and South Vietnam a handy foreign target. It weakened the power of South Vietnamese officials and, in the eyes of many nationalists, smeared them for working with the foreigners. In a classic form of political jujitsu, the Communists could use the buildup of U.S. strength to defeat the American effort.

The Communists also matched Johnson's buildup on the ground. U.S. ground forces grew from 14,000 in 1963 to 267,000 in 1966. Regular Vietcong (often referred to as the National Liberation Front) strength grew during those years from 25,000 to 101,000, with another 170,000 irregulars in reserve by 1966. North Vietnam regular army units grew in the South from zero in 1963 to 30,000 by 1966. The U.S. bombing had only accelerated the infiltration of Communist troops.

Politically and militarily Johnson could not solve the revolution. In December 1965 he announced with fanfare that he was dispatching diplomats to world capitals in a search for peace. This "flying circus," as it was soon labeled, meant little. The two opponents disagreed too fundamentally and the U.S. negotiating position was too weak to allow meaningful talks. As American resources disappeared into an apparently bottomless pit, debate sharpened in the United States. Senator J. William Fulbright (Dem.-Ark.), a longtime advocate of a strong presidency, turned against his former close friend in the White House. Fulbright concluded that Johnson had deliberately misled Congress on several foreign policy issues, especially Vietnam. In early 1966 the senator summoned Secretary of State Dean Rusk before the Foreign Relations Committee. Americans now heard a full debate by Washington officials. It occurred as South Vietnamese troops deserted in greater numbers.

America's European allies also quietly withdrew, especially as Johnson's fixation on China tightened. Quoting Theodore Roosevelt that this was to be the "Pacific era," the President warned that a "hostile China must be discouraged from aggression." That remark made at least three questionable assumptions: that China, whom the North Vietnamese had fought and feared for a thousand years, controlled the Vietnamese Communists; that China, not mass revolution, was thwarting U.S. efforts; and that China, bitterly divided internally by its own problems, wanted to fight the United States. The Peking government did provide large supplies of war matériel to North Vietnam. But the Chinese carefully explained in 1967 that they would intervene in Vietnam with combat troops only if Americans invaded North Vietnam and approached "our borders," or if there was a highly unlikely "sell-out" peace by Ho Chi Minh. A great irony appeared: Johnson focused on the Chinese threat, but in 1967 also moved toward lessening tensions with the Soviet Union. It was the Russians, however, who supplied increasingly larger amounts of war matériel to North Vietnam than did the Chinese.

The battle at home went no better and had as much irony. As war costs spiraled upward, Johnson frantically pushed for completion of his Great Society programs. "This may be the last chance we have to get some of these things done," he prophetically told an aide in 1966. At the same time, he had to admit publicly, "Because of Vietnam we cannot do all that we should, or all that we would like to do." As battle costs soared, he cut nearly every budget item but defense. Having gone into Vietnam partly to save the Great Society program, Johnson now sacrificed the program to Vietnam. But the irony did not stop there. Key sections of the program that were passed to help blacks and other minorities in 1965–66 failed to prevent riots that killed thirty-four blacks in Watts (a suburb of Los Angeles) and spread to other ghettos. By 1967 antiwar protests that disrupted college campuses were accompanied by race riots in Tampa, Cincinnati, Atlanta, and then in Detroit, where forty-three people died and parts of the city were destroyed. Devastation in American urban areas mirrored on a much smaller scale the destruction of Vietnamese towns. Johnson wanted to end "that bitch of a war" so he could court "the woman I really loved"—the Great Society. In the end, he lost both.

Meanwhile the world's greatest economy stumbled. It was being victimized by war costs that produced a startling inflation rate of nearly 5 percent and large budget deficits. The value of the dollar, the currency that had long undergirded world trade, began to crumble under the burden of war. In 1966 the New York Stock Exchange panicked when it appeared that an economy increasingly dependent on military contracts might be damaged by possible peace in Vietnam. The peace scare soon passed, however. As an exchange between Johnson and Ho Chi Minh indicated in early 1967, an end to the war was not in sight.

A lack of U.S. power did not cause these dilemmas. Johnson increased his own authority until top aides could taunt Congress with the "imperial presidency." The President could also call upon an ever-larger storehouse of military might. But such power was not ending the conflict on Johnson's terms. As an increasingly discouraged McNamara secretly told a Senate committee, "We could take out all their power systems, all of their oil, all of their harbors, destroy their dams," and the North Vietnamese could still send in "men and equipment necessary to support some level of operations in the South." By late 1967, however, Johnson believed the right moment might have arrived to make a deal. The U.S. presidential campaign of 1968 appeared on the horizon. The massive U.S. effort had come closer to stabilizing the military situation than during the previous two years. Something had to be done, moreover, to stop what some were calling the "Vietnamization" of American cities and campuses.

In September 1967 Johnson proposed in San Antonio, Texas, that he would halt the bombing if Ho Chi Minh would negotiate and not attempt to build up militarily in South Vietnam during the halt. The speech was also notable for the absence of references to China. The Administration was finally glimpsing Asian realities: the growing hatred between China and Russia, growing mistrust between China and North Vietnam, and growing Vietnamese dependence on Russia as U.S. military efforts escalated. These realities were unfortunately glimpsed at least several years too late. The great difference—whether South Vietnam was to be in the U.S. camp or part of a unified, Communist Vietnam—continued to divide Johnson and Ho. But U.S. military policies were reported (erroneously as it turned out) to be more successful, and a happy Administration passed all the good news on to the American people.

In this context occurred the turning point of the United States involvement. On January 31, 1968, the Communists launched an offensive during the Tet (New Year's) holiday. For a remarkable moment, Ho's forces actually controlled parts of Saigon. They captured provincial capitals as well as the ancient capital of Hue. Only intense U.S. bombing of those cities and bloody battles waged by South Vietnamese and American troops finally repulsed the Communists. (It was during these terrible days that U.S. officials offered a famous explanation of how they were having to fight the war: "We had to destroy the village to save it.") Ho's forces lost 30,000 to 40,000 men. Many Communist cadres were wiped out. The South Vietnamese, moreover, had refused to join in an uprising against the Saigon Government.

General William Westmoreland, commander of U.S. forces in Vietnam, declared a triumph, but then secretly asked Johnson for 206,000 more troops to win a final victory. The President was stunned. Publicly he said the Tet offensive had been "anticipated . . . and met," but privately he and his advisers were shocked. They had believed Westmoreland's upbeat speeches of late 1967 and discounted McNamara's warning that, despite U.S. efforts, Ho's ability to fight on had not been weakened. Johnson's top advisers now wondered whether accomplishing their goals required 500,000 to one million additional Americans in Vietnam. McNamara agreed that such numbers at least focused on the price that might have to be paid. He had little use for Westmoreland's recommendation, for 206,000 men "is neither enough to do the job, nor an indication that our role must change." Johnson's former NSC adviser, McGeorge Bundy, agreed: "We must also prepare for the worst. [South Vietnam] is very weak."

Many Americans shared the shock felt in Washington. The general feeling was well expressed by Benjamin Read, a top aide to Rusk. "The fact that screamed at you . . ." Read later observed, "was [the Communists'] ability to just romp at will over that much of the landscape of that miserable country." In such a context, Westmoreland's request for 206,000 more Americans made Vietnam look "like an endless engagement and an endless rathole."

In the years since the Tet disaster, U.S. officials and many of their supporters have blamed the American media, especially television, for misrepresenting the results of the offensive and thus undermining Johnson's effort in Vietnam. As the McNamara, Bundy, and Read quotes indicate, however, the media did not shape the pessimism of Johnson's top aides. Blaming television neglects more fundamental realities both in Washington and Vietnam. American public opinion appears to have had little if any effect on Johnson's decision to change course sharply after the Tet offensive. That decision was shaped by other forces. His own top military officers warned him that Tet had been "a very near thing," and that the war could become much more costly than it had been before Tet. The South Vietnamese people doubted now that Americans could protect them, while their government remained unsteady and sharply divided between the factions of President Nguyen Van Thieu and Vice-President Nguyen Cao Ky.

Johnson heard some of the most surprising news from the home front. McNamara, about to leave the Defense Department, warned the President that U.S. forces had to be kept at home "to meet the possibility of widespread civil disorder in the United States in the months ahead." Inflation, race riots, antiwar protests threatened to rip apart the society. McNamara's successor, Clark Clifford (an influential Washington lawyer whose deep involvement in White House politics went back to the 1940s), then discovered that for all their outward optimism, the military chiefs had no plan to win the war in Vietnam. The chiefs complained bitterly about civilian restraints not allowing them to fight the war as they wished, but Clifford learned that—restraints or no restraints— the Pentagon had no tenable ideas about gaining victory, at least short of destroying most of the country that Johnson had promised to save. Clifford also knew firsthand that the war was devastating the American economy and business community, as well as the crucial alliance system with Western Europe and Japan. His view was shared by a group of so-called Wisemen whom Johnson had begun to consult in 1967. Powerful members of the corporate community, former top government officials, and men who had been instrumental in waging the Cold War since the 1940s, they had wanted no retreat from Vietnam just six months earlier. In March 1968, however, they warned Johnson that an independent South Vietnam could not be built, at least not without unacceptable costs.

On March 31, 1968, the President told a nationwide television audience that he was stopping the bombing of North Vietnam in the hope that this gesture would lead Ho to begin negotiations. To show his earnestness, Johnson dramatically announced he would not run for a second term so that he could instead concentrate on bringing peace to Southeast Asia. Preliminary talks did begin, but ground fighting continued. Johnson even secretly raised the level of U.S. troops from 486,000 to 535,000 during the summer. North Vietnam matched the buildup until by early 1969, one year after their terrible losses of Tet, the Communists had their party structure and/or important influence in 80 percent of South Vietnam's hamlets, and among 65 percent of the total population. Neither side had given up hope of winning South Vietnam.

Negotiations quickly deadlocked on three key issues that killed hopes for peace during the next four years: the U.S. insistence that Ho withdraw all his troops from South Vietnam; Ho's insistence that U.S. forces fully withdraw before he would agree to a cease-fire; and the Thieu-Ky regime's insistence that it not have to enter into any governing coalition with the more powerful Communists. The peace talks appeared as fruitless as the battlefield action. The military draft of young Americans continued. Then in late spring 1968 Martin Luther King and Robert Kennedy were murdered—King as he led blacks and whites alike toward change through nonviolence, Kennedy as he seemed about to win the Democratic presidential nomination on an antiwar platform. Riots erupted throughout the nation. Among the worst were those in Chicago during the Democrats' presidential nominating convention.

In November, Republican nominee Richard Nixon barely defeated Vice-President Hubert Humphrey by 0.7 percent of the popular vote. Stressing law and order in American streets, Nixon refused to discuss Vietnam. He would only say he had a "plan" for handling the war. Nixon privately admitted, however, "I've come to the conclusion that there's no way to win the war. But we can't say that, of course." The pessimism of the new President and his National Security Adviser, Henry Kissinger, deepened when they surveyed the facts and possible policy alternatives in early 1969. One survey revealed that knowledge-able State Department officials estimated it could take thirteen more years to control the Communists in South Vietnam. The war was costing Americans $30 billion a year and two hundred dead each week by this time.

Given such a sad assessment, Nixon could have begun rapid withdrawal of those forces. He instead decided on a two-prong policy that aimed at conclud-ing the war on his terms. First, the President tried to work through Russia and China in the hope that the two Communist giants, who now hated and feared each other, could somehow force North Vietnam to make peace. This policy assumed, wrongly as it turned out, that Moscow and Peking could pressure Hanoi to follow their wishes. Second, Nixon attempted to salvage South Viet-nam and—of much greater importance to him and Kissinger—what they be-lieved to be the credibility of U.S. global commitments, by slowly withdrawing Americans while beefing up South Vietnam's army to do the fighting. In addi-tion, Nixon decided to rely on massive air strikes, the kind that in three years would give him the name of "the mad bomber." (Nixon actually did not mind the label because he believed the Communists would be more careful if they thought he was indeed slightly unbalanced.) The President's overall policy be-came known as "Vietnamization."

Vietnamization required more time. As it turned out, the policy required four years and 26,000 more American lives, as well as hundreds of thousands of Vietnamese casualties, before the last U.S. combat troops left in 1973. Nixon believed he could buy time. Despite massive antiwar protests, polls showed that nationwide some 58 percent of those surveyed approved his policies. Pub-lic opinion was not forcing the President's hand. His appeal to the "great silent majority of Americans" won him time, even as he laid out a Nixon Doctrine that explained how the United States would remain deeply involved in Asian affairs. . . .

The President withdrew the first contingent of U.S. troops during 1969. He thus set in motion an irreversible policy. South Vietnamese forces could now be protected only by their own efforts or U.S. bombing. During that year Nixon followed this logic by ordering repeated bombing raids on Cambodia, which Communist troops used for supplies and passage into South Vietnam. The President wanted the raids to be kept secret (he was, after all, devastating parts of a neutral country friendly to the United States). The Pentagon even kept two sets of records so that if the press or Congress became too curious, they could be satisfied with lies supported by hollow figures. When news of the raids did leak in May 1969, Nixon created a "plumbers' unit" to fix the leaks and spy on the Administration's supposed enemies. His decision led directly to the break-in of Democrat Party headquarters in 1972 at the Watergate Hotel in Washing-ton, and, when Nixon tried to cover up that crime, his resignation in 1974. Vietnamization, much like Dr. Frankenstein's monster, turned on its creator. Nixon could not keep the effects of the war limited to Southeast Asia.

That lesson appeared tragically in April–May 1970. Claiming that North Vi-etnamese and Vietcong bases in Cambodia could be destroyed, the President launched a major assault into South Vietnam's neighbor. . . . The operation failed either to capture the Communists' headquarters or to stop their use of Cambodian bases. But the effects rippled to American campuses. Four students were killed by Ohio National Guardsmen during antiwar protests at Kent State University. . . . A new protest group, Vietnam veterans, began to attack U.S. policy at home as well as in Asia, and did so with a passion and insight unsurpassed by other antiwar voices. These veterans illustrated how the costs of the war went far beyond casualty figures. Some of the costs even escaped accurate calculation. Nixon himself nearly lost control during one night of the Cambodian–Kent State crisis. He made forty-nine phone calls after 10:30 P.M., then, in early morning light, drove to the Lincoln Memorial to talk with protesting students. Kissinger feared the president was "on the edge of a nervous breakdown."

The full impact of the war, however, was only beginning to be felt. For the first time Congress passed laws tying the President's hands in Asia. He could not again send troops into Cambodia. In 1971 Nixon nevertheless tried to save his Vietnamization policy by attacking Communist bases and trails in neighboring Laos with South Vietnamese troops backed by U.S. artillery and air power. The assault again failed to destroy the camps. The South's troops performed so poorly that Vietnamization appeared doomed. Nixon had brought nearly 300,000 U.S. men home and, by 1971, silenced part of the antiwar movement by halting the draft. But he left behind a crippled ally whose prices skyrocketed because of uncontrollable inflation, whose population suffered spreading hunger, whose economy crumbled under deficits and corruption. All that remained for Nixon to do was to bomb massively, as he had hoped to do in 1969.

First, however, he and Kissinger tried to protect Vietnamization by making deals with the North's two giant allies. The President extended better relations and valued U.S. goods to the Soviets, while offering a reversal of twenty-two years of enmity and a new relationship to China if the two nations would help, as Kissinger phrased it, "in settling the war." A strange reversal had taken place: Eisenhower, Kennedy, and Johnson had argued that the defeat of North Vietnam was necessary to contain China and Russia. Now Nixon and Kissinger argued that the friendship of China and Russia was necessary to contain North Vietnam. The second approach, however, worked no better than the first. Neither Peking nor Moscow could force Hanoi to bend to U.S. wishes, even if the two giants wished to do so. Kissinger discovered North Vietnamese stubbornness firsthand when he conducted a series of secret talks with Hanoi's diplomats in 1970–71 and made little progress.

The logjam broke in 1972. In the spring the Communists launched a full-scale conventional assault complete with 120,000 men and Soviet-made tanks. The South Vietnamese and U.S. forces drove back the invasion, inflicting casualties that may have run as high as 100,000. Nixon proceeded to put his 1969 plan into effect. He launched large-scale B-52 attacks on civilian as well as military areas in the North, and even mined Haiphong harbor, despite Russian and other foreign shipping unloading at the docks. He did all this without massive protests in the United States. The Communists had suffered a major military and political defeat. Such a setback again misled, however: the war was one of revolution, not conventional battle (as in Korea or World War II), and in this struggle the Communists continued to display amazing strength.

U.S. leverage was, meanwhile, hardly growing. The presidential election loomed and Nixon needed to show that his Vietnamization plans had produced peace, not merely military stalemate. Kissinger and the North Vietnamese negotiated feverishly during 1972 and finally struck a deal that required a cease-fire, final withdrawal of U.S. troops, the return of all American prisoners of war, and elections administered by a group made up of Communists, the South Vietnam Government, and neutralists.

Kissinger obtained the deal just days before Nixon faced the Democratic (and antiwar) nominee for President, Senator George McGovern of South Dakota. The agreement helped undercut McGovern's campaign. But in late October, Nixon suddenly decided he wanted no agreement. Public opinion polls showed that nearly half those surveyed opposed any U.S. recognition of Communist political power in South Vietnam, but to obtain his agreement Kissinger had recognized the North Vietnamese Communists' right to stay in the area. The President wanted to appear tough. He was also becoming jealous of Kissinger's growing fame. Nixon passed the word to his negotiator that "it will hurt—not help us—to get the settlement before the election." He also used General Alexander Haig, Kissinger's top aide in the talks, as an agent to undercut Kissinger's attempt to make peace. The critical blow was finally struck by President Thieu of South Vietnam. He flatly refused to accept any deal that left the North's troops in his country. Kissinger was furious with Thieu: "We'll kill the son-of-a-bitch if we have to," he supposedly told his aides late one night. Nixon, however, now had it both ways: a peace to demonstrate the success of his Vietnamization policies, and an ongoing war to show his toughness. McGovern went down to one of the greatest defeats in U.S. political history.

Nixon proceeded to launch another massive bombing attack. His purpose was twofold: to soften up the Communists for new talks, and—perhaps more important—to show Thieu that South Vietnam could accept peace in full confidence that in a crisis the Americans would be fully willing to act, in Nixon's words, like a "mad man." American military officers became deeply concerned at the number of bombers lost during the raids. Some U.S. airmen rebelled against flying the missions. "My conscience told me not to," was the way one pilot explained it. Court-martials were secretly ordered and at least one officer found guilty. Against this background, Kissinger and the North Vietnamese hammered out a final accord in Paris during January 1973.

The agreement included: (1) a cease-fire; (2) U.S. recognition of the "unity" of all Vietnam; (3) withdrawal of U.S. forces and the dismantling of American bases in Indochina; (4) the return of U.S. prisoners and the intention of working out an agreement between the Vietnamese parties to exchange political prisoners; (5) South Vietnam's right to self-determination; (6) Thieu's remaining in power in Saigon until an election could be held by a "National Council" that included representatives of his government, the Communists, and neutralists; (7) a demilitarized zone between North and South that would act as a provisional military demarcation line; and (8) allowing North Vietnamese troops to remain in the South. Thieu now accepted the deal. He had to accept it: Nixon was prepared to desert his regime if he did not. But the American President also offered a carrot. In a secret agreement, he assured Thieu that "we will respond with full force should the settlement be violated by North Vietnam." He also offered a carrot to the Communists: billions of dollars for economic reconstruction if they followed through on the settlement.

The deal reflected the military and political realities in South Vietnam. The Communists were an accepted force in the country, and they built their strength by moving heavy reinforcements down the Ho Chi Minh Trail into South Vietnam. Nixon could do little in response. In July and August 1973 the U.S. Congress prohibited the use of funds to "support directly or indirectly combat activities in or over Cambodia, Laos, North Vietnam, and South Vietnam." In Kissinger's words, "any American military action anywhere in or around Indochina became illegal." Nor was the President in any position to ignore Congress and carry through his secret deal with Thieu. Investigations of the break-in at the Watergate Hotel complex revealed that Nixon and some of his top aides had tried to cover up the crime. In August 1974 he became the first U.S. President to resign from office.

By that time the South Vietnamese were on their own. To drive home that point, the U.S. Congress, besieged by other crises and a faltering domestic economy, cut back assistance to Thieu's government. The fighting meanwhile escalated. Thieu's forces, fearful of competing politically with the Communists, tried to salvage their position by ignoring the cease-fire and attacking the Communists in order to expand their territorial control. In late 1973 the Communists began retaliating. The 160,000 Communist troops of early 1973 became a 220,000-man force by January 1975 when it launched an offensive that aimed to conquer all of South Vietnam in two years. After initial resistance, Thieu's forces began to disintegrate. Kissinger, now Secretary of State for President Gerald Ford, asked Congress for more aid. Everyone understood this was only a gesture, but it gave Kissinger and Congress an opportunity to reflect on how the United States had ended up in such a dead end. The Communists needed only four months, not two years, before they marched into Saigon. By May 1975, Vietnam was united and Communist. So was Laos. Cambodia fell under the control of the Khmer Rouge, a brutal Communist group that hated the Vietnamese and within three years were driven out of power by an invading Vietnamese force.

So ended the quarter-century-long U.S. war in Southeast Asia. It was the longest war in U.S. history. The conflict cost over 57,000 American men and women, but the price also included beliefs—the very beliefs that Americans had long accepted without question as they grew into the world's leading power. Because of those lives lost, that power wasted, and those beliefs threatened, the debate over the U.S. role in Vietnam will long continue. That debate will revolve around the beliefs—the views of U.S. history and values—that carried Americans into the struggle.

One belief dated to the 1950s and before: only U.S. power could keep Southeast Asia open, free from Chinese control, and safe for allied (especially Japanese) investments and markets. By the 1980s, however, Vietnam itself excluded Chinese power from the area, while the Japanese—who had criticized U.S. policy during the post-1961 years—profited more handsomely from Southeast Asia after the United States departed than while the war went on. A second belief assumed that if Vietnam fell to communism, all of Southeast Asia, and perhaps even Japan, would follow in what Eisenhower had called a "domino" effect. Laos and Cambodia did become Communist, but the United States as well as South Vietnam had made those two small nations part of the war in the post-1961 years. The dominoes could fall in a certain direction, journalist Richard Rovere warned in 1967, *because we set them up that way.* Other nations that refused to become dominoes (Thailand, Malaysia, and Singapore, not to mention Japan), never wobbled. The domino theory was (and remains) one of the most dangerous of ideas that attract Americans. As experts on Asia tried to tell Johnson in 1965, "A first reality to bear in mind: Despite elements of similarity, no Southeast Asian nation is a replica of any other."

American supporters of the effort in Vietnam also held to a third idea: that if the United States did not respond to the situation, American "credibility" would disappear. Allies would stop trusting U.S. commitments. The Soviets and Chinese would then take advantage of this U.S. loss of will (or what Nixon called the "pitiful, helpless giant") and expand their power indefinitely. A variation of this view was that the Chinese (or Soviets, or North Vietnamese) resembled Hitler's Germany. If the aggressor was "appeased" as Hitler had been in the 1930s, he would only move on insatiably to new conquests. In the Vietnam War, however, U.S. allies questioned Washington's credibility for quite different reasons. As Professor Lawrence Kaplan has phrased it, "The apparent American obsession with the defense of South Vietnam raised doubts [among allies] about the wisdom of American leadership in any part of the world." Henry Kissinger recognized this truth by 1972: "We have fought for four years, have mortgaged our whole foreign policy to the defense of one country."

A fourth idea is especially important because it has become increasingly popular years after the war: the United States lost because it did not use enough power. A variation of this view is that civilian officials never allowed the U.S. military to win the war. Another variation is that the antiwar, pro-peace movement of the 1960s undermined the military effort and prevented a U.S. victory.

It should be pointed out, however, that the United States dropped three times the amount of bombs on these small Southeast Asian countries than it dropped on both Europe and Asia during all of World War II. Two million Vietnamese, Cambodians, and Laotians died in the post-1946 era, and twice that number were wounded. The United States, according to recently released documents, did not escalate rapidly in 1964–65 because Johnson feared the weak

South Vietnamese Government would collapse and China might retaliate. The supposed limits of U.S. military power and the actions of antiwar protesters did not restrain him. By 1968–69 the United States had committed over a half-million men who controlled the most advanced technology for killing in a conventional war that science had ever devised. As journalist Michael Herr observed, "There was such a dense concentration of American energy there, American and essentially adolescent, if that energy could have channeled into anything more than noise, waste and pain, it would have lighted up Indochina for a thousand years."

Those who believe that greater force should have been applied might recognize that such an application would have required either invading North Vietnam (thus running the risk of Chinese response) or—more likely—that the United States would have had to send in a million or more men, employ nuclear weapons, and remove all bombing restrictions. McNamara saw those possibilities as early as 1965. The United States would have literally had to destroy Vietnam to save it. Fortunately no U.S. policy-maker in the 1960s and 1970s was that irrational. Officials instead hoped to raise force levels until they found a point at which the North Vietnamese would "break" and agree to negotiate on U.S. terms. That point could never be found. The Vietnamese were willing to take one of the highest casualty rates in proportion to population in history—indeed, at twice the rate of the supposedly suicidal Japanese forces of World War II. By 1971, Dean Rusk admitted he had "underestimated the resistance and determination of the North Vietnamese." They had taken the killing of "almost the equivalent of—what? Ten million Americans? And they continue to come."

The United States never lost a major battle against North Vietnamese troops, but it lost the war because the struggle was a revolution, not just a war. It involved political ideals for which Vietnamese Communists were willing to die in large numbers: the ideals of national unity and independence from foreign domination. The Communists constructed a totalitarian regime that efficiently used those ideals as the dynamic to drive out the French, then the Americans. The United States had no comparable ideals to appeal to the mass of Vietnamese. The more U.S. officials tried to impose their values, the more they Americanized the war, thus giving the Communists "foreign devils" to target. As early as 1966, Senator Fulbright worried over the U.S. ability "to go into a small, alien, undeveloped Asian nation and create stability where there is chaos, the will to fight where there is defeatism, democracy where there is no tradition of it, and honest government where corruption is almost a way of life."

The United States tried to impose its values on Vietnam in such a way that it succeeded only in corrupting those values at home. The Nixon years, the "imperial presidency," the Watergate scandal that shocked the political and economic system, were all products of Vietnam. So was the inflation that tore apart the U.S. economy, destroyed much of the dollar's value by 1971, and helped bring on the quadrupling of gasoline prices in 1973–74 as oil producers tried to maintain the dollar value of their mineral. Some 200,000 Americans became draft evaders rather than go to Vietnam. The duty of dying in the war, moreover, fell disproportionately on blacks and poor whites.

The U.S. failure in Vietnam had little to do with the use or the lack of American military power. It had much to do with Americans' failure to understand their own history, their own two-century-old revolution, and their own long relationship with Asia.

QUESTIONS FOR DISCUSSION

1. Why did Lyndon Johnson believe that his actions in Vietnam were not aberrant, but in line with the foreign policy actions of the presidents that had preceded him? Do you agree with him?

2. LaFeber concludes his essay by stating that the U.S. failure in Vietnam had less to do with the use or lack of American military power and more "to do with Americans' failure to understand their own history." What does he mean by this? Do you agree with him?

Chapter Eight

Toward the Twenty-First Century

WILLIAM H. CHAFE

The New Feminism

Among the most visible and effective of the protest and reform movements of the second half of the twentieth century was the women's movement of the 1960s and 1970s. In the following essay, William Chafe shows us how this movement was both related to, and different from, earlier crusades for women's rights. Feminism, he reminds us, was not born in the second half of the twentieth century.

Contemporary feminism, Chafe argues, "operated in tandem with long-range social developments which made [the goals of the movement] more objectively feasible." Feminist complaints about inequality in American society made more sense than ever before as more women entered the work force in the 1960s and 1970s and discovered firsthand the inequalities in their weekly paychecks.

Though the movement may have had its greatest impact on the college campuses and drawn most support from white, middle-class women, it appealed to a broad range of women, black and white, young and old, middle class and working class. This is not to say that there was a consensus of opinion in favor of all or even some of the demands raised by the feminists. For many women and men, the demands made by the movement were not only distasteful but dangerous.

It is impossible to quantify the measure of support for the women's movement of the 1960s and 1970s or define "the exact nature of the change" it brought about. Still, if the polls and surveys Chafe cites are at all reliable, the movement's effect on American beliefs, behaviors, and consciousness was enormous.

William Chafe is a professor of history at Duke University and the author of a number of books on the civil rights movement, the women's movement, and contemporary United States history. The following excerpt is taken from *Women and Equality: Changing Patterns in American Culture.*

The resurgence of feminism in the 1960s represented the third incarnation of a dynamic women's rights movement in American history. The first . . . grew out of the abolitionist struggle of the 1830s and featured the legendary leadership of people like Elizabeth Cady Stanton and Susan B. Anthony. The second developed out of the social reform ethos of the early 1900s, and though the lineal descendant of the first movement, exhibited a style of leadership and a tactical approach significantly different from its antecedent. Cresting with the battle over the suffrage amendment, it succumbed to factionalism and public indifference in the 1920s and 1930s. The contemporary movement, like its predecessors, has grown out of a period of generalized social ferment, both drawing upon and reflecting a widespread sensitivity toward discrimination and injustice. The contemporary drive for women's liberation, however, differs from its forerunners in at least three ways: it is grounded in and moving in the same direction as underlying social trends at work in the society; it has developed an organizational base that is diverse and decentralized; and it is pursuing a wide range of social objectives that strike at many of the root causes of sex inequality. Although some of these distinctive characteristics are a source of weakness as well as strength, no previous feminist movement has attempted so much, and none has been better situated to make progress toward the goal of equality.

Probably the chief advantage of contemporary feminism lies in the extent to which its goals and programs have meshed with, or addressed directly, prevailing trends in society. In the past, the demands of women's rights organizations had often been far removed from the experience and immediate concerns of most women in the population. Although the Seneca Falls Declaration of Sentiments and Resolutions was bold in its vision, it bore little relationship to the world most women found themselves in—a world that was non-urban, populated by large families, and increasingly suffused with the precepts of Victorian morality. The notions of equal access to careers, or being able to preach from the pulpit, appealed to only a select group of women. Indeed, feminist objectives were so far outside the realm of most people's experience that females and males alike tended to dismiss early women's rights advocates as a lunatic fringe.

In a slightly different way, the suffrage movement of the 20th century also displayed misunderstanding of, and lack of contact with, some of the basic realities of the day. In their quest for one of the most fundamental rights of citizenship—the vote—the suffragists overestimated the extent to which a breakthrough in one area would lead to liberation in others as well. By expecting all women to vote together for the same candidates and programs on the basis of loyalty to their sex, the suffragists profoundly misread the degree to which ethnic, class, and family allegiances undermined the prospect of sex-based political behavior. Similarly, in thinking that winning the vote would encourage women to carry the fight for equality into the economic arena as well, the suffragists underestimated significantly the power of traditional forces of socialization. In both cases the fundamental error was to exaggerate the ability of a political reform to transform an entire structure of roles and activities based on gender.

The one area where "emancipation" did take hold—that of sex—also illustrated the extent to which the suffragists were out of touch with some of the trends in society. Throughout the first three decades of the twentieth century, a sexual revolution was in progress. For women born after 1900, rates of premarital and extra-marital intercourse were approximately double those of women born before 1900. A new awareness of contraceptive devices and an increased recognition of female sexuality signified an important expansion of sexual freedom for middle-class women of the flapper era. Yet many feminists were repelled by the "revolution in manners and morals." To most women's rights advocates, the flapper seemed frivolous and irresponsible. At a time when there were political battles to be fought and careers to be opened up, concern with the libido and sexual freedom appeared counter-productive. Sex was meant for procreation, Charlotte Perkins Gilman remarked, and her views seemed to reflect the generalized dismay of suffrage leaders about the new morality. Improving the status of women in government and the economy required discipline, dedication, and sacrifice—attributes seemingly inconsistent with the concerns dominating the lives of younger women.

In the end, of course, it was the social environment rather than the shortcomings of women activists which prevented the realization of feminist hopes. As long as the day-to-day structure of most women's lives reinforced the existing distribution of sex roles, there was little possibility of developing a feminist constituency committed to far-reaching change. Women in large numbers might support the effort to win the suffrage, but there was no frame of reference in experience, and little support in the culture, for seeking the kind of full-scale equality that would revolutionize the social structure. Although the suffragists participated in the general "progressive" tendency to equate limited reforms with basic change, the real problem was a social milieu which proved inhospitable to more far-reaching change.

In this context, the feminism of the 1960s and 1970s differed from previous women's movements precisely because it grew out of and built upon prevailing social trends. For the first time ideological protest and underlying social and economic changes appeared to be moving in a similar direction. Female work patterns were virtually transformed in the years after 1940. Prior to World War II, female employment was limited primarily to young, single women or poor, married women. Few middle-class wives held jobs. By 1975, in contrast, the two-income family had become the norm; 49 percent of all wives worked; and the median income of families where wives were employed was nearly $17,000. Although the employment changes did not signify progress toward equality, they ensured that social norms about a woman's "place" no longer had a base in reality.

As a result, feminist programs spoke more directly than ever before to the daily experience of millions of women. Female workers might not consider themselves feminists; indeed, they might shun any kind of association with the abstract cause of women's rights. But the same workers knew that they did not receive equal pay with men and that most of the higher paying jobs carried a "male only" tag. Similarly, the large number of women workers who had school-age and pre-school children understood the problems caused by inadequate day-care and after-school facilities. Discontented homemakers, who yearned for a more diverse life but saw all the barriers in the way, had a comparable sense of recognition. Thus there developed a common ground on which feminist activists and their potential constituency could stand, and that common ground provided the starting point from which some women moved toward greater collective consciousness of a sense of grievance.

A second social trend which coincided with the revival of feminism was the decline in the birth rate during the 60s and 70s. After World War II a "baby boom" swept the country, peaking in 1957 with a birth rate of 27.2 children per thousand people. There then ensued a prolonged downturn, which in 1967 resulted in a birth rate of 17.9, the lowest since the Great Depression. At the time demographers disagreed about the reasons for the decline, some citing the development of oral contraceptives, others economic and social instability. But all agreed that there would be a new baby boom in the early 1970s when the children born twenty years earlier would begin to reproduce. Instead of rising, though, the birth rate continued to plummet, reaching an all-time low by the mid-70s and achieving the reproduction level required—over time—for Zero Population Growth.

Although many forces contributed to the continuing decline, the interaction of female employment with changing attitudes toward women's roles appears to have been decisive. Throughout the 1960s, women married later, delayed the birth of their first child, and bore their last child at an earlier age. Whether as cause or effect, this trend coincided with many women finding occupations and interests away from the home. The rewards of having a job, as well as the desire for extra money to meet rising living standards, tended to emphasize the advantages of a small family. These values, in turn, were reinforced in the late 60s by the ideology of feminism and the population control movement. Two Gallup polls in 1967 and 1971 highlighted the shift in values. The earlier survey showed that 34 percent of women in the prime childbearing years anticipated having four or more children. By 1971, in contrast, the figure dropped to 15 percent. Two years later 70 percent of the nation's 18- to 24-year-old women indicated that they expected to have no more than two children. Thus feminist emphasis on personal fulfillment and freedom from immersion in traditional sex roles operated in tandem with long-range social developments which made such goals more objectively feasible.

Finally, changing attitudes and behavior in the realm of human sexuality meshed closely with feminist values concerning personal and bodily liberation. Although suffrage leaders in the early 20th century had exhibited little understanding or tolerance of the sexual revolution, supporters of women's liberation emphasized as one of their strongest themes the importance of women knowing their own bodies and having the freedom to use them as they saw fit. One manifestation of this emphasis was the publication by a women's health collective of *Our Bodies Our Selves,* a handbook which urged women to understand and appreciate their bodies. (The book had sold 850,000 copies from 1971 through 1976.) Still another manifestation was a generally supportive attitude toward "liberated" personal lifestyles, including lesbianism, communal living, and sexual relationships outside of marriage.

Significantly, such attitudes reinforced many of the social trends already developing in the culture, particularly among the young. In the eyes of many observers, a second sexual revolution occurred starting in the mid-60s. One study of women students at a large urban university showed a significant increase after 1965 in the number of women having intercourse while in a "dating" or "going steady" relationship; at the same time guilt feelings about sex sharply declined. Another nation-wide sample of freshmen college women in 1975 disclosed that one third endorsed causal sex based on a short acquaintance, and over 40 percent believed a couple should live together before getting married. Most indicative of changing mores, perhaps, was a survey of eight colleges in 1973 which showed not only that 76 percent of women had engaged in intercourse by their junior year (the male figure was 75 percent), but that women were appreciably more active sexually than men. Daniel Yankelovich's public opinion polls of college and non-college young people in the 60s and 70s appeared to confirm the major departure in sexual behavior and attitudes. Only a minority of women disapproved morally of pre-marital sex, homosexual relations between consenting adults, or having an abortion. Although women's liberation advocates warned that women could be victimized anew as sex objects under the guise of sexual freedom (just as they had been under a system of more repressive mores), the fact remained that the movement's support for abortion, homosexual rights, and free bodily expression placed it more in harmony with emerging cultural attitudes toward sexuality than in opposition.

In each of these areas, it seemed clear that the women's liberation movement was both drawing upon and reinforcing important changes taking place in the society. Shifts in employment patterns, demography, and sexual mores may have had a momentum of their own, but feminism introduced a powerful ingredient of ideology and activism that sought to transform these impersonal social trends and create new values and attitudes toward sex roles. In that sense, for the first time a dynamic relationship existed between "objective" social changes and feminist efforts to shape those changes in a particular direction. In contrast with each of the previous women's movements, the women's liberation drive of the 1960s and 1970s operated in a context where the social preconditions for ideological change were present. No longer was feminism irrelevant to most people's daily lives. Instead, its message spoke to many of the realities of the contemporary society. As a result, the possibility of an audience being able to respond was greater than ever before.

The second major distinctive quality of the new feminism is that as a result of a broader social base, the organization and structure of the movement differ significantly from that of the past. When women's rights advocates were on the margin of society and alienated from the world of most women, the organizational basis of the movement was narrow. Supporters of feminism, for the most part, came from the same social class and economic background. To maximize impact, the organizations they formed were national in scope. The women's liberation movement of the 60s and 70s, in contrast, almost defied categorization. Although feminist groups such as NOW and the Women's Equity Action League (WEAL) operated out of national offices in a style similar to that of other reform groups, the grass roots supporters of the movement fit less easily into an organizational niche. Some observers described women's liberation as a "guerrilla movement," its headquarters located in every kitchen or bedroom where women developed a more critical and independent sense of self. Whether or not the description was fully accurate, the new feminism appeared both diverse and decentralized, its strength more likely to be found in local communities than in national hierarchies. Since the movement had emerged in response to social conditions affecting a large number of women, it tended to reflect the different backgrounds of its supporters and the special concerns which were of greatest interest to them.

The distinction between the various feminist movements was reflected in their different constituencies. Through most of the 19th century, feminism drew its support primarily from a scattering of upper- and upper-middle-class women who were angered at the growing tendency to deny women the opportunity to use their abilities on the same basis as men. Although occasional working-class women or black heroines like Sojourner Truth joined the movement, feminism was generally identified with radical, alienated members of the cultural elite. Toward the beginning of the 20th century, the movement softened its rhetoric and broadened its base, becoming part of the larger effort of Progressive reform. But it remained overwhelmingly native white and middle class. Suffrage organizations shared the anti-black and anti-immigrant prejudices of their age, passing resolutions that disparaged both groups. Despite achieving a remarkable amount of support from club women and church women, the suffragists, like the Progressives generally, represented a homogeneous middle-class constituency.

With some justification, the same charge of being narrow, elitist, and white middle class has also been leveled at the women's liberation movement. In the late 60s feminism was generally associated with "liberal" university towns, student enclaves, the affluent suburbs, or the cosmopolitan urban centers of the East and West Coasts. Many supporters of the movement did come from the best universities and from well-off families, even if in the latter case, they had rejected some of the paraphernalia of affluence. (In a survey of its readers, *Ms.* magazine found that 84 percent had been to college, and that 71 percent worked, mostly in higher level jobs.) Others supposedly were disaffected suburban housewives and mothers, bored by bridge parties and chauffeuring children to dance lessons. From the point of view of some critics, such women were indulging a fantasy desire to join the world of social protest, and in the absence of exposure to the real injustices of hunger, poverty, and racial violence had "invented" the superficial issue of sex discrimination.

Still, the charge of elitism appeared less applicable to the women's movement of the 60s and 70s than to prior manifestations of feminism. Most supporters of the movement identified with the political left and were highly conscious of the issues of class and race, seeking wherever possible to find ways of transcending those barriers. Rather than criticize or remain aloof from other dissident groups, women liberationists supported organizations like the United Farm Workers and aligned themselves with other groups seeking social change. (The early women's rights movement had done the same, but the concern with racism faded by the late 19th century.) Many of the substantive demands of the movement, in turn, promised to help the poor as well as the rich and middle class. Most well-off women could afford to send their children to nursery school or hire service help. It was working-class women who would benefit most from universal day-care, equal pay, an end to job discrimination, and the availability of inexpensive abortions and birth control assistance.

In addition, there was some evidence to contradict the popular image of the women's movement as a white middle-class preserve. Despite major differences in priority and perspective between black and white women, a National Black Feminist Organization formed in 1973 both to assert the distinctive interests of black women in the struggle for women's rights and to provide a base for cooperative action on those issues which affected women across racial lines. By 1974 the NBFO had a membership of 2,000 women in ten chapters. Similarly, working-class women affirmed some identification with the concerns of the women's movement through the creation of the Coalition of Labor Union Women (CLUW). When the new organization met in Chicago in 1973 over 3,000 women from a wide range of unions united on a platform with clear feminist overtones. Although most of the issues were economic, the dominant theme was that women, as women, shared a reason to organize and fight for their collective interest. Earlier in the 20th century the Women's Trade Union League (WTUL) sought to achieve objectives which sounded similar but, despite some attention to unionizing activities, the WTUL was primarily a Progressive, middle-class organization devoted to persuading middle-class citizens to support social welfare legislation. CLUW, in contrast, excluded non-union members and seemed committed to a working-class perspective tied to relevant feminist issues. Significantly, a poll by Social Research, Inc. showed substantial support for feminist goals (though not feminist tactics) among working-class women. Thus, even if most avowed feminists were white and middle class in origin, the nature of the movement's involvement with women of diverse social and economic backgrounds suggested a more varied constituency than had existed in the past.

Perhaps more important, the new social base of feminism produced a thoroughly decentralized structure. When feminism had a narrower constituency, activity tended to focus on a national or state level. Hoping to maximize their influence, women reformers joined together in committees dedicated to securing specific goals such as the suffrage, or a minimum wage bill for women. A few devoted activists would work out of a regional or national headquarters, and in the name of all women, seek to persuade legislators or public opinion leaders of the virtue of their cause. Even when the popular base of the movement broadened in the early 20th century, the structure remained hierarchical, with coordination starting from state and national levels and working down to local branches. Indeed, through most of the 19th and 20th centuries, feminist groups were characterized by a vertical structure in which activity centered in coordinating committees at the top.

The women's liberation movement of the 60s and 70s, in contrast, was almost without any overarching structure. Despite the existence of groups like the National Organization for Women (NOW), the movement functioned primarily through small, informal groups on a local level. Its energy came from the bottom, not the top, and from the immediate ongoing concern of women with the quality of their own lives. Events or issues which were national in scope (such as the Equal Rights Amendment, or the march for equality on the 50th anniversary of the suffrage victory) were certainly not ignored, but the day-to-day direction of the movement grew out of local conditions which were central to the lives of the women most involved. Thus, as long as people in the immediate environment shared a common sense of grievance and a common desire for change, the movement was largely self-sustaining. It did not depend on national leadership. Indeed, many feminists believed deeply that "leaders" were unnecessary, that women could make decisions collectively, and that concepts of hierarchy and command were products of a male culture, hence to be avoided. In this context, the movement was decentralized for two reasons: it was rooted in local communities where women came together to deal with issues in their own lives; and it represented an ideology that viewed large organizations and leadership structures as part of the problem rather than the solution.

Not surprisingly, the absence of conventional leadership structures proved a source of considerable controversy. Some observers criticized the movement for its lack of direction and focus, implying that a disciplined national organization could mobilize a concerted following and secure more immediate results. Women's liberation theorist Jo Freeman warned about a potential "tyranny of structurelessness," arguing that the deliberate rejection of structure by feminists could create situations where a few women with staying power would dominate the movement because of the absence of regularized procedures to guarantee fairness and order. The latter criticism, in particular, spoke to a perennial problem. The entire Judeo-Christian tradition was premised on the imperfection of human nature, and the tendency of people, in the absence of external restraints, to seek their own ends. Reliance on collective good will, without resort to institutionalized checks and balances, tested severely people's ability to withstand the temptation to take advantage of others and impose their own will. Indeed, among some student radical groups, outlasting the opposition during interminable meetings provided a basic technique for controlling—and abusing—the process of participatory democracy.

In addition, the absence of structure helped to narrow the movement's class base, and limit its political effectiveness. Informal meetings worked well when people were skillful with words, confident about handling social tension, and at ease with complex and open-ended relationships. But not everyone fit such a category. Working-class people in particular favored meetings of limited duration with a specific agenda and a structured format. Moreover, the emphasis of movement supporters on intra-group compatibility unintentionally reinforced a tendency toward middle-class homogeneity. Also, an absence of structure made effective political action less likely. Not only was there no identifiable hierarchy to speak for the movement in developing coalitions or negotiating issues; the emphasis on "personal" issues sometimes diverted attention from public policy.

On balance, though, it seemed that decentralization and the lack of structure were central to the movement's strength as well as its distinctiveness. An ideal social movement might combine the discipline of a national organization with the energy of local grass roots efforts, yet such a combination appeared inconsistent—even contradictory—to the internal dynamics of the women's liberation movement. The vitality of the movement lay precisely in the proliferation of local organizations, each growing out of a particular concern or experience of different groups of women. Because such organizations reflected the immediate priorities of the women who created them, they commanded substantial loyalty and energy. It seemed at least possible, if not likely, that such an investment of local energy and initiative would be difficult to sustain in a hierarchical organization with established policies and strict procedures.

Finally, the pattern of decentralization ensured that the women's liberation movement would not rise or fall on the basis of one organization's activities or decisions. When all attention was riveted on a single national group as the embodiment of a cause, there was always the danger of defeat through internal divisions or the independent action of third parties. Thus some movements have been judged dead or alive on the basis of a single vote in Congress, or a series of public relations maneuvers. A social movement rooted in diverse local situations, however, and organized around a variety of issues, was less vulnerable to symbolic defeats. Thus, just as the movement's relevance to social trends helped to reinforce its ideological vitality, its decentralized structure accentuated its organizational strong point—grass roots support in the local community.

This, in turn, leads to the third distinguishing characteristic of the women's liberation movement, the variety and scope of its objectives. Through most of the 19th and 20th centuries, the women's movement tended to focus on a single issue, showing a tendency characteristic of nearly all American reform efforts. Although the Seneca Falls feminists sought far-reaching change in almost every area relevant to sex discrimination, their approach was too radical, and in a basically uncongenial political atmosphere it made sense to select one issue to effectively symbolize the movement. The problem was that the suffrage gradually became identified *in toto* with the larger issues. In a similar way, the National Women's Party (NWP) became obsessed with the belief that an Equal Rights Amendment (ERA) would prove to be a panacea. Beginning in 1923 the

NWP devoted its entire energies to the fight for an ERA, eschewing identification with other questions such as birth control or maternal and infant health care. Clearly, the ERA was an important issue, and its incorporation into the Constitution would have provided a valuable lever for seeking change in women's status wherever questions of law were involved. But in the process of seeking the ERA, the NWP, already a small elitist organization, alienated most working women (the ERA prior to 1941 would have brought invalidation of protective legislation for working women such as minimum-wage laws), spent an excessive amount of energy battling other women's organizations, and tended to ignore the extent to which the roots of sex inequality went beyond the reach of even the most powerful constitutional amendment.

The supporters of women's liberation, in the other hand, appeared to recognize the pitfalls of thinking there was any single answer to inequality or sex role stereotyping. The result was a plethora of related but separate activities, giving each individual group maximum leeway to work on the specific aspect of inequality that concerned it most. Although ratification of the proposed Equal Rights Amendment to the Constitution, repeal of abortion laws, or women's political caucuses represented the most visible items on the feminist agenda, most activists understood that success in one venture only meant there would be a new problem to work on. In this sense, feminists seemed to have learned a great deal from the civil rights movement, where the achievement of some goals such as the Voting Rights Act simply disclosed the existence of additional layers of racism to be combated. Implicit in feminist activities was the perception that, as in the Chinese proverb, the problem of inequality was a box within a box within a box, with no single answer.

The spectrum of activities in one university community during the early 1970s illustrated the diversity of objectives pursued by different groups. One group of women came together to plan a course for public school teachers on eliminating sexism in the classroom. Another met weekly to edit and publish children's books which were free of invidious sex stereotypes. Still another group worked on a coalition of citizens concerned with day care. While a local woman's center sponsored a meeting for the purpose of starting a union of household workers, a NOW chapter worked to counter employment discrimination. Counseling on sexuality, birth control, and abortion occupied still others. Lesbian discussion groups provided a forum for homosexual women to talk about the politics of sex, and a socialist feminist group addressed the junction of class and sex issues. Consciousness-raising groups for divorced or widowed women attempted to deal with the specific problems growing out of those situations. Although such diversity produced conflict over priorities as well as opportunities for cooperation, it illustrates the pluralistic approach which the women's movement of the 60s and 70s brought to the problem of sex inequality—an approach which maximized the possibility of local women becoming involved in an issue important to their own immediate lives.

In the end, therefore, each of the distinctive qualities of feminism in the 60s and 70s was inextricably connected to the next. Because feminist ideas directly addressed contemporary social realities, more people perceived the movement as relevant to their own circumstances. This, in turn, helped to produce involvement in local activities which seemed pertinent to the larger issue. The extent to which the movement grew out of and related back to the immediate experience of large numbers of women made unnecessary the centralized and hierarchical structures of the past, and the absence of such structures encouraged the development of multiple activities, each dealing with a particular aspect of sex inequality. In this sense, the women's liberation movement of the 60s and 70s was more similar to the Southern Farmer's Alliance of the 1880s or the civil rights movement of the 1960s than to earlier manifestations of feminism. It took its direction and vitality from the experience of people in local communities.

As in the history of all social movements, however, contemporary feminism faced serious obstacles. Some reflected internal tensions that emerged from the very diversity and decentralization which distinguished the movement from its predecessors. Others derived from outside sources and mirrored the opposition, tacit as well as organized, which the ideas of women's liberation engendered. Together, they highlighted both the dimensions of the challenge confronting the movement and the scope of its quest for change.

Perhaps the most profound obstacle was the extent to which the movement threatened the sense of identity millions of people had derived from the culture and from the primary transmitter of social values, the family. The words "masculine" and "feminine" were as emotionally powerful in the meanings they conveyed as any other terms, including "white" and "black." People were raised to identify as almost sacred the attributes attached to each phrase, and to view any deviation as a mark of shame. For a boy to be called a "fairy," for example, represented a crushing insult, to be avoided at all costs.

Those who were deeply committed to prevailing values, such as the author George Gilder, believed that such networks of attributes derived from a sexual constitution found in all civilized societies. Within that constitution, women controlled otherwise intemperate male drives by tying men to the family, giving them a bond of fatherhood to their progeny, building up the masculine role of provider, and rewarding the male sex drive through the act of genital intercourse. (Genital intercourse was important because it affirmed male dominance, was tied directly to procreation, and thus supported the maintenance of the sexual constitution.) Within this social system, all work found its "ultimate test in the quality of the home," and woman's role as housewife made hers the "central position in all civilized society." This position, in turn, derived from woman's part in procreation and the primary tie of mother and child. Thus, according to Gilder:

> The woman's sexual life and how she manages it is crucial to this process of male socialization. The males have no ties to women and children—or to long-term human community—so deep or tenacious as the mother's to her child. That is primary in society; all else is contingent and derivative. . . . The woman assumes charge of . . . the domestic values of the community. . . . all those

matters that we consider of such importance that we do not ascribe a financial worth to them.

In this context, an assault on any components of the sexual constitution—childbirth, the male role as provider, or genital sex—threatened to destroy civilized society itself by unleashing the previously harnessed antisocial drives of males.

Whether or not others would agree with Gilder's description of the sources of civilized society, it seemed clear that feminism was attacking the entire spectrum of traditional male and female roles. Women's liberation advocates argued that the culture had denied females their right to be human, first, by insisting that they be "feminine" and then, by defining "feminine" in such a way that women were deprived of the freedom to shape their own lives and choose their own careers. The same culture, it was charged, had denied males the right to be fully human by ruling out of bounds the idea of fatherhood as a full-time vocation and defining as inappropriate for men the expression of vulnerability, gentleness, or dependence. To correct these errors, feminists proposed to dismantle or radically alter some of the fundamental institutions of the culture. Instead of the traditional marriage ceremony, feminists suggested a marital contract, specifying the responsibilities of each partner and the prerequisites that had to be maintained for the relationship to be continued. Women's liberation advocates argued that women and men should be equally free to pursue careers, care for children, initiate sex, and select social companions. Public day-care services, they contended, should be available to assume part of the responsibility previously borne solely by parents. And individuals should be free—as individuals—to determine their own life style, sexual preference, occupation, and personal values.

Not surprisingly, both the indictment and the proposed solutions deeply offended people who had been raised to believe that existing norms of behavior were not only functional but morally inviolable. If not everyone went as far as George Gilder in seeing feminist views as leading to "sexual suicide," many nevertheless felt threatened. To women who had spent a lifetime devoting themselves to the culturally sanctioned roles of homemaker and helpmate, the feminist charge that women had been enslaved frequently appeared as a direct attack on their own personal experience. Such women did not believe that they had wasted their lives or had been duped by malevolent husbands. Many enjoyed the nurturant and supportive roles of wife and mother, believed that the family should operate with a sexual division of labor, and profoundly resented the suggestion that the life of a homemaker somehow symbolized failure. From their point of view, the women's liberation movement was often guilty of arrogance and contempt toward the majority of women, and some expressed that view by voting against local Equal Rights amendments in New Jersey and New York or by supporting the traditional values celebrated in the "Total Woman" movement.

In a somewhat similar way, many men believed that the movement was conducting an insidious campaign to undermine their strength, deny their authority, and destroy their self-image. As they looked at feminist demands for equal sharing of household responsibilities, affirmative action in employment, and complete freedom over personal lives, it seemed that women activists were trying to take away their role as breadwinners and sabotage their position of leadership in the home. Instead of helping women, many men believed, feminists were intent on wrecking the family, turning wife against husband, and transforming men into dishwashers and baby-sitters. Nothing threatened men more than the belief that in movement groups women told each other intimate details of their respective experiences with men and hatched plans to subvert traditional marital relationships. From such a vantage point, women's liberation symbolized anarchic and amoral forces at work in the society, seeking to untie all the knots and loosen the bonds that gave life its security and stability.

Although such fears were exaggerated, concern about the challenge to traditional "masculine" and "feminine" roles ran deep in the society. The issues raised by feminism went to the root of people's personal as well as social identity. At best such questions had the potential of making people vulnerable and insecure. At worst, they produced bitter hostility. Moreover, there existed a generalized anxiety that the triumph of women's liberation might mean the destruction of human relationships as they had been known, with impersonal competition replacing the warmth associated with woman's traditional role, and a unisex sameness overcoming the rich distinctiveness of previous male-female relationships. Part nostalgia and part legitimate concern about depersonalization, the anxiety provided important kindling for those forces seeking to build a political backfire against women's liberation on such issues as opposition to abortion and the Equal Rights Amendment. Thus the greatest obstacle feminism faced was the commitment of millions of people to the institutions, values, and personal self-images which were associated with traditional sex roles. As conservatives mobilized the political potential implicit in that commitment, feminists found some of their objectives increasingly endangered.

The second major obstacle faced by the movement was that of internal dissension. Though the absence of a centralized structure and focus on a single issue proved to be assets in most respects, the resulting diversity of aims and priorities constituted a seedbed of ideological conflict. Intense factional disputes erupted over both goals and methods. Some feminists believed that only the total abolition of the nuclear family could bring freedom to women. Others accepted the family institution but sought to change its structure to make it more equitable. While some traced discrimination against women to an inherent and irrevocable male malevolence, others saw men as parallel victims of a warped socialization process. Similar divisions developed over the issue of style or political tactics. Should movement supporters denounce the status quo in uncompromising terms and demand immediate radical change? Or should they moderate their rhetoric, seek a common ground with their audience, and

attempt to move one step at a time? Clearly, such questions had no easy answers, but they produced a continuing tension which on occasion resulted in
internal disputes even more ferocious and embittered than conflicts with outside opponents.

A conference of socialist feminists held at Yellow Springs, Ohio, in the summer of 1975 highlighted some of the factional difficulties created by the diverse
make-up of the movement. The more than 1500 participants at the conference
were for the most part self-defined Marxists who supposedly agreed that all
oppression, whether based on class, sex, race, or lesbianism, was inter-related,
and that socialist feminism, operating through an autonomous women's movement, provided the best strategy for revolution. With the aim of recognizing
variety and at the same time bringing unity out of diversity, the conference
planners scheduled workshops on subjects ranging from women in prison to
women in farming and anarchist feminist experiments. Informal caucuses of
Jewish women, older women, and mothers also sprang up, each focusing on
the particular concerns of most significance to the particular group—older
women, for example, asking that attention be paid to the crises of employment,
health, and family that frequently accompanied middle age.

The major conflicts at the conference, however, erupted over the radically
different perceptions of the underlying problem held by lesbian feminists, a
third world caucus, and an "anti-imperialist, Marxist-Leninist" caucus. The last-
named group insisted that class was the basic problem, that women's organizations had to be subsumed within the revolutionary struggle of the proletar-
iat, and that efforts to develop alternative life-styles to the family or an
autonomous women's movement were a *petit bourgeois* escape from the real
issue. Within this view, male supremacy and hierarchical rule were simply a
function of capitalism and once capitalism was overthrown oppression of
women and lesbians would cease. Lesbian feminists, by contrast, argued that
homosexuality represented more than a personal sexual preference and was a
political act against the institutional source of all women's oppression, hetero-
sexuality. Within this perspective, male supremacy constituted the basic problem, and its primary instrument of control was the heterosexual relationship.
Although capitalism was implicated in the problem, male supremacy also existed in socialist countries like Cuba, where homosexuals were oppressed and
"macho" values remained largely intact. Thus only a direct attack on the source
of male oppression could bring liberation for women; for that reason, all feminists had to identify, politically at least, with the lesbian struggle. Finally, the
third world panel asserted the primacy of race and imperialism as fundamental
questions. Pointing out the absence of many conference participants from third
world backgrounds, the caucus warned of the dangers of generalizing from
white middle-class experience, particularly involving the family, to third world
cultures with different priorities and perspectives. A poor black woman, one
speaker remarked, cared more about food and decent medical care than sophisticated feminist theorizing. By the end of the conference, therefore, instead
of arriving at a "unified understanding of women's oppression," the women
participants had been forced to grapple with most of the conflicts inherent in

a movement which sought to speak for a group divided into multiple class, racial, and cultural constituencies. No event could have dramatized more the potential for factionalism.

For the most part, supporters of the movement attempted to deal with the danger of dissension in two ways. First, there developed early in the movement a general policy of not excluding groups or points of view for reasons of political unorthodoxy or social unpopularity. The issue surfaced quickly on the question of endorsing the struggles of lesbians; despite deep concern among some that identification with homosexuality would harm the prospect of gaining legislative and political reform, most activists made common cause on the indivisibility of women's rights. In part this reflected the absence of a monolithic organization seeking to impose a party line, and in part an ideological conviction that disavowing one group of women for reasons of political expediency would lead to the death of the movement. A second approach—growing out of the first—was a belief that women could resolve conflict through understanding and conciliation. While men might go to war rather than admit the possibility of error, women, it was argued, could work through a problem to a collective solution. Thus observers at the Yellow Springs conference reported a desire on the part of the conflicting groups to deal with their differences "in the context of the whole," rather than to secede into separate bastions.

Not surprisingly, though, the depth of feeling sometimes divided the movement into warring camps. Gloria Steinem, identified in the public eye as a major feminist figure because of her writing and the attention paid her by the media, became a symbol of such divisions when she was accused by some "radical" feminists of having been a CIA agent for ten years. Because of her association with the "moderate" *Ms.* magazine and her reluctance to adopt an uncompromisingly radical stance on some issues, Steinem unwittingly became a scapegoat in the fight over who would control the movement. Conflicts between lesbians and non-lesbians also frequently reached the stage of no-holds-barred battle, and some feminists like Betty Friedan viewed the so-called "lavender menace" as more an enemy to the movement than male chauvinism. Even more established organizations like NOW split over the reform/radical issue, and when the 1975 NOW convention adopted as its slogan "out of the mainstream and into the revolution," some members withdrew in protest to start their own organization.

Together with resistance to change within the dominant culture, then, the constant threat of internecine warfare plagued the movement's efforts to make inroads among its potential constituency. The questions at issue were neither trivial nor simple, and the distinction between compromise and surrender was not always clear. Yet there was a profound difference between viewing the contented homemaker as a deluded Sambo and reaching out to make contact with her on her own ground. Similarly, a tremendous chasm separated those who viewed men as congenitally oppressive and those who saw males as people in need of support as well as prodding in coming to grips with their attitudes. In the presence of such conflicts, the potential existed that the women's movement of the 1960s and 1970s would fall victim to the same polarization that had torn apart its predecessor in the 1920s, and that energies needed for positive action would be diverted into sectarian feuding.

Still, what remained impressive was the degree of change that appeared to be taking place notwithstanding the obstacles. Although most American women might disavow any overt association with the movement *per se* ("I'm no women's libber," "They're too radical for my taste"), the same women supported many of the substantive programs of the movement. Day-care centers, availability of abortion services, equal career opportunities, and greater sharing of household tasks all received substantial approval in public opinion surveys of women. As late as 1962 a Gallup poll showed that a majority of female respondents did not believe American women were discriminated against. Eight years later women divided down the middle on the question of whether they supported the movement to secure greater equality. By 1974 those responding to the same question endorsed the efforts toward more equality by two to one.

The greatest impact of the movement appeared among the young and on college campuses. The Yankelovich survey of the early 70s showed a doubling in two years of the number of students viewing women as an oppressed group, with a large majority endorsing concepts of equality in sexual relations, the importance of women's relation to other women, and the notion that men and women were born with the same talents. Two thirds of college women agreed that "the idea that a woman's place is in the home is nonsense," and only one third felt that having children was an important personal value. Other polls showed similar results, including a rapid change over time. A 1970 survey of college freshmen indicated that half of the men and more than one third of the women endorsed the idea that "the activities of married women are best confined to the home and family." Five years later only one third of the men and less than one fifth of the women took the same position.

Not surprisingly, changing attitudes toward traditional roles in the home were accompanied by shifting expectations about careers. In the 1970 survey of freshmen, males out-numbered females 8 to 1 in expressing an interest in the traditionally "masculine" fields of business, engineering, medicine, and law. By 1975, in contrast, the ratio was down to 3 to 1. In the same period, moreover, the number of women expecting to enter the "feminine" fields of elementary and secondary school teaching plummeted from 31 percent to 10 percent. Indicative of the general trend was one survey of eight colleges in 1973 which showed that 82 percent of the women considered a career very important or important for their self-fulfillment, while only 67 percent put marriage in the same category. Although such survey data described theoretical expectations rather than actual behavior, the evidence suggested that many women were following through on their announced intentions. The proportion of women in the entering classes of law school skyrocketed by 300 percent from 1969 to 1974, and many law schools anticipated that women would

make up half of each class by 1980. Women doctorates also increased significantly, with the share of Ph.D.'s earned by women growing from 11 percent in
1970 to 21 percent in 1975. Although working-class and older women did not
share completely all the new ideas, they too seemed to be undergoing change.
Non-college young women were less convinced of the value of sisterhood or
the reality of discrimination than college women, but the Yankelovich survey
showed them endorsing feminist ideas on greater equality in family decision-
making, women's rights to sexual pleasure, and skepticism toward the traditional homemaker ideal. Older women, in turn, displayed their involvement in
change by enrolling in growing numbers in continuing education programs
and seeking graduate training for new careers.

The exact nature of the change that had taken place was not easy to define.
At its roots, it was a shift of consciousness, a new awareness or sensibility
among women about women, and about their relation to men. The consciousness surfaced to some extent in public opinion polls, but it also appeared
frequently in more personal and direct encounters—in the comment of a middle-aged woman who said in a phone conversation, "I'll have to check with my
husband," and then felt called upon to add: "We're a traditional couple." Or in
the remark of a young woman, not an active feminist, who was angered because the epilogue to the film *American Graffiti* ignored women: "Why did
they tell us just what happened to the boys ten years later? What about the
girls?" Or finally, in the bitter comment of a forty-year-old mother: "I need to
be recycled, only no one wants to give me the chance. I gave away my career
fifteen years ago when I dropped out of graduate school to stay home with
the kids."

There is no way to quantify such consciousness, or to know with certainty
what it meant. Yet it seemed to be a palpable reality—taking root, growing,
spreading. It appeared in public school brochures where the traditional "he"
as the description for everyone was replaced with "he or she." In offices it
sometimes blossomed when male bosses, without thinking, automatically assumed that the "girls" would get coffee or buy a Christmas present for a female
relative. And in discussions of rape, gynecological practices, who would watch
the children, drive the car, or fold the laundry, it could suddenly emerge.
Wherever the consciousness appeared, change began to occur because in one
way or another, every activity of the day, from interaction with co-workers to
reading a night-time story to children, took on a new significance. Social revolutions, to be sure, do not develop full blown from the simple emergence of
a new idea. Yet heightened awareness of a set of social conditions is a prereq-
uisite for a change in values, and it seemed likely that as consciousness of sex
role stereotyping and discrimination mounted, other social relationships
would be cast in a new light also, sparking a rethinking process about one's
entire life—work, family, spouse, children, and friends.

Much of the change that had taken place, of course, could be traced to non-
ideological forces. Long-term trends in the economy, demographic patterns,
and cultural values all contributed substantially. In addition, only a relatively

small proportion of the total female population participated, either directly or indirectly, in the women's movement. If a majority identified with some feminist ideas, only a few were activists. Indeed, many of those who were involved in changing their own lives might have done so regardless of the movement, as a natural byproduct of the underlying changes in the society and economy.

Yet the women's movement of the 60s and 70s seems, on balance, to have been decisive to the heightened consciousness of the younger generation. Behavioral change, prompted by impersonal social forces, can go only so far. At some point ideological forces must intervene to spur a transformation of the values which help to shape and define behavioral options. In the late 60s and 70s the women's movement provided such a spur, criticizing the assumptions, values, and images that had prevailed in the past and offering an alternative vision of what might prevail in the future. Although most men and women did not align themselves vigorously on the side of feminism, political discussions, media coverage, decisions on public school curriculum, employment practices, and the dynamics of family living all reflected the impact of the movement's existence. It had raised questions, presented demands, and introduced ideas which compelled discussion. And even when the discussion was hostile, people were considering issues central to self and society in a way that had not happened before.

QUESTIONS FOR DISCUSSION

1. Why did the movement arouse such passionate opposition?
2. What do you believe has been the effect of the women's movement on American beliefs, behaviors, and consciousness?

RICHARD WADE

The New Urban Crisis

Although the phrase urban crisis *has crept into our public conversation only in the past few decades, violence, racial conflict, and the perception of our cities as ungovernable are not newcomers to the American scene.*

In the early 1900s, urban slums were, if anything, dirtier, more violent, and more crowded than they are today. Still, there was hope for the future. Immigrant families looked upon the slums as temporary, not permanent, residences, while increasing prosperity and population growth provided city governments with the resources they required to attack "even the most vexing problems." These conditions changed dramatically after World War II as "two divisive elements entered the metropolis, destroying its economic and governmental unity and profoundly altering its social structure. The first division was between suburb and city; the second between black and white." The fiscal crisis of the 1970s and the urban "riots" of the 1960s, each in its own way, highlighted the existence and the consequences of these divisions.

In 1979, when Richard Wade published the following essay, he could discern hopeful signs for the future. Nonetheless, he warned at the time—and his warning may hold true today—that if Americans did not begin to unite their divided metropolises and disperse their ghettoes, the decades to come would be filled with "renewed tension and turmoil."

More than a decade ago the phrase "urban crisis" crept into our public conversation. Since then it has become a cliché, connoting a wide range of persistent and dangerous problems confronting our cities. Moreover, the phrase, like "missile crisis" or "energy crisis," suggests both newness and immediate danger. The rioting, arson, and looting that erupted in the 1960s fortified this general impression. Presumably something unprecedented had

---

Richard Wade is a Distinguished Professor of History at the Graduate Center of the City University of New York and the author of a number of books on urban history. The following article was originally published in *American Heritage*.

happened. Urban life had become unmanageable; in the professional and popular view, cities were "ungovernable."

Something new, indeed, had happened. It was not that American cities had not known violence and race conflict before. They ran like thick red lines through the history of many cities. But the scale and ubiquity of the modern outbreaks had no earlier analogue. Large and small cities, both north and south, witnessed almost simultaneous explosions; the number of dead and injured and the amount of property damage easily exceeded those of anything previous. Few people predicted the rioting, hence most sought for an explanation in very recent developments—black migrations, the slow pace of desegregation, unemployment, broken families, and the Vietnam War.

Yet the fires of the 1960s were not the arson of a single decade or generation. Urban society had been accumulating combustibles for well over a century. The seventies have simply tamped down the flames while the ashes still smolder and unless the historical sources of the present crisis are better understood and public policy changed, a recurrence, next time probably worse, is almost inevitable. New York City's experience during the 1977 blackout ought to have served as the first alarm for the nation.

What baffled most commentators in the sixties was that the convulsions came at a time when urban experts confidently had asserted that the nation's cities were overcoming their afflictions. There had been, for example, a marked decline in the percentage of substandard housing; there were relatively fewer urban poor than ever before; hospital beds had caught up with need; federal programs were bringing health care to an unprecedented number of people; schools had reduced class size; new skylines attested to renewed downtown vitality; municipal government, though scarred by occasional scandals, was demonstrably more competent than it once had been.

To the historian the argument had a superficial validity. One only had to compare the city of 1970 with the city of 1900 to measure municipal progress. At the turn of the century every city had its concentrations of wretched neighborhoods where poor people huddled in run-down or jerry-built houses and in tenements lacking even toilets or running water. Primitive coal stoves provided the heat; kerosene lamps the light. Family cohesiveness, always fragile, often cracked under the weight of these oppressive circumstances. Nor were these conditions exceptional. Jacob Riis's *How the Other Half Lives* described the festering slums on New York's Lower East Side in 1890; but as the title suggests, he was also discussing the predicament of over 50 percent of the city's population. Indeed, a congressional inquiry into urban housing at about the same time demonstrated that every metropolis matched New York's dilapidated, unsanitary, and dangerous dwellings.

Nor was there much in the neighborhood to compensate for the miseries of home life. The droppings of thousands of horses made even crossing the street hazardous. Garbage clogged thoroughfares; sanitation carts picked their way through congested avenues and alleys once a week at best. Cheap shops and uninspected markets lined the sidewalks. No traffic regulations prevented horse-drawn trucks and carts, electric trolleys, and private hacks from creating a continual cacophony, day and night. And dense smoke from coal-burning factories and office buildings rolled darkly through downtown. Worse still, crime and violence were constant companions of slum dwellers.

Three institutions attenuated the misery of the slum—the church, the school, and the saloon. And they were attractive precisely because they provided what the tenement and neighborhood lacked. The church was clean and uncongested; its friendly priest, minister, or rabbi cared about the parishioners and their families. Even the most primitive schools took the children out of the tenement and into rooms that were at least heated in the winter. The saloon was bright and congenial, and the husband could meet with friends and neighbors away from the oppressive crowding of the apartment. Yet these oases could not conceal—indeed they only magnified—the grinding deprivation of the lives of these people. Later commentators would invest the "good old neighborhood" with charm, conviviality, and livability; but to most of its residents, life was a losing struggle against filth, noise, and disorder.

The whole family was drawn into the contest. Jobs for anyone were scarce and irregular. Good, steady work that permitted the father to feed, clothe, and shelter his family on his own was very rare. The wife and children usually had to enter the already overcrowded job market. Mothers and daughters sewed, packaged nuts, made artificial flowers. Young boys sold newspapers, picked coal, collected rags, ran errands. Frequent depressions did away with even these menial tasks.

Schooling was brief. Children dropped out, not at fourteen or fifteen, but at eight or nine. Even so, education was often inadequate: classrooms were crowded, teachers poorly trained and politically selected. No audiovisual aids or paraprofessional help assisted the beleaguered instructor; the truant officer became a familiar figure in the neighborhood. Reformers sought vainly to get class sizes down to fifty and replace patronage appointments with professionals.

Conditions in the area were tolerable only because those who lived there considered them temporary. Residential turnover was high; one of every five families had a different address each year. Most, of course, moved only a short distance and often because they could not pay the rent. But a significant number found housing in more pleasant communities away from the old slum. Scholars later argued over the percentage who "made it" out; yet every resident knew someone who did; a relative, perhaps, or someone on the block or in the parish. But the possibility of escape was as much a part of the experience as confinement.

The change over the subsequent three-quarters of a century was dramatic. In 1902 Robert Hunter estimated that over half the urban population lived beneath the poverty line. By 1970 that figure had fallen to less than 20 percent, even though the definition of poverty has been raised substantially. Density in the inner city dropped drastically; Jacob Riis found over 300,000 people per square mile living in New York's tenth ward; today, any concentration over 75,000 a square mile is considered intolerable. Public policy and private development removed the most visible downtown slums, though cancerous nodes remained behind. Public housing, with all its problems, replaced the most depressed and dilapidated areas. New building in the outer city and suburbs provided modern accommodations for an exploding urban population. In the sixties, experts argued over whether "substandard" housing composed 15 or 18 percent of the total stock; judged by the same standards seventy years earlier, it would have composed more than half.

Even the crime rate was probably higher in 1900, though there is no way to prove it. Police organization was primitive, and systematic reporting of crime was still decades away. Politicians hired and fired the force; collusion between criminals and police was common. Constant gang warfare jeopardized the peace of nearly every downtown area. Political reformers always promised the "restoration of law and order."

Municipal governments were too weak to control matters. State governments granted cities only modest powers, and then only grudgingly. Corruption riddled most city halls and municipalities. Political bosses and special interests united to plunder the public till. Lincoln Steffens made a national reputation with the book entitled *The Shame of the Cities,* which chronicled the boodle, bribery, and chicanery that he contended characterized nearly every American city. Good government forces occasionally broke the unseemly ring, but usually not for long.

In short, the present city, for all its problems, is cleaner, less crowded, safer, and more livable than its turn-of-the-century counterpart. Its people are more prosperous, better educated, and healthier than they were seventy years ago.

The slow but steady improvement in municipal affairs was the result of both particular historical conditions of the twentieth century and the efforts of many generations of urban dwellers. American cities enjoyed continued growth and expansion for most of the period. They were also the vital centers of a surging national economy. As the country became increasingly urban, the best talent and greatest wealth gravitated to the metropolis, where a huge pool of skilled and unskilled labor could be easily tapped. This combination made it possible for the United States to become the most powerful industrial nation in the world.

Technological changes, themselves largely products of the urban explosion, permitted new advances in municipal management. Subways, elevateds, and automobiles facilitated the movement of people throughout the expanding metropolis, retiring horses to the country. Modern medicine increased the effectiveness of public health measures. Electricity and central heating improved the comfort of new housing, and the long-term mortgage made home ownership easier to manage. Movies, radios, and television democratized entertainment, if they did not always elevate it. New laws forced more children into schools and kept them there longer.

Though progress was often sporadic, city government widened its competence and improved its performance. Tensions between reformers and urban machines resulted in permanent gains, for after each revolt was beaten back, some improvements were always retained. Civil service slowly produced a bureaucracy that, for all its clumsiness, was distinctly superior to the earlier rampant patronage system. Zoning put a measure of predictability, if not control, into land use. And nearly everywhere the quality of urban leadership was noticeably better than before. A few old-time bosses persisted, but they were viewed as quaint anachronisms rather than as the logical expressions of city politics.

This considerable achievement rested on two historical conditions—the general prosperity of the period and the ample municipal limits which permitted expanding economic activity to take place within a single political jurisdiction. Except for the Great Depression and occasional sharp dips in the business index, American cities generally witnessed sustained growth. Even wartime did not interrupt the expansion; indeed, immense military spending acted as a swift stimulus to urban economies. Municipal progress cost money—a lot of it—and American cities generally had it to spend. And when they did not, they borrowed, confident that the future would be even more prosperous.

This was, moreover, the age of the self-sufficient city. Municipal boundaries were wide and continually enlarging. In 1876 St. Louis reached out into neighboring farm land and incorporated all the area now within its city limits. In one swift move in 1889 Chicago added over 125 square miles to its territory. And in 1898 New York absorbed the four surrounding counties—including Brooklyn, the nation's fourth largest city—making it the world's Empire City.

In 1900 municipal boundaries were generous, almost always including unsettled and undeveloped land. As populations grew, there were always fresh areas to build up. This meant that all the wealth, all the commerce, all the industry, and all the talent lay within the city. When serious problems arose, all the resources of the metropolis could be brought to bear to solve them. More prosperous than either the state or federal governments, the cities needed no outside help; indeed they met any interference with the demand for home rule.

For as long as these historical conditions prevailed, American cities could make incremental progress in attacking even the most vexing problems. But after the Second World War, two divisive elements entered the metropolis, destroying its economic and governmental unity and profoundly altering its social structure. The first division was between suburb and city; the second between black and white. Actually, these fissures always had been present, but not on the same scale or with the same intensity, and certainly not with the same significance.

Suburbanization is almost as old as urbanization. American cities always have grown from the inside out; as population increased, it spilled outside municipal limits. Initially these suburbs were not the exclusive resort of the wealthy; many poor lived there to avoid city taxes and regulations. But railroad development in the mid-nineteenth century produced modern commuting suburbs: Chicago had fifty-two of them by 1874. Though suburbs grew rapidly, their numbers were always relatively small and their locations governed by rail lines. By the 1920s the automobile spawned a second generation of suburbs, filling in the areas between the older ones and setting off an unprecedented building boom beyond the municipal limits.

The crash of 1929 put an end to suburban expansion for fifteen years. During the Depression, people could not afford new housing, and when war came, the military consumed all available construction material. But the pent-up demand broke loose with the coming of peace. By 1970, the census reported that more people in the metropolitan regions lived outside the municipal boundaries than within. All cities, even smaller ones, were surrounded by numerous small jurisdictions, self-governing, self-taxing—and growing.

The historical remedy to this problem—annexation of surrounding areas— was no longer available. In most states the process required a majority of the voters in both the cities and the suburbs to support consolidation, and after 1920 the outlying areas were increasingly against incorporation. The cities, now with fixed boundaries, gradually lost population, while the suburbs experienced steady growth.

Moreover, this demographic change profoundly altered the social structure of the metropolis. The middle class rapidly evacuated the old city in favor of the suburbs. In turn, they were replaced by migrants from the South and from Latin America. The newcomers were mostly poor and racially distinct. With little education or skills, they were tax consumers rather than tax producers. They needed help on a large scale. Most of all they needed jobs. But industry and commerce had followed the outward movement of people. At just the time municipal government faced additional responsibilities, it saw its revenue base shrinking. Inevitably, various groups fell to quarreling over these limited resources, producing new tensions and anxieties.

The rioting of the 1960s revealed another fissure in the metropolis—the division between black and white. Some blacks always had lived in cities, even under slavery. But the "peculiar institution" had confined most to the Southern countryside. After the Civil War, former slaves without land or urban skills drifted into Southern cities, where they quickly composed a large portion of the population. The urban South accommodated the newcomers within an elaborate system of segregation. The separation of the races was accomplished both by custom and, after 1896, under Jim Crow statutes.

The massive Northern migration of rural Southern blacks in this century, however, slowly altered the racial composition of nearly every city across the country. Municipal governments adopted no new policies to deal with the influx. Indeed, they assumed that the same process that had incorporated millions of immigrants into the metropolitan mainstream would also be available to blacks. That is, the newcomers initially would congregate at the heart of town, increase their numbers, get an economic foothold, and then gradually disperse into more pleasant residential neighborhoods away from the congested center. This process, though often cruel and painful, had served the immigrants, the city, and the country well.

But the black's experience was fundamentally different. They did, indeed, gather at the center, and there they found what immigrants always had found: wretched housing, overcrowded neighborhoods, high unemployment, inadequate schools, littered streets, garbage-strewn alleys, rampant crime, and endemic disorder. However, the new ghetto, unlike the old, did not loosen and disperse. Rather it simply spread block by block, oozing out over adjacent communities. White residents retreated while blacks moved into new areas beyond downtown. Later a generation would grow up that knew only the ghetto and its debilitating life.

The immigrant ghetto had been tolerable because it was thought to be temporary, a rough staging ground for upward and outward mobility. Blacks increasingly perceived the ghetto to be their permanent home. And each federal census fortified this apprehension as the index of racial segregation moved steadily upward. There was, of course, some modest leakage here and there, but the barriers to escape remained formidable.

This confinement had two consequences that were different from those of the old ghetto. The first was the alienation of its black middle class. They, after all, had done what they were supposed to do: stayed in school, kept out of serious trouble, got higher education, and made good money. But they were still denied, by color of their skin alone, that most important symbol of success in America—the right to live in a neighborhood of their own choosing with schools appropriate to their ambitions for their children.

The size of this black middle class is large; indeed, no other group has had a success story quite equal to it. In 1950 the federal census listed about 10 percent of American blacks as "middle class"; by 1960 that figure had climbed to nearly 18 percent; by 1970 it had jumped above one-third. To be sure, it often required two breadwinners in the family to achieve this status; that, plus ambition and hard work. For these people, continued *de facto* residential segregation was especially cruel. Even in fashionable black neighborhoods, hope turned into resentful bitterness.

For the less successful, the situation was much worse. The black ghetto contained the city's worst housing, schools, and community institutions. It generated few jobs and experienced soaring unemployment. Crime rates were high, gang warfare common, and vice rampant. All this contributed to the breakdown of family life and the encouragement of dependency. Newcomers always found it difficult to adjust to the ghetto; race compounded the problem. In the sixties, daily frustrations spilled over into violence. The young struck out against the symbols of their oppression that were closest at hand, reducing large ghetto areas to ashes.

Race, then, greatly widened the already yawning gap between city and suburb. Every important issue that arose within the metropolis reflected this division. School busing became the symbolic question: without residential segregation, no busing would be necessary. "Affirmative action" became a euphemism for introducing minorities into employment areas previously monopolized by whites. The collapse of mass transit left blacks riding in the front of the bus but with diminishing numbers of white companions. While crime rates rose in the suburbs, popular stereotypes still associated violence with inner-city minorities. In short, uniting the metropolis would have been difficult enough; the addition of race introduced an enormously complicating factor.

In the seventies the inner cities quieted down. But the new tranquillity came from black resignation rather than from a larger measure of justice. The unemployment figures contained the warning: 10 percent in older cities; 20 percent in the ghettoes; 40 percent among minority youth. In addition, middle-class blacks ran into all kinds of obstacles when trying to escape to the suburbs. The courts were ambivalent about legal restrictions, especially zoning, which had the effect of exclusion. And social pressures in the suburbs were often not very subtle. As a result, the ghetto still festered; indeed, its boundaries expanded each week.

Yet certain factors hold out some hope for the future. For example, suburbs are finding that they are no more self-sufficient than the cities. The same forces that led to urban decay earlier are now spreading into the surrounding communities. This is particularly true of those suburbs adjacent to the city limits. Indeed, the phrase "inner suburbs" surely will join "inner city" as shorthand for the long list of urban ills in the eighties. And for much the same reasons. They are the oldest part of suburban America. In order to keep taxes down, they allowed most of their land to be developed. Now there is no room for expansion. The new suburbanites go farther out; new industrial and commercial installations also bypass the closer-in suburbs. Large numbers of older residents, their children now gone, head for retirement areas or back to the city. Newer shopping centers in outlying suburbs skim off dollars from local merchants. Worse still, crime rates grow faster in these communities than in any other part of the metropolis.

In addition, suburban government is the weakest link in our governmental system. Until recently, residential participation in local affairs was low; most communities hired professional managers to make budgets and administer day-to-day affairs. Voting was light for local offices, and though suburbanites vote heavily Republican in national elections, suburban politics remain consciously nonpartisan. Hence, when the crisis moved in, most suburbs lacked the tradition or tools to grapple with it. By the 1970s new suburban newspapers began to reveal the often scandalous relations between some developers and many town halls. Voters increasingly turned down bond issues, even for schools. The inner suburbs' one trump card is that they still control the suburban lobby in most states. They played that card to get some relief for all local governments, hence they became the major beneficiaries. Yet neither this nor federal revenue-sharing programs could do more than postpone the inevitable fiscal impasse. When New York City slid toward bankruptcy, Yonkers, located in one of the nation's richest suburban counties, was placed in receivership.

The extension of city problems into the suburbs poked large holes in the crabgrass curtain that previously had separated the two parts of the metropolis. Now their common predicament created the possibility of a new cooperation to replace the hostility that historically had divided city and suburb. The inner suburbs were reluctant to recognize their own decline, but by the seventies they recognized that they had to trade part of their independence for outside help.

For the first time, a substantial suburban population has a stake in a united metropolis. The inner ring is no longer self-sufficient. It relies increasingly on state and federal aid rather than on its indigenous tax base. Hence, its most serious problems cannot be solved without cooperation with the city as well as with neighboring suburbs. In the 1950s the movement for metropolitan government was essentially a big-city strategy; now that concept has natural allies. To be sure, the notion of a single governmental jurisdiction is politically impossible except in a few places.

A consolidation of effort by function, however, is already imperative. In housing, education, transportation, water, pollution, and police, control depends on devising programs that employ a concentrated, cooperative regional approach. Even this requires a change in state and federal policies, which presently funnel funds into old governmental units rather than into intergovernmental ones. But the crisis of the inner suburbs has produced the necessary condition for a fundamental shift in public policy based on metropolitan realities rather than on anachronistic political jurisdictions.

New demographic changes also brought some easing of racial tensions. The massive movement of blacks from the South to Northern cities virtually has stopped; indeed, some experts detect a slight reverse of the flow. The breaking of segregation and the availability of jobs in Southern cities made them at least as attractive as Northern ones. Moreover, urban black birth rates dropped rapidly. This reduced ghetto tensions somewhat but not ghetto conditions. In addition, the election of black mayors in many parts of the country lessened the feeling of isolation and powerlessness of urban blacks. The relative quiet of the ghetto in the seventies was somewhat deceptive but did provide some breathing space for the nation if the nation had the ingenuity and will to seize it.

But time is running out and we have not used it wisely to heal racial divisions or reduce urban-suburban tensions. Federal policy has neglected cities in favor of surrounding communities. Revenue-sharing formulas were based largely on population rather than on need; government installations usually were placed in outlying areas; special programs for the inner cities were either reduced or dismantled. Worse still, urban economies, historically the nation's most resilient, recovered more slowly from recurring recessions than the suburbs with their newer facilities. And the outward flow of jobs and middle-class city dwellers continued unabated. The problem is more severe in the older areas of the Northeast and Midwest. Yet the "Sunbelt" cities show the same symptoms. The acids of urban decay do not recognize the Mason-Dixon line.

The persistence of the urban crisis has led many Americans to look elsewhere for solutions. But a look outward indicates that what some thought was a peculiarly American question is, in fact, an international urban crisis. Rome's fiscal management makes New York's look frugal; the inadequacy of London's inner-city schools is more than a match for their American counterparts; Frankfurt's pollution experts travel to Pittsburgh for advice; few American housing commissioners would trade jobs with their opposite numbers in Sydney. Russian urban experts see their limited growth policies overwhelmed by illegal migration; the smog in Sarajevo would frighten even an Angelino; Rumania's ambitious satellite city plan has not inhibited the growth of Bucharest or produced any "new towns"; more than three decades after World War II, no major city in Eastern Europe has dented its housing shortage.

The record of foreign cities on race is no more instructive. British urban centers are producing their own "New Commonwealth" ghettoes; not a single black sits in Parliament. Amsterdam cannot handle its old colonists of different color. Paris and Marseilles have been unable to assimilate their French Algerians. Moscow couldn't manage even a small number of African students; in Bucharest, urban renewal is gypsy removal. In Sydney and Auckland, the aborigines, though small in number, face the usual range of discrimination. Indeed, the immigration policies of Canada and Australia are designed to avoid the issue.

The fact is that no society has learned to manage a large metropolis, nor has any society succeeded in solving the question of race. If these problems are to be solved, it will be done here in the United States. Perhaps that is the way it should be. Our national history has been almost conterminous with the rise of the modern city; racial diversity always has been a part of the American experience. We have managed in the past to take millions of people with different backgrounds, languages, and religions and incorporate them into the metropolitan mainstream.

In facing the present urban crisis, we need only draw upon our best traditions. But if we do not begin to unite the metropolis and to disperse the ghetto in the next few years, the eighties will be a decade of renewed tension and turmoil and will bear out Wendell Phillips' grim prophecy of a hundred years ago: "The time will come when our cities will strain our institutions as slavery never did."

QUESTIONS FOR DISCUSSION

1. This article was written in 1979. Is the "urban crisis" Wade describes still with us? How, if at all, has it changed, for better or worse?

2. Explain how and why the postwar metropolitan divisions between suburb and city and black and white exacerbated the "urban crisis."

Ronald Reagan, the master campaigner, accepts the cheers and happy demonstration of his supporters at the 1984 Dallas Convention of the Republican Party. The enthusiasm generated here amplified into one of the greatest electoral triumphs in the history of the presidency. *(Bettmann Newspbotos)*

Ronald Reagan's
Second Acceptance Speech
to Republican Nominating
Convention

Commentary by James Gilbert

American political conventions are ritual events. Every four years delegates from each party gather at a city chosen for its symbolic significance to nominate candidates and mark the beginning of the official campaign season. Since, by the time the opening gavel sounds, the nominees have usually built commanding leads and most of the behind-the-scenes-deals have been struck, the most important business is presenting the candidates and launching the campaign. The presidential acceptance speech is the central event in these proceedings. It sets the tone of the campaign, establishes the issues and momentum, and gives full exposure to a candidate who will subsequently be seen by most Americans only in very brief and carefully planned campaign advertisements.

President Ronald Reagan's acceptance speech in Dallas, Texas, on August 23, 1984, was both typical of speeches by incumbent presidents before him and unique in the ways that it revealed the style of his leadership and the sources of his political strength. As the jewel in the crown of public relations events during the week, it reflected the efforts of the president's political managers to establish the tone of the campaign. As the central event of the long renomination process, it ratified the choice of the Republican party: a brilliant speaker, a vibrant television personality, a man whose instinctive reactions to events were so canny that his opponents were reduced to lamenting his "good luck."

Like other aspects of political campaigning, conventions are filled with self-conscious "Americana" and references to history. Deeply imbedded in democratic traditions, they resound with state and national pride and exhibit the energy and showmanship characteristic of American politics. Delegates representing party, principle, and locale, sometimes wearing garb to symbolize their area (ten-gallon hats from Texas, for example), whoop merrily at the mention of their states.

As events whose function has changed largely because of television, the conventions retain vestiges of well-worn traditions—nominating speeches, debates over platforms, and demonstrations for candidates—though most of the decisions are made off camera. They also express an inherent populism that has so often in American history pitted "the people" against "the government" in Washington, as exemplified in Ronald Reagan's call to "get government off our backs."

The convention delegates who gathered in Dallas in the sweltering late summer of 1984 came together to renominate Ronald Reagan and reaffirm their enthusiasm for him in a ceremony scheduled for the prime-time evening television hours of August 24. The delegates represented each American state and territory. Racial groups such as blacks were underrepresented (less than 5 percent of the delegates were black), but there was a large contingent of women. Invited guests and speakers included Jeane Kirkpatrick, a Democrat, United Nations representative, and a staunch Reagan supporter; former President Gerald Ford; Senator Barry Goldwater, the father of the conservative movement that brought Reagan to the White House; evangelist Reverend Jerry Falwell; and a variety of television personalities and Gold Medal winners from the summer Olympics in Los Angeles. This was decidedly not a cross section of the American population, but then, few political conventions really are.

The Republicans broke with the past by renominating the president in a new format. Following a traditional political speech delivered by Senator Paul Laxalt of Nevada, the convention was treated to an eighteen-minute biographical/political film of Ronald Reagan's career narrated by the president himself. Featuring scenes of family and political life, the film projected a happy, confident, and accomplished man, surrounded by an adoring wife and effective associates. It was both intimate and detached—a skillful blend designed to attract voters to the image of success. Its message suggested that the president was a phenomenon and not a politician, and that his candidacy represented a news event, not a struggle between two political parties. Reagan struck the pose of a man beyond politics—a major theme of his campaign. Unprecedented and clearly intended as a partisan commercial and not a nominating speech, the film segment provoked controversy among network television stations. ABC and CBS only showed excerpts from it, although NBC ran it in its entirety.

Immediately following this film, at 9:11 P.M. Dallas time, to the cheers of the delegates, the president stepped before the microphones and television cameras to begin his address. His speech evoked a long personal history, filled with words, phrases, and images he had employed countless times before. It was also a document dotted with contemporary allusions: to the prior Democratic Convention at San Francisco that had nominated Walter Mondale and Geraldine Ferraro as president and vice president and to events during the first four years of his presidency. Written principally by Ken Khachigian, passed for approval to advisers and aides, and finally agreed to by the president, it reflected the collective wisdom of the Reagan phenomenon and the essence of the president's political philosophy. That philosophy may be summarized in the slogan adopted for the campaign and characteristic of the public posture of the Republican party: "Bringing America Back, Prouder, Stronger, and Better." By this the Republicans signaled that they meant to resume in 1984 their successful 1980 campaign against former President Jimmy Carter. In that campaign they had convinced voters that the Democratic president stood for a distorted economic program, a weak defense, and indecisiveness in foreign policy.

Once in office in 1981, Reagan had continued his attack on Carter and the practices of the postwar Democratic party. Those policies, he contended, had brought big government and special interest-group politics to Washington, generated rules, taxes, and regulations that stifled creativity and growth, and resulted in the inflation, shortages of raw materials, and slower economic growth of the 1970s. In defining Americans as members of groups (blacks, union members, women, elderly, and so on), the Democratic party, Reagan contended, had built a huge, sloppy, and divided governing coalition that rewarded each of its constituent groups with special legislation. The result was a sluggish, overregulated economy. This accusation reflected far more than sloganeering. Reagan's label of "interest group politics" stuck to the Democrats like phosphorescent strips. At the same time, the president's appeal to individuals rather than groups meant that he could avoid making hard and politically compromising choices. An appeal to individuals was an appeal to everyone.

When the president finished his address to applause and shouts of "four more years!" a huge American flag descended behind him. White balloons drifted down from the rafters and red balloons rose from the floor. The band played merry patriotic songs.

Renomination speeches such as Reagan's have a particular and significant role to play in American political life. Pronounced from the pinnacle of incumbency and written from success, they are, as a rule, happy reaffirmations. They express the very essence of political optimism and project the hopes of a winning candidate; a president who, having gained victory once, has every reason to expect to win again.

Acceptance speeches by incumbents inevitably include a strong appeal to American nationalism, for it is the duty of the successful candidate to surround himself, his party, and his platform with the symbols of an American political consensus. Incumbent candidates for renomination blur any sharp distinctions made by the convention and aim their campaigns at the political center. This is often accomplished by accusing the opposition party of extremism, of having sold its soul to narrow, selfish interests, while proclaiming that one's own party expresses true American ideals.

Renomination speeches also focus on the future; the use of the word "new" is as old a political staple as exists. Addressed toward the unfolding future, filled with promise for a better life, these speeches are aimed at the young voters, a special constituency of enormous importance and one assumed to be the most volatile segment of the electorate.

Emphasis upon the future carries with it the burden of speaking about the past. Incumbent presidents, unlike other candidates, cannot (logically) run a populist campaign against government, since they themselves represent government. But they can use history to identify opposition forces with former administrations or with economic interests, narrow parties, or opposing candidates tarnished by prior political actions. They may also use history to identify themselves or their party with the march of progress and their opponents with reaction. Appealing to history allows them to continue their criticism of already defeated opponents.

In the recent past, presidents have chosen two strategies to rally support for their reelection: they have either defended their own records or attacked the opposition. The first strategy is best represented by Franklin Roosevelt's 1936 speech, "A Rendezvous with Destiny." In this renomination speech, Roosevelt presented a tightly argued interpretation of American history pointing to the necessity for the New Deal programs initiated during his administration. Defending his philosophy of government, Roosevelt employed a poetic language, strewn with Biblical cadences. He proceeded logically from point to point in a rhetorical mode intended for listening and reading. The second format is best illustrated by Democrat Harry S. Truman's acceptance speech of 1948 (technically his first election as president since he succeeded to the office in 1945 at Roosevelt's death). Truman took a very different tack, arguing in highly partisan terms about specific programs opposed by the Republicans. He accused the Republicans, who then controlled Congress, of opposing all progress—as evidenced by their failure to ratify his specific proposals for legislative reform. It was a belligerent, but highly effective beginning to a successful uphill victory.

Ronald Reagan's speech of 1984 took something from both models. The first half of the address is pugnacious, accusatory, and highly partisan, recalling Truman's, or more recently, Richard Nixon's words of 1972. But the final portion exhibits traces of Franklin Roosevelt's visionary style—with one telling difference. Whereas Roosevelt's speech proceeds by argument, Reagan's imagination works in symbols. His points are tied together by images of Olympic torch bearers passing through and illuminating different American patriotic elements: "Gotham City," "The City of the Big Shoulders, Chicago," "the greening Northwest," and so on. Rather like a television montage, these images, pronounced like the dialogue to accompany a documentary film, end with a final view of the Statue of Liberty, promise for the future, a golden door, and "a springtime of hope."

Interpreters who concentrate on either the partisan overture or the euphoric ending of Reagan's acceptance speech will not see the way in which each part depends upon the other. In the first half, Reagan drew upon the traditions of his predecessors. In the second, his sweeping and cinematic invocation of the American nation may have appeared trite and without logical progression, but symbolically, it solidified the visionary elements of his candidacy. He pronounced strong partisan judgments, running against a discredited past and against his current opponent, Walter Mondale, whom he linked to that past. But despite the unusual narrowness of his own party's platform, his description of the future transcended politics. It presented a picture of nationalism drawn in the textbook language of the American dream.

Some commentators have noted in criticism that parts of the speech had been delivered hundreds of times before. Even the format recalled other times and other places. With its opening warm up compliment to Dallas, Texas, and its obligatory joke, the speech resembled countless after-dinner talks Reagan had given during decades of proselytizing for General Electric and supporting conservative issues. Yet this repetition had a virtue, for it emphasized the familiar. Reagan's vocabulary, after four years of success, had become the accepted and standard language of political discourse; that is precisely the position of strength from which any incumbent president wishes to run.

Of all recent presidents, Ronald Reagan is perhaps the most optimistic, projecting an open and ebullient personality. Yet his optimism covered over a fundamentally pessimistic, almost haunted view of history. His vision of hope was ultimately more apocalyptic than optimistic. On two fronts, the president's sense of threat ran deep. His view of the tide of communism, inexorable until his election and inevitable without his reelection, carried a powerful overtone of doubt. Inside the United States, he raised a muted but similar fear: decades of willful and profligate spending—once again held off and reversed by his presidency. Without him, he implied, America might renew its slide from welfare state towards totalitarianism.

The president did not resolve the tensions he raised by proposing specific actions to counter them. Instead, his vision of the Olympics provided the optimistic tone of his speech—a patriotism based upon winning to lighten the shades of pessimism.

In the long history of American political campaigns, and as a reflection of Reagan's extraordinary presidency, this is a remarkable and central document. It demonstrates the spirit of a man who has baffled many political experts. It reflects the skills of a remarkable politician. And it summarizes and makes vivid the issues that brought this conservative ideologue, moralist, and movie actor to the presidency.

RONALD REAGAN

Second Acceptance Speech to Republican Nominating Convention

*M*r. *Chairman, Mr. Vice President, delegates to this convention, and fellow citizens:*

In 75 days, I hope we enjoy a victory that is the size of the heart of Texas. Nancy and I extend our deep thanks to the Lone Star State and the "Big D"—the city of Dallas—for all their warmth and hospitality.

Four years ago I didn't know precisely every duty of this office, and not too long ago, I learned about some new ones from the first-graders of Corpus Christi School in Chambersburg, Pennsylvania. Little Leah Kline was asked by her teacher to describe my duties. She said: "The President goes to meetings. He helps the animals. The President gets frustrated. He talks to other Presidents." How does wisdom begin at such an early age?

Tonight, with a full heart and deep gratitude for your trust, I accept your nomination for the Presidency of the United States.

I will campaign on behalf of the principles of our party which lift America confidently into the future.

America is presented with the clearest political choice of half a century. The distinction between our two parties and the different philosophy of our political opponents are at the heart of this campaign and America's future.

I've been campaigning long enough to know that a political party and its leadership can't change their colors in four days.[1] We won't, and no matter how hard they tried, our opponents didn't in San Francisco. We didn't discover our values in a poll taken a week before the convention. And we didn't set a

---

[1]San Francisco, California, site of the Democratic National Convention which met in the Moscone Center from July 16 through 19, 1984.

Source: The speech is quoted from Office of the Federal Register, National Archives and Records Service, Government Services Agency, "Remarks Accepting the Presidential Nomination at the 1984 Republican National Convention, August 23, 1984," *Weekly Compilation of Presidential Documents,* pp. 1167–74.

weathervane on top of the Golden Gate Bridge before we started talking about the American family.

The choices this year are not just between two different personalities or between two political parties. They're between two different visions of the future, two fundamentally different ways of governing—their government of pessimism, fear and limits, or ours of hope, confidence, and growth.

Their government sees people only as members of groups; ours serves all the people of America as individuals. Theirs lives in the past, seeking to apply the old and failed policies to an era that has passed them by. Ours learns from the past and strives to change by boldly charting a new course for the future. Theirs lives by promises, the bigger, the better. We offer proven, workable answers.

Our opponents began this campaign hoping that America has a poor memory. Well, let's take them on a little stroll down memory lane. Let's remind them of how a 4.8 percent inflation rate in 1976 became back-to-back years of double-digit inflation—the worst since World War I—punishing the poor and the elderly, young couples striving to start their new lives, and working people struggling to make ends meet.

Inflation was not some plague borne on the wind; it was a deliberate part of their official economic policy, needed, they said, to maintain prosperity. They didn't tell us that with it would come the highest interest rates since the Civil War. As average monthly mortgage payments more than doubled, home building nearly ground to a halt; tens of thousands of carpenters and others were thrown out of work. And who controlled both Houses of the Congress and the executive branch at that time? Not us—not us.

Campaigning across America in 1980, we saw evidence everywhere *of industrial decline.* And in rural America, farmers' costs were driven up by inflation. They were devastated by a wrongheaded grain embargo[2] and were forced to borrow money at exorbitant interest rates just to get by. And many of them didn't get by. Farmers have to fight insects, weather, and the marketplace; they shouldn't have to fight their own government.

The high interest rates of 1980 were not talked about in San Francisco. But how about taxes? They were talked about in San Francisco. Will Rogers once said he never met a man he didn't like. Well, if I could paraphrase Will, our friends in the other party have never met a tax they didn't like—[applause]—they didn't like or hike.

Under their policies, tax rates have gone up three times as much for families with children as they have for everyone else over these past three decades. In just the 5 years before we came into office, taxes roughly doubled.

Some who spoke so loudly in San Francisco of fairness were among those who brought about the biggest single, individual tax increase in our history in 1977, calling for a series of increases in the social security payroll tax and in

---

[2]The grain embargo was instituted in January 1980 by President Jimmy Carter. This policy which cut off shipments of U.S. grain to the Soviet Union was a response to that nation's invasion of Afghanistan.

the amount of pay subject to that tax. The bill they passed called for two additional increases between now and 1990, increases that bear down hardest on those at the lower income levels.

The Census Bureau confirms that, because of the tax laws we inherited, the number of households at or below the poverty level paying Federal income tax more than doubled between 1980 and 1982. Well, they received some relief in 1983, when our across-the-board tax cut was fully in place. And they'll get more help when indexing goes into effect this January.

Our opponents have repeatedly advocated eliminating indexing.[3] Would that really hurt the rich? No, because the rich are already in the top brackets. But those working men and women who depend on a cost-of-living adjustment just to keep abreast of inflation would find themselves pushed into higher tax brackets and wouldn't even be able to keep even with inflation because they'd be paying a higher income tax. That's bracket creep; and our opponents are for it, and we're against it.

It's up to us to see that all our fellow citizens understand that confiscatory taxes, costly social experiments, and economic tinkering were not just the policies of a single administration. For the 26 years prior to January of 1981, the opposition party controlled both Houses of Congress. Every spending bill and every tax for more than a quarter of a century has been of their doing.

About a decade ago, they said Federal spending was out of control, so they passed a budget control act and, in the next 5 years, ran up deficits of $260 billion. Some control.

In 1981 we gained control of the Senate and the executive branch. With the help of some concerned Democrats in the House we started a policy of tightening the Federal budget instead of the family budget.

A task force chaired by Vice President George Bush—the finest Vice President this country has ever had—it eliminated unnecessary regulations that had been strangling business and industry.

And while we have our friends down memory lane, maybe they'd like to recall a gimmick they designed for their 1976 campaign. As President Ford told us the night before last, adding the unemployment and inflation rates, they got what they called a misery index. In '76 it came to 12½ percent. They declared the incumbent had no right to seek reelection with that kind of a misery index. Well, 4 years ago, in the 1980 election, they didn't mention the misery index, possibly because it was then over 20 percent. And do you know something? They won't mention it in this election either. It's down to 11.6 and dropping.

By nearly every measure, the position of poor Americans worsened under the leadership of our opponents. Teenage drug use, out-of-wedlock births, and crime increased dramatically. Urban neighborhoods and schools deteriorated. Those whom government intended to help discovered a cycle of dependency that could not be broken. Government became a drug, providing temporary relief, but addiction as well.

---

[3]Indexing is a procedure that changes income tax categories by the rate of inflation to prevent increases in taxes due solely to cost-of-living adjustments in wages.

And let's get some facts on the table that our opponents don't want to hear. The biggest annual increase in poverty took place between 1978 and 1981—over 9 percent each year, in the first two years of our administration. Well, I should—pardon me—I didn't put a period in there. In the first 2 years of our administration, that annual increase fell to 5.3 percent. And 1983 was the first year since 1978 that there was no appreciable increase in poverty at all.

Pouring hundreds of billions of dollars into programs in order to make people worse off was irrational and unfair. It was time we ended this reliance on the government process and renewed our faith in the human process.

In 1980 the people decided with us that the economic crisis was not caused by the fact that they lived too well. Government lived too well. It was time for tax increases to be an act of last resort, not of first resort.

The people told the liberal leadership in Washington, "Try shrinking the size of government before you shrink the size of our paychecks."

Our government was also in serious trouble abroad. We had aircraft that couldn't fly and ships that couldn't leave port. Many of our military were on food stamps because of meager earnings, and reenlistments were down. Ammunition was low, and spare parts were in short supply.

Many of our allies mistrusted us. In the 4 years before we took office, country after country fell under the Soviet yoke. Since January 20th, 1981, not one inch of soil has fallen to the Communists.

Audience. 4 more years! 4 more years! 4 more years! . . .

The President. All right,

Audience. 4 more years! 4 more years! 4 more years! . . .

The President. But worst of all, Americans were losing the confidence and optimism about the future that has made us unique in the world. Parents were beginning to doubt that their children would have the better life that has been the dream of every American generation.

We can all be proud that pessimism is ended. America is coming back and is more confident than ever about the future. Tonight, we thank the citizens of the United States whose faith and unwillingness to give up on themselves or this country saved us all.

Together, we began the task of controlling the size and activities of the government by reducing the growth of its spending while passing a tax program to provide incentives to increase productivity for both workers and industry. Today, a working family earning $25,000 has about $2,900 more in purchasing power than if tax and inflation rates were still at the 1980 level.

Today, of all the major industrial nations of the world, America has the strongest economic growth; one of the lowest inflation rates; the fastest rate of job creation—6½ million jobs in the last year and a half—a record 600,000 business incorporations in 1983; and the largest increase in real, after-tax personal income since World War II. We're enjoying the highest level of business investment in history, and America has renewed its leadership in developing the vast new opportunities in science and high technology. America is on the move again and expanding toward new eras of opportunity for everyone.

Now, we're accused of having a secret.[4] Well, if we have, it is that we're going to keep the mighty engine of this nation revved up. And that means a future of sustained economic growth without inflation that's going to create for our children and grandchildren a prosperity that finally will last.

Today our troops have newer and better equipment; their morale is higher. The better armed they are, the less likely it is they will have to use that equipment. But if, heaven forbid, they're ever called upon to defend this nation, nothing would be more immoral than asking them to do so with weapons inferior to those of any possible opponent.

We have also begun to repair our valuable alliances, especially our historic NATO alliance. Extensive discussions in Asia have enabled us to start a new round of diplomatic progress there.

In the Middle East, it remains difficult to bring an end to historic conflicts, but we're not discouraged. And we shall always maintain our pledge never to sell out one of our closest friends, the State of Israel.

Closer to home, there remains a struggle for survival for free Latin American states, allies of ours.[5] They valiantly struggle to prevent Communist takeovers fueled massively by the Soviet Union and Cuba. Our policy is simple: We are not going to betray our friends, reward the enemies of freedom, or permit fear and retreat to become American policies—especially in this hemisphere.

None of the four wars in my lifetime came about because we were too strong. It's weakness that invites adventurous adversaries to make mistaken judgments. America is the most peaceful, least warlike nation in modern history. We are not the cause of all the ills of the world. We're a patient and generous people. But for the sake of our freedom and that of others, we cannot permit our reserve to be confused with a lack of resolve.

Ten months ago, we displayed this resolve in a mission to rescue American students on the imprisoned island of Grenada. Democratic candidates have suggested that this could be likened to the Soviet invasion of Afghanistan—

Audience. Boo-o-o!

The President. —the crushing of human rights in Poland or the genocide in Cambodia.

Audience. Boo-o-o!

The President. Could you imagine Harry Truman, John Kennedy, Hubert Humphrey, or Scoop Jackson making such a shocking comparison?[6]

Audience. No!

---

[4]The "secret" refers to Walter Mondale's charge, made in his nomination acceptance speech of July 19, 1984, that the Republicans had an unannounced and unacknowledged plan to raise federal taxes to reduce the enormous federal debt.

[5]In citing the "Latin American states," the president meant El Salvador, which the United States was aiding in its war against guerrillas, and Nicaragua, where the United States was helping guerrillas seeking to overthrow the government.

[6]Harry Truman et al. are prominent Democrats, all deceased, whom Reagan enlists as supporters of his foreign policy.

The President. Nineteen of our fine young men lost their lives on Grenada, and to even remotely compare their sacrifice to the murderous actions taking place in Afghanistan is unconscionable.

There are some obvious and important differences. First, we were invited in by six East Caribbean states. Does anyone seriously believe the people of Eastern Europe or Afghanistan invited the Russians?

Audience. No!

The President. Second, there are hundreds of thousands of Soviets occupying captive nations across the world. Today, our combat troops have come home. Our students are safe, and freedom is what we left behind in Grenada.

There are some who've forgotten why we have a military. It's not to promote war; it's to be prepared for peace. There's a sign over the entrance to Fairchild Air Force Base in Washington State, and that sign says it all: "Peace is Our Profession."

Our next administration—

Audience. 4 more years! 4 more years! 4 more years! . . .

The President. All right.

Audience. 4 more years! 4 more years! 4 more years! . . .

The President. It's—I heard you.

And that administration will be committed to completing the unfinished agenda that we've placed before the Congress and the Nation. It is an agenda which calls upon the national Democratic leadership to cease its obstructionist ways.

We've heard a lot about deficits this year from those on the other side of the aisle. Well, they should be experts on budget deficits. They've spent most of their political careers creating deficits. For 42 of the last 50 years, they have controlled both Houses of Congress.

Audience. Boo-o-o!

The President. And for almost all of those 50 years, deficit spending has been their deliberate policy. Now, however, they call for an end to deficits. They call them ours. Yet, at the same time, the leadership of their party resists our every effort to bring Federal spending under control. For 3 years straight, they have prevented us from adopting a balanced budget amendment to the Constitution. We will continue to fight for that amendment, mandating that government spend no more than government takes in.

And we will fight, as the Vice President told you, for the right of a President to veto items in appropriations bills without having to veto the entire bill. There is no better way than the line-item veto, now used by Governors in 43 States to cut out waste in government. I know. As Governor of California, I successfully made such vetos over 900 times.

Now, their candidate, it would appear, has only recently found deficits alarming. Nearly 10 years ago he insisted that a $52 billion deficit should be allowed to get much bigger in order to lower unemployment, and he said that sometimes "we need a deficit in order to stimulate the economy."

Audience. Boo-o-o!

The President. As a Senator, he voted to override President Ford's veto of billions of dollars in spending bills and then voted "no" on a proposal to cut the 1976 deficit in half.

Audience. Boo-o-o!

The President. Was anyone surprised by his pledge to raise your taxes next year if given the chance?[7]

Audience. No!

The President. In the Senate, he voted time and again for new taxes, including a 10 percent income tax surcharge, higher taxes on certain consumer items. He also voted against cutting the excise tax on automobiles. And he was part and parcel of that biggest single, individual tax increase in history—the social security payroll tax of 1977. It tripled the maximum tax and still didn't make the system solvent.

Audience. Boo-o-o!

The President. If our opponents were as vigorous in supporting our voluntary prayer amendment as they are in raising taxes, maybe we could get the Lord back in the schoolrooms and drugs and violence out.

Something else illustrates the nature of the choice Americans must make. While we've been hearing a lot of tough talk on crime from our opponents, the House Democratic leadership continues to block a critical anticrime bill that passed the Republican Senate by a 91-to-1 vote. Their burial of this bill means that you and your families will have to wait for even safer homes and streets.

There's no longer any good reason to hold back passage of tuition tax credit legislation. Millions of average parents pay their full share of taxes to support public schools while choosing to send their children to parochial or other independent schools. Doesn't fairness dictate that they should have some help in carrying a double burden?

When we talk of the plight of our cities, what would help more than our enterprise zones bill, which provides tax incentives for private industry to help rebuild and restore decayed areas in 75 sites all across America? If they really wanted a future of boundless new opportunities for our citizens, why have they buried enterprise zones over the years in committee?

Our opponents are openly committed to increasing our tax burden.

Audience. Boo-o-o!

The President. We are committed to stopping them, and we will.

They call their policy the new realism, but their new realism is just the old liberalism. They will place higher and higher taxes on small businesses, on family farms, and on other working families so that government may once again grow at the people's expense. You know, we could say they spend money like drunken sailors, but that would be unfair to drunken sailors—[*laughter*]

Audience. 4 more years! 4 more years! 4 more years! . . .

The President. All right. I agree.

---

[7]Candidate Mondale promised, if elected, to raise taxes to lower the federal budget deficit.

Audience. 4 more years! 4 more years! 4 more years! . . .

The President. I was going to say, it would be unfair, because the sailors are spending their own money. [*Laughter*]

Our tax policies are and will remain pro-work, pro-growth, and pro-family. We intend to simplify the entire tax system—to make taxes more fair, easier to understand, and, most important, to bring the tax rates of every American further down, not up. Now, if we bring them down far enough, growth will continue strong; the underground economy will shrink; the world will beat a path to our door; and no one will be able to hold America back; and the future will be ours.

Audience. U.S.A.! U.S.A.! . . .

The President. All right.

Another part of our future, the greatest challenge of all, is to reduce the risk of nuclear war by reducing the levels of nuclear arms. I have addressed parliaments, have spoken to parliaments in Europe and Asia during these last 3½ years, declaring that a nuclear war cannot be won, and must never be fought. And those words, in those assemblies, were greeted with spontaneous applause.

There are only two nations who by their agreement can rid the world of those doomsday weapons—the United States of America and the Soviet Union. For the sake of our children and the safety of this Earth, we ask the Soviets— who have walked out of our negotiations—to join us in reducing and, yes, ridding the Earth of this awful threat.

When we leave this hall tonight, we begin to place those clear choices before our fellow citizens. We must not let them be confused by those who still think that GNP stands for gross national promises. [*Laughter*] But after the debates, the position papers, the speeches, the conventions, the television commercials, primaries, caucuses, and slogans—after all this, is there really any doubt at all about what will happen if we let them win this November?

Audience. No!

The President. Is there any doubt that they will raise our taxes?

Audience. No!

The President. That they will send inflation into orbit again?

Audience. No!

The President. That they will make government bigger than ever?

Audience. No!

The President. And deficits even worse?

Audience. No!

The President. Raise unemployment?

Audience. No!

The President. Cut back our defense preparedness?

Audience. No!

The President. Raise interest rates?

Audience. No!

The President. Make unilateral and unwise concessions to the Soviet Union?

Audience. No!

The President. And they'll do all that in the name of compassion.

Audience. Boo-o-o!

The President. It's what they've done to America in the past. But if we do our job right, they won't be able to do it again.

Audience. Reagan! Reagan! Reagan! . . .

The President. It's getting late.

Audience. Reagan! Reagan! . . .

The President. All right.

In 1980 we asked the people of America, "Are you better off than you were 4 years ago?" Well, the people answered then by choosing us to bring about a change. We have every reason now, 4 years later, to ask that same question again, for we have made a change.

The American people joined us and helped us. Let us ask for their help again to renew the mandate of 1980, to move us further forward on the road we presently travel, the road of common sense, of people in control of their own destiny; the road leading to prosperity and economic expansion in a world at peace.

As we ask for their help, we should also answer the central question of public service: Why are we here? What do we believe in? Well for one thing, we're here to see that government continues to serve the people and not the other way around. Yes, government should do all that is necessary, but only that which is necessary.

We don't lump people by groups or special interests. And let me add, in the party of Lincoln, there is no room for intolerance and not even a small corner for anti-Semitism or bigotry of any kind.[8] Many people are welcome in our house, but not the bigots.

We believe in the uniqueness of each individual. We believe in the sacredness of human life.[9] For some time now we've all fallen into a pattern of describing our choice as left or right. It's become standard rhetoric in discussions of political philosophy. But is that really an accurate description of the choice before us?

Go back a few years to the origin of the terms and see where left or right would take us if we continued far enough in either direction. Stalin. Hitler. One would take us to Communist totalitarianism—the other to the totalitarianism of Hitler.

Isn't our choice really not one of left or right, but of up or down? Down through the welfare state to statism, to more and more government largesse accompanied always by more governmental authority, less individual liberty and, ultimately, totalitarianism, always advanced as for our own good. The al-

---

[8]This is a somewhat disguised reference to speeches by Louis Farrakhan, leader of the Nation of Islam, and a supporter of the Reverend Jesse Jackson, a prominent black leader and candidate for the Democratic presidential nomination. Farrakhan made several scurrilous references to Jews and Israel in speeches.

[9]The phrase, "sacredness of human life," is probably meant as support for the "right-to-life" movement which proposed to make abortions illegal in the United States.

ternative is the dream conceived by our Founding Fathers, up to the ultimate in individual freedom consistent with an orderly society.

We don't celebrate dependence day on the Fourth of July. We celebrate Independence Day.

Audience. U.S.A.! U.S.A.! U.S.A.! . . .

The President. We celebrate the right of each individual to be recognized as unique, possessed of dignity and the sacred right to life, liberty, and the pursuit of happiness. At the same time, with our independence goes a generosity of spirit more evident here than in almost any other part of the world. Recognizing the equality of all men and women, we're willing and able to lift the weak, cradle those who hurt, and nurture the bonds that tie us together as one nation under God.

Finally, we're here to shield our liberties, not just for now or for a few years but forever.

Could I share a personal thought with you tonight, because tonight's kind of special to me. It's the last time, of course, that I will address you under these same circumstances. I hope you'll invite me back to future conventions. Nancy and I will be forever grateful for the honor you've done us, for the opportunity to serve, and for your friendship and trust.

I began political life as a Democrat, casting my first vote in 1932 for Franklin Delano Roosevelt. That year, the Democrats called for a 25 percent reduction in the cost of government by abolishing useless commissions and offices and consolidating departments and bureaus, and giving more authority to State governments. As the years went by and those promises were forgotten, did I leave the Democratic Party, or did the leadership of that party leave not just me but millions of patriotic Democrats who believed in the principles and philosophies of that platform?

One of the first to declare this was a former Democratic nominee for President—Al Smith, the Happy Warrior, who went before the Nation in 1936 to say, on television—or on radio that he could no longer follow his party's leadership and that he was "taking a walk." As Democratic leaders have taken their party further and further away from its first principles, it's no surprise that so many responsible Democrats feel that our platform is closer to their views, and we welcome them to our side.

Four years ago we raised a banner of bold colors—no pale pastels. We proclaimed a dream of an America that would be "a shining city on a hill."[10]

We promised that we'd reduce the growth of the Federal Government, and we have. We said we intended to reduce interest rates and inflation, and we have. We said we would reduce taxes to provide incentives for individuals and business to get our economy moving again, and we have. We said there must be jobs with a future for our people, not government make-work programs, and, in the last 19 months, as I've said, 6½ million new jobs in the private

---

[10]The "city on a hill" is a quotation from "A Model of Christian Charity," delivered by John Winthrop in 1630 on board the *Arbella*. The ship was en route to establish a Puritan outpost in the new world as an example for the religious conversion of other societies. (See Chapter 1.)

sector have been created. We said we would once again be respected throughout the world, and we are. We said we would restore our ability to protect our freedom on land, sea, and in the air, and we have.

We bring to the American citizens in this election year a record of accomplishment and the promise of continuation.

We came together in a national crusade to make America great again, and to make a new beginning. Well, now it's all coming together. With our beloved nation at peace, we're in the midst of a springtime of hope for America. Greatness lies ahead of us.

Holding the Olympic games here in the United States began defining the promise of this season.[11]

Audience. U.S.A.! U.S.A.! U.S.A.! . . .

The President. All through the spring and summer, we marveled at the journey of the Olympic torch as it made its passage east to west. Over 9,000 miles, by some 4,000 runners, that flame crossed a portrait of our nation.

From our Gotham City, New York, to the Cradle of Liberty, Boston, across the Appalachian springtime, to the City of the Big Shoulders, Chicago. Moving south toward Atlanta, over to St. Louis, past its Gateway Arch, across wheatfields into the stark beauty of the Southwest and then up into the still snowcapped Rockies. And, after circling the greening Northwest, it came down to California, across the Golden Gate and finally into Los Angeles. And all along the way, that torch became a celebration of America. And we all became participants in the celebration.

Each new story was typical of this land of ours. There was Ansel Stubbs, a youngster of 99, who passed the torch in Kansas to 4-year-old Katie Johnson. In Pineville, Kentucky, it came in at 1 A.M., so hundreds of people lined the streets with candles. At Tupelo, Mississippi, at 7 A.M. on a Sunday morning, a robed church choir sang "God Bless America" as the torch went by.

That torch went through the Cumberland Gap, past the Martin Luther King, Jr., Memorial, down the Santa Fe Trail, and alongside Billy the Kid's grave.

In Richardson, Texas, it was carried by a 14-year-old boy in a special wheelchair. In West Virginia the runner came across a line of deaf children and let each one pass the torch for a few feet, and at the end these youngsters' hands talked excitedly in their sign language. Crowds spontaneously began singing "America the Beautiful" or "The Battle Hymn of the Republic."

And, then, in San Francisco a Vietnamese immigrant, his little son held on his shoulders, dodged photographers and policemen to cheer a 19-year-old black man pushing an 88-year-old white woman in a wheelchair as she carried the torch.

My friends, that's America.

Audience. U.S.A.! U.S.A.! U.S.A.! . . .

---

[11]The Olympic games were held in Los Angeles in late July 1984. The Soviet Union and most of its allies declined to participate in response to U.S. refusal to join the games in Moscow four years earlier.

The President. We cheered in Los Angeles as the flame was carried in and the giant Olympic torch burst into a billowing fire in front of the teams, the youth of 140 nations assembled on the floor of the Coliseum. And in that moment, maybe you were struck as I was with the uniqueness of what was taking place before a hundred thousand people in the stadium, most of them citizens of our country, and over a billion worldwide watching on television. There were athletes representing 140 countries here to compete in the one country in all the world whose people carry the bloodlines of all those 140 countries and more. Only in the United States is there such a rich mixture of races, creeds, and nationalities—only in our melting pot.

And that brings to mind another torch, the one that greeted so many of our parents and grandparents. Just this past Fourth of July, the torch atop the Statue of Liberty was hoisted down for replacement. We can be forgiven for thinking that maybe it was just worn out from lighting the way to freedom for 17 million new Americans. So, now we'll put up a new one.

The poet called Miss Liberty's torch the "lamp beside the golden door."[12] Well, that was the entrance to America, and it still is. And now you really know why we're here tonight.

The glistening hope of that lamp is still ours. Every promise, every opportunity is still golden in this land. And through that golden door our children can walk into tomorrow with the knowledge that no one can be denied the promise that is America.

Her heart is full; her door is still golden, her future bright. She has arms big enough to comfort and strong enough to support, for the strength in her arms is the strength of her people. She will carry on in the eighties unafraid, unashamed, and unsurpassed.

In this springtime of hope, some lights seem eternal; America's is.

Thank you, God bless you, and God bless America.

=============== Commentary: Part II ===============

🎴 🎴 🎴

Ronald Reagan's remarks to the vast television audience and the cheering Dallas delegates provide important insights into his campaign and his presidency. His acceptance speech is also significant because it articulated the themes of his presidency. Of these, perhaps the most important was his decisive and clear response to economic crisis. The problems that beset America in the late 1970s were extraordinarily complex, but they had a singular effect upon the electorate. High interest and inflation rates combined with slow economic growth and spot shortages of critical materials such as oil made voters nervous about the future. The years of rapid growth following World War II

---

[12]The poet is Emma Lazarus, whose 1883 verse, "The New Colossus" appears on a plaque attached to the Statue of Liberty.

and the euphoric expansion of the 1960s had turned to years of uncertainty, increased world competition, and, most troubling, a major decline of the manufacturing sector of the economy. Ronald Reagan proposed to solve these problems by restoring the creativity of the individual entrepreneur.

Beyond rejecting this past (or rather, offering a reconstruction of a new past), the acceptance speech was significant for its effectiveness in rallying support. As the central document of the campaign, it provided a cornerstone of reelection strategy by clarifying Reagan's image of decisiveness. The huge audience of voters responded by reelecting the president with a resounding landslide in November.

In a sense, the speech prefigured the basic strategy of the Reagan camp. A great many subsequent speeches delivered by the president during the next two months reiterated the tone and recalled the content of his remarks at Dallas. From this point onward the president set the agenda of both parties. The Democratic ticket, headed by former Vice President Fritz Mondale (under Jimmy Carter) and Representative Geraldine Ferraro of New York (the first woman nominated by a major party for such high office) failed to establish or define its own independent issues. Mondale, in his acceptance speech, criticized Reagan for abandoning the poor and underprivileged in society, for floundering on foreign policy, and for creating a disastrous federal debt that could only be eliminated by higher taxes.

In his acceptance speech and in all subsequent strategy, Reagan used these accusations to prove his contention that the Democrats represented special interests and the "Great Society" programs of social benevolence begun in the late 1960s under President Lyndon Johnson. Over and over he stressed the strength and clarity of his foreign policy, in particular his tough stance against communism, and he accused the Democrats of fighting to renew their policy of "tax and spend" at the federal level. By defining his own priorities as positive and those of the Democratic party as negative, parochial, and reactionary, he made the Democratic party's every effort to seize the initiative into an issue in itself.

Of course, Ronald Reagan's acceptance speech was not, in itself, decisive in swinging votes to the Republican ticket. But it established momentum, presented the issues on which Reagan would campaign, and symbolized the appeal of his presidency.

This latter point is made clear in looking at the results of the federal election. Reagan and Vice President Bush won 59 percent of the vote to 41 percent for Mondale and Ferraro. Expressed in electoral votes this amounted to 552 to 10, with all states save Minnesota and the District of Columbia on the Republican side. Yet this landslide failed to carry over into congressional results. The Republican majority in the Senate (established in 1980) diminished by two. In the House of Representatives the Republicans gained several seats from the 1982 elections, but still trailed the Democrats 253 to 182. If nothing else this suggests two characteristics of the Reagan presidency. The first is the inherent conservatism of the electorate which, though supportive of the president, was unwilling to give him the working majority of Republicans in both houses that he required to carry out his radical proposals for dismantling federal programs. The second represents the elevation of the president above considerations of the specific issues and interests which often determine state and local elections.

Indeed, everything in the Dallas speech, and the Reagan presidency, underscored the president's attempts to separate his office from politics. By defining himself in terms of traditional American aspirations, by stressing the cultural symbolism of success, and by appealing to patriotism, he effectively converted the presidency into a kind of head of state at the ceremonial pinnacle of American government. Thus he successfully appropriated the unlikely symbol of the Olympic Games to symbolize America's and his own success. He could refuse to debate substantive issues like those contained in the Republican platform because he was not running on them.

Does this mean, as some commentators have suggested, that campaigns for the presidency have changed forever? Will American voters only pull a lever for symbols and not substance in coming elections? Perhaps not. But this particular election, this speech, and this candidate represented a significant evolution in American politics away from traditional parties. As party loyalties and political participation have declined since the late 1950s, decisions are less likely to be made in the "smoke-filled rooms." They are now made by pollsters, advertisers, and media consultants. Because political history in the United States is as much cyclical as anything else, with trends advancing and subsiding, it would be wrong to guess that this or any recent trend is permanent. Yet it may well be that the 1984 election symbolizes a profound shift in American presidential elections in which the appeal to popular culture is as important and persuasive as more traditional appeals to political issues.

Index

A

American Social Hygiene Association, 118, 130, 131
American Society of Sanitary and Moral Prophylaxis, 118
American Supremacy (Kitchell), 159
American Youth Congress, 276
Anderson, Marian, 277
Anthony, Susan B., 380
Anti-imperialists, 169–70
Antilynching legislation, 276–78
Anti-Saloon League, 115–16, 122, 124, 126
Anti-Semitism, 245
Antoine, C. C., 90
Argersinger, Peter H., 101
Ashby, Stump, 101
Atlantic Charter, 292
Atkinson, Edward, 170
Atomic bomb
    destabilizing effect on international system, 293
    used against Japan, 285
Atomic energy, 294
Austria, 291
Abbott, Edith, 138, 150
Abbott, Grace, 138
Abernathy, Gertrude, 198
Abernathy, Ralph, 336
Abortion, 321, 383
Acheson, Dean, 286, 289, 294, 298–303, 312 n
Adams, Henry C., 137, 364
Adams, John, 36
Addams, Jane, 118, 123, 127, 131–32, 134
    "Subjective Necessity for Social Settlements," 135–51
    text, 141–51
Advertising, 213–14
    importance in social order, 218–19

Affirmative action, 404
The Age of Reform (Hofstadter), 99
Agricultural Adjustment Administration, 264, 268
Agricultural production, 157, 166–67
Agiunaldo, Emilio, 169, 177, 186–87
Ahmann, Mathew, 349, 353
Alexander, Edward Porter, 16
Alexander, Will, 271
Alger, Horatio, 223
American Asiatic Association, 166
American Association of University Women, 137
American expansionism
    colonialism, 168–71
    investment, 156–61
    missionaries, 161–62
    national interest and international mission, 165–68
    trade, 154–58
American Invaders (McKenzie), 158
American Issue, 116
American Manufacturers Export Association, 166
American Purity Alliance, 115, 118
American Psychological Association, 320

B

Bacon, Francis, 256
Baker, Ella, 337, 338
Baker, Newton D., 118, 129–30, 133
Baker, Purley A., 122
Ball, Lucille, 322–23
Bank Holiday (1933), 263
Banking Act (1933), 264
Banks, Nathaniel P., 10
Barton, Bruce, 214–22
Barton, William Eleazar, 215
Baruch, Bernard M., 204
Bates, Daisy, 339, 340
Bates, Edward, 87

Beard, Charles A., 119
Batten, Barton, Durstine and Osborne
    (BBD&O), 217
Beecher, Lyman, 115
Bell, Alexander Graham, 158
Berle, A. A., 294
Berlin, 283
Besant, Walter, 146
Berry, Fanny, 51
Berry, Mary Frances, 81
Bethune, Mary McLeod, 274, 338, 346
Beveridge, Albert, 158, 167
Bird, Caroline, 237
Birney, James G., 85
Birth control, 243
Black, Hugo, 275
The Black Bourgeoisie (Frazier), 341–42
Black cabinet (Black brain Trust), 274
"Black codes", 69, 77
Black Over White (Holt), 93
Blacks
    civil rights; see Civil rights for blacks
    Democratic party affiliation, 279
    family, 324
    infant and maternal mortality, 272
    longevity, 325
    New Deal, 266–80
    political participation, 82
    political power during
        Reconstruction, 88–96
    reaction to freedom after Civil War,
        48–63
    segregation, 79–80, 267, 269, 270
    sexual liberalism, 326
    suffrage, 69, 79–80, 82, 86, 92
    troops in Civil War, 5, 7–9, 28–30, 86
    unemployment in Great Depression,
        244
    women in civil rights movement,
        332–49
Black, Eugene Carson, 353
Blassingame, John W., 81
Bliss, W. D. P., 120
Bohlen, Charles, 301
Bonus Army, 250–51
Boorstin, Daniel, 159
Borah, William E., 200
Border states, 4
Boston Red Sox, 233
Bourget, Paul, 154

Boxer uprising, 162, 193
Boyer, Paul, 113
Brandeis, Louis, 119
Brando, Marlon, 327
Breckinridge, Sophonisba, 138
Bromley, Dorothy Dunbar, 243
Brotherhood of Sleeping Car Porters,
    276, 333, 352
Brown, William Wells, 6, 62
Brown v. Topeka, 332
Bruce, Blanche K., 90
Bryan, William Jennings, 101, 177–78,
    193–94, 220
    public ownership of railroads, 203
    World War I, 199
Bryce, James, 209
Buffalo Bill's Wild West Show, 163–64
Bundy, McGeorge, 365, 369
Bureau of Social Hygiene (N.Y.), 118
Burgess, John W., 169
Burke, Katherine, 346
Burke, Mary, 335
Burlingame, Roger, 223, 225
Burma, 291–292
Bush, George, 416
Business
    American idea of, 222
    Barton's defense of, 221
    Busse, Fred, 117
    Butler, Benjamin, 10
    Byrd, Harry, 333
    Byrnes, James, 275

C

Cable, George Washington, 270
Cain, Richard H., 76
Calhoun, John C., 176
Calkins, Raymond, 130–31
Cambodia, 372
    bombing in Vietnam War, 372
    Communist takeover, 375
    Khmer Rouge, 374
Capen, Samuel, 162
Capone, Al, 213–14
Capote, Truman, 329
Cardozo, Francis L., 76, 89, 91
Carpetbaggers, 78
Cartavio Sugar Company, 160
Carter, Jimmy, 314, 410
Cary, Mary Ann Shadd, 333

Catcher in the Rye (Salinger), 317
Ceylon, 292
Chafe, William, 379
Chain letters, 248–49
The Challenge of the City, 114, 123
Chamberlain, Daniel, 94
Chase, Salmon P., 87
Chestnut, John A., 79
Chiang Kai-shek, 291
Chicago Tribune, 263
Chicago as vice center, 117
  Vice Commission report, 125–26
Chicago Vice Commission, 121–22,
  124–25
Chicago White Sox, 233
China, 161–62, 179, 191–92
  Boxer uprising, 162, 193
  Civil War, 291
  Vietnam, 363, 367
Christian Recorder, 86
Churchill, Winston S., 282, 289, 299
Cities, 113
  moral reform of, 114–29
  social forces shaping, 135
  social reform, 129–33
City Vigilance League, 117
Civilian Conservation Corps (CCC), 268,
  270
Civil Rights Act of 1866, 89
Civil rights for blacks
  black women, 332–49
  bus boycott in Montgomery, Alabama,
    333–38
  demonstrations, 339
  Eleanor Roosevelt, 276–77
  New Deal, 261, 270–80
  school integration, 339–40
  student movement, 340–47
    financial resources, 344
    interstate transportation integrated,
      345–47
    sit-in at lunch counters, 342–43
  white pressure for, 269–70
Civil War
  advantages of North
    industrial potential, 22
    manpower, 19–20
    sea power, 22
    transportation, 21–22
  black troops, 5, 7–8, 28–30

Civil War—*Cont.*
  centralization of government, 17
  conscription, 15–18, 24–28
    exemptions, 26
  Davis, 23–25
  first of modern wars, 18
  Gettysburgh, battle of, 35
  Lincoln, 23–24
  preservation of union, 17
  war of ideas, 18–19
  weapons and tactics, 30–32
Civil Works Administration, 261
Clanton, Gene, 102
Clay, Lucius, 283
Cleveland, Grover, 157
Clifford, Clark, 300–301, 370
Coalition of Labor Union Women
  (CLUW), 385
Cochrane, John, 12
Cold War, 282, 288
  origins of, 289
Collier's Five Foot Shelf of Harvard
  Classics, 217
Collins, Lucretia, 346–47
Colonial empires after World War II,
  291–92
Colonialism, U.S.
  Philippines, 169
  protectorates, 170–71
  Spanish-American War, 168
Columbian Exposition of 1893, 153–54
Committee of Fifteen (New York),
  117–18, 123, 125, 129
Committee of Fifty for the Investigation
  of the Liquor Problem, 121
Committee on Public Information,
  201–2
Commons, John R., 227
"Companionship family," 325
Conant, Charles, 159
Confederate States of America
  advantages of North in War, 19–22
  advantages of the South, 20, 23
  conscription, 18, 25–28
  Davis' leadership, 23–25
  Gettysburgh, battle of, 35
Confiscation Act of 1862, 86
Confiscation radicals, 78
Congressional Reconstruction, 76–79,
  89–92

Congress of Industrial Organizations, 269
Congress of Racial Equality (CORE), 342–43
Connor, Eugene "Bull," 346, 351
Conscription
  Civil War, 15–18, 24–28
  World War I, 199
Containment, doctrine, 363
Contraception, 321
Cooke, Alastaire, 218
Coolidge, Calvin, 214, 222
Costigan, Edward, 278
Couples (Updike), 327
"Creed of an Advertising Man" (Barton), 218
Creel, George, 202
Croker, Richard, 117
Croly, Herbert, 119
Crook, D. F., 22
Cuba, 168–71
  ethics of acquisition, 176
  Spanish-American War 168, 175
  United States considers annexation, 168–69
  U.S. protectorate, 170, 175
Cudahy, Joseph, 163

D

Dance marathons, 249
Darby, Mary, 55
Daughters of the American Revolution, 276–77
Davies, Robert, 159
Davis, Angela, 340–41, 344
Davis, Cyclone, 101
Davis, Jefferson, 17, 23–25
  problems with Congress, 24
  rumors of capture, 51
Davis, J. W. H., 110
Dean, James, 317, 327–28
Dearborn Independent, 227
Defender, 244
de Gaulle, Charles, 291
Delany, Martin R., 10, 65, 95
DeLarge, R. C., 77, 89
Democratic party
  call for peace, 11
  denied rights to Negroes, 85

Democratic party—*Cont.*
  destroyed Reconstruction government in South Carolina, 95–96
  split over civil rights, 269
Democratic Promise (Nugent), 100
Destler, Chester McArthur, 99
Detroit *Advertiser and Tribune,* 42
Devine, Edward T., 132
Dewey, John, 318
Dickinson, Anna E., 6
Dilke, Emilia, 139
Dominican Republic, 171
Domino theory, 300, 312 n, 363, 375
Dorr, Thomas, 84
Douglas, Stephen A., 11, 85
Douglas, William O., 275
Douglass, Ambrose, 54
Douglass, Frederick, 244
  black suffrage, 84, 87
  interview with Lincoln, 9
  Lincoln myth, 13–14
  objections to President's Reconstruction plans, 86
  opposes Lincoln' renomination, 12
  recruitment of black troops, 7–8, 86
  support of Republicans, 86
Douglass, H. Ford, 85
Dred Scott decision, 85
Dr. Eliot's Five Foot Shelf of Books, 217
Drummond, Henry, 113
DuBois, W. E. B., 278
Dudley, Helena, 135
Dugger, Ronnie, 364
Dulles, Allen, 290
Dumbarton Oaks conference, 292
Dunn, Oscar James, 90, 92
Durkheim, Emil, 242
Durr, Clifford, 335

E

Early, Jubal, 12
Eastland, James, 347
Edison, Thomas A., 158, 224
Eisenhower, Dwight D., 315
Elderly
  longevity, 324–25
  political power, 325
Elliott, Robert B.; 90
El Salvador, 418
Emancipation Proclamation, 6, 42, 86

England after World War II, 290
Englehardt, N. L., Jr., 294
Enrollment Act (1863), 25
Equal Rights Amendment (ERA), 386–88
Erskine, Albert R., 242
Espionage Act of 1917, 205
Ethical Culture Societies, 135
Evans, Hiram, 214
Expansionism; see American
    expansionism
Everleigh, Ada and Minna, 116
Everleigh Club, 116
Evers, Medgar, 349

F

Falwell, Jerry, 410
Family
  baby boom, 1940s, 319–20
  birth control, 321
  blacks, households, 323–24
  changing economy, 318
  delinquency blamed on, 328
  divorce rate, 319, 323
  experimental relationships, 329–30
  ideology in 1940s and 1950s, 317
  illegitimacy rate, 323
  impact of war, 319–20
  legislation affecting, 325
  longevity affecting, 324–25
  public opinion, 320
  shattered, 327
  women's movement threatened,
      389–91
  women's role, 321
  working women, 318, 323
Family planning, 320–21
Farm Security Administration, 271
Farmer, James, 345
Farrakhan, Louis, 422 n
Faulkner, William, 210
Federal Emergency Relief
    Administration, 268
Federal Housing Administration, 269
Feldman, Egal, 119
Feminine mystique, 322
Ferraro, Geraldine, 410, 426
Fifteenth Amendment, 83
Filene, Peter, 119
Flower, Benjamin, 121
Foner, Eric, 65

Ford, Henry, 222–29
  anti-Semitism, 227
  wages and hours programs for
      workers, 226–27
Ford, William, 223
Fordismus, 222
Ford Motor Company, 225
  assembly lines, 226
  Education Department, 227
  Model A, 228
  Model T, 226
Forrestal, James, 301
Fortune, T. Thomas, 93
Fortune magazine, 287
Fourteen Points, 206
Fourteenth Amendment, 89
France, 291
Frankfurter, Felix, 275
Free blacks
  disagreement with Lincoln's plan for
      disposition of blacks, 86
  disenfranchisement before the Civil
      War, 83–85
  Louisiana, 87
  political participation, 82–88
  support for Lincoln, 86
Freedmen's Bureau, 58, 65–67
Freedmen's Bureau Extension Bill, 89
Freedom Riders, 346–47, 351
Free labor ideology, 67
Freeman, Jo, 386
Free Soil party, 85
Frémont, John C., 12, 85
Freud, Sigmund, 318
Friedan, Betty, 322
Friedenberg, Edgar, 328
Froebel, Friedrich, 144
Frontier
  new frontiers after 1890, 154
  Turner's thesis, 154
Fulbright, William J., 289, 315, 367, 376
Fuller, Alfred C., 240
Fuller Brush Company, 240

G

Gaither, Gerald B., 101
Galbraith, J. K., 248
Gambling, 249
Gardner, Lloyd, 175, 262
Garnet, Henry Highland, 83–84

Garrow, David J., 351
Gehrig, Lou, 231–32
Germany after World War II, 283–84, 290
Gettysburgh, battle of, 35
Gettysburgh Address, 34–45
    defined meaning of war, 42
    press reaction, 41–43
    public's reaction, 42–43
    text, 40
Gibbs, Jonathan, 65, 76
Giddings, Paula, 332
Gilbert, James, 316, 409
Gilder, George, 389–90
Gilman, Charlotte Perkins, 381
Gleason, Jackie, 322
Golden Age movement, 325
Goldwater Barry, 364, 410
Good neighbor policy, 256, 261
Goodwyn, Lawrence, 100–101
Grace, W. R. and Company, 160
Grant, Ulysses S., 35
Grapes of Wrath (Steinbeck), 250
Great Awakening, 111
Great Depression, 237
    birthrate, 243
    blacks and Jews, mob discrimination, 244–45
    dance marathons, 249
    gambling, 249
    psychological effect, 246–47
    suicide, 242–43
    superfluous people, 238
    unemployment; *see* Unemployment
Great Society, 367–68
Greece, 291, 298–99, 313
    Truman Doctrine, 299–315
Greenfield Village, 229
Guest, Edgar, 218
Gulf of Tonkin Resolution, 364–65

H

Hackney, Sheldon, 101
Hahn, Michael, 87
Haig, Alexander, 373
Hair, William, Ivy, 102
Hall, Newton M., 123
Hamburg massacre, 96
Hamer, Fannie Lou, 347–49
Hamilton, Alice, 138

Hampton, Wade, 96
Harding, Vincent, 67
Harding, Warren G., 196, 210, 214
Harrison-Fletcher-Thomas federal aid to education bill, 275
Harvard Classics, 217
Hastie, William, 274
Hearst, William Randolph, 173
Hefner, Hugh, 326
Held, Jon, 214
Helper, Hinton Rowan, 3
Hemingway, Ernest, 210
Henderson, Lucy, 300
Hendrickson, Robert C., 328
Henley, William Ernest, 179
Henry Street Settlement, 150
Herr, Michael, 376
Hickerson, John, 293
Hicks, John D., 99, 109
Highways to Progress (Hill), 156
Hill, James J., 155–57
Hill, Napoleon, 239
Hiroshima, 285
Ho Chi Minh, 368
Hodgson, Claire, 235
Hofstadter, Richard, 99–100, 119
Holmes, Hamilton, 339
Holmes, Oliver Wendell, 205
Holt, Thomas, 93
Home Owners Loan Company, 264
Homosexual relations, 383
Hoover, Herbert, 250–51, 253
Hoovervilles, 254
Hopkins, Harry, 268
Howe, Frederick, 114, 120
Howe, Louis, 256
Hubbard, H. H., 336
Huber, Richard M., 219, 220
Hudson, Rock, 316
Huggins, Miller, 235
Huggins, Nathan Irvin, 2
Hughes, Charles Evans, 255
Huizinga, Johan, 236
Hull House, 135
    activities, 136–49
    labor movement links, 136
    social settlement, 141
    subjective necessity for social settlements, 135–51
Hunter, Charlayne, 339

Hull House—*Cont.*
   Hunter, Robert, 399
   Hurley, Ruby, 339

I

If Christ Came to Chicago (Stead), 138
I Love Lucy Show, 322–23
Immigration, 114
The Impending Crisis of the South
   (Helper), 4
Imperialism, 176–79, 193–94
In Cold Blood (Capote), 329
Income tax, 203
Indexing of taxes, 416
India, 292
Indochina, 292
Inflation after Vietnam war, 376
In Friendship (civil rights organization),
   337
Intemperance, 115
Inter-Collegiate Alumni Association, 137
Investment, 159–61
Ismay, H. L., 283
Israel, 292
Italy, 290

J

James, Henry, 200
Japan after World War II, 285, 290
Jefferson, Thomas, 36, 178
Jerome, William T., 117
Jews, discrimination in employment,
   244–45
Johnson, Andrew, 13
   Reconstruction, 89
Johnson, Henry, 79
Johnson, Hiram, 200
Johnson, Lyndon, 315, 362, 426
Johnston, Eric A., 288
Johnston, Parke, 59
Jones, Charles, 345
Jones, Joseph M., 312 n
Juvenile delinquency, 324, 328

K

Kaplan, Lawrence, 375
Karl, Barry, 196
Kefauver, Estes, 328
Keith, Minor C., 160
Kelley, Florence, 136, 138

Kemp, Jack, 267
Keniston, Kenneth, 329
Kennan, George, 301
Kennedy, John F., 175, 329, 342, 346, 352
Kennedy, Robert, 352, 370
Kerouac, Jack, 328
Khachigian, Ken, 410
Kiernan, John, 231
King, Coretta Scott, 342
King, Martin Luther, Jr., 332, 336, 345,
   350
   assassination, 370
   "I Have a Dream" speech, 251–61
   text, 355–61
Kinsey, Alfred, 325
Kirkpatrick, Jeane, 410
Kissinger, Henry, 371–74
Kitchell, J. G., 159
Kneeland, George J., 117, 127
Korea, 291
Kresge, S. S., 116
Ku Klux Klan, 79, 214

L

Labor movement, 209
LaFeber, Suzanne, 362
LaFeder, Walter, 297, 362
LaFollette, Robert M., 200
Lampasas People's Journal, 108–10
Landis, James Kenesaw Mountain, 233
Laos, 375
Lardner, Ring, 231
Large-policy, 176
Lathbury, Vincent T., 327
Lathrop, Julia, 135, 138
Lazarus, Emma, 425 n
Laxalt, Paul, 410
League of Nations, 210–11
   mandate system, 194
Leahy, William, 313
Lee, George, 333
Lee, Robert E., 35
Lee, Samuel J., 90
Legalized segregation, 79
Lenin, Vladimir, 223
Lesbianism, 392–93
Leuchtenberg, William E., 235
Lewis, C. Day, 284
Lewis, Hylan, 341
Lewis, John, 350, 353

Lewis, Sinclair, 222
Liberty Party, 85
Lincoln, Abraham
   assassination, 3
   Civil War, 23–24
   Dred Scott decision, 85
   Emancipation Proclamation, 6
   Frederick Douglass and, 2–14
   Gettysburgh Address, 35–45
   myth of, 13–14
   program of reconstruction, 13, 88
   Union more important than abolition
      of slavery, 2, 4–6, 47
Lippman, Walter, 119, 200, 299, 313
Little Rock, Arkansas, school
      desegregation, 339–40
Litwack, Leon, 47
Localists versus Cosmopolitans, 111
Locke, John, 145
Lodge, Henry Cabot, 174–75, 177–78
   speech to the U.S. Senate on the
      Philippine Islands, 175–95
   text, 180–93
Lomax, Louis, 333, 338
London *Daily Mail,* 164
London *Times,* 42
Louisiana
   blacks in legislature (1886–96), 90
   black suffrage, 87
Louisville Vice Commission, 125, 131
Low, Seth, 117
Lucy, Autherine, 329
Lumpkin, Robert, 48
Lusitania, 199
Lynch, John R., 91
Lynching, 276–78
Lynd, Helen and Robert, 247

M

McAdoo, William Gibbs, 204
McArthur, Douglas, 251, 285, 293
McCarthy, Joe, 314
McClure's, 117
McCormick, Thomas, 362
McDonald, Margaret, 139
McDowell, John R., 115
McGeehan, Bill, 234
McGovern, George, 373
McGuffy *Reader,* 223, 229
Mack, Julian W., 133

McKenzie, Fred A., 158
McKinley, William, 101, 167–68, 175, 178
McKissick, Floyd, 350
MacMahon, Brian, 242
McNamara, Robert, 364, 366, 368–70,
      376
McVeagh, Lincoln, 301
Mahan, Alfred Thayer, 170–71
Mailer, Norman, 329
Main, Jackson Turner, 111–12
Maine, sinking of, 175
Malone, Vivian, 339
Manifest Destiny, 3
Mann, James, 115
Mann Act, 115, 118
The Man Nobody Knows (Barton),
      219–21
Mao Tse-tung, 291
Marburg, Theodore, 167
Marshall, George C., 294, 298, 301
Marshall Plan, 295
Mass culture, 163–65
   journalism, 164
Mayne, Richard, 284
Mazzini, Guiseppe, 144
Menard, John W., 90
Methodist Board of Temperance and
      Morals, 122
"Middletown" (Lynds), 247
Miller, Arthur, 222
Miller, Loren, 275
Misery and Its Causes (Devine), 132
Missionaries, 161–62
   Philippines, 169
"Model of Christian Charity"
      (Winthrop), 423 n
Moley, Raymond, 255
Molotov, V. M., 288
Mondale, Walter, 410, 418 n, 420 n, 426
Montgomery, Alabama, bus boycott,
      333–38
Montgomery Improvement Association,
      336–37
Moral reform, 114
   battling saloon and brothel, 115–18
   links between coercive crusade and
      Progressivism, 119–24
   negative environmentalism, 114–29
   positive environmentalism, 129–33
   secularization of, 122–23

Moral reform—*Cont.*
  settlement movement; *see* Settlement
    movement
  symbolic component of coercive
    crusade, 124–29
Morrill Act of 1862, 157
Morrow, Prince A., 118, 124
Mulato, 93–94
Munro, William B., 113
Murphy, Frank, 275
Murphy, Robert, 283
Muscle Shoals, 227

N

Nagasaki, 285
Nash, Beverly, 92
Nash, Diane, 341, 344, 346
Nash, William Beverly, 79
Nashville Banner, 263
Nashville *Colored Tennessean,* 88
Nation, 263
National Advisory Committee on
  Education (1938), 274
National Association for the
  Advancement of Colored People
  (NAACP), 269, 333, 343, 352
National Association of Manufacturers,
  166
National Association of Women Lawyers,
  245
National Black Feminist Organization,
  385
National Council of Negro Women, 276
National Grange, 166
National Labor Relations Act, 269
National Liberation Front, 365
National Negro Congress, 269
National Organization for Women
  (NOW), 384, 386
  split over reform/radical issue, 393
National Recovery Administration (NRA),
  268
National Union Party, 13
National Urban League, 269
National Vigilance Society, 117
National War Labor Board, 204
National Women's Party (NWB), 387
National Youth Organization, 264,
  270–72
Natural law, 3

Negative environmentalists, 114
Negro American Labor Council, 352
Negro National Convention, 1843, 83
Netherlands, 291
A New Conscience and an Ancient Evil
  (Addams), 132
New Deal, 256, 263–65
  blacks, 266–80
  creative period in American political
    history, 264
  Democratic coalition, 265
  expanded federal government
    authority, 275
  unemployment, 264
New Encyclopedia of Social Reform, 118
New feminism
  birth rate affecting, 382
  constituency, 384–86
  Equal Rights Amendment, 386–88
  internal dissension, 391–94
  objectives, 387–89
  organization and structure of
    movement, 383–87
  prevailing social trends, 381–82
  sexuality, 382–83
  social base, 385
  social changes brought on by
    movement, 394–96
  threat to family and women's role,
    389–91
New Republic, 199
Newsweek, 299
New York as vice center, 117
New York *Colored American,* 83
New York *Globe,* 93
New York Herald Tribune, 263
New York State Convention of Colored
  Men, 83
New York Times, 178, 222, 229
New York Yankees, 231, 233
Ngo-yen Cao Ky, 369
Nguyen Khanh, 365
Nicaragua, 171, 418
Nineteenth Ward Improvement Club,
  136
Nixon, E. D., 333, 335–337
Nixon, Richard, 362, 370
Nkrumah, Kwame, 342
Norris, Frank, 155
Norris, George, 227

NOW; *see* National Organization for
Women
Nugent, Walter T. K., 100

O

Older, Fremont, 120
Oldfield, Barney, 225
Olds, Ransome E. 225
Olympic games, 424n
O'Neill, Eugene, 222
On the Road (Kerouac), 328
O'Ryan, John E., 243
Our Bodies Our Selves, 382–83
Overman Act (1918), 206

P

Pakistan, 292
Panama, 171
Parke Davis Company, 160
Parkhurst, Charles, 117
Parks, Rosa, 333–38, 351
Parsons, Stanley B., 101
Paterson, Thomas G., 282
Patman, Wright, 364
Patman Bill, 250, 251
Peabody, Endicott, 255
Peabody, Francis G., 123
Peace Corps, 150
People's party, 98; *see also* Populism
Pestalozzi, Johann, 145
Philadelphia *Inquirer,* 41
Philanthropists, 162–63
  overseas relief, 163
Philippines, 169–70, 75
  ethics of acquisition, 176
  Lodge's speech to the U.S. Senate,
    175–95
    text, 180–95
  value to U.S., 188–90
Phillips, David Graham, 118
Pinchback, P. B. S., 90–91
Pittsburgh Courier, 273
Platt Amendment, 170–71
Playboy, 326
Pleasant, Mary Ellen, 333
Plessy v. Ferguson, 167, 275
Poland, 291
Political Parties Before the Constitution
  (Main), 111

Poll tax, 276–77
Ponder, Annelle, 349
Populism, 98
  anti-Semitism, 100
  cooperative commonwealth ideology,
    100
  economic hardship, 99–101, 104, 106
  farm income, 104
  frontier movement, 99
  historical views, 99–102
  ideology, 100
  industrial populism, 101–2
  isolation from economic and social
    mainstream, 101–7, 109
  motivation, 101
  organized religion, 105
  plains states and the South, 99
  pseudo-Populists, 100
  rebellion against plutocracy, 108
  Texas Democratic and Populist
    countries compared, 102–10
Porter, Katherine Anne, 210
Positive environmentalists, 114
Potter, Henry C., 116
Powell, Aaron Macy, 115
"The Prayer Pilgrimage" (civil rights
  demonstration), 339
President Hoover's Committee on
  Recent Social Trends (1929), 329
Presidential Reconstruction, 68–69, 76,
  78, 88
President's Commission on Fair
  Employment Practices, 271
Prinz, Joachim, 350, 353
Progressives, 113
  programs of urban reform, 114
    negative environmentalists, 114–29
    positive environmentalists, 114,
      129–33
  reform movement, 167–68
  wage and hour laws, 121
Prohibition, 115–16, 119, 126
  18th Amendment, 115, 205
Prostitution, 115–16, 122, 124–27, 129,
  132
Pseudo-Populists, 100
The Psychic Factors of Civilization
  (Ward), 138
Public Works Administration (PWA),
  271

Prohibition—*Cont.*
  Public works program in Hoover
    administration, 253
Puerto Rico, 175
Pugh, Thomas, 242
Pure Food and Drug Act, 160
Pure Radicals, 92

R

Racism, 167, 178
  diminishing, 273–74
  discrimination in New Deal relief
    programs, 266–67
  student frustration at, 342
  whites pressing for civil rights,
    169–70
Radical Reconstruction, 76–77
Railroads
  American exports, 155–57
  Civil War, 21–22
  World War I, 203–5
Raines Law, 116, 128
Rainey, James H., 77, 91
Randolph, A. Philip, 350, 352–53
Ransier, Alonzo J., 90
Rauschenbusch, Walter, 131
Read, Benjamin, 369
Reagan, Ronald, 315, 408
  foreign policy, 426
  importance of renomination
    speeches, 411–12
  second acceptance speech at
    Republican National Convention,
    409–27
    text, 414–25
  speech prefigured basic strategy, 426
  symbols versus substance, 427
Reason, Charles, 83
Rebel Without a Cause, 327
Reciprocity Treaty of 1902, 170
Reconstruction
  Congressional, 76–79, 89–92
  Lincoln-Johnson plan, 88
  overthrow of, 79–80, 92–93
  political participation of blacks, 82
  power of blacks in the South, 88–92
  Presidential, 68–69, 76, 88
  South Carolina, 93–96
  state constitutions, 89–90
Reconstruction Act of 1867, 81, 83

Reconstruction Finance Corporation,
  253
"Red Shirts," 96
Reedy, George, 363
Regulator movements, 111
Republican party
  betrayal of blacks, 92, 95–96
  black support, 86
  carpetbaggers and scalawags, 78
  reconstruction, 88, 92, 95–96
  southern blacks dependent on, 78
Reuther, Walter, 353
Revels, Hiram R., 90
Rice, Grantland, 230–31
Richardson, Gloria, 344
Right-to-life movement, 422 n
Riis, Jacob, 398–99
Roberts, Owen, 276
Robinson, Cleveland, 350
Robinson, Elsie, 251
Robinson, Joanne, 335
Rock, John, 87
Rockefeller, John D., Jr., 116, 118
"Rock Hill Four", 345
Rockwell, Norman, 322
Roe, Clifford G., 117–18, 127
Roosevelt, Eleanor, 244, 254, 256, 266
  civil rights, 276–77
Roosevelt, Franklin D., 237, 252
  First Inaugural Address, 253–65
    response to, 263
    text, 259–63
  1932 election, 254
  nomination acceptance speech, 412
Roosevelt, Theodore, 118, 129, 167
  colonialism, 170
  imperialism, 176
Rosenberg, Emily, 153
Rosenman, Samuel J., 259
"Rotten apple" effect, 312
Rovere, Richard, 375
Ruef, Abraham, 120
Ruppert, Jacob, 231, 235
Rusk, Dean, 367, 376
Russett, Bruce M., 289
Russian famine of 1891, 163
Rustin, Bayard, 337, 352
Ruth, George Herman Jr. (Babe), 229–36
Rutledge, Wiley, 275

S

Salesmanship, 221–22
Salinger, J. D., 317
Saloons, 116
    Anti-Saloon League, 116
    link with prostitution, 127
    Prohibition Amendment, 115
    substitute for, 130
Sanders, Elias, 105
School busing for integration, 403–4
School desegregation, 339–46
School of Civics and Philanthropy, 150
Schultz, Stanley K., 120
Schurman, Jacob Gould, 169
Schurz, Carl, 170
Scientific racism, 167
A Scientific Temperance Journal, 121
Scudder, Vida, 135
Second Confiscation Act, 6
Segregation, 79–80, 267
    New Deal, 269, 270–80
    white American approval of, 270
Selden, George, 224
Seneca Falls Declaration of Sentiments
    and Resolutions, 380
Senior citizen, 325
Settlement house, 132
Settlement movement, 131–35, 137, 138
    appeal to young women, 138–39, 143
    England, 139
    Hull House, 141
    legacy, 150–51
    motives for establishing, 141
    peace movements, 151
    provisional nature, 149
    social democracy, 151
Sexual Behavior in the Human Male
    (Kinsey), 325–26
Sexual liberalism, 326
    after 1900, 381
    women's movement of 1960s and
        1970s, 383–83
Seward, William H., 4
Shame of the Cities (Steffens), 120
Sherman, William T., 13, 21
Sherrod, Charles, 345
Shuttlesworth, Fred, 347, 352
Simkhovitch, Mary Kingsbury, 132

Simkins, George, 342
Sitkoff, Harvard, 266
Skinner, B. F., 318
Sklar, Kathryn Kish, 135
Slavery
    blacks reaction to freedom, 48–63
    Lincoln, 2, 4–6, 47
    Northern public, 5
    root cause of Civil War, 5
    white reaction to freedom of slaves,
        50, 55–57
Smalls, Robert, 55, 91
Smith, Alfred E., 253–54
Smith, Jean, 340–41, 344
Smith, Ruby Doris, 344–45
Smith, Silas, 56
Sobol, Ken 232
Social Darwinism, 138, 167, 176, 194
Social democracy, 140, 151
The Social Evil in Chicago, 117, 122,
    125
Social Gospel, 131
Social Hygiene, 118, 123, 128–29
Social Security Act, 269
Social Security Administration, 264
South Carolina black Reconstruction, 77
    reasons for failure
        disunity among Republicans, 96
        divisions among blacks, 93–94
        failure to take governorship, 94–95
        inexperience of blacks, 94
        refusal to confiscate and
            redistribute land, 95
        reliance on Northern Republicans,
            95–96
South Carolina Colored State
    Convention, 65–80
    delegates, 65, 67
    political concerns, 66–67
    texts of addresses
        Address to Legislature of State of
            South Carolina, 73–74
        Address to the People of the State
            of South Carolina, 70–72
        Memorial to Senate and House of
            Representatives of the U.S.,
            75–80
    South Carolina Constitutional
        Convention of 1868, 77

Southern Christian Leadership Conference (SCLC), 338–39, 343, 351
Southern Conference for Human Welfare, 276
Southern Electoral Reform League, 276
Southern Manifesto, 333
Southern Negro Youth Congress, 269
Southern Regional Council, 349
Soviet Union, Cold War, 289
Spanish-American War, 168, 175
    peace treaty, 176–77
The Spirit of Youth and the City Streets (Addams), 131
Spock, Benjamin, 317–18
Stalin, Josef, 287, 289, 298–99
Stanton, Edwin M., 9
Stanton, Elizabeth Cady, 380
Starr, Ellen Gates, 135, 141
Stead, William, 138, 155
Stearns, G. L., 8
Steinbeck, John, 250
Steinem, Gloria, 393
Steffens, Lincoln, 120, 400
Stevens, George, 317
Stevens, Thaddeus, 78
Stimson, Henry J., 293
Stoddard, Cora Frances, 121–22
Strecker, Vincent, 327
Strong, Josiah, 114, 120, 127, 131
Student Nonviolent Coordinating Committee (SNCC), 340, 343–44, 353
Student Volunteer Movement, 161
Subasic, Ivan, 291
"Subjective Necessity for Social Settlements" (Addams), 135–51
    text, 141–51
Subsistence homestead program, 269
Suburbs, 401–6
    crime, 404
    government, 404–5
    lack of self-sufficiency, 404
Suffrage
    blacks, 69, 79–80, 82, 86
    women's movement, 380–81
Sumner, Dean, 122
Sumner, Walter T., 117
Sumner, William Graham, 171, 221

Supreme Court
    court packing, 275
    Roosevelt's appointment, 275
Susman, Beatrice, 213
Susman, Warren, 213

T

Taft, Robert, 313
Taft, William Howard, 205
Taney, Roger B., 82
Taylor, Elizabeth, 316
Taylor, Frederick Winslow, 207
Taylor, Graham, 132
Technology, 157–58
Teller Amendment, 175
Temperance, 115
Tennessee Valley Authority (TVA), 268
Texas
    cotton economy, 102–3
    Populism, 102–10
Texas Farmers' Alliance, 100
Thieu, Nguyen Van, 309, 373
Thirteenth Amendment, 88
Till, Emmett, 333
Tito, Josip Broz, 291, 299
Tolerant Populists, 100
Towsendites, 325
Toynbee Hall, 135, 139
Trade
    agricultural products, 157
    exports, 155–59
    new frontier, 155
    overseas, 165–66
    railroads, 155–57
    technology, 157–58
Trade associations, 166
Traffic in Souls, 118
Transportation Act of 1920, 204
Trenholme, George A., 57
Truman, Harry S., 283, 285–86, 289, 295, 418n
    acceptance speech, 1948, 412
    Foreign Economic Policy Address at Baylor University, 297–307
    text, 304–7
Truman Doctrine, 297, 299–315
    text of special message to Congress, 308–13
Truth, Sojourner, 333, 384

Turkey, 298, 301, 313
    Truman Doctrine, 299–315
Turner, Frederick Jackson, 99, 112, 153
    "frontier" thesis, 154
Turner, George Kibbe, 117–18, 121,
    124–25, 127
Turner, James 98
Twain, Mark, 177
Twenty Years at Hull House (Addams),
    135

U

Unemployment
    blacks and Jews, job discrimination,
        244–45
    crime, 248
    exploitation of self by unemployed,
        240
    Great Depression, 237–64
    job-hunting, 241
    leisure activity, 247
    numbers of unemployed, 238
    women, 245–46
Union
    Lincoln's view, 2, 4–6, 47
    Northern objective in Civil War, 17
Union League, 77
United Fruit Company, 160
United Nations, 292–93
    San Francisco Conference, 292–93
United States Chamber of Commerce,
    166
University Extension movement, 144
Updike, John, 327
Urban crisis
    division between blacks and whites,
        402–5
    division between city and suburb,
        401–2, 405
    foreign cities compared to United
        States, 406
    ghettos of today compared to 1900s,
        398–400
    metropolitan government, 405–6
Urban population, 114
U.S. Housing Authority, 271

V

Van Buren, Martin, 85
Vandenburg, Arthur, 300

Vanderlip, Frank, 169
Vanishing Adolescent (Friedenburg),
    328
Van Wyck, Robert, 117
Venereal disease, 123–24
Viorst, Milton, 333
Vietnam War, 362–77
    anti-war protests, 370–72
    costs of war affecting U.S. economy,
        368, 376
    reasons for loss of war, 375–77
    Tet offensive, 366–69
    Vietcong, 367
    Vietnamization policy, 371–72
Voting rights; *see* Suffrage

W

Wade, Richard, 397
Wade-Davis Bill, 12
Wagner, Robert, 278
Wagner-Van Nuys-Gavagan
    antidelinquency bill, 276
Wald, Lillian, 150
Walden Two (Skinner), 318
Wallace, George C., 354
Walls, J. T., 91
Walsh, Christy, 234
Walsh, Frank P., 204
Ward, Lester, 138
Ware, Susan, 253
War Finance Corporation, 204
War Industries Board, 204, 208
War Labor Policies Board, 204
Warmoth, Henry C., 90
War Revenue Act of 1917, 203
Washington, Booker T., 55, 60
Watch and Ward Society, 123
Watergate scandal, 371, 374, 376
Waters, Walter W., 250
Watts, 368
Wears, Isaiah, 86
Webb, Beatrice, 139
Westmoreland, William, 369
Westward expansion, frontier thesis,
    134, 155
White, Garland H., 49
White, Viola, 334
White-slave traffic, 115, 118
Wiebe, Robert, 128
Wilcox, Delos F., 130

Wilder, Thornton, 222
Williams, Roy, 274, 350, 352
Williams, Aubrey, 270
Williams, T. Harry, 15
Williams, William Appleman, 362
Wilson, R. Jackson, 35
Wilson, Woodrow, 197–99, 201, 206–7,
    225
  League of Nations, 210
  war to end war, 206
Wittner, Lawrence S., 310 n
Wolfe, Tom, 329
Women; *see also* New feminism
  civil rights movement, 332–49
  discrimination in employment, 245
  family; *see* family
  1960s and 1970s women's rights
      movement, 379–96
  support of families during
      depression, 246
  unemployment, 245–46
  working, 324, 381
Women's Christian Temperance Union
    (WCTU), 115, 121, 139
Women's Equity Action League (WEAL),
    384
Women's magazines, 321–22
Women's Political Council
    (Montgomery, Ala.), 335
Women's rights movement; *see* New
    feminism
Women's Trade Union League (WTUL),
    385
Wood, Leonard, 170
Woods, Robert A., 135
World War I
  American industrial system, 201, 208
  blockade, 198
  centralization of power in federal
      government, 209–10
  farm prices, 205
  financing, 202–3

World War I—*Cont.*
  hostility to German-Americans, 202
  influenza epidemic, 209
  international trade, 197, 198
  men under arms, 207
  neutrality, 197
  private managerial sector, 201
  Prohibition, 205
  railroad takeover by government,
      203–4
  submarine warfare, 198
  U.S. declaration of war, 201–2
  U.S. entry into war, 207
  war debts, 211
World War II
  colonial empires, 291–92
  destruction
    economic, 290
    physical, 296
  domestic political turmoil, 290
  Germany, 283–84
  growth of global outlook, 294
  Japan, 285
  U.S. reconversion after war, 287–88
Works Progress Administration, 264
Wright, Jonathan J., 76
Wyler, William, 319
Wylie, Philip, 327
Wyman v. *James,* 325

Y–Z

Yalta Conference, 293
Yankelovich, Daniel, 383, 394
Young, Robert, 322
Young, Whitney, 350, 352
Young Negroes' Cooperative League,
    337
Yugoslavia, 291, 299
Zero population growth, 382
Ziegfeld, Flo, 214
Zimmerman note, 206
Zweig, James, 347

ABOUT THE CONTRIBUTORS

Eric Foner is Professor of History at Columbia University. He is the author of several books, including *Free Soil, Free Labor, Free Men: The Ideology of the Republican Party before the Civil War; Nothing but Freedom: Emancipation and Its Legacy*; and *Politics and Ideology in the Age of the Civil War*.

Lloyd Gardner is Professor of History at Rutgers University. He is the author of several books including *A Covenant with Power: American and World Order from Wilson to Reagan; Economic Aspects of New Deal Diplomacy; Safe for Democracy: The Anglo-American Response to Revolution, 1913–1923; Wilson and Revolutions, 1913–1921;* and *Imperial America: American Foreign Policy since 1898*.

David Garrow is Associate Professor of Political Science at the City College of New York and the City University Graduate Center. He has written *Protest at Selma: Martin Luther King, Junior and the Voting Rights Act of 1965;* and *The FBI and Martin Luther King, Junior*. His forthcoming biography *Bearing the Cross: Martin Luther King, Junior and the Southern Christian Leadership Conference* will be published in October 1986.

James Gilbert is Professor of History at the University of Maryland. He has taught at Teachers College, Columbia University, and the Center for Social History at Warwick University, Coventry, England. He is the author of several books, including *A Cycle of Outrage: Juvenile Delinquency and Mass Media in the 1950s; Writers and Partisans: Designing the Industrial State; Work Without Salvation*; and *Another Chance: Postwar America, 1945–1985*. He is co-author of *The Pursuit of Liberty: A History of the American People*.

Walter LaFeber is Professor of History at Cornell University and a well-known lecturer on American foreign policy. He is the author of many books on U.S. history including *America, Russia, and the Cold War; Inevitable Revolutions: The United States in Central America;* and *The New Empire: An Interpretation of American Expansion*, 1860–1898. Professor LaFeber is also the co-author of *The American Century: A History of the United States since the 1890s*.

Kathryn Kish Sklar is Professor of History at the University of California at Los Angeles. She is the author of *Catharine Beecher: A Study in American Domesticity,* and a forthcoming biography on Florence Kelley.

(continued)

Susan Ware is Assistant Professor of History at New York University and the author of several books including *Beyond Suffrage: Women in the New Deal*; *Holding Their Own: American Women in the 1930s*; and co-author of *America's History*.

R. Jackson Wilson is Professor of History at Smith College, where he also teaches American studies and philosophy. His special field of interest is cultural history, and he is currently at work on a study of nineteenth-century American writers. He has written several books including *In Quest of Community: Social Philosophy in the United States*; and *Darwinism and the American Intellectual*. He is co-author of *The Pursuit of Liberty: A History of the American People*; and *Freedom and Crisis: An American History*. Professor Wilson was editor of *America's History* by Henretta, Brody, Brownlee, and Ware.

ABOUT THE EDITOR

David Nasaw received his doctoral degree from Columbia University in 1972. He is currently a Professor of History at the City University of New York, the College of Staten Island. Professor Nasaw is the author of *Schooled to Order: A Social History of Public Schooling in the United States* (Oxford University Press, 1979), and *Children of the City: At Work and At Play* (Oxford University Press, 1986).

A NOTE ON THE TYPE

The text of this book was set in 10/12 Garamond via computer-driven cathode ray tube. Claude Garamond (1480–1561), the respected French type designer and letter cutter, produced this beautiful typeface for François I at the king's urging. Garamond is a fine example of the Old Style typeface, characterized by oblique stress and relatively little contrast between thicks and thins. Full of movement and charm, this elegant face influenced type design down to the end of the eighteenth century.

Composed by Weimer Typesetting Co., Inc., Indianapolis, Indiana.

Printed and bound by Maple Press, York, Pennsylvania.